Rockwright. N Raug

3 Elsworthy Terrace
London, N.W.3
30. X. 70

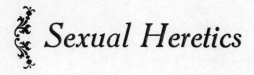 *Sexual Heretics*

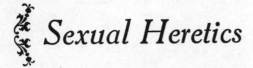

Sexual Heretics

*Male Homosexuality
in English Literature
from 1850 to 1900*

*An Anthology Selected
with an Introduction
by Brian Reade*

Routledge & Kegan Paul   London

First published in 1970
by Routledge & Kegan Paul Ltd
Broadway House, 68–74 Carter Lane
London E.C.4.
Printed in Great Britain by
Cox & Wyman Ltd, Reading

I.S.B.N. 0 7100 6797 6

Contents

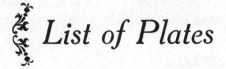

List of Plates

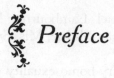

Preface

Perhaps the fashion for books on homosexuality is passing, and it will be only with previously unco-ordinated inferences that future writers on this subject will be anxious to concern themselves. The present book may be regarded as attempting to close a gap – a gap I myself could have filled years ago, I think, if circumstances had permitted. As it happens, it is a gap greatly reduced by Mr. Croft-Cooke in his very readable *Feasting with Panthers*, except that the author dealt there with prominent Victorian figures and he made no attempt to cover homosexual literature generally during the period. Moreover, aiming to cut everybody and everything down to size, as he confessed, he abetted himself with the slang of our time – which must have given younger generations an odd impression of Victorian vocabulary and manners. I would emphasize willingly my indebtedness to Mr. Croft-Cooke, if I felt any – that is, apart from places in the text where he is mentioned. Unfortunately the present work was more or less finished when his book came out in 1967.

I am however distinctly indebted to a few people: first to Dr. W. H. Bond, Librarian of the Houghton Library, Harvard University, by whose permission I am able to quote from the library's collection of privately printed poems by John Addington Symonds. I am indebted also to Mr. Donald Weeks, of Detroit and London, a leading authority on Frederick Rolfe (Baron Corvo), who lent me several photographs from his collection and responded most patiently to my enquiries about such comparatively little-known writers as John Gambril Nicholson and Charles Kains-Jackson. Equally I would have fared worse without Mr. Timothy d'Arch Smith and Mr. W. G. Good at hand, willing to impart bibliographical and other information essential to the subject; and to Mr. d'Arch Smith moreover for lending me rare books from his library. To these friends I can add Mr. Anthony Symondson, who sent some material of his for reproduction and who engaged in helpful correspondence.

It is a pleasure to recall the names of others who took an interest in this compilation while it was under way; including Mr. John Adlard,

Dr. Ian Fletcher, Mr. Peter Gunn, Mr. Lionel Lambourne, Mr. Ronald Lightbown, Mr. Henry Maas, Mr. Jonathan Mayne, Miss Sybil Pantazzi, and my wife Mrs. Margaret Reade.

An all-embracing study of nineteenth-century homosexuality was not what I projected, nor was there scope for it in the introduction. This introduction is a guide to the anthology; and while some of the material included here is of merit, some of it may be considered merely amusing. That is not the point, however: all of it seems to me to be of particular interest.

London   Brian Reade

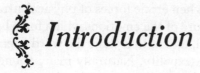# Introduction

It was during 1964 while I was doing researches in the life of Aubrey Beardsley and his friends that I found something was taking shape in the distance which amounted to the beginnings of the anthology presented here. In the introduction to a book on Beardsley published in 1967 I suggested that this artist was not 'a homosexual' in one of the current senses of the word, but rather an ironist who mocked the impulses in himself which responded to homosexual young men in the art world of his time.

It is unwise, perhaps, to use the word homosexual in this way as a noun, with the suggestion that anyone so-called has sexual feelings only for persons of the same sex. Many people who are homosexual are heterosexual too, though either at different times in their lives, or with one or another state in the ascendant. Of these again, some like Lord Alfred Douglas grow out of a youthful phase, or become like Oscar Wilde more homosexual as they grow older. Here we are not concerned with these personal transitions, only with the literary evidence of homosexual moods and with the idea of homosexuality as a romantic stimulus.

But the sexual element in a homosexual condition is less important than it is in a heterosexual condition, which offers wider and longer developments – as in family life for example. Why then not avoid using the word 'sexual' and keep to the word 'friendship' for attachments between persons of the same sex? This indeed was done in the days when homosexual males were legally persecuted, and the phrase 'romantic friendship' was used for relationships of the kind inspiring so many of the poems in the present anthology. But as soon as psychologists evolved the idea of sex underlying many other springs of emotion, homosexuality began to be seen as a normal but unresolved state, abnormal perhaps in persons who habitually imitated functional (that is to say heterosexual) acts.

The result of this considerable change in the values of the words sex and friendship makes it harder than ever to draw a firm line where homosexuality begins. What is it that distinguishes it from friendship today? Eroticism, perhaps. For, when erotic forces of physical attraction motivate a friendship, some tincture of the emotions which form hetero-sexual relationships will be found, and at that stage the word friendship is superseded by the word homosexuality. Naturally many friendships are, and were, thus motivated, often quite unconsciously.

This book is not concerned with female homosexuality, or les-bianism. A similar anthology might be made out of literature with lesbian qualities, though this would be less easy to achieve out of English than out of French or German literature of the period 1850–1900. So far as England goes in this context, therefore, it is true to say that homosexual literature for all practical purposes is male homo-sexual literature. Our concern is with male homosexuality alone, and this includes pederasty, or the love of boys by men. Sodomy, a word often used unwittingly with reference to male homosexuality, means nothing more than anal penetration and applies heterosexually too.

Homosexuality breeds readily in environments that exclude mem-bers of the opposite sex; schools, prisons, military units remote from towns or villages, ships at sea, and so forth. But pederasty has the peculiar distinction of being once practised in ancient Greece, where it was a respected relationship between teacher and taught, senior and junior, the soldier and his page. And the cult of homosexuality in its pederastic form gained support from the arguments of Plato and other Greek philosophers who took this educational pattern in their lives as they found it, only maintaining that the less physical it was the more philosophical, and therefore the better. Platonic Love became a glib phrase for attachments both homo- and heterosexual which by evasion or restraint excluded physical expression.

What interested me particularly in studying Victorian homosexual literature was the problem of how much we all were indebted to it. In a similar way one might legitimately wonder how much the French were indebted to the homosexual court of Henri III. As a result, the selection here has been made from literary works revealing certain cultural ideals, and with one or two debatable exceptions (such as the novel *Teleny*), works openly published, or like the 'peccant pamphlets' of John Addington Symonds published for circulation among sympa-thetic friends. *Teleny* – issued in an edition of two hundred copies in 1893 – was partly in the above category and partly in the category of pornography, which developed along lines of its own, reflecting social values maybe, but cultural issues only in the most fossilized forms. In spite of contrary assertions,[1] homosexual pornography was not altogether rare in our period in England, and the Parisian Depot in Holborn and

[1] See Steven Marcus, *The Other Victorians*, London, 1964, p. 261.

similar places in London, and in the country too, existed for its distribution. Into this class falls a novel like *The Adventures of a Mary-Ann*, which exploited the subject of transvestism as it was revealed to the public in 1870 in the trial of Boulton and Park. Some years ago one might even have hoped to see passages from *Don Leon* (1866) in an anthology like this, but the poem is now dated well before 1850 and its authorship is still a matter for doubt. Homosexual literature after 1900 has been equally excluded from this book. In fact chronological convenience agrees with what I believe to be a discernible wave of homosexual subculture, beginning around 1850 and closing shortly after the Wilde trials of 1895. When after that date homosexual literature revived in England, it seems to have changed with the changing scene.

While everything in this anthology was written in English, including the only Colonial example I was able to find, which was Australian (No. 85), it could not be claimed that I have represented all late nineteenth-century homosexual literature in English without including American–English examples. But to have done this would have overbalanced the book. Homosexual literature in the United States was not uncommon, and the influence of Walt Whitman's *Leaves of Grass*, published in 1855, can be traced in England and in other parts of the English-speaking world. In Whitman's famous series of poems pederasty had no place, but in the sections 'Adam' and 'Calamus' especially, what Whitman called adhesiveness – which could be interpreted as the state of loving anybody of either sex – was especially recommended, and illustrated in his own life, as an emotional heightening of friendships between men. When challenged by his admirer, John Addington Symonds, to say once and for all whether eroticism was comprehended in Whitman's adhesiveness, the American poet denied such a thing had occurred to him. It has been generally felt in later years that he was disingenuous, partly because his message was the message of a democratic egalitarianism of the spirit; and he could scarcely have wished himself a prophet of 'crimes against nature'. To do Whitman the justice of the doubt, it is possible that when he spoke ardently of embraces and other physical contacts between men, he did not see that gestures like these could, in certain cases, lead to some kind of climax. Whitman himself was by no means entirely homosexual. There are men who must be counted the masculine equivalents of *demi-vierges*; and Whitman may have been one of them. We do not know. What we do know is that erotic relationships between persons of the same sex may continue without physical contact, so that everybody is happy to believe in their 'chastity'. Recognizing at least a potential of men like this in the world, we are astounded perhaps less at the apparent restraint in some of the nineteenth-century homosexuals whose lives are remembered, and whose works appear again in these pages.

Oddly enough it was in England – in the realm of a state Church – that three homosexual men made their conspicuous bows to the tottering altars. These men were John Henry Newman; his close friend Richard Hurrell Froude, who died young; and another friend, Frederick William Faber, whose dog-like devotion to Newman was inspired and resented by the older man. Froude's diaries reveal his recognition of, and worry over, his own sexual orientations, while Faber's collected poems in an edition of 1856 include many emotional verses to men and to youths, written for the most part before 1850. Newman's poems, although never erotic except in a generally symbolic sense, are none the less emotional secretions of a mind in which female images counted for little. The most famous of these, *The Pillar of the Cloud* (1833) and *The Dream of Gerontius* (1865), are best understood in an all-male context: women have no place in such poetry. It is not difficult therefore to understand the transition from the repressed homosexuality of certain Tractarians to the emphasis on Christ, not the Virgin Mary, in the poems of Newman and Faber after both men had been converted to the Roman faith.

Since Geoffrey Faber wrote *Oxford Apostles* in 1933, a book in which he disclosed underlying or repressed homosexuality in New-man's make-up, it should have been plausible to see in Newman an archetype of Englishmen passing through homosexual and religious crises during the period reviewed. Throughout that period he was much admired as a prose stylist. But when a style is admired it is often that the admiration obscures from admirers psychological links between themselves and the author.

Apart from that, if we are to believe Canon J. M. Wilson in his address to the Education Society in 1881 on *Morality in Public Schools and its Relation to Religion*, 'there is, and aways has been an undoubted coexistence of religiosity and animalism'.[2]

A further significance in the link between the Oxford Movement and the Roman Church should not be overlooked. And that is to be found in the romantic revival of chivalry. The first half of the nineteenth century in England saw a notable awakening of interest in this subject, stimulated partly no doubt by Walter Scott's novels. An early convert to Roman Catholicism, Kenelm Henry Digby, had brought out in 1822 his book, *The Broad Stone of Honour, or Rules for the Gentlemen of England*, which afterward went into several larger editions; and the

[2] *Morality in Public Schools and its Relation to Religion*, a fragment by the Rev. J. M. Wilson, Headmaster, Clifton College. Delivered as the Presidential Address to the Education Society, 1 November 1881. Printed in the Supplement to the *Journal of Education*, 1 November 1881, pp. 253–9.

Eglinton Tournament of 1839, a kind of pastiche tournament in the mediaeval style, described by Disraeli in *Endymion*, was the most spectacular expression of this revival. It is interesting to note that Edward Fitzgerald, who later translated *Omar Khayyam* and is known to have been homosexual, published his anonymous essay *Euphranor, A Dialogue on Youth* in 1851, and in this little book he gave perhaps currency to the romantic notion of bringing chivalrous values to male friendships. If Fitzgerald knew Faber I have no information of it. But already, about then, Faber revealed that a friend of his had arrived at a similar notion.[3] This quiet combination of Platonic and Neo-Gothic ideals had of course associations with the monastic institutions of that very Church towards which Faber and his friend were drawn.

The confluence of Romantic and Tractarian chivalry was later to reach a related stream in the ideals of John Addington Symonds, whose poem in honour of Walt Whitman, 'The Song of Love and Death' (c. 1875), contained one passage which went through Whitman's adhesiveness and on into a Graeco-Mediaeval chivalrous fantasy.[4]

There shall be comrades thick as flowers that crown
Valdarno's gardens in the morn of May;
On every upland and in every town
Their dauntless imperturbable array,
Serried like links of living adamant
By the sole law of love their wills obey,
Shall make the world one fellowship, and plant
New Paradise for nations yet to be.
O nobler peerage than that ancient vaunt
Of Arthur or of Roland! Chivalry
Long sought, last found! Knights of the Holy Ghost!
Phalanx Immortal! True Freemasonry,
Building your temples on no earthly coast,
But with star-fire on souls and hearts of man!
Stirred from their graves to greet your Sacred Host
The Theban lovers, rising very wan,
By death made holy, wave dim palms, and cry:
'Hail, Brothers! who achieve what we began!'

Women, it will be noted, did not come into this fantasy. Nor had they anything to do with the political amours that Symonds conceived. Farther back in the same poem he apostrophized Whitman:

[3] The relevant quotation from this letter is given by Geoffrey Faber in *Oxford Apostles*, London, 1933, p. 231.
[4] 'The Song of Love and Death' formed part of 'Love and Death – A Symphony' in *Studies in Terza Rima etc.*, privately printed, Clifton, c. 1875.

Thou dost establish – and our hearts receive –
New laws of Love to link and intertwine
Majestic peoples; Love to weld and weave
Comrade to comrade, man to bearded man,
Whereby indissoluble hosts shall cleave
Unto the primal truths republican.

All that is very well; but knowing, as we do, about John Addington
Symonds, it is difficult not to repress a smile at the thought of clashing
beards and tinkling watch-chains as the comrades became more and
more republican. Symonds was not without a sense of humour; yet
here he shared with the French generals of fifty years back a solemn
innocence of the English Eye.

The idea of chivalry between men, and between men and youths
or boys, or even between boys, survived a whole half-century, to
emerge again in Kains-Jackson's article 'The New Chivalry', published
in 1894 and included in this anthology (No. 68). Finally, Dr. Edwin
Emmanuel Bradford made *The New Chivalry* the title of one of his
books of homosexual poems in 1918.

Let us see a little more of what Canon Wilson had to say in 1881
upon what was, for him apparently, a terrifying subject. 'It must I
believe be admitted as a fact,' he emphasized, with no more than
rhetorical relish maybe, 'that immorality, used in a special sense, which
I need not define, has been of late increasing among the upper classes
in England, and specially in the great cities. Those who have the best
opportunities of knowing, who can from personal knowledge compare
the tone of society now with that of twenty, thirty, forty years ago,
speak most positively of this deterioration. This is not the place to give
details or evidence. There is amply sufficient ground for alarm that the
nation may be on the eve of an age of voluptuousness and reckless
immorality.'

Canon Wilson therefore bears out, in that estimate of his, my own
suspicion that an increase in homosexuality was observable in England
from about the middle of the nineteenth century onward – or if we
work from 1841, that is forty years from 1881, from just before 1850.
Less voluptuous forms of the menace he envisaged had for a long time
been possible and accepted, as we can see from Leigh Hunt's *Autobiography* (No. 1), in which this author looked back from 1850 to his
passionate feelings for a school friend in Regency days.

Means for the gratification of homosexual impulses in eighteenth-
century England were not rare, and probably not much rarer in proportion to the size of the population than in the Victorian age. But
literary references to homosexuality during that century and until the

beginning of our own period were generally satirical: Churchill in *The Times* and Smollett in *Roderick Random* refer to it for example with detachment as a vice, and not as an interesting phenomenon or as stimulus to aesthetic experience. It may be easy now to see, with the light of psychological analysis behind us, that many a passage in the writings of Beckford and Isaac Bickerstaffe suggests the background of a homosexual mental pattern – though this is not overtly disclosed by the words themselves. What is never felt in English literature since the seventeenth century up to about 1850 is that homosexual emotions were taken seriously, with the support of some aesthetic or some moral principle which might be a rationalization of an author's obsession, but which provided none the less an orientation affecting the whole tone (let alone the substance) of a literary production, helping thereby to set up a chain of cause and effect, of imitation and expansion, that turned what was motivated by one author into a cult expounded by his successors. Whatever we may discover about its vices, this process is not to be discovered in eighteenth-century England; but from 1850 onward it is notable in a growing spate of literary effusions, some long recognized as of merit (such as poems by Hopkins and Housman), some of historical interest chiefly, and some merely curious as laboured expressions of a wave in group psychology.

This wave broke in the Wilde trials of 1895, a climax due in part to the publicity which developments in popular journalism during the 1890s made feasible. Yet, assuming it can be discerned, how did the wave start moving in the first place? The purpose of the present anthology is to show that the existence of the wave can certainly be assumed, and that it had a high – as opposed to a vicious or pornographic – level of expression. How it came into being is a large question and one which lies beyond the scope of this introduction.

None the less I will try to summarize a few of the forces which appear to have nourished the growth of homosexuality in Victorian England. These were contingent on the changes in relations between the sexes. Among them was the presence of the sexually inhibitive matriarch as she prompted and controlled the behaviour of her young in a jealous world of unplanned families. Joined to this presence was an increase in the numbers of upper-middle-class people alongside the expansion of enterprise after the Industrial Revolution, and the desire of this class as a whole to give to its children the training that had been offered to the sons of prosperous gentry by schools like Winchester and Harrow, where homosexuality flourished because it was expedient. Then in alignment with sociological forces like these should be seen the aesthetic values inherited from eighteenth-century Neo-Classicism – those associated with the homosexual Winckelmann in fact – and the contribution of all public and grammar schools to a growing familiarity with homosexual themes in classical literature. A dependent force at work was the alternating current in the Oxford Movement, the subsequent evolution of High Anglicanism, and its persistent temptation to conversion in a very English and psychosomatic form of Romanism.

It can be argued I think that the Roman Church had greater attractions than any Protestant Church for the homosexual – both male and female – in that its theology and teaching were not based on empirical studies of the Bible. In spite of former tirades by early Fathers against sodomy, and in spite of the Aristotelian growth of Schoolmen in the Middle Ages, this teaching embodied elements of Platonism, inherited as parts of the primitive philosophical structure. Such strains permitted on the one hand, the charitable classification of homosexual emotions as mental events, leading to celibacy and dedication to the monastery or nunnery (no one need be deceived about this, or about the opportunities provided in mediaeval times for the integration of what might now be called schizoid personalities); on the other hand as mental events extending, if they extended at all in physical expression, to venial sins. By the time the Jesuits were widely established all over the world, sins of this order were accounted easy to forgive. In the Protestant communities homosexuality was more hypocritically tolerated, more deceptively expressed and less obviously waylaid in the dedicated abstention from involvement with the opposite sex which a celibate priesthood and the monastic system provided. Herbert Horne struck a chord in this key in 1891 in his poem 'Non Delebo Propter Decem' (No. 48).

The year of the publication of Hunt's *Autobiography* was also the year when *In Memoriam* was published, a long poem in which Tennyson commemorated the death of his friend Arthur Hallam in 1833. Certain chapters of *In Memoriam* have been selected here and set in sequence, though they are separated in the poem, sometimes quite widely. From this it will be seen that Tennyson used the language of deprivation, both prophetic and unconscious – 'Something it is which thou hast lost, some pleasure from thine early years' – alongside references associated with, and henceforth to be associated repeatedly with, the Shakespeare of the *Sonnets* and with Arcady and its innocent pleasures. For John Addington Symonds the word Arcadian meant homosexual, and little more; and the Greek conditions of life, the old philosophy and so on, as mentioned by Tennyson, do not differ in kind from similar references by overt homosexuals later in the same century. If some of the better passages in the poem, and some of its best-known lines, have not been included in my quotations, that is because they do not help to bring out unequivocally the allegorical elements in it which made it a vehicle for homosexual feeling. Even the figure of Urania gave a foot-hold to that association; while the consciousness of sin, together with such phrasing as 'loved deeplier, darklier understood', whatever they may have meant to Tennyson himself, contributed to the notion of a kind of attachment awkwardly close to the pederasty discussed in Plato's *Symposium* and familiar to undergraduates and even to school-boys of the period. I say awkwardly close, because unless it were main-tained at the Platonic or philosophic level (or, as earlier psychiatrists used to say, unless it were sublimated) it might have been the inspiration to a gust of unnatural vice – to use an expression even more outmoded. In this respect Tennyson, indignant though he would have been to be linked thus, might be classified as the author of *In Memoriam* with the hero of *Teleny*, in the context of erotic relationships between males.

We differ from him chiefly in this: that we believe it is a physical orientation which counts, not the degree of its expression. And the fact that Tennyson evolved an emphatically heterosexual image in later life does nothing to disqualify him as homosexual when he wrote *In Memoriam*, or in that part of his temperament he kept sensitive to the memory of Hallam; so that the love of his friend became greater than it had been when he was alive, and the object of this attachment became identified with the cosmos – not God – at the same time helping the author, in his sadness, to justify the inscrutable ways of God to Man.

A lot of the imagery of the poem is that of the conventional lover, as when Tennyson writes of the bereavement of the widower, or when the intimacy between himself and Hallam is illustrated by a reference to thought leaping out 'to wed with Thought e'er Thought could wed itself with speech'. The symbols of desire are conveyed archly in the 'secrets of the Spring (moving) in the chambers of the blood'; and in the possessive chant of 'Mine, mine for ever, ever mine'.

When the poem was published it was taken apparently at its face value, and so provided both a relief and a language of lament for those readers who were either committed to unrequited homosexual feeling in place of all other sexual instinct, or, while passing through a phase of such feeling, remained in ignorance of its true implications. *In Memoriam* was reviewed in *The Times* with a certain reserve; and the occasion was not let slip to point out that the undertones of the poem were, at least from the reviewer's standpoint, unconventional. But its popularity, which was not long in arriving, suggests that others besides Tennyson could be swayed by the author's unconventional symbolism, which either was, or soon became, the symbolism of unexplained emotions in numerous readers. Queen Victoria, who much admired the poem, presumably skated over the undertones and applied the general sense to her own situation as a widow. *In Memoriam* was so frequently quoted in print during the years 1850–1900 that a pursuit of the references would be both easy and tiresome. This popularity was due not only to the length of the poem, to its skilful versification, or to the moralistic reflections it contained. It was due also, I have little doubt, to the relevance of the undertones to the condition of certain readers (No. 2).

Whereas Tennyson's friendship with Hallam had been one between young men of approximate ages, the friendships of William Johnson, better known by the name he adopted, William Cory, were formed among pupils he taught at Eton where he became an assistant master in 1845. As author of the Eton Boating Song, Cory can scarcely be said to have been forgotten by his own school; and as author of the lines beginning 'They told me, Heraclitus, they told me you were dead', he has been represented in anthologies, as he is represented here again. But as the author of a collection of verses, *Ionica*, containing some of the best examples of classical prosody in English, he is likely still to be underrated. The earliest group of these poems, first published in 1858, addressed to Charles Wood and reflecting his pederastic tastes, began to be disparaged around 1920; since when the discreet but sincere feelings expressed in them have been, all too crudely, dismissed as sentimental (Nos. 4, 5, 6).

While it would be difficult to come anywhere near gauging the extent of Cory's influence on his pupils at Eton, this was undoubtedly great, especially when he became emotionally involved with them; which he did on the analogy of the ancient Greek pupil-teacher relationship. Naturally he had his favourites. With such a system all his pupils could not be equally favoured, and complaints from a parent that Cory had gone too far with one of them caused his downfall in 1872. Cory left Eton under a cloud; but as time went by he discovered that he also could be involved with persons of the other sex. His later poems showed this. At length he married and had a son. Several generations of boys, remembering him with affection as a master, included Algernon Drummond, R. B. Brett (Lord Esher), Henry Scott Holland, Francis Eliot, W. O. Burrows, Charles Wood (Lord Halifax), Lord Rosebery, Lord Chichester, and many others – and some of these did little to restrain their pederastic habits in later years. The romantic, rather chauvinistic, Cory was commemorated in Henry Newbolt's poem 'Ionicus' (1898).

One Eton boy exceptionally impressed Cory, not as a budding statesman or as a noble ornament of society but as a poet simply; and that was Digby Mackworth Dolben (Plate 1), who proved in his short life how a passion for the Oxford Movement could be inlaid with a vital passion for romantic friendships. And with Dolben this was indeed a passion, as anyone may feel in the verses he showed to Cory and to his senior at Eton, Robert Bridges. It was not until 1911 that Bridges published Dolben's poems.[5] But before that time many of them were known already to a limited circle at Oxford including Gerard Manley Hopkins and Canon Richard Watson Dixon. Cory went to the length of copying out some of these poems, and in other ways warmly encouraging the young Christian – whose emotionalism had a quality somewhere between Tennyson's idealism and Faber's effusiveness. Both Cory and Dolben were admirers of Tennyson: the Faber element in Dolben's verses was deplored by Bridges, however. At the same time, and unlike Henry Newman and Hurrell Froude, both of whom were repressed homosexuals, Faber counted as the popular poet of the Oxford Movement, and later of the Perverts (as converts to Rome were called in those days). He was the one who expressed almost blatantly in his poems and in his hymns a mixture of that homosexual sentiment and religiosity on which the Oxford Movement was to some extent nourished. With less facile accomplishments than Faber, Dolben – 'readier to turn symbols into flesh than flesh into symbols', as Bridges said – was moving in a similar direction when he was drowned in 1867 at the age of 19, just before going up as an undergraduate to Oxford. This tragedy affected the young Hopkins, who had met Dolben once in 1863 at Oxford and had been strongly attracted to him (No. 9).

Of the three sonnets by Hopkins included here, the earliest drafts date from 6–8 May in 1865; that is, at a time not very long after Hopkins had met Dolben in the previous February and following his religious crisis in March.[6] According to Gardner, a poem 'Where art thou, friend', dating from 25–27 April 1865, could have alluded to Dolben or to 'some fascinating stranger'. Anyhow, all four poems seem to allude to men and not to women, and Dolben's struggles with his own homosexual passions might well have had an effect of causing sympathetic vibrations in Hopkins. This probability is strengthened in the evidence of Robert Bridges, the first editor of Hopkins, noting in a later manuscript version of the first and third sonnets that they 'must *never* be printed'. It is difficult to believe his directive referred to the workmanship, because that is not inferior to the workmanship of certain other early poems edited by Bridges.

The sonnets concentrate on the pain of withdrawal from an infatuation, and there seem to be undercurrents of realization that this state was linked with the religious crisis, yet in conflict with that crisis.

[5] *The Poems of Digby Mackworth Dolben,* edited with a Memoir by Robert Bridges, London, 1911.
[6] See *Poems of Gerard Manley Hopkins,* edited by W. H. Gardner, London, 1948, pp. 214, 215, Nos. 8, 9.

It may have been the conflict rather than any literal rebuff to his approaches that induced Hopkins to see himself in the eyes of his friend as a despicable person; for it was unlikely that Dolben of all people would have encouraged him in such a belief.

At the end of the third sonnet a line was drawn in the 1865 manuscript and a new and incomplete sequence of verses was begun, apparently on a heterosexual theme.

Except for some pieces published in anthologies, Hopkins's poetry, as a body of work, was not presented to the public until 1918, and its hermetic character could have had small bearing in his lifetime on any but a few friends like Canon Dixon and Robert Bridges. The poems introduced into the present anthology are here mainly to indicate what links arise, or may have arisen then, between homosexual emotional crises and religious emotional crises. It is not hard to see how the difficulty of gratifying erotic emotions on one plane – the difficulty of *l'amour de l'impossible* – led by imaginative extensions to a vanishing point of safety in 'God'. For the 'love of God', a predominantly Christian conception, can only be communicated in figures of speech inspired originally by erotic sensations; and this spiritual love on the part of men for a masculine force can thus be rendered backwards into homosexual emotion which has taken refuge in the clouds of intellect. However religious we may be, we should recognize that the idea of God is arrived at by argument supported by feeling, and not by demonstration. The word 'God' may well stand for an idea based on, or emanating from, an awareness of a superior or 'supernatural' force. But whether our emotions reveal it to us or not, the existence of such a force is irrelevant to the verbal convenience of 'God'. This idea of 'God' is the fruit of intellectual acts which rationalize the experience of inhibiting erotic emotions from human (or animal) objectives, and the equally curious experience of attempting to anthropomorphize the unknown, or what we do not understand. As it is, we have to describe and discuss not the emotions of God in regard to us, of which we can know nothing, but our emotions in respect of God, which have to be framed in words of all too human limitation.

When Hopkins composed his poem on 'The Bugler's First Communion' (No. 21), therefore, he gave a description of his excitement at the prospect of a youth willing to enter by means of the ritual act into quasi-tangible relationship with God. This relationship is sanctioned as one of love; and Hopkins's excitement is partly, indeed largely, one of discovering that the bugler and he are both involved in an emotional triangle; but also that the bugler happens to be a young male 'breathing bloom of chastity in mansex fine'. The erotic nature of the poet's excitement may be left to extrude itself if we imagine him faced with the task of writing a comparable piece on the first communion of some hideous, some delinquent, butcher. As it was, Hopkins accounted disingenuously for the feelings inspired in him by the bugler in transferring them to an orthodox excitement at the bugler's awakening piety.

Concealed or indirect homosexual emotion was behind several more of Hopkins's poems; 'The Brothers', for instance and 'Epithalamion' (No. 39), the second of which hinges upon a vision of boys in the same region of experience as Corvo's 'Ballade of Boys Bathing' (No. 43) and numerous other pederastic bathing verses of the 1890s. For in this poem a peak of excitement is reached in describing the natural beauties of a place in 'the loins of hills', where a bevy of boys 'with down-dolphinry and bellbright bodies' are seen to plunge into a river. In order to extend this excitement, Hopkins introduces a stranger who observes the boys, and is inspired thereby to take off his clothes and imitate them by plunging into a neighbouring pool. And if the symbolism of this were not enough, Hopkins ends the passage by asking what is water; and concluding that it is spousal love. The poem was intended as an ode on the occasion of his brother's marriage in 1888. But the symbol of the water in this case – water that is shared and entered by boys and stranger – is the symbol of a current which links the bellbright bodies of all concerned. And only by courtesy can we allow it to be, in any sense, either feminine or asexual.

Literary influences, it will be agreed, are not simply stylistic, but also psychological, moral and sentimental (in the sense of suggesting sentiments). Important factors in the establishing of a homosexual climate in our period were those of the poetry, and, also in some degree, the personality of Algernon Swinburne. One feature that readers took from his poetry – by which I mean one that impressed them, one they remembered sometimes unconsciously and reproduced sometimes in their verses – was the concentration of his own peculiar mental erethism in vivid imagery. This vividness was not so much the vividness of precision as the vivid quality of verbal intoxication; and those who let themselves be partly intoxicated by it found themselves introduced sideways, as it were, to various deviations from routine eroticism.

The poems of Swinburne which deal most consistently with homosexual subjects are 'Anactoria', 'Fragoletta' and 'Hermaphroditus'.[7] As regards 'Hermaphroditus', a point of interest, especially to homosexually-inclined readers, was that it stood alone in being the first openly published English *poem* on such a subject since the seventeenth

[7] These three poems by Swinburne appeared in *Poems and Ballads*, London, 1866.

century in which the 'argument' was sensual and not satirical nor, as in Cory's poems, sentimental. The effect on such a reader in 1866 when the poem was published must have been one in which thoughts, visions, feelings were aroused and fused into a mood having a primary aesthetic justification – not, as in the eighteenth century, an aesthetically satirical justification. In the opinion of Alice Meynell the poem was one of Swinburne's worst: in the view of John D. Rosenburg, in a recent paper on the poet, it is called 'one of his earliest and finest poems'.[8] It consists of a four-sonnet sequence, ostensibly inspired by a statue in the Louvre in 1863. But the Louvre inspiration was itself suggested by a stream of French literature dealing with hermaphroditism – clearly well-known to Swinburne (No. 8).

Chronological priority in this stream must be given to Henri de Latouche's *Fragoletta*, which became also the title of one of Swinburne's poems in the particular group. Latouche's *Fragoletta* had less of the female than the male in her make-up; and since this is true as well of Swinburne's 'Fragoletta', the balance of sense seems to be toward male homosexuality rather than toward lesbianism. The second example known to Swinburne of an epicene character in French literature was Balzac's Séraphita in his romance of the same name. According to Randolph Hughes,[9] Swinburne had read *Séraphita* before he left Oxford, because the title appears in a list of books borrowed by him from the library of the Taylorian Institute in 1859–60. Balzac also wrote one straightforward lesbian story *La Fille aux Yeux d'Or*, and one novel *Sarrasine*, which is the story of Zambinella, a castrated male: and with both of these works Swinburne seems to have been well acquainted. But anxiety to combine certain aesthetic qualities of males with certain attributes of females found its best exponent in Théophile Gautier, who in the poem 'Contralto' provided a close antecedent to Swinburne's 'Hermaphroditus'. And in the romance *Mademoiselle de Maupin* Gautier wrote a source-book for homosexuals of either sex for many years afterwards.

The idea that a preoccupation with lesbianism proved the exclusively heterosexual nature of both Gautier and Swinburne, which Hughes maintained, seems altogether too simple to let pass. That they were at the same time horrified, or supposed to be horrified, at pederasty implied a state of guilt about this subject. And the fact that they sought hermaphrodite ideals suggests that femininity in any sort of excess was unsatisfactory for them. In so far as they were interested at all in

[8] Alice Meynell's opinion was given in *Hearts of Controversy*, London, 1917, p. 71. John D. Rosenberg's opinion is to be found in *Victorian Studies*, December 1967, Vol. XI, No. 2, 'Swinburne', p. 149.

[9] Randolph Hughes (ed.), Swinburne's *Lesbia Brandon*, London, 1952, p. 403.

combining various attributes of the sexes, we can infer that their orientations were not fixed but in transit, and, at least part of the time, still automatically registering the attractions of their own sex.

It is tempting therefore to see Swinburne as a bridge-builder for the cult of French 'hermaphroditism' as he knew it in the form of a literary obsession. And if something of French literary hermaphroditism was transmitted by Swinburne into England, it would perhaps have had small growth in this country, were it not that conditions for it thrived already. We discover two of these, as we might expect, in the boyish libertinism of the boarding schools, and in the pupil-teacher relationship glorified by Cory.

As most people know by this time, Swinburne was a masochist visiting a brothel in Regent's Park at intervals to get himself flagellated. Ever since he left Eton he seems to have indulged in visions of being beaten; and in his doggerel manuscripts *The Flogging Block, The Whip-pingham Papers* and other unpublished pieces, he left evidence of that side of his nature.[10] The poems deal with schoolmasters flogging school-boys. It might be argued therefore that here was a transition in the objectives of his aberration, in its Etonian form within homosexual limits, to its Regent's Park form, which meant beatings by women. But on the many occasions Swinburne referred to this subject in letters to friends,[11] it will be noted that the preoccupation with schoolboy floggings persisted, and that he seemed to have carried the memory of early experiences in homosexual terms, at the same time extending his interest to the urbane fashion of gratifying masochism which, from the few records we have on such a subject, appears to have been hetero-sexual. Two planes of masochism in Swinburne are thus revealed: a homosexual one for retrospective verses on schoolboys, and a hetero-sexual one for being beaten by women in Regent's Park. As a poet with a wide acquaintance he acted as propagandist for tastes on both these planes.

Eton can scarcely be held accountable for making Swinburne what he was; otherwise his contemporaries who went to the same school would have shared his obsessions. Some shared them perhaps; but we can safely conclude the majority did not. And in any case his early life was not all passed at Eton. We cannot overlook factors contributing to what may be accepted as early masochistic conditioning. This is for somebody else to work out; here I am simply emphasizing Swinburne's awareness of homosexuality and the reflection of this awareness in what he wrote. Enlightenment could have sprung from his readings of

[10] The manuscripts of Swinburne's flogging pieces are in the British Museum, but do not appear in the published catalogues.

[11] See Swinburne's letters of the 1860s and 1870s in *The Swinburne Letters*, edited by Cecil Y. Lang, New Haven, 1959.

Gautier and Baudelaire, or from those passages in Balzac's *Comédie Humaine* describing the homosexual relationship between Vautrin and Rubempré. Yet hints emerge that Swinburne may have had glimmerings of some earlier enlightenment before he read any works by these authors. Indeed, nobody in considering him seems to have stressed the importance of the times spent as a guest of his grandfather, Sir John Swinburne, at Capheaton, near Newcastle. There it was that he visited for long periods during his holidays from school; and if his grandfather had anything in common with his father these visits would have had little significance. Sir John, however, was not at all like Algernon's father. For one thing, the old baronet undertook to fill the gaps in his grandson's education by teaching him French and Italian, and by preventing him from reading any fiction. In the article by Gosse in the *Dictionary of National Biography* we learn that the grandfather had a strong influence upon the grandson. Curiosity about this baronet becomes especially relevant.

So far as we are concerned, the chief point of interest about Sir John Swinburne was that, as a young man, he had spent an impressionable period in Paris during the last years of the *ancien régime*. Here he had got to know various radical thinkers and libertines of that time and place. Memories of his youth seemed to guide him through life, and even as an old man when his grandson knew him he still preserved views and prejudices of those long-dead *Encyclopédistes*, cultivating, as Gosse says, the memory of Mirabeau. It was not a far cry from cultivating the memory of Mirabeau to cultivating the sexual licence of that republican voluptuary, if not in practice, for which we have no evidence, then perhaps in theory – which possibility we have nothing to contradict. Around the time when his grandson was staying with him, Sir John was still friendly with William Mulready the painter, whose pederastic activities appear to have wrecked his marriage in the 1820s.[12] That a particle of Sir John's devotion to Mirabeau, or of his friendship with Mulready, should have brushed off on Algernon Swinburne as a youth is, of course, conjecture. But to this conjecture we join the known facts: that Swinburne took shape later as a radical in politics, somewhat in the manner of certain French eighteenth-century nobles; and that his obsession with the Marquis de Sade, whose works he had read by the end of 1861, fitted loosely into the background presented by his grandfather, who died in 1860. Was there a chain of association running from Mirabeau to Algernon Swinburne? Was the near-impotent erethism of the poet a thriving development alongside his memory of the punishments at school?

[12] A letter dated 1827 from Mulready's wife complaining of his pederastic activities is in the Library of the Victoria and Albert Museum.

In 1865 Swinburne went to Oxford, and in the following year he met Rossetti and the other Pre-Raphaelite artists engaged on painting the walls of the Union there. It was in these Pre-Raphaelite circles that he made the acquaintance of the young Jewish painter Simeon Solomon. With Solomon he was on terms of friendship by the early 1860s. During his stay with Rossetti in Cheyne Walk he and his new friend were supposed to have chased each other naked down the staircase at Number 16, much to Rossetti's annoyance. In these years too he seems to have introduced Solomon to Walt Whitman's *Leaves of Grass* which had appeared in 1855: the attractions of the section 'Calamus' in this bookful of poems lay precisely in its marked homosexual character.

Solomon was perhaps destined to be homosexual whether he met Swinburne or not; but his deference in correspondence and his indebtedness to the poet for all kinds of sexual lore leave one with the impression that Swinburne acted towards him as an agent provocateur, as we shall note. Meanwhile Solomon was subjected to another sophisticated influence, from Oscar Browning, a pupil of William Cory at Eton and a master there, who met the young Jewish painter as a guest at Fryston, Lord Houghton's country house in Yorkshire. Lord Houghton, with his library of erotica, was a formative influence on all these men: it was from him that Swinburne borrowed the works of the Marquis de Sade in 1861. Moreover, Houghton's collected poems – many written in the pre-Victorian years – were published in 1859 and included one or two with sufficiently ambiguous undertones to suggest the likelihood of a homosexual phase in their author. Swinburne had been introduced to Houghton in 1861; and he fostered the affair between Browning and Solomon to which Houghton provided a background at Fryston. Another person whose orbit for a time crossed that of Solomon was Edward Poynter, the artist, for whom in 1865 Solomon made a series of allegorical drawings with homosexual insinuations, one of which showed schoolboys embracing (Plate 2). In the following year Solomon went with Browning for a tour in Italy, an experience which may have disinhibited the young painter profoundly.

Surviving correspondence between Swinburne and Solomon shows them to have been mutually excited by a variety of sexual subjects, mostly deviant, the poet for example making his by this time facetious comments about Sade, and with Solomon sharing great excitement over the transvestites Boulton and Park who were brought to trial and acquitted in 1870. As yet Swinburne had shown no repugnance for homosexual themes: his first series of *Poems and Ballads* had appeared in 1866 and included the one lesbian and two hermaphrodite vignettes already mentioned – all tributes to French pioneers. At some date before 1865 he had got to know George Powell, a fellow ex-Etonian, with whom he stayed in Wales and in France during the later 1860s and 1870. The Goncourt brothers recorded in 1875 that Guy de Maupassant told them he had met the poet and his friend Powell in 1870 at Étretat, where the two men were living in a hired cottage. In the course of several visits to this romantic hideout Maupassant was shown erotic photographs of youthful males; and also he noticed that Powell had fourteen-year-old boys as servants from England. There was a monkey as well, which slept in Powell's bed. Maupassant assumed both Englishmen to be pederasts. Even if this were untrue of Swinburne, his obvious enjoyment of Powell's way of living supports a belief that, as Sade's disciple, he was willing to foster the homosexual spirit in others, before 1873. Indeed it was during this period, in the late 1860s probably, that he asked Solomon especially to provide him with drawings of boys being flogged by schoolmasters.

Solomon had visited Italy again with Browning in 1868 and 1869, and according to Edmund Gosse he was threatened with legal proceedings for sexual acts at some time in the following year, when he went off once more to Italy, this time presumably to avoid unpleasant consequences.[13] His one literary adventure, the allegorical prose poem *A Vision of Love Revealed in Sleep* (No. 15), had been written in Rome in 1869 and was published in 1871. It was shot through with homosexual masochism, reflecting perhaps in its serious way something of Swinburne's flippant obsessions at the time. Anyhow, Swinburne gave it a long puff in *The Dark Blue* magazine, not without critical comments which annoyed its author. The first signs of estrangement began to show. A period of indiscretions was at hand. Early in 1873 Solomon was caught with a man called Roberts in a public urinal north of Oxford Street, and sentenced to eighteen months' imprisonment in Clerkenwell House of Correction.[14] The sentence was suspended and police supervision was imposed. In due course, after hearing of this, Swinburne went to Oxford about 23 May, Gosse recalled, largely to discuss Solomon with his friend Walter Pater. His attitude to the young artist changed very quickly.[15] He began to think of Solomon with horror; but this did not prevent him from viewing George Powell as before with approval, and continuing to pester, or to amuse, his friends with jokes about whipping and the Eton Block. Indignation against Solomon rose to screaming point when the poet discovered his former companion was selling his letters.[16] It is possible that Solomon would

[13] See Margery Ross, *Robert Ross, Friend of Friends*, London, 1952. Letter to Robert Ross from Edmund Gosse, 20 August 1917, p. 315.
[14] Detailed information on this subject was kindly sent to me by Mr. Lionel Lambourne, who has made a close study of the life and art of Simeon Solomon.
[15] See Margery Ross, op. cit., p. 315.
[16] See Cecil Y. Lang (ed.), op. cit., pp. 253, 261, 264 etc.

never have sunk to expedients like this had Swinburne behaved to him with ordinary charity, instead of what was extraordinary and hysterical inconsistency.

Meanwhile Swinburne's natural afflatus had fanned another spark, this time in the mysterious heart of Walter Pater.

Pater had first met Swinburne at Oxford as a member of the Old Mortality club in 1858. From the date of the poet's first published work in 1860, *The Queen Mother and Rosamund*, he was vulnerable to a combined fascination of style and eroticism in Swinburne's writings. The next stage, in the 1860s, was for Solomon, through Swinburne, to make friends with Pater and to stay with him in Oxford; and moreover to draw his portrait, which he gave to him.

Now Pater was a grey sheep from another flock. In his earlier years his ambition had been to take orders, and through life he retained an interest in ecclesiastical ritual. From the paths of the Oxford Movement he strayed, or rather crossed over, to the Renaissance – to what, for comparison's sake, we might nickname Vanity Fair. Influenced by Swinburne's style and the strange moods conveyed in the poet's manner of writing and also by Jahn's life of the German antiquary Winckelmann, Pater came forward in 1867 with an article in *The Westminster Review* about this eighteenth-century scholar (No. 12), and in November 1869 with another one in *The Fortnightly Review* on Leonardo da Vinci. Yet another appeared in November 1871, again in *The Fortnightly Review*, on Michelangelo. It can be supposed that his interest in the slant of these subjects was markedly buttressed by Swinburne, both as a writer and as a character, and by the friendship which Pater enjoyed, through Swinburne, with the young Solomon. Pater also became an admirer of Solomon's drawings and paintings of youths, conceived at this date somewhat in the manner of Rossetti's paintings of idealized women.

Hearing that Solomon had been charged in London, Swinburne wrote to Powell to say that Pater knew something about it. Whatever Pater may have known about it, he must have felt it was unfortunate to be associated with a classified deviant, even if the senior dons, other than Swinburne's friend Benjamin Jowett, were unaware of Solomon's existence. In which case it was equally unfortunate that hard on the heels of the London scandal there should arrive by the autumn of 1873 the first copies of *Studies in the History of the Renaissance*, containing the above articles collected between covers, with some other essays of Pater's on contingent matters. He seems to have been affected by a sense of guilt; or maybe by the caricature of himself as Mr. Rose in W. H. Mallock's *New Republic*, which came out soon afterwards in the magazine *Belgravia*. Or perhaps Oxford innuendos were too much for

him. The fact remains that in the second edition of *Studies*, published
in 1877, he cut out the famous 'Conclusion' to the essays. He conceived,
so he said in a note in the third edition (1888), 'it might possibly mislead
some of those young men into whose hands it might fall . . . (and) I have
dealt more fully in *Marius the Epicurean* with the thoughts suggested
by it' (No. 29).

By doing that, of course, Pater dissociated himself a little from the
parlour hedonism of the Aesthetic movement. And it was true that
much of what he wrote in the 'Conclusion', as far back as 1868, was
echoed and amplified in this later book *Marius the Epicurean* (1885).
In that novel it will be noted how male friendships were among the
more powerful emotions described; and not only were these dependent
on physical attractiveness and therefore strictly erotic, but they were
linked dramatically to religious crises. Pater's personal crisis, however,
occurred in an opposite sense to that of almost everybody else who had
then encountered the Oxford Movement; whereas their conflicts drove
them on – in Faber's case to a fulsome Catholicism – Pater's drove him
out, to become the apostle of a form of aestheticism in which religion
had a secondary, if not a subordinate, place. He became, it appears, an
addictive cigarette-smoker.[17]

The most difficult passage in the 'Conclusion', from Pater's viewpoint, was this: 'While all melts under our feet, we may well catch at
any exquisite passion, or any contribution to knowledge that seems, by
a lifted horizon, to set the spirit free for a moment, or any stirring of
the senses, strange dyes, strange flowers, and curious odours, or work
of the artist's hands, or the face of one's friend'.

It was not much. But whatever it was, it was a significant gesture
in the Victorian moral continuum.

I would advocate here that the influence of Cory's *Ionica* on Pater,
which has, so far as I know, never been considered, is hinted at in the
even more famous passage on the Gioconda, by the reference there to
her 'fallen day'. The image is striking, since after all there would occur
to most of us certain other conditions which might be 'about her';
while at the same time the use of the phrase 'fallen day' provides a very
particular and mysterious effect. Yet, as we can see in No. 5, the
phrase was used by Cory in 1858 before Pater used it, and this may be
the only evidence which remains to suggest that Pater read *Ionica*,
or was clearly, if quietly, impressed by this book of poems. John
Addington Symonds noted that it was making a stir in Oxford in
1859. So Cory's importance as a coach, so to say, in the cult of Victorian pederasty had at least one side-effect – that is in matters of
style, often no doubt in the works of those very persons whose

[17] See Louise Jopling, *Twenty Years of My Life*, London, 1925, p. 273.

enthusiasm for *Ionica* sprang from some emotional coincidence: like Pater perhaps.

Certainly Cory had an influence, and a more direct influence, on John Addington Symonds. Indeed Symonds took the trouble to write specially to the Eton poet, whose *Ionica* had been given to him by Professor Conington at Oxford.[18] In his letter he frankly admitted his pederastic inclinations, and asked to be advised. The reply he received from Cory included 'a long and passionate defence of pederasty'. 'I used to dote on that book (*Ionica*) when I was a lad at Oxford', wrote Symonds to his daughter Madge in 1892. His early years had been distressed by a powerful struggle between duty and inclination, between his father's morality and his own fixations on choirboys and male genitals. *Ionica* gave him the encouragement he needed first of all to write poetry, and second of all to externalize in this poetry his constantly accumulating sexual urges. An early example of this is 'What Cannot Be' (No. 7), written in 1861 about a Bristol choirboy named Alfred Brooke. In republishing this poem for ordinary distribution in later years, Symonds altered the word 'he' in line 12 to 'she'.[19]

In what Symonds called the 'peccant pamphlets' of his verses, often limited to ten or twenty copies, which he distributed among such friends as Arthur and Henry Sidgwick, F. W. H. Myers and Graham Dakyns – like himself all repressed pederasts – there is, in the earlier ones, some imitation of Cory's Grecian manner, on a different plane of accomplishment. Symonds's virtues as a poet, like Cory's usually ignored by modern commentators, were none the less dissimilar from Cory's own: he was less resigned, less careful of the texture of his verse, more determined to have out with it, that he possessed all the secrets of Arcadian or Greek love, as he called the homosexual emotions in general. In 1878 his poem 'Eudiades', inspired ten years earlier by Norman Moor, a boy at Clifton College (near which Symonds lived), was printed in one of these pamphlets entited *Tales of Ancient Greece, No. 1*. The poem expressed Symonds's worries around 1868, and tells of an affair between a young man and a boy, the boy becoming so anxious to please that he offers himself for copulation. But the man resists, and later the two die in battle having never sullied their ideal of love by 'shame' (No. 13).

Mrs. Grosskurth, in her life of Symonds, leaves us with the impression that he restrained himself from physical intimacy with the boys he knew until he met Roden Noel the poet, when he threw off his timidity and let himself go, first with the uninhibited Noel, and later

[18] Phyllis Grosskurth, *John Addington Symonds*, London, 1964, p. 48.
[19] 'What Cannot be' appeared on p. 32 of *Crocuses and Soldanellas* by John Addington Symonds, privately printed, Clifton, c. 1879.

SH- C

in London with male prostitutes. Symonds's own account of his sexual life which appears as Case XVIII in Havelock Ellis's *Sexual Inversion* (1897) implies that his first collaborative orgasm was shared with a soldier; while Noel himself, in the contribution he made to the same book under Case XXVII, insists that he was not particularly keen on the consummation of aggressive drives, but mainly on courting the admiration of younger people, male or female. 'Eudiades' shows Symonds advancing from the 'platonic' verses of the early 1860s to more physiological themes; and by 1875 when he printed 'Midnight at Baiae' in *Lyra Viginti Cordarum*[20] he had come to the point of being able to imagine sadistic lusts (No. 18). In the 1870s however his objectives changed, and as he grew older he became less interested in boys and more interested in young men, and receptive also to the idea of 'adhesiveness' recommended by Whitman as a binding medium of democracy. It was then that Symonds turned his attention to Swiss peasants and, in the following decade, to Venetian gondoliers. The long poem 'Stella Maris', though addressed to a female (even in the peccant pamphlets before reprinting), was really inspired by his Venetian experiences (No. 25).[21] It shows that he had come a long way from the position maintained by Cory. Like Swinburne before he began to disparage Whitman, Symonds was an admirer of the American poet, to whom he paid tribute in his long poem 'The Song of Love and Death: A Symphony'.[22] But when he corresponded with Whitman about the implications of 'Calamus' the other refused to admit that he had condoned any kind of eroticism in his references to friendship between males.[23] At the end of 'Stella Maris' Symonds revealed that by this time he was prepared to get what he wanted on any terms, however sordid such terms might have seemed to him in younger days. As he struggled with religious precepts, not to speak of conventional mores, he contradicted himself time and again; yet in his determination to share himself with the world he showed courage.

Roden Noel on the other hand, credited though he is with having helped Symonds towards homosexual self-expression, had a patrician indifference to self-justification, believing, according to his own account of himself, that he had inherited from his mother's family a tendency

[20] 'Midnight at Baiae' was first printed privately by J. A. Symonds in *Lyra Viginti Cordarum*, Clifton, c. 1875. Another version was printed in *The Artist*, March 1893, with the first ten lines of the 1875 version omitted and certain tactful amendments introduced. Symonds claimed the poem recorded an actual dream of his (see *The Artist*, March 1893, p. 70).

[21] 'Stella Maris' was a sonnet sequence originally printed privately in *The Sea Calls*,(?) London, c. 1884, and in the same year in *Vagabunduli Libellis*. The poem was inspired between September 1881 and April 1882 by the gondolier Angelo Fusato (see Grosskurth, op. cit., p. 242).

[22] 'Love and Death – A Symphony'. See Note 4 to the introduction.

[23] Grosskurth, op. cit., pp. 233–5, 272–4.

to homosexuality.[24] His great-uncle had been the famous Percy Jocelyn, Bishop of Clogher, who in 1822 was caught with a soldier in a tavern in St. Alban's Place, and then broke bail to fly to Scotland. Noel's amativeness was almost an inverted parody of Whitman's adhesiveness, since he confessed to being somewhat vain. What he enjoyed most was for young men or women to express admiration for him physically; and if he was bold in pursuing this pleasure he may not have been otherwise sexually aggressive. Walt Whitman's creed of democracy through adhesiveness suited him well, and he was among the earliest of Englishmen to write at any length on *Leaves of Grass*, which he did in *The Dark Blue* in 1871. In spite of his background he prided himself on being an unaffected disciple of the American poet.

While the shape of versification in the 'Ganymede' of 1868 links Noel clearly with eighteenth-century poems in the Miltonic tradition, the visual imagery of the subject has a parallel and a pretext in the vogue for nude boy-children associated with Raphael and his school. In Noel's 'Water Nymph' of 1872 pederastic images were presented through the fictional thoughts of a mermaid. An odd, apparently deliberate, omission of commas, an occasionally remarkable phrase – these two features together distinguish the works of this now forgotten poet. In a large part of his published work there seems to be a consistent ambivalent glow, suggesting that here was a man, happily married and with a family, who throughout adult life was beset strongly by both homosexual and heterosexual feelings (Nos. 14, 47).

After 1855, when *Leaves of Grass* was published, Walt Whitman counted as the most influential of the poets who brought forms of homosexual sentiment prominently into their writings. In America the effect of Whitman's message on younger generations was evident enough during the last half of the nineteenth century. In England he had staunch supporters from Roden Noel to Richard Le Gallienne, while some of the pioneers of socialism, who were also homosexual, found in 'Calamus' the arguments for expressing libidos alongside political doctrines.

If Edward Carpenter (Plate 3) gave priority to his emotions of love over his political feelings, none the less his gospel of brotherliness could be said, in his eyes, to have been the essence of a true democracy. In this of course he was guided by Whitman, whose *Leaves of Grass* fell into his hands some years before he published *Narcissus and Other Poems*, after a visit to Italy in 1873. In 1874 he gave up a curateship of St. Edwards in Cambridge and his Fellowship at Trinity Hall, and in the same year became a University Extension Lecturer. But within four

---

[24] Havelock Ellis and John Addington Symonds, *Sexual Inversion*, London, 1897, Case XXVII, pp. 75–6.

years after meeting Whitman in 1877 in the United States, Carpenter broke with his former background, and turned to market-gardening, then to sandal-making, and to working-class companionship in the North of England. Among these 'comrades' of his were Albert Fearnehough and George Merrill; while a poetic disciple emerged in the 1880s in James Morgan Brown of Glasgow (No. 62), of whom he wrote an account.

Carpenter's lecture on homosexuality, which he called *Homogenic Love*, given in Manchester in 1894, was printed for wider distribution than Symonds's *A Problem in Modern Ethics* (1891), and, indebted to the former work though it was, it deserves to be reprinted here because it was the third of the pioneering essays on the subject to be delivered in English (No. 70). Like Symonds and the Prussian writer Ulrichs in the 1860s, Carpenter tended to glorify overt homosexual behaviour among Urnings (Ulrichs' word) or congenital inverts as if they were a race apart. Symonds's notion of a third sex, even as a convenient classification of the sexually intermediate, has long been rejected since Freud, among others, pointed out its untenability in the face of psychological and biological advances. Since then the notion of a third sex, privileged to live and to behave like some in-group of hermaphrodites, never regained the attraction that it had for Urnings at the close of the nineteenth century (No. 51).

The first phase of the movement outlined here may be said to have been punctuated by the indiscretions of the 1870s. Thus we have Cory's resignation from Eton in 1872; Oscar Browning's resignation from the same school in 1875; Solomon's encounter with the law in 1873; Pater's publication of *Studies in the History of the Rennaissance* later in the same year; Swinburne's collapse and his reform undertaken by Watts Dunton in 1879. All these men were stimulated by views and literature of the 1860s or earlier. The second phase, or what for convenience we may understand as a second phase, appeared during the 1880s, in the wake of the Aesthetic cult; and it had behind it the force of the writings and personalities of those who had been mentioned in the first phase.

The second phase opened neatly with the publicity accorded to Oscar Wilde, during and after his visit to America; and it closed with the noise of a trial amplified to extremes by publicity again, and prejudicial to its victim in the events of 1895.

A belief that Wilde was first seriously initiated in homosexual practices only as late as 1886, when he met Robert Ross, then an undergraduate at King's College, Cambridge – this belief asserted by Arthur Ransome in his critical study of 1912 – is no longer held. It seems more likely that Wilde's initiation took place during his Oxford period, about the time when he made friends with Francis Miles, a young dilettante artist of ambisexual tastes; and also with Miles's friend Lord Ronald Gower, a notorious homosexual, one of the models for Lord Henry Wotton in *The Picture of Dorian Gray*. When Wilde began to live in London he took rooms with Miles in Salisbury Street near to the Embankment at Charing Cross, and it might be guessed it was then that he came to know Henry Marillier, a boy friend of Miles's, with whom he may have had some kind of connection.[25] What concerns us here is that a similar kind of connection may have linked Wilde and Rennell Rodd, the young poet who had taken a lead in the production of the Oxford magazine *Waifs and Strays*, and the winner of the Newdigate Prize two years after Wilde himself. Some of Wilde's earliest poems appeared in *Waifs and Strays* during 1879 and 1880, and in 1880 Rodd was his companion in a tour along the river Loire in France.

James Rennell Rodd (1858–1941), later knighted and given a peerage, went to Balliol College, Oxford, at the same time as Wilde was at Magdalen.[26] When he published his first collection of poems, entitled *Songs in the South*, he sent a copy to Wilde, retrospectively dated July 1880 (the publication date was November 1881), having inscribed the paper-covered pamphlet with a significant prophecy. This inscription consisted of verses in Italian which have been translated to read: 'At thy Martyrdom the greedy and cruel crowd to which thou speakest will assemble; all will come to see thee on thy cross, and not one will have pity on thee!'

Now why should Rodd have written such ominous lines? Clearly Wilde had impressed him in the role of prophet – in his assumed role of Aesthetic prophet perhaps, though this is doubtful. Had he also impressed him as an advocate of *l'amour de l'impossible*? Writing in November 1880, Wilde recalled the Loire holiday, spent with 'a delightful Oxford friend'.

Early in 1882, while on his American tour, Wilde arranged with J. M. Stoddart of Philadelphia to re-issue the bulk of the contents of *Songs in the South* as *Rose Leaf and Apple Leaf*, with a new dedication to himself, which (it has been suggested) he copied from the dedication inscribed by Rodd, either in the copy with the prophetic verses, or in another copy Wilde brought with him to the United States. The dedication ran: 'To Oscar Wilde – "Heart's Brother" – These Few Songs

[25] See Rupert Hart-Davis, *The Letters of Oscar Wilde*, London, 1962, pp. 180–1, pp. 184–6.
[26] These observations on Rennell Rodd are based upon references to him in Hart-Davis, *The Letters of Oscar Wilde*, 1962; the Bibliographical Note by T. B. Mosher in his edition of *Rose Leaf and Apple Leaf*, Portland, Maine, 1906; and Stuart Mason's *Bibliography of Oscar Wilde*, edited by Timothy d'Arch Smith, London, 1967.

and Many Songs to Come'. Wilde's plan was a generous one, and a letter survives in which he asked Stoddart for an advance of £25 to be sent to Rodd through him; while to encourage his Oxford friend, whom he described as 'a young fellow of . . . great poetical promise', he wrote an essay, which he called 'L'Envoi', to precede the poems.

About the time all this was being planned on Rodd's behalf, Rodd himself was putting his name to a letter written by Whistler, along with two other acquaintances of Wilde's, Lady Archibald Campbell and Mat Elden.

> 4 February, 1882.
>
> Oscar! We of Tite Street and Beaufort Gardens joy in your triumphs, and delight in your success, but – we think that, with the exception of your epigrams, you talk like Sidney Colvin in the Provinces, and that, with the exception of your knee-breeches, you dress like 'Arry Quilter.
>
> Signed J. McNeil Whistler, Janey Campbell, Mat Elden, Rennell Rodd.
>
> New York papers please copy.

This letter, over Whistler's signature alone, was soon afterwards published in *The World*, provoking Wilde to reply in a telegram: 'I admit knee-breeches, and acknowledge epigrams, but reject Quilter and repudiate Colvin'.

Already by then, therefore, the relationship between Rodd and Wilde had declined sufficiently for Rodd to join with Whistler in poking fun at the 'Aesthete'.

Rose Leaf and Apple Leaf was published in an ornate Aesthetic style in both an ordinary edition and in an edition *de luxe* during the autumn of 1882; and Rodd complained to Stoddart of the way in which he had been identified, so he felt, with Wilde's Aesthetic philosophy in 'L'Envoi', and also of the effusive dedication, which 'annoyed [him] excessively'. He wanted the dedication removed from all copies sold thereafter, but it was too late for this to be done: the edition was a small one and no reprint was required.

Writing to Stoddart on 7 August 1882, when he had received advance copies of the book, Wilde still spoke enthusiastically of Rodd – which was strange, considering that often he took offence at much less than the aforesaid unpleasant letter. However, by April in the following year the friendship between them had been scuttled; even then, in a letter to R. H. Sherard accompanying *Rose Leaf and Apple Leaf*, Wilde was still able to discriminate between Rodd as a 'true poet' and as a 'false friend'.

Of the two poems by Rodd included here, the first (No. 23) was included in Part III of 'Ave Atque Vale' in *Poems in Many Lands* in 1883. Part I dated from 1882–3, Part II from 1879, and Part III from 1881. Part III was originally entitled 'Requiescat' and had possible affinities with Wilde's poem of the same name, written in memory of his sister who died in 1867 – affinities not of prosody but of imagery, towards the end. Wilde's poem was published for the first time in his collection issued in June 1881; Rodd's poem appeared, dated 1881, first as 'Requiescat' in *Songs in the South*, issued in November 1881; and then again in *Rose Leaf and Apple Leaf*, issued in 1882; and in *Poems in Many Lands*, issued in 1883, in the last of which the title 'Requiescat' was omitted. Wilde's poem may well have been written in 1877 since it is annotated as written at Avignon that is, during Wilde's journey to Rome and to Greece with Mahaffy. His next trip abroad was down the Loire with Rodd, and if they went to Avignon together this is not recorded. The connection seems more likely to be Wilde–Rodd than Rodd–Wilde, which again lends weight to the possibility of Wilde inveigling Rodd into some sort of emotional state, which the younger man disacknowledged later. The relationship broke up because of Rodd's unilateral hostility; and this suggests the kind of revulsion that follows sometimes after a state of emotional dependence.

There is a chronological support at least for the possibility of Rodd's two poems included here deriving something of their homosexual signature from his association with Wilde. In other respects they owe little or nothing to Wilde as a poet, and this would apply to all subsequent verse published by Rodd until he settled for being a diplomat. In Wilde's own verse, and indeed in his literary remains as a whole, we seem to be aware of homosexuality like something radio-active, invisible except when the diction is loaded with Mediterranean patinae from ancient Greece. That he himself was aware of this quality is shown probably by his alteration of the sex of the subject of 'Wasted Days', first printed in 1877,[27] when in 1881 the sonnet was republished with

---

[27] Stuart Mason's *Bibliography of Oscar Wilde*, edited by Timothy d'Arch Smith, London, 1967, the page facing p. 96. On this page is reproduced the 'picture' that occasioned the poem, which consisted of a tile six inches square and painted by Miss V.T., who is not identified. A line divides the design of the decoration of the tile into two panels, one on the right showing a fair-haired youth wearing hose, smock and peaked hat, leaning against a tree trunk, while in the distance reapers are at work in a cornfield; the other panel on the left showing the same youth wearing a jerkin and torn hose, sitting on the steps outside the window of a house through which are seen people feasting within. On the left panel is inscribed, over the bricks of the house, 'He must hunger in frost,' and on the right panel, over the stubble of the cornfield, 'That will not worke in heate'.

major amendments in his collected poems. The theme of this poem, as first conceived, is that the 'fair slim boy' (one is reminded of the famous letter produced at the trials in which he called Alfred Douglas a 'slim gilt soul'), who is still 'in fear of love', dreams away a summer afternoon instead of toiling with the reapers, and has never noticed that night is approaching – the night in which reaping, or gathering 'fruit', will be equally impracticable. Having descanted on the physical attractions of this youth, Wilde exclaims 'Alas! if all should be in vain.' Then, as the sun sinks, the boy still dreams; and 'in the night-time no man gathers fruit'. In calling the poem 'Wasted Days' and bringing in the subject of Love, its author showed he was not concerned so much with the youth's idleness as with his charm. This lay in his separateness and the inhibitions, the fear of love, which prevented him from enjoying life before the coming of night, here a negative symbol for a time when no *man* gathered fruit – that is, could enjoy the love of the youth, or the act of loving the youth, and so on. In default of a reference to any female, the 'waste' can be interpreted as waste of homosexual opportunity (No. 19).

References to, or hints at, homosexual entanglements can be found in *Salome* and in *The Picture of Dorian Gray*; and these works are so well known I have not considered it necessary to include quotations from them. But Wilde's story 'The Portrait of Mr. W. H.', first appearing in *Blackwood's Edinburgh Magazine* in 1889, has the distinction of being the first story in English published for ordinary and unlimited distribution which involved romantic pederasty, touched on with impeccable discretion. The problem of Shakespeare's sonnets and the theory that he was in love with a boy actor fascinated Wilde, and by 1895 he had another and longer version of the story ready for publication by John Lane at the Bodley Head. It missed being published by Lane however because of the scandal of the trials, and Wilde's manuscript was filched from his house in Tite Street when the sale of

---

Wilde's poem appeared while he was at Oxford in Vol. III, No. 2 of *Kottabos*, the magazine of Trinity College, Dublin, during the Michaelmas Term, 1877. A corrigendum substituted the word 'glow', as here, for 'rays' in line 12. In copies issued later a printed slip of corrigenda was issued, dated 30 October, at Oxford; these amounted to an altered version of the last six lines as follows:

Cornfields behind, and reapers all a-row
In weariest labour toiling wearily,
To no sweet sound of laughter, or of lute;
And careless of the crimson sunset-glow
The boy still dreams: nor knows that night is nigh:
And in the night-time no man gathers fruit.

When, however, Wilde's collected poems appeared in Bogue's edition of 1881, the author had evidently thought fit to change the sex of its subject, and indeed the sense of the whole, which was now entitled 'Madonna Mia', omitting any reference to the painted tile and including at the end a comparison with Dante beholding the Seventh Crystal.

his effects took place on 24 April 1895. Years later it turned up again, to be published for the first time by Mitchell Kennerley in New York; and it is from this 1921 edition that the text has been reprinted here.

By 1870 two contrasted streams of homosexual sentiment were especially noteworthy: one from the Oxford Movement with its undercurrent of emotional friendship as expressed by Newman and Faber; the other from the muscular Christianity of Dr. Arnold at Rugby School, a somewhat inarticulate trend. Although these two streams were opposed, in fact they were joined at the point in a friendship where emphasis is placed on overtones of self-sacrifice, and not on the practical advantages accruing. At this point Dr. Arnold's athletic comradeships, with their socially cohesive values, could interweave with Faber's religious comradeships which justified a kind of promiscuous affection among males. And the relative unimportance of women in relation to these two streams of sentiment could be seen as sometimes the cause, sometimes the effect of the unisexual conditions in which they made any sense.

The disciples of Arnold were usually aware how easy it was for emotional friendships which they recommended as Christian to swerve into the conventional paths of schoolboy homosexuality. Readers were warned in *Tom Brown's Schooldays* and in *Eric, or Little by Little*, and in other school stories of the period, about the unhealthiness of the beaten tracks. The authors of such books were frightened by vice, however. The clergyman Edward Cracroft Lefroy, who died young, seems to have been checked in his development precisely when 'platonic' homosexuality was a real temptation.[28] He was not frightened of vice in himself, so much as of morbid growths, of indulging emotions associated with pagan literature and incompatible with the Pauline Christian teaching. Antinous, he declared, could, 'on purely artistic grounds', bear away the palm from Helen; but doubtless he would

[28] Wilfrid Austin Gill, *Edward Cracroft Lefroy, His Life and Poems including a Reprint of 'Echoes of Theocritus,'* with a critical estimate of the Sonnets by the late John Addington Symonds, London, 1897.

A plagiarism by Beardsley (as often, probably unconscious) is suggested by the last lines in the first paragraph of his romance 'Under the Hill' (*The Savoy*, Vol. I et seq., 1896; reprinted 1904; in its unexpurgated version *The Story of Venus and Tannhäuser* 1907) '. . . from point to point . . . the fingers wandered, quelling the little mutinies of cravat and ruffle'.

Here is one of those striking passages which the reader may be tempted to remember. The same applied to Beardsley. It seems that he was tempted to remember a line in Lefroy's poem 'A Palaestral Study' which goes: 'Whisper of mutinies divinely quelled'. This poem had been published first in 1885 in *Echoes from Theocritus and Other Sonnets* by Lefroy. Would Beardsley have encountered such a work? Very likely not. But it was very likely indeed that he read John Addington Symonds's prestigious book *In the Key of Blue* (London, 1893) which contained his 'Critical Estimate' of Lefroy, reprinted with additions from an article in *The New Review*. In this essay Symonds quoted 'A Palaestral Study' in full.

have been annoyed to learn that the symbolism of his flute of Daphnis, which thinks of the lips that pressed it, might be interpreted as a symbol of fellatio. In spite of an essay of his directed against the questionable hedonism, as he saw it, of John Addington Symonds and of the Aesthetic movement, he succumbed to the one undeclared force in this Aesthetic hedonism that made it so deeply suspect. But although he was a parson he admired athletes, not choirboys (Nos. 26, 27).

Lefroy's *Echoes from Theocritus* (1885) brought him letters of praise from Tennyson, Sir Frederick Leighton, Frederick Myers and Edmund Gosse, all in differing ways familiar with some of his problems. And after his death Symonds forgave him the hostility and recognized in his poems the special merit of a fellow Arcadian.

'Damned impostor!' So thought an irate clubman giving his views on Sir Richard Burton, whom he had once known in India.[29] The old gentleman, in his way, was venting the kind of suspicion that comes naturally to any conformist, when he finds himself affronted by egocentric, provocative colleagues; or by acquaintances whose company at times, in the limited scope of an English colony, he has been obliged to endure. In his professional career Burton's impatience with conventions and red tape certainly made him a difficult man, either to contend with or to understand (Plate 6).

After a good start in the Indian Army Burton fell foul of officialdom, when his confidential report on various aspects of Indian life, including homosexuality, drawn up for Sir Charles Napier, his chief, fell into the hands of the Secretariat at Bombay. Promotion beyond the rank of captain in the Army in India evaded him, so from 1861 onward he found employment in the British consular service. But amid all his preoccupations with oriental religions and philosophies, the subject of homosexuality seems to have retained its appeal, for by 1885–8, during which time he was publishing his translation of the *Arabian Nights*, not only did he include previously omitted passages and even whole stories in which pederasty raised its head, but he took the opportunity of adding a 'Terminal Essay' on the history of pederasty all over the world up to the year of writing. Being the first account in English of any length or breadth devoted entirely to this matter, it has been included complete in the present anthology (No. 28).

Burton's craft as a translator has been highly praised: his literary style is none the less strangely informal. This style has been called macaronic, partly on account of the home-made neologisms; while his assurance has an exhibitionist quality justifying in some degree the old

[29] See *The Anti-Philistine*, No. II, 15 July, 1897: 'Romancing Lady Burton's Romances', p. 118.

gentleman's view of its author. For Burton was perhaps something of an impostor: he was also something of a pioneer. Though much of what he wrote on the nature of homosexuality is no longer acceptable, he had the merit of cutting no corners when it came to laying out what he had discovered, and at that date it took a mischievous and ruthless mind like his to discuss, and even to dwell upon, such a subject at all. His chief contention that male homosexuality was to be found, and had always flourished, in what he called the Sotadic Zones of the globe – which coincided roughly with the land between latitudes 43° and 30° – amounted to little more than the application of Taine's theory of climatic and geographical factors directly affecting the growth and character of races and civilizations; but it is of little guidance finally because the zones coincide also with the most populated places in the world.

At first it may seem surprising that this world could be so small that Burton should find himself in the same literary groove along with Swinburne, but so it was. He was also known to Lord Houghton and to most of the Pre-Raphaelites, who soon discovered his gifts as a raconteur, as well as that ruggedness, that flamboyance which graced a bohemianism more professional than theirs. Whether or not at some time in his adventurous life in the East he had enjoyed homosexual experiences, he certainly had more than a casual knowledge of the subject, and like Swinburne he should count, I believe, as one of the solvents acting on the oblique inhibitions of upper-class literary coteries.

We have now reached a position in our second phase when, in the mid-1880s, the pace established in the 1860s was beginning to alter its momentum. This was due mainly to the arrival of younger generations of literary men accepting homosexual sentiment as part of the whole range of feeling which waited to be explored. The next stage was when the admission of such sentiments, albeit only among a few people who were haunted by them, grew into a belief that the more acute sensibility of the 'artistic temperament' was often allied to the frustrated senses of the homosexual. To be homosexually inclined thus became one of the secondary qualifications for declaring oneself an 'artist', and the easiest way to show what an 'artist' one could be, as in Wilde's case, was to record one's feelings in some literary medium – which after all was the medium which came readily to hand at universities.

A connection between homosexuality and the supposed views of the Aesthetes in 1881 was possibly hinted at by W. S. Gilbert in his comic opera *Patience*, wherein the poet Bunthorne, modelled on Rossetti and others but later identified with Wilde, sings obscurely about 'an attachment à la Plato for a bashful young potato or a not too French, French bean!' An attachment à la Plato, to the Victorians, could of course mean any kind of attachment that was not physical. From Gilbert's song the public might get an impression that poets could be sexually deviant; but equally the impression might capsize, so that deviants could be poets.

Here it should be emphasized that in considering popular notions like these we are not accepting anything precise or logical; only prejudices, coloured by one or other of those vast reservoirs of feeling which contain, for instance, aggression towards minorities. For those persons in the 1880s who were determined not to be taken for Aesthetes, the Aesthetes were stigmatized with – among other things – 'Platonic' habits. But the younger men who admitted to such ill-defined habits gravitated naturally towards the stigmatized group, and we can watch this process taking place throughout the 1880s. Wilde already in his private life was heading towards a final exposition of Gilbert's idea of the Aesthete. More quietly, in his well-appointed Mayfair house, a rich young dilettante of Russo-Jewish origin was courageously and laboriously exemplifying the new notion of the homosexual as poet. This was Mark André Raffalovich, of whom Wilde once said he had come to London to found a salon and succeeded in opening a saloon.

Some of the references to Raffalovich in memoirs and correspondence are unflattering, especially those of Violet Paget, who wrote under the name of Vernon Lee.[30] In reading Miss Paget's letters a suspicion arises that, after detecting what he was looking for in *Marius the Epicurean*, the young Raffalovich decided that friendship with the man whom George Moore called a 'Vicarage Verlaine' would bring him into contact with other disciples. And there, very probably, he was not much mistaken; even if those disciples were not perhaps so rich, nor so arriviste, as Raffalovich, that they could lay siege to Pater with dinner parties.

Before he was converted to Roman Catholocism in 1896 and renounced worldly and literary ambitions, Raffalovich had published five volumes of verse, two novels, a playlet and numerous articles – though some of these were intended for limited circulation only. But nobody seems to have taken much notice of them, or to have given him in printed reviews the recognition he deserved. In spite of English not being his native tongue, he acquired dexterity in the writing of it: his novels are cats' cradles of obsolete social nuances; his poems betray overtly the kinds of emotion that Symonds would have limited to twenty-five copies. And he had the added distinction of becoming by the 1890s an experimental craftsman: internal and feminine rhymes,

[30] *Vernon Lee's Letters*, edited by Irene Cooper Willis, London, 1937, pp. 147–8, 207, 221, 224.

bad rhymes, no rhymes, odd rhymes – he tried all such devices, with results that were occasionally marred by weakness of syntax. In 'Tulip of the Twilight', however, (No. 79), published in 1895, there comes a curious foretaste of the flavour of the 'Song of Lilli Marlene', with the salt of homosexual persecution and pride in place of the heterosexual stoicism of 1942.

Raffalovich has another claim to notice in our particular context; which was his long attachment to John Gray, the author of *Silverpoints* – that remarkable collection of 'Decadent' verses published by Elkin Mathews and John Lane in 1893 with letterpress and covers designed by Charles Ricketts. The son of a Woolwich carpenter and one of a large family, Gray's diligence had brought him a job in the Foreign Office Library when about 1890 he met Wilde at the Playgoers Club. But Gray had literary ambitions, and Wilde must take some credit for promoting these.

Meanwhile *The Picture of Dorian Gray* appeared in 1890 as a magazine story, and in book form in the following year. In 1892 its hero was rashly identified in *The Star* as Wilde's young protégé. As it happened Gray had facetiously called himself 'Dorian' in letters to Wilde, but he was scarcely comparable to the hero of the story. And the story being what it was, he threatened the paper with an action for libel. The affair was settled out of court. By that time Gray had encountered Raffalovich, who seems to have attracted him away from Wilde's entourage in which Lord Alfred Douglas was then the favoured member. In due course Gray became the intimate friend of Raffalovich, remaining so until his death in 1934.[31]

Gray converted to Catholicism in 1890. In 1892 he experienced some sort of psychological crisis. After being a candidate for holy orders in 1898 he entered the priesthood in 1901, settling in Edinburgh with Raffalovich for the rest of his life. The young decadent emerged as Father Gray; then as Canon Gray, his literary ambitions dwindling into the work of editing Beardsley's letters to André, publishing essays and verses, mainly pious, and ending in a short allegorical novel, *Park*, which came out in 1932. Raffalovich, who had followed Gray into the Catholic church in 1896, likewise ceased after 1897 to publish anything except minor articles. Thereafter he contented himself with his social life in Edinburgh and with his prolonged, and perhaps always platonic, relationship with John Gray – a relationship referred to during those years a little uneasily as 'inverted'. Like the friendship between Ricketts and Shannon, it enjoyed the fortune of success; which means it did

---

[31] Brocard Sewell (ed.) *Two Friends*, London, 1963, p. 10. A more recent account of these men will be found in Brocard Sewell's *A Footnote to the Nineties*, London, 1969.

not break down.[32] How in other ways it resembled the Shannon–Ricketts ménage it would be hard to discover. What is of special interest yet is the personality of John Gray in comparison with that of Raffalovich (Plates 7, 8 and 9).

Here we touch upon the old controversy of environment versus heredity. Are homosexual tendencies the result of influences to which the subject is sensitive; or are they congenital? These questions were debated exhaustively at the end of last century, when the idea of homosexuality as congenital was useful to men like Symonds who sought an apology for it. Various continental psychiatrists discounted this idea and Havelock Ellis in *Sexual Inversion* (1897), deferring to the views of his collaborator Symonds, gave it somewhat half-hearted recognition. Later sexologists have theorized on most of the possible queries that arise, from the exact meaning of the word *congenital* to the possibility of inheriting genetic patterns which at least pre-dispose the subject to homosexuality. The fact remains that, as far as we know, the majority of English male homosexuals have not been congenitally orientated so much as swayed in that direction by parental relationships in early childhood, or by habits formed at school, or in reaction from early heterosexual rebuffs – or by all three factors. From Raffalovich's monograph *Uranisme et Unisexualité*, published in French at Lyon in 1896, we might infer that he considered himself congenitally homosexual, along with numerous eminent men from Socrates to the poet August von Platen; and the likelihood is, if we disregard the semantic problem, that his condition was indeed one from which he was never consciously free; in other words that it dated back to very early childhood, to a stage in life well before he could have acquired homosexual tastes by imitation or emulation.

There is no evidence that the same could be said of John Gray, however. In the opinion of one who knew both men in their Edinburgh period, Gray's homosexual history was inseparable from his drive for self-betterment in the 1890s.[33] For an introverted literary aspirant, toying with luxurious French Decadent and Symbolist writings, the opportunities of acquaintance with Wilde and his friends were too tempting to reject. If Raffalovich spitefully removed Gray from proximity to Wilde, it was only to confirm any homosexual feelings Gray might have entertained; and that Gray was by no means inflexible in this matter we can judge by the poems in *Silverpoints*, some of which

[32] Charles de Sousy Ricketts, R.A. (1866–1931) and Charles Hazelwood Shannon, R.A. (1863–1937), painters and designers. No biographical records that I know shed much light on the friendship of these two men, which was none the less held to be a 'romantic friendship' during their life together and never openly criticized.
[33] Mr. Charles Ballantyne of Edinburgh communicated verbally to me many opinions on his friends John Gray and André Raffalovich in 1966.

are at least quasi-heterosexual. Two poems which had been intended for the book were finally thrown out, but these were not homosexual.[34] A manuscript poem entitled 'Passing the Love of Women', once in the possession of A. J. A. Symons, has been attributed to Gray, but this cannot be confirmed.

The word to be stressed here is 'introvert'; and this word should be linked with the psychological crisis of 1892. The probability is that Gray had no strong sexual inclinations at all, and that by his subsequent chastity he exploited what was already there – a kind of incipient sexual anaesthesia. None the less, the most important human relationship in his life from the early 1890s onward was the one with Raffalovich. It looks then as if he may have been a clear case of a man being influenced by his environment, not the environment of school or university, but of literary suggestion and association, followed by the effects of flattery and affection from a dedicated homosexual rich enough to make life easy for them both.

Raffalovich, as we have seen, was an admirer of Pater, whose prose style even affected his own. Two other men for whom Pater was important are represented in the present book: Richard Jackson by a poem in honour of Pater himself; and A. C. Benson by a passage from his earliest novel, *The Memoirs of Arthur Hamilton* (1886) (No. 34).

Richard Charles Jackson, who died in 1923, was a lay-brother and so-called Professor of Ecclesiastical History in the High Anglican Priory of St. Austin's, an institution in the New Kent Road, London, organized by Father Nugée in the interests of the poor of Walworth, and not recognized officially by the English Church.[35] Jackson's claim to notice is the one he put forward himself of being the model for *Marius the Epicurean*. From what can be gathered in Wright's account of him, this seems at best to be an exaggeration. He published many poems but the fulsome manner of his verses to Pater, and of his recorded utterances, suggest that Pater would never have taken him seriously. His tribute is little more than a document – though not a negligible document – of gush, with physical strings attached. In this respect it is welcome, because it reveals the sort of Platonism, garnished with High Church Faberism, in which Pater relaxed after stretches of unobtrusive eccentricity at Brasenose College, Oxford. And his own aesthetic posture may be felt to have contributed indirectly to the sentiment of Jackson's poem (No. 40).

[34] The two poems by John Gray excluded from *Silverpoints* were published in John Gawsworth's *Known Signatures*, London, 1932.

[35] See Thomas Wright, *The Life of Walter Pater*, London, 1907, especially Vol. II, pp. 19 and 89; also the Victoria and Albert Museum copy of this book which contains an inscription by Richard C. Jackson. Robin Ironside's remarkable essay on Pater in the *Cornhill Magazine*, No. 962, May 1944, contains a scornful account of Jackson.

Arthur Christopher Benson on the other hand owed a great deal directly to Pater. One of three homosexually inclined sons of an Archbishop of Canterbury, he settled down to being a Fellow, and ultimately Master, of Magdalen College, Cambridge, and to working out in simple faith some of the precepts of the Oxford don. He also wrote a sympathetic account of William Cory in an introduction to *Ionica*, as reprinted in 1905. Arthur Hamilton's portrayal includes several references to a type of purely mental homosexuality similar to that hinted at in Pater's writings. The passage quoted from this book is a literary landmark, and one that could be placed beside the sections of Hall Caine's *The Deemster* (1888) which concern a David and Jonathan relationship of unconscious sexuality, nearer to the manner favoured by muscular Christians of Dr. Arnold's persuasion (No. 37).

Hall Caine, being a best seller and somewhat sententious, was roughly handled by both the Aesthetes of his own period and by almost everybody since. So too was his friend, the poet T. E. Brown, whose comments on *The Deemster* prove that this novel could, at the time, be taken seriously by someone of intelligence.[36] The truth is of course that the works of both men have been over-disparaged. The inclusion of the homosexual portions of *The Deemster* here is intended to draw attention to the author's awareness of emotions which Victorian readers of circulating-library books were willing to accept, on a Biblical precedent.

A poet not to be overlooked was Francis William Bourdillon, whose earliest collections date from the 1870s, but who was still publishing verse, some of it homosexual in tone, during the 1890s. The theme of 'The Legend of the Water Lilies' (1878) would appear to be an early example of the bathing symbolism which became epidemic fifteen years afterwards (No. 20). Another poet, and one who has decidedly been overlooked, possibly for good reason – though he was an astonishing character – was Eric, Count Stenbock, an Estonian of Swedish family brought up in England and dying from the effects of drink aggravated by drugs at the age of thirty-five.[37] Stenbock spent a short time at Balliol College, Oxford, in 1879, without taking a degree, and published limited editions of homosexual poems in 1881, 1883 and 1893 (No. 63). Simeon Solomon, with whom he made friends, described him about 1886 in a letter to Frederick Hollyer,[38] the photographer, whose portrait of him is reproduced at Plate 10.

[36] See *Thomas Edward Brown*, a memorial volume, Cambridge, 1930, pp. 116–18.
[37] I am indebted to Mr. John Adlard, the biographer of Stenbock, for my information on this subject.
[38] A photocopy of this letter from Solomon to Hollyer was sent to me by Mr. Lionel Lambourne (see Note 14 to the introduction). The letter has been impossible to transcribe in print without slight repunctuation.

13, Newton Street,
Holborn, W.C.

Dear Mr. Hollyer,

I received a letter from Count Stenbock asking me to go to
him as soon as possible; I have spent the day with him and
it has been in every way a delightful one to me – his
kindness is most singular and he certainly is singular – he
received me with a low and truly Oriental salute. He had on
a magnificent blood red silk robe embroidered in gold and
silver. He was swinging a silver censer before an altar
covered with lilies, myrtles, lighted candles and a sanctuary
lamp burning with scented oil. The air was so heavy with
incense, sandalwood and the scent of flowers that I felt quite
faint. His appearance was that of a tall, graceful intellectual
looking girl and although he is not exactly good-looking,
his eyes and expression are very beautiful; he began to talk
about everything that interests me, and played beautiful
religious music on the piano and harmonium; he began then
to talk about my affairs rather as if I were his age and he
mine – he said his room was entirely at my disposal and
apologized for offering me *only* a £5 note (a sum of great
value to me just now). He then asked me not to be offended
if he gave me a coat and waistcoat, which I, of course,
accepted and which suit me perfectly – all was done in so
kind and courteous a way that it more than doubled the
gifts. He then went to get shaved and buy more flowers.
We then went to the Grosvenor where I much enjoyed
myself. The Cophetua is wonderfully beautiful and good
with the exception of the disagreeable colour of the drapery
the maid is sitting on. He then took me to the News Room
and I am sorry to say after so much pleasure that I found
I had lost a drawing I had very carefully begun of 'Perseus
with the Head of Medusa', and the little one I brought to
you, it is extremely vexatious but I am so dreadfully forgetful.
I am going to dine with the Count tomorrow to talk over
a design he wants for an altar piece. I am greatly indebted
to you for being the means of procuring for me an introduction to so kind, generous and desirable a friend; I had no
idea he had so many of my drawings. He wishes me to take
a room near him but I fear it would be too dear for me
but I should like to work with him playing to me.
Believe me,

   Truly yours,
    (Sgd) S. Solomon

He has adopted my old monogram but I have made him a
new one.

Solomon's prose style had certainly decayed since the days in 1869
when he had written *A Vision of Love Revealed in Sleep*. Among
Stenbock's papers there has survived a pastiche of this literary work of
Solomon. The ageing and now discredited painter had found in the
young count a patron in a thousand. Many stories have been told of
Stenbock, whom W. B. Yeats thought worthy of a favourable reference
in his introduction to an anthology of modern poetry.[39] He has been
unsympathetically interpreted, nevertheless, first by Arthur Symons,
then by others – none of whom admit to finding any clues in the meaning
of the death-wish pervading so many of his verses.[40] It seems to me
anyhow that apart from Stenbock's sense of parental deprivation, his
guilt in being homosexual and his profound desire to escape any
responsibility for it were probably represented in this symbolism.

Unlike Raffalovich, whose native tongue was not English but
French, Stenbock was actually brought up to speak English as well as
other languages, but he had an uneven streak of imagination and very
little sense of verse. His prose stories on the other hand, collected under
the title of *Studies of Death* and published in 1894, the year before he
died, were considerably better. The Oedipal morbidity is in them
throughout; and yet the story 'Narcissus' seems worthy of salvage.
It is tempting to take this account of a blind boy's cure as fortuitously
anticipating an episode in André Gide's novel *La Symphonie Pastorale*,
published in 1919. When the blind boy in 'Narcissus' gains his sight
and sees for the first time the man who has befriended him, he projects
his single affection into accepting the appearance of this friend as
'beautiful'. We alone know that the friend, once a handsome man, has
features scarred from the liquid thrown at him by an envious fiancée.
In Gide's novel there is a different irony in that the pastor who befriends
the blind girl is not the one she falls in love with on gaining her sight,
but his son (No. 69).

Another of Stenbock's tales in the same book is of vampirism in a
homosexual form. The practice of the Black Mass, which he boasted,
as well as a description of it here, are evidence more of traumata in the
author than of a wish to shock.

'Flung roses, roses, riotously with the throng.' This well-known line
in Ernest Dowson's poem 'Non Sum Qualis Eram Bonae Sub Regno
Cynarae' looks like some fragment from the Greek Anthology. However

[39] W. B. Yeats (ed.), *The Oxford Book of Modern Verse 1892–1935*,
Oxford, 1936, p. x.
[40] See Rupert Croft-Cooke, *Feasting with Panthers*, London, 1967,
pp. 256 and 257.

it is not. The first three words of it would seem to have been lifted, perhaps unconsciously, from a homosexual poem by Charles Sayle (No. 36) who was at New College, Oxford, when his friend Dowson was at Queen's. Also at New College in the 1870s, before Sayle's period there, was Horatio Brown, already from his schooldays at Clifton a friend of John Addington Symonds, and best known as a writer on Venice, but also the author of *Drift*, a little book of poems issued in 1900 for limited circulation – one copy being presented to Sayle, as it happened[41] (No. 89). With a house on the Zattere in Venice, Horatio Brown became a figure the English colony there, and we need never doubt that he followed the footsteps of Symonds in his partiality for gondoliers.[42]

Lionel Johnson, who is much better-remembered as a writer of the nineties, was also at New College and at the same time as Sayle. He had fallen in love with Lord Alfred Douglas at Winchester, and before his life ended in 1902 he had published several homosexual poems, including the well-known 'The Dark Angel', and the one directed against Wilde for enticing Douglas away from him (No. 56). It has been solemnly averred that 'The Dark Angel' is about alcoholic indulgence, to which poor Johnson was subject. But alcoholism in his case, as in most cases, was the symptom of emotional conflict; and 'The Dark Angel' can barely be read correctly if the anguish expressed in it is not grasped as a fantasy of starved affection. The poem is so familiar that it has been left out of this anthology, but the sonnet on jealous hatred is included for comparison with the slightly earlier and more forthright poem on a similar theme by Rensham, a London bachelor it seems, about whom little is known (No. 38).

The comparison presents another problem always facing the student of Victorian homosexuality. I cannot say from external evidence that Rensham was homosexual. What is advanced here is that the adoption of a homosexual mood is implied by wishing to write a poem in which strong feelings of love and resentment are directed on a man. This, it may be countered, is an imaginative act that anybody is capable of, and most male dramatists and novelists assume the habit of it as a necessary qualification in writing about female emotions. But the point about the Victorians is that male crypto-homosexuality found relief in the excuse to write from a woman's viewpoint. Rensham's poem may, or may not, be an example of this. He did not make it clear; and it did not prevent him from writing poems about women – although the verse of John Gray is sufficient reminder that homosexual poets could do this plausibly. There is always the threat from some quarters

[41] Information from Mr. Donald Weeks.
[42] Phyllis Grosskurth, op. cit., London, 1964, p. 241.

to reduce the whole of such delicate problems of interpretation to generalities about the polymorphism of sex.

Mention of Lionel Johnson and Charles Sayle leads inevitably to three magazines which could be described as pilots of a cult, if not open organs of propaganda. Two of these were *The Spirit Lamp* and *The Chameleon*, both Oxford journals, with no opposite numbers in Cambridge. The third was a London magazine, *The Artist, or Journal of Home Culture*, which was older and more firmly established than any undergraduate magazine could hope to be. *The Artist* was also important in the sense that it reached a greater number of readers, especially in the provinces. It had been in circulation for many years when *The Studio* began its long innings as a leading art journal. Yet in spite of having no illustrations, *The Artist* was useful in that it provided notices of current art exhibitions; and it recorded art gossip of every kind. Its net was, in fact, spread to cover not only visual arts, but literature and music and the theatre, in which respect it was unlike *The Studio* or anything else. But the key to its link with the expanding articulation of homosexuality in England was to be found in the person of Charles Kains-Jackson, a young lawyer who was appointed editor of *The Artist* in 1888.

It is in retrospect that one realizes how crucial that appointment was. *The Artist* was founded in 1880. From 1888 onwards small poems were pushed in to fill empty spaces in the columns of the magazine, and within a year or so the regularity of these features might be supposed to have established feelings of expectancy among certain readers. And as we go on from 1890 to 1891, 1892, 1893, 1894, a homosexual note is repeatedly sounded. The authorship of some of the verses remains anonymous; in others initials are used, and sometimes these are found only in the Contents List, not underneath the poem itself. Thus we find the initials P.C., C.K.J., E.B.S. and J.G.W. in the years 1888–9. From a study of all the other Contents Lists for the years 1888–94 it becomes evident that the initials P.C. and C.K.J refer to the same person, who was Charles Philip Castle Kains-Jackson, the editor aforesaid, sometimes using his middle names Philip Castle separately. E.B.S. stood for E. Bonney-Steyne and J.G.W. for Joseph Gleeson White – of whom more later. During the same period verse contributions appeared from Charles Sayle, the Oxford poet mentioned above (pp. 39, 40) who took a job in Cambridge University Library (to which he bequeathed a journal revealing his lifelong homosexual inclination); from Horatio Brown, J. A. Symonds, Edward Cracroft Lefroy, Rennell Rodd, F. W. Bourdillon, John Gray and André Raffalovich, who again have been discussed above (pp. 21, 22 and 33–39); from George Gillet and 'Bertram Lawrence' (J. F. Bloxam), who were Oxford undergraduates contributing at the same time to *The Spirit Lamp* and to *The Chameleon*.

By 1890 there could be no doubt at all that there was a selective principle at work behind the ordinary affairs of editorship. The verses published in the magazine up to the spring of 1894 were more often homosexual than not, and they introduced the reader to various sympathetic authors such as Lord Henry Somerset, a well-known song writer of the day, who went to live in Italy to escape scandal in 1879; Lord Alfred Douglas, the friend of Oscar Wilde and still an undergraduate; Arthur Marvell, whose real name was Clifton, a young lawyer friend of Robert Ross and a contributor to *The Woman's World* under Wilde's editorship; Palgrave Morrison; and many others. An ambiguous poem from Lord Francis Hervey's *The Taking of Alba*, first published in 1873, was adopted as though it had just been composed (No. 16). If a pederastic poem appeared in an American magazine it was loyally praised; and Justin Huntly McCarthy was rebuked for substituting girls for boys in his translations from the poems of Hafiz. By 1893 the frequent presence of homosexually-slanted matter in *The Artist* was making it suspect in certain quarters as a source of moral infection. A minor incident in that year shows this.

One of the magazine's most useful contributors, whose poems, essays and reviews were identified by initials, was Theodore Wratislaw, son of a Rugby master and a pupil in Arnold's old school, who later succeeded his father as a titular hereditary count of the Holy Roman Empire. Wratislaw went to Oxford where he belonged to the set which included John Francis Bloxam, George Gillet and Edmund Backhouse.[43] Being a contributor to *The Spirit Lamp*, it is not surprising that he contributed to *The Artist* as well, and in the number for 1 August 1893 there appeared his short poem 'To a Sicilian Boy', as bold and as matter-of-fact as a slightly earlier example of the same genus by Lord Alfred Douglas, already published in the magazine. But when in the autumn of the same year Wratislaw included 'To a Sicilian Boy' and another poem, 'L'Eternel féminin', in *Caprices*, his third collection of verses, a man on the staff of the *Pall Mall Gazette* threatened to stir up ostracism against him. So while in a few advance copies of the book these poems were retained, in the remainder a fresh leaf with substitute poems had to be incorporated[44] (No. 61).

[43] See the manuscript letter beginning 'My dear Cottam', attached to the British Museum copy of Wratislaw's *Caprices*. In the opinion of Mr. Timothy d'Arch Smith this letter, which is illegibly signed, was from George Ives.

[44] See Charles Kains-Jackson's inscription on the fly-leaf of the British Museum copy of *Caprices*. Strong criticism of Wratislaw by a contributor to the September number of *The Artist* was perhaps another reason for the publishers to withdraw the poems.

At some date in the 1880s Kains-Jackson, the editor of *The Artist*, made the acquaintance of Joseph Gleeson White, the son of a bookseller and stationer at Christchurch near Bournemouth, where White himself continued to live. He was a man of many gifts – designer, critic, journalist and wit. When Lewis Hind, the editor presumptive of *The Studio* at its foundation, laid down this post, it was offered to White, who became the first substantive editor of the magazine. This was early in 1893, by which time he had left Christchurch for Chiswick. It was just before then, roughly from 1889 to 1892, that this little coastal town in Hampshire became a sort of holiday centre for members of the set attached to *The Artist*. Some of these were brought along by Kains-Jackson: others were friends of Gleeson White, who presided as a kind of informal host to the artistic community there. At Christchurch the visitors met other visitors with similar tastes, including a love of the arts motivated by homosexuality mainly in the pederastic mode.

Gleeson White himself was married and had a family, which did not of course prevent him from contributing ambiguous poems, sometimes, to *The Artist*. One of his friends, whom he introduced to Kains-Jackson, was Frederick Rolfe, then using the pseudonym of Baron Corvo and at work on murals in the local Catholic church. For the figures in the murals Rolfe took photographs of Cecil Castle, a cousin of Kains-Jackson and one of the visiting coterie, and projected the photographic images on to his working canvas so that he could draw outlines around them.[45] In due course he contributed to *The Artist* poems on Saint Sebastian and similar subjects.

Today it is easy to see Rolfe as a typically repressed homosexual, abandoning himself in middle age to the pederastic joys described in his famous letters from Venice to the Falmouth timber merchant.[46] These letters were written in 1909–10. At the time he was staying in Christchurch, however, he still believed in his vocation for the priesthood, and there is no evidence that he risked this redoubtable image by showing his deeper feelings. The verses he wrote for *The Artist* and *The Art Review* (No. 43), and the murals and banners he painted, all declared the nature of his fantasy life, even in those days – so one would have thought. In that sense he might have found the environment at Christchurch sympathetic. It is of course possible that the underlying preoccupations of Kains-Jackson and his friends did something to modify Rolfe's inhibitions, and to detach him a little from his obstinate view of himself as a priest in the making. But this remains surmise.

There was pathos in Rolfe's determination to strike a dent in the community. If he could not be a priest, he would be a painter; or a

[45] Information from Mr. Donald Weeks.
[46] Information from Mr. Donald Weeks.

nobleman; or a man-of-letters; or, if nothing better, he could be a pioneer photographer. He had come back from Italy at the end of 1890 after an inconclusive five months' training at the Scots College in Rome and a short time as the guest of an elderly Englishwoman, the Duchess Sforza-Cesarini. And it was while he was in Italy that he got to know 'Toto', a small peasant boy who figures as the narrator of the 'Stories Toto Told Me', later published in *The Yellow Book* during 1895–6. Rolfe took photographs of Toto and his friends, and after his return to England gave prints of these to Kains-Jackson.[47] When allowances have been made for the comparatively primitive apparatus available to him, the picture of the boys on lake Nemi looks years ahead of its actual date (Plates 11, 12). And evidently Gleeson White was sufficiently impressed to include some reproductions of photographs of boys by Rolfe in an article on 'The Nude in Photography' in *The Studio*, No. 3, June 1893. In the article Rolfe is referred to as Baron Corvo. A less discreet type of pederastic photograph was the stock in trade of another baron, a real one this time, the Baron von Gloeden, a German who established his studio at Taormina in Sicily, entirely to accommodate the rising demand from homosexuals. Yet another photographer, Guglielmo Pluschow, plied a similar trade in Rome, and an example of the somewhat overposed groups so typical of his output (and of the whole craft) can be seen in Plate 13.[48]

To return to Corvo, or Rolfe. In an earlier period, about 1880 to 1886, he had been a master at Saffron Walden Grammar School, and there he seems to have favoured a boy called John Gambril Nicholson.[49] What brought the two together again is not recorded, but at the time that Rolfe was working on murals in Christchurch, Nicholson was visiting the town. He had been an undergraduate at Oxford, and he was earning his living then as a schoolmaster, meanwhile composing sonnets in the Italian style introduced by Rossetti. His first collection of verses was published in 1892 as *Love in Earnest*. It was entirely and wholly pederastic in content. Charles Sayle – another visitor to Christchurch – reviewed it in the *Century Guild Hobby Horse*, very favourably, as might be expected. None the less, difficulties arose over a sonnet titled 'St. William of Norwich', originally composed it seems by Rolfe, and 'improved' and adopted in his book by Nicholson (No. 55). Rolfe was so annoyed that the leaf on which the sonnet had been printed had to be cut out before the book was issued.[50]

[47] Information from Mr. Donald Weeks. The photographs are his property.

[48] The photograph formerly belonged to an eminent architect, and was acquired around 1900.

[49] Information from Mr. Donald Weeks.

[50] Information from Mr. W. G. Good.

Apart from this single incident, Nicholson remained on better terms with Rolfe than any of the older man's early friends. He is mentioned by A. J. A. Symons in *The Quest for Corvo* (1934) without being identified, in a passage describing a meeting with Rolfe in 1904, just before the publication of Rolfe's best-known book *Hadrian the Seventh*. That was the last time they saw each other.

Some of the journals which took Nicholson's poems for publication in the first instance were juveniles, like *Chums*, *Boys*, and *Old and Young*. Otherwise they seem to have been regular journals of the day, such as the *Universal Magazine*, *Chambers'*, *Home Chimes*, *Black and White*, the *Athenaeum* and *Brighton Society*. Among the pederastic poets of this period he stands aside like Cory, a schoolmaster whose role as a teacher depended on his homosexual temperament. Naturally he was selective, and photographs survive of two of his boyish Muses, W. A. Melling (Plate 14) and J. A. Simon.[51] To Simon he addressed the last, and to Melling most of the rest of the poems in his second collection, entitled *A Chaplet of Southernwood*, published quietly at Derby in 1896.

Rolfe's quarrel with Gleeson White, described in *The Quest for Corvo*, arose ostensibly from his offer to buy Caxton House, White's property in Christchurch – White having decided to live in London. At that time, towards the end of 1891, both Rolfe and Kains-Jackson had rooms in a large boarding establishment at 16 Bridge Street, named Tyneham House. This name appeared on Rolfe's visiting cards in what he must have considered its proper and archaic form, 'Toinham House'.[52] Kains-Jackson, being a lawyer, acted as Gleeson White's legal adviser. In that capacity he advised against negotiations with Rolfe who was badly in debt and in no position to buy property. Rolfe was offended; and Mrs. White, like most women who met him, disliked him so strongly that her influence was probably decisive in bringing matters to a head – though Rolfe on his part maintained her hostility arose from his rejection of her advances. Rolfe left Christchurch for Aberdeen in 1892; while Gleeson White sold Caxton House to someone else and moved to Chiswick, where he lived until his death in 1898.

One friend of Kains-Jackson, who became an important unit in the Christchurch set associated with *The Artist*, was Henry Scott Tuke, the son of Hack Tuke, a noted doctor specializing in insanity. Henry Tuke was a painter and a member of the New English Art Club, who lived at Falmouth in Cornwall where he evolved a bold, *plein-air* type of picture in which boys or young men were shown bathing, boating,

[51] Information and photographs from Mr. Donald Weeks.
[52] Information from Mr. Donald Weeks.

lying in the sun, or otherwise displaying their nude bodies. *The Artist* was not long in taking him up. In the number for 1 May 1889 a reference to Tuke, then twenty-nine years old, contains the opinion that 'nobody has painted boys better than this Cornish artist since the days of Fred Walker'. And in the same number Kains-Jackson placed a sonnet of his own, 'On a Picture by H. S. Tuke in the present exhibition at the New English Art Club'. He was constantly mentioned in the magazine thereafter. In the number dated 1 September 1893 we find an anonymous poet addressing 'A Ballade of Falmouth' to the admired young painter. In the next year, when his picture 'August Blue' (Plate 15) won acclamations after it was hung at the Royal Academy, a writer Alan Stanley, not known as a member of the *Artist* coterie however, produced verses about bathing boys using that very same title (No. 71). Bathing boys had come into a respectable vogue – for a time. The next year was 1895.

Rolfe also was doubtless an admirer of Tuke's art. It is believed that he stood close enough to the painter to get help from him in drawing some of the boy-figures in his murals in the Catholic Church at Christchurch.[53] In any case, both men had a mutual friend in Charles Masson Fox, the Falmouth timber-merchant, who received letters from Rolfe describing pederastic life in Venice during 1909–10.[54] After the 1914–18 War Tuke's reputation as an artist declined, though there have been signs recently of a revival of interest in his work.

At length the publication of an article called 'The New Chivalry' by Kains-Jackson, signing himself with his two middle names, Philip Castle, in the April number of *The Artist* in 1894, provoked an indignant sermon directed against him,[55] and it probably accounted for his resignation of the editorship soon afterwards. In May Lord Mountmorres replaced him in this office and the tone and style of the journal rapidly altered.

But 'The New Chivalry' was an unusual essay, and Kains-Jackson is entitled to any credit that may be due to his originality. At the same time, as I pointed out earlier (p. 5), this essay developed ideas associated formerly with Faber, Fitzgerald and Symonds. It was significant not only in the history of homosexuality in England, but also in the history of men's conception of women, which was gradually changing. Kains-Jackson was going even further than Carpenter was to do in his *Homogenic Love* published in the same year. He was recommending in 'The New Chivalry' that the conventions of special courtesy to women should apply to men and to boys, particularly to

[53] Information from Mr. Donald Weeks.
[54] Information from Mr. Timothy d'Arch Smith.
[55] Information from Mr. Timothy d'Arch Smith.

those distinguished in mind or in body (which was a little invidious). In other words he was adapting the relics of a mediaeval Courtly convention to the romantic exigencies of homosexuals in his own period. He had hopes, too, that the future would endorse his views of the matter; and in some respects the future did just that, but not in the way he meant. It endorsed them to the extent that some of the physical and mental characteristics of youthful males were imitated by women as the years passed, so that by the middle of the twentieth century young women had come to look more like the boys than the females of former times. This curious change, and the politics, slimming, leg-showing, independence and sport that have gone with it, had a psychological parallel in the changing tastes of men over the same period, whereby the aesthetic ideals of pederasts have contributed to the heterosexual standards of recent times (No. 68).

Another person who provoked hostility from conformists was George Ives, one of Kains-Jackson's friends and contemporaries, a contributor to *The Artist*, and also a friend of Wilde. In October of that same year, 1894, he was attacked in the *Review of Reviews* for an article in *The Humanitarian* in which he had criticized Grant Allen for evading the problem of homosexuality in his essay 'The New Hedonism'. 'The New Morality . . .' observed the *Review of Reviews*, 'might . . . have gone elsewhere for its ideal than to Sodom and Gomorrah.'[56] Before the end of the century two collections of poems by Ives were published: *A Book of Chains* (1897) without the author's name; and *Eros' Throne* (1900) with his name on the title-page. For the rest of his life he remained something of a crusader for what he imagined the Greek way of life.

The two other magazines mentioned previously were Oxford magazines. Of these, *The Spirit Lamp* was founded and edited from May 1892 by Sandys Wason of Christ Church, a clergyman-to-be. The editorship passed in November of the next term to Lord Alfred Douglas, who remained editor until the magazine came to an end in June 1893, after having changed into an irregular monthly.

To turn the pages of *The Spirit Lamp* is to discover numerous homosexual poems throughout – some translated from the French, for in France at this time parallel developments in quite different environments were afoot. Not all the contributors were undergraduates however: Stenbock for instance had long ceased to be. Some of the contributors must have been made much happier by the fact that compositions like theirs were appearing in successive numbers of the magazine. Apart from Douglas, Stenbock and Lionel Johnson, and Robert Ross of Cambridge, there were also, *de la bande*, George Gabriel Scott Gillett

[56] See Hart-Davis, *The Letters of Oscar Wilde*, London, 1962, p. 375.

of Keble (who became a clergyman); 'Bertram Lawrence' (J. F. Bloxam), Oscar Wilde, Pierre Louÿs, Charles Kains-Jackson, John Gambril Nicholson, Theodore Wratislaw, E. Bonney-Steyne, Percy Osborn, Stanley Addleshaw (another curate in later life) and William Percy Addleshaw; of whom Lionel Johnson, Wilde, Kains-Jackson and W. P. Addleshaw either were, or became, frequenters of the Crown pub in the Charing Cross Road.[57]

The short-lived *Chameleon*, edited by John Francis Bloxam of Exeter College and lasting for only one number, acquired notoriety in the year following its single emergence in December 1894 because of the unscrupulous use of three of its contents made by the prosecution in the Wilde case. These items were the poems by Douglas entitled 'Two Loves' and 'In Praise of Shame', and a story, 'The Priest and the Acolyte', by Bloxam (another clergyman-to-be). The last being unsigned was attributed to Wilde, and with indignation disacknowledged by him. Nevertheless he had read the story when it had appeared in the magazine and had not found fault with it then (No. 73).

Mr. Croft-Cooke in *Bosie*, his life of Lord Alfred Douglas, calls the story disgusting and blasphemous. Technically indeed it may be blasphemous; but disgusting? – surely not! The word that would be thrown at it today would be 'embarrassing'. If Wilde's 'Portrait of Mr. W. H.' counted as the first short story in English to dwell upon a pederastic note, then Bloxam's was the second. But Wilde was speculating about events in the life of Shakespeare, a national institution; whereas Bloxam was writing about a contemporary situation, and was quite frank about the sexual tone of the affection he was describing. The humorist Jerome K. Jerome in the London Journal *Today* drew attention to the 'unnatural' subject of the story, with some heat. But the pleas put forward by Bloxam to justify his boy-loving priest would be confirmed by most apologists for homosexuality still. Oddly enough the story would be unprintable in the routine publishing of our time, not on account of the subject, but on account of the emotions expressed by its author. The fact is that tenderfoot sentimentality of the past, or of this particular past, has come to be regarded since as more indecent than sentimental brutality of the present.

After a record of good service in the 1914 War, Bloxam continued life as a clergyman in the East End of London. He seems never to have published anything after 1894, and within the confines of this anthology he has his place on the strength of his pathetic *cris de cœur*.

In the literary treatment of male homosexuality certain Oxford graduates and undergraduates, as I have outlined, took conspicuous

[57] See Grant Richards, *Memoirs of a Misspent Youth*, London, 1932, p. 339.

parts in the years just before 1895. Over the half century from 1850 to 1900 some of the leading figures in the cultivation of this subject were in fact Cambridge men such as Cory and Carpenter and Oscar Browning. But the sister university never witnessed anything so fully-fashioned as *The Spirit Lamp* or *The Chameleon*. There was, no doubt, just as much practical homosexuality at Cambridge – but who can say? The expression of it was more individuated. Thus Howard Overing Sturgis, an American born in England, went to Eton where he was Cory's pupil; and then on to Cambridge, but nobody would be the wiser for that. His first novel *Tim* was the story of a romantic affair between a sensitive small boy and his slightly older and more conventional friend. The description of the younger boy as he died gave the author an opportunity to pitch the emotive passages high. It is another example of the kind of writing that would never get printed today: in the story are allusions to sentiments for which the English language seems no longer right. As a novel of childhood, *Tim* belongs to the same group as Florence Montgomery's *Misunderstood* or Anna Sewell's *Black Beauty* – a group now considered to be morbid. But at the back of this hard-faced approach lies an oversimplified concept of 'maturity'. In 1891 that was not a factor to be reckoned with, and on the strength of his friends' approval of *Tim*, Sturgis proceeded to write two other novels of a totally different character. E. M. Forster has written the most memorable portrait of him: '. . . heavily built . . . strong, [with] brilliantly white hair, forehead tall and narrow eyes soft and rather prominent, his moustache heavy and well-trimmed, the complexion delicate, the voice grave and low . . . something of a muff but far, far, far from a fool' (No. 52).[58]

Oxford was the alma mater, but Cambridge the refuge, of the one poet, A. E. Housman, who stands out from among the rest as capable of exploiting the depression experienced by homosexuals in that curiously inconsistent half-tolerant, half-hostile atmosphere of late Victorian England. Housman's *A Shropshire Lad* was published in 1896, not long after the Wilde trials of the previous year: the author even sent a copy of the book to Wilde soon after he came out of prison. But the sensuality which had inspired so many of the verses in *The Artist* had no place in Housman's poetry. His sadness was the sadness of one who was doomed to live with unsuitable emotions in a community where these were tacitly recognized but officially condemned.

A Shropshire Lad is like a beautiful ruin built over an invisible framework, and Housman obscured the framework so well that until recently not many readers of the poems seemed to guess that it was

[58] E. M. Forster, *Abinger Harvest*, London, 1936. The essay on H. O. Sturgis therein is dated 1935.

l'amour de l'impossible which haunted many of them, the same that haunted *In Memoriam* and *Ionica*. The untitled poem numbered XLIV (No. 83) has for its theme the kind of suicide Edward VII recommended in 1903 to Sir Hector Macdonald when that unfortunate general was under suspicion of homosexual practices. This was a suicide in order to preserve honour. In a related sense Housman's melancholy was an 'honourable' melancholy, arising from the suppression of his natural inclinations; and in that sense the context of some of the poems, if perceived at all, was properly understood. The melancholy of course may have had physiological origins apart from, but ultimately linked with, the depression in Housman which sprang from renunciation.

In contrast to the acceptance of social conventions which provided the tension for Housman's fatalism, a Cambridge student of the period exerted himself to defy all reticence about sexual emotions and all conventions of morality. This was Aleister Crowley, soon afterwards graduating into an Occultist, but in the 1890s still writing poems for *The Cambridge Magazine*, alongside more flagrant verses like the ones he had printed privately in his *White Stains*. This early phase of Aleister Crowley's was associated indirectly with Aubrey Beardsley, through their mutual friend Herbert Pollitt; except that what Crowley learnt from Beardsley was not the irony, which he was incapable of, but the provocation, which delighted him. It is in *White Stains* that we notice for the first time since the eighteenth century the promise – not so long after the Wilde scandal – of a brutal, burlesque approach to sexual intimacies and emotions which was to become common in our century; in a word, ribaldry. This approach is less evident in the two poems from *White Stains* included here than in others in the book which would not suit this anthology (Nos. 86, 87).

The only novel available in England before the 1914–18 War which had anything like the outspokenness of Crowley's *White Stains* was *Teleny, or the Reverse of the Medal*, written apparently about 1890, and published by Leonard Smithers in 1893. This book was scarcely more than a pornographic compilation, part of it following the formulae set out for such productions in the nineteenth century. It was redeemed however by being the one English novel until then in which the main story was concerned with homosexuality at its fullest extent. Some of the under-counter literature of the period included transvestite and homosexual incidents, both feminine and masculine; and *My Secret Life* contained more than one graphic description of exactly what happened when the author chose to experiment with 'sodomitical practices'. But the author, or authors, of *Teleny* were alone in their day in England in attempting to record the special atmosphere of homo-sexual intrigue and the emotions of men involved in what the police call a liaison. As such, therefore, the book has a certain literary réclame, though there are too many passages in it which look as if they were written to shock (No. 46).

I said 'author or authors', because nobody knows now who wrote the book. Wilde was associated with it, in that he brought the manuscript of it to Hirsch's shop in Coventry Street in 1890 and asked him to pass it on to a friend who would call for it. The friend duly called and took it away, returning it to be again called for by someone else. This process was repeated several times until the manuscript was returned to Wilde. Hirsch concluded that the novel was a compilation by several hands, among them that of Wilde. When it was published in an edition of 200 copies by Smithers the action of the story was moved from London to Paris in an attempt to avoid shocking his subscribers – or at least that is what Smithers told Hirsch. Anyway, it is easy to see that the locale of the novel is London and nowhere else.[59]

But it is hard to believe that Wilde had any hand in the writing of *Teleny*, though it is conceivable he may have made one or two corrections. Certainly there is little in the book that is much like any passage known to be by him. And the passages selected here show the novel at its best. The lurid portions are still too lurid for general publication and seem to have been dragged in to accord with pornographic expectations. A significant point is made, however, in the Foreword, where there is mention of 'the subtle influence of music *and the musician* in connection with perverted sexuality'. This was one of the superstitions referred to by Raffalovich in his *Uranisme et Unisexualité*, and a part of the total superstition that homosexuals were somehow more gifted than other persons, especially in the arts. One other significant point is that the novel is subtitled *A Physiological Romance of Today*; and in comparison with others that went before, the book is indeed physiological, with circumstantial descriptions of all the acrobatics a homosexual man is supposed to enjoy.

[59] An expurgated edition of *Teleny* was published by Icon Books, London, 1966, with an Introduction by Mr. Montgomery Hyde. The extracts in the present anthology have not been taken from that edition but from a copy of the 1893 edition published at 'Cosmopoli' by Leonard Smithers. The subtitle, *or The Reverse of the Medal*, did not appear with the name-title until Smithers published the book. By that time it had suffered many corrections and alterations. But Smithers claimed that a definitive edition would be issued when the 1893 edition was exhausted. Smithers' death prevented this project from being carried out. The manuscript passed into the hands of a friend of Hirsch, named Duringe, who permitted Hirsch to arrange for a French translation of the book, later issued in 300 copies at Paris in 1934.

Des Grieux. A Prelude to Teleny was announced by the Erotica Biblion Society in 1908.

Mr. Timothy d'Arch Smith was kind enough to let me take notes of the above and other information on *Teleny* from a manuscript by C. R. Dawes, the first English biographer of the Marquis de Sade.

The author of *Jaspar Tristram*, Edward Ashley Walrond Clarke, seems to have published nothing else, and to have left no reputation behind him as the begetter of one of the most interesting novels of the 1890s. But so it was. One can be carried away by the measured prose of this book, as developments in the career of Jaspar are described relentlessly from his first schooldays to his self-destructive rejection of Nita at the finish. The accurate analysis of each stage in the evolution of his unhappy passion for a school friend, from ecstasy to bitterness; of the transference of this passion for the friend to the friend's sister – surely an enlightened detail; and of the pride in which, at certain crises of emotion, he rejects whatever good fortune may arrive; all this has seldom been done so well or so vividly (No. 88).

The characters in many novels of the period seem to be made to overplay their parts, like actors in a silent film. *Jaspar Tristram* has none of this contemporary vice of professionalism. Presumably it was an autobiographical novel. It must have been one of the last read by Wilde, and a letter exists in which he recommended it to Louis Wilkinson, remarking that Radley was the model for the school in the story.[60]

John Gambril Nicholson's copy of *Jaspar Tristram* survives. In it he inscribed a poem of his own and another by Kains-Jackson, both on the subject of the book; and in the same note he revealed that he too suffered from the 'Pride and Sloth' that afflicted Clarke's hero.[61] Today we should perhaps emphasize not the pride and the sloth but the strain of conflicts arising in those who, by no fault of their own, have to encounter and reduce to the practical terms of a boarding school, their most formative, most urgent, years. Certainly no one who has been to a school like Radley in the earlier part of this century could fail to recognize the truth of Clarke's exposition of the tricks and subterfuges played by adolescent emotions in their concern with affection, and with the objects of affection.

In this introduction to the literary material that follows I can scarcely avoid a conclusion which might otherwise be taken for granted; and that is how everything points to an increase in the cultural manifestation of homosexuality between the years 1850 and 1895; and that the final stages of the increase can be associated with *The Artist*, its editor and contributors, and with Wilde and his friends – although among his friends only Douglas, at that time, had published anything much. Some of the movement of public opinion against Wilde in 1895[62]

---

[60] See Hart-Davis, *The Letters of Oscar Wilde*, London, 1962, p. 812.
[61] Information from Mr. Timothy d'Arch Smith.
[62] There was also resistance on principle in certain quarters to the newspaper-fed public indignation against Wilde. We find a memory of this in a book by an unnamed woman, *Anonymous 1871–1935*, London, 1936.

can be understood more easily if we remember certain incidents in the previous two years; the Wratislaw rumpus, esoteric though that was, the 'New Chivalry' article, Bloxam's story, and Ives's article on Grant Allen in 1894, all of which inspired hostile publicity. 1894 was also the year in which Carpenter gave his lecture on *Homogenic Love* at Manchester (a thing unimaginable until it happened); and the year too when Wilde's acquaintance, Alfred Taylor, was arrested with others in a brothel

---

[Hermann] Vezin's excitement at the trial, his horror and indignation at the sentence were Titanic. He looked like a tortured God. All of that circle were indignant, declaring openly and without fear of consequence that others were far more guilty and yet went unscathed. Names were bandied about as fitting for the crime list with a freedom of utterance that even after this lapse of time I dare not imitate. A famous artist – perhaps the most famous here in England in his time – a popular actor-manager – titled names – household words – were vociferously suggested as substitutes more deserving of the Law's attention, and it is to the credit of that little circle of great Bohemians that not a voice was hushed through any fear of shame or personal inconvenience. They felt Oscar was 'finished' socially, but his tragedy made no difference to their loyalty and value of him, and this was the more remarkable because they did not love him overmuch. On the contrary, until trouble fell on him they were something antagonistic. . . .
. . . Then his particular vice was abominated. James Welch, in particular, whose head of flaming red hair had a special attraction for Oscar, used to screw up his whimsical little face into a look of blazing scorn when Wilde tried to pull his bushy locks through his fingers. But all this was forgotten when the trial came and a deep, breathless spell seemed to fall on them. Newspapers were snatched from the boys' hands – coins scattered on the pavement to save the second it would take to select one, even by those with whom coins were not plentiful, while all who could went to the courts, not out of curiosity, but from a spirit of suspense and anxious expectation. I was waiting in his chambers for Vezin's return. He came in – shut the door – half held out his hand – dropped it and said nothing. But he looked years older.
There is an idea that Wilde was shameless and that he flaunted his vices. This is not quite the truth; he posed and advertised his whims, but it may have been from the same motive that I become aggressive – to cover humiliation. I know that when Welch winced away from his hand he flinched and turned first fiery red and then livid. He was ashamed. It was that same penetrating shame that broke him up. A man of harder metal might have weathered the storm, but he wilted under it. It was not lack of courage, for he faced the trial. It was, as I believe, his sense of the Greek that carried him through, as it had brought him to its cause. He felt himself Socrates perhaps; but it is easier to drink hemlock than to return from prison. Our justice was the more cruel.
Wilde was 'done'. They all said he was done. They all knew it. He would never come back. His name was removed from the programmes of the St. James' Theatre, where *The Importance of Being Earnest* was being played. Vezin had seats and took me, and when he saw that altered programme he crushed it in his hand and threw it away with an exclamation of disgust. And after a little he said:
'I'm sorry. I can't stay.' We left the theatre.
Yet now, when Cambridge youths hear by chance that I knew Oscar Wilde they gather round me.
'Did you know him well?' they ask and ply me with eager questions.

It is interesting to note that Louise Jopling recorded how she heard a newsboy shouting news of the trial. She stopped her hansom, 'and could not refrain from saying, "What is it?" The boy made a gesture of pity, and said, "Two years!" and we looked sorrowfully at each other' Louise (Jopling, *Twenty Years of My Life*, London, 1925, p. 82).

in Fitzroy Street. It was also the year in which Robert Hichens published his novel *The Green Carnation*, a satire on Douglas and Wilde with obvious insinuations. Thus 1894 could be described as a golden year for homosexuals in England, for the very reason that it was the last year for a long time in which they could take shelter in public ignorance or tolerance to propagate a non-hostile climate of taste and opinion.

But a majority verdict against whoever might be the scapegoat for this cultural manifestation was being steadily built up from a series of minor provocations, until in the trials of 1895 the show-down occurred, with Wilde as scapegoat. The force of public opinion, worked on by the press for financial-sensational reasons, had an effect of suppressing very notably and for a number of years the emergence of a climate like the one before 1895. What Frank Harris said in his biography of Wilde, about every train to Dover being crowded and every steamer to Calais being thronged with prudent homosexuals after the news of the arrest, is not quite true. On the other hand it is not quite false, for it is well known that Wilde's friends either went abroad or kept their heads well down in this dangerous period. As for the *Artist* coteries, these were already dispersed; Christchurch days were over and the journal under new management. Men who had formerly written homosexual poems either ceased to publish them, like Raffalovich and Kains-Jackson; or else had them published for limited circulation, like John Gambril Nicholson; or they took good care that their art concealed their craft, like A. E. Housman. An exception was Edward Clarke, whose *Jaspar Tristram* was published in 1899; which only goes to show that majority prejudices may not be quite so formidable as they seem. By 1901 it was possible for Percy Osborn to get away with *Rose Leaves from Philostratus*, which included some of his *Spirit Lamp* poems of eight years before.[63] Yet, even as late as 1906, Frank Danby (Julia Frankau) could produce a novel about Ada Leverson called *The Sphinx's Lawyer* in which homosexuality was referred to, but was none the less still referred to in a mysterious fashion. Younger men like Ronald Firbank in the Edwardian years reflected the stigmata of Wilde's martyrdom in novel and self-conscious flippancies. And it was not until 1908 that pederasty of the platonic sort became safe again with the *Sonnets, Songs and Ballads* of E. E. Bradford; like Bloxam, formerly of Exeter College, Oxford, and also a clergyman. Dr. Bradford's Crabbe-like stories in verse, in which he combined something of the padre and a little of the

[63] *Rose Leaves from Philostratus and other Poems*, written by Percy Osborn and published at The Sign of the Unicorn, vii Cecil Court, A.D. mdcccci. Even so, a few tactful amendments were made. The sonnet 'Heartsease and Orchid', dated December 1892 in the *Spirit Lamp*, Vol. 3, No. II, 17 February 1893, appeared again in *Rose Leaves from Philostratus*; but 'tender' replaced 'dainty' in line 2, and 'childhood' replaced 'boyhood' in line 3; and there were alterations of punctuation.

scoutmaster, flowed on into the 1930s with remarkable facility – one was even called *The New Chivalry*.[64] But what had evidently gone underground were the sensuous, dreamy, Greece-haunted and luxurious ideas of the Aesthetic school, and the over-handled images of Antinous and Ganymede, seen through a Renaissance gauze. By the middle of this century the treatment of homosexual fixation in terms of a Christian crisis was also outmoded, together with the primary worries which had disturbed Symonds and other devotees in the nineteenth century.

In the aftermath of the 1914 War the accent on 'femininity' in women was removed, and ever since then there has been a recurring tendency towards boyishness in form and clothes, up to the Dick Whittington figure of the later 1960s. A new permissiveness greeted the popularization of Freud and the objective treatment of sex questions. And of our own period the Victorians would very likely have said that the objective treatment had overbalanced into a calculated indulgence of the squalors as against the brilliancies of sexual adventure; yet of course they could be wrong. In any case, each generation has its own kind of collective ignorance, and it may be that for all our objectivity we know little about sexual problems and sexual possibilities.

Another point which becomes clear, I think, from this anthology and the study of its contents, is that a cultural condition can certainly influence sexual behaviour. It suited Wilde to maintain in the Old Bailey that books do not influence anybody. Yet they certainly influenced him. In all the arts the processes of imitation, assimilation and competition are essential and not to be overlooked in assessing the element of fashion by means of which the public, or portions of it, are kept in touch with actual artists of whatever sort. And when social and economic reasons are adduced for the increase of homosexuality in the second half of the nineteenth century in England, these should be multiplied by the imitative principle which made homosexuality of various kinds a vogue within certain small but widening circles.

The interest in this vogue for us today lies in the fact that 'Nature', in whatever scientific discipline we care to persuade her, was not in the long run on the side of the big battalions in 1895. With the passing of time since then it should be clear that some of the ideals which wrought changes in women, from garments to accomplishments, were ideals which came (unconsciously maybe) from the homosexual culture of the late nineteenth century. As women began to rival men, so they adopted male attributes, and in the United States, according to Vance Packard and other writers, confusion in the masculine role has resulted. But

[64] Early writings by Bradford date from the 1890s and so fall within the period covered by this book. A story by him, 'Boris Orloff', was published in *The Boy's Own Paper*, Nos. 2 and 9, September 1893, and was reprinted in a limited edition by Timothy d'Arch Smith in 1968.

just as changes like these are dependent partly on cultural influences, the position can be reversed in part, also by cultural influences, so that when the present ideas and ideals offer no future we can advance by brainwashing the public, or whatever minority it sanctions, to discourage all homosexuality and demoralize all homosexual emotion. Only, if we do this, the line between sex and friendship should be re-drawn compulsively by enough people to change the meaning of the words.

The chief difficulty for homosexuals, and for some of them a sovereign charm, is the fact that they travel together in the same direction. They share the same tastes; yet these are not complementary. True, they can stay balanced on the same path, until physical relations have no point, or until they swerve out; but if they imitate the polarities of heterosexuals they reach what is still regarded as an abnormal condition, in which one partner, or either alternately, takes over a para-female role. And although transvestites are not necessarily homosexual, a homosexual may acquire a 'female' temperament and so become, in some degree, transvestite. Meanwhile the popular and legal approach to pederasty is too severe. It has to be a very small child who can be said to be literally 'damaged' by such a relationship. The only kinds of sexual damage for which there can be any evidence, as in heterosexual instances, are rape and violence.

Walt Whitman, in his way, was right. The striving for security and power is planned at the cost of unconscious life: so that discords arising from this strain bring vitality too soon and too often to a deterioration of mind and body. In later, and now familiar, terms it amounts to the conflict of the Id and the Super-Ego destroying the Ego between them.

Centrifugally we lengthen ourselves from old beliefs which threaten our progress. The rise of homosexuality as a cultural phenomenon in the Victorian age, as well as its more recent development, were parts of this various enterprise; nor can they be separated from a struggle between men and women which ethical assumptions brought to a new urgency. In one related field we see it as only a question of time before the principles on which the empire of Great Britain were founded and sustained were produced to a meeting point, whence the assurance necessary to maintain an empire by force was not possible because this contradicted the new faith of equity. Within the same period it became clear how women should take, or be given, very much of what was held to be the right of all yet was enjoyed by men alone. The masculine protest of suffragettes, and the still closer approach to men from later emancipated women, both in order to fulfil and to compete with male desires, were affronted, chronologically at least, by the goose-steps of brutal and bewildering wars.

There came about another protest too, what for brevity's sake we may call the feminine protest of men, haunted by the will for a psychic unity, a state analogous to that state before a child realizes what sex it has, which the Greeks expressed in the legend of hermaphrodites; from which humanity was thought to be divided; at which homosexuals, male and female, by virtue of their handicaps, dreamed sometimes they were arriving. In a different sense the heterosexual shares the same dream. While the art of reconciling ourselves to existence remains mislaid, it is a dream that everybody craves. This was not always so. The Pantocrators of Byzantium, the Virgins of Giotto, the reassurance that runs through European music from Palestrina to Bach, often hint by religious means at the redemption of mankind; of the security and power, not of this immediate world but of another region within us and beside us, which comprises the unknown. But there are few demotic words for this region today, and no logic.

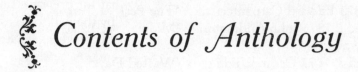

Contents of Anthology

C = date of composition P = date of first publication

Throughout the anthology, quotation marks around a title indicate that the following passage is simply an extract from a longer work. The title of the extract is not necessarily that of the complete work. Full details of the complete work and original title are given at the head of each extract.

1 Schooldays

Leigh Hunt. From *The Autobiography of Leigh Hunt*. Published 1850. The extract is taken from Chapter IV.

If I had reaped no other benefit from Christ-Hospital, the school would be ever dear to me from the recollection of the friendships I formed in it, and of the first heavenly taste it gave me of that most spiritual of the affections. I use the word 'heavenly' advisedly; and I call friendship the most spiritual of the affections, because even one's kindred, in partaking of our flesh and blood, become, in a manner, mixed up with our entire being. Not that I would disparage any other form of affection, worshipping, as I do, all forms of it, love in particular, which, in its highest state, is friendship and something more. But if ever I tasted a disembodied transport on earth, it was in those friendships which I entertained at school, before I dreamt of any maturer feeling. I shall never forget the impression it first made on me. I loved my friend for his gentleness, his candour, his truth, his good repute, his freedom even from my own livelier manner, his calm and reasonable kindness. It was not any particular talent that attracted me to him, or anything striking whatsoever. I should say, in one word, it was his goodness. I doubt whether he ever had a conception of a tithe of the regard and respect I entertained for him; and I smile to think of the perplexity (though he never showed it) which he probably felt sometimes at my enthusiastic expressions; for I thought him a kind of angel. It is no exaggeration to say, that, take away the unspiritual part of it, – the genius and the knowledge – and there is no height of conceit indulged in by the most romantic character in Shakespeare, which surpassed what I felt towards the merits I ascribed to him, and the delight which I took in his society. With the other boys I played antics, and rioted in fantastic jests; but in his society, or whenever I thought of him, I fell into a kind of Sabbath state of bliss; and I am sure I could have died for him.

I experienced this delightful affection towards three successive schoolfellows, till two of them had for some time gone out into the world and forgotten me; but it grew less with each, and in more than one instance, became rivalled by a new set of emotions, especially in regard to the last, for I fell in love with his sister – at least, I thought so. But on the occurrence of her death, not long after, I was startled at finding myself assume an air of greater sorrow than I felt, and at being willing to be relieved by the sight of the first pretty face that turned towards me. I was in the situation of the page in Figaro:

> Ogni donna cangiar di colore;
> Ogni donna mi fa palpitar.

My friend, who died himself not long after his quitting the University, was of a German family in the service of the court, very refined and musical. I likened them to the people in the novels of Augustus La Fontaine; and with the younger of the two sisters I had a great desire to play the part of the hero in the *Family of Halden*.

2   *In Memoriam*

Alfred, Lord Tennyson. Published 1850. The verses are taken from various sections.

IV

To Sleep I give my powers away;
   My will is bondsman to the dark;
   I sit within a helmless bark,
And with my heart I muse and say:

O heart how fares it with thee now,
   That thou should'st fail from thy desire,
   Who scarcely darest to inquire,
'What is it makes me beat so low?'

Something it is which thou hast lost,
   Some pleasure from thine early years.
   Break, thou deep vase of chilling tears,
That grief hath shaken into frost!

Such clouds of nameless trouble cross
   All night below the darken'd eyes;
   With morning wakes the will, and cries,
'Thou shalt not be the fool of loss'.

V

I sometimes hold it half a sin
   To put in words the grief I feel;
   For words, like Nature, half reveal
And half conceal the Soul within.

But, for the unquiet heart and brain,
   A use in measured language lies;
   The sad mechanic exercise,
Like dull narcotics, numbing pain.

In words, like weeds, I'll wrap me o'er,
  Like coarsest clothes against the cold:
  But that large grief which these enfold
Is given in outline and no more.

XIII

Tears of the widower, when he sees
  A late-lost form that sleep reveals,
  And moves his doubtful arms, and feels
Her place is empty, fall like these;

Which weep a loss for ever new,
  A void where heart on heart reposed;
  And, where warm hands have prest and closed,
Silence, till I be silent too.

Which weep the comrade of my choice,
  An awful thought, a life removed,
  The human-hearted man I loved,
A Spirit, not a breathing voice.

XVIII

Tis Well; 'tis something; we may stand
  Where he in English earth is laid,
  And from his ashes may be made
The violet of his native land.

'Tis little; but it looks in truth
  As if the quiet bones were blest
  Among familiar names to rest
And in the places of his youth.

Come then, pure hands, and bear the head
  That sleeps or wears the mask of sleep,
  And come, whatever loves to weep,
And hear the ritual of the dead.

Ah yet, ev'n yet, if this might be,
  I, falling on his faithful heart,
  Would breathing thro' his lips impart
The life that almost dies in me;

That dies not, but endures with pain,
    And slowly forms the firmer mind,
    Treasuring the look it cannot find,
The words that are not heard again.

XXIII

Now, sometimes in my sorrow shut,
    Or breaking into song by fits,
    Alone, alone, to where he sits,
The Shadow cloak'd from head to foot,

Who keeps the keys of all the creeds,
    I wander, often falling lame,
    And looking back to whence I came,
Or on to where the pathway leads;

And crying, How changed from where it ran
    Thro' lands where not a leaf was dumb;
    But all the lavish hills would hum
The murmur of a happy Pan:

When each by turns was guide to each,
    And Fancy light from Fancy caught,
    And Thought leapt out to wed with Thought
Ere Thought could wed itself with Speech;

And all we met was fair and good,
    And all was good that Time could bring,
    And all the secret of the Spring
Moved in the chambers of the blood;

And many an old philosophy
    On Argive heights divinely sang,
    And round us all the thicket rang
To many a flute of Arcady.

XXXVII

Urania speaks with darken'd brow:
    'Thou pratest here where thou art least;
    This faith has many a purer priest,
And many an abler voice than thou.

'Go down beside thy native rill,
    On thy Parnassus set thy feet,
    And hear thy laurel whisper sweet
About the ledges of the hill.'

And my Melpomene replies,
    A touch of shame upon her cheek:
    'I am not worthy ev'n to speak
Of thy prevailing mysteries;

'For I am but an earthly Muse,
    And owning but a little art
    To lull with song an aching heart,
And render human love his dues;

'But brooding on the dear one dead,
    And all he said of things divine,
    (And dear to me as sacred wine
To dying lips is all he said),

'I murmur'd, as I came along,
    Of comfort clasp'd in truth reveal'd;
    And loiter'd in the master's field,
And darken'd sanctities with song.'

XLIII

If Sleep and Death be truly one,
    And every spirit's folded bloom
    Thro' all its intervital gloom
In some long trance should slumber on;

Unconscious of the sliding hour,
    Bare of the body, might it last,
    And silent traces of the past
Be all the colour of the flower:

So then were nothing lost to man;
    So that still garden of the souls
    In many a figured leaf enrolls
The total world since life began;

And love will last as pure and whole
    As when he loved me here in Time,
    And at the spiritual prime
Reawaken with the dawning soul.

LXI

If, in thy second state sublime,
    Thy ransom'd reason change replies
    With all the circle of the wise,
The perfect flower of human time;

And if thou cast thine eyes below,
    How dimly character'd and slight,
    How dwarf'd a growth of cold and night,
How blanch'd with darkness must I grow!

Yet turn thee to the doubtful shore,
    Where thy first form was made a man;
    I loved thee, Spirit, and love, nor can
The soul of Shakespeare love thee more.

CXXIX

Dear friend, far off, my lost desire,
    So far, so near in woe and weal;
    O loved the most, when most I feel
There is a lower and a higher;

Known and unknown; human, divine;
    Sweet human hand and lips and eye;
    Dear heavenly friend that canst not die,
Mine, mine, for ever, ever mine;

Strange friend, past, present, and to be;
    Loved deeplier, darklier understood;
    Behold, I dream a dream of good,
And mingle all the world with thee.

CXXX

Thy voice is on the rolling air;
    I hear thee where the waters run;
    Thou standest in the rising sun,
And in the setting thou art fair.

What art thou then? I cannot guess;
 But tho' I seem in star and flower
 To feel thee some diffusive power,
I do not therefore love thee less:

My love involves the love before;
 My love is vaster passion now;
 Tho' mix'd with God and Nature thou,
I seem to love thee more and more.

Far off thou art, but ever nigh:
 I have thee still, and I rejoice;
 I prosper, circled with thy voice;
I shall not lose thee tho' I die.

3 'Half a Heart'

Frederick William Faber. From *Poems*. Published 1856.

Come, I will give thee half a heart
 If that will do to love;
And if I give thee all, dear friend,
 It would but worthless prove.

Thou art too good to see or know
 The ills that in me dwell:
It is most right to keep our faults
 From those we love so well.

So then I warn thee, do not think
 My fitful love untrue:
I have another, darker self,
 Which thou must sometimes view.

Men take me, change me, if they may,
 And love me if they can;
Few can do that; few choose, like thee,
 A double-hearted man.

My better self shall be thy friend,
　　My worse self not thy foe,
And to love light in time perchance,
　　May make my darkness go.

If I should seem to play thee false,
　　Then pour thy love through prayer:
It is the fit; my better heart
　　Withdraws itself elsewhere.

And weary not if I do still
　　New light or gloom disclose:
What else in sooth can poets be
　　But men whom no one knows?

4   'Heraclitus'

William Cory. From *Ionica*. Published 1858.

They told me, Heraclitus, they told me you were dead,
They brought me bitter news to hear and bitter tears to shed.
I wept, as I remembered, how often you and I
Had tired the sun with talking and sent him down the sky.

And now that thou art lying, my dear old Carian guest,
A handful of grey ashes, long long ago at rest,
Still are thy pleasant voices, thy nightingales awake;
For Death, he taketh all away, but them he cannot take.

5   'Preparation'

William Cory. From *Ionica*. Published 1858.

Too weak am I to pray, as some have prayed,
That love might hurry straightway out of mind,
And leave an ever-vacant waste behind.
I thank thee rather, that through every grade
Of less and less affection we decline,
As month by month thy strong importunate fate

Thrusts back my claims, and draws thee toward the great,
And shares amongst a hundred what was mine.
Proud heroes ask to perish in high noon:
I'd have refractions of the fallen day,
And heavings when the gale hath flown away,
And this slow disenchantment: since too soon,
Too surely, comes the death of my poor heart,
Be it inured to pain, in mercy, ere we part.

6   'Parting'

William Cory. From *Ionica*. Published 1858.

As when a traveller, forced to journey back,
    Takes coin by coin, and gravely counts them o'er,
Grudging each payment, fearing lest he lack,
    Before he can regain the friendly shore;
So reckoned I your sojourn, day by day,
So grudged I every week that dropt away.

And as a prisoner, doomed and bound, upstarts
    From shattered dreams of wedlock and repose,
At sudden rumblings of the market-carts,
    Which bring to town the strawberry and the rose,
And wakes to meet sure death; so shuddered I,
To hear you meditate your gay Good-bye.

But why not gay? For, if there's aught you lose,
    It is but drawing off a wrinkled glove
To turn the keys of treasuries, free to choose
    Throughout the hundred-chambered house of love,
This pathos draws from you, though true and kind,
Only bland pity for the left-behind.

We part; you comfort one bereaved, unmanned;
    You calmly chide the silence and the grief;
You touch me once with light and courteous hand,
    And with a sense of something like relief
You turn away from what may seem to be
Too hard a trial of your charity.

So closes in the life of life; so ends
    The soaring of the spirit. What remains?
To take whate'er the Muse's mother lends,
    One sweet sad thought in many soft refrains
And half-reveal in Coan gauze of rhyme
A cherished image of your joyous prime.

7   'What Cannot Be'

John Addington Symonds. From *Crocuses and Soldanellas*. Written October 1861, published *c*. 1879.

1

Oh! what a pain is here! All through the night
I yearned for power, and nursed rebellious scorn,
Striving against high heaven in hot despite
Of feeble nerves and will by passion torn.
I dreamed; and on the curtain of the gloom
False memory drew an idyll of old hope,
Singing a lullaby to mock my doom
With love far off and joy beyond my scope.
I woke; the present seemed more sad than hell;
On daily tasks my sullen soul I cast;
But, as I worked, a deeper sorrow fell
Like thunder on my spirit, for he passed
Before the house with wondering wide blue eye
That said 'I wait: why will you not reply?'

2

My heart was hot and answered 'What might be!
Love, peace, content, the brotherhood of strength;
He offers it of all convention free:
Wilt thou not take and eat and rest at length?
His brow is framed of beauty, and his soul
Sits throned within his eyelids orbed in light;
And from his parted lips harmonious roll
Full floods of music, rivers of delight!'
Oh, heart! false heart! why tear'st thou me again?
'To touch, to handle, stretching forth thy palm;

To sleep forgetful of sharp self-disdain:
It were so easy, and so sweet the calm!'
Calm as the dead salt sea; easy as sin;
Sweet as love-apples hiding dust within.

8   *'Hermaphroditus'*

Algernon Swinburne. From *Poems and Ballads*. Written 1863, published 1866.

I

Lift up thy lips, turn round, look back for love,
    Blind love that comes by night and casts out rest;
    Of all things tired thy lips look weariest,
Save the long smile that they are wearied of.
Ah sweet, albeit no love be sweet enough,
    Choose of two loves and cleave unto the best;
    Two loves at either blossom of thy breast
Strive until one be under and one above.
Their breath is fire upon the amorous air,
    Fire in thine eyes and where thy lips suspire:
And whosoever hath seen thee, being so fair,
    Two things turn all his life and blood to fire;
A strong desire begot on great despair,
    A great despair cast out by strong desire.

II

Where between sleep and life some brief space is,
    With love like gold bound round about the head,
    Sex to sweet sex with lips and limbs is wed,
Turning the fruitful feud of hers and his
To the waste wedlock of a sterile kiss;
    Yet from them something like as fire is shed
    That shall not be assuaged till death be dead,
Though neither life nor sleep can find out this.
Love made himself of flesh that perisheth
    A pleasure-house for all the loves his kin;
But on the one side sat a man like death,
    And on the other a woman sat like sin.
So with veiled eyes and sobs between his breath
    Love turned himself and would not enter in.

III

Love, is it love or sleep or shadow or light
        That lies between thine eyelids and thine eyes?
        Like a flower laid upon a flower it lies,
Or like the night's dew laid upon the night.
Love stands upon thy left hand and thy right,
        Yet by no sunset and by no moonrise
        Shall make thee man and ease a woman's sighs,
Or make thee woman for a man's delight.
To what strange end hath some strange god made fair
        The double blossom of two fruitless flowers?
Hid love in all the folds of all thy hair,
        Fed thee on summers, watered thee with showers,
Given all the gold that all the seasons wear
        To thee that art a thing of barren hours?

IV

Yea, love, I see; it is not love but fear.
        Nay, sweet, it is not fear but love, I know;
        Or wherefore should thy body's blossom blow
So sweetly, or thine eyelids leave so clear
Thy gracious eyes that never made a tear –
        Though for their love our tears like blood should flow,
        Though love and life and death should come and go,
So dreadful, so desirable, so dear?
Yea, sweet, I know; I saw in what swift wise
        Beneath the woman's and the water's kiss
        Thy moist limbs melted into Salmacis,
And the large light turned tender in thine eyes,
And all thy boy's breath softened into sighs;
        But Love being blind, how should he know of this?

9   *'The Beginning of the End'*

Gerard Manley Hopkins. Written 1865, first published 1918.

My love is lessened and must soon be past,
I never promised such persistency
In its condition. No, the tropic tree

Has not a charter that its sap shall last
Into all seasons, though no Winter cast
The happy leafing. It is so with me:
My love is less, my love is less for thee.
I cease the mourning and the abject fast,
And rise and go about my works again
And, save by darting accidents, forget.
But ah! if you could understand how then
That *less* is heavens higher even yet
Than treble-fervent *more* of other men,
Even your unpassioned eyelids might be wet.

I must feed fancy. Show me any one
That reads or holds the astrologic lore,
And I'll pretend the credit given of yore;
And let him prove my passion was begun
In the worst hour that's measured by the sun,
With such malign conjunctions that before
No influential heaven ever wore;
That no recorded devilish thing was done
With such a seconding, nor Saturn took
Such opposition to the Lady-star
In the most murderous passage of his book;
And I'll love my distinction: Near or far
He says his science helps him not to look
At hopes so evil-heaven'd as mine are.

You see that I have come to passion's end;
This means you need not fear the storms, the cries,
That gave you vantage when you would despise:
My bankrupt heart has no more tears to spend.
Else I am well assured I should offend
With fiercer weepings of these desperate eyes
For poor love's failure than his hopeless rise.
But now I am so tired I soon shall send
Barely a sigh to thought of hopes foregone.
Is this made plain? What have I come across
That here will serve me for comparison?
The sceptic disappointment and the loss
A boy feels when the poet he pores upon
Grows less and less sweet to him, and knows no cause.

10   'A Letter'

Digby Mackworth Dolben. Written 1866, published 1911.

My Love, and once again my Love,
And then no more until the end,
Until the waters cease to move,
Until we rest within the Ark,
And all is light which now is dark,
And loves can never more descend.
And yet – and yet be just to me
At least for manhood; for the whole
Love-current of a human soul,
Though bent and rolled through fruitless ways,
Tho' marred with slime and choked with weed,
(Long lost the silver ripple-song,
Long past the sprouting water-mead,)
Is something awful, broad and strong.
Remember that this utterly,
With all its waves of passion, set
To you; that all the water store,
No second April shall restore,
Was so to broken cisterns poured,
And lost, or else long since had met
The ocean-love of Christ the Lord.
My Brother, hear me; for the Name
Which is as fire in my bones
Has burned away the former shame;
Held I my peace, the very stones
Would cry against me; hear me then,
Who will not bid you hear again.
Hear what I saw, and why I fled,
And how I lost and how I won,
I, who between the quick and dead,
Once chose corruption for my own.
     I saw, where heaven's arches meet,
One stand in awfulness alone,
With folded robe and gleaming feet
And eyes that looked not up nor down.
It was the archangel, drawing breath
To blow for life, to blow for death.
The glow and soft reality

Of love and life grew cold and grey,
And died before the Eternity
That compasseth the Judgement day.
I said, 'My sin is full and ended';
While down the garden that we tended,
As in a heavy dream, I turned
Thro' lilied glades that once were sweet,
Trampling the buds that kissed my feet,
Until the sword above me burned.
My hair was shrivelled to my head,
My heart as ashes scorched, and dead
As his who ere its beating died.
The life imprisoned in my brain
Burst to my eyes in throbs of pain,
And all their tender springs were dried.
For miles and miles the wilds I trod,
Drunk with the angry wine of God;
Until the nets of anguish broke,
Until the prisoner found release.
    I mused awhile in quietness
Upon that strangest liberty:
Then other fires intolerably
Were kindled in me – and I spoke;
And so attained the hidden Peace,
The land of Wells beyond the fire,
The Face of loveliness unmarred,
The Consummation of desire.
    O vesper-light! O night thick-starred!
O five-fold springs, that upward burst
And radiate from Calvary
To stay the weary nations' thirst,
And hide a world's impurity! –
How one drew near with soiled feet,
Through all the Marah overflow,
And how the waters were made sweet
That night Thou knowest, – only Thou.
    Repent with me, for judgement waits.
Repent with me, for Jesus hung
Three hours upon the nails for you.
Rise, bid the angels sing anew
At every one of Sion's gates
The song which then for me they sung.

11   'Sonnet'

Digby Mackworth Dolben. Written 1866, published 1911.

> One night I dreamt that in a gleaming hall
> You played, and overhead the air was sweet
> With waving kerchiefs; then a sudden fall
> Of flowers; and jewels clashed about your feet.
> Around you glittering forms, a starry ring,
> In echo sang of youth and golden ease:
> You leant to me a moment, crying – 'Sing,
> 'If, as you say, you love me, sing with these.' –
>   In vain my lips were opened, for my throat
> Was choked somewhence, my tongue was sore and dry,
> And in my soul alone the answering note;
> Till, in a piercing discord, one shrill cry,
> As of a hunted creature, from me broke.
> You laughed, and in great bitterness I woke.

12   'Winckelmann'

Walter Pater. From *The Westminster Review*, 1867. Included in *Studies in the History of the Renaissance*, 1873.

Goethe's fragments of art criticism contain a few pages of strange pregnancy on the character of Winckelmann. He speaks of the teacher who had made his career possible, but whom he had never seen, as of an abstract type of culture, consummate, tranquil, withdrawn already into the region of ideals, yet retaining colour from the incidents of a passionate intellectual life. He classes him with certain works of art possessing an inexhaustible gift of suggestion, to which criticism may return again and again with undiminished freshness. Hegel, in his Lectures on the Philosophy of Art, estimating the work of his predecessors, has also passed a remarkable judgement on Winckelmann's writings. 'Winckelmann by contemplation of the ideal works of the ancients received a sort of inspiration through which he opened a new sense for the study of art. He is to be regarded as one of those who in the sphere of art have known how to initiate a new organ for the human spirit.' That it has given a new sense, that it has laid open a new organ, is the highest that can be said of any critical effort. It is interesting then to ask what kind of man it was who thus laid open a new organ? Under what conditions was that effected?

Johann Joachim Winckelmann was born at Stendal, in Brandenburg, in the year 1717. The child of a poor tradesman, he passed through many struggles in early youth, the memory of which ever remained in him as a fitful cause of dejection. In 1763, in the full emancipation of his spirit, looking over the beautiful Roman prospect, he writes, 'One gets spoiled here; but God owed me this; in my youth I suffered too much.' Destined to assert and interpret the charm of the Hellenic spirit, he served first a painful apprenticeship in the tarnished intellectual world of Germany in the earlier half of the eighteenth century. Passing out of that into the happy light of the antique he had a sense of exhilaration almost physical. We find him as a child in the dusky precincts of a German school hungrily feeding on a few colourless books. The master of this school grows blind; Winckelmann becomes his famulus. The old man would have had him study theology. Winckelmann, free of the master's library, chooses rather to become familiar with the Greek classics. Herodotus and Homer win, with their 'vowelled' Greek, his warmest cult. Whole nights of fever are devoted to them; disturbing dreams of an Odyssey of his own come to him. 'Il se sentit attiré vers le Midi, avec ardeur,' Madame de Staël says of him; 'on retrouve encore souvent dans les imaginations Allemandes quelques traces de cet amour du soleil, de cette fatigue du Nord, qui entraîna les peuples septentrionaux dans les contrées méridionales. Un beau ciel fait naître des sentiments semblables à l'amour de la patrie.'

To most of us, after all our steps towards it, the antique world, in spite of its intense outlines, its perfect self-expression, still remains faint and remote. To him, closely limited except on the side of the ideal, building for his dark poverty a house not made with hands, it early came to seem more real than the present. In the fantastic plans of travel continually passing through his mind, to Egypt, for instance, and France, there seems always to be rather a wistful sense of something lost to be regained, than the desire of discovering anything new. Goethe has told us how, in his eagerness to handle the antique, he was interested in the insignificant vestiges of it which the neighbourhood of Strasburg contained. So we hear of Winckelmann's boyish antiquarian wanderings among the ugly Brandenburg sandhills. Such a conformity between himself and Winckelmann, Goethe would have gladly noted.

At twenty-one he enters the University of Halle, to study theology, as his friends desire; instead he becomes the enthusiastic translator of Herodotus. The condition of Greek learning in German schools and universities had fallen, and Halle had no professors who could satisfy his sharp, intellectual craving. Of his professional education he always speaks with scorn, claiming to have been his own teacher from first to last. His appointed teachers did not perceive that a new source of culture was within their hands. 'Homo vagus et inconstans,' one of them pedantically reports of the future pilgrim to Rome, unaware on which side his irony was whetted. When professional education confers nothing but irritation on a Schiller, no one ought to be surprised; for Schiller and such as he are primarily spiritual adventurers. But that Winckelmann, the votary of the gravest of intellectual traditions, should get nothing but an attempt at suppression from the professional guardians of learning, is what may well surprise us.

In 1743 he became master of a school at Seehausen. This was the most wearisome period of his life. Notwithstanding a success in dealing with children, which seems to testify to something simple and primeval in his nature, he found the work of teaching very depressing. Engaged in this work, he writes that he still has within a longing desire to attain to the knowledge of beauty; 'sehnlich wünschte zur Kenntniss des Schönen zu gelangen.' He had to shorten his nights, sleeping only four hours, to gain time for reading. And here Winckelmann made a step forward in culture. He multiplied his intellectual force by detaching from it all flaccid interests. He renounced mathematics and law, in which his reading had been considerable, all but the literature of the arts. Nothing was to enter into his life unpenetrated by its central enthusiasm. At this time he undergoes the charm of Voltaire. Voltaire belongs to that flimsier, more artificial, classical tradition, which Winckelmann was one day to supplant by the clear ring, the eternal outline of the genuine antique. But it proves the authority of such a gift as Voltaire's, that it allures and wins even those born to supplant it. Voltaire's impression on Winckelmann was never effaced; and it gave him a consideration for French literature which contrasts with his contempt for the literary products of Germany. German literature transformed, siderealized, as we see it in Goethe, reckons Winckelmann among its initiators. But Germany at that time presented nothing in which he could have anticipated 'Iphigenie' and the formation of an effective classical tradition in German literature.

Under this purely literary influence, Winckelmann protests against Christian Wolf and the philosophers. Goethe, in speaking of this protest, alludes to his own obligations to Emmanuel Kant. Kant's influence over the culture of Goethe, which he tells us could not have been resisted by him without loss, consisted in a severe limitation to the concrete. But he adds, that in born antiquaries like Winckelmann, constant handling of the antique, with its eternal outline, maintains that limitation as effectually as a critical philosophy. Plato however, saved so often for his redeeming literary manner, is excepted from

Winckelmann's proscription of the philosophers. The modern most often meets Plato on that side which seems to pass beyond Plato into a world no longer pagan, based on the conception of a spiritual life. But the element of affinity which he presents to Winckelmann is that which is wholly Greek, and alien from the Christian world, represented by that group of brilliant youths in the Lysis, still uninfected by any spiritual sickness, finding the end of all endeavour in the aspects of the human form, the continual stir and motion of a comely human life.

This new-found interest in Plato's writings could not fail to increase his desire to visit the countries of the classical tradition. 'It is my misfortune,' he writes, 'that I was not born to a great place, wherein I might have had cultivation and the opportunity of following my instinct and forming myself.' Probably the purpose of visiting Rome was already formed, and he silently preparing for it. Count Bünau, the author of an historical work then of note, had collected at Nöthenitz, near Dresden, a valuable library, now part of the library of Dresden. In 1784 Winckelmann wrote to Bünau in halting French: 'He is emboldened,' he says, 'by Bünau's indulgence for needy men of letters.' He desires only to devote himself to study, having never allowed himself to be dazzled by favourable prospects in the church. He hints at his doubtful position 'in a metaphysical age, when humane literature is trampled under foot. At present,' he goes on, 'little value is set on Greek literature, to which I have devoted myself so far as I could penetrate, when good books are so scarce and expensive.' Finally, he desires a place in some corner of Bünau's library. 'Perhaps at some future time I shall become more useful to the public, if, drawn from obscurity in whatever way, I can find means to maintain myself in the capital.'

Soon after we find Winckelmann in the library at Nöthenitz. Thence he made many visits to the collection of antiques at Dresden. He became acquainted with many artists, above all with Oeser, Goethe's future friend and master, who, uniting a high culture with a practical knowledge of art, was fitted to minister to Winckelmann's culture. And now there opened for him a new way of communion with the Greek life. Hitherto he had handled the words only of Greek poetry, stirred indeed and roused by them, yet divining beyond the words an unexpressed pulsation of sensuous life. Suddenly he is in contact with that life still fervent in the relics of plastic art. Filled as our culture is with the classical spirit, we can hardly imagine how deeply the human mind was moved when at the Renaissance, in the midst of a frozen world, the buried fire of ancient art rose up from under the soil. Winckelmann here reproduces for us the earlier sentiment of the Renaissance. On a sudden the imagination feels itself free. How facile and direct, it seems to say, is this life of the senses and the understanding when once we have apprehended it! That is the more liberal life we have been seeking so long, so near to us all the while. How mistaken and roundabout have been our efforts to reach it by mystic passion and religious reverie; how they have deflowered the flesh; how little they have emancipated us! Hermione melts from her stony posture, and the lost proportions of life right themselves. There, is an instance of Winckelmann's tendency to escape from abstract theory to intuition, to the exercise of sight and touch. Lessing, in the *Laocoon*, has finely theorized on the relation of poetry to sculpture; and philosophy can give us theoretical reasons why not poetry but sculpture should be the most sincere and exact expression of the Greek ideal. By a happy, unperplexed dexterity, Winckelmann solves the question in the concrete. It is what Goethe calls his 'Gewahrwerden der griechischen Kunst,' his *finding* of Greek art.

Through the tumultuous richness of Goethe's culture, the influence of Winckelmann is always discernible as the strong regulative under-current of a clear antique motive. 'One learns nothing from him,' he says to Eckermann, 'but one becomes something.' If we ask what the secret of this influence was, Goethe himself will tell us: elasticity, wholeness, intellectual integrity. And yet these expressions, because they fit Goethe, with his universal culture, so well, seem hardly to describe the narrow, exclusive interest of Winckelmann. Doubtless Winckelmann's perfection is a narrow perfection; his feverish nursing of the one motive of his life is a contrast to Goethe's various energy. But what affected Goethe, what instructed him and ministered to his culture, was the integrity, the truth to its type of the given force. The development of this force was the single interest of Winckelmann, unembarrassed by anything else in him. Other interests, religious, moral, political, those slighter talents and motives not supreme, which in most men are the waste part of nature, and drain away their vitality, he plucked out and cast from him. The protracted longing of his youth is not a vague romantic longing; he knows what he longs for, what he wills. Within its severe limits his enthusiasm burns like lava. 'You know,' says Lavater, speaking of Winckelmann's countenance, 'that I consider ardour and indifference by no means incompatible in the same character. If ever there was a striking instance of that union, it is in the countenance before us.' 'A lowly childhood,' says Goethe, 'insufficient instruction in youth, broken, distracted studies in early manhood; the burden of school-keeping! He was thirty years old before he enjoyed a single favour of fortune, but as soon as he had attained to an adequate condition of freedom, he appears before us consummate and entire, complete in the ancient sense.'

But his hair is turning grey, and he has not yet reached the south.

The Saxon court had become Roman Catholic, and the way to favour at Dresden was through Romish ecclesiastics. Probably the thought of a profession of the Romish religion was not new to Winckelmann. At one time he had thought of begging his way to Rome, from cloister to cloister, under the pretence of a disposition to change his faith. In 1751 the papal nuncio, Archinto, was one of the visitors at Nöthenitz. He suggested Rome as a stage for Winckelmann's attainments, and held out the hope of a place in the papal library. Cardinal Passionei, charmed with Winckelmann's beautiful Greek writing, was ready to play the part of Maecenas, on condition that the necessary change should be made. Winckelmann accepted the bribe and visited the nuncio at Dresden. Unquiet still at the word 'profession,' not without a struggle, he joined the Romish Church, July the eleventh, 1754.

Goethe boldly pleads that Winckelmann was a pagan, that the landmarks of Christendom meant nothing to him. It is clear that he intended to deceive no one by his disguise; fears of the inquisition are sometimes visible during his life in Rome; he entered Rome notoriously with the works of Voltaire in his possession; the thought of what Bünau might be thinking of him seems to have been his greatest difficulty. On the other hand, he may have had a sense of something grand, primeval, pagan, in the Catholic religion. Casting the dust of Protestantism off his feet – Protestantism which at best had been one of the *ennuis* of his youth – he might reflect that while Rome had reconciled itself to the Renaissance, the Protestant principle in art had cut off Germany from the supreme tradition of beauty. And yet to that transparent nature, with its simplicity as of the earlier world, the loss of absolute sincerity must have been a real loss. Goethe understands that Winckelmann had made this sacrifice. He speaks of the doubtful charm of renegadism as something like that which belongs to a divorced woman, or to 'Wildbret mit einer kleinen Andeutung von Fäulniss.' Certainly at the bar of the highest criticism Winckelmann is more than absolved. The insincerity of his religious profession was only one incident of a culture in which the moral instinct, like the religious or political, was lost in the artistic. But then the artistic interest was that by desperate faithfulness to which Winckelmann was saved from the mediocrity which, breaking through no bounds, moves ever in a bloodless routine, and misses its one chance in the life of the spirit and the intellect. There have been instances of culture developed by every high motive in turn, and yet intense at every point; and the aim of our culture should be to attain not only as intense but as complete a life as possible. But often the higher life is only possible at all on condition of a selection of that in which one's motive is native and strong; and this selection involves the renunciation of a crown reserved for others. Which is better; to lay open a new sense, to initiate a new organ for the human spirit, or to cultivate many types of perfection up to a point which leaves us still beyond the range of their transforming power? Savonarola is one type of success; Winckelmann is another; criticism can reject neither, because each is true to itself. Winckelmann himself explains the motive of his life when he says, 'It will be my highest reward if posterity acknowledges that I have written worthily.'

For a time he remained at Dresden. There his first book appeared, *Thoughts on the Imitation of Greek Works of Art in Painting and Sculpture*. Full of obscurities as it was, obscurities which baffled but did not offend Goethe when he first turned to art-criticism, its purpose was direct, an appeal from the artificial classicism of the day to the study of the antique. The book was well received, and a pension was supplied through the king's confessor. In September, 1755, he started for Rome, in the company of a young Jesuit. He was introduced to Raphael Mengs, a painter then of note, and found a home near him, in the artists' quarter, in a place where he could 'overlook far and wide the eternal city.' At first he was perplexed with the sense of being a stranger on what was to him native soil. 'Unhappily,' he cries in French, often selected by him as the vehicle of strong feeling, 'I am one of those whom the Greeks call ὀψιμαθεῖς. I have come into the world and into Italy too late.' More than thirty years afterwards, Goethe also, after many aspirations and severe preparation of mind, visited Italy. In early manhood, just as he, too, was *finding* Greek art, the rumour of that high artist's life of Winckelmann in Italy had strongly moved him. At Rome, spending a whole year drawing from the antique, in preparation for 'Iphigenie,' he finds the stimulus of Winckelmann's memory ever active. Winckelmann's Roman life was simple, primeval, Greek. His delicate constitution permitted him the use only of bread and wine. Condemned by many as a renegade, he had no desire for places of honour, but only to see his merits acknowledged and existence assured to him. He was simple, without being niggardly; he desired to be neither poor nor rich.

Winckelmann's first years in Rome present all the elements of an intellectual situation of the highest interest. The beating of the intellect against its bars, the sombre aspect, the alien traditions, the still barbarous literature of Germany, are far off; before him are adequate conditions of culture, the sacred soil itself, the first tokens of the advent of the new German literature, with its broad horizons, its boundless intellectual promise. Dante, passing from the darkness of the 'Inferno,' is filled with a sharp and joyful sense of light which makes him deal with it in the opening of the 'Purgatorio' in a wonderfully touching and penetrative way. Hellenism, which is pre-eminently intellectual light –

modern culture may have more colour, the mediaeval spirit greater heat and profundity, but Hellenism is pre-eminent for light – has always been most successfully handled by those who have crept into it out of an intellectual world in which the sombre elements predominate. So it had been in the ages of the Renaissance. This repression, removed at last, gave force and glow to Winckelmann's native affinity to the Hellenic spirit. 'There had been known before him,' says Madame de Staël, 'learned men who might be consulted like books: but no one had, if I may say so, made himself a pagan for the purpose of penetrating antiquity.' '*On exécute mal ce qu'on n'a pas concu soi-même*'[1] – words spoken on so high an occasion – are true in their measure of every genuine enthusiasm. Enthusiasm – that, in the broad Platonic sense of the *Phaedrus*, was the secret of his divinatory power over the Hellenic world. This enthusiasm, dependent as it is to a great degree on bodily temperament, gathering into itself the stress of the nerves and the heat of the blood, has a power of reinforcing the purer motions of the intellect with an almost physical excitement. That his affinity with Hellenism was not merely intellectual, that the subtler threads of temperament were inwoven in it, is proved by his romantic, fervid friendships with young men. He has known, he says, many young men more beautiful than Guido's archangel. These friendships, bringing him in contact with the pride of human form, and staining his thoughts with its bloom, perfected his reconciliation with the spirit of Greek sculpture. A letter on taste, addressed from Rome to a young nobleman, Friedrich von Berg, is the record of such a friendship.

'I shall excuse my delay,' he begins, 'in fulfilling my promise of an essay on the taste for beauty in works of art, in the words of Pindar. He says to Agesidamus, a youth of Locri, ἰδέᾳ τε καλὸν, ὥρᾳ τε κεκραμένον, whom he had kept waiting for an intended ode, that a debt paid with usury is the end of reproach. This may win your good-nature on behalf of my present essay, which has turned out far more detailed and circumstantial than I had at first intended.

'It is from yourself that the subject is taken. Our intercourse has been short, too short both for you and me; but the first time I saw you the affinity of our spirits was revealed to me. Your culture proved that my hope was not groundless, and I found in a beautiful body a soul created for nobleness, gifted with the sense of beauty. My parting from you was, therefore, one of the most painful in my life; and that this feeling continues our common friend is witness, for your separation from me leaves me no hope of seeing you again. Let this essay be a memorial of our friendship, which, on my side, is free from every

[1] Words of Charlotte Corday before the *Convention*. (The note here, and those throughout this essay, are Pater's.)

selfish motive, and ever remains subject and dedicate to yourself alone.'

The following passage is characteristic:

'As it is confessedly the beauty of *man* which is to be conceived under one general idea, so I have noticed that those who are observant of beauty only in women, and are moved little or not at all by the beauty of men, seldom have an impartial, vital, inborn instinct for beauty in art. To such persons the beauty of Greek art will ever seem wanting, because its supreme beauty is rather male than female. But the beauty of art demands a higher sensibility than the beauty of nature, because the beauty of art, like tears shed at a play, gives no pain, is without life, and must be awakened and repaired by culture. Now, as the spirit of culture is much more ardent in youth than in manhood, the instinct of which I am speaking must be exercised and directed to what is beautiful before that age is reached at which one would be afraid to confess that one had no taste for it.'

Certainly, of that beauty of living form which regulated Winckelmann's friendships, it could not be said that it gave no pain. One notable friendship, the fortune of which we may trace through his letters, begins with an antique, chivalrous letter in French, and ends noisily in a burst of angry fire. Far from reaching the quietism, the bland indifference of art, such attachments are nevertheless more susceptible than any others of equal strength of a purely intellectual culture. Of passion, of physical stir, they contain just so much as stimulates the eye to the last lurking delicacies of colour and form. These friendships, often the caprices of a moment, make Winckelmann's letters, with their troubled colouring, an instructive but bizarre addition to the *History of Art*, that shrine of grave and mellow light for the mute Olympian family. Excitement, intuition, inspiration, rather than the contemplative evolution of general principles, was the impression which Winckelmann's literary life gave to those about him. The quick, susceptible enthusiast, betraying his temperament, even in appearance, by his olive complexion, his deep-seated, piercing eyes, his rapid movements, apprehended the subtlest principles of the Hellenic manner not through the understanding, but by instinct or touch. A German biographer of Winckelmann has compared him to Columbus. That is not the happiest of comparisons; but it reminds one of a passage in which M. Edgar Quinet describes Columbus's famous voyage. His science was often at fault; but he had a way of estimating at once the slightest indication of land in a floating weed or passing bird; he seemed actually to come nearer to nature than other men. And that world in which others had moved with so much embarrassment, seems to call out in Winckelmann new senses fitted to deal with it. He is *en rapport* with it; it penetrates him, and becomes part of his temperament. He remodels his writings with constant renewal of insight; he catches the thread of a whole sequence of laws in some hollowing of the hand, or dividing of the hair; he seems to realize that fancy of the reminiscence of a forgotten knowledge hidden for a time in the mind itself, as if the mind of one φιλοσοφήσας πότε μέτ᾽ ἔρωτος, fallen into a new cycle, were beginning its intellectual culture over again, yet with a certain power of anticipating its results. So comes the truth of Goethe's judgement on his works; they are *ein Lebendiges für die Lebendigen geschrieben, ein Leben selbst.*

In 1758, Cardinal Albani, who possessed in his Roman villa a precious collection of antiques, became Winckelmann's patron. Pompeii had just opened its treasures; Winckelmann gathered its first fruits. But his plan of a visit to Greece remained unfulfilled. From his first arrival in Rome he had kept the *History of Ancient Art* ever in view. All his other writings were a preparation for it. It appeared, finally, in 1764; but even after its publication Winckelmann was still employed in perfecting it. It is since his time that many of the most significant examples of Greek art have been submitted to criticism. He had seen little or nothing of what we ascribe to the age of Phidias; and his conception of Greek art tends, therefore, to put the mere elegance of Imperial society in place of the severe and chastened grace of the palaestra. For the most part he had to penetrate to Greek art through copies, imitations, and later Roman art itself; and it is not surprising that this turbid medium has left in Winckelmann's actual results much that a more privileged criticism can correct.

He had been twelve years in Rome. Admiring Germany had made many calls to him; at last, in 1768, he set out on a visit with the sculptor Cavaceppi. As he left Rome a strange inverted home-sickness came upon him. He reached Vienna; there he was loaded with honours and presents; other cities were awaiting him. Goethe, then nineteen years old, studying art at Leipsic, was expecting his coming with that wistful eagerness which marked his youth, when the news of Winckelmann's murder arrived. All that *fatigue du Nord* had revived with double force. He left Vienna, intending to hasten back to Rome. At Trieste a delay of a few days occurred. With characteristic openness Winckelmann had confided his plans to a fellow-traveller, a man named Arcangeli, and had shown him the gold medals which he had received at Vienna. Arcangeli's avarice was roused. One morning he entered Winckelmann's room under pretence of taking leave; Winckelmann was then writing 'memoranda for the future editor of the *History of Art*,' still seeking the perfection of his great work; Arcangeli begged to see the medals once more. As Winckelmann stooped down to take them from the chest, a cord was thrown round his neck. Some time after, a child

whose friendship Winckelmann had made to beguile the delay, knocked
at the door, and receiving no answer, gave an alarm. Winckelmann was
found dangerously wounded, and died a few hours later, after receiving
the sacraments of the Romish church. It seemed as if the gods, in
reward for his devotion to them, had given him a death which, for its
swiftness and its opportunity, he might well have desired. 'He has,'
says Goethe, 'the advantage of figuring in the memory of posterity as
one eternally able and strong, for the image in which one leaves the
world is that in which one moves among the shadows.' Yet, perhaps,
it is not fanciful to regret that that meeting with Goethe did not take
place. Goethe, then in all the pregnancy of his wonderful youth, still
unruffled by the press and storm of his earlier manhood, was awaiting
Winckelmann with a curiosity of the noblest kind. As it was, Winckelmann became to him something like what Virgil was to Dante. And
Winckelmann, with his fiery friendships, had reached that age and that
period of culture at which emotions, hitherto fitful, sometimes concentrate themselves in a vital unchangeable relationship. German literary
history seems to have lost the chance of one of those famous friendships
the very tradition of which becomes a stimulus to culture, and exercises
an imperishable influence.

In one of the frescoes of the Vatican, Raffaelle has commemorated the
tradition of the Catholic religion. Against a strip of peaceful sky, broken
in upon by the beatific vision, are ranged the great personages of
Christian history, with the Sacrament in the midst. The companion
fresco presents a very different company, Dante alone appearing in
both. Surrounded by the muses of Greek mythology, under a thicket of
myrtles, sits Apollo, with the sources of Castalia at his feet. On either
side are grouped those on whom the spirit of Apollo descended, the
classical and Renaissance poets, to whom the waters of Castalia come
down, a river making glad this other city of God. In this fresco it is the
classical tradition, the orthodoxy of taste, that Raffaelle commemorates.
Winckelmann's intellectual history authenticates the claims of this
tradition in human culture. In the countries where that tradition arose,
where it still lurked about its own artistic relics, and changes of language
had not broken its continuity, national pride might often light up anew
an enthusiasm for it. Aliens might imitate that enthusiasm, and classicism become from time to time an intellectual fashion; but Winckelmann was not farther removed by language than by local aspects and
associations from the vestiges of the classical spirit, and he lived at a
time when, in Germany, classical studies were out of fashion. Yet,
remote in time and place, he feels after the Hellenic world, divines the
veins of ancient art, in which its life still circulates, and, like Scyles in

the beautiful story of Herodotus, is irresistibly attracted by it. This testimony to the authority of the Hellenic tradition, its fitness to satisfy some vital requirement of the intellect, which Winckelmann contributes as a solitary man of genius, is offered also by the general history of culture. The spiritual forces of the past, which have prompted and informed the culture of a succeeding age, live, indeed, within that culture, but with an absorbed, underground life. The Hellenic element alone has not been so absorbed or content with this underground life; from time to time it has started to the surface; culture has been drawn back to its sources to be clarified and corrected. Hellenism is not merely an element in our intellectual life; it is a conscious tradition in it.

Again, individual genius works ever under conditions of time and place: its products are coloured by the varying aspects of nature and type of human form and outward manners of life. There is thus an element of change in art; criticism must never for a moment forget that 'the artist is the child of his time.' But besides these conditions of time and place, and independent of them, there is also an element of permanence, a standard of taste which genius confesses. This standard is maintained in a purely intellectual tradition; it acts upon the artist, not as one of the influences of his own age, but by means of the artistic products of the previous generation, which in youth have excited, and at the same time directed into a particular channel, his sense of beauty. The supreme artistic products of each generation thus form a series of elevated points, taking each from each the reflection of a strange light, the source of which is not in the atmosphere around and above them, but in a stage of society remote from ours. This standard takes its rise in Greece at a definite historical period. A tradition for all succeeding generations, it originates in a spontaneous growth out of the influences of Greek society. What were the conditions under which this ideal, this standard of artistic orthodoxy, was generated? How was Greece enabled to force its thought upon Europe?

Greek art, when we first catch sight of it, is entangled with Greek religion. We are accustomed to think of Greek religion as the religion of art and beauty, the religion of which the Olympian Zeus and the Athena Polias are the idols, the poems of Homer the sacred books. Thus Dr. Newman speaks of 'the classical polytheism which was gay and graceful, as was natural in a civilized age.' Yet such a view is only a partial one; in it the eye is fixed on the sharp bright edge of high Hellenic culture, but loses sight of the sombre world across which it strikes. Greek religion, where we can observe it most distinctly, is at once a magnificent ritualistic system, and a cycle of poetical conceptions. Religions, as they grow by natural laws out of man's life, are modified by whatever modifies his life. They brighten under a bright sky, they become liberal as the social range widens, they grow intense and shrill in the clefts of human life, where the spirit is narrow and confined, and the stars are visible at noonday; and a fine analysis of these differences is one of the gravest functions of religious criticism. Still, the broad characteristic of all religions, as they exist for the greatest number, is a universal pagan sentiment, a paganism which existed before the Greek religion, and has lingered far onward into the Christian world, ineradicable, like some persistent vegetable growth, because its seed is an element of the very soil out of which it springs. This pagan sentiment measures the sadness with which the human mind is filled whenever its thoughts wander far from what is here, and now. It is beset by notions of irresistible natural powers, for the most part ranged against man, but the secret also of his luck, making the earth golden and the grape fiery for him. He makes wilful Gods in his own image, gods smiling and drunken, or bleeding by a sad fatality, to console him by their wounds, never closed from generation to generation. It is with a rush of home-sickness that the thought of death presents itself. He would remain at home for ever on the earth if he could: as it loses its colour, and the senses fail, he clings ever closer to it; but since the mouldering of bones and flesh must go on to the end, he is careful for charms and talismans that may chance to have some friendly power in them when the inevitable shipwreck comes. Such sentiment is the eternal stock of all religions, modified indeed by changes of time and place, but indestructible, because its root is so deep in the earth of man's nature. The breath of religious initiators passes over them; a few 'rise up with wings as eagles,' but the broad level of religious life is not permanently changed. Religious progress, like all purely spiritual progress, is confined to a few. This sentiment fixes itself in the earliest times to certain usages of patriarchal life, the kindling of fire, the washing of the body, the breaking of bread, the slaughter of the flock, the gathering of harvest, holidays and dances. Here are the beginnings of a ritual, at first as occasional and unfixed as the sentiment which it expresses, but destined to become the permanent element of religious life. The usages of patriarchal life change; but this germ of ritual remains, developing, but always in a religious interest, losing its domestic character, and therefore becoming more and more inexplicable with each generation. This pagan cult, in spite of local colouring, essentially one, is the base of all religions. It is the anodyne which the religious principle, like one administering opiates to the incurable, has added to the law which makes life sombre for the vast majority of mankind.

More definite religious conceptions come from other sources, and fix themselves upon this cult in various ways, changing it and giving it new meanings. With the Hebrew people they came from individuals of genius, the authors of the prophetic literature. In Greece they were derived from mythology, itself not due to a religious source at all, but developing in the course of time into a body of anthropomorphic religious conceptions. To the unprogressive ritual element it brought these conceptions, itself the πτεροῦ δύναμις, an element of refinement, of ascension, with the promise of an endless destiny. While the cult remains fixed, the aesthetic element, only accidentally connected with it, expands with the freedom and mobility of the things of the intellect. Always the fixed element is the religious observance; the fluid unfixed element is the myth, the religious conception. This religion is itself pagan, and has on a broad view of it the pagan sadness. It does not at once and for the majority become the higher Hellenic religion. That primeval pagan sentiment, as it is found in its most pronounced form in Christian countries where Christianity has been least adulterated by modern ideas, as in Catholic Bavaria, is discernible also in the common world of Greek religion, against which the higher Hellenic culture is in relief. In Greece, as in Catholic Bavaria, the beautiful artistic shrines, with their chastened taste, are far between. The wilder people have wilder gods; which, however, in Athens or Corinth, or Lacedaemon, changing ever with the worshippers in whom they live and move and have their being, borrow something of the lordliness and distinction of human nature there. The fiery, stupefying wine becomes in a happier region clear and exhilarating. In both, the country people cherish the unlovely idols of an earlier time, such as those which Pausanias found still devoutly preserved in Arcadia. Athenaeus tells the story of one who, coming to a temple of Latona, had expected to see a worthy image of the mother of Apollo, and who laughed on finding only a shapeless wooden figure. In both, the fixed element is not the myth or religious conception, but the cult with its unknown origin and meaning only half understood. Even the mysteries, the centres of Greek religious life at a later period, were not a doctrine but a ritual; and one can imagine the Catholic church retaining its hold through the 'sad mechanic exercise' of its ritual, in spite of a diffused criticism or scepticism. Again, each adjusts but imperfectly its moral and theological conceptions; each has its mendicants, its purifications, its Antinomian mysticism, its garments offered to the gods, its statues worn with kissing,[2] its exaggerated superstitions for the vulgar only, its worship of sorrow, its addolorata, its mournful mysteries. There is scarcely one wildness of the Catholic church that has not been anticipated by Greek polytheism. What should we have thought of the vertiginous prophetess at the very centre of Greek religion? The supreme Hellenic culture is a

---

[2] Hermann's *Gottesdienstliche Alterthümer der Griechen*. Th. ii. c. ii. § 21, 16.

sharp edge of light across this gloom. The Dorian cult of Apollo, rational, chastened, debonair, with his unbroken daylight, always opposed to the sad Chthonian divinities, is the aspiring element, by force and spring of which Greek religion sublimes itself.[3] Religions have sometimes, like mighty streams, been diverted to a higher service of humanity as political institutions. Out of Greek religion under happy conditions arises Greek art, *das Einzige, das Unerwartete*, to minister to human culture. The claim of Greek religion is that it was able to transform itself into an artistic ideal. Unlike that Delphic Pythia, old but clothed as a maiden, this new Pythia is a maiden, though in the old religious vesture.

For the thoughts of the Greeks about themselves and their relation to the world were ever in the happiest readiness to be turned into an object for the senses. In this is the main distinction between Greek art and the mystical art of the Christian middle age, which is always struggling to express thoughts beyond itself. Take, for instance, a characteristic work of the middle age, Angelico's 'Coronation of the Virgin,' at San Marco, in Florence. In some strange halo of a moon sit the Virgin and our Lord, clad in mystical white raiment, half shroud, half priestly linen. Our Lord, with rosy nimbus and the long pale hair, *tanquam lana alba et tanquam nix*, of the figure in the Apocalypse, sets, with slender finger tips, a crown of pearl on the head of his mother, who, corpse-like in her refinement, bends to receive it, the light lying like snow upon her forehead. Certainly it cannot be said of Angelico's fresco that it throws into a sensible form our highest thoughts about man and his relation to the world; but it did not do this adequately even for Angelico. For him all that is outward or sensible in his work – the hair like wool, the rosy nimbus, the crown of pearl – is only the symbol or type of an inexpressible world to which he wishes to direct the thoughts; he would have shrunk from the notion that what the eye apprehended was all. Such forms of art, then, are inadequate to the matter they clothe; they remain ever below its level. Something of this kind is true also of Oriental art. As in the middle age from an exaggerated inwardness, so in the East from a vagueness, a want of definition in thought, the matter presented to art is unmanageable: forms of sense struggle vainly with it. The many-headed gods of the East, the orientalized Ephesian Diana with its numerous breasts, like Angelico's fresco, are at best overcharged symbols, a means of hinting at an idea which art cannot adequately express, which still remains in the world of shadows.

But take a work of Greek art, the Venus of Melos. That is in no sense a symbol, a suggestion of anything beyond its own victorious

[3] Hermann, Th. i. § 5.

fairness. The mind begins and ends with the finite image, yet loses no part of the spiritual motive. That motive is not lightly and loosely attached to the sensuous form, as the meaning to the allegory, but saturates and is identical with it. The Greek mind had advanced to a particular stage of self-reflection, but was careful not to pass beyond it. In Oriental thought there is a vague conception of life everywhere, but no true appreciation of itself by the mind, no knowledge of the distinction of man's nature; in thought he still mingles himself with the fantastic indeterminate life of the animal and vegetable world. In Greek thought the 'lordship of the soul' is recognized; that lordship gives authority and divinity to human eyes and hands and feet; nature is thrown into the background. But there Greek thought finds its happy limit; it has not yet become too inward; the mind has not begun to boast of its independence of the flesh; the spirit has not yet absorbed everything with its emotions, nor reflected its own colour everywhere. It has indeed committed itself to a train of reflection which must end in a defiance of form, of all that is outward, in an exaggerated idealism. But that end is still distant; it has not yet plunged into the depths of Christian mysticism.

This ideal art, in which the thought does not outstrip or lie beyond its sensible embodiment, could not have arisen out of a phase of life that was uncomely or poor. That delicate pause in Greek reflection was joined by some supreme good luck to the perfect animal nature of the Greeks. Here are the two conditions of an artistic ideal. The influences which perfected the animal nature of the Greeks are part of the process by which the ideal was evolved. Those 'Mothers' who in the second part of *Faust* mould and remould the typical forms which appear in human history, preside at the beginning of Greek culture over such a concourse of happy physical conditions as ever generates by natural laws some rare type of intellectual or spiritual life. That delicate air, 'nimbly and sweetly recommending itself' to the senses, the finer aspects of nature, the finer lime and clay of the human form, and modelling of the bones of the human countenance, – these are the good luck of the Greek when he enters into life. Beauty becomes a distinction like genius or noble place.

'By no people,' says Winckelmann, 'has beauty been so highly esteemed as by the Greeks. The priests of a youthful Jupiter at Aegae, of the Ismenian Apollo, and the priest who at Tanagra led the procession of Mercury, bearing a lamb upon his shoulders, were always youths to whom the prize of beauty had been awarded. The citizens of Egesta, in Sicily, erected a monument to a certain Philip, who was not their fellow-citizen, but of Croton, for his distinguished beauty; and the people made offerings at it. In an ancient song, ascribed to Simonides, or Epicharmus, of four wishes, the first was health, the second beauty. And as beauty was so longed for and prized by the Greeks, every beautiful person sought to become known to the whole people by this distinction, and above all to approve himself to the artists, because they awarded the prize; and this was for the artists an opportunity of having supreme beauty ever before their eyes. Beauty even gave a right to fame; and we find in Greek histories the most beautiful people distinguished. Some were famous for the beauty of one single part of their form; as Demetrius Phalereus, for his beautiful eyebrows, was called χαριτοβλέφαρος. It seems even to have been thought that the procreation of beautiful children might be promoted by prizes; this is shown by the existence of contests for beauty, which in ancient times were established by Cypselus, King of Arcadia, by the river Alpheus; and at the feast of Apollo of Philae a prize was offered to the youths for the deftest kiss. This was decided by an umpire; as also at Megara by the grave of Diocles. At Sparta, and at Lesbos in the temple of Juno, and among the Parrhasii, there were contests for beauty among women. The general esteem for beauty went so far, that the Spartan women set up in their bed-chambers a Nireus, a Narcissus, or a Hyacinth, that they might bear beautiful children.'[4]

So from a few stray antiquarianisms, from a few faces cast up sharply from the waves, Winckelmann, as his manner is, divines the temperament of the antique world, and that in which it had delight. It has passed away with that distant age, and we may venture to dwell upon it. What sharpness and reality it has, is the sharpness and reality of suddenly arrested life. Gymnastic originated as part of a religious ritual. The worshipper was to recommend himself to the gods by becoming fleet and serpentining, and white and red, like them. The beauty of the palaestra and the beauty of the artist's studio reacted on each other. The youth tried to rival his gods, and his increased beauty passed back into them. Ὄμνυμι πάντας θεοὺς μὴ ἐλέσθαι ἂν τὴν Βασιλέως ἀρχὴν ἀντὶ τοῦ καλὸς εἶναι. That is the form in which one age of the world chose 'the better part' – a perfect world, if our gods could have seemed for ever only fleet and serpentining, and white and red – not white and red as in Francia's 'Golgotha.' Let us not say, would that that unperplexed youth of humanity, seeing itself and satisfied, had never passed into a mournful maturity; for already the deep joy was in store for the spirit of finding the ideal of that youth still red with life in its grave.

It followed that the Greek ideal expressed itself pre-eminently in sculpture. All art has a sensuous element, colour, form, sound – in poetry a dexterous recalling of these together with the profound joyful

[4] *Geschichte der Kunst des Alterthums*, Th. i. Kap. iv.

sensuousness of motion; each of these may be a medium for the ideal; it is partly accident which in any individual case makes the born artist, poet or painter rather than sculptor. But as the mind itself has had an historical development, one form of art, by the very limitations of its material, may be more adequate than another for the expression of any one phase of its experience. Different attitudes of the imagination have a native affinity with different types of sensuous form, so that they combine easily and entirely. The arts may thus be ranged in a series which corresponds to a series of developments in the human mind itself.[5] Architecture, which begins in a practical need, can only express by vague hint or symbol the spirit or mind of the artist. He closes his sadness over him, or wanders in the perplexed intricacies of things, or projects his purpose from him clean-cut and sincere, or bares himself to the sunlight. But these spiritualities, felt rather than seen, can but lurk about architectural form as volatile effects, to be gathered from it by reflection; their expression is not really sensuous at all. As human form is not the subject with which it deals, architecture is the mode in which the artistic effort centres when the thoughts of man concerning himself are still indistinct, when he is still little preoccupied with those harmonies, storms, victories of the unseen intellectual world, which wrought out into the bodily form, give it an interest and significance communicable to it alone. The art of Egypt, with its supreme architectural effects, is, according to Hegel's beautiful comparison, a Memnon waiting for the day, the day of the Greek spirit, the humanistic spirit, with its power of speech. Again, painting, music, poetry, with their endless power of complexity, are the special arts of the romantic and modern ages. Into these, with the utmost attenuation of detail, may be translated every delicacy of thought and feeling incidental to a consciousness brooding with delight over itself. Through their gradations of shade, their exquisite intervals, they project in an external form that which is most inward in humour, passion, sentiment. Between architecture and the romantic arts of painting, music, and poetry, is sculpture, which, unlike architecture, deals immediately with man, while it contrasts with the romantic arts, because it is not self-analytical. It deals more exclusively than any other art with the human form, itself one entire medium of spiritual expression, trembling, blushing, melting into dew with inward excitement. That spirituality which only lurks about architecture as a volatile effect, in sculpture takes up the whole given material and penetrates it with an imaginative motive; and at first sight sculpture, with its solidity of form, seems more real and full than the faint abstract manner of poetry or painting. Still the fact is the reverse. Discourse and action show man as he is more directly than the

[5] Hegel, *Aesthetik*, Theil. ii. Einleitung.

springing of the muscles and the moulding of the flesh; and these poetry commands. Painting, by the flushing of colour in the face and dilation of light in the eye, and music by its subtle range of tones, can refine most delicately upon a single moment of passion, unravelling its finest threads.

But why should sculpture thus limit itself to pure form? Because by this limitation it becomes a perfect medium of expression for one peculiar motive of the imaginative intellect. It therefore renounces all those attributes of its material which do not help that motive. It has had, indeed, from the beginning an unfixed claim to colour; but this colour has always been more or less conventional, with no melting or modulation of tones, never admitting more than a very limited realism. It was maintained chiefly as a religious tradition. In proportion as sculpture ceased to be merely decorative and subordinate to architecture it threw itself upon pure form. It renounces the power of expression by sinking or heightening tones. In it no member of the human form is more significant than the rest; the eye is wide, and without pupil; the lips and brow are not more precious than hands, and breasts, and feet. The very slightness of its material is part of its pride; it has no backgrounds, no sky or atmosphere, to suggest and interpret a train of feeling; a little of suggested motion, and much of pure light on its gleaming surfaces, with pure form – only these. And it gains more than it loses by this limitation to its own distinguishing motives; it unveils man in the repose of his unchanging characteristics. Its white light purged from the angry blood-like stains of action and passion, reveals not what is accidental in man, but the god, as opposed to man's restless movement. It records the first naïve unperplexed recognition of man by himself; and it is a proof of the high artistic capacity of the Greeks that they apprehended and remained true to these exquisite limitations, yet in spite of them gave to their creations a vital, mobile individuality.

Heiterkeit, blitheness or repose, and *Allgemeinheit*, generality or breadth, are, then, the supreme characteristics of the Hellenic ideal. But that generality or breadth has nothing in common with the lax observation, the unlearned thought, the flaccid execution which have sometimes claimed superiority in art on the plea of being 'broad' or 'general.' Hellenic breadth and generality come of a culture minute, severe, constantly renewed, rectifying and concentrating its impressions into certain pregnant types. The base of all artistic genius is the power of conceiving humanity in a new, striking, rejoicing way, of putting a happy world of its own creation in place of the meaner world of common days, of generating around itself an atmosphere with a novel power of refraction, selecting, transforming, recombining the images it transmits, according to the choice of the imaginative intellect. In exercising this power, painting and poetry have a choice of subject almost unlimited. The range of characters or persons open to them is as various as life itself; no character, however trivial, misshapen, or unlovely, can resist their magic. This is because those arts can accomplish their function in the choice and development of some special situation, which lifts or glorifies a character in itself not poetical. To realize this situation, to define in a chill and empty atmosphere the focus where rays, in themselves pale and impotent, unite and begin to burn, the artist has to employ the most cunning detail, to complicate and refine upon thought and passion a thousand-fold. The poems of Robert Browning supply brilliant examples of this. His poetry is pre-eminently the poetry of situations. The characters themselves are always of secondary importance; often they are characters in themselves of little interest; they seem to come to him by strange accidents from the ends of the world. His gift is shown by the way in which he accepts such a character and throws it into some situation, apprehends it in some delicate pause of life, in which for a moment it becomes ideal. Take an instance from 'Dramatis Personae.' In the poem entitled 'Le Byron de nos Jours' we have a single moment of passion thrown into relief in this exquisite way. Those two jaded Parisians are not intrinsically interesting; they only begin to interest us when thrown into a choice situation. But to discriminate that moment, to make it appreciable by us, that we may 'find it,' what a cobweb of allusions, what double and treble reflections of the mind upon itself, what an artificial light is constructed and broken over the chosen situation – on how fine a needle's point that little world of passion is balanced! Yet, in spite of this intricacy, the poem has the clear ring of a central motive; we receive from it the impression of one imaginative tone, of a single creative act.

To produce such effects at all requires the resources of painting, with its power of indirect expression, of subordinate but significant detail, its atmosphere, its foregrounds and backgrounds. To produce them in a pre-eminent degree requires all the resources of poetry, language in its most purged form, its remote associations and suggestions, its double and treble lights. These appliances sculpture cannot command. In it, therefore, not the special situation, but the type, the general character of the subject to be delineated, is all-important. In poetry and painting, the situation predominates over the character; in sculpture, the character over the situation. Excluded by the limitations of its material from the development of exquisite situations, it has to choose from a select number of types intrinsically interesting, interesting that is, independently of any special situation into which they may be thrown. Sculpture finds the secret of its power in presenting these types in their broad, central, incisive lines. This it effects not by accumulation of detail, but by abstracting from it. All that is accidental, that distracts the simple effect of the supreme types of humanity, all traces in them of the commonness of the world, it gradually purges away.

Works of art produced under this law, and only these, are really characterized by Hellenic generality or breadth. In every direction it is a law of limitation; it keeps passion always below that degree of intensity at which it is necessarily transitory, never winding up the features to one note of anger, or desire, or surprise. In the allegorical designs of the middle ages, we find isolated qualities portrayed as by so many masks; its religious art has familiarized us with faces fixed obdurately into blank types of religious sentiment; and men and women, in the hurry of life, often wear the sharp impress of one absorbing motive, from which it is said death sets their features free. All such instances may be ranged under the 'grotesque'; and the Hellenic ideal has nothing in common with the 'grotesque.' It lets passion play lightly over the surface of the individual form, which loses by it nothing of its central impassivity, its depth and repose. To all but the highest culture, the reserved faces of the gods will ever have something of insipidity. Again, in the best Greek sculpture, the archaic immobility has been thawed, its forms are in motion; but it is a motion ever kept in reserve, which is very seldom committed to any definite action. Endless as are the attitudes of Greek sculpture, exquisite as is the invention of the Greeks in this direction, the actions or situations it permits are simple and few. There is no Greek Madonna; the goddesses are always childless. The actions selected are those which would be without significance, except in a divine person, binding on a sandal or preparing for the bath. When a more complex and significant action is permitted, it is most often represented as just finished, so that eager expectancy is excluded, as Apollo just after the slaughter of the Python, or Venus with the apple of Paris already in her hand. The Laocoon, with all that patient science through which it has triumphed over an almost unmanageable subject, marks a period in which sculpture has begun to aim at effects legitimate only in painting. The hair, so rich a source of expression in painting, and, as we have lately seen, in poetry, because relatively to the eye or to the lip it is mere drapery, is withdrawn from attention; its texture, as well as its colour, is lost, its arrangement faintly and severely indicated, with no enmeshed or broken light. The eyes are wide and directionless, not fixing anything with their gaze, nor riveting the brain to any special external object; the brows without hair. It deals almost exclusively with youth, where the moulding of the bodily organs is still as if suspended between growth and completion, indicated but not emphasized; where the transition from curve to curve is so delicate and elusive that

Winckelmann compares it to a quiet sea, which, although we understand it to be in motion, we nevertheless regard as an image of repose; where, therefore, the exact degree of development is so hard to apprehend. If one had to choose a single product of Hellenic art, to save in the wreck of all the rest, one would choose from the 'beautiful multitude' of the Panathenaic frieze that line of youths on horses, with their level glances, their proud patient lips, their chastened reins, their whole bodies in exquisite service. This colourless unclassified purity of life, with its blending and interpenetration of intellectual, spiritual, and physical elements, still folded together, pregnant with the possibilities of a whole world closed within it, is the highest expression of that indifference which is beyond all that is relative or partial. Everywhere there is the effect of an awaking, of a child's sleep just disturbed. All these effects are united in a single instance – the Adorante of the museum of Berlin, a youth who has gained the wrestler's prize, with hands lifted and open in praise for the victory. Naïve, unperplexed, it is the image of man as he springs first from the sleep of nature; his white light taking no colour from any one-sided experience, characterless so far as character involves subjection to the accidental influences of life. In dealing with youth, Greek art betrays a tendency even to merge distinctions of sex. The Hermaphrodite was a favourite subject from early times. It was wrought out over and over again, with passionate care, from the mystic terminal Hermaphrodite of the British Museum, to the perfect blending of male and female beauty in the Hermaphrodite of the Louvre.[6]

'This sense,' says Hegel, 'for the consummate modelling of divine and human forms was pre-eminently at home in Greece. In its poets and orators, its historians and philosophers, Greece cannot be conceived from a central point, unless one brings, as a key to the understanding of it, an insight into the ideal forms of sculpture, and regards the images of statesmen and philosophers as well as epic and dramatic heroes from the artistic point of view; for those who act, as well as those who create and think, have in those beautiful days of Greece this plastic character. They are great and free, and have grown up on the soil of their own individuality, creating themselves out of themselves, and moulding themselves to what they were and willed to be. The age of Pericles was rich in such characters: Pericles himself, Phidias, Plato, above all Sophocles, Thucydides also, Xenophon and Socrates, each in his own order, without the perfection of one being diminished by that of the others. They are ideal artists of themselves, cast each in one flawless mould – works of art which stand before us as an immortal presentment of the gods. Of this modelling also are those bodily works of art, the

[6] Hegel, *Aesthetik*, Th. iii. Absch. 2, Kap. 1.

victors in the Olympic Games; yes, and even Phryne, who, as the most beautiful of women, ascended naked out of the water in the presence of assembled Greece.'

This key to the understanding of the Greek spirit, Winckelmann possessed in his own nature, itself like a relic of classical antiquity laid open by accident to our alien modern atmosphere. To the criticism of that consummate Greek modelling he brought not only his culture but his temperament. We have seen how definite was the leading motive of his culture; how, like some central root-fibre, it maintained the well-rounded unity of his life through a thousand distractions. Interests not his, nor meant for him, political, moral, religious, never disturbed him. In morals, as in criticism, he followed the clue of an unerring instinct. Penetrating into the antique world by his passion, his temperament, he enunciates no formal principles, always hard and one-sided; it remained for Hegel to formulate what in Winckelmann is everywhere individualized and concrete. Minute and anxious as his culture was, he never became one-sidedly self-analytical. Occupied ever with himself, perfecting himself and cultivating his genius, he was not content, as so often happens with such natures, that the atmosphere between him and other minds should be thick and clouded; he was ever jealously refining his meaning into a form, express, clear, objective. This temperament he nurtured and invigorated by friendships which kept him ever in direct contact with the spirit of youth. The beauty of the Greek statues was a sexless beauty; the statues of the gods had the least traces of sex. Here, there is a moral sexlessness, a kind of impotence, an ineffectual wholeness of nature, yet with a divine beauty and significance of its own.

One result of this temperament is a serenity, a *Heiterkeit*, which characterizes Winckelmann's handling of the sensuous side of Greek art. This serenity is, perhaps, in a great measure, a negative quality; it is the absence of any sense of want, or corruption, or shame. With the sensuous element in Greek art he deals in the pagan manner; and what is implied in that? It has been sometimes said that art is a means of escape from 'the tyranny of the senses.' It may be so for the spectator; he may find that the spectacle of supreme works of art takes from the life of the senses something of its turbid fever. But this is possible for the spectator only because the artist in producing those works has gradually sunk his intellectual and spiritual ideas in sensuous form. He may live, as Keats lived, a pure life; but his soul, like that of Plato's false astronomer, becomes more and more immersed in sense, until nothing else has any interest for him. How could such an one ever again endure the greyness of the ideal or spiritual world? The spiritualist is satisfied in seeing the sensuous elements escape from his conceptions; his interest grows, as the dyed garment bleaches in the keener air. But the artist steeps his thought again and again into the fire of colour. To the Greek this immersion in the sensuous was indifferent. Greek sensuousness, therefore, does not fever the blood; it is shameless and childlike. But Christianity, with its uncompromising idealism, discrediting the slightest touch of sense, has lighted up for the artistic life, with its inevitable sensuousness a background of flame. 'I did but taste a little honey with the end of the rod that was in mine hand, and lo, I must die.' It is hard to pursue that life without something of conscious disavowal of a spiritual world; and this imparts to genuine artistic interests a kind of intoxication. From this intoxication Winckelmann is free; he fingers those pagan marbles with unsinged hands, with no sense of shame or loss. That is to deal with the sensuous side of art in the pagan manner.

The longer we contemplate that Hellenic ideal in which man is at unity with himself, with his physical nature, with the outward world, the more we may be inclined to regret that he should ever have passed beyond it, to contend for a perfection that makes the blood turbid, and frets the flesh, and discredits the actual world about us. But if he was to be saved from the *ennui* which ever attaches itself to realization, even the realization of perfection, it was necessary that a conflict should come, that some sharper note should grieve the perfect harmony, in order that the spirit, chafed by it, might beat out at last a broader and profounder music. In Greek tragedy this conflict has begun; man finds himself face to face with rival claims. Greek tragedy shows how such a conflict may be treated with serenity, how the evolution of it may be a spectacle of the dignity, not of the impotence, of the human spirit. But it is not only in tragedy that the Greek spirit showed itself capable of thus winning joy out of matter in itself full of discouragements. Theocritus too, often strikes a note of romantic sadness. But what a blithe and steady poise above these discouragements in a clear and sunny stratum of the air!

Into this stage of Greek achievement Winckelmann did not enter. Supreme as he is where his true interest lay, his insight into the typical unity and repose of the sculpturesque seems to have involved limitation in another direction. His conception of art excludes that bolder type of it which deals confidently and serenely with life, conflict, evil. Living in a world of exquisite but abstract and colourless form, he could hardly have conceived of the subtle and penetrative, but somewhat grotesque art of the modern world. What would he have thought of Gilliatt, or of the bleeding mouth of Fantine in that first part of *Les Misérables*, penetrated as it is with a sense of beauty as lively and transparent as that of a Greek? There is even a sort of preparation for the romantic temper within the limits of the Greek ideal itself, which Winckelmann failed to see. For Greek religion has not merely its mournful mysteries of Adonis, of Hyacinthus, of Ceres, but it is conscious also of the fall of earlier divine dynasties. Hyperion gives way to Apollo, Oceanus to Poseidon. Around the feet of that tranquil Olympian family still crowd the weary shadows of an earlier, more formless, divine world. Even their still minds are troubled with thoughts of a limit to duration, of inevitable decay, of dispossession. Again, the supreme and colourless abstraction of those divine forms, which is the secret of their repose, is also a premonition of the fleshless consumptive refinements of the pale mediaeval artists. That high indifference to the outward, that impassivity, has already a touch of the corpse in it; we see already Angelico and the 'Master of the Passion' in the artistic future. The crushing of the sensuous, the shutting of the door upon it, the flesh-outstripping interest, is already traceable. Those abstracted gods, 'ready to melt out their essence fine into the winds,' who can fold up their flesh as a garment, and remain themselves, seem already to feel that bleak air in which, like Helen of Troy herself, they wander as the spectres of the middle age.

Gradually as the world came into the church, as Christianity compromised its earlier severities, the native artistic interest reasserted its claims. But Christian art was still dependent on pagan examples, building the shafts of pagan temples into its churches, perpetuating the form of the basilica, in later times working the disused amphitheatres as quarries. The sensuous expression of conceptions which unreservedly discredit the world of sense, was the delicate problem which Christian art had before it. If we think of mediaeval painting as it ranges from the early German schools, still with the air of a charnel-house about them, to the clear loveliness of Perugino, we shall see that the problem was met. Even in the worship of sorrow the native blitheness of art asserted itself; the religious spirit, as Hegel says, 'smiled through its tears.' So perfectly did the young Raffaelle infuse that *Heiterkeit*, that pagan blitheness, into religious works, that his picture of Saint Agatha at Bologna became to Goethe a step in the evolution of *Iphigenie*.[7] But in proportion as this power of smiling was refound, there came also an aspiration towards that lost antique art, some relics of which Christian art had buried in itself, ready to work wonders when their day came.

The history of art has suffered as much as any history by trenchant and absolute divisions. Pagan and Christian art are sometimes harshly opposed, and the Renaissance is represented as a fashion which set in at a definite period. That is the superficial view; the deeper view is that which preserves the identity of European culture. The two are really

[7] *Italiänische Reise*. Bologna, 19 Oct. 1786.

continuous: and there is a sense in which it may be said that the Renaissance was an uninterrupted effort of the middle age, that it was ever taking place. When the actual relics of the antique were restored to the world, it was to Christian eyes as if an ancient plague-pit had been opened: all the world took the contagion of the life of nature and the senses. Christian art allying itself with that restored antiquity which it had ever emulated, soon ceased to exist. For a time art dealt with Christian subjects as its patrons required; but its true freedom was in the life of the senses and the blood – blood no longer dropping from the hands in sacrifice, as with Angelico, but, as with Titian, burning in the face for desire and love. And now it was seen that the mediaeval spirit too had done something for the destiny of the antique. By hastening the decline of art, by withdrawing interest from it, and yet keeping the thread of its traditions, it had suffered the human mind to repose, that it might awake when day came, with eyes refreshed, to those antique forms.

The aim of a right criticism is to place Winckelmann in an intellectual perspective, of which Goethe is the foreground. For, after all, he is infinitely less than Goethe; it is chiefly because at certain points he comes in contact with Goethe that criticism entertains consideration of him. His relation to modern culture is a peculiar one. He is not of the modern world; nor is he of the eighteenth century, although so much of his outer life is characteristic of it. But that note of revolt against the eighteenth century, which we detect in Goethe, was struck by Winckelmann. Goethe illustrates that union of the Romantic spirit, its adventure, its variety, its deep subjectivity, with Hellenism, its transparency, its rationality, its desire of beauty – that marriage of Faust and Helena, of which the art of the nineteenth century is the child, the beautiful lad Euphorion, as Goethe conceives him, on the crags in the 'splendour of battle,' 'in harness as for victory,' his brows bound with light.[8] Goethe illustrates, too, the preponderance in this marriage of the Hellenic element; and that element, in its true essence, was made known to him by Winckelmann.

Breadth, centrality, with blitheness and repose, are the marks of Hellenic culture. Is that culture a lost art? The local, accidental colouring of its own age has passed from it; the greatness that is dead looks greater when every link with what is slight and vulgar has been severed; we can only see it at all in the reflected, refined light which a high education creates for us. Can we bring down that ideal into the gaudy, perplexed light of modern life?

Certainly for us of the modern world, with its conflicting claims, its entangled interests, distracted by so many sorrows, so many pre-

[8] *Faust*, Th. ii. Act 3. (Pater's note.)

occupations, so bewildering an experience, the problem of unity with ourselves in blitheness and repose, is far harder than it was for the Greek within the simple terms of antique life. Yet, no: less than ever, the intellect demands completeness, centrality. It is this which Winckelmann prints on the imagination of Goethe, at the beginning of his culture, in its original and simplest form, as in a fragment of Greek art itself, stranded on that littered, indeterminate shore of Germany in the eighteenth century. In Winckelmann this type comes to him, not as in a book or a theory, but importunately, in a passionate life and personality. For Goethe, possessing all modern interests, ready to be lost in the perplexed currents of modern thought, he defines in clearest outline the problem of culture-balance, unity with oneself, consummate Greek modelling.

It could no longer be solved, as in Phryne ascending naked out of the water, by perfection of bodily form, or any joyful union with the world without; the shadows had grown too long, the light too solemn for that. It could hardly be solved as in Pericles or Phidias, by the direct exercise of any single talent; amid the manifold claims of modern culture that could only have ended in a thin, one-sided growth. Goethe's Hellenism was of another order, the *Allgemeinheit* and *Heiterkeit*, the completeness and serenity of a watchful, exigent intellectualism. *Im Ganzen, Guten, Wahren, resolut zu leben*, is Goethe's description of his own higher life; and what is meant by life in the whole, *im Ganzen*? It means the life of one for whom, over and over again, what was once precious has become indifferent. Every one who aims at the life of culture is met by many forms of it, arising out of the intense, laborious, one-sided development of some special talent. They are the brightest enthusiasms the world has to show. They do not care to weigh the claims which this or that alien form of culture makes upon them. But the pure instinct of self-culture cares not so much to reap all that these forms of culture can give, as to find in them its own strength. The demand of the intellect is to feel itself alive. It must see into the laws, the operation, the intellectual reward of every divided form of culture; but only that it may measure the relation between itself and them. It struggles with those forms till its secret is won from each, and then lets each fall back into its place in the supreme, artistic view of life. With a kind of passionate coldness such natures rejoice to be away from and past their former selves. Above all, they are jealous of that abandonment to one special gift which really limits their capabilities. It would have been easy for Goethe, with the gift of a sensuous nature, to let it overgrow him. It is easy with the other-worldly gifts to be a *schöne Seele*; but to the large vision of Goethe that seemed to be a phase of life that a man might feel all round and leave behind him. Again, it is easy to indulge the commonplace metaphysical instinct. But a taste for metaphysics may be one of those things which we must renounce if we mean to mould our lives to artistic perfection. Philosophy serves culture not by the fancied gift of absolute or transcendental knowledge, but by suggesting questions which help one to detect the passion and strangeness and dramatic contrasts of life.

But Goethe's culture did not remain 'behind the veil'; it ever abutted on the practical functions of art, on actual production. For him the problem came to be – Can the *Allgemeinheit* and *Heiterkeit* of the antique be communicated to artistic productions which contain the fulness of the experience of the modern world? We have seen that the development of the various forms of art has corresponded to the development of the thoughts of man concerning himself, to the growing relation of the mind to itself. Sculpture corresponds to the unperplexed, emphatic outlines of Hellenic humanism; painting to the mystic depth and intricacy of the middle age; music and poetry have their fortune in the modern world. Let us understand by poetry all literary production which attains the power of giving pleasure by its form as distinct from its matter. Only in this varied literary form can art command that width, variety, delicacy of resources, which will enable it to deal with the conditions of modern life. What modern art has to do in the service of culture is so to rearrange the details of modern life, so to reflect it, that it may satisfy the spirit. And what does the spirit need in the face of modern life? The sense of freedom. That naïve, rough sense of freedom, which supposes man's will to be limited, if at all, only by a will stronger than his, he can never have again. The attempt to represent it in art would have so little verisimilitude that it would be flat and uninteresting. The chief factor in the thoughts of the modern mind concerning itself is the intricacy, the universality of natural law even in the moral order. For us necessity is not as of old an image without us, with whom we can do warfare; it is a magic web woven through and through us, like that magnetic system of which modern science speaks, penetrating us with a network subtler than our subtlest nerves, yet bearing in it the central forces of the world. Can art represent men and women in these bewildering toils so as to give the spirit at least an equivalent for the sense of freedom? Goethe's *Wahlverwandtschaften* is a high instance of modern art dealing thus with modern life; it regards that life as the modern mind must regard it, but reflects upon it blitheness and repose. Natural laws we shall never modify, embarrass us as they may; but there is still something in the nobler or less noble attitude with which we watch their fatal combinations. In *Wahlverwandtschaften* this entanglement, this network of law, becomes a tragic situation, in which a group of noble men and women work out a

supreme *dénouement*. Who, if he foresaw all, would fret against circumstances which endow one at the end with so high an experience?

13 'Eudiades'

John Addington Symonds. From *Tales of Ancient Greece, No. 1, Eudiades and
a Cretan Idyll*. Written December 1868, published 1878.

IN ILLUSTRATION OF PLATO AND ARISTOPHANES

ἀεὶ διὰ λαμπροτάτου βαίνοντες ἁβρῶς αἰθέρος

Praeludium

A wave that toward the longing lingering shore
      Floats on the surge of the resistless tide,
That seems to shrink and quail and faint before
      The strong slow force that may not be denied;
      Vainly it loiters, like a blushing bride,
Vainly recedes, yet ever onward moves
To break with tears upon the beach it loves.

A rose all radiant 'neath the moon of May:
      Shyly she droops her head, and seems in thought
Sequestered; while the nightingale alway
      Sings for her love, and pants with passion wrought
      To rapture: for the amorous air is fraught
With her full fragrance, eloquently dumb,
To the night crying, 'Come, my love, oh, come!'

A lute wherein soft melody is mocked
      With silence conscious of delicious song,
In whose still strings the soul of love lies locked
      For want of one to touch who tarries long;
      Yet, even ere he sweep the chords, a throng
Scarce heard of preluding notes her bosom shake,
And the love-pulses at a breath awake.

A face that visits us in dreams, whose eyes,
      Instinct with inward light mysterious, seem
To take from us their life; a strange surprise

Lurks in their innocent lightning, and the dream
    Moves with our motion, quivering on the stream
Of sleep's swift minutes; till we wake and find
A deathless image left upon the mind.

A pawn that in the player's skilful hand
    Trembles irresolute o'er the fatal square
Round which king, knight, queen, bishop, castle stand
    In strength impregnable: once planted there,
    He daunts their goodly fellowship; – the fair
Band before which he trembled, breaks, and he
Is victor crowned of all their chivalry.

A little girl, who half in fear, half led
    By curious impulse, at her mother's knee
Stands, while a stranger bends and strokes her head
    And whispers kind words in a tender key,
    Till with quick step at last confidingly,
Still blushing, to his lap she flies, and smiles,
And coaxes him with winning artless wiles.

Fuga

Away with metaphor! In years of old
There lived the boy of whom this tale is told,
Fair-haired Eudiades, upon the hill
Which bears the sacred name of Athens still.
Nurtured he was in all the ancient ways
Of nobleness which brought his fathers praise,
What time at Marathon they stained the sea
And broad corn-land with Persian butchery.
He from his couch at earliest break of day
Arising, prayer and orison would pay
To Phoebus and to Hermes, and with pure
Cold baths would brace his beauty to endure
Rough winds and scorching suns, and on his bloom
Flung the broad chlamys: then he left his room,
And with grave earnest eyes and glistening face
Joined his school-fellows in the open place.
They walking in due order hand in hand,
With laughter and low-vowelled words, that fanned
The drooping boughs of rose and myrtle-rods,

Went singing, smiled upon by marble gods,
In the clear level sunlight, on their way
Down to the harper's school. There many a lay
Was learned of praise to Pallas, and war songs,
Wherethrough the trumpet shrilled and hurtling throngs
Of warriors tramped, made blood leap boundingly
Through dainty limbs, rousing the flashing eye
Of boyhood. But when songs were still, they read
Of mighty heroes, whose stern hardihead
Yet lives in valorous breasts and breeds the scorn
Of baseness.
        Then while yet the maiden morn
Shook dewdrops from her tresses, that bright band
Of playfellows, the fairest in the land,
Ran to the wrestling-ground; and off they threw
Their mantles, and their white flesh in the new
Light of the morning shone like ivory,
Which the skilled workman hath wrought daintily
With rosy hues or golden; and their hair
Floating upon their shoulders, like the rare
Curls of the crested hyacinth, made sport
For winds, that wandering through porch and court
Spread summer coolness.
        Now the games began:
Here through the long straight course their races ran
Phaedrus and Phaedon and Agathocles;
Here, rubbed with oil and sand, Eudiades
Wrestled with sturdy Pheidias. Long they strove
In the dry dust beneath the olive grove,
And from the farthest peristyles a throng
Of athletes, like young gods, stately and strong,
Gazed on the goodly pair matched equally
With even issue struggling, arm and knee
Close locked; until Eudiades, by sleight
Of cunning and quick nimbleness, like light
Flickering on vexed waves, while stout Pheidias bowed
His knitted thews in vain, thrice from the crowd
Won swift applause; then panting stood and took
The firm hand of his conquered friend, and shook
The fine dust from his limbs; and laughing they
Inarmed went slowly to the bath away.
Nor, though the eyes of many lovers burned
Upon them, from their forward course they turned;

But modestly, with calm clear brows, whereon
The light of innocence and honour shone,
Sunbright, they passed; then in the water wan
From their pure stainless forms the trace of toil
Purging, they rubbed their breasts with fragrant oil,
And on their forehead wreathed the flowering rush,
Sweet to the scent, whose faint fair petals blush
Like bloom of maidens.
              Next, what time the day
Flamed in his zenith, on the grass they lay
Of Academe, beneath the olive shade;
And of their pulse and sweet dried figs they made
A frugal meal, low murmuring till the sun
Began to wester. Then once more they run
Through light and shadow of thin branches, fleet
With moon-white breasts and merry twinkling feet, –
Smelling of springtime, and sweet health, and flowers,
And pure white poplar boughs, and idle hours,
And youthful happiness; while overhead
The elms and limes and olives mingling shed
Soft wind-stirred murmurs, and a breeze above
Told wordless tales of longing and of love.
Yet of these songs they recked not, only joyed
In supple strength of life, and child-like toyed
With their own amorous beauty, as a thing
Worthless, whereon they set no reckoning.

Yea, and when now the shadows from the hill
Crept lengthening o'er the meadow, and the still
Of afternoon by rising winds was stirred,
They homeward paced, and stood, and silent heard
The elders in the housegate, how they told
Of Zeus-born warriors of the age of gold,
Or deeds ancestral, or far distant lands,
Carthage or Sicily, or treacherous sands
Of sun-burned Libya: till, whenas the wan
Light of love's star upon the spear-point shone
Of guardian Pallas, their tired limbs they laid,
After due prayer, each on his narrow bed,
And sleep like dew upon their eyes was shed.

Leave we awhile of these fair friends to tell,
And turn to one on whom the miracle

Of boyhood in Eudiades had brought
The wonder of a swift change passion-wrought
From loveless life to love's uncertain good.
For while the striplings strove, Melanthias stood –
Himself of athletes mightiest – and saw,
With unaccustomed eyes and wildering awe,
The form of Beauty, visible and bright,
An effluence of ineffable sunlight,
In the boy's flawless lineaments. The sweat
Rose on his brow, his knees quaked, and his great
Man's bosom throbbed with heart-aches, and his eyes
Swam in a sudden painful sweet surprise.
Nor could he rest from thought; but in the boy
His soul lay sphered; nor was there any joy
Prized hitherto wherein he had delight.
But through the day he pined; and when the night
Came with her dew-drops and live stars and smell
Of strengthened flowers, on the thin grass he fell
Limb-length, where he had seen Eudiades
Lie at noontide beneath the sacred trees.
For there, so fancy feigned or dreamed the man,
Some trace still lingered on crushed herbs and wan
Leaves of pressed asphodel, of each dear limb
Which with its radiance had enraptured him.
The broken flowers he kissed, the grass, the boughs
Brushed by the passing boy, and on his brows,
Hot with quick thoughts, he bound those cool bruised leaves,
And in the twilight that the full moon weaves
Of olive branches, lay drinking the bowl
Of new-born longing, till his languid soul
Sank drowsed with sweetness, and beneath the tree
Endymion-like he slumbered tranquilly.

Fair and full-formed he was, like Hermes, in
The first free dawn of manhood; for his chin
Was woolly as the peach, and bright as bloom
Of hillset galingale, whose pure perfume
Scarce matched his breath. Above his level brow,
Wherein great deep blue eyes were set, the snow
Was overshadowed by crisp curls of brown,
Brightening to golden; and the wavy down
That on his smooth white thighs and perfect breast
Lay soft as sleep was coloured like the west

At sunset, when the silver star shines through
Pale amber spaces spread beneath the blue.
Sweet as spring flowers and blossoming with the fresh
Hues of young health unsullied was his flesh:
Wide shoulders, knitted arms, and narrow waist
Between the broad reins and the massive chest;
Firm feet, and ankles like the wingéd heels
Of Jove's own messenger, who lightly steals
From cloud to cloud, from mountain peak to peak,
On the king's errand. Slow he was to speak,
Yet swift to do; nor of his words had lack
If aught of speech were needed, nor was slack
In jest or song, or when the cups were filled
For merry-making guests; but nothing skilled
In grave discourse or staid philosophy,
Of sage and priest he lived unheedingly.

Such was the youth, Melanthias, the first
Of Attic athletes, on whose soul had burst
The sunrise of Eudiades, the spring
Of sudden love's unlooked-for blossoming.

But when the first grey streak of dawning broke
Over Hymettus, from his dreams awoke
That longing man, and the delicious pain
Of memory in his bosom stirred again
The thirst of yester-eve. Then on the sward,
Still wan, but now with dews of night restored,
He pressed warm lips, and rising like a god
Through the still avenues of olives trod
Down to the sacred stream, and bathed, and prayed,
What time the sungod's ruddy lips were laid
On the fair marble porches far above,
To the white queen of joy and lord of love,
That he might do some mighty deed to please
The bright soul of the boy Eudiades.
The boy meanwhile had risen, and that day
In the same golden round of work and play
Glided; nor ever o'er his innocent eyes
Trembled the vision of that strange surprise
Which gave new life and loveliness of limb
To the great man who yearned athirst for him.
But, wheresoe'er he moved, at work or play,

Close like a shadow followed on his way
Love-lost Melanthias, feeding with the sight
Of that new-found unrealized delight
His longing; and the soul-wings throbbed and grew
Within his breast; until dark night withdrew
His darling from his eyes.
                And so three days
Were fully spent, nor had the listening bays
Or olives of the garden told the boy
The secret of the strong man's eager joy.
But on the fourth night, when the silver moon
Paled in the west, and wakeful birds of June
Sang to the gliding silent stars, there crept
Melanthias to the little house where slept,
Rose-latticed from night winds, Eudiades;
And thus with song his amorous soul did ease:

Arise! arise!
See how the starry skies
Keep breathing through the night their breath of love!
The nightingale above,
In myrtle boughs
Close-shrouded, sleepeth not but sings;
And on the faint air flings
The delicate rose her perfume. Rouse
From slumber, darling: see,
I stand and wait for thee!
Come to thy lattice; from thy curtained bed
Arise, and shed
Thy light of brightest eyes upon my head!

Ah me, relentless lord
Of Love! whose hands are stored
With bitter biting arrows keen!
Why have I seen
The lustre-lighted limbs of young Eudiades?
O, cruel Queen
Of Beauty! does thou please
To mock me with the bloom more sweet than flowers,
Softer than summer hours,
Of him who cannot care, –
He is so fair, –
For his poor lover?

Yet arise!
Show forth thy silvery eyes!
I die for thee, and melt
Like wax away,
Or like spring violets, which, having felt
The strong relentless ray
Of Phoebus, fade in premature decay.

Shine forth, my golden sun,
My little lovely one!
Sweet bud of beauty, nursling of heaven's grace!
Thou fairest face
Of all that shine upon the smiling earth!
Why wilt thou shun
These words that wake thee to a happier birth,
Thou thoughtless one?

Nay, slay me not! but rise!
And let thy living eyes
Be to me as the light
Which envious night
For all her clouds and shadows cannot chase away!
It is Melanthias cries:
Arise, arise!
And beam upon him with thy spirit's day!
Nay, ere he dies,
Be pitiful, and ease
The languor of his love, Eudiades!

So to the low lute with a sobbing tune
He made his plaint through the still night of June;
And the boy heard, and knew whose voice it was,
And murmured in his heart:
                              'Melanthias
Loves me! Ye gods! what thing is love? I know
No more of love than when my sisters throw
Their arms about my neck and kiss me. Lo!
Some dream deceives me!'
                              Then he rose, and through
The red rose-blossoms peeping saw the man
Stand in the starlight very tall and wan.
Whereat the boy blushed, and new thoughts were stirred
Within his soul; yet uttered he no word;

But silent hung upon the sill and breathed
Low, lest the frail and thin rose-tendrils wreathed
Around the trellis, quaking should give sign
Of aught that lived and heard that song divine:
Nor slept he till the morn, but lay wide-eyed
And listened. On the night the music died,
And the man's lingering feet had passed away
Ere from the hills smiled forth the jocund day.

But when he rose and from the lattice leant,
The boughs beneath his window-eaves were bent
With more than weight of roses, bud or bloom;
For there a branch of golden blossoming broom
Was set, wherefrom there hung a parsley crown
With fillets interwoven, fluttering down,
Snow-white and scarlet, through the leaves like flame,
Whereon was wrought with silver thread a name –
'Melanthias, thrice victor in the race!'
Then stole a red blush o'er the sweet boy's face,
And scarcely dared he breathe for great delight;
Yet in his breast he laid the splendour bright
Of those tale-telling ribbands, but the wreath
Forthwith he placed with trembling hands beneath
His lowly bed, grey rushes strewing o'er
Its dark green leaves upon the chamber floor.

Then ran amain, kissed by the rising sun,
Down to the school, and, when the tasks were done,
With Pheidias, their arms round neck and waist
Close-twining, to the wrestling-ground he paced,
And spake of many things, but nought of love;
For not as yet did that young bosom move
With restless yearnings, and he scarce could frame
His secret of the night in speech for shame.
But while they wrestled, and the strain was still
Even between them, though the stronger will
Of stubborn Pheidias bent toward mastery,
Lo! on a sudden from the poplar tree
Where he lay hidden, leaned the mighty breast
Of great Melanthias, and his eyes expressed
Such depth of longing that the fair boy quailed,
And blushed, and lost his footing, and nigh failed
With faintness of excessive shame and fear;

So that the meed of victory was clear
For Pheidias, who shouted, knowing not
That Love himself had striven in that bout.
Then rose Eudiades; but on his brow
There lingered still some shade of thought, as though
His mind far off perplexed were wandering
Enwrapped in dreams and mazy questioning;
Nor on the athlete did he gaze. Nathless
Melanthias, who marked that dizziness,
Triumphed:
         'He hath remembered last night's song!
He keeps my garland! it will not be long
Ere he shall listen to my words, and learn
Some pity.'
       While the lover thus in turn
Hoped after fear, one glance Eudiades
Cast from his eyelids soft and meant to please
On the broad-chested hero. Then demure,
With rosy cheek and downcast forehead pure,
He with his friend pursued the wonted way
To the cool shades of Academe, and lay
Till evening.
       There the stripling Chariton
Beside them winged with words the summer sun,
Talking of love and lovers. He was fair,
Of old Aristocles the wealthy heir,
Noble of speech and manners, and beloved
By one who with his fiery music moved
The souls of hardy men, well skilled to teach
By changeful moods and subtlety of speech,
Whate'er in love or fate or death or life
Can stir the soul or quell her eager strife.

'Nay, prithee, tell me,' cried Eudiades,
'What thing is love?'
       'Art thou a child of Greece
And knowest not love?' said Chariton: 'the best
Of gods, the wisest, youngest, tenderest!
Fairest he is and happiest – if a god
May rightly be called happy – who ne'er trod
Rough places with soft foot, but ever wends
Over the yielding hearts of happy friends;
Who makes his palace in the souls of men,

Dwelling with those are loved and love again;
Whose thoughts are fresh and fragrant, ever new,
Like deathless flowers that bud and blossom through
Unending years: of nobleness the sire
And lofty deeds, he lights the living fire
In breasts of heroes; nay, a bard is he;
For who that loves, but sings unceasingly?
His whole life is a poem!' –
                                    Here a smile
Brightened Eudiades who thought the while
Of that low song his lover sang, then cried:

'All this, fair Chariton, hath been denied
By men who loved unhappily; but they
Who are beloved, how shall they profit? Say!'
'Ah me!' blushed Chariton, 'what thing is this
You ask? What profit is there in a kiss,
A song, a flower, a face, a voice, the sky
When the clear stars fade in the dawn and die?
Nay, seek, Eudiades: taste this sweet thing,
And smile thereafter at thy questioning.'

Much mused Eudiades, and his dreaming eyes
Were saddened with the wistfulness that tries
To fathom depths of half forbidden things,
Made wonderful by vague imaginings
Of untried sweetness – visionary bliss
Mingled with doubts and drear uncertainties.
But while he pondered, o'er his wavering soul,
Swift as a lightning flash, the strong control
Of those wide earnest eyes of deepest blue
That gazed on him, was carried; and he flew
In spirit forth to greet the unknown love
They offered him; therewith he longed to prove
What Chariton had promised, and his brain
Burned with the strange hope, and a pleasant pain
Shot through his limbs, and what he once held dear
Seemed now far off and worthless in the clear
Bright light of the intoxicating bliss
Which for one word of kindness might be his.
All was so new, so wonderful, so dim,
He thought another sun had dawned for him;
With altered eyes he saw his friends of old,

Pheidias and Chariton: their love seemed cold;
Their hand-touch had no charm; their kisses lay
Like snow-flakes on his lips; nor could he say
What wrought the change, save that the passionate song
And eager eyes and strong man's strength had strung
His soul to subtler music. So he dreamed.

But now the day was dying. Rosy streamed
The sunset splendour on the sculptured snow
Of statues – gods and men in gleaming row
Set mid the olive trees; and as he went
Between them, sphered in strange bewilderment,
He, with his comrades silent on each hand,
A melody he scarce dared understand
Breathed from the stately limbs and brows sublime,
And his calm soul was troubled, and the time
Of eventide fell hallowed. Up the hill
Slowly they paced, and, as they journeyed, still
Converse of daily things between them fell,
That stirred but did not scathe the miracle
Of that pure vision.
              To his home at last
He came, and there his father's eyes were cast
Upon him, and his mother cried:
                     'My son,
Where hast thou tarried? Lo, the summer sun
Hath set, and thou art fasting!'
                      Nought he said,
But, seated at the table, broke his bread
With amber honey sweetened, and was fain
To be once more alone with his delicious pain.

But while he supped, nor they who loved him knew
What thoughts were in his soul, deep words like dew
Fell on his ear; for, so it chanced, that day
Black-browed Ameinias with his father lay,
The Thurian stranger, skilled in ancient lore
Of love-tales and great deeds of men of yore.
He with a low voice rhythmically grave
Chaunted in many an antique measured stave
The tale of Hylas. Then like flame the joy
Of that great love of heroes through the boy
Burned, and he crept beneath his father's knee,

And listened for a long hour patiently.
Nor did he now doubt any more, but sighed
For very pleasure that on him the pride
Of beauty like an aureole had been
Set by the white hands of the awful queen.
Till at the last his father said:
                                        'My son,
Learn thou to follow after fame; but shun
The feet of amorous songsters. Love was great
In those good days when heroes conquered fate.
But now the times are changed. Scarce fit for thee
Are these sweet whisperings of minstrelsy,
That hide the soul of truth and sacred things
Under feigned forms and false imaginings.'

Over the poet's face there stole a smile,
And on the boy he gazed a little while,
Seeming to say –
                        'Eudiades, nathless
Thou shalt be loved: yea, thou shalt live to bless
The hour that shows thee all love's godliness.'

Whereat the boy rose, and with blushing face
Moved in the twilight from the silent place,
And laid him on his couch, and from his breast
Drew the bright scarlet bands, nor thought of rest;
But longed with eager longing for the sound
Of those fair feet, which o'er the garden ground,
He doubted not, with music and with song
Would bring his lover through the dews ere long.
Nay, nor in vain he lingered; for the night
Still with young stars and rising moon was bright,
When through the cypress trees the prelude sweet
Of that low lute he heard, and soon the feet
Stayed at his window, and he saw the man
Stand in the starlight very tall and wan.

        Oh, happy wreath
            And crown of flowers!
        Doth my love breathe
            Through the still hours
            Upon thee now?
            Or on his brow,

Or better in his breast,
Hast thou found rest?
I left thee here with tears and dew
Wet through:
Last night I left thee, when the moon
Sank all too soon;
And in the skies
The starry eyes
Were cold and keen.
Now thou art vanished; and I know
That he hath cherished thee; between
Thy petals and thy silk-enwoven sheen
The rose of love hath deigned to blow.
Yea, from his brow serene
There flashed on me –
Oh thou most mighty Queen
Of Joy, thou smilest! – one
Bright arrow, like the sun;
Wherewith I warm myself, and wait till he
Wake from his sleep and live and love with me!

So thrilled the voice and lute. Behind the screen
Of rose-buds, white and red, with delicate green
Of tender foliage twined, Eudiades
Lay listening, till the tender melodies
Softened his soul, and from the boughs he broke
One ruddy flower, nor stirred therefore nor spoke,
But dropped it silently. It fell and breathed
Its perfume on the lover's breast, who sheathed
The pure gift in his trembling palms and sighed
For rapture. But the boy, confused with pride
And shame, now that the very deed was done
And that he saw no little way to shun
The mighty love that thus encompassed him,
Wavered, and weeping in the twilight dim
Of his once innocent room, now made the shrine
Of this new sacrament, while the divine
Voice sang of love and laughter, silent lay
Till the moon sank and from the hills the day
Again sprang joyous.
                    Then with heavy head
He rose; and lo! the grace of morning shed
New blessings on his heart, and he was ware

Of love's delightfulness, and cast off care
And fear: – or only feared, perchance, lest he
Might by his coyness have grieved utterly
That longed-for lover, and so lost the bliss
Of falling on his breast with the first kiss
Of those who sob and tell their yearnings. Then
Forth with his fellows to the school again
He fared, and at his task sat patient, while
The morning wore to noon; nor did a smile
Brighten his face as in the days gone by
With the mere light of life's felicity;
But o'er his books he mused, and singing seemed
As one who slept and sang the while he dreamed;
And when he stood or sat, his fingers played
With the bright ribbands in his bosom laid;
And much he longed for the man's ardent eyes.

Thence, rising with the rest in simple wise,
Down to the wrestling-field he went, and lay
Veiled by the thick shade of an olive grey.
It was a still and lonely place, where stood
A statue, wrought of old in cedar wood,
Of the young Love-God and fair Anteros,
Set 'neath a marble canopy. The gloss
Of gold was on a palm branch, which the boy
Held in his right hand; and the glittering toy
Moved the quick wish of Anteros, who strove
To steal it from the powerful lord of love.
But Eros smiled upon him, and the pair,
Hand locked in hand and hair with golden hair
Twined in a labyrinth of brightness, held
Perpetual strife, which never might be quelled
Till from the shrine those lovely shapes were thrust
Or the wise carver's work had fallen to dust.

Here stayed Eudiades, obscure, alone;
For of his friends and comrades everyone
Joined in the race or quoiting-match, or tried
New wrestling-feats, or boxed, or leaped; the wide
Garden around them ringing.
                                    Then there came
Who made the stripling's forehead burn like flame:
Yea, to the tree he crept and clung and cowered

Into its shadow; for his lover towered
Before his dazzled eyes, Melanthias,
White and large-limbed, bruising the thin wan grass.
He by the statue stood with arms outstretched
And moving lips that murmured; then he fetched
From that deep chest a sigh, but not of grief,
And with a rose thorn on a broad palm leaf
Pricked the plain words:
     'Eudiades the fair!'
And underneath again:
     'Thrice fair, most fair!'
As though he could not tire of writing 'fair.'

Upon the pedestal of Love he placed
The votive branch; then lightly turning faced
Eudiades, unseen before, who shrank
Close to the tree, while on his bosom sank
The beautous weight of blushing head, and heaved
The fluttering heart that scarcely still conceived
Its overmeasure of excessive bliss.
Melanthias stooped, and took one hand in his,
And stroking those soft tresses murmured low
Such little words as all true lovers know,
Nor need my tale to teach them: then he kissed
The rosy fingers, and to his bosom pressed
At last the boy, who now, more bold, dared lift
Quick furtive eyes, yet still away would shift,
To hide, if so might be, the strong delight
That swayed him.
    As he moved, the ribbands white
And scarlet fell: Melanthias laughed outright;
Nor could Eudiades refuse a smile: –
What further need had he of craft or guile?
Thus by the Love-God's shrine, beneath the trees,
Fragrant with summer, musical with bees,
While in the boughs the loud cicada sang,
And through the field glad boyish laughter rang,
These lovers vowed unspoken vows and blent
Their throbbing souls in love's accomplishment.
All was so calm, so fair, they scarce could think
'Twas but this morn had brought them to the brink
Of that full stream from which they slaked at will
The strange sweet thirst that burned and pleased them still

But – so they feigned – the years before had been
Some tedious prologue to this blissful scene,
Through which their joy before them ever moved
And told them it was life to be beloved –
The rest mere death and dark monotony
Tried by the light of their felicity.

Enough! Joy needs no words. I cannot tell –
Though of Love's dear delights I wot full well –
What strain of bliss between these lovers fell,
What bloom of kisses, what soul-nourishing sighs,
What long unutterable gazing of great eyes,
What silences like stars that in clear skies
Tremble with mute and eloquent ecstasies!
Ah me! words fail. I bow my head and seem
To be but singing in a golden dream.
I cannot bring again the days of Greece,
Or raise to life beloved Eudiades:
I cannot make superb Melanthias grow
In glory of orbed manhood here, or glow
Before your aching eyes; or teach you how
No shame or fear obscured his lucid brow,
No sin was in his soul, no dull distress
Marred the calm sunlight of his comeliness:
But in his breast sat aweful sense of good,
And his strong heart was armed with hardihood
To do and dare all things that might not shame
The boy he loved or taint his own proud name.

Do ye believe – dull generations, dead
In the cold mire of ignorance and dread –
Do ye believe the pure and lofty love
That stirred these children of the seed of Jove?
Oh! that in fact and deed I might rebuild
Those spacious shrines, now marred, I can but gild –
Bruised statues, ruined walls, fast fading forms,
Blurred with dank mists and soaked with ceaseless storms!
In vain. I faint. Yet listen, and endure:
The men of whom I speak were strong and pure.
No shame oppressed them: they could fight and fall;
And the whole earth mourned at their funeral.

One little hour in these delights flew by.
Then from the grass the lovers silently
Rising, lest eyes too curious should scan
The joy they still would hold from every man,
Went on their way; but ere they parted, words
Fluttered between them, winged with smiles, like birds
Who bear love-letters on their downy side;
And he who wooed and now had conquered, cried:

'To-night, my love! To-night, Eudiades!
Thou shalt not leave me till the dawn to freeze
Under thy window. Make full broad thy bed,
For henceforth we together will be laid.'

Nor more he spake, but hurried thence straightway,
Lest haply the too timid boy might pray
For respite and dear hours of bliss delay.
Nor was the fear vain; for the love that burned
Within the strong man's heart of steel and spurned
All idle dread of any ill to be,
Was soft as yet and slumbered dreamily
In the boy's breast, more like a future good
Which the still pondering soul scarce understood.
Yea, and he trembled with the passionate pain
Of those white winding arms, whose eager strain
Yet made him flutter like a bird just caught,
Who in the fowler's hand most gently brought
Must struggle still and pant and long to be
Once more at large in woodland liberty.
His father's words too on his heart like lead
Lay with a dull unapprehended dread.
This passion was so new, so terrible;
He tried, but tried in vain the strife to quell
Of his o'erburdened bosom. The good thing
Which he had longed for with such sorrowing,
How all untried, immeasurable, full
It was of wild pain and joy wonderful!
Nor could he guess why love like flame could dart
Through the man's marble limbs, or why his heart
Throbbed with the ravening furnace-breath of fire,
His flesh quaked with the fierce tongues of desire.
It was enough for him, the boy, to dream
Of coming days, in fancy down the stream

Of life to glide or rest among its flowers
And rushes on the bank through slumbrous hours
With that unrealized and vague delight
He called his lover. Then the thought of night
Oppressed him, and he cried:
                                   'What shall be done?
I have heard strange tales told! 'Twere well to shun
The sweetness that brings shame!'
                                          And yet again
Thrilled in his soul that swift delicious pain
Of love's anticipation.
                              Thus all day
He parleyed with his spirit, till the grey
Shadows of evening fell, and on his bed,
Tired out with tears and smiles, he laid his head,
And slumbered. It was scarce the noon of night
When to his window in the pale starlight
Melanthias came, and pushed aside the boughs
Of blossoming rose, and, careful not to rouse
The sleeping boy, doffed cloak and shoes, and hid
His light of limbs beneath the coverlid.
Then the boy stirring in his dream was ware
Of that loved presence, feeling round his bare
Smooth ivory breast the warm arms laid; yet he
Feigned in his guile and wise simplicity
To sleep, and watched with fear what should befall.
But nought befell; nor was he moved at all
Save with new longing, for the lover kissed
His forehead with pure lips and gently pressed
The little swelling softness of his breast.
Then turned Eudiades, and laughed, and cried:
'Didst think me sleeping?' and to the man's side
Nestled, and lay there dreaming, half awake,
While wakeful birds of June sweet sounds did make
Among the cypresses. But at daybreak
Uprose Melanthias, and the boy could see
His beauty naked in the mystery
Of morning; and thenceforth, I ween, no dread
Stayed in his soul where love was harbouréd:
But day by day living with him he learned
New sweetness, and the fire divine that burned
In the man's heart was mirrored in the boy's,
So that he thirsted for the self same joys,

And knew what passion was, nor could abide
To be one moment severed from the side
Of him in whom whatever maketh sweet
The life of man was centred and complete.
Yea, but the joy that grew between them wove
Their very bodies in a web of love,
So that they seemed to breathe one air and drew
The same delights dropping like honeydew
From all glad things – from scent of summer skies,
From sleep and toil and whispered melodies
Of music.

       Stay! what fierce and fiery thing
Is this that threatens them with withering?
The love that hitherto above them hovered
On wings angelical and lightly covered
Their brows with blooming olive wreaths and bay,
Now flames, a shape of dread, ruthless to slay
And shrivel their young veins in dry decay!
With ash-white flowers of poison crowned, he shoots
Through the thin air; and from his hands the fruits
Of pomegranate, whose harsh and bitter shell
Enspheres a blood-red heart of pain and hell,
Tempt the parched lips that gape and crack with drouth
Blown from the furnace-breath of that fierce mouth.
Ah me! relentless Love! and is it thus
With coals of fire you prove and temper us?
Must they be left, these lovers, to be caught
In the sly snare their wealth of love has wrought?
Will you, blind god and pitiless, be fain
To change for loss their great and golden gain?
It was in still September nights that this
Shadow of change o'erlaid their happiness:
For when Eudiades had learned to long,
When in his soul the fire of amorous song
Quivered with swift unrest, and love began
To mould the calm boy to a passionate man;
Then by his side, Melanthias, grown bold
Through weeks of joy, mourned that their love was cold,
Nursing the fever of a hidden want,
Till in his wish he waxed extravagant –
Why from the fruits should they their hands withold
Which strewed the paths of loving men with gold?

Nor spake thereof, but often sighed and turned
Wrestling with thoughts that in his bosom burned,
And from his side sometimes the sleeping boy was spurned.
But he, with young desire intoxicate,
Deeming no gift, no sacrifice, too great
For him he worshipped; yea, much pondering
To prove his service by some painful thing,
Offered the pleasure none may touch and live
Thenceforth unshamed:
                           'Lo, lover, I will give,'
Said he, 'whatever joy is mine. Nay, take
And drink my soul! from my life's fountain slake
Thy thirsty lips! fear not to shed my blood;
For I will die to do thee any good,
Or in my body bear thy mark of shame
To all men visible, cherish the blame
That falls on me for blessings! Only say
That I have gladdened thee! this word will pay
For grief or anguish in all years to come.'

So spake he; and the mighty man was dumb,
Marvelling at innocence wherein the fire
Flamed of immaculate white-winged desire,
Till love became a momentary bliss
Of tears and rapture and forgetfulness.
Then from the still depths of his soul there soared
A mist most wonderful, and spread, and poured
Her passion of pure raindrops through his eyes:
And, as before the painful sweet surprise
Of sudden beauty's vision had o'erborne
All thoughts within his soul, so now a scorn
Of baseness, god-begotten, bright with awe,
Subdued his spirit to the perfect law.
Once more he sank and trembled, and the sweat
Rose on his forehead – yea, once more his great
Man's bosom throbbed with heartaches. Then he stood
Self-conquered, slave thenceforth to only good,
In the wide eyes of young Eudiades
Threefold transfigured.
                           Lo! if men like these
Peopled this world with selfless deeds and gave
Their longings for a sacrifice to save
Bright honour, we should little need to dream

Of fabled heaven, but earth herself would gleam
With all that souls of mortal man can guess
Of love divine and God's great blessedness.
That night when love thus triumphed, ere the morn
A storm rose, and the cypress boughs were torn
With winds that swept the vexed skies clear: and they,
Lying with passionate tears tired in the grey
Light of the weeping dawn, felt love so sore,
So tested in the fiery furnace-core,
That nought might stand between them any more.

Eudiades, arising, all that day
Thought not of music or of amorous play
As heretofore, but pondered how that he,
Sphered in his fullness of felicity,
Might to his father bare the joy till this
Veiled from all eyes like a forbidden bliss.

But when eve came, black-browed Ameinias,
Who in the lore of love most cunning was,
And still, as other men know gold, could tell
By certain signs true love from false full well,
Supped with his sire; and lo, their converse ran
On love and great deeds, and that ardent man,
Glowing with fire poetic, swore that nought
Tempered the soul of man to lofty thought,
Or nerved his heart to suffer, but the stress
Of love's sublime god-sent deliriousness.
Yea, and with many an old mysterious line
Of sage and bard, on whose blind eyes the shine
Of heaven sight-searing with swift vision
Branded the shapes of things unseen, he won
Proof for his paradox; then turned and read
The boy's face like a book, and raised his head
In both his hands, and through his eyes like flame
Searching his soul found neither spot nor shame,
Nor any little corner that was free
From the pure fire of love's insanity.
He to the father cried:
                    'Behold thy son!
On him the light whereof I sang hath shone;
And he walks splendour-clad, a priest and king.'

Then was the boy bold, and the mighty wing
Of Love spread broad above him, and he spake
In the dim twilight words of force to shake
The hearts of hard men; and his father's eyes
Were troubled; but when silence fell, the wise
Soul of the old man pondered, and at length,
Seeing that nought may strive against the strength
Of Love, and that on earth no better fate
Is found for man than pure love passionate,
He kissed the boy, and blessed him, and, with prayer
To the great king of spirits, cast off care;
And so the night fell calm with stars and fair
Upon them.

      Ah! the vision fades! I clasp
Vain forms, and at an empty image grasp!
Yet stay; once more I see them! There they stand –
Eudiades a man, and in the hand
Of great Melanthias a conquering palm,
Gilded and wreathed with myrtle! Very calm
Are his blue eyes, like Love's, in which the deep
Oceans of amorous thoughts for ever sleep.
Eudiades, like Anteros, with curls
That stream upon his lover's neck, unfurls
The folds of the Olympian garland wound
About the athlete's brow, while trumpets sound
Their triumph in the porches, and the press
Of men crowd round to greet their goodliness.

Yea, and once more the shapes of dreams arise! –
Will no god shield my weak and shrinking eyes
From this fierce furnace-glare of agonies?
See, where the sun of Syracuse hath set
His dying lips, that scorch and tremble yet,
On a square space hemmed in by straight stone walls,
And thick with olive trees. The splendour falls
Crimson on grey gnarled stems and hoary leaves,
Shedding a baptism of blood that cleaves
To each fine spike of foliage, and beneath
Drenches a death-locked crowd that scarce can breathe.
There have they stood from morn as in a pen
For slaughter set by cruel cunning men;
Sheep howled around by ravening wolves, who bay

And bite, until at last woe-wearied they,
Worn out with hunger, cold, and slow disease,
Wavering beneath the weight of miseries,
Seek rest in shame; of Athens once the flower,
Sent forth to triumph, now in evil hour
The prey of scornful foes.
                But ah, why thus
Lengthen the tale oft told and piteous?
It is enough that there, beneath the trees,
Lies wounded unto death Eudiades,
Clasped in his lover's arms: – oh, pale and wan
Is the smooth forehead of the dying man!
And from his lips the slow few words are sighed
In whispers; while, around, the hideous tide
Of carnage and of mocking triumph roars
Like wind-frothed steely waves on weary shores.

'So dearest! Death hath found me; and our bliss
Ends in this last embrace and holy kiss,
Calm as the star – our star – that even now
Begins to shine on the day's tortured brow,
Bringing her promise of still dews and rest,
Cradled within the cool night's soothing breast.
I know not what hath rocked me into peace
Here in these Hell waves; but the torments cease
Of strife that kept me waking, and with thee,
Though ringed around with fire, I seem to be
Sphered in the arms of love inviolably.
The gall of death is past. Again the night
Of June, upon whose wings our dear delight
Was borne, a new and young-eyed thing of joy,
Descends upon me, and with thee, a boy,
I seem to lie drinking the delicate air.
Ah, dearest! do not grieve: those sighs that tear
Thy heart – those wide and anguished eyes that strain
Their tearless orbits – stir my soul again
To sorrow. Listen, lover; for I know –
Death teaches me – hear how he murmurs low
Between us – saying, nought can sever those
Whom love hath joined.'
                He swooned, and in the throes
Of dying trembled; then his breath was still,
And the fair limbs were very pale and chill.

Melanthias stirred not, though the trumpet shrill
Spake through the trees; and in his ears the tread
Of heavy men, who passed with hearts like lead
Forth to their doom of slavery and disgrace,
Wakened the echoes of that hideous place;
But on the corpse he bent, and he could hear
Who cried:
       'Thrice blest! yea, safe from shame and fear
Are these dead lovers! would that we had died
Like them! see how they slumber side by side,
Nor of the woes that wait for us are ware!
But surely in some shadowy valley fair
Of Hades they drink Lethe, and for them
Nepenthe blooms upon the poppy-stem.'

Then was he wrapped in silence; and his eyes
Searching the twilight of the darkening skies,
Saw sleep and death, twin brothers, on the knees
Of night, who hovered o'er the dim grey trees
And beckoned him. Nor did they wait, but he
Kissed the dear lips he loved most tenderly,
And, stretched beside Eudiades, with breast
Still warm upon that frozen bosom pressed,
Unsheathed his sword, and leaned on it, and died:
For sleep and death bent over him, with wide
Smooth downy wings, and raised him up, and breathed
Swift peace upon his quivering limbs, and wreathed
His forehead with the boughs of rest, and bore
His slumbering spirit to the blissful shore.
So was dear Love in Death accomplishéd.

Then they who on the morrow found them dead
Deemed that they were twin gods, for never yet
Had mortal souls in forms so fair been set;
And though their arms bewrayed them, though they lay
Among the slain Athenians, whom that day
Just fate had smitten for their insolent pride,
Yet were they nobly buried where they died.
And on their grave a shrine was set, and prayer
By the poor laity of love was there
Offered through many years, until at length
Time, who is stronger even than the strength
Of love and beauty, who with dust o'erlays

The names of mighty kings and breaks the bays
Of poets, breathed upon them with his breath
So that none held remembrance of their death.

Now all is dark – now there remains for me
Nought but the weak and wavering memory
Of what through lonely hours of night I drew
Forth from the grave, and tricked with form and hue
Delusive. Ah, farewell! for me ye were
More than mere dreams: and lo, my life is bare.

Postludium

A brief night-blossoming flower, that all day through
    Sleeps; but when eve descends, from her blue veil
Shaking the shower of stars and drift of dew,
    Exhales strong perfume, and its petals pale
    Spread in the twilight: – such is the dim tale
Which I have striven in vain with words to dress
Not all unworthy of its loveliness.

A star that thwart the midmost gloom of night
    Shoots through the firm fixed lamps of heaven and dies,
Yet on the darkness leaves a streak of light
    That for a while delays our lingering eyes,
    Making a novel lustre in the skies: –
Such is the joy that in my story shines,
And with a fading splendour gilds the lines.

A dream that hovers on the twilight-bar
    Of sleep and waking, very fair to see,
Yet very frail, scarce felt, like some small star
    That in the growing sunrise silently
    Is swallowed, and we grieve amid our glee: –
So fair, so frail, so transient is the thought
Which my poor fancy dreamingly hath wrought.

A cloud that sailing o'er the sunset shows
    Strange heavenly hues and many a changeful shape
But when the day is dead, and the last rose
    Hath faded, and grey mists descend and drape
    Its pearly rondure, then the thoughts escape

Which lent it life, and all is dead and dull: –
So are the forms I feigned so beautiful.

Yea, they are fled and vanished. Night and day
  Alike have slain them, But the stars that shine
Studding the clear ethereal skies for aye
  Of mighty poets, fail not; their divine
  Calm sculptured forms will stand and smile when mine
Like clouds dissolve to nothing; and their flowers
Fear not the kisses of the amorous hours.

Yet ere I leave you – ere the vision dies
  Returning to its nothingness – behold,
I kiss you on the lips and on the eyes,
  And bless you for the gift more dear than gold
  I held of you, who in midwinter cold
Have made for me three summer days of peace,
Radiance reflected from the sun of Greece.

Yea, boy and lover! Phantoms though ye be,
  Brain-born, of music woven and rose-leaves
And nightingales and moonlight, fair to see,
  But lifeless, lustreless! my bosom heaves
  At parting, and a stony sadness cleaves
Here to my heart, and for some unknown good
I pine perplexed with pain and solitude.

Oh, I am dazed and utterly undone.
  My soul hath drunk of sweetness – lo, she dies!
The wholesome light of day I have foregone
  To dote on old delusive mysteries.
  Farewell, Melanthias! Eudiades,
Farewell! You fade, and fading filch away
Some portion of my heart, that still must stay

And, howsoe'er her longings pass, live on,
  A broken maimed and desecrated thing,
Born out of time, by cross fate cast upon
  A sandy tract of sloth and sorrowing.
  Yet, dearest, grieve I not: 'tis you who fling
The radiance years can never wholly blight
Athwart the dimness of descending night.

14   'Ganymede'

Hon. Roden Noel. From *Beatrice and Other Poems*, 1868.

Azure the heaven with rare a feathery cloud;
Azure the sea, far-scintillating light,
Soft rich like velvet yielding to the eye;
Horizons haunted with some dreamlike sails;
A temple hypaethral open to sweet air
Nigh on the height, columned with solid flame,
Of flutings and acanthus-work instinct
With lithe green lizards and the shadows sharp
Slant barring golden floor and inner wall.

A locust-tree condensing all the light
On glossy leaves, and flaky spilling some
Sparkling among cool umbrage underneath;
There magically sobered mellow soft
At unaware beholding gently laid
A youth barelimbed the loveliest in the world,
Gloatingly falling on his lily side,
Smoothing one rounded arm and dainty hand
Whereon his head conscious and conquering
All chesnut-curled rests listless and superb;
Near him and leaning on the chequered bole
Sits his companion gazing on him fond,
A goat herd whose rough hand on bulky knee
Holds a rude hollow reeden pipe of Pan,
Tanned clad with goatskin rudely-moulded huge;
While yonder, browsing in the rosemary
And cytisus, you hear a bearded goat,
Hear a fly humming with a droning bee
In yon wild thyme and in the myrtles low
That breathe in every feebly-blowing air;
Whose foamy bloom fair Ganymede anon
Plucks with a royal motion and an aim
Toward his comrade's tolerant fond face.
Far off cicada shrills among the pine,
And one may hear low tinkling where a stream
Yonder in planes and willows, from the beam
Of day coy hiding, runs with many a pool
Where the twain bathe how often in the cool!

And so they know not of the gradual cloud
That stains the zenith with a little stain,
Then grows expansive, nearing one would say
The happy earth – until at last a noise
As of a rushing wind invades the ear,
Gathering volume, and the shepherd sees,
Amazed forth-peering, dusking closing all
Startled and tremulous rock-roses nigh,
Portentous shadow; and before he may
Rise to explore the open, like a bolt
From heaven a prodigy descends at hand,
Absorbing daylight; some tremendous bird,
An eagle, yet in plumage as in form
And stature far transcending any bird
Imperial inhabiting lone clefts
And piny crags of this Idaean range.

But lo! the supernatural dread thing,
Creating wind from cavernous vast vans,
Now slanting swoops toward them, hovering
Over the fair boy smitten dumb with awe.
A moment more, and how no mortal knows,
The bird hath seized him, if it be a bird,
And he though wildered hardly seems afraid,
So lightly lovingly those eagle talons
Lock the soft yielding flesh of either flank,
His back so tender, thigh and shoulder pillowed
How warmly whitely in the tawny down
Of that imperial eagle amorous!
Whose beakèd head with eyes of burning flame
Nestles along the tremulous sweet heave
Of his fair bosom budding with a blush,
So that one arm droops pensile all aglow
Over the neck immense, and hangs a hand
Frail like a shell, pink like an apple bloom;
While shadowy wings expansive waving wind
Jealously hide some beauty from the sun.

Poor hind! he fancied as the pinions clanged
In their ascent, he looking open-mouthed
Distraught yet passive, that the boy's blue eye
Sought him in soaring; his own gaze be sure
Wearied not famished feeding upon all

The youth's dear charms for ever vanishing
From his poor longing, hungered for in heaven –
Took his last fill of delicate flushed face,
And swelling leg and rose-depending foot,
Slim ankle, dimpling body rich and full.
Behold! he fades receding evermore
From straining vision misting dim with tears,
Gleaming aloft swanwhite into the blue
Relieved upon the dusky ravisher,
Deeper and deeper glutting amorous light,
That cruel swallows him for evermore.

15 A Vision of Love Revealed in Sleep

Simeon Solomon. Extracts from *A Vision* etc. Written 1869, published 1871.

Then I sought my Soul in trembling, for I knew that there was one present on whom I had not yet dared to look, and my Soul said to me by the spirit, *Behold him whom we seek, but we are not yet prepared.* Then I turned my gaze upon him; in the gloom of the unremembered temple he sat in all lowliness upon the fragment of a broken frieze, whereon the sculptured histories of his ancient glory crumbled and fell away, forgotten and uncared for, blighted by the breath of ages, stained with the rust of storms that know no mercy; his red and golden raiment hung loose about his limbs, and the blossoms from his hair had fallen crisped and dead upon his shoulders; the tears of a divine agony yet lay upon his cheek; the radiance which I had seen by my spirit, before my feet had gained the threshold of the temple, sprang from the wound upon his heart; and when I looked upon and saw it illumine the dim eyes of my Soul, my spirit abased itself, and my gaze fell upon the earth. Then I knew that this vision had been fulfilled, and my heart, ringing with the inner voices of the things that had been revealed to us, and my eyes laden with their images, I again turned unto my Soul, and saw that upon his countenance rested the light that came forth of Love's wound, and made it shine; and, as we departed from the temple, I rejoiced secretly at this; also I felt strengthened and gladdened at heart because of Sleep; and my spirit was softened by reason of his smile. And we turned our steps towards the waning stars.

And the awe which comes upon man at the passing away of night fell upon us, and I bethought me again of the words of the wise king, *Until the day break, and the shadows flee away.* And a strong yearning was begotten within me, and a sob burst forth from my mouth up out of my heart, and my lips said inaudibly, *Ah, that the day would break, and the shadows verily and indeed flee away*; and the spirit essayed to escape, and in travail I sought help of my Soul, and it was given unto me, and he spoke these words: *Put thy sorrowing away from thee, for the sword shall not again cruelly cleave thy spirit; yet, as I told thee before we stood upon the threshold of the ruined temple we have erewhile left, another trial shall be laid upon thee, and the spirit must needs crouch beneath the weight of it; but, albeit sorrow shall go up as a mist before thee, when thou beholdest what is at hand, thou shalt see, as behind a thick cloud, the presence of light; in the coming vision shall be dimly heralded his effulgence; it shall appear in thine eyes as it were the strong weeping that goes before joy; and as the springing forth of hope from despair: it shall not be seen of thee as a dark mystery; thy spirit will look into it and know it.* He made an end of speaking, and by the pale beams of the sinking stars I saw an image dimly mirrored in his eyes. I removed my gaze from his face, and looked abroad, and beheld, dark against the wan air of the dying night, Love seated upon a throne lowly and poor, and not worthy to bear him, – no longer, indeed, wounded and bleeding, but still bereft of his perfect glory; in his eyes there shone a soft light of suffering not yet past, but on his brow, where poppies were mingled with the myrtles, there lay the shadow which falls upon one not remembered; upon his parted lips hovered the half-formed smile of a child who halts between weeping and laughter; he was fully clothed in raiment of dim and sullied red and gold; in one hand he bore a poppy branch bound about the myrtle, from which the stars had fallen one by one, and in the other a golden globe whose brightness was obscured and shamed by dust; his feet were wholly hidden in the thick growth of weeds and poppies that crowded round his throne; he spoke no word, only the faint sounds in the air about him and the grief-dimmed eyes of my Soul told me that he was Love imprisoned in an alien land of oblivion – forgotten, put away.

Again my heart sank, and the flowing of its streams waxed dull, and the words of him bound by the sea burned upon it with a more ardent flame, and the vision we passed from filled my eyes, and came forth of them in bitter tears; yet I forgot not the saying of my Soul, that this should be as the darkly revealed sign of the joy to come, for was not Love enthroned – poorly indeed – and had not the shadow of suffering well-nigh lifted, albeit indeed its sear remained? But I called up strength, and bound it as a girdle about me, and looked upon the countenance of him beside me; and behold, upon it, despite the eyelids drooping with foregone grief, I saw the longed-for smile, and I took content upon me.

Our course now lay along an upward slope, whereon the poppies waxed scantier, and the weeds less rank; a soft mossy grass soothed our wayworn feet, and I could see by the light of the dying stars that small golden blossoms lay in a pattern upon the sward. As we neared the brow of the hill, I knew that a yet unseen and mysterious presence was about to be revealed to us; soft breezes bore his light to us upon their wings, and voices from the passing Night spoke to us of him; he was half-seated, half-lying, upon a height beyond which was stretched out the faintly glimmering sea; there lay upon him yet the shadow of the Night, but his face had upon it the radiance of an expected glory, the light of glad things to come; his eyes were yet soft with the balm of Sleep, but his lips were parted with desire; his breath was as that of blossoms that awake and lift up their heads and give forth their odours; his dusky limbs were drawn up as if in readiness to depart, and his great and goodly wings softly beat the air; with one hand he cast away his dim and dewy mantle from him, and with the other he put aside the poppies that had clustered thickly about him; as he turned his head to the East, the poppies fell from his hair, and the light rested upon his face; the smile it kindled made the East to glow, and Dawn spread forth his wings to meet the new-born Day. And when the Day was seated on his throne, we passed along a pleasant land that lay beneath the light of a great content; and the radiance yet lingered on the countenance of my Soul. And the sadness that had made the curves of his mouth heavy, and had dimmed his eye, now gradually departed, and there came upon him an aspect of calm, as of one certain of a good thing shortly to befall, although he knows not fully what it may be; and when I looked upon his eyes my spirit took heart, and I girded myself and set forward with my head no more bent; and we were met by many who had been shown me in my former dreams, and who all bore the reflection of a light upon their faces.

Also I saw with great joy many whom I knew by name, and who were dear to me, and they were clad in garments of beauty, so that it joyed my eyes to behold them. And it appeared to me as though I felt beating upon my breast the warmth that came from theirs towards me; and youth was set as a crown upon their heads, and they bore branches blossoming from the breath of youth, and its divine essence coloured all the air about them; and I discerned one face in that company beloved of me beyond the rest; a northern sun had set a ruddy sweetness upon it, and southern suns had kissed it into perfect bloom; from the depths of the grey eyes welled up and sprang forth the spirit of Love, and, most loath to depart, yet brooded upon them as the dove in early time upon the waters; a sacred light, as of the guileless dreams of childhood, looked out from them and gladdened my own, and the softness of Sleep was bound upon the head. When I looked upon the face, I felt, indeed, that my travail was well-nigh over, and as it passed from me, and was lost to me, my spirit bathed its dusty wings in the warm, glad tears that bubbled from my heart, and was refreshed. And when the throne of day was set well-nigh above our heads, and there was that in the air which moves the heart of nature, we rested ourselves beside a running stream, whose waters brought joyous sounds from afar, as it were the long-forgotten songs and gentle voices of our childhood, yet laden with a heavier and fuller harmony from a source we knew not yet; and as we journeyed on in the dawn of the evening, an awe fell upon me, as when one enters upon a new and unknown way, and all the air about teemed with the echoes of things past and the vague intimations of things to come.

Then my Soul turned towards me and spoke these words: *Lay upon thy spirit a glad humility, and essay to strengthen thine eyes, that they may bear to behold the things which shall shortly be brought before thee to thy comfort and solace. As thou hast hitherto only seen him we seek sinking beneath the burdens that have been laid upon him by thee and by the like of thee; as thou hast seen the glory about him shattered and made dull by reason of the wounds and weakness the bitter darkness of the world has inflicted, so shalt thou now behold him gathering his natural power about him, and clothed with light; but not yet shall it be given to thee to see him in the plenitude of his glory. I will support thee. Look up.*

And now I raised my eyes and looked upon the stream, and it seemed to me as though the waters were cleft apart, and there was a hollow in their midst; and lo, the air about it appeared changed, and its pulses stood still, and the sounds I had heard borne on its wave collected themselves together and took form; and the form was of the colour of the sun-lighted sea, and within it I saw one borne gently upward, naked, and glowing exceedingly; the stars of the living myrtles burned fresh upon his hair, and his countenance was as the supreme excellence of youth transfigured, the wound upon his heart was healed, and on its place I saw burning a ruddy flame, whereof the tongues came forth to me and touched my own, whereon were engraven the words which I heard Love speak when we saw him bound to the tree, and in their stead the flame wrought this saying, letter by letter, *Many waters cannot quench Love, neither can the floods drown it;* and now the radiant mist wherein he was lifted up rose and enfolded him, and hid his aspect from me, and its form was dispersed, and it was changed to gentle sounds in the stream, and all the air about became as it was before.

Then I turned my eyes upon my Soul and saw that he appeared well pleased, and the sparkling light sent up from the ripples of the stream whereby we sat played across his brow and illumined his dusky hair. Then I knew that I should be gladdened by what he was going to tell me. He spoke and said, *Thou hast well seen that the travail of Love is past and gone by, and content and joy are spread over the whole air because of it. Now there will arise upon thy vision a mystery which thou wilt, of thy nature, comprehend but dimly; yet fail not to look well upon it, for by it the springs of the heart of the universe are fed and made glad; and because Love is thus gone up from the wave in thy sight, it is given to thee to look upon it.*

He ceased to speak, and I turned my gaze in the direction where I had seen the last vision; and behold, again the air seemed changed, and I saw a happy light gathering itself there, and it seemed, as it were, to be formed of the warmth which makes the earth bring forth its fruit; and there appeared to me within the light an inner living glow, and the glow divided itself in twain, and became two Holy Ones, each having six wings; their limbs moved not, but the ardour wherewith their spirits were endued bore them along. As one sees in a soft air two flower-laden branches bend one towards the other, and, mingling, send forth a two-fold fragrance, so I saw one of these impelled towards his fellow and lightly touch him, and a living pulse seemed to beat in the flame that went forth from them, and a form was given to it, and a heart informed it, and all the fire-coloured air about it breathed hymns at this marvellous birth. Albeit, my spirit had not yet been fully purified, so that I should clearly know what this mystery showed forth; yet I was greatly rejoiced in that it was given me to see it. And now my Soul turned towards me and spoke these words, *What thou hast just beheld it is vouchsafed to no man to comprehend, save he see the glory that comes forth of the Holy Place; therefore gird up thy spirit that thou be ready for the call of him who shall lead thee thereunto. What thou hast seen it was given to the three Holy Ones to know fully when they were cast into the furnace; for as the serpent-rod which the prophet threw forth swallowed its fellows, the greater eating the lesser, so did the fiercer flames of that Charity which thou hast erewhile seen wonderfully and mystically begotten go forth of the righteous children's hearts, and devour and utterly dry up the heat that burned about them.*

He ceased to speak, and then I turned my gaze upon his eyes, and rejoiced greatly through my spirit to see a brighter glow upon them, as from the expected coming of the long-desired; and when I cast my eyes upon the earth I discerned there many happy creatures, joyous and beautiful, and such as have no existence in the neighbourhood of evil. After a space, and when my eyes had been gladdened by reason of these things, I again turned them upon my Soul, and I knew that what we sought would now shortly be revealed to us. A weakness fell upon me, but my Soul supported me; we looked forward, and saw one approaching clothed about with a soft light; he moved towards us, gently lifted by the spirit from the ground, neither flying nor running. Ever and again his feet, wherefrom sprang glowing wings, touched the earth and caused it to bring forth flowers; his head was bound with a fillet of violet, and violet blossoms breathed upon by Love; he carried a mystic veil of saffron colour, which depended from his head upon his shoulders even to the ground, and his shining body was half girt with fawn-skin; in his hand he carried a staff, which was as the rod of the high priest, for as I looked upon it its barrenness burst forth in almond bloom; and, as when the prophet put away his shoes from off his feet before the Holy Place, and beheld the bush burning with fire but not consumed, even so I saw upon the staff the dancing tongues of flame cling round the wood, but leave it scatheless; and this thing appeared marvellous in my eyes, and I thought upon the words my Soul had spoken to me concerning the three Holy Ones, and how the fires which wrapped them about did but make them stronger and fairer than before.

And now, looking upon the face of him who came towards us, it appeared as the face of one dwelling in the Holy Place, glowing with the perfect peace which is shed of Love, for he had borne the Very Love within his hands, therefore upon him the shadow of the burden of humanity had not rested; and now, encouraged by his gentle mien, and by the strengthened light upon the eyes of my Soul, I went forward until I set myself in front of him who bore the saffron veil; the waves of Love that moved about him laved my face, they refreshed me, and appeared to make my self-consciousness sit lightly upon me, and to loosen me from the grip of my humanity, but it was not yet vouchsafed to me to cast it from me.

As the holy seer prayed to be purged of his transgressions by the burning coal of Charity, so I too desired that my lips should be touched, and my eyes made clear and worthy to behold those things whence flow the springs of life. When the aspect of him who bore the blossoming staff fell full upon me it generated a stronger yearning towards the Beatific Vision, and the distant harmonies of the spheres became clearer unto me; I then first felt conscious that a faint light hovered about my own head, like that upon the head of my Soul, and the voice of him who bore the mystic veil spoke to me by the spirit, and I heard these words, *Before thou art worthy to behold Him whom thou hast so long sought in the perfect fulness of His glory, thou must be purged of all grossness, thou must be clothed utterly with change of raiment, and the dead fruit of thy heart and of thy lips must be put away from thee; and when these things shall have been done, yea, even then thou shalt not see His full effulgence with none between it and thee, but through the veil of Sleep shall it be revealed unto thee. Follow me.* Then, chastened by these words, I again bent my head, and my Soul led me forward.

Then I turned unto him and bent a look upon him as of one questioning, and, seeing my aspect, he turned towards me and spoke these words: *Wouldst thou learn who is this thus leading us on towards Him we seek; thou sawest his name upon his brow, but the lingering darkness of thy spirit forbade thee to decipher it aright; he it is whom thou hast known since first thou camest away from thy mother's breast, for with what thou receivedst therefrom, thou acceptedst him; looking upon him thou lookest upon what has ever dwelt within thy heart of hearts, for by him shall the Very Love be revealed unto thee; he has no beginning, for throughout all ages has he stood by and ministered to Him we seek and shown Him forth: it has been desired of many from the first years unto this day to put him aside and even to slay him, but, like the flame-girt, unconsumed staff he bears, he passed through the fire, and even in these latter days gives forth the light that has first been shed upon him. The violets upon his brow are those of young time, yet the dew is fresh upon them; and though it was believed of many that his staff was sapless and withered, behold how the air about it is made fragrant by the blossoms that it bears. Faithful is he through all; he holds on high his lamp so that those who look above the low fogs that cling about the earth may be led of it, and the flames about him penetrate the thick darkness of the waking world. Many have sought to tear the wings from off his feet that they may not see the light that springs forth from them; yet still the radiance of Him whom he shows forth makes his feet shed light abroad, and still the earth yields flowers at his approach. Let us follow him.*

He who bore the flame-girt staff floated lightly along his path of flowers, and the glow about his winged feet made their petals to expand. And now in all humility I stood upon the threshold of a glowing temple; the air about it was moved by the breath of Him who dwelt within, its waves were heavy with the odours that came forth of His presence, and its pulses echoed with the voices of the worlds that revolve because of Him. Within the court of the temple I heard the sound of wings that ceased not to beat the air; then a tremor came upon my hands and feet, for remembrance brought to me the image of him we saw by the grey sea, bound hand and foot, and the voice from his heart sounded yet in my ears. Then one came unto me, having six wings, which overshadowed my Soul and me, and, though I looked not upon his face, I knew he touched my forehead and lips with it, and they were purified by fire, but not seared with its sting. Then his fellow came unto me, and put away my traveller's garb from off me, and clothed me with a vestment in colour like the heart of an opal, and over my left shoulder he laid a stole tinted like a flame seen through water, and he placed upon my head a veil which covered my eyes, but did not dim my spiritual vision; and now again the words which came from Love's mouth, when I saw him bound by the sea, rang in my ears, *Thou hast wounded my heart*, and a deeper humility fell upon me. Then I heard him of the winged feet say unto my Soul, *He is prepared, come*; and I was borne along by the spirit through the outer court and toward the Holy Place, and ever the rushing sound of the wings became louder and louder, and I knew that the temple was filled with seraphim, for the veil which hung over my eyes but shielded them from a light which, when it should fall upon them, would blind them; also I knew that he whose head was bound with violets had left us, and consigned me to the care of my Soul.

Now there arose before me the image of him whom we had seen sleeping in the ruined temple; his arms were wound about his head, which lay back upon them; he was naked, but his form was wrapped about with the soft star-lighted air; his lashes were no longer moist with tears, but his face shone as became one through whom the Very Love was to be revealed. And now I felt the heart of the universe beat, and its inner voices were made manifest unto me, the knowledge of the coming presence of the Very Love informed the air, and its waves echoed with the full voices of the revolving spheres. Then my Soul spoke to me and said, *In the beginning of time the universe and all that was therein was grey, and its springs were without life, as a fair body, joyless and lacking beauty, because no spirit stirs it; light had not come upon it; and, as when one is in a trance, the pulses are dead, and await the aid of that which shall enter them and make the dead alive; even so, there sprang forth, of its own power and holy ardour, a light over the face of all things, and the heat of it made them glow, and the grey became green: the golden air sang over all, and an universal hymn arose and went up, and its voice yet gladdens the circling worlds. As the prophet saw in the dark valley the dead bones come together and take life upon them, even so Love, who was the light, smiled upon the uninformed countenance of things, and it was kindled because of it; and there went from him a two-fold essence, whereof the streams have flowed for ever, and cease not to flow; and by them are we upheld, and our spirits replenished; and, as the priest holds the flower-starred crown over the heads of the bridegroom and the bride, so now and again do the streams unite within us, and Love, whence they go forth, is the crown over us and the light about us. But through the thick veil of the darkness of the world this is not seen or known of men, but only through the spirit may it be made clear unto us; and the spirit soars aloft rejoicing, and is girt about with delight because of it.*

And now the image of Sleep filled the orbit of my sight, and through the veil of his form I saw him who bore the mystic saffron raiment wherewith he had covered his hands. My spirit well-nigh fainting, I turned unto my Soul, and knew by the increasing glow upon him that strength was given me yet again to lift my eyes. Well was it for me that what came was revealed to me through the veil of Sleep, else I could not have borne to look upon it.

From out the uplifted hands of him who stood within the Holy Place there sprang forth a radiance of a degree so dazzling that what else of glory there was within the temple was utterly obscured; as one seeing a thin black vapour resting before the face of the mid-day sun, so I saw upon the radiance the brooding cherubim, their wings meeting, their faces hidden; I saw within the glory, one who seemed of pure snow and of pure fire, the Very Love, the Divine Type of Absolute Beauty, primaeval and eternal, compact of the white flame of youth, burning in ineffable perfection.

For a moment's space I shielded my eyes from the blinding glow, then once more raised them upon the Beatific Vision. It seemed to me as though my spirit were drawn forth from its abiding place, and dissolved in unspeakable ardours; anon fiercely whirled round in a sphere of fire, and swiftly borne along a sea of throbbing light into the Very Heart. Ah, how may words shew forth what it was then vouchsafed to me to know? As when the thin, warm tears upon the cheek of the sleeping bride are kissed away by him who knows that she is wholly his, and one with him; as softly as his trembling lips are set upon the face transfigured on his soul, even so fell upon my heart, made one with the Heart of Love, its inmost, secret flame: my spirit was wholly swallowed up, and I knew no more.

Then all this wondrous vision was fulfilled, and looking upon the sky, I saw that the stars had set and the dawn had spread his wings over the world; and again the words of the sage King, *Until the day break and the shadows flee away*, came into my mind.

16 'Song'

Lord Francis Hervey. From *The Taking of Alba and Other Poems and Translations*, 1873.

> We sat, my true love sat and I,
> Beneath the tall oak tree;
> The wind above piped mournfully,
> My whole soul swooned with agony, –
> O pain! does he love me?

His head upon my neck he laid:
    His keen eyes I could see –
Twin stars that flashed amid the shade;
His warm breath on my forehead played –
    O heaven! does he love me?

His lips touched mine, O joy, O bliss!
    The wind sang in the tree;
I knew his long-drawn rapturous kiss,
I felt his wild, wild, burning kiss; –
    O joy! he loveth me.

17   'The Peak of Terror'

Edward Carpenter. From *Narcissus and Other Poems*, 1873.

Upward all day we toiled athwart the rain,
Henry and I, through Alpine pastures green
And great firwoods that overhung the vale
Far spread below; but ever, as evening fell
Day's cloudy curtain parted, and the mists
Thinned more and more, and fled among the hills,
Or dropped beneath, or clung in silver threads
To tresses of dim forest; and we saw
A clear blue arch of space spanned high above,
And, burning behind the utmost mountain edge,
Gold altar-glories of the stricken sun.

And high amid the snows we found a crag,
Hung darkly on that argent slope, within
Stamped hollows as by rage of Titan tost;
And there we lit the flame, and made ourselves
Good cheer, while round us dreamed a silent world.
But ere we slept he, my beloved, arose
And lightly left our firelit cave and stood
Night circled on a jutting rock beyond;
And with the setting stars about his head
And at his feet that purple vale profound,
He sang the song he sings me evermore.
He sang to watchful heaven and weary earth,
To glittering peak and star and crescent moon,

And high Love, and the lovelorn Heart of all.
And all the vales were filled with melody,
And o'er the wide wide night and clear profound,
And over the blank snows and barren crags,
His song came floating back unto his feet:
Unto his feet, and deep into my heart,
There as I lay by the fire and saw him stand,
Saw him there in the night, and see him now,
Now, and for ever,
                        For he came not back.
At morning dawn, when earth was dashed with light,
Beside the golden summit he slipped and fell,
And slid, and passed to his own home beyond.

18   'Midnight at Baiae'

John Addington Symonds. From 'Three Visions of Imperial Rome', in
Lyra Viginti Cordarum c. 1875.

It is a night of summer: overhead
Pale stars are slumbering in a liquid sky;
And from the journeying moon blue splendours spread
O'er breathing earth and sea's serenity.
I hear a kissing ripple on some shore
Unseen, not far below me: thick and high
Shoot laurel boughs above: the marble floor,
Laid smooth and cool beneath, like frozen snow,
Gives back no sound; as from the gilded door
Furtive I steal, and with hushed footsteps slow
Glide through the palace between painted wall
And pillared aisle and flowering shrubs arow.
Where am I? Thwart my path dim glimmerings fall
From one tall narrow portal: onward still
It lures me breathless through a silent hall:
Still onward: sense and thought and shrinking will
Are drawn by irresistible control
Unto that core of light that sharp and chill
Shines like the loadstar of my shuddering soul.
Yet would I fain draw back: all is so dark,
So ominously tranquil; and the goal
To which I tend is but one tiny spark
Cleaving the dreamy twilight terrible.

What sound? Nay, quiver not! The watch dogs bark
Far off in farm-yards where men slumber well.
Here stillness broods; save when a cricket chirrs,
Or wheeling on slant wing the black bat shrill
Utters her thin sharp scream. No night wind stirs
The sleeping foliage of the stately bays.
Forward I venture. On warm silky furs
My feet fall muffled now; and now I raise
The latchet of the door that stands ajar.
I enter: with a fixed and frozen gaze
What is within I reckon: – near and far,
Things small and great, sights terrible and strange,
Alike in equal vision, on that bar
Of blackness standing, with firm eyes I range.
It is a narrow room: walls high and straight
Enclose it: here the lights that counterchange
Pale midnight shadows, scarce can penetrate
The fretwork of far rafters rough with gold.
The lamps are silver – Cupids love-elate
Upraising cressets: phallic horns that hold
Pure essences and oils. From gloom profound
Shine shapes of mural gods and heroes old,
Gleaming with hues auroral on the ground
Of ebon blackness: Hylas, Hyacinth,
And heaven-rapt Ganymede: – I know them. Crowned
With lilies dew-bedrenched upon a plinth
Of jasper stands Uranian Love, a god
Carved out of marble for some labyrinth
Of Acadêmic grove where sages trod: –
Here, breathless, in his beauty-bloom, he smiled,
Making more grim the ghastly solitude.
Amid the chamber was a table piled
With fruits and flowers. Thereon there blazed a cup,
Sculptured of sardonyx, where Maenads wild
With wine and laughter, shrieking, seemed to sup
The blood of mangled Pentheus: it was full
Of dark Falernian; the draught bubbling up
From blackness into crimson, rich and cool,
Glowed in the bowl untasted. Wreathes of rose,
Such as the shepherd lads of Paestum pull,
Circled two smaller murrhine cups: but these
Were empty, and no hand the flowers had shed.
Then was I ware how neath the gleaming rows

Of cressets a fair ivory couch was spread:
Rich Tyrian silks and gauzes hyaline
Were bound with jewelled buckles to the bed:
Thereon I saw a naked form supine.
It was a youth from foot to forehead laid
In slumber. Very white and smooth and fine
Were all his limbs; and on his breast there played
The lambent smiles of lamplight. But a pool
Of blood beneath upon the pavement stayed.
There, where blue cups of lotos-lilies cool
With reeds into mosaic-wreathes were blent,
The black blood grew and curdled; and the wool
Whereon his cloudy curls were pillowed, sent
Thick drops slow-soaking down o'er gold and gem.
Yet was the raiment ruffled not nor rent.
Spell-bound I crept, and closer gazed at him:
And lo! from side to side his throat was gashed
With some keen blade; and every goodly limb,
With marks of crispéd fingers marred and lashed,
Told the fierce strain of tyrannous lust that here
Life's crystal vase of youth divine had dashed.
It is enough. Those glazed eyes, wide and clear;
Those lips by frantic kisses bruised; that cheek
Whereon foul teeth-dints blackened; the tense fear
Of that white innocent forehead; – vain and weak
Are words, unutterably weak and vain,
To paint how madly eloquent, how meek,
Were those mute signs of dire soul-shattering pain!

19   'Wasted Days'

Oscar Wilde. From *Kottabos*, Vol. III, Dublin, 1877. The poem is subtitled
'From a picture painted by Miss V.T.'.

A fair slim boy not made for this world's pain,
With hair of gold thick clustering round his ears,
   And longing eyes half veil'd by foolish tears
Like bluest water seen through mists of rain;
Pale cheeks whereon no kiss hath left its stain,
   Red under-lip drawn in for fear of Love,
   And white throat whiter than the breast of dove –
Alas! alas! if all should be in vain.

Behind, wide fields, and reapers all a-row
In heat and labour toiling wearily,
To no sweet sound of laughter or of lute.
The sun is shooting wide its crimson glow,
Still the boy dreams: nor knows that night is nigh,
And in the night-time no man gathers fruit.

20   'The Legend of the Water Lilies'

Francis William Bourdillon. From *Among the Flowers and Other Poems*, 1878.

Far out from land fair lilies lie,
That gaze into the Eastern sky,
Upon a mighty river borne,
The worship of the lands of morn.
Far out from land, like some soft isle,
  The broad green leaves are laid;
And over them the lilies smile,
Or bow their beauteous heads awhile,
  With sweetness overweighed.
Yet perfect though is their repose
From morns that ope to eves that close,
Something there is, more deep and high,
That wins upon the wistful eye;
Such holiness as makes men yearn
For some forgotten life's return;
Ev'n as, when heaven with stars is set,
  The starred snow-flakes would fain
Rise to the life remembered yet,
  And float in heaven again.
Then, flowers of wonder, let me seek,
Not a presumptuous praise to speak, –
Ye need no praise, – but if I may,
  To ease the burden of desire,
By wafting lightest verse away,
  Sweet with the sweetness you inspire;
As wafts the rich Seringa bloom,
To ease her passionate love, perfume.

The roughest hills take tender haze
  From distance; so my tale

Comes softened down the vista'd days,
    Till passion's self is pale.
So not of sadness let it seem,
Save like the sorrows of a dream!

The sun was halfway to the West,
When to the river bank there pressed,
So long long back, a band of boys,
Intoxicate with summer joys.
Fair were they all in face and limb;
But one, – all left the prize to him,
For loveliness of boyish face,
And sinuous body's tender grace.
With happy laughter through the sedge
They burst, that hemmed the river's edge,
Parting with outstretched arms the reeds,
And feathered o'er with silken seeds.
And one would cast the brittle cane
At other, who returned again;
Or with the plumy-pointed rush
Would seek the warded face to brush.
So with their bare limbs rosier grown
    With boyish play, they pass
Throughout the fringing river-zone
    Of tall and tangled grass,
And came upon a tiny bay,
Girt with a shell-set shingle-way.
And there were sands that wooed their feet
With warm soft kisses; for the beat
Of lisping waves had left the form
Of carved lips, where the sun lay warm,
But now no tiniest wavelet played
    On all the water wide;
Nor showed the line, by light or shade,
Where first the sand was overlaid
    With crystal of the tide.
For not the lightest wind went by
To mar that mirror of the sky.
But soon with glowing foot and palm
Was shivered all the glassy calm,
As each on each, with joyous shout,
The flashing waters flung about,
With spray that, dancing down the air,

Made mimic rainbows everywhere.
Then down the shining water-floor
    They wandered, seeking deeper waves,
Though scarcely higher than before
    By foot or foot the current laves;
And nigh a furlong from the land,
Washed only to the waist they stand.
But then, as though the water lent
    New life to every limb,
No longer listlessly they went,
    But swiftly dive and swim;
More like some buoyant water-birth,
Than creatures wont to walk the earth.
Now silver-clad one dives below,
To seize his fellow ere he know;
Now one will stand apart a space,
A goal to which the rest shall race,
    But ere they touch him, turns and flies,
Like hunted bird from place to place,
    Till to the dearest in his eyes
    He yields himself an easy prize.

So gay it was, beneath the smile
Of loving skies to play awhile;
When winds above and waves beneath
Seemed of a world forgot by Death.
But deeper still would venture out
    The fairest, bravest boy;
The silk-soft waters curled about
    His rosy shape with joy,
And leaped to kiss his laughing face,
And clove to give him close embrace.
The water seemed itself for him
To grow more firm, since he would swim,
Itself to cleave a sliding way
Before his lithe limbs' easy play;
Until, upon a deeper tide,
He turns, to see the waters wide,
That part him from his fellows' side.
They, in their eager play, forgot
That he was gone, or noticed not,
Till far away they heard his shout,
    And gazed the water o'er;

There saw his form so far far out,
And marked he now has turned about
    And struggles for the shore.
For now his limbs a languor held,
And with sharp pain the nerves rebelled;
And for his boldness, growing fear
Came o'er him, as beneath him clear
He saw how far far under lay
The sands and shells and fish at play.
So not for help, – what help, alas,
In time that tedious space could pass!
Nor was there one of stronger limb,
Nor abler than himself to swim; –
But in desire of sympathy
    In danger and distress,
Came from his lips that terror-cry,
    That roused their carelessness.
Then heedless of the hopeless length,
Forgetting toils and failing strength,
Forgetting life, and breath and all,
Save their despairing comrade's call,
They flung themselves in earnest race,
To reach, before he sink, the place.
So easily does boyhood bear,
    In hearts that seem so light,
Such courage as Death's self will dare,
    Nor count the cost of fight.

O noble Sun! if heart benign
As thy world-cheering smile be thine,
How dark and sad with grief must seem
The world to thine unclouded beam!
So ceaselessly the rolling earth,
With every day thou giv'st to birth,
In every clime, before thine eye
Bids pageantry of pain pass by.
How must thou mourn for woes displayed
Thine eye must see, but cannot aid!
What heart can wonder, if thou call
The soft rain-clouds, with tearful pall,
To veil from thee the sights of pain,
More sad, because to see is vain?
What human heart could bear the throne,

Whence must his eye behold alone
All misery from zone to zone?
Did not thy head untimely hide
That day in earlier eventide,
When helplessly thine eye beheld,
        From thy lone height above,
Those struggling lives; how long hope swelled
In their young breasts, while they rebelled
Against the doom the dark waves knelled
        To happy life and love!
For scarce the strongest swimmer came
        There to his fellow's aid,
When Death put forth his stronger claim,
        That needs must be obeyed;
And downward the light body sank
To sleep upon the sanded bank.
There, for their weary limbs they gain
To find their labour waste and vain,
And see in deathly rest beneath
The form that seemed too fair for death.
The water, of such burial proud,
Had lent the soft limbs silver shroud,
And like a death-flame in calm air,
Streamed, shadowing his shut eyes, his hair.
Like birds that, spite of weary wing,
        Long hover round and round,
With useless cries, far echoing,
        High o'er the hateful ground,
When taloned hawk, or hunter's shaft
The life-blood of their mate has quaffed;
So long and vainly hung the swarm
On tired limbs o'er their fellow's form,
Nor for spent strength could any dare
To dive where each so fain would fare;
Nor yet for love would leave the place, –
Gain land and life, but lose his face.
So one by one his strength and breath
Left powerless to the might of Death;
Till, like a flowered bier, below,
The sand lay strewn with forms of snow,
As each bestowed for burial dower
        Upon their best beloved, first dead,
His own bright body, fairer flower

Than blooms in grassy graveyards shed.
What god, save Love, could launch such doom,
Could crave such cruel hecatomb?

Ah, who can tell, when even came,
Red for such guilty horror's shame,
How, one by one, by brake and fen,
    Through traces of the reeds uptorn,
With eager eyes burst down the men,
      And women, seeking eldest-born,
      And fairest-born, and dearest-born,
      In vain, until the vacant morn!
Then, with the light, each saw their love
Laid cold, the cruel depths above,
Lapped calmly in the pulseless deep,
Like flowers the night-flood drowns in sleep.
Then, as his own love each beheld,
Cry upon cry the anguish swelled,
Till bore the winds so wild a wail,
As blanched the blushing morn to pale,
And there were tender feet, that tore
    Through the resisting water-way,
To the sad spoil the river bore,
    Now careless of its costly prey.
And there were lips, whose blood was fled
In hopeless kisses of the dead.
Some beat in passionate woe their breast,
    Or rent their locks of gold,
Or fain beside their dead would rest,
    As pale as them, and cold.
In vain, in vain! What profiteth
Love's treasure in the wastes of death?
What profiteth in death the sight
Of that, where life has chief delight?
The face, where no emotion plays,
The eyes, that give not back our gaze,
The hands, that cannot clasp again, –
Love's old delights, – how all in vain!
And oh! last comfort! that reveals, –
    As one faint spark but deepens gloom, –
How darkly Death all comfort steals,
    Love's hands must deck for Death the tomb!
So by the river bank was raised

A monument, whereon was blazed
In golden letters all the tale;
And lest in time such record fail,
By cunning hands was carved the base,
Four-sided, with four scenes, – the race,
The lonely swimmer, far from aid,
The bodies on the water laid,
And last, the weepers on the shore,
And white limbs stilled for evermore.
But a more fitting monument
To those young lives the river lent.
For suddenly above the spot,
    Far in mid-waves, where fell their fate,
A cluster of bright lilies shot,
    And burst in blossoms delicate.
And all who saw in wonder stood;
    And soon the legend sprung,
That human was the lily-brood,
    Born of the souls that clung
In love of boyish life to earth,
Till God had given them back to birth,
New-clothed in shapes as pure as they
Had purely lived their passing day.
So sweet a grace did fancy twine
    About the tearful tale,
As grows around the ruined shrine
    The graceful ivy veil.
And when the fancy fits so well,
Who on its emptiness would dwell?
So, Lilies fair, forgive my verse,
    Nor let the fancy seem
O'erclouded with too dark a curse,
    To suit so light a theme!
For spite of that your tranquil grace,
And simple innocence of face;
Ay, though your petals love to lie
All peace, beneath the loving sky,
And in the soft waves' stillest spot
To find a world that Death knows not;
Still seems your peacefulness to be
Not from death's tears but terrors free;
Nor you from death have passed to peace.
Hence, in your sight, our hearts, that yet

Go on to death, their fears forget;
And in your beauties deem they see,
But half unveiled, a Heaven to be.

21 'The Bugler's First Communion'

Gerard Manley Hopkins. Written 27 July (?) 1879, first published 1918.

A bugler boy from barrack (it is over the hill
There) – boy bugler, born he tells me, of Irish
    Mother to an English sire (he
Shares their best gifts surely, fall how things will),

This very very day came down to us after a boon he on
My late being there begged of me, overflowing
    Boon in my bestowing,
Came, I say, this day to it – to a First Communion.

Here he knelt then in regimental red.
Forth Christ from cupboard fetched, how fain I of feet
    To his youngster take his treat!
Low-latched in leaf-light housel his too huge godhead.

There! and your sweetest sendings, ah divine,
By it, heavens, befall him! as a heart Christ's darling, dauntless;
    Tongue true, vaunt- and tauntless;
Breathing bloom of a chastity in mansex fine.

Frowning and forefending angel-warder
Squander the hell-rook ranks sally to molest him;
    March, kind comrade, abreast him;
Dress his days to a dexterous and starlight order.

How it does my heart good, visiting at that bleak hill,
When limber liquid youth, that to all I teach
    Yields tender as a pushed peach,
Hies headstrong to its wellbeing of a self-wise self-will!

Then though I should tread tufts of consolation
Days after, so I in a sort deserve to
    And do serve God to serve to
Just such slips of soldiery Christ's royal ration.

Nothing else is like it, no, not all so strains
Us: fresh youth fretted in a bloomfall all portending
      That sweet's sweeter ending;
Realm both Christ is heir to and there reigns.

O now well work that sealing sacred ointment!
O for now charms, arms, what bans off bad
      And locks love ever in a lad!
Let me though see no more of him, and not disappointment

Those sweet hopes quell whose least me quickenings lift,
In scarlet or somewhere of some day seeing
      That brow and bead of being,
An our day's God's own Galahad. Though this child's drift

Seems by a divine doom channelled, nor do I cry
Disaster there; but may he not rankle and roam
      In backwheels though bound home? –
That left to the Lord of the Eucharist, I here lie by;

Recorded only, I have put my lips on pleas
Would brandle adamantine heaven with ride and jar, did
      Prayer go disregarded:
Forward-like, but however, and like favourable heaven heard
  these.

22 'A Love Song'

'Sigma'. From *Kottabos*, Vol. III, Dublin, 1881. Signed with a capital sigma.

When noontide's azure turns to gold,
    And evening's gold to grey;
When heaven-wrought tapestries enfold
    The throne of parted day;
When through the twilight's falling veil
    Peeps out Love's rising star –
Oh! fairer than its light I hail
    The light of your cigar.

When woodbines to the night disclose
    Their trumpet's weight of dew;

When lilies droop, and violets close,
    And daphnes breathe – of you;
Mid all a summer night e'er gave
    Of fragrance wandering far;
Still, still my aching breast would crave
    One whiff of your cigar.

23   'If Any One Return'

Rennell Rodd (Lord Rennell). From *Songs in the South*, 1881.

I would we had carried him far away
    To the light of this south sun land,
Where the hills lean down to some red-rocked bay
And the sea's blue breaks into snow-white spray
    As the wave dies out on the sand.

Not there, not there, where the winds deface!
    Where the storm and the cloud race by!
But far away in this flowerful place
Where endless summers retouch, retrace
    What flowers find heart to die.

And if ever the souls of the loved, set free,
    Come back to the souls that stay,
I could dream he would sit for a while with me
Where I sit by this wonderful tideless sea
    And look to the red-rocked bay,

By the high cliff's edge where the wild weeds twine,
    And he would not speak or move,
But his eyes would gaze from his soul at mine,
My eyes that would answer without one sign,
    And that were enough for love.

And I think I should feel as the sun went round
    That he was not there any more,
But dews were wet on the grass-grown mound
On the bed of my love lying underground,
    And evening pale on the shore.

24   'Requiescat'

Rennell Rodd (Lord Rennell). From *Songs in the South*, 1881.

> He had the poet's eyes,
>   – Sing to him sleeping, –
> Sweet grace of low replies,
>   – Why are we weeping?
>
> He had the gentle ways,
>   – Fair dreams befall him! –
> Beauty through all his days,
>   – Then why recall him? –
>
> That which in him was fair
>   Still shall be ours:
> Yet, yet my heart lies there
>   Under the flowers.

25   'Stella Maris XLV'

John Addington Symonds. From *The Sea Calls*, 1884. Written September 1881–April 1882.

> Take it, oh take it, take thy gold! The shame
>   Shall rest with me, the bitter barren bliss
>   Of dreaming on a joy so brief as this.
>   Thou hast no suffering, and, I think, no blame.
> Abide for me the everlasting flame,
>   The worm that dies not, and the snakes that hiss
>   Round souls that seek impossibilities,
>   Lost in their lake of longing without aim.
> Is there no spell then to assuage this smart?
>   None; for we truly know not what we crave.
>   Knowing, we might appease the clamorous heart:
> But lust contents it not; and storms that rave
>   O'er the soul's seas, are stilled by no fine art.
>   Ah God, will peace be found even in the grave?

26 'The Flute of Daphnis'

Edward Cracroft Lefroy. From *Echoes from Theocritus and Other Sonnets*, 1885.
Written 1883.

Epigram ii

I am the flute of Daphnis. On this wall
He nailed his tribute to the great god Pan,
What time he grew from boyhood, shapely, tall,
And felt the first deep ardours of a man.
Through adult veins more swift the song-tide ran, –
A vernal stream whose swollen torrents call
For instant ease in utterance. Then began
That course of triumph reverenced by all.
Him the gods loved, and more than other men
Blessed with the flower of beauty, and endowed
His soul of music with the strength of ten.
Now on a festal day I see the crowd
Look fondly at my resting-place, and when
I think those lips have pressed me, I am proud.

27 'A Palaestral Study'

Edward Cracroft Lefroy. From *Echoes from Theocritus and Other Sonnets*, 1885.
Written 1883, it is No. XXXI of 'Miscellaneous Sonnets'.

The curves of beauty are not softly wrought:
These quivering limbs by strong hid muscles held
In attitudes of wonder, and compelled
Through shapes more sinuous than a sculptor's thought,
Tell of dull matter splendidly distraught,
Whisper of mutinies divinely quelled, –
Weak indolence of flesh, that long rebelled,
The spirit's domination bravely taught.
And all man's loveliest works are cut with pain.
Beneath the perfect art we know the strain,
Intense, defined, how deep soe'er it lies.
From each high master-piece our souls refrain,
Not tired of gazing, but with stretchèd eyes
Made hot by radiant flames of sacrifice.

28   'Terminal Essay'

Sir Richard Burton. From *The Arabian Nights*, Sir Richard Burton's translation, 1885. This is Section D, 'Pederasty'.

The 'execrabilis familia pathicorum' first came before me by a chance of earlier life. In 1845, when Sir Charles Napier had conquered and annexed Sind, despite a fraction (mostly venal) which sought favour with the now defunct 'Court of Directors to the Honourable East India Company,' the veteran began to consider his conquest with a curious eye. It was reported to him that Karàchi, a townlet of some two thousand souls and distant not more than a mile from camp, supported no less than three lupanars or bordels, in which not women but boys and eunuchs, the former demanding nearly a double price,¹ lay for hire. Being then the only British officer who could speak Sindi, I was asked indirectly to make enquiries and to report upon the subject; and I undertook the task on express condition that my report should not be forwarded to the Bombay Government, from whom supporters of the Conqueror's policy could expect scant favour, mercy or justice. Accompanied by a Munshi, Mirza Mohammed Hosayn of Shiraz, and habited as a merchant, Mirza Abdullah the Bushiri² passed many an evening in the townlet visited all the porneia and obtained the fullest details which were duly despatched to Government House. But the 'Devil's Brother' presently quitted Sind leaving in his office my unfortunate official: this found its way with sundry other reports³ to Bombay and produced the expected result. A friend in the Secretariat informed me that my summary dismissal from the service had been formally proposed by one of Sir Charles Napier's successors, whose decease compels me parcere sepulto. But this excess of outraged modesty was not allowed.

Subsequent enquiries in many and distant countries enabled me to arrive at the following conclusions:

¹ This detail especially excited the veteran's curiosity. The reason proved to be that the scrotum of the unmutilated boy could be used as a kind of bridle for directing the movements of the animal. I find nothing of the kind mentioned in the Sotadical literature of Greece and Rome; although the same cause might be expected everywhere to have the same effect. But in Mirabeau (Kadhésch) a grand seigneur moderne, when his valet-de-chambre de confiance proposes to provide him with women instead of boys, exclaims, 'Des femmes! eh! c'est comme si tu me servais un gigot sans manche.' See also infra for 'Le poids du tisserand.' [The notes here and throughout this essay are Burton's.]

² See *Falconry in the Valley of the Indus*, London, John Van Voorst, 1852.

³ Submitted to Government on Dec. 31, '47 and March 2, '48, they were printed in *Selections from the Records of the Government of India*. Bombay, New Series, No. xvii, Part 2, 1855. These are (1) Notes on the Population of Sind, etc., and (2) Brief Notes on the Modes of Intoxication, etc., written in collaboration with my late friend Assistant-Surgeon John E. Stocks, whose early death was a sore loss to scientific botany.

1   There exists what I shall call a 'Sotadic Zone,' bounded westwards by the northern shores of the Mediterranean (N. Lat. 43°) and by the southern (N. Lat. 30°). Thus the depth would be 780 to 800 miles including meridional France, the Iberian Peninsula, Italy and Greece, with the coast-regions of Africa from Marocco to Egypt.

2   Running eastward the Sotadic Zone narrows, embracing Asia Minor, Mesopotamia and Chaldaea, Afghanistan, Sind, the Punjab and Kashmir.

3   In Indo-China the belt begins to broaden, enfolding China, Japan and Turkistan.

4   It then embraces the South Sea Islands and the New World where, at the time of its discovery, Sotadic love was, with some exceptions, an established racial institution.

5   Within the Sotadic Zone the Vice is popular and endemic, held at the worst to be a mere peccadillo, whilst the races to the North and South of the limits here defined practise it only sporadically amid the opprobium of their fellows who, as a rule, are physically incapable of performing the operation and look upon it with the liveliest disgust.

Before entering into topographical details concerning Pederasty, which I hold to be geographical and climatic, not racial, I must offer a few considerations of its cause and origin. We must not forget that the love of boys has its noble sentimental side. The Platonists and pupils of the Academy, followed by the Sufis or Moslem Gnostics held such affection, pure as ardent, to be the beau idéal which united in man's soul the creature with the Creator. Professing to regard youths as the most cleanly and beautiful objects in this phenomenal world, they declared that by loving and extolling the chef-d'œuvre, corporeal and intellectual, of the Demiurgus, disinterestedly and without any ad-mixture of carnal sensuality, they are paying the most fervent adoration to the Causa causans. They add that such affection, passing as it does the love of women, is far less selfish than fondness for and admiration of the other sex which, however innocent, always suggest sexuality;[4] and Easterns add that the devotion of the moth to the taper is purer and more fervent than the Bulbul's love for the Rose. Amongst the Greeks of the best ages the system of boy-favourites was advocated on considerations of morals and politics. The lover undertook the education of the beloved through precept and example, while the two were con-joined by a tie stricter than the fraternal. Hieronymus the Peripatetic

---

[4] Glycon the Courtesan in *Athen.* xiii. 84 declares that 'boys are hand-some only when they resemble women;' and so the Learned Lady in *The Nights* (vol. v, 160) declares 'Boys are likened to girls because folks say, Yonder boy is like a girl.' For the superior physical beauty of the human male compared with the female, see *The Nights*, vol. iv. 15; and the boy's voice before it breaks excels that of any diva.

strongly advocated it because the vigorous disposition of youths and the confidence engendered by their association often led to the overthrow of tyrannies. Socrates declared that 'a most valiant army might be composed of boys and their lovers; for that of all men they would be most ashamed to desert one another.' And even Virgil, despite the foul flavour of Formosum pastor Corydon, could write:

Nisus amore pio pueri.

The only physical cause for the practice which suggests itself to me and that must be owned to be purely conjectural, is that within the Sotadic Zone there is a blending of the masculine and feminine temperaments, a crasis which elsewhere occurs only sporadically. Hence the male *féminisme* whereby the man becomes patiens as well as agens, and the woman a tribade, a votary of mascula Sappho,[5] Queen of Frictrices or Rubbers.[6] Prof. Mantegazza claims to have discovered the cause of this pathological love, this perversion of the erotic sense, one of the marvellous list of amorous vagaries which deserve, not prosecution but the pitiful care of the physician and the study of the psychologist. According to him the nerves of the rectum and the genitalia, in all cases closely connected, are abnormally so in the pathic who obtains, by intromission, the venereal orgasm which is usually sought through the sexual organs.

[5] 'Mascula,' from the priapiscus, the over-development of clitoris (the veretrum muliebre, in Arabic Abu Tartur, habens cristam) which enabled her to play the man. Sappho (nat. 612 B.C.) has been retoillée like Mary Stuart, La Brinvilliers, Marie Antoinette and a host of feminine names which have a savour not of sanctity. Maximus of Tyre (Dissert. xxiv.) declares that the Eros of Sappho was Socratic and that Gyrinna and Atthis were as Alcibiades and Chermides to Socrates: Ovid, who could consult documents now lost, takes the same view in the Letter of Sappho to Phaon and in Tristia ii. 265.
      Lesbia quid docuit Sappho nisi amare puellas?
Suidas supports Ovid. Longinus eulogises the ἐρωτικὴ μανία (a term applied only to carnal love) of the far-famed Ode to Atthis:
      Ille mî par esse Deo videtur . . .
      Heureux! qui près de toi pour toi seule soupire . . .
      (Blest as th' immortal gods is he, etc.)
By its love symptoms, suggesting that possession is the sole cure for passion, Erasistratus discovered the love of Antiochus for Stratonice. Mure (*Hist. of Greek Literature*, 1850) speaks of the Ode to Aphrodite (Frag. 1) as 'one in which the whole volume of Greek literature offers the most powerful concentration into one brilliant focus of the modes in which amatory concupiscence can display itself.' But Bernhardy, Bode, Richter, K. O. Müller and esp. Welcker have made Sappho a model of purity, much like some of our dull wits who have converted Shakespeare, that most debauched genius, into a good British bourgeois.
      [6] The Arabic Sahhákah, the Tractatrix of Subigitatrix, who has been noticed in vol. iv. 134. Hence to Lesbianise (λεσβίζειν) and tribassare (τρίβεσθαι); the former applied to the love of woman for woman and the latter to its mécanique: this is either natural, as friction of the labia and insertion of the clitoris when unusually developed; or artificial by means of the fascinum, the artificial penis (the Persian 'Mayájang'); the patte de chat, the banana-fruit and a multitude of other succedanea. As this feminine perversion is only glanced at in *The Nights* I need hardly enlarge upon the subject.

So amongst women there are tribads who can procure no pleasure except by foreign objects introduced a posteriori. Hence his threefold distribution of sodomy; (1) Periphic or anatomical, caused by an unusual distribution of the nerves and their hyperaesthesia; (2) Luxurious, when love a tergo is preferred on account of the narrowness of the passage; and (3) the Psychical. But this is evidently superficial: the question is what causes this neuropathy, this abnormal distribution and condition of the nerves.[7]

As Prince Bismarck finds a moral difference between the male and female races of history, so I suspect a mixed physical temperament effected by the manifold subtle influences massed together in the word climate. Something of the kind is necessary to explain the fact of this pathological love extending over the greater portion of the habitable world, without any apparent connection of race or media, from the polished Greek to the cannibal Tupi of the Brazil. Walt Whitman speaks of the ashen grey faces of onanists: the faded colours, the puffy features and the unwholesome complexion of the professed pederast with his peculiar cachectic expression, indescribable but once seen never forgotten, stamp the breed, and Dr. G. Adolph is justified in declaring 'Alle Gewohnneits-paederasten erkennen sich einander schnell, oft mit einen Blick.' This has nothing in common with the féminisme which betrays itself in the pathic by womanly gait, regard and gesture: it is a something sui generis; and the same may be said of the colour and look of the young priest who honestly refrains from women and their substitutes. Dr. Tardieu, in his well-known work, 'Etude Medico-légale sur les Attentats aux Mœurs,' and Dr. Adolph note a peculiar infundibuliform disposition of the 'After' and a smoothness and want of folds even before any abuse has taken place, together with special forms of the male organs in confirmed pederasts. But these observations have been rejected by Caspar, Hoffman, Brouardel and Dr. J. H. Henry Coutagne

[7] Plato (*Symp.*) is probably mystical when he accounts for such passions by there being in the beginning three species of humanity, men, women and men-women or androgynes. When the latter were destroyed by Zeus for rebellion, the two others were individually divided into equal parts. Hence each division seeks its other half in the same sex; the primitive man prefers men and the primitive woman women. C'est beau, but – is it true? The idea was probably derived from Egypt which supplied the Hebrews with androgynic humanity; and thence it passed to extreme India, where Shiva as Ardhanárí was male on one side and female on the other side of the body, combining paternal and maternal qualities and functions. The first creation of humans (Gen. i. 27) was hermaphrodite (= Hermes and Venus) masculum et foeminam creavit eos – male and female created He them – on the sixth day, with the command to increase and multiply (ibid. v. 28) while Eve the woman was created subsequently. Meanwhile, say certain Talmudists, Adam carnally copulated with all races of animals. See L'Anandryne in Mirabeau's *Erotika Biblion*, where Antoinette Bourgnon laments the undoubling which disfigured the work of God, producing monsters incapable of independent self-reproduction like the vegetable kingdom.

(Notes sur la Sodomie, Lyon 1880), and it is a medical question whose discussion would here be out of place.

The origin of pederasty is lost in the night of ages; but its historique has been carefully traced by many writers, especially Virey,[8] Rosenbaum[9] and M. H. E. Meier.[10] The ancient Greeks who, like the modern Germans, invented nothing but were great improvers of what other races invented, attributed the formal apostolate of Sotadism to Orpheus, whose stigmata were worn by the Thracian women;

> – Omnemque refugerat Orpheus
> Foemineam venerem; –
> Ille etiam Thracum populis fuit auctor, amorem
> In teneres transferre mares: citraque juventam
> Aetatis breve ver, et primos carpere flores.
>
> Ovid Met. x. 79–85.

Euripides proposed Laïus father of Oedipus as the inaugurator, whereas Timaeus declared that the fashion of making favourites of boys was introduced into Greece from Crete, for Malthusian reasons said Aristotle (Pol. ii, 10) attributing it to Minos. Herodotus, however, knew far better, having discovered (ii. c. 80) that the Orphic and Bacchic rites were originally Egyptian. But the Father of History was a traveller and an annalist rather than an archaeologist and he tripped in the following passage (i. c. 135), 'As soon as they (the Persians) hear of any luxury, they instantly make it their own, and hence, among other matters, they have learned from the Hellenes a passion for boys' ('unnatural lust' says modest Rawlinson). Plutarch (De Malig. Herod. xiii.)[11] asserts with much more probability that the Persians used eunuch boys according to the *Mos Graeciae*, long before they had seen the Grecian main.

In the Holy Books of the Hellenes, Homer and Hesiod, dealing with the heroic ages, there is no trace of pederasty, although, in a long subsequent generation, Lucian suspected Achilles and Patroclus as he did Orestes and Pylades, Theseus and Pirithous. Homer's praises of beauty are reserved for the feminines, especially his favourite Helen. But the Dorians of Crete seem to have commended the abuse to Athens and Sparta and subsequently imported it into Tarentum, Agrigentum and

[8] *De la Femme*, Paris, 1827.
[9] *Die Lustseuche des Alterthum's*, Halle, 1839.
[10] See his exhaustive article on (Grecian) 'Paederastie' in the *Allgemeine Encyclopaedie* of Ersch and Gruber, Leipzig, Brockhaus, 1837. He carefully traces it through the several states, Dorians, Aeolians, Ionians, the Attic cities and those of Asia Minor. For these details I must refer my readers to M. Meier; a full account of these would fill a volume not the section of an essay.
[11] Against which see Henri Estienne, *Apologie pour Hérodote*, a society satire of xvith century, lately reprinted by Liseux.

other colonies. Ephorus in Strabo (x. 4 § 21) gives a curious account of the violent abduction of beloved boys (παραστοθέντες) by the lover (ἐραστής); of the obligations of the ravisher (φιλήτωρ) to the favourite (κλεινός)[12] and of the 'marriage-ceremonies' which lasted two months. See also Plato *Laws* i. c. 8. Servius (Ad Aeneid. x. 325) informs us 'De Cretensibus accepimus, quod in amore puerorum intemperantes fuerunt, quod postea in Laconas et in totam Graeciam translatum est.' The Cretans and afterwards their apt pupils the Chalcidians held it disreputable for a beautiful boy to lack a lover. Hence Zeus the national Doric god of Crete loved Ganymede;[13] Apollo, another Dorian deity, loved Hyacinth, and Hercules, a Doric hero who grew to be a sun-god, loved Hylas and a host of others: thus Crete sanctified the practice by the examples of the gods and demigods. But when legislation came, the subject had qualified itself for legal limitation and as such was undertaken by Lycurgus and Solon, according to Xenophon (*Lac.* ii. 13), who draws a broad distinction between the honest love of boys and dishonest (αἴχιοτος) lust. They both approved of pure pederastía, like that of Harmodius and Aristogiton; but forbade it with serviles because degrading to a free man. Hence the love of boys was spoken of like that of women (Plato: *Phaedrus*; *Repub.* vi. c. 19 and Xenophon, *Synop.* iv. 10) *e.g.*, 'There was once a boy, or rather a youth, of exceeding beauty and he had very many lovers' – this is the language of Hafiz and Sa'adi. Aeschylus, Sophocles and Euripides were allowed to introduce it upon the stage, for 'many men were as fond of having boys for their favourites as women for their mistresses; and this was a frequent fashion in many well-regulated cities of Greece.' Poets like Alcaeus, Anacreon, Agathon and Pindar affected it and Theognis sang of a 'beautiful boy in the flower of his youth.' The statesmen Aristides and Themistocles quarrelled over Stesileus of Teos; and Pisistratus loved Charmus who first built an altar to Puerile Eros, while Charmus loved Hippias son of Pisistratus. Demosthenes the Orator took into keeping a youth called Cnosion greatly to the indignation of his wife. Xenophon loved Clinias

---

[12] In Sparta the lover was called εἰσπνήλας or εἰοπνηλος and the beloved as in Thessaly ἀῖτας or ἀῖτης.

[13] The more I study religions the more I am convinced that man never worshipped anything but himself. Zeus, who became Jupiter, was an ancient king, according to the Cretans, who were entitled liars because they showed his burial-place. From a deified ancestor he would become a local god, like the Hebrew Jehovah as opposed to Chemosh of Moab; the name would gain amplitude by long time and distant travel and the old island chieftain would end in becoming the Demiurgus. Ganymede (who possibly gave rise to the old Lat. 'Catamitus') was probably some fair Phrygian boy ('son of Tros') who in process of time became a symbol of the wise man seized by the eagle (perspicacity) to be raised amongst the Immortals; and the chaste myth simply signified that only the prudent are loved by the gods. But it rotted with age as do all things human. For the Pederastia of the Gods see Bayle under Chrysippe.

and Autolycus; Aristotle, Hermeas, Theodectes[14] and others; Empedocles, Pausanias; Epicurus, Pytocles; Aristippus, Eutichydes and Zeno with his Stoics had a philosophic disregard for women, affecting only pederastía. A man in Athenaeus (iv. c. 40) left in his will that certain youths he had loved should fight like gladiators at his funeral; and Charicles in Lucian abuses Callicratidas for his love of 'sterile pleasures.' Lastly there was the notable affair of Alcibiades and Socrates, the 'sanctus paederasta'[15] being violemment soupçonné when under the mantle: – non semper sine plagâ ab eo surrexit. Athanaeus (v. c. 13) declares that Plato represents Socrates as absolutely intoxicated with his passion for Alcibiades.[16] The ancients seem to have held the connection impure, or Juvenal would not have written –

Inter Socraticos notissima fossa cinaedos,

followed by Firmicus (vii. 14) who speaks of 'Socratici paedicones.' It is the modern fashion to doubt the pederasty of the master of Hellenic Sophrosyne, the 'Christian before Christianity;' but such a world-wide term as Socratic love can hardly be explained by the lucus-a-non-lucendo theory. We are overapt to apply our nineteenth century prejudices and prepossessions to the morality of the ancient Greeks who would have specimen'd such squeamishness in Attic salt.

[14] See *Dissertation sur les idées morales des Grecs et sur les danger de lire Platon*. Par M. Audé, Bibliophile, Rouen, Lemonnyer, 1879. This is the pseudonym of the late Octave Delepierre, who published with Gay, but not the Editio Princeps – which, if I remember rightly, contains much more matter.

[15] The phrase of J. Matthias Gesner, *Comm. Reg. Soc. Gottingen* i. 1–32. It was founded upon Erasmus' 'Sancte Socrate, ora pro nobis,' and the article was translated by M. Alcide Bonmaire, Paris, Liseux, 1877.

[16] The subject has employed many a pen, *e.g. Alcibiade Fanciullo a Scola*, D. P. A. (supposed to be Pietro Aretino – ad captandum?), Oranges, par Juann VVart, 1652: small square 8vo. of pp. 102, including 3 preliminary pp. and at end an unpaged leaf with 4 sonnets, almost Venetian, by V. M. There is a re-impression of the same date, a small 12mo. of longer format, pp. 124 with pp. 2 for sonnets: in 1862 the Imprimerie Raçon printed 102 copies in 8vo. of pp. iv.–108, and in 1863 it was condemned by the police as a liber spurcissimus atque execrandus de criminis sodomici laude et arte. This work produced *Alcibiade Enfant à l'école*, traduit pour la première fois de l'Italien de Ferrante Pallavicini, Amsterdam, chez l'Ancien Pierre Marteau, mdccclxvi. Pallavicini (nat. 1618), who wrote against Rome, was beheaded, aet. 26(March 5, 1644) at Avignon in 1644 by the vengeance of the Barberini: he was a bel esprit déréglé, nourri d'études antiques and a Memb. of the Acad. Degl' Incogniti. His peculiarities are shown by his *Opere Scelte*, 2 vols. 12mo, Villafranca, mdclxiii.; these do not include *Alcibiade Fanciullo*, a dialogue between Philotimus and Alcibiades which seems to be a mere skit at the Jesuits and their Péché philosophique. Then came the *Dissertation sur l'Alcibiade fanciullo a scola*, traduit de l'Italien de Giambattista Baseggio et accompagnée de notes et d'une post-face par un bibliophile français (M. Gustave Brunet, Librarian of Bordeaux), Paris. J. Gay, 1861 – an octavo of pp. 78 (paged), 254 copies. The same Baseggio printed in 1850 his *Disquisizioni* (23 copies) and claims for F. Pallavicini the authorship of *Alcibiades* which the Manuel du Libraire wrongly attributes to M. Girol. Adda in 1859. I have heard of but not seen the *Amator fornaceus, amator ineptus* (Palladii, 1633) supposed by some to be the origin of *Alcibiade Fanciullo*; but most critics consider it a poor and insipid production.

1 Digby Mackworth Dolben. From
the memoir and poems edited by
Robert Bridges, Oxford, 1911

2 Edward Carpenter. From a photograph by Frederick Hollyer, c. 1890
(Victoria and Albert Museum, London)

3 'Love Talking to Boys', a pen and ink drawing by Simeon Solomon, 1865. (From a
photograph in the Victoria and Albert Museum, London)

4 Oscar Wilde. From *The Sunday Chronicle*, 23 April 1893 (Victoria and Albert Museum, London)

5 Oscar Wilde. From the *Yorkshire Weekly Post*, 22 April 1893 (Victoria and Albert Museum, London). Note: Wilde is shown testing the nostalgia awakened through an old-fashioned box of Noah's Ark toys by sucking the paint from Noah's head in a Regent Street shop

NOAH'S HEAD.

The Spartans, according to Agnon the Academic (confirmed by Plato, Plutarch and Cicero), treated boys and girls in the same way before marriage: hence Juvenal (xi. 173) uses 'Lacedaemonius' for a pathic and other writers apply it to a tribade. After the Peloponnesian War, which ended in 404 B.C., the use became merged in the abuse. Yet some purity must have survived, even amongst the Boeotians who produced the famous Narcissus,[17] described by Ovid (*Met.* iii. 339):

> Multi illum juvenes, multae cupiere puellae;
> Nulli illum juvenes, nullae tetigere puellae:[18]

for Epaminondas, whose name is mentioned with three beloveds, established the Holy Regiment composed of mutual lovers, testifying the majesty of Eros and preferring to a discreditable life a glorious death. Philip's reflections on the fatal field of Chaeroneia form their fittest epitaph. At last the Athenians, according to Aeschines, officially punished Sodomy with death; but the threat did not abolish bordels of boys, like those of Karáchi; the Porneia and Pornoboskeia, where slaves and pueri venales 'stood,' as the term was, near the Pnyx, the city walls and a certain tower, also about Lycabettus (Aesch. contra Tim.); and paid a fixed tax to the state. The pleasures of society in civilized Greece seem to have been sought chiefly in the heresies of love – Hetairesis[19] and Sotadism.

It is calculated that the French of the sixteenth century had four hundred names for the parts genital and three hundred for their use in coition. The Greek vocabulary is not less copious and some of its pederastic terms, of which Meier gives nearly a hundred, and its nomenclature of pathologic love are curious and picturesque enough to merit quotation.

To live the life of Abron (the Argive) *i.e.* that of a πάσχων, pathic or passive lover.

---

[17] The word is from νάρκη, numbness, torpor, narcotism: the flowers, being loved by the infernal gods, were offered to the Furies. Narcissus and Hippolytus are often assumed as types of morosa voluptas, masturbation and clitorisation for nymphomania: certain mediaeval writers found in the former a type of the Saviour; and Mirabeau a representation of the androgynous or first Adam: to me Narcissus suggests the Hindu Vishnu absorbed in the contemplation of his own perfections.

[18] The verse of Ovid is parallel'd by the song of Al-Zahir al-Jazari (*Ibn Khall.* iii. 720).
Illum impuberem amaverunt mares; puberem feminae.
Gloria Deo! nunquam amatoribus carebit.

[19] The venerable society of prostitutes contained three chief classes. The first and lowest were the Dicteriads, so called from Diete (Crete) who imitated Pasiphaë, wife of Minos, in preferring a bull to a husband; above them was the middle class, the Aleutridae who were the Almahs or professional musicians, and the aristocracy was represented by the Hetairai, whose wit and learning enabled them to adorn more than one page of Grecian history. The grave Solon, who had studied in Egypt, established a vast Dicterion (Philemon in his Delphica), or bordel, whose proceeds swelled the revenue of the Republic.

SH–M

The Agathonian song.

Aischrourgía = dishonest love, also called Akolasía, Akrasía, Arrenokoitía, etc.

Alcinoan youths, or 'non-conformists,'

> In cute curandâ plus aequo operata Juventus.

Alegomenos, the 'unspeakable,' as the pederast was termed by the Council of Ancyra: also the Agrios, Apolaustus and Akolastos.

Androgyne, of whom Ansonius wrote (*Epig.* lxviii. 15):

> Ecce ego sum factus femina de puero.

Badas and badízein = clunes torquens: also Bátalos = a catamite.

Catapygos, Katapygosyne = puerarius and catadactylium from Dactylion, the ring, used in the sense of Nerissa's, but applied to the corollarium puerile.

Cinaedus (Kínaidos), the active lover (ποιών) derived either from his kinetics or quasi κύων αἴδως = dog-modest. Also Spatalocinaedus (lasciviâ fluens) = a fair Ganymede.

Chalcidissare (Khalkidizein), from Chalcis in Euboea, a city famed for love a posteriori; mostly applied to le léchement des testicules by children.

Clazomenae = the buttocks, also a sotadic disease, so called from the Ionian city devoted to Aversa Venus; also used of a pathic,

> —et tergo femina pube vir est.

Embasicoetas, prop. a link-boy at marriages, also a 'night-cap' drunk before bed and lastly an effeminate; one who perambulavit omnium cubilia (Catullus). See Encolpius' pun upon the Embasicete in Satyricon, cap. iv.

Epipedesis, the carnal assault.

Geiton lit. 'neighbour' the beloved of Encolpius, which has produced the Fr. Giton = Bardache, Ital. bardascia from the Arab. Baradaj, a captive, a slave; the augm. form is Polygeiton.

Hippias (tyranny of) when the patient (woman or boy) mounts the agent. Aristoph. Vesp. 502. So also Kelitizein = peccare superne or equum agitare supernum of Horace.

Mokhthería, depravity with boys.

Paidika, whence paedicare (act) and paedicari (pass): so in the Latin poet:

> PEnelopes primam DIdonis prima sequatur,
> Et primam CAni, syllaba prima REmi.

Pathikos, Pathicus, a passive, like Malakos (malacus, mollis, facilis), Malchio, Trimalchio (Petronius), Malta, Maltha and in Hor. (Sat. ii. 25)

Malthinus tunicis demissis ambulat.

Praxis = the malpractice.

Pygisma = buttockry, because most actives end within the nates, being too much excited for further intromission.

Phœnicissare (*φοινικίζειν*) = cunnilingere in tempore menstruum, quia hoc vitium in Phoenicia generata solebat (Thes. Erot. Ling. Latinae); also irrumer en miel.

Phicidissare, denotat actum per canes commissum quando lambunt cunnos vel testiculos (Suetonius): also applied to pollution of childhood.

Samorium flores (Erasmus, Prov. xxiii.) alluding to the androgynic prostitutions of Samos.

Siphniassare (*σιφνιάζειν*, from Siphnos, hod. Sifanto Island) = digito podicem fodere ad pruriginem restinguendam, says Erasmus (see Mirabeau's Erotika Biblion, Anoscopie).

Thrypsis = the rubbing.

Pederastía had in Greece, I have shown, its noble and ideal side: Rome, however, borrowed her malpractices, like her religion and polity, from those ultra-material Etruscans and debauched with a brazen face. Even under the Republic Plautus (*Casin.* ii. 21) makes one of his characters exclaim, in the utmost sang-froid, 'Ultro te, amator, apage te a dorso meo!' With increased luxury the evil grew and Livy notices (xxxix. 13), at the Bacchanalia, plura virorum inter sese quam foeminarum stupra. There were individual protests; for instance, S. Q. Fabius Maximus Servilianus (Consul U.C. 612) punished his son for dubia castitas; and a private soldier, C. Plotius, killed his military Tribune, Q. Luscius, for unchaste proposals. The Lex Scantinia (Scatinia?), popularly derived from Scantinius the Tribune and of doubtful date (226 B.C.?), attempted to abate the scandal by fine and the Lex Julia by death; but they were trifling obstacles to the flood of infamy which surged in with the Empire. No class seems then to have disdained these 'sterile pleasures:' l'on n'attachoit point alors à cette espèce d'amour une note d'infamie, comme en pais de chrétienté, says Bayle under 'Anacreon.' The great Caesar, the Cinaedus calvus of Catullus, was the husband of all the wives and the wife of all the husbands in Rome (Suetonius, cap. lii.); and his soldiers sang in his praise Gallias Caesar subegit, Nicomedes Caesarem (Suet. cies. xlix.); whence his sobriquet 'Fornix Bithynicus.' Of Augustus the people chaunted

Videsne ut Cinaedus orbem digito temperet?

Tiberius, with his pisciculi and greges exoletorum, invented the Symplegma or nexus of Sellarii, agentes et patientes, in which the spinthriae (lit. women's bracelets) were connected in a chain by the bond of flesh[20] (Seneca Quaest. Nat.): Of this refinement, which in the earlier part of the nineteenth century was renewed by sundry Englishmen at Naples, Ausonius wrote (*Epig.* cxix. 1),

> Tres uno in lecto: stuprum duo perpetiuntur;

And Martial had said (xii. 43)

> Quo symplegmate quinque cupulentur;
> Qua plures teneantur a catena; etc.

Ausonius recounts of Caligula he so lost patience that he forcibly entered the priest M. Lepidus, before the sacrifice was completed. The beautiful Nero was formally married to Pythagoras (or Doryphoros) and afterwards took to wife Sporus who was first subjected to castration of a peculiar fashion; he was then named Sabina after the deceased spouse and claimed queenly honours. The 'Othonis et Trajani pathici' were famed; the great Hadrian openly loved Antinoüs and the wild debaucheries of Heliogabalus seem only to have amused, instead of disgusting, the Romans.

Uranopolis allowed public lupanaria where adults and meritorii pueri, who began their career as early as seven years, stood for hire: the inmates of these cauponæ wore sleeved tunics and dalmatics like women. As in modern Egypt pathic boys, we learn from Catullus, haunted the public baths. Debauchees had signals like freemasons whereby they recognized one another. The Greek Skematízein was made by closing the hand to represent the scrotum and raising the middle finger as if to feel whether a hen had eggs, tâter si les poulettes ont l'œuf: hence the Athenians called it Catapygon or sodomite and the Romans digitus impudicus or infamis, the 'medical finger[21]' of Rabelais and the Chiromantists. Another sign was to scratch the head with the minimus – digitulo caput scabere (Juv. ix. 133).[22] The prostitution of boys was first forbidden by Domitian; but Saint Paul, a Greek, had formally expressed his abomination of Le Vice (Rom. i. 26; i. Cor. vi. 8); and we may agree with Grotius (de Verit. ii. c. 13) that early Christianity did much to suppress it. At last the Emperor Theodosius punished it with fire as a profanation, because sacro-sanctum esse debetur hospitium virilis animae.

[20] This and Saint Paul (Romans i. 27) suggested to Caravaggio his picture of St. Rosario (in the museum of the Grand Duke of Tuscany), showing a circle of thirty men turpiter ligati.

[21] Properly speaking 'Medicus' is the third or ring-finger, as shown by the old Chiromantist verses,
Est pollex Veneris; sed Jupiter indice gaudet,
Saturnus medium; Sol *medicum*que tenet.

[22] So Seneca uses digito scalpit caput. The modern Italian does the same by inserting the thumb-tip between the index and medius to suggest the clitoris.

In the pagan days of imperial Rome her literature makes no difference between boy and girl. Horace naïvely says (*Sat.* ii. 118):

> Ancilla aut verna est praesto puer;

and with Hamlet, but in a dishonest sense:

> – Man delights me not
> Nor woman neither.

Similarly the Spaniard Martial, who is a mine of such pederastic allusions (xi. 46):

> Sive puer arrisit, sive puella tibi.

That marvellous Satyricon which unites the wit of Molière[23] with the
debaucheries of Piron, whilst the writer has been described, like
Rabelais, as purissimus in impuritate, is a kind of Triumph of Pederasty.
Geiton the hero, a handsome curly-pated hobbledehoy of seventeen,
with his câlinerie and wheedling tongue, is courted like one of the sequor
sexus: his lovers are inordinately jealous of him and his desertion leaves
deep scars upon the heart. But no dialogue between man and wife in
extremis could be more pathetic than that in the scene where shipwreck
is imminent. Elsewhere everyone seems to attempt his neighbour: a
man alte succinctus assails Ascyltos; Lycus, the Tarentine skipper,
would force Encolpius and so forth: yet we have the neat and finished
touch (cap. vii.): – 'The lamentation was very fine (the dying man
having manumitted his slaves) albeit his wife wept not as though
she loved him. *How were it had he not behaved to her so well?*'

Erotic Latin glossaries[24] give some ninety words connected with
Pederasty and some, which 'speak with Roman simplicity,' are peculiarly

[23] What can be wittier than the now trite 'Tale of the Ephesian Matron',
whose dry humour is worthy of *The Nights*? No wonder that it has made the
grand tour of the world. It is found in the neo-Phaedrus, the tales of Musaeus
and in the Septem Sapientes as the 'Widow which was comforted'. As the
'Fabliau de la Femme qui se fist putain sur la fosse de son Mari,' it tempted
Brantôme and La Fontaine; and Abel Rémusat shows in his Contes Chinois
that it is well known to the Middle Kingdom. Mr. Walter K. Kelly remarks,
that the most singular place for such a tale is the *Rule and Exercise of Holy
Dying* by Jeremy Taylor, who introduces it into his chapt. v – 'Of the
Contingencies of Death and Treating our Dead.' But in those days divines
were not mealy-mouthed.

[24] Glossarium eroticum linguae Latinae, sive theogoniae, legum et
morum nuptialium apud Romanos explanatio nova, auctore P. P. (Parisiis,
Dondey-Dupré, 1826, in 8vo). P. P. is supposed to be Chevalier Pierre
Pierrugues, an engineer who made a plan of Bordeaux and who annotated the
Erotica Biblion. Gay writes, 'On s'est servi pour cet ouvrage des travaux
inédits de M. le Baron de Schonen, etc. Quant au Chevalier Pierre Pierrugues,
qu'on désignait comme l'auteur de ce savant volume, son existence n'est pas
bien avérée, et quelques bibliographes persistent à penser que ce nom cache la
collaboration du Baron de Schonen et d'Éloi Johanneau.' Other glossicists as
Blondeau and Forberg have been printed by Liseux, Paris.

expressive. 'Aversa Venus' alludes to women being treated as boys: hence Martial, translated by Piron, addresses Mistress Martial (x. 44):

Teque puta, cunnos, uxor, habere duos.

The capillatus or comatus is also called calamistratus, the darling curled with crisping-irons; and he is an Effeminatus *i.e.* qui muliebria patitur; or a Delicatus, slave or eunuch for the use of the Draucus, Puerarius (boy-lover) or Dominus (Mart. xi. 71). The Divisor is so called from his practice Hillas dividere or caedere, something like Martial's cacare mentulam or Juvenal's Hesternae occurrere caenae. Facere vicibus (Juv. vii. 238), incestare se invicem or mutuum facere (Plaut. Trin. ii. 437), is described as 'a puerile vice,' in which the two take turns to be active and passive: they are also called Gemelli and Fratres = compares in paedicatione. Illicita libido is = praepostera seu postica Venus, and is expressed by the picturesque phrase indicare (seu incurvare) aliquem. Depilatus, divellere pilos, glaber, laevis and nates pervellere are allusions to the Sotadic toilette. The fine distinction between demittere and dejicere caput are worthy of a glossary, while Pathica puella, puera, putus, pullipremo, pusio, pygiaca sacra, quadrupes, scarabaeus and smerdalius explain themselves.

From Rome the practice extended far and wide to her colonies especially the Provincia now called Provence. Athenaeus (xii. 26) charges the people of Massilia with 'acting like women out of luxury'; and he cites the saying 'May you sail to Massilia!' as if it were another Corinth. Indeed the whole Keltic race is charged with Le Vice by Aristotle (*Pol.* ii. 66), Strabo. (iv. 199) and Diodorus Siculus (v. 32). Roman civilization carried pederasty also to Northern Africa, where it took firm root, while the negro and negroid races to the South ignore the erotic perversion, except where imported by foreigners into such kingdoms as Bornu and Haussa. In old Mauritania, now Morocco,[25] the Moors proper are notable sodomites; Moslems, even of saintly houses, are permitted openly to keep catamites, nor do their disciples think worse of their sanctity for such license: in one case the English wife failed to banish from the home 'that horrid boy'.

[25] This magnificent country which the petty jealousies of Europe condemn, like the glorious regions about Constantinople, to mere barbarism, is tenanted by three Moslem races. The Berbers, who call themselves Tamazight (plur. of Amazigh), are the Gaetulian indigenes speaking an Africo-Semitic tongue (see Essai de Grammaire Kabyle, etc. par A. Hanoteau, Paris, Benjamin Duprat). The Arabs, descended from the conquerors in our eighth century, are mostly nomads and camel-breeders. Third and last are the Moors proper, the race dwelling in towns, a mixed breed originally Arabian but modified by six centuries of Spanish residence and showing by thickness of feature and a parchment-coloured skin, resembling the American Octaroon's, a negro innervation of old date. The latter are well described in *Morocco and the Moors*, etc. (Sampson Low and Co., 1876), by my late friend Dr. Arthur Leared, whose work I should like to see reprinted.

Yet pederasty is forbidden by the Koran. In chapter iv. 20 we read; 'And if two (men) among you commit the crime, then punish them both,' the penalty being some hurt or damage by public reproach, insult or scourging. There are four distinct references to Lot and the Sodomites in chapters vii. 78; xi 77–84; xxvi. 160–174 and xxix. 28–35. In the first the prophet commissioned to the people says, 'Proceed ye to a fulsome act wherein no creature hath foregone ye? Verily ye come to men in lieu of women lustfully.' We have then an account of the rain which made an end of the wicked and this judgement on the Cities of the Plain is repeated with more detail in the second reference. Here the angels, generally supposed to be three, Gabriel, Michael and Raphael, appeared to Lot as beautiful youths, a sore temptation to the sinners and the godly man's arm was straitened concerning his visitors because he felt unable to protect them from the erotic vagaries of his fellow townsmen. He therefore shut his doors and from behind them argued the matter: presently the riotous assembly attempted to climb the wall when Gabriel, seeing the distress of his host, smote them on the face with one of his wings and blinded them so that all moved off crying for aid and saying that Lot had magicians in his house. Hereupon the 'cities' which, if they ever existed, must have been Fellah villages, were uplifted: Gabriel thrust his wing under them and raised them so high that the inhabitants of the lower heaven (the lunar sphere) could hear the dogs barking and the cocks crowing. Then came the rain of stones: these were clay pellets baked in hell-fire, streaked white and red, or having some mark to distinguish them from the ordinary and each bearing the name of its destination like the missiles which destroyed the host of Abrahat al-Ashram.[26] Lastly the 'Cities' were turned upside down and cast upon earth. These circumstantial unfacts are repeated at full length in the other two chapters; but rather as an instance of Allah's power than as a warning against pederasty, which Mohammed seems to have regarded with philosophic indifference. The general opinion of his followers is that it should be punished like fornication unless the offenders made a public act of penitence. But here, as in adultery, the law is somewhat too clement and will not convict unless four credible witnesses swear to have seen rem in re. I have noticed (vol. i. 211) the vicious opinion that the Ghilmán or Wuldán, the beautiful boys of Paradise, the counterparts of the Houris, will be lawful catamites to the True Believers in a future state of happiness: the idea is nowhere countenanced in Al-Islam; and, although I have often heard debauchees refer to it, the learned look upon the assertion as scandalous.

[26] Thus somewhat agreeing with one of the multitudinous modern theories that the Pentapolis was destroyed by discharges of meteoric stones during a tremendous thunderstorm. Possible, but where are the stones?

As in Morocco so the Vice prevails throughout the old regencies of Algiers, Tunis and Tripoli and all the cities of the South Mediterranean seaboard, whilst it is unknown to the Nubians, the Berbers and the wilder tribes dwelling inland. Proceeding Eastward we reach Egypt, that classical region of all abominations which, marvellous to relate, flourished in closest contact with men leading the purest of lives, models of moderation and morality, of religion and virtue. Amongst the ancient Copts Le Vice was part and portion of the Ritual and was represented by two male partridges alternately copulating (Interp. in Priapi Carm. xvii). The evil would have gained strength by the invasion of Cambyses (524 B.C.), whose armies, after the victory over Psammenitus, settled in the Nile-Valley, and held it, despite sundry revolts, for some hundred and ninety years. During these six generations the Iranians left their mark upon Lower Egypt and especially, as the late Rogers Bey proved, upon the Fayyum the most ancient Delta of the Nile.[27] Nor would the evil be diminished by the Hellenes who, under Alexander the Great, 'liberator and saviour of Egypt' (332 B.C.), extinguished the native dynasties: the love of the Macedonian for Bagoas the Eunuch being a matter of history. From that time and under the rule of the Ptolemies the morality gradually decayed; the Canopic orgies extended into private life and the debauchery of the men was equalled only by the depravity of the women. Neither Christianity nor Al-Islam could effect a change for the better; and social morality seems to have been at its worst during the past century when Sonnini travelled (A.D. 1717). The French officer, who is thoroughly trustworthy, draws the darkest picture of the widely-spread criminality especially of the bestiality and the sodomy (chapt. xv.) which formed the 'delight of the Egyptians.' During the Napoleonic conquest Jaubert in his letter to General Bruix (p. 19) says, 'Les Arabes et les Mamelouks ont traité quelques-uns de nos prisonniers comme Socrate traitait, dit-on, Alcibiade. Il fallait périr ou y passer.' Old Anglo-Egyptians still chuckle over the tale of Sa'id Pasha and M. de Ruyssenaer, the high-dried and highly respectable Consul-General for the Netherlands, who was solemnly advised to make the experiment, active and passive, before offering his opinion upon the subject. In the present age extensive intercourse with Europeans has produced not a reformation but a certain reticence amongst the upper classes: they are as vicious as ever, but they do not care for displaying their vices to the eyes of mocking strangers.

[27] To this Iranian domination I attribute the use of many Persic words which are not yet obsolete in Eygpt. 'Bakhshish,' for instance, is not intelligible in the Moslem regions west of the Nile-Valley and for a present the Moors say Hadiyah, regalo or favor.

Syria and Palestine, another ancient focus of abominations, borrowed from Egypt and exaggerated the worship of Androgynic and hermaphroditic deities. Plutarch (De Iside) notes that the old Nilotes held the moon to be of 'male-female sex,' the men sacrificing to Luna and the women to Lunus.[28] Isis also was a hermaphrodite, the idea being that Aether or Air (the lower heavens) was the menstruum of generative nature; and Damascius explained the tenet by the all-fruitful and prolific powers of the atmosphere. Hence the fragment attributed to Orpheus, the song of Jupiter (Air) –

> All things from Jove descend
> Jove was a male, Jove was a deathless bride;
> For men call Air, of two-fold sex, the Jove.

Julius Firmicus relates that 'The Assyrians and part of the Africans' (along the Mediterranean seaboard?) 'hold Air to be the chief element and adore its fanciful figure (imaginata figura), consecrated under the name of Juno or the Virgin Venus. . . . Their companies of priests cannot duly serve her unless they effeminate their faces, smooth their skins and disgrace their masculine sex by feminine ornaments. You may see men in their very temples amid general groans enduring miserable dalliance and becoming passives like women (viros muliebria pati) and they expose, with boasting and ostentation, the pollution of the impure and immodest body.' Here we find the religious significance of eunuchry. It was practised as a religious rite by the Tympanotribas or Gallus,[29] the castrated votary of Rhea or Bona Mater, in Phrygia called Cybele, self-mutilated but *not* in memory of Atys; and by a host of other creeds: even Christianity, as sundry texts show,[30] could not altogether cast out

[28] Arnobius and Tertullian, with the arrogance of their caste and its miserable ignorance of that symbolism which often concealed from vulgar eyes the most precious mysteries, used to taunt the heathen for praying to deities whose sex they ignored: 'Consuistis in precibus "Seu tu Deus seu tu Dea," dicere!' These men would know everything; they made God the merest work of man's brains and armed him with a despotism of omnipotence which rendered their creation truly dreadful.

[29] Gallus lit.=a cock, in pornologic parlance is a capon, a castrato.

[30] The texts justifying or conjoining castration are Matt. xviii. 8–9; Mark ix. 43–47; Luke xxiii. 29 and Col. iii. 5. St. Paul preached (I Corin. vii. 29) that a man should live with his wife as if he had none. The Abelian heretics of Africa abstained from women because Abel died virginal. Origen mutilated himself after interpreting too rigorously Matth. xix. 12, and was duly excommunicated. But his disciple, the Arab Valerius founded (A.D. 250) the castrated sect called Valerians who, persecuted and dispersed by the Emperors Constantine and Justinian, became the spiritual fathers of the modern Skopzis. These eunuchs first appeared in Russia at the end of the xith century, when two Greeks, John and Jephrem, were metropolitans of Kiew: the former was brought thither in 1089 A.D. by Princess Anna Wassewolodowna and is called by the chronicles Nawjè or the Corpse. But in the early part of the last century (1715–33) a sect arose in the circle of Uglitseh and in Moscow, at first called Clisti or flagellants which developed into the modern Skopzi. For this extensive subject see De Stein (Zeitschrift für Ethn. Berlin, 1875) and Mantegazza, chapt. vi.

the old possession. Here too we have an explanation of Sotadic love in its second stage, when it became, like cannibalism, a matter of super-stition. Assuming a nature-implanted tendency, we see that like human sacrifice it was held to be the most acceptable offering to the God-goddess in the Orgia or sacred ceremonies, a something set apart for peculiar worship. Hence in Rome as in Egypt the temples of Isis (Inachidos limina, Isiacae sacraria Lunae) were centres of sodomy and the religious practice was adopted by the grand priestly castes from Mesopotamia to Mexico and Peru.

We find the earliest written notices of the Vice in the mythical destruction of the Pentapolis (Gen. xix.), Sodom, Gomorrah (= 'Ámirah, the cultivated country), Adama, Zeboïm and Zoar or Bela. The legend has been amply embroidered by the Rabbis who make the Sodomites do everything à l'envers: e.g. if a man were wounded he was fined for bloodshed and was compelled to fee the offender; and if one cut off the ear of a neighbour's ass he was condemned to keep the animal till the ear grew again. The Jewish doctors declare the people to have been a race of sharpers with rogues for magistrates, and thus they justify the judgement which they read literally. But the traveller cannot accept it. I have carefully examined the lands at the North and at the South of that most beautiful lake, the so-called Dead Sea, whose tranquil loveli-ness, backed by the grand plateau of Moab, is an object of admiration to all save patients suffering from the strange disease 'Holy Land on the Brain.'[31] But I found no traces of craters in the neighbourhood, no signs of vulcanism, no remains of 'meteoric stones': the asphalt which named the water is a mineralized vegetable washed out of the limestones, and the sulphur and salt are brought down by the Jordan into a lake without issue. I must therefore look upon the history as a myth which may have served a double purpose. The first would be to deter the Jew from the Malthusian practices of his pagan predecessors, upon whom obloquy was thus cast, so far resembling the scandalous and absurd legend which explained the names of the children of Lot by Pheiné and Thamma as 'Moab' (Mu-ab) the water or semen of the father, and 'Ammon' as mother's son, that is, bastard. The fable would also account for the abnormal fissure containing the lower Jordan and the Dead Sea, which the late Sir R. I. Murchison used wrong-headedly to call a 'Volcano of Depression': this geological feature, that cuts off the river-basin from its natural outlet the Gulf of Eloth (Akabah), must date from myriads of years before there were 'Cities of the Plains.' But the main object of the ancient lawgiver, Osarsiph, Moses or the Mosei-dae, was doubtless to discountenance a perversion prejudicial to the

---

[31] See the marvellously absurd description of the glorious 'Dead Sea' in the Purchas v. 84.

increase of population. And he speaks with no uncertain voice, Whoso lieth with a beast shall surely be put to death (Exod. xxii. 19): If a man lie with mankind as he lieth with a woman, both of them have committed an abomination: they shall surely be put to death; their blood shall be upon them (Levit. xx. 13; where vv. 15–16 threaten with death man and woman who lie with beasts). Again, There shall be no whore of the daughters of Israel nor a sodomite of the sons of Israel (Deut. xxii. 5).

The old commentators on the Sodom-myth are most unsatisfactory *e.g.* Parkhurst, *s.v.* Kadesh. 'From hence we may observe the peculiar propriety of this punishment of Sodom and of the neighbouring cities. By their sodomitical impurities they meant to acknowledge the Heavens as the cause of fruitfulness independently upon, and in opposition to Jehovah;[32] therefore Jehovah, by raining upon them not genial showers but brimstone from heaven, not only destroyed the inhabitants, but also changed all that country, which was before as the garden of God, into brimstone and salt that is not sown nor beareth, neither any grass groweth therein.' It must be owned that to this Pentapolis was dealt very hard measure for religiously and diligently practising a popular rite which a host of cities even in the present day, as Naples and Shiraz, to mention no others, affect for simple luxury and affect with impunity. The myth may probably reduce itself to very small proportions, a few Fellah villages destroyed by a storm, like that which drove Brennus from Delphi.

The Hebrews entering Syria found it religionized by Assyria and Babylonia, whence Accadian Ishtar had passed west and had become Ashtoreth, Ashtaroth or Ashirah,[33] the Anaitis of Armenia, the Phoenician Astarte and the Greek Aphrodite, the great Moon-goddess,[34] who is queen of Heaven and Love. In another phase she was Venus Mylitta = the Procreatrix, in Chaldaic Mauludatá and in Arabic Moawallidah, she who bringeth forth. She was worshipped by men habited as women and vice versâ; for which reason in the Torah (Deut. xx. 5) the sexes are forbidden to change dress. The male prostitutes were called Kadesh

[32] Jehovah here is made to play an evil part by destroying men instead of teaching them better. But, 'Nous faisons les Dieux à notre image et nous portons dans le ciel ce que nous voyons sur la terre.' The idea of Yahweh, or Yah is palpably Egyptian, the Ankh or ever-living One: the etymon, however, was learned at Babylon and is still found amongst the cuneiforms.

[33] The name still survives in the Shajarát al-Asharà, a clump of trees near the village Al-Ghájar (of the Gypsies?) at the foot of Hermon.

[34] I am not quite sure that Astarte is not primarily the planet Venus; but I can hardly doubt that Prof. Max Müller and Sir G. Cox are mistaken in bringing from India Aphrodite the Dawn and her attendants, the Charites identified with the Vedic Harits. Of Ishtar in Accadia, however, Roscher seems to have proved that she is distinctly the Moon sinking into Amenti (the west, the Underworld) in search of her lost spouse Izdubar, the Sun-god. This again is pure Egyptianism.

the holy, the women being Kadeshah, and doubtless gave themselves up to great excesses. Eusebius (De bit. Const. iii. c. 55) describes a school of impurity at Aphac, where women and 'men who were not men' practised all manner of abominations in honour of the Demon (Venus). Here the Phrygian symbolism of Kybele and Attis (Atys) had become the Syrian Ba'al Tammuz and Astarte, and the Grecian Dionaea and Adonis, the anthropomorphic forms of the two greater lights. The site, Apheca, now Wady al-Afik on the route from Bayrut to the Cedars, is a glen of wild and wondrous beauty, fitting frame-work for the loves of goddess and demigod: and the ruins of the temple destroyed by Constantine contrast with Nature's work, the glorious fountain, splendidior vitro, which feeds the River Ibrahim and still at times Adonis runs purple to the sea.[35]

The Phoenicians spread this androgynic worship over Greece. We find the consecrated servants and votaries of Corinthian Aphrodite called Hierodouli (Strabo viii. 6), who aided the ten thousand courtesans in gracing the Venus-temple: from this excessive luxury arose the proverb popularized by Horace. One of the headquarters of the cult was Cyprus where, as Servius relates (Ad Aen. ii. 632), stood the simulacre of a bearded Aphrodite with feminine body and costume, sceptered and mitred like a man. The sexes when worshipping it exchanged habits and here the virginity was offered in sacrifice: Herodotus (i. c. 199) describes this defloration at Babylon but sees only the shameful part of the custom which was a mere consecration of a tribal rite. Everywhere girls before marriage belong either to the father or to the clan and thus the maiden paid the debt due to the public before becoming private property as a wife. The same usage prevailed in ancient Armenia and in parts of Ethiopia; and Herodotus tells us that a practice very much like the Babylonian 'is found also in certain parts of the Island of Cyprus:' it is noticed by Justin (xviii. c. 5) and probably it explains the 'Succoth Benoth' or Damsels' booths which the Babylonians transplanted to the cities of Samaria.[36] The Jews seem very

[35] In this classical land of Venus the worship of Ishtar-Ashtaroth is by no means obsolete. The Metáwali heretics, a people of Persian descent and Shiite tenets, and the peasantry of 'Bilád B'sharrah,' which I would derive from Bayt Ashirah, still pilgrimage to the ruins and address their vows to the Sayyidat al-Kabírah, the Great Lady. Orthodox Moslems accuse them of abominable orgies and point to the lamps and rags which they suspend to a tree entitled Shajarat al-Sitt – the Lady's tree – an Acacia Albida which, according to some travellers, is found only here and at Sayda (Sidon) where an avenue exists. The people of Kasrawán, a Christian province in the Libanus, inhabited by a peculiarly prurient race, also hold high festival under the farfamed Cedars and their women sacrifice to Venus like the Kadashah of the Phoenicians. This survival of old superstition is unknown to missionary 'Handbooks,' but amply deserves the study of the anthropologist.

[36] Some commentators understand 'the tabernacles sacred to the reproductive powers of women;' and the Rabbis declare that the emblem was the figure of a setting hen.

successfully to have copied the abominations of their pagan neighbours, even in the matter of the 'dog.'[37] In the reign of wicked Rehoboam (975 B.C.) 'There were also sodomites in the land and they did according to all the abominations of the nations which the Lord cast out before the children of Israel' (1 Kings xiv. 20). The scandal was abated by zealous King Asa (958 B.C.) whose grandmother[38] was high-priestess of Priapus (princeps in sacris Priapi): he 'took away the sodomites out of the land' (1 Kings xv. 12). Yet the prophets were loud in their complaints, especially the so-called Isaiah (760 B.C.), 'except the Lord of Hosts had left to us a very small remnant, we should have been as Sodom' (i. 9); and strong measures were required from good King Josiah (641 B.C.) who amongst other things, 'brake down the houses of the sodomites that were by the house of the Lord, where the women wove hangings for the grove' (2 Kings xxiii. 7). The bordels of boys (pueris alienis adhaeseverunt) appear to have been near the Temple.

Syria has not forgotten her old 'praxis.' At Damascus I found some noteworthy cases amongst the religious of the great Amawi Mosque. As for the Druses we have Burckhardt's authority (Travels in Syria, etc., p. 202) 'unnatural propensities are very common amongst them.'

The Sotadic Zone covers the whole of Asia Minor and Mesopotamia now occupied by the 'unspeakable Turk,' a race of born pederasts; and in the former region we first notice a peculiarity of the feminine figure, the mammae inclinatae, jacentes et pannosae, which prevails over all this part of the belt. Whilst the women to the North and South have, with local exceptions, the mammae stantes of the European virgin,[39] those of Turkey, Persia, Afghanistan and Kashmir lose all the fine curves of the bosom, sometimes even before the first child; and after it the hemispheres take the form of bags. This cannot result from climate only; the women of Marathá-land, inhabiting a damper and hotter region than Kashmir, are noted for fine firm breasts even after parturition. Le Vice of course prevails more in the cities and towns of Asiatic Turkey than in the villages; yet even these are infected; while the nomad Turcomans contrast badly in this point with the Gypsies, those Badawin of India. The Kurd population is of Iranian origin, which means that the evil is deeply rooted: I have noted in The

[37] 'Dog' is applied by the older Jews to the Sodomite and the Catamite; and thus they understand the 'price of a dog' which could not be brought into the Temple (Deut. xxiii. 18). I have noticed it in one of the derivations of cinaedus and can only remark that it is a vile libel upon the canine tribe.

[38] Her name was Maachah and her title, according to some, 'King's mother': she founded the sect of Communists who rejected marriage and made adultery and incest part of worship in their splendid temple. Such were the Basilians and the Carpocratians, followed in the xith century by Tranchelin, whose sectarians, the Turlupins, long infested Savoy.

[39] A noted exception is Vienna, remarkable for the enormous development of the virginal bosom which soon becomes pendulent.

Nights that the great and glorious Saladin was a habitual pederast. The Armenians, as their national character is, will prostitute themselves for gain but prefer women to boys: Georgia supplied Turkey with cata-mites whilst Circassia sent concubines. In Mesopotamia the barbarous invader has almost obliterated the ancient civilization which is ante-dated only by the Nilotic: the mysteries of old Babylon nowhere survive save in certain obscure tribes like the Mandaeans, the Devil-worshippers and the Alí-iláhi. Entering Persia we find the reverse of Armenia; and, despite Herodotus, I believe that Iran borrowed her pathologic love from the peoples of the Tigris-Euphrates Valley and not from the then insignificant Greeks. But whatever may be its origin, the corruption is now bred in the bone. It begins in boyhood and many Persians account for it by paternal severity. Youths arrived at puberty find none of the facilities with which Europe supplies fornication. Onanism[40] is to a certain extent discouraged by circumcision, and meddling with the father's slave-girls and concubines would be risking cruel punishment if not death. Hence they use each other by turns, a 'puerile practice' known as Alish-Takish, the Lat. facere vicibus or mutuum facere. Temperament, media, and atavism recommend the custom to the general; and after marrying and begetting heirs, Paterfamilias returns to the Ganymede. Hence all the odes of Hafiz are addressed to youths, as proved by such Arabic exclamations as 'Afáka 'llah = Allah assain thee (masculine)[41]: the object is often fanciful but it would be held coarse and immodest to address an imaginary girl.[42] An illustration of the penchant is told at Shiraz concerning a certain Mujtahid, the head of the Shi'ah creed, corresponding with a prince-archbishop in Europe. A friend once said to him, 'There is a question I would fain address to your Eminence but I lack the daring to do so.' 'Ask and fear not,' replied the Divine. 'It is this, O Mujtahid! Figure thee in a garden of roses and hyacinths with the evening breeze waving the cypress-heads, a fair youth of twenty sitting by thy side and the assurance of perfect privacy. What, prithee, would be the result?' The holy man bowed the chin of doubt upon the collar of meditation; and, too honest to lie, presently whispered, 'Allah defend me from such temptation of Satan!' Yet even in Persia men have not been wanting who have done their utmost to uproot the Vice: in the same Shiraz they speak of a father who, finding his son in flagrant delict, put him to death like Brutus or

[40] Gen. xxxviii. 2–11. Amongst the classics Mercury taught the 'Art of le Thalaba' to his son Pan who wandered about the mountains distraught with love for the Nymph Echo and Pan passed it on to the pastors. See Thalaba in Mirabeau.

[41] The reader of The Nights has remarked how often the 'he' in Arabic poetry denotes a 'she'; but the Arab, when uncontaminated by travel, ignores pederasty, and the Arab poet is a Badawi.

[42] So Mohammed addressed his girl-wife Ayishah in the masculine.

Lynch of Galway. Such isolated cases, however, can effect nothing. Chardin tells us that houses of male prostitution were common in Persia whilst those of women were unknown: the same is the case in the present day and the boys are prepared with extreme care by diet, baths, depilation, unguents and a host of artists in cosmetics.[43] Le Vice is looked upon at most as a peccadillo and its mention crops up in every jest-book. When the Isfahan man mocked Shaykh Sa'adi, by comparing the bald pates of Shirazian elders to the bottom of a lotá, a brass cup with a wide-necked opening used in the Hammam, the witty poet turned its aperture upwards and thereto likened the well-abused podex of an Isfahani youth. Another favourite piece of Shirazian 'chaff' is to declare that when an Isfahan father would set up his son in business he provides him with a pound of rice, meaning that he can sell the result as compost for the kitchen-garden, and with the price buy another meal: hence the saying Khakh-i-pái káhú = the soil at the lettuce-root. The Isfahanis retort with the name of a station or halting-place between the two cities where, under pretence of making travellers stow away their riding-gear, many a Shirázi had been raped: hence 'Zín o takaltú tú bi-bar' = carry within saddle and saddle-cloth! A favourite Persian punishment for strangers caught in the Harem or Gynaeceum is to strip and throw them and expose them to the embraces of the grooms and negro slaves. I once asked a Shirázi how penetration was possible if the patient resisted with all the force of the sphincter muscle: he smiled and said, 'Ah, we Persians know a trick to get over that; we apply a sharpened tent-peg to the crupper-bone (os coccygis) and knock till he opens.' A well-known missionary to the East during the last generation was subjected to this gross insult by one of the Persian Prince-governors, whom he had infuriated by his conversion-mania: in his memoirs he alludes to it by mentioning his 'dishonoured person;' but English readers cannot comprehend the full significance of the confession. About the same time Skaykh Nasr, Governor of Bushire, a man famed for facetious blackguardism, used to invite European youngsters serving in the Bombay Marine and ply them with liquor till they were insensible. Next morning the middies mostly complained that the champagne had caused a curious irritation and soreness in la parte-poste. The same Eastern 'Scrogin' would ask his guests if they had ever seen a man-cannon (Adami-top); and, on their replying in the negative, a grey-beard slave was dragged in blaspheming and struggling with all his strength. He was presently placed on all fours and firmly held by the

[43] So amongst the Romans we have the Iatroliptae, youths or girls who wiped the gymnast's perspiring body with swan-down, a practice renewed by the professors of 'Massage'; Unctores who applied perfumes and essences; Fricatrices and Tractatrices or shampooers; Dropacistae, corn-cutters; Alipilarii who plucked the hair, etc.

extremities; his bag-trousers were let down and a dozen peppercorns were inserted ano suo: the target was a sheet of paper held at a reasonable distance; the match was applied by a pinch of cayenne in the nostrils; the sneeze started the grapeshot and the number of hits on the butt decided the bets. We can hardly wonder at the loose conduct of Persian women perpetually mortified by marital pederasty. During the unhappy campaign of 1856–7 in which, with the exception of a few brilliant skirmishes, we gained no glory, Sir James Outram and the Bombay army showing how badly they could work, there was a formal outburst of the Harems; and even women of princely birth could not be kept out of the officers' quarters.

The cities of Afghanistan and Sind are thoroughly saturated with Persian vice, and the people sing

> Kadr-i-kus Aughán dánad, kadr-i-kunrá Kábuli:
> The worth of coynte the Afghan knows: Cabul prefers the
> other *chose*![44]

The Afghans are commercial travellers on a large scale and each caravan is accompanied by a number of boys and lads almost in woman's attire with kohl'd eyes and rouged cheeks, long tresses and henna'd fingers and toes, riding luxuriously in Kajáwas or camel-panniers: they are called Kúch-i safari, or travelling wives, and the husbands trudge patiently by their sides. In Afghanistan also a frantic debauchery broke out amongst the women when they found incubi who were not pederasts; and the scandal was not the most insignificant cause of the general rising at Cabul (Nov. 1841), and the slaughter of Macnaghten, Burnes and other British officers.

Resuming our way Eastward we find the Sikhs and the Moslems of the Panjab much addicted to Le Vice, although the Himalayan tribes to the north and those lying south, the Rájputs and Marathás, ignore it. The same may be said of the Kashmirians who add another Kappa to the tria Kakista, Kappadocians, Kretans, and Kilicians: the proverb says,

> Agar kaht-i-mardum uftad, az ín sih jins kam gírí;
> Eki Afghán, dovvum Sindí,[45] siyyum badjins-i-Kashmírí:
> Though of men there be famine yet shun these three –
> Afghan, Sindi and rascally Kashmírí.

[44] It is a parody on the well-known song, Roebuck i. sect. 2, No. 1602: The goldsmith knows the worth of gold, jewellers worth of jewelry; The worth of rose Bulbul can tell and Kambar's worth his lord, Ali.
[45] For 'Sindi' Roebuck (*Oriental Proverbs* Part i. p. 99) has Kunbu (Kumboh) a Panjábi peasant and others vary the saying ad libitum. See vol. vi. 156.

6 Captain (later Sir) Richard Burton. From a photograph, c. 1860 (Victoria and Albert Museum, London)

7 Mark André Raffalovich. From a photograph, c. 1880 (Mr. Charles Ballantyne)

8 Mark André Raffalovich. From the photograph of a painting by Sydney Starr, c. 1889 (Mr. Charles Ballantyne)

9 John Gray. From a
lithograph by Charles
Shannon, 1896

10 Eric, Count
Stenbock. From a
photograph by
Frederick Hollyer,
c. 1886 (Victoria and
Albert Museum,
London)

M. Louis Daville describes the infamies of Lahore and Lakhnau where he found men dressed as women, with flowing locks under crowns of flowers, imitating the feminine walk and gestures, voice and fashion of speech, and ogling their admirers with all the coquetry of bayadères. Victor Jacquemont's *Journal de Voyage* describes the pederasty of Ranjít Singh, the 'Lion of the Panjáb,' and his pathic Guláb Singh whom the English inflicted upon Cashmir as ruler by way of paying for his treason. Yet the Hindus, I repeat, hold pederasty in abhorrence and are as much scandalized by being called Gánd-márá (anus-beater) or Gándú (anuser) as Englishmen would be. During the years 1843–4 my regiment, almost all Hindu Sepoys of the Bombay Presidency, was stationed at a purgatory called Bandar Ghárrá,[46] a sandy flat with a scatter of verdigris-green milk-bush some forty miles north of Karáchi the headquarters. The dirty heap of mud-and-mat hovels, which represented the adjacent native village, could not supply a single woman; yet only one case of pederasty came to light and that after a tragical fashion some years afterwards. A young Brahman had connection with a soldier comrade of low caste and this had continued till, in an unhappy hour, the Pariah patient ventured to become the agent. The latter, in Arab Al-Fá'il = the 'doer,' is not an object of contempt like Al-Mafúl = the 'done'; and the high-caste sepoy, stung by remorse and revenge, loaded his musket and deliberately shot his paramour. He was hanged by court martial at Hyderabad and, when his last wishes were asked he begged in vain to be suspended by the feet; the idea being that his soul, polluted by exiting 'below the waist,' would be doomed to endless transmigrations through the lowest forms of life.

Beyond India, I have stated, the Sotadic Zone begins to broaden out embracing all China, Turkistan and Japan. The Chinese, as far as we know them in the great cities, are omnivorous and omnifutuentes: they are the chosen people of debauchery and their systematic bestiality with ducks, goats, and other animals is equalled only by their pederasty. Kaempfer and Orlof Torée (Voyage en Chine) notice the public houses for boys and youths in China and Japan. Mirabeau (L'Anandryne) describes the tribadism of their women in hammocks. When Pekin was plundered the Harems contained a number of balls a little larger than the old musket-bullet, made of thin silver with a loose pellet of brass inside somewhat like a grelot:[47] these articles were placed by the women between the labia and an up-and-down movement on the bed gave a pleasant titillation when nothing better was to be procured. They have every artifice of luxury, aphrodisiacs, erotic perfumes and singular

---

[46] See *Sind Revisited* i. 133–35.

[47] They must not be confounded with the *grelots lascifs*, the little bells of gold or silver set by the people of Pegu in the prepuce-skin, and described by Nicolo de Conti who however refused to undergo the operation.

applications. Such are the pills which, dissolved in water and applied to the glans penis, cause it to throb and swell: so according to Amerigo Vespucci American women could artificially increase the size of their husbands' parts.[48] The Chinese bracelet of caoutchouc studded with points now takes the place of the Herisson, or Annulus hirsutus,[49] which was bound between the glans and prepuce. Of the penis succedaneus, that imitation of the Arbor vitae or Soter Kosmou, which the Latins called phallus and fascinum,[50] the French godemiché and the Italians passatempo and diletto (whence our 'dildo'), every kind abounds, varying from a stuffed 'French letter' to a cone of ribbed horn which looks like an instrument of torture. For the use of men they have the 'merkin,'[51] a heart-shaped article of thin skin stuffed with cotton and slit with an artificial vagina: two tapes at the top and one below lash it to the back of a chair. The erotic literature of the Chinese and Japanese is highly developed and their illustrations are often facetious as well as obscene. All are familiar with that of the strong man who by a blow with his enormous phallus shivers a copper pot; and the ludicrous contrast of the huge-membered wights who land in the Isle of Women and presently escape from it, wrinkled and shrivelled, true Domine Do-littles. Of Turkistan we know little, but what we know confirms my statement. Mr. Schuyler in his *Turkistan* (i. 132) offers an illustration of a 'Batchah' (Pers. bachcheh = catamite), 'or singing-boy surrounded by his admirers.' Of the Tartars Master Purchas laconically says (v. 419), 'They are addicted to Sodomie or Buggerie.' The learned casuist Dr. Thomas Sanchez the Spaniard had (says Mirabeau in Kadhésch) to decide a difficult question concerning the sinfulness of a peculiar erotic perversion. The Jesuits brought home from Manilla a tailed man whose moveable prolongation of the os coccygis measured from 7 to 10 inches: he had placed himself between two women, enjoying one naturally while the other used his tail as a penis succedaneus. The verdict was incomplete sodomy and simple fornication. For the islands north of Japan, the 'Sodomitical Sea,' and the 'nayle of tynne' thrust through the prepuce to prevent sodomy, see Lib. ii. chap. 4 of Master Thomas

[48] *Relation des découvertes faites par Colomb etc.* p. 137, Bologna 1875: also Vespucci's letter in *Ramusio* (i. 131) and Paro's *Recherches philosophiques sur les Américains.*

[49] See Mantegazza loc. cit. who borrows from the *Thèse de Paris* of Dr. Abel Hureau de Villeneuve, 'Frictiones per coitum productae magnum mucosae membranae vaginalis turgorem, ac simul hujus cuniculi coarctationem tam maritis salacibus quaeritatam afferunt.'

[50] Fascinus is the Priapus-god to whom the Vestal Virgins of Rome, professed tribades, sacrificed; also the neck-charm in phallus-shape. Fascinum is the male member.

[51] Captain Grose (Lexicon Balatronicum) explains merkin as 'counterfeit hair for women's privy parts. See *Bailey's Dict.*' The Bailey of 1764, an 'improved edition,' does not contain the word which is now generally applied to a cunnus succedaneus.

Caudish's Circumnavigation, and vol. vi. of Pinkerton's Geography translated by Walckenaer.

Passing over to America we find that the Sotadic Zone contains the whole hemisphere from Behring's Straits to Magellan's. This prevalence of 'mollities' astonishes the anthropologist, who is apt to consider pederasty the growth of luxury and the especial product of great and civilized cities, unnecessary and therefore unknown to simple savagery where the births of both sexes are about equal and female infanticide is not practised. In many parts of the New World this perversion was accompanied by another depravity of taste – confirmed cannibalism.[52] The forests and campos abounded in game from the deer to the pheasant-like penelope, and the seas and rivers produced an unfailing supply of excellent fish and shell-fish;[53] yet the Brazilian Tupis preferred the meat of man to every other food.

A glance at Mr. Bancroft[54] proves the abnormal development of sodomy amongst the savages and barbarians of the New World. Even his half-frozen Hyperboreans 'possess all the passions which are supposed to develop most freely under a milder temperature' (i. 58). 'The voluptuousness and polygamy of the North American Indians, under a temperature of almost perpetual winter is far greater than that of the most sensual tropical nations' (*Martin's Brit. Colonies* iii. 524). I can quote only a few of the most remarkable instances. Of the Koniagas of Kadiak Island and the Thinkleets we read (i. 81–82), 'The most repugnant of all their practices is that of male concubinage. A Kadiak mother will select her handsomest and most promising boy, and dress and rear him as a girl, teaching him only domestic duties, keeping him at women's work, associating him with women and girls, in order to render his effeminacy complete. Arriving at the age of ten or fifteen years, he is married to some wealthy man who regards such a companion as a great acquisition. These male concubines are called Achnutschik or Schopans' (the authorities quo ed being Holmberg, Langsdorff, Billing, Choris, Lisiansky and Marchand). The same is the case in Nutka Sound and the Aleutian Islands, where 'male concubinage obtains throughout, but not to the same extent as amongst the Koniagas.' The objects of 'unnatural' affection have their beards carefully plucked out as soon as the face-hair begins to grow, and their chins are tattooed like those of the women. In California the first missionaries found the same practice, the youths being called Joya (Bancroft, i. 415 and authorities Palon, Crespi,

[52] I have noticed this phenomenal cannibalism in my notes to Mr. Albert Tootle's excellent translation of *The Captivity of Hans Stade of Hesse*, London, Hakluyt Society, mdccclxxiv.
[53] The Ostreiras or shell mounds of the Brazil, sometimes 200 feet high, are described by me in *Anthropologia* No. i. Oct. 1873.
[54] *The Native Races of the Pacific States of South America*, by Herbert Howe Bancroft, London, Longmans, 1875.

Boscana, Mofras, Torquemada, Duflot and Fages). The Comanches unite incest with sodomy (i. 515). 'In New Mexico according to Arlegui, Ribas, and other authors, male concubinage prevails to a great extent, these loathsome semblances of humanity, whom to call beastly were a slander upon beasts, dress themselves in the clothes and perform the functions of women, the use of weapons being denied them' (i. 585). Pederasty was systematically practised by the peoples of Cueba, Careta, and other parts of Central America. The Caciques and some of the headmen kept harems of youths who, as soon as destined for the un-clean office, were dressed as women. They went by the name of Camayoas, and were hated and detested by the goodwives (i. 773–4). Of the Nahua nations Father Pierre de Gand (alias de Musa) writes, 'Un certain nombre de prêtres n'avaient point de femmes, *sed eorum loco pueros quibus abutebantur*. Ce péché était si commun dans ce pays que, jeunes ou vieux, tous étaient infectés; ils y étaient si adonnés que mêmes les enfants de six ans s'y livraient' (Ternaux-Campans, *Voyages*, Série i. Tom. x. p. 197). Among the Mayas of Yucatan Las Casas declares that the great prevalence of 'unnatural' lust made parents anxious to see their progeny wedded as soon as possible (Kings-borough's Mex. Ant. viii. 135). In Vera Paz a god, called by some Chin and by others Cavial and Maran, taught it by committing the act with another god. Some fathers gave their sons a boy to use as a woman, and if any other approached this pathic he was treated as an adulterer. In Yucatan images were found by Bernal Diaz proving the sodomitical propensities of the people (Bancroft v. 198). De Pauw (*Recherches Philosophiques sur les Américains*, London, 1771) has much to say about the subject in Mexico generally: in the northern provinces men married youths who, dressed like women, were forbidden to carry arms. Accord ing to Gomara there were at Tamalipas houses of male prostitution; and from Diaz and others we gather that the *pecado nefando* was the rule. Both in Mexico and in Peru it might have caused, if it did not justify, the cruelties of the Conquistadores. Pederasty was also general throughout Nicaragua, and the early explorers found it amongst the indigenes of Panama.

We have authentic details concerning Le Vice in Peru and its adjacent lands, beginning with Cieza de Leon, who must be read in the original or in the translated extracts of Purchas (vol. v. 942, etc.), not in the cruelly castrated form preferred by the Council of the Hakluyt Society. Speaking of the New Granada Indians he tells us that 'at Old Port (Porto Viejo) and Puna, the Deuill so farre prevayled in their beastly Deuotions that there were Boyes consecrated to serue in the Temple; and at the times of their Sacrifices and Solemne Feasts, the Lords and principall men abused them to that detestable filthinesse;'

i.e. performed their peculiar worship. Generally in the hill-countries the Devil, under the show of holiness, had introduced the practice; for every temple or chief house of adoration kept one or two men or more which were attired like women, even from the time of their childhood, and spake like them, imitating them in everything; with these, under pretext of holiness and religion, their principal men on principal days had commerce. Speaking of the arrival of the Giants[55] at Point Santa Elena, Cieza says (chap. lii.), they were detested by the natives, because in using their women they killed them, and their men also in another way. All the natives declare that God brought upon them a punishment proportioned to the enormity of their offence. When they were engaged together in their accursed intercourse, a fearful and terrible fire came down from Heaven with a great noise, out of the midst of which there issued a shining Angel with a glittering sword, wherewith at one blow they were all killed and the fire consumed them.[56] There remained a few bones and skulls which God allowed to bide unconsumed by the fire, as a memorial of this punishment. In the Hakluyt Society's bowdler-ization we read of the Tumbez Islanders being 'very vicious, many of them committing the abominable offence' (p. 24); also, 'If by the advice of the Devil any Indian commit the abominable crime, it is thought little of and they call him a woman.' In chapters lii. and lviii. we find exceptions. The Indians of Huancabamba, 'although so near the peoples of Puerto Viejo and Guayaquil, do not commit the abominable sin;' and the Serranos, or island mountaineers, as sorcerers and magicians inferior to the coast peoples, were not so much addicted to sodomy.

The Royal Commentaries of the Yncas shows that the evil was of a comparatively modern growth. In the early period of Peruvian history the people considered the crime 'unspeakable:' if a Cuzco Indian, not of Yncarial blood, angrily addressed the term pederast to another, he was held infamous for many days. One of the generals having reported to the Ynca Ccapacc Yupanqui that there were some sodomites, not in all the valleys, but one here and one there, 'nor was it a habit of all the inhabitants but only of certain persons who practised it privately,' the ruler ordered that the criminals should be publicly burnt alive and their houses, crops and trees destroyed: moreover, to show his abomination, he commanded that the whole village should so be treated if one man fell into this habit (Lib. iii. cap. 13). Elsewhere we learn, 'There were sodomites in some provinces, though not openly nor universally, but some particular men and in secret. In some parts they had them in their temples, because the Devil persuaded them that the Gods took great

---

[55] All Peruvian historians mention these giants, who were probably the large-limbed Caribs (Caraibes) of the Brazil: they will be noticed in page 186.

[56] This sounds much like a pious fraud of the missionaries, a Europeo-American version of the Sodom legend.

delight in such people, and thus the Devil acted as a traitor to remove the veil of shame that the Gentiles felt for this crime and to accustom them to commit it in public and in common.'

During the times of the Conquistadores male concubinage had become the rule throughout Peru. At Cuzco, we are told by Nuno de Guzman in 1530, 'The last which was taken, and which fought most couragiously, was a man in the habite of a woman, which confessed that from a childe he had gotten his liuing by that filthinesse, for which I caused him to be burned.' V. F. Lopez[57] draws a frightful picture of pathologic love in Peru. Under the reigns which followed that of Inti-Kapak (Ccapacc) Amauri, the country was attacked by invaders of a giant race coming from the sea: they practised pederasty after a fashion so shameless that the conquered tribes were compelled to fly (p. 271). Under the pre-Yncarial Amauta, or priestly dynasty, Peru had lapsed into savagery and the kings of Cuzco preserved only the name. 'Toutes ces hontes et toutes ces misères provenaient de deux vices infâmes, la bestialité et la sodomie. Les femmes surtout étaient offensées de voir la nature frustrée de tous ses droits. Elles pleuraient ensemble en leurs réunions sur le misérable état dans lequel elles étaient tombées, sur le mépris avec lequel elles étaient traitées. . . . Le monde était renversé, les hommes s'aimaient et étaient jaloux les uns des autres. . . . Elles cherchaient, mais en vain, les moyens de remédier au mal; elles employaient des herbes et des recettes diaboliques qui leur ramenaient bien quelques individus, mais ne pouvaient arrêter les progrès incessants du vice. Cet état de choses constitua un véritable moyen âge, qui dura jusqu'à l'établissement du gouvernement des Incas' (p. 277).

When Sinchi Roko (the xcvth of Montesinos and the xcist of Garcilazo) became Ynca, he found morals at the lowest ebb. 'Ni la prudence de l'Inca, ni les lois sévères qu'il avait promulguées n'avaient pu extirper entièrement le péché contre nature. Il reprit avec une nouvelle violence, et les femmes en furent si jalouses qu'un grand nombre d'elles tuèrent leurs maris. Les devins et les sorciers passaient leurs journées à fabriquer, avec certaines herbes, des compositions magiques qui rendaient fous ceux qui en mangaient, et les femmes en faisaient prendre, soit dans les aliments, soit dans la chicha, à ceux dont elles étaient jalouses' (p. 291).

I have remarked that the Tupi races of the Brazil were infamous for cannibalism and sodomy; nor could the latter be only racial as proved by the fact that colonists of pure Lusitanian blood followed in the path of the savages. Sr. Antonio Augusto da Costa Aguiar[58] is outspoken upon this point. 'A crime which in England leads to the gallows,

---

[57] *Les Races Aryennes du Pérou*, Paris, Franck, 1871.
[58] *O Brazil e os Brazileiros*, Santos, 1862.

and which is the very measure of abject depravity, passes with impunity amongst us by the participating in it of almost all or of many (*de quasi todos, ou de muitos*). Ah! if the wrath of Heaven were to fall by way of punishing such crimes (*delictos*), more than one city of this Empire, more than a dozen, would pass into the category of the Sodoms and Gomorrahs' (p. 30). Till late years pederasty in the Brazil was looked upon as a peccadillo; the European immigrants following the practice of the wild men who were naked but not, as Columbus said, 'clothed in innocence.' One of Her Majesty's Consuls used to tell a tale of the hilarity provoked in a 'fashionable' assembly by the open declaration of a young gentleman that his mulatto-'patient' had suddenly turned upon him, insisting upon becoming agent. Now, however, under the influences of improved education and respect for the public opinion of Europe, pathologic love amongst the Luso-Brazilians has been reduced to the normal limits.

Outside the Sotadic Zone, I have said, Le Vice is sporadic, not endemic: yet the physical and moral effect of great cities where puberty, they say, is induced earlier than in country sites, has been the same in most lands, causing modesty to decay and pederasty to flourish. The Badawi Arab is wholly pure of Le Vice; yet San'á the capital of Al-Yaman and other centres of population have long been and still are thoroughly infected. History tells us of Zú Shanátir, tyrant of 'Arabia Felix,' in 478, A.D. who used to entice young men into his palace and cause them after use to be cast out of the windows: this unkindly ruler was at last poinarded by the youth Zerash, known from his long ringlets as 'Zú Nowás.' The negro race is mostly untainted by sodomy and tribadism. Yet Joan dos Sanctos[59] found in Cacongo of West Africa certain 'Chibudi, which are men attyred like women and behaue themselves womanly, ashamed to be called men; are also married to men, and esteem that vnnaturale damnation an honor.' Madagascar also delighted in dancing and singing boys dressed as girls. In the Empire of Dahomey I noted a corps of prostitutes kept for the use of the Amazon-soldieresses.

North of the Sotadic Zone we find local but notable instances. Master Christopher Burrough[60] describes on the western side of the Volga 'a very fine stone castle, called by the name Oueak, and adioyning to the same a Towne called by the *Russes, Sodom,* . . . which was swallowed into the earth by the iustice of God, for the wickednesse of the people.' Again: although as a rule Christianity has steadily opposed pathologic love both in writing and preaching, there have been remarkable exceptions. Perhaps the most curious idea was that of certain

[59] *Aethiopia Orientalis*, Purchas ii. 1558.
[60] Purchas iii. 243.

medical writers in the middle ages: 'Usus et amplexus pueri, bene temperatus, salutaris medicina' (Tardieu). Bayle notices (under 'Vayer') the infamous book of Giovanni della Casa, Archbishop of Benevento, 'De laudibus Sodomiae,'[61] vulgarly known as 'Capitolo del Forno.' The same writer refers (under 'Sixte iv') to the report that the Dominican Order, which systematically decried Le Vice, had presented a request to the Cardinal di Santa Lucia that sodomy might be lawful during three months per annum, June to August; and that the Cardinal had underwritten the petition 'Be it done as they demand.' Hence the Faeda Venus of Battista Mantovano. Bayle rejects the history for a curious reason, venery being colder in summer than in winter, and quotes the proverb 'Aux mois qui n'ont pas d' R, peu embrasser et bien boire.' But in the case of a celibate priesthood such scandals are inevitable: witness the famous Jesuit epitaph Ci-gît un Jésuite, etc.

In our modern capitals, London, Berlin and Paris for instance, the Vice seems subject to periodical outbreaks. For many years, also, England sent her pederasts to Italy, and especially to Naples whence originated the term 'Il vizio Inglese.' It would be invidious to detail the scandals which of late years have startled the public in London and Dublin: for these the curious will consult the police reports. Berlin, despite her strong flavour of Phariseeism, Puritanism and Chauvinism in religion, manners and morals, is not a whit better than her neighbours. Dr. Gaspar,[62] a well-known authority on the subject, adduces many interesting cases especially an old Count Cajus and his six accomplices. Amongst his many correspondents one suggested to him that not only Plato and Julius Caesar but also Winckelmann and Platen (?) belonged to the Society; and he had found it flourishing in Palermo, the Louvre, the Scottish Highlands and St. Petersburg, to name only a few places. Frederick the Great is said to have addressed these words to his nephew, 'Je puis vous assurer, par mon expérience personelle, que ce plaisir est peu agréable à cultiver.' This suggests the popular anecdote of Voltaire and the Englishman who agreed upon an 'experience' and found it far from satisfactory. A few days afterwards the latter informed the Sage of Ferney that he had tried it again and provoked the exclamation, 'Once a philosopher: twice a sodomite!' The last revival of the kind in Germany is a society at Frankfort and its neighbourhood, self-styled Les Cravates Noires in opposition, I suppose, to Les Cravates Blanches of A. Belot.

Paris is by no means more depraved than Berlin and London; but,

[61] For a literal translation see 1re Série de la Curiosité Littéraire et Bibliographique, Paris, Liseux, 1880.
[62] His best known works are (1) Praktisches Handbuch der Gechtlichener Medecin, Berlin, 1860; and (2) Klinische Novellen zur gerechtlichen Medicin, Berlin, 1863.

whilst the latter hushes up the scandal, Frenchmen do not: hence we see a more copious account of it submitted to the public. For France of the xviith century consult the *Histoire de la Prostitution chez tous les Peuples du Monde*, and *La France devenue Italienne*, a treatise which generally follows *L'Histoire Amoureuse des Gaules* by Bussy, Comte de Rabutin.[63] The headquarters of male prostitution were then in the Champ Flory, *i.e.*, Champ de Flore, the privileged rendezvous of low courtesans. In the xviiith century, 'quand le Français à tête folle,' as Voltaire sings, invented the term 'Péché philosophique,' there was a temporary recrudescence; and, after the death of Pidauzet de Mairobert (March, 1779), his *Apologie de la Secte Anandryne* was published in L'Espion Anglais. In those days the Allée des Veuves in the Champs Elysées had a 'fief reservé des Ebugors'[64] – 'veuve' in the language of Sodom being the maîtresse en titre, the favourite youth.

At the decisive moment of monarchical decomposition Mirabeau[65] declares that pederasty was reglementée and adds, 'Le goût des pédérastes, quoique moins en vogue que du temps de Henri III. (the French Heliogabalus), sous le règne desquel les hommes se provoquaient mutuellement[66] sous les portiques du Louvre, fait des progrès considérables. On sait que cette ville (Paris) est un chef-d'œuvre de police; en conséquence, il y a des lieux publics autorisés a cet effet. Les jeunes gens qui se destinent à la profession, sont soigneusement enclassés; car les systèmes réglementaires s'étendent jusques-là. On les examine; ceux qui peuvent être agents et patients, qui sont beaux, vermeils, bien faits, potelés, sont réservés pour les grands seigneurs, ou se font payer très-cher par les évêques et les financiers. Ceux qui sont privés de leurs testicules, ou en termes de l'art (car notre langue est plus chaste qui nos mœurs), qui n'ont pas le *poids du tisserand*, mais qui donnent et reçoivent, forment la seconde classe; ils sont encore chers, parceque les

[63] The same author printed another imitation of Petronius Arbiter, the 'Larissa' story of Théophile Viand. His cousin, the Sévigné, highly approved of it. See Bayle's objections to Rabutin's delicacy and excuses for Petronius' grossness in his 'Éclaircissement sur les obscénités' (Appendice au *Dictionnaire Antique*).

[64] The Boulgrin of Rabelais, which Urquhart renders Ingle for Boulgre, an 'indorser,' derived from the Bulgarus or Bulgarian, who gave to Italy the term bugiardo – liar. Bougre and Bougrerie date (Littré) from the xiiith century. I cannot however, but think that the trivial term gained strength in the xvith when the manners of the Bugres or indigenous Brazilians were studied by Huguenot refugees in La France Antartique and several of these savages found their way to Europe. A grand Fête in Rouen on the entrance of Henri II and Dame Katherine de Medicis (June 16, 1564) showed, as part of the pageant, three hundred men (including fifty 'Bugres' or Tupis) with parroquets and other birds and beasts of the newly explored regions. The procession is given in the four-folding woodcut 'Figure des Brésiliens' in Jean de Prest's Edition of 1551.

[65] *Erotika Biblion* chapt. Kadésch (pp. 93 et seq.) Edition de Bruxelles with notes by the Chevalier P. Pierrugues of Bordeaux, before noticed.

[66] Called Chevaliers de Paille because the sign was a straw in the mouth, à la Palmerston.

femmes en usent tandis qu'ils servent aux hommes. Ceux qui ne sont plus susceptibles d'érection tant ils sont usés, quoiqu'ils aient tous ces organes nécessaires au plaisir, s'inscrivent comme *patiens purs*, et composent la troisieme classe: mais celle qui préside à ces plaisirs, vérifie leur impuissance. Pour cet effet, on les place tout nus sur un matelas ouvert par la moitié inférieure; deux filles les caressent de leur mieux, pendant qu'une troisième frappe doucement avec des orties naissantes le siège des désirs vénériens. Après un quart d'heure de cet essai, on leur introduit dans l'anus un poivre long rouge qui cause une irritation considérable; on pose sur les échauboulures produites par les orties, de la moutarde fine de Caudebec, et l'on passe le *gland* au camphre. Ceux qui résistent à ces épreuves et ne donnent aucun signe d'érection, servent comme patiens à un tiers de paie seulement'.[67]

The Restoration and the Empire made the police more vigilant in matters of politics than of morals. The favourite club, which had its mot de passe, was in the Rue Doyenne, old quarter St. Thomas des Louvre; and the house was a hôtel of the xviith century. Two street-doors, on the right for the male gynaeceum and the left for the female, opened at 4 p.m. in winter and 8 p.m. in summer. A decoy-lad, charmingly dressed in women's clothes, with big haunches and small waist, promenaded outside; and this continued till 1826 when the police put down the house.

Under Louis Philippe, the conquest of Algiers had evil results, according to the Marquis de Boissy. He complained without ambages of mœurs Arabes in French regiments, and declared that the result of the African wars was an éffrayable débordement pédérastique, even as the vérole resulted from the Italian campaigns of that age of passion, the xvith century. From the military the fléau spread to civilian society and the Vice took such expansion and intensity that it may be said to have been democratized in cities and large towns; at least so we gather from the Dossier des Agissements des Pédérastes. A general gathering of 'La Sainte Congrégation des glorieux Pédérastes' was held in the old Petite Rue des Marais where, after the theatre, many resorted under pretext of making water. They ranged themselves along the walls of a vast garden and exposed their podices: bourgeois, richards and nobles came with full purses, touched the part which most attracted them and were duly followed by it. At the Allée des Veuves the crowd was dangerous from 7 to 8 p.m.: no policeman or ronde de nuit dared venture in it; cords were stretched from tree to tree and armed guards drove away strangers amongst whom, they say, was once Victor Hugo. This nuisance was at length suppressed by the municipal administration.

The Empire did not improve morals. Balls of sodomites were held

---

[67] I have noticed that the eunuch in Sind was as meanly paid and have given the reason.

at No. 8 Place de la Madeleine where, on Jan. 2, '64, some one hundred and fifty men met, all so well dressed as women that even the landlord did not recognize them. There was also a club for sotadic debauchery called the Cent Gardes and the Dragons de l'Impératrice.[68] They copied the imperial toilette and kept it in the general wardrobe: hence 'faire l'Impératrice' meant to be used carnally. The site, a splendid hotel in the Allée des Veuves, was discovered by the Procureur-Général who registered all the names; but, as these belonged to not a few senators and dignitaries, the Emperor wisely quashed proceedings. The club was broken up on July 16, '64. During the same year *La Petite Revue*, edited by M. Loredan Larchy, son of the General, printed an article, 'Les échappés de Sodome': it discusses the letter of M. Castagnary to the Progrès de Lyons and declares that the Vice had been adopted by plusieurs corps de troupes. For its latest developments as regards the *chantage* of the *tantes* (pathics), the reader will consult the last issues of Dr. Tardieu's well-known *Etudes*.[69] He declares that the servant-class is most infected; and that the Vice is commonest between the ages of fifteen and twenty-five.

The pederasty of *The Nights* may briefly be distributed into three categories. The first is the funny form, as the unseemly practical joke of masterful Queen Budúr (vol. iii. 300–306) and the not less hardi jest of the slave-princess Zumurrud (vol. iv. 226). The second is in the grimmest and most earnest phase of the perversion, for instance where Abu Nowas[70] debauches the three youths (vol. v. 64–69); whilst in the

[68] *Centuria Librorum Absconditorum* (by Pisanus Fraxi) 4to, p. lx. and 593. London. Privately printed, mdccclxxix.

[69] A friend learned in these matters supplies me with the following list of famous pederasts. Those who marvel at the wide diffusion of such erotic perversion, and its being affected by so many celebrities, will bear in mind that the greatest men have been some of the worst: Alexander of Macedon, Julius Caesar and Napoleon Buonaparte held themselves high above the moral law which obliges common-place humanity. All three are charged with the Vice. Of Kings we have Henri iii., Louis xiii. and xviii., Frederick ii. of Prussia, Peter the Great, William ii. of Holland and Charles ii. and iii. of Parma. We find also Shakespeare (i., xv., Edit. François Hugo) and Molière, Theodorus Beza, Lully (the Composer), D'Assoucy, Count Zintzendorff, the Grand Condé, Marquis de Villette, Pierre Louis Farnèse, Duc de la Vallière, De Soleinne, Count D'Avaray, Saint Mégrin, D'Epernon, Admiral de la Susse, La Roche-Pouchin Rochfort S. Louis, Henne (the Spiritualist), Comte Horace de Viel Castel, Lerminin, Fievée, Théodore Leclerc, Archi-Chancellier Cambacèrés, Marquis de Custine, Sainte-Beuve and Count D'Orsay. For others refer to the three volumes of Pisanus Fraxi: *Index Librorum Prohibitorum* (London, 1877), *Centuria Librorum Absconditorum* (before alluded to) and *Catena Librorum Tacendorum*, London, 1885. The indices will supply the names.

[70] Of this peculiar character Ibn Khallikan remarks (ii. 43), 'There were four poets whose works clearly contraried their character. Abu al-Atahíyah wrote pious poems himself being an atheist; Abú Hukayma's verses proved his impotence, yet he was more salacious than a he-goat; Mohammed ibn Házim praised contentment, yet he was greedier than a dog; and Abú Nowás hymned the joys of sodomy, yet he was more passionate for women than a baboon.'

third form it is wisely and learnedly discussed, to be severely blamed, by the Shaykhah or Reverend Woman (vol. v. 154).

To conclude this part of my subject, the éclaircissement des obscénités. Many readers will regret the absence from *The Nights* of that modesty which distinguishes *Amadis de Gaul*; whose author when leaving a man and a maid together says, 'And nothing shall be here related; for these and suchlike things which are conformable neither to good conscience nor nature, man ought in reason lightly to pass over, holding them in slight esteem as they deserve.' Nor have we less respect for Palmerin of England who after a risqué scene declares, 'Herein is no offence offered to the wise by wanton speeches, or encouragement to the loose by lascivious matter.' But these are not oriental ideas and we must e'en take the Eastern as we find him. He still holds 'Naturalia non sunt turpia,' together with 'Mundis omnia munda'; and, as Bacon assures us the mixture of a lie doth add to pleasure, so the Arab enjoys the startling and lively contrast of extreme virtue and horrible vice placed in juxtaposition.

Those who have read through these ten volumes will agree with me that the proportion of offensive matter bears a very small ratio to the mass of the work. In an age saturated with cant and hypocrisy, here and there a venal pen will mourn over the 'Pornography' of *The Nights*, dwell upon the 'Ethics of Dirt' and the 'Garbage of the Brothel'; and will lament the 'wanton dissemination (!) of ancient and filthy fiction.' This self-constituted Censor morum reads Aristophanes and Plato, Horace and Virgil, perhaps even Martial and Petronius, because 'veiled in the decent obscurity of a learned language;' he allows men Latinè loqui; but he is scandalized at stumbling-blocks much less important in plain English. To be consistent he must begin by bowdlerizing not only the classics, with which boys' and youths' minds and memories are soaked and saturated at schools and colleges, but also Boccaccio and Chaucer, Shakespeare and Rabelais; Burton, Sterne, Swift and a long list of works which are yearly reprinted and republished without a word of protest. Lastly, why does not this inconsistent puritan purge the Old Testament of its allusions to human ordure and the pudenda; to carnal copulation and impudent whoredom, to adultery and fornication, to onanism, sodomy and bestiality? But this he will not do, the whited sepulchre! To the interested critic of the *Edinburgh Review* (No. 335 of July, 1886), I return my warmest thanks for his direct and deliberate falsehoods: – lies are one-legged and short-lived, and venom evaporates.[71] It appears to me that when I show to such men,

[71] A virulently and unjustly abusive critique never yet injured its object: in fact it is generally the greatest favour an author's unfriends can bestow upon him. But to notice in a popular Review books which have been printed and not published is hardly in accordance with the established courtesies of literature.

so 'respectable' and so impure, a landscape of magnificent prospects whose vistas are adorned with every charm of nature and art, they point their unclean noses at a little heap of muck here and there lying in a field-corner.

29 Marius the Epicurean

Walter Pater. The death of Flavian from *Marius the Epicurean*, 1885.

. . . Flavian lay at the open window of his lodging, with a burning pain in the head, fancying no covering light and thin enough to be applied to his body. His head being relieved after a time, there was distress at the chest. It was but the fatal course of the strange new sickness, under many disguises; travelling from the brain to the feet, like a material resident, weakening one after another of the organic centres; often, when it did not kill, depositing various degrees of lifelong infirmity in this member or that; and after that descent, returning upwards again, now as a mortal coldness, leaving the entrenchments of the fortress of life overturned, one by one, behind it.

Flavian lay there, with the enemy at his breast now, in a painful cough, but relieved from that burning fever in the brain, amid the rich-scented flowers – rare Paestum roses, and the like – procured by Marius for his solace, in a fancied convalescence; and would, at intervals, return to work at his verses, with a great eagerness to complete and transcribe the poem, while Marius sat and wrote at his dictation, one of the latest but not the poorest specimens of genuine Latin poetry.

It was in truth a kind of nuptial hymn, which, taking its start from the thought of nature as the universal mother, celebrated the preliminary pairing, and mating together, of all fresh things, in the hot and genial spring-time – the immemorial nuptials of the soul of spring itself and the brown earth; and was full of a delighted, mystic sense of what passed between them in that fantastic marriage. And the mystic burden was relieved, at intervals, by a familiar playfulness of the Latin verse-writer in dealing with mythology, which, coming at so late a day, had still a wonderful freshness in its old age – '*Amor* has put his weapons by and will keep holiday. He has been bidden to go unclad, that none may be wounded by his bow and arrows. But take care! In truth he is none the less armed than usual, though he be all unclad.'

In the expression of all that Flavian seemed, while making it his

---

At the end of my work I propose to write a paper 'The Reviewer Reviewed' which will, amongst other things, explain the motif of the writer of the critique and the editor of the Edinburgh.

chief aim to retain the opulent, many-syllabled vocabulary of the Latin genius, at some points even to have advanced beyond it, in anticipation of wholly new laws of taste as regards sound – of a new range of sound itself; the note of which, associating itself with certain other fancies or experiences of his, was to Marius like the foretaste of an entirely novel world of poetic beauty to come. Flavian had caught, in fact, something of the rhyming cadence, the sonorous organ-music of the medieval Latin, and therewithal something of its unction and mysticity of spirit. There was in his work, along with the last splendour of the classical language, a touch, almost prophetic, of that transformed life it was to have in the rhyming middle age, just about to dawn. The impression thus forced upon Marius connected itself with a feeling, the precise inverse of that, known to every one, which seems to say – *You have been just here, just thus, before!* – a feeling in his case not reminiscent but prescient, which passed over him many times afterwards, coming across certain people and places; as if he detected there the process of actual change to a wholly undreamed of and renewed condition of human body and soul. It was as if he saw the heavy, yet decrepit old Roman architecture about him, rebuilding on an intrinsically better pattern – Could it have been actually on a new musical instrument that Flavian had first heard those novel accents of his verse? And still Marius noticed there, amid all that richness of impression and imagery, the firmness of outline he had always relished so much, in the composition of Flavian – Yes! a firmness like that of some master of noble metal-work, manipulating tenacious bronze or gold. Even then, the haunting refrain, with its *impromptu* variations, from the throats of those strong young men, floated in at the window.

> Cras amet qui nunquam amavit!
> Quique amavit cras amet!

– repeated Flavian, tremulously dictating yet one stanza more.

What he was losing, his freehold of a soul and a body so fortunately endowed, the mere liberty of life itself above-ground, 'those sunny mornings in the cornfields, by the sea,' as he recollected them one day, when the window was thrown open upon the early freshness – his sense of all that, was from the first very sharp and clear, yet still rather as of something he was but deprived of for a time than finally bidding farewell to. That was while he was still with no very grave misgivings as to the issue of his sickness, and felt the sources of life still springing essentially unadulterate within him. From time to time indeed Marius, working eagerly at the poem from his dictation, was haunted by a feeling of the triviality of such work just then. The recurrent sense of some obscure danger beyond the mere danger of death, vaguer than that and by so much the more terrible, like the menace of some shadowy adversary in the dark with whose mode of attack they were unacquainted, confused him now and again, through those hours of excited attention to his manuscript, and to the merely physical wants of Flavian. Still, for those three days there was much hope and cheerfulness, and even jesting. Half-consciously Marius tried to prolong one or another relieving circumstance of the day, the preparations for rest and for morning refreshment for instance; somewhat sadly making the most of the little luxury of this or that, with something of the feigned cheer of the mother who sets her last morsels before her famished child as for a feast, but really that he 'may eat it and die.'

It was on the afternoon of the seventh day that he allowed Marius finally to put the unfinished manuscript aside. For the enemy, leaving the chest quiet at last though exhausted, had made itself felt with full power again in a painful vomiting, which seemed to shake his body asunder, with great consequent prostration. From that time the distress increased rapidly downwards – *omnia tum vero vitai claustra labatant* – and soon the cold was mounting, with sure pace, from the dead feet to the head.

And now Marius began more than to suspect what the issue must be, and henceforward could but watch with a sort of agonized fascination the rapid but systematic work of the destroyer, faintly relieving a little the mere accidents of the sharper forms of the suffering. Flavian himself seemed with full consciousness at last – with a clear, concentrated, jealous estimate of the actual crisis – to be doing battle with his enemy. His mind surveyed, with great distinctness, the various suggested modes of relief. He would certainly get better, he fancied, could he be removed to a certain place on the hills where as a child he had once recovered from sickness; but found that he could scarcely raise his head from the pillow without giddiness. And then, as if now clearly foreseeing the end, he would set himself, with an eager effort, and with that eager and angry look, which is noted as one of the premonitions of death in this disease, to fashion out, without formal dictation, still a few more broken verses of his unfinished work, in hard-set determination, defiant of pain, to arrest this or that little drop at least, from the river of sensuous imagery rushing so quickly past him.

But at length *delirium* – symptom that the enemy's work was done, and the last resort of life yielding to the plague – broke the coherent order of words and thoughts; and Marius, dwelling intently on the coming agony, found his best hope in the increasing dimness of the patient's mind. In intervals of clearer consciousness the visible signs of cold, of sorrow and desolation, were very painful. No longer battling with the disease, he seemed to be yielding himself, as it were, to the disposal of the victorious foe, and dying passively, like some dumb creature, in hopeless acquiescence at last. That old, half-pleading peevishness, actually unamiable, yet seeming only to need conditions of life a little happier than they had been, to become refinement of affection, and a delicate grace in its demand on the sympathy of others, had changed in those moments of full intelligence to a tremulous, clinging gentleness, as he lay – 'on the very threshold of death' – with his sharply contracted hand in that of Marius, to his almost surprised happiness, winning him now to an absolutely self-forgetful devotion. There was a new sort of pleading in the misty eyes just because they took such unsteady note of him which made Marius feel as if *guilty*; anticipating a form of self-reproach which surprises sometimes even the tenderest ministrant after death, when the sudden cessation of affectionate labour gives time for the suspicion of some failure of love, perhaps, at one or another minute point in it. Marius almost longed to take his share in the suffering that he might understand so the better how to relieve it.

It seemed that the light of the lamp distressed the patient, and Marius extinguished it. The thunder which had sounded all day among the hills, with a heat not unwelcome to Flavian, had given way at nightfall to steady rain; and in the darkness Marius lay down beside him, faintly shivering now in the sudden cold, to lend him his own warmth, undeterred by the fear of contagion which had kept other people from passing near the house. At length about day-break he perceived that the last effort had come with a restoration of mental clearness which recognized him (Marius understood this in the contact, light as it was) there, beside him. 'Is it a comfort,' he whispered then, 'that I shall often come and weep over you?' – 'Not unless I am aware of you there, and hear you weeping!'

The sun shone out on the people going to work for a long hot day, and Marius was standing by the dead, watching, with the deliberate purpose of fixing in his memory every detail, that he might have that picture in reserve, should any day of forgetfulness ever hereafter come to him with the temptation to feel completely happy again. A blind feeling of outrage, of resentment against nature itself, mingled with an agony of pity, as he noted on the now placid features a certain touching look of humility, almost of abjectness, like the expression of a smitten child or animal, as of one, fallen at last, after a bewildering struggle, wholly under the power of a remorseless adversary. Out of mere tenderness he would not forget one circumstance of all that; as a man might piously stamp on his memory the death-scene of a brother wrongfully condemned, against a time that may come.

The fear of the corpse, which surprised him at last in his effort to watch by it at night, was a hint of his own failing strength, just in time. The first night after the washing of the body, he bore stoutly enough the tax which affection seemed to demand, throwing the incense from time to time on the little altar placed beside the bier. It was the re-currence of the thing – that unchanged outline below the coverlet, amid a silence in which the faintest rustle seemed to speak – that finally over-came his determination. Surely here, in this alienation, in this sense of distance between them, which had come over him before in a minor degree when the mind of Flavian had wandered in his sickness, was another of the pains of death. Yet he was able to make all due prepara-tions, and go through the ceremonies, shortened a little because of the infection, when, on a cloudless evening, the funeral procession went forth; himself, when the flames of the pyre had done their work, carrying away the urn of the deceased, in the folds of his toga, to its last resting-place in the cemetery beside the highway –

> Quis desiderio sit pudor aut modus
> Tam cari capitis? –

and so turning home to sleep in his own lonely lodging.

30   'Rose Leaves When the Rose is Dead'

Mark André Raffalovich. From *In Fancy Dress*, 1886.

> VIII
> Young but not youthful he thou lovest not
> Will cease to love thee if thou love not soon:
> But he would never weary of thy thought
> Did thy hand yield to his this very noon.
> His love is pure as thy own life is pure,
> And passionate as thy dreams are passionate,
> And there is none thou canst so much allure,
> And none thou couldst so little satiate.
> So much belovèd, love who loves thee so,
> Glad to be chosen to do love's commands,
> Beloved be loving also, straightway go
> With graceful footsteps and with gracious hands,
> And pale with pleasure or the sense of doom,
> Knock loudly once and enter thy friend's room.

SH–O

31   'The World Well Lost IV'

Mark André Raffalovich. From *In Fancy Dress*, 1886.

Because our world has music, and we dance;
Because our world has colour, and They gaze;
Because our speech is tuned, and schooled our glance,
And we have roseleaf nights and roseleaf days,
And we have leisure, work to do, and rest;
Because They see us laughing when we meet,
And hear our words and voices, see us dressed
With skill, and pass us and our flowers smell sweet: –
They think that we know friendship, passion, love!
Our peacock Pride! And Art our nightingale!
And Pleasure's hand upon our dogskin glove!
And if They see our faces burn or pale,
    It is the sunlight, think They, or the gas,
    – Our lives are wired like our gardenias.

32   'The World Well Lost XVIII'

Mark André Raffalovich. From *In Fancy Dress*, 1886.

You are to me the secret of my soul
And I to you what no man yet has been.
I, your Prometheus, fire from Heaven stole
And for my theft the world's revenge is keen.
What I have done for you no man has done;
I have nor begged nor bought a common bliss,
But what you are to me you were to none.
And I will suffer this, and more than this,
And much beyond that more, a martyrdom
Without the crown of a celestial birth,
Or any hope of any world to come
Exalting most what lowest was on Earth,
    The passion purest of all out of Heaven,
    The love in Hell least easily forgiven.

33   'Lovelace'

Mark André Raffalovich. From *In Fancy Dress*, 1886.

'Why did you come to-night, to-night,
So many miles of cold and rain?'

– O but I come with much delight
To warm your sheltering nest again.

'Why did you come to-night, to-night,
It may be death to both of us!'

– O but I come with much delight,
All things I love are dangerous.

'Why did you come? Do you forget
Who broke my heart so long ago?'

– O but since then my lips have met
No sweetness like your saying 'No.'

34   Arthur Hamilton at Cambridge

Arthur Christopher Benson. Extract from *The Memoirs of Arthur Hamilton*,
1886, by Christopher Carr (pseudonym of A. C. Benson).

[Arthur] had been at Cambridge about two years, when, in the common
consent of all his friends, his habits and behaviour seemed to undergo
a complete and radical change.

I have never discovered what the incident was that occasioned this
change; all I know is that suddenly, for several weeks, his geniality of
manner and speech, his hilarity, his cheerfulness, entirely disappeared;
a curious look of haunting sadness, not defined, but vague, came over
his face; and though he gradually returned to his old ways, yet I am
conscious myself, and others would support me in this, that he was
never quite the same again; he was no longer young.

The only two traces that I can discover in his journals, or letters,
or elsewhere, of the facts are these.

He always in later diaries vaguely alludes to a certain event which
changed his view of things in general; 'ever since,' 'since that November,' 'for now nearly five years I have felt.' These and similar phrases

constantly occur in his diary. I will speak in a moment of what nature I should conjecture it to have been.

A packet of letters in his desk were marked 'to be burnt unopened;' but at the same time carefully docketed with dates: these dates were all immediately after that time, extending over ten days.

The exact day was November 8, 1872. It is engraved in a small silver locket that hung on his watch-chain, where he was accustomed to have important days in his life marked, such as the day he adopted his boy, his mother's death. It is preceded by the Greek letters B *Π*, which from a certain entry in his diary I conceive to be βάπτισμα πυρὸς, 'the baptism of fire.'

Lastly, in a diary for that year, kept with fair regularity up till November 8, there here intervenes a long blank, the only entry being November 9: 'Salvum me fac, Dñe.'

I took the trouble, incidentally, to hunt up the files of a Cambridge journal of that date, to see if I could link it on to any event, and I found there recorded, in the course of that week, what I at first imagined to be the explanation of the incidents, and I own I was a good deal surprised.

I found recorded some Revivalist Mission Services, which were then held in Cambridge with great success. I at once concluded that he underwent some remarkable spiritual experience, some religious fright, some so-called conversion, the effects of which only gradually disappeared. The contagion of a Revivalist meeting is a very mysterious thing. Like a man going to a mesmerist, an individual may go, announcing his firm intention not to be influenced in the smallest degree by anything said or done. Nay more, he may think himself, and have the reputation of being, a strong, unyielding character, and yet these are the very men who are often most hopelessly mesmerized, the very men whom the Revival most absolutely – for the occasion – enslaves. And thus, knowing that one could form no *prima facie* judgements on the probabilities in such a matter, I came to the conclusion that he had fallen, in some degree, under the influence of these meetings.

But in revising this book, and carefully recalling my own and studying others' impressions, I came to the conclusion that it was impossible that this should be the case.

1   In the first place, he was more free than any man I ever saw from the influence of contagious emotions; he dissembled his own emotions, and contemned the public display of them in other people.

2   He had, I remember, a strange repugnance, even abhorrence, to public meetings in the later days at Cambridge. I can now recall that he would accompany people to the door, but never be induced to enter. A passage which I will quote from one of his letters illustrates this.

'The presence of a large number of people has a strange, repulsive physical effect on me. I feel crushed and overwhelmed, not stimulated and vivified, as is so often described. I can't listen to a concert comfortably if there is a great throng, unless the music is so good as to wrap one altogether away. There is undoubtedly a force abroad among large masses of people, the force which forms the basis of the principle of public prayer, and I am conscious of it too, only it distresses me; moreover, the worst and most afflicting nightmare I have is the sensation of standing sightless and motionless, but with all the other senses alert and apprehensive, in the presence of a vast and hostile crowd.'

3   He never showed the least sign of being influenced in the direction of spiritual or even religious life by this crisis. He certainly spoke very little at all for some time to any one on any subject; he was distrait and absent-minded in society – for the alteration was much observed from its suddenness – but when he gradually began to converse as usual, he did not, as is so often the case in similar circumstances, do what is called 'bearing witness to the truth.' His attitude towards all enthusiastic forms of religion had been one, in old days, of good-natured, even amused tolerance. He was now not so good-natured in his criticisms, and less sparing of them, though his religious-mindedness, his seriousness, was undoubtedly increased by the experience, whatever it was.

On the whole, then, I should say that the coincidence of the revival is merely fortuitous. It remains to seek what the cause was.

We must look for it, in a character so dignified as Arthur's, in some worthy cause, some emotional failure, some moral wound. I believe the following to be the clue; I cannot develop it without treading some rather delicate ground.

He had formed, in his last year at school, a very devoted friendship with a younger boy; such friendships like the εἰσπνήλας and the ἀϊτάς of Sparta, when they are truly chivalrous and absolutely pure, are above all other loves, noble, refining, true; passion at white heat without taint, confidence of so intimate a kind as cannot even exist between husband and wife, trust such as cannot be shadowed, are its characteristics. I speak from my own experience, and others will, I know, at heart confirm me, when I say that these things are infinitely rewarding, unutterably dear.

Arthur left Winchester. A correspondence ensued between the two friends. I have three letters of Arthur's, so passionate in expression that for fear of even causing uneasiness, not to speak of suspicion, I will not quote them. I have seen, though I have destroyed, at request, the letters of the other.

This friend, a weak, but singularly attractive boy, got into a bad set at Winchester, and came to grief in more than one way; he came to

Cambridge in three years, and fell in with a thoroughly bad set there. Arthur seems not to have suspected it at first, and to have delighted in his friend's society; but such things as habits betray themselves, and my belief is that disclosures were made on November 8, which revealed to Arthur the state of the case. What passed I cannot say. I can hardly picture to myself the agony, disgust, and rage (his words and feelings about sensuality of any kind were strangely keen and bitter), loyalty fighting with the sense of repulsion, pity struggling with honour, which must have convulsed him when he discovered that his friend was not only yielding, but deliberately impure.

The other's was an unworthy and brutal nature, utterly corrupted at bottom. He used to speak jestingly of the occurrence. 'Oh yes!' I have heard him say; 'we were great friends once, but he cuts me now; he had to give me up, you see, because he didn't approve of me. Justice, mercy, and truth, and all the rest of it.'

It was certainly true; their friendship ended. I find it hard to realize that Arthur would voluntarily have abandoned him; and yet I find passages in his letters, and occasional entries in his diaries, which seem to point to some great stress put upon him, some enormous burden indicated, which he had not strength to attempt and adopt. 'May God forgive me for my unutterable selfishness; it is irreparable now,' is one of the latest entries on that day in his diary. I conceive, perhaps, that his outraged ideal was too strong for his power of forgiveness. He was very fastidious, always.

How deep the blow cut will be shown by these following extracts:
'I once had my faith in human nature rudely wrecked, and it has never attempted a long voyage again. I hug the coast and look regretfully out to sea; perhaps the day may come when I may strike into it . . . believe in it always if you can; I do not say it is vanity . . . the shock blinded me: I cannot see if I would.'

And again –
'Moral wounds never heal; they may be torn open by a chance word, by a fragment of print, by a sentence from a letter; and there we have to sit with pale face and shuddering heart, to bleed in silence and dissemble it. Then, too, there is that constant dismal feeling which the Greeks called ὕπουλος the horrible conviction, the grim memory lurking deep down, perhaps almost out of sight, thrust away by circumstance and action, but always ready to rise noiselessly up and draw you to itself.'

' "A good life, and therefore a happy one," says my old aunt, writing to me this morning; it is marvellous and yet sustaining what one can pass through, and yet those about you – those who suppose that they have the key, if any, to your heart – be absolutely ignorant of it. "He looks a little tired and worn: he has been sitting up late;" "all young men are melancholy: leave him alone and he will be better in a year or two," was all that was said when I was actually meditating suicide – when I believe I was on the brink of insanity.'

All these extracts are from letters to myself at different periods. Taking them together, and thus arranged, my case seems irresistible; still I must concede that it is all theory – all inference: I do not wholly know the facts, and never shall.

35   'Muscovy'

Charles Edward Sayle. From *Erotion*, 1889. Written 1884–8.

> In Muscovy when a corpse they bury
>   And round in a group the mourners stand,
> Instead of an obol for Charon's ferry
>   They place a Script in the dead man's hand:
>
> 'To Holy Nicholas, Saint of God. –
>   Here is a man who loved you well
> When on the earth with us he trod.
>   Save him now from the Gates of Hell.'
>
> If, when I die, I have still bewailers,
>   While over me swings the cresset-glass,
> Open this book where these letters stand
> And write again in a bold, round hand: –
> 'He loved boys and thieves and sailors,
>   Servant of Thine, St. Nicholas!'

36   'Amor Redux'

Charles Edward Sayle. From *Erotion*, 1889. Written 1888.

> Dead Love, new born, nor born to die again
> Or, dying, nevermore to cherish pain; –
> Nay, dying not, though Time past come again.
>
> Fast asleep, new waked, nor waked again in sleep,
> Or, sleeping, nevermore sad dreams to keep;
> Yea, sleeping now, sacring eternal sleep.

Fling roses, roses down before Love's feet. –
'After long years I shall be with you, sweet,' –
As when we kissed, O Love, God's shining feet.

37   The Deemster

Sir Henry Hall Caine. From *The Deemster*, 1887. The first extract is from the
chapter entitled 'Passing the Love of Women', the second from that entitled
'Blind Passion and Pain'.

Now the facts of this history must stride on some six years, and in that
time the Deemster had lost nearly all the little interest he ever felt in
his children. Mona had budded into womanhood, tender, gracious,
quiet, a tall, fair-haired maiden of twenty, with a drooping head like a
flower, with a voice soft and low, and the full blue eyes with their depths
of love and sympathy shaded by long fluttering lashes as the trembling
sedge shades the deep mountain pool. It was as ripe and beautiful a
womanhood as the heart of a father might dream of, but the Deemster
could take little pleasure in it. If Mona had been his son, her quiet ways
and tractable nature might have counted for something; but a woman
was only a woman in the Deemster's eyes, and the Deemster, like the
Bedouin chief, would have numbered his children without counting
his daughter. As for Ewan, he had falsified every hope of the Deemster.
His Spartan training had gone for nothing. He was physically a weak-
ling; a tall, spare youth of two and twenty, fair-haired like his sister,
with a face as spiritual and beautiful, and hardly less feminine. He was
of a self-torturing spirit, constantly troubled with vague questionings,
and though in this regard he was very much his father's son, the
Deemster held his temperament in contempt.

The end of all was that Ewan showed a strong desire to enter the
Church. The Deemster had intended that his son should study the law
and follow him in his place when his time came. But Ewan's womanly
temperament co-existed with a manly temper. Into the law he would
not go, and the Church he was resolved to follow. The Bishop had then
newly opened at Bishop's Court a training college for his clergy, and
Ewan sought and obtained admission. The Deemster fumed, but his
son was not to be moved even by his wrath. This was when Ewan was
nineteen years of age, and after two more years the spirituality of his
character overcame the obstacle of his youth, and the Bishop ordained
him at twenty-one. Then Ewan was made chaplain to the household at
Bishop's Court.

Hardly had this been done when Ewan took another step in life. With the knowledge of the Bishop, but without consulting the Deemster, he married, being now of age, a pretty child of sixteen, the daughter of his father's old foe, the vicar of the parish. When knowledge of this act of unwisdom reached the Deemster his last remaining spark of interest in his son expired, and he sent Mona across to Bishop's Court with a curt message saying that Ewan and his wife were at liberty, if they liked, to take possession of the old Ballamona. Thus he turned his back upon his son, and did his best to wipe him out of his mind.

Ewan took his young wife to the homestead that had been the place of his people for six generations, the place where he himself had been born, the place where that other Ewan, his good grandfather, had lived and died.

More than ever for these events the Deemster became a solitary man. He kept no company; he took no pleasures. Alone he sat night after night in his study at Ballamona, and Ballamona was asleep before he slept, and before it awoke he was stirring. His daughter's presence in the house was no society for the Deemster. She grew beside him like her mother's youth, a yet fairer vision of the old days coming back to him hour by hour, but he saw nothing of all that. Disappointed in his sole hope, his son, whom truly he had never loved for love's sake, but only for his own sorry ambitions, he sat down under his disappointment a doubly-soured and thrice-hardened man. He had grown noticeably older, but his restless energy suffered no abatement. Bi-weekly he kept his courts, but few sought the law whom the law did not first find, for word went round that the Deemster was a hard judge, and deemed the laws in rigour. If men differed about money, they would say, 'Och, why go to the Deemster? It's throwing a bone into the bad dog's mouth,' and then they would divide their difference.

The one remaining joy of the Deemster's lonely life was centred in his brother's son, Dan. That lusty youth had not disappointed his expectations. At twenty he was a braw, brown-haired, brown-eyed lad of six feet two inches in stature, straight and upright, and with the thews and sinews of an ox. He was the athlete of the island, and where there was a tough job of wrestling to be had, or a delightful bit of fighting to be done, there was Dan in the heart of it. 'Aw, and middling few could come anigh him,' the people used to say. But more than in Dan's great stature and great strength the little Deemster took a bitter pleasure in his daring irreverence for things held sacred. In this regard Dan had not improved with improving years. Scores of tricks his sad pugnacity devised to help the farmers to cheat the parson of his tithe, and it added not a little to the Deemster's keen relish of freaks like these that it was none other than the son of the Bishop who perpetrated them. As for the Bishop himself, he tried to shut his eyes to such follies. He meant his son to go into the Church, and, in spite of all outbursts of spirits, notwithstanding wrestling matches and fights, and even some tipsy broils of which rumour was in the air, he entered Dan as a student at the college he kept at Bishop's Court.

In due course the time of Dan's examination came, and then all further clinging to a forlorn hope was at an end. The Archdeacon acted as the Bishop's examining chaplain, and more than once the little man had declared in advance his conscientious intention of dealing with the Bishop's son as he would deal with any other. The examination took place in the library of Bishop's Court, and besides the students and the examiner there were some six or seven of the clergy present, and Ewan Mylrea, then newly ordained, was among them. It was a purely oral examination, and when Dan's turn came the Archdeacon assumed his loftiest look, and first tackled the candidate where he was known to be weakest.

'I suppose, sir, you think you can read your Greek Testament?'

Dan answered that he had never thought anything about it.

'I dare say for all your modesty that you have an idea that you know it well enough to teach it,' said the Archdeacon.

Dan hadn't an idea on the subject.

'Take down the Greek Testament, and imagine that I'm your pupil, and proceed to expound it,' said the Archdeacon.

Dan took the book from the bookcase and fumbled it in his fingers.

'Well, sir, open at the parable of the tares.'

Dan scratched his big head leisurely, and he did his best to find the place. 'So I'm to be tutor – is that it?' he said, with a puzzled look.

'That is so.'

'And you are to be the pupil?'

'Precisely – suppose yourself my tutor – and now begin.'

At this Ewan stepped out with a look of anxiety. 'Is not that a rather difficult supposition, Archdeacon?' he said timidly.

The Archdeacon glanced over his grandson loftily and made no reply.

'Begin, sir, begin,' he said, with a sweep of his hand towards Dan, and at that he sat down in the high-backed oak chair at the head of the table.

Then on the instant there came into Dan's quick eyes a most mischievous twinkle. He was standing before the table with the Greek Testament open at the parable of the tares, and he knew too well he could not read the parable.

'When do we change places, Archdeacon?' he asked.

'We have changed places – you are now the tutor – I am your pupil – begin, sir.'

'Oh! we have changed places, have we?' said Dan, and at that he lifted up the Archdeacon's silver-tipped walking cane which lay on the table and brought it down again with a bang. 'Then just you get up off your chair, sir,' he said with a tone of command.

The Archdeacon's russet face showed several tints of blue at that moment, but he rose to his feet. Thereupon Dan handed him the open book.

'Now, sir,' he said, 'first read me the parable of the tares.'

The clergy began to shuffle about and look into each other's faces. The Archdeacon's expression was not amiable, but he took the book and read the parable.

'Very fair, very fair indeed,' said Dan in a tone of mild condescension – 'a few false quantities, but very fair on the whole.'

'Gentlemen, gentlemen, this is going too far,' said one of the clergy.

'Silence, sir,' said Dan, with a look of outraged authority.

Then there was dire confusion. Some of the clergy laughed outright, and some giggled under their breath, and some protested in white wrath, and the end of it all was that the examination came to a sudden termination, and, rightly or wrongly, wisely or foolishly, Dan was adjudged to be unfit for the ministry of the Church.

When the Bishop heard the verdict his pale face whitened visibly, and he seemed to see the beginning of the end. At that moment he thought of the Deemster with bitterness. This blow to his hopes did not cement the severed lives of the brothers. The forces that had been dividing them year by year since the days of their father appeared to be drawing them yet wider apart in the lives and fortunes of their children. Each felt that the other was frustrating his dearest expectations in his son, and that was an offence that neither could forgive. To the Deemster it seemed that the Bishop was bearing down every ambition of his life, tearing him up as a naked trunk, leaving him a childless man. To the Bishop it seemed that the Deemster was wrecking the one life that was more to him than his own soul, and standing between him and the heart that with all its follies was dearer than the world beside. From this time of Ewan's marriage and Dan's disgrace the Bishop and the Deemster rarely met, and when they passed on the road they exchanged only the coldest salutation.

But if the fates were now more than ever fostering an unnatural enmity between the sons of old Ewan, they were cherishing at the same time the loves of their children. Never were cousins more unlike or more fondly attached. Between Dan, the reckless scapegrace, and

Mona, with the big soft eyes and the quiet ways, the affection was such as neither understood. They had grown up side by side, they had seen each other daily, they had scampered along the shore with clasped hands, they had screamed at the seagulls with one voice, and still they were boy and girl together. But once they were stooking the barley in the glebe, and, the day being hot, Mona tipped back her white sun bonnet, and it fell on to her shoulders. Seeing this, Dan came stealthily behind and thought very craftily to whisk it away unobserved; but the strings by which it was tied caught in her hair and tugged at its knot, and the beautiful wavy shower fell rip-rip-rippling down her back. The wind caught the loosened hair and tossed it about her, and she stood up erect among the corn with the first blush on her cheeks that Dan had ever brought there, and turned full upon him all the glorious light of her deep blue eyes. Then, then, oh then, Dan seemed to see her for the first time a girl no longer, but a woman, a woman, a woman! And the mountains behind her were in one instant blotted out of Dan's eyes, and everything seemed to spin about him. When next he knew where he was, and what he was doing, behold there were Mona's rosy lips under his, and she was panting and gasping for breath.

But if the love of Dan and Mona was more than cousinly, though they knew it not as yet, the love of Ewan for Dan was wonderful and passing the love of women. That pure soul, with its vague spiritual yearnings, seemed to have nothing in common with the jovial roysterer, always fighting, always laughing, taking disgrace as a duck takes water, and losing the trace of it as easily. Twenty times he stood between the scapegrace and the Bishop, twenty times he hid from the good father the follies of the son. He thought for that thoughtless head that never had an ache or a care under its abundant curls; he hoped for that light heart that hoped for nothing; he trembled for the soul that felt no fear. Never was such loyalty between man and man since David wept for Jonathan. And Ewan's marriage disturbed this affection not at all, for the love he bore to Dan was a brotherly passion for which language has yet no name.

Let us tell one story that shall show this friendship in its double bearings – Ewan's love and temper and Dan's heedless harshness and the great nature beneath it, and then we will pass on with fuller knowledge to weightier matters.

Derry, the white-eyed collie that had nestled on the top of his master's bed the night Dan sneaked home in disgrace from the Oiel Verree, was a crafty little fox, with cunning and duplicity bred in his very bones. If you were a tramp of the profession of Billy the Gawk, he would look up at you with his big innocent eyes, and lick your hand, and thrust his nose into your palm, and the next moment he would seize you by the hindmost parts and hold on like a leech. His unamiable qualities grew as he grew in years, and one day Dan went on a long journey, leaving Derry behind, and when he returned he had another dog with him, a great shaggy Scotch collie, with bright eyes, a happy phiz, and a huge bush of a tail. Derry was at the gate when his master came home, and he eyed the newcomer with looks askance. From that day Derry turned his back on his master, he would never answer his call, and he did not know his whistle from the croak of a corn-crake. In fact, Derry took his own courses, and forthwith fell into all manner of dissolute habits. He went out at nights alone, incognito, and kept most un-christian hours. The farmers around complained that their sheep were found dead in the field, torn and worried by a dog's teeth. Derry was known to be a dog that did not live a reputable life, and suspicion fell on him. Dan took the old fox in hand, and thenceforward Derry looked out on the world through a rope muzzle.

One day there was to be a sheep-dog match, and Dan entered his Scotch collie, Laddie. The race was to be in the meadow at the foot of Slieu Dhoo, and great crowds of people came to witness it. Hurdles were set up to make all crooks and cranks of difficulty, and then a drift of sheep were turned loose in the field. The prize was to the dog that would, at the word of its master, gather the sheep together and take them out at the gate in the shortest time. Ewan, then newly married, was there, and beside him was his child-wife. Time was called, and Dan's turn came to try the mettle of his Laddie. The dog started well, and in two or three minutes he had driven the whole flock save two into an alcove of hurdles close to where Ewan and his wife stood together. Then at the word of his master Laddie set off over the field for the stragglers, and Dan shouted to Ewan not to stir a hand or foot or the sheep would be scattered again. Now just at that instant who should pop over the edge but Derry in his muzzle, and quick as thought he shot down his head, put up his paws, threw off his muzzle, dashed at the sheep, snapped at their legs, and away they went in twenty directions.

Before Ewan had time to cry out Derry was gone, with his muzzle between his teeth. When Dan, who was a perch or two up the meadow, turned round and saw what had happened, and that his dog's chances were gone, his anger overcame him, and he turned on Ewan with a torrent of reproaches.

'There – you've done it with your lumbering – curse it.'

With complete self-possession Ewan explained how Derry had done the mischief.

Then Dan's face was darker with wrath than it had ever been before.

'A pretty tale,' he said, and his lip curled in a sneer. He turned to the people around. 'Anybody see the dog slip his muzzle?'

None had seen what Ewan affirmed. The eyes of everyone had been on the two stragglers in the distance pursued by Dan and Laddie.

Now when Ewan saw that Dan distrusted him, and appealed to strangers as witness to his word, his face flushed deep, and his delicate nostrils quivered.

'A pretty tale,' Dan repeated, and he was twisting on his heel when up came Derry again, his muzzle on his snout, whisking his tail, and frisking about Dan's feet with an expression of quite lamb-like simplicity.

At that sight Ewan's livid face turned to a great pallor, and Dan broke into a hard laugh.

'We've heard of a dog slipping his muzzle,' he said, 'but who ever heard of a dog putting a muzzle on again?'

Then Ewan stepped from the side of his girl-wife, who stood there with heaving breast. His eyes were aflame, but for an instant he conquered his emotion, and said, with a constrained quietness, but with a deep pathos in his tone, 'Dan, do you think I've told you the truth?'

Dan wheeled about. 'I think you've told me a lie,' he said, and his voice came thick from his throat.

All heard the word, and all held their breath. Ewan stood a moment, as if rooted to the spot, and his pallid face whitened every instant. Then he fell back, and took the girl-wife by the hand and turned away with her, his head down, his very heart surging itself out of his choking breast. And, as he passed through the throng, to carry away from that scene the madness that was working in his brain, he overheard the mocking comments of the people. 'Aw, well, well, did ye hear that now? – called him a liar, and not a word to say agen it.' 'A liar! Och, a liar? and him a parzon, too!' 'Middling chicken-hearted anyways – a liar! Aw, well, well, well!'

At that Ewan flung away the hand of his wife, and, quivering from head to foot, he strode towards Dan.

'You've called me a liar,' he said in a shrill voice that was like a cry. 'Now, you shall prove your word – you shall fight me – you shall, by God.'

He was completely carried away by passion.

'The parzon, the parzon!' 'Man alive, the young parzon!' the people muttered, and they closed around.

Dan stood a moment. He looked down from his great height at Ewan's quivering form and distorted face. Then he turned about and glanced into the faces of the people. In another instant his eyes were swimming in tears; he took a step towards Ewan, flung his arms about him, and buried his head in his neck, and the great stalwart lad wept like a little child. In another moment Ewan's passion was melted away, and he kissed Dan on the cheek.

'Blubbering cowards!' 'Aw, blather-skites!' 'Och, man alive, a pair of turtle-doves!'

Dan lifted his head, and looked around, raised himself to his full height, clenched his fists, and said:

'Now, my lads, you did your best to make a fight, and you couldn't manage it. I won't fight my cousin, and he shan't fight me; but if there's a man among you would like to know for himself how much of a coward I am, let him step out – I'm ready.'

Not a man budged an inch.

Dan moved uneasily, and presently awoke, opened his eyes, and saw Ewan, and betrayed no surprise at his presence there.

'Ah! Is it you, Ewan?' he said, speaking quietly, partly in a shame-faced way, and with some confusion. 'Do you know, I've been dreaming of you – you and Mona?'

Ewan gave no answer. Because sleep is a holy thing, and the brother of death, whose shadow also it is, therefore Ewan's hideous purpose had left him while Dan lay asleep at his feet; but now that Dan was awake, the evil passion came again.

'I was dreaming of that Mother Carey's chicken – you remember it? when we were lumps of lads, you know – why, you can't have forgotten it – the old thing I caught in its nest just under the Head?'

Still Ewan gave no sign, but looked down at Dan resting on his elbows. Dan's eyes fell from Ewan's face, but he went on in a confused way.

'Mona couldn't bear to see it caged, and would have me put it back. Don't you remember I clambered up to the nest, and put the bird in again? You were down on the shore, thinking sure I would tumble over the Head, and Mona – Mona – '

Dan glanced afresh into Ewan's face, and its look of terror seemed to stupefy him; still he made shift to go on with his dream in an abashed sort of way.

'My gough! if I didn't dream it all as fresh as fresh, and the fight in the air, and the screams when I put the old bird in the nest – the young ones had forgotten it clean, and they tumbled it out, and set on it terrible, and drove it away – and then the poor old thing on the rocks sitting by itself as lonesome as lonesome – and little Mona crying and crying down below, and her long hair rip-rip-rippling in the wind, and – and – '

Dan had got to his feet, and then seated himself on a stool as he rambled on with the story of his dream. But once again his shifty eyes came back to Ewan's face, and he stopped short.

'My God, what is it?' he cried.

Now Ewan, standing there with a thousand vague forms floating in his brain, had heard little of what Dan had said, but he had noted his confused manner, and had taken this story of the dream as a feeble device to hide the momentary discomfiture.

'What does it mean?' he said. 'It means that this island is not large enough to hold both you and me.'

'What?'

'It means that you must go away.'

'Away!'

'Yes – and at once.'

In the pause that followed after his first cry of amazement, Dan thought only of the bad business of the killing of the oxen at the ploughing match that morning, and so in a tone of utter abasement, with his face to the ground, he went on; in a blundering, humble way, to allow that Ewan had reason for his anger.

'I'm a blind headstrong fool, I know that – and my temper is – well, its damnable, that's the fact – but no one suffers from it more than I do, and if I could have felled myself after I had felled the oxen, why down. . . . Ewan, for the sake of the dear old times when we were good chums, you and I and little Mona, with her quiet eyes, God bless her! – '

'Go away, and never come back to either of us,' cried Ewan, stamping his foot.

Dan paused, and there was a painful silence.

'Why should I go away?' he said, with an effort at quietness.

'Because you are a scoundrel – the basest scoundrel on God's earth – the foulest traitor – the blackest-hearted monster – '

Dan's sunburnt face whitened under his tawny skin.

'Easy, easy, man veen, easy,' he said, struggling visibly for self-command while he interrupted Ewan's torrent of reproaches.

'You are a disgrace and a by-word. Only the riff-raff of the island are your friends and associates.'

'That's true enough, Ewan,' said Dan, and his head fell between his hands, his elbows resting on his knees.

'What are you doing? Drinking, gambling, roystering, cheating – yes – '

Dan got on his feet uneasily and took a step to and fro about the little place; then sat again, and buried his head in his hands as before.

'I've been a reckless, self-willed, mad fool, Ewan, but no worse than that. And if you could see me as God sees me, and know how I suffer for my follies and curse them, for all I seem to make so light of them, and how I am driven to them one on the head of another, perhaps – perhaps – perhaps you would have pity – ay, pity.'

'Pity? Pity for you? You who have brought your father to shame? He is the ruin of the man he was. You have impoverished him; you have spent his substance and wasted it. Ay, and you have made his grey head a mark for reproach. "Set your own house in order" – that's what the world says to the man of God, whose son is a child of the – '

'Stop,' cried Dan.

He had leapt to his feet, his fist clenched, his knuckles showing like nuts of steel.

But Ewan went on, standing there with a face that was ashy white above his black coat. 'Your heart is as dead as your honour. And that is not all, but you must outrage the honour of another.'

Now, when Ewan said this, Dan thought of his forged signature, and of the censure and suspension to which Ewan was thereby made liable.

'Go away,' Ewan cried again, motioning Dan off with his trembling hand.

Dan lifted his eyes. 'And what if I refuse?' he said in a resolute way.

'Then take the consequences.'

'You mean the consequences of that – that – that forgery?'

At this Ewan realized the thought in Dan's mind, and perceived that Dan conceived him capable of playing upon his fears by holding over his head the penalty of an offence which he had already taken upon himself. 'God in heaven!' he thought, 'and this is the pitiful creature whom I have all these years taken to my heart.'

'Is that what your loyalty comes to?' said Dan, and his lip curled.

'Loyalty,' cried Ewan, in white wrath. 'Loyalty, and you talk to me of loyalty – you who have outraged the honour of my sister – '

'Mona!'

'I have said it at last, though the word blisters my tongue. Go away from the island for ever, and let me never see your face again.'

Dan rose to his feet with rigid limbs. He looked about him for a moment in a dazed silence, and put his hand to his forehead as if he had lost himself.

'Do you believe *that*?' he said in a slow whisper.

'Don't deny it – don't let me know you for a liar as well,' Ewan said eagerly; and then added in another tone, 'I have had her own confession.'

'Her confession!'

'Yes, and the witness of another.'

'The witness of another!'

Dan echoed Ewan's words in a vague, half-conscious way.

Then, in a torrent of hot words that seemed to blister and sting the man who spoke them no less than the man who heard them, Ewan told all, and Dan listened like one in a stupor.

There was silence, and then Ewan spoke again in a tone of agony. 'Dan, there was a time when in spite of yourself I loved you – yes, though I'm ashamed to say it, for it was against God's own leading; still I loved you, Dan. But let us part for ever now, and each go his own way, and perhaps, though we can never forget the wrong that you have done us, we may yet think more kindly of you, and time may help us to forgive – '

But Dan had awakened from his stupor, and he flung aside.

'Damn your forgiveness!' he said hotly, and then, with teeth set and lips drawn hard and eyes aflame, he turned upon Ewan and strode up to him, and they stood together face to face.

'You said just now that there was not room enough in the island for you and me,' he said in a hushed whisper. 'You were right, but I shall mend your words: if you believe what you have said – by Heaven, I'll not deny it for you! – there is not room enough for both of us in the world.'

'It was my own thought,' said Ewan, and then for an instant each looked into the other's eyes and read the other's purpose.

The horror of that moment of silence was broken by the lifting of the latch. Davy Fayle came shambling into the tent on some pretended errand. He took off his militia belt with the dagger in the sheath attached to it, and hung it on a long rusty nail driven into an upright timber at one corner. Then he picked up from among some ling on the floor a waterproof coat and put it on. He was going out, with furtive glances at Dan and Ewan, who said not a word in his presence, and were bearing themselves towards each other with a painful constraint, when his glance fell on the hatchet which lay a few feet from the door. Davy picked it up and carried it out, muttering to himself, 'Strange, strange, uncommon!'

Hardly had the boy dropped the latch of the door from without than Ewan took the militia belt from the nail and buckled it about his waist. Dan understood his thought; he was still wearing his own militia belt and dagger. There was now not an instant's paltering between them – not a word of explanation.

'We must get rid of the lad,' said Dan.

Ewan bowed his head. It had come to him to reflect that when all was over Mona might hear of what had been done. What they had to do was to be done for her honour, or for what seemed to be her honour in that blind tangle of passion and circumstance. But none the less, though she loved both of them now, would she loathe that one who returned to her with the blood of the other upon him.

'She must never know,' he said. 'Send the boy away. Then we must go to where this work can be done between you and me alone.'

Dan had followed his thought in silence, and was stepping towards the door to call to Davy when the lad came back, carrying a log of driftwood for the fire. There were some small flakes of snow on his waterproof coat.

'Go up to the shambles, Davy,' said Dan, speaking with an effort at composure, 'and tell Jemmy Curghey to keep me the ox-horns.'

Davy looked up in a vacant way, and his lip lagged low. 'Aw, and didn't you tell Jemmy yourself, and terrible partic'lar, too?'

'Do you say so, Davy?'

'Sarten sure.'

'Then just slip away and fetch them.'

Davy fixed the log on the fire, tapped it into the flame, glanced anxiously at Dan and Ewan, and then in a lingering way went out. His simple face looked sad under its vacant expression.

The men listened while the lad's footsteps could be heard on the shingle, above the deep murmur of the sea. Then Dan stepped to the door and threw it open.

'Now,' he said.

It was rapidly growing dark. The wind blew strongly into the shed. Dan stepped out, and Ewan followed him.

They walked in silence through the gully that led from the creek to the cliff head. The snow that had begun to fall was swirled about in the wind that came from over the sea, and, spinning in the air, it sometimes beat against their faces.

Ewan went along like a man condemned to death. He had begun to doubt, though he did not know it, and would have shut his mind to the idea if it had occurred to him. But once when Dan seemed to stop as if only half resolved, and partly turn his face towards him, Ewan mistook his intention. 'He is going to tell me that there is some hideous error,' he thought. He was burning for that word. But no, Dan went plodding on again, and never after shifted his steadfast gaze, never spoke, and gave no sign. At length he stopped, and Ewan stopped with him. They were standing on the summit of Orris Head.

It was a sad, a lonesome, and a desolate place, in sight of a wide waste of common land, without a house, and with never a tree rising above the purple gorse and tussocks of long grass. The sky hung very low over it; the steep red cliffs, with their patches of green in ledges, swept down from it to the shingle and the sharp shelves of slate covered with sea-weed. The ground swell came up from below with a very mournful noise, but the air seemed to be empty, and every beat of the foot on the soft turf sounded near and large. Above their heads the sea-fowl kept up a wild clamour, and far out, where sea and sky seemed to meet in the gathering darkness, the sea's steady blow on the bare rocks of the naze sent up a deep, hoarse boom.

Dan unbuckled his belt, and threw off his coat and vest. Ewan did the same, and they stood there face to face in the thin flakes of snow, Dan in his red shirt, Ewan in his white shirt open at the neck, these two men whose souls had been knit together as the soul of Jonathan was knit to the soul of David, and each ready to lift his hand against his heart's best brother. Then all at once a startled cry came from near at hand.

It was Davy Fayle's voice. The lad had not gone to the shambles. Realizing in some vague way that the errand was a subterfuge and that mischief was about, he had hidden himself at a little distance, and had seen when Dan and Ewan came out of the tent together. Creeping through the ling, and partly hidden by the dusk, he had followed the men until they had stopped on the Head. Then Davy had dropped to his knees. His ideas were obscure, he scarcely knew what was going on before his eyes, but he held his breath and watched and listened. At length, when the men threw off their clothes, the truth dawned on Davy; and though he tried to smother an exclamation, a cry of terror burst from his husky throat.

Dan and Ewan exchanged glances, and each seemed in one moment to read the other's thoughts. In another instant, at three quick strides, Dan had taken Davy by the shoulders.

'Promise,' he said, 'that you will never tell what you have seen.'

Davy struggled to free himself, but his frantic efforts were useless. In Dan's grip he was held as in a vice.

'Let me go, Mastha Dan,' the lad cried.

'Promise to hold your tongue,' said Dan; 'promise it, promise it.'

'Let me go, will you? let me go,' the lad shouted sullenly.

'Be quiet,' said Dan.

'I won't be quiet,' was the stubborn answer.' 'Help! help! help!' and the lad screamed lustily.

'Hold your tongue, or by G—'

Dan held Davy by one of his great hands hitched into the lad's guernsey, and he lifted the other hand threateningly.

'Help! help! help!' Davy screamed still louder, and struggled yet more fiercely, until his strength was spent, and his breath was gone, and then there was a moment's silence.

The desolate place was still as desolate as before. Not a sign of life around; not an answering cry.

'There's nobody to help you,' said Dan. 'You have got to promise never to tell what you have seen to man, woman, or child.'

'I won't promise, and I won't hould my tongue,' said the lad stoutly. 'You are goin' to fight, you and Mastha Ewan, and – '

Dan stopped him. 'Hearken here. If you are to live another hour you will promise – '

But Davy had regained both strength and voice.

'I don't care – help! help! help!' he shouted.

Dan put his hand over the lad's mouth, and dragged him to the cliff head. Below was the brant steep, dark and jagged and quivering in the deepening gloom, and the sea-birds were darting through the mid air like bats in the dark.

'Look,' said Dan, 'you've got to swear never to tell what you have seen to-night, so help you God.'

The lad, held tightly by the breast and throat, and gripping the arms that held him with fingers that clung like claws, took one horrified glance down into the darkness. He struggled no longer. His face was very pitiful to see.

'I cannot promise,' he said in a voice like a cry.

At that answer Dan drew Davy back from the cliff edge, and loosed his hold of him. He was abashed and ashamed. He felt himself a little man by the side of this half-daft fisher-lad.

All this time Ewan had stood aside looking on while Dan demanded the promise, and saying nothing. Now he went up to Davy, and said in a quiet voice:

'Davy, if you should ever tell anyone what you have seen, Dan will be a lost man all his life hereafter.'

'Then let him pitch me over the cliff,' said Davy in a smothered cry.

'Listen to me, Davy,' Ewan went on; 'you're a brave lad, and I know what's in your head, but – '

'Then what for do you want to fight him?' Davy broke out. The lad's throat was dry and husky, and his eyes were growing dim.

Ewan paused. Half his passion was spent. Davy's poor dense head had found him a question that he could not answer.

'Davy, if you don't promise, you will ruin Dan – yes, it will be you who will ruin him, you, remember that. He will be a lost man, and my sister, my good sister Mona, she will be a broken-hearted woman.'

Then Davy broke down utterly, and big tears filled his eyes, and ran down his cheeks

'I promise,' he sobbed

'Good lad – now go.'

Davy turned about, and went away, at first running, and then dragging slowly, then running again, and then again lingering.

What followed was a very pitiful conflict of emotion. Nature, who looks down pitilessly on man and his big, little passions, that clamour so loud but never touch her at all – even Nature played her part in this tragedy.

When Davy Fayle was gone, Dan and Ewan stood face to face as before, Dan with his back to the cliff, Ewan with his face to the sea. Then, without a word, each turned aside and picked up his militia belt.

The snowflakes had thickened during the last few moments, but now they seemed to cease and the sky to lighten. Suddenly in the west the sky was cloven as though by the sweep of a sword, and under a black bar of cloud and above a silvered water-line the sun came through very red and hazy in its setting, and with its ragged streamers around it.

Ewan was buckling the belt about his waist when the setting sun rose upon them, and all at once there came to him the Scripture that says, 'Let not the sun go down on your wrath.' If God's hand had appeared in the heavens, the effect on Ewan could not have been greater. Already his passion was more than half gone, and now it melted entirely away.

'Dan,' he cried, and his voice was a sob, 'Dan, I cannot fight – right or wrong I cannot,' and he flung himself down, and the tears filled his eyes.

Then Dan, whose face was afire, laughed loud and bitterly. 'Coward,' he cried, 'coward and poltroon!'

At that word all the evil passion came back to Ewan and he leapt to his feet.

'That is enough,' he said; 'the belts – buckle them together.'

Dan understood Ewan's purpose. At the next breath the belt about Dan's waist was buckled to the belt about the waist of Ewan, and the two men stood strapped together. Then they drew the daggers, and an awful struggle followed.

With breast to breast until their flesh all but touched, and with thighs entwined, they reeled and swayed, the right hand of each held up for thrust, the left for guard and parry. What Dan gained in strength Ewan made up in rage, and the fight was fierce and terrible. Dan still with his back to the cliff, Ewan still with his face to the sea.

At one instant Dan, by his great stature, had reached over Ewan's shoulder to thrust from behind, and at the next instant Ewan had wrenched his lithe body backwards and had taken the blow in his lifted arm, which forthwith spouted blood above the wrist. In that encounter they reeled about, changing places, and Ewan's back was henceforward towards the cliff, and Dan fought with his face towards the sea.

It was a hideous and savage fight. The sun had gone down, the cleft in the heavens had closed again, once more the thin flakes of snow were falling, and the world had dropped back to its dark mood. A stormy petrel came up from the cliff and swirled above the men as they fought and made its direful scream over them.

Up and down, to and fro, embracing closely, clutching, guarding, and meantime panting hoarsely, and drawing hard breath, the two men fought in their deadly hate. At last they had backed and swayed to within three yards of the cliff, and then Ewan, with the gasp of a drowning man, flung his weapon into the air, and Dan ripped his dagger's edge across the belts that bound them together, and at the next breath the belts were cut, and the two were divided, and Ewan, separated from Dan, and leaning heavily backward, was reeling, by force of his own weight, towards the cliff.

Then Dan stood as one transfixed with uplifted hand, and a deep groan came from his throat. Passion and pain were gone from him in that awful moment, and the world itself seemed to be blotted out. When he came to himself, he was standing on the cliff head alone.

The clock in the old church was striking. How the bell echoed on that lonely height! One – two – three – four – five. Five o'clock! Everything else was silent as death The day was gone. The snow began to fall in thick, large flakes. It fell heavily on Dan's hot cheeks and bare neck. His heart seemed to stand still, and the very silence itself was awful. His terror stupefied him. 'What have I done?' he asked himself. He could not think. He covered his eyes with his hands, and strode up and down the cliff head, up and down, up and down. Then in a bewildered state of semi-consciousness he looked out to sea, and there far off, a league away, he saw a black thing looming large against the darkening sky. He recognized that it was a sail, and then perceived that it was a lugger, and quite mechanically he tried to divide the mainmast and mizzen, the mainsail and yawlsail, and to note if the boat were fetching to leeward or beating down the Channel.

All at once sea and sky were blotted out, and he could not stand on his legs, but dropped to his knees, and great beads of perspiration rolled down his face and neck. He tried to call 'Ewan! Ewan!' but he could not utter the least cry. His throat was parched; his tongue swelled and filled his mouth. His lips moved, but no words came from him. Then he rose to his feet, and the world flowed back upon him: the sea-fowl crying over his head, the shrillness of the wind in the snow-capped gorse, and the sea's hoarse voice swelling upwards through the air, while its heavy, monotonous blow on the beach shook the earth beneath him. If anything else had appeared to Dan at that moment, he must have screamed with terror.

Quaking in every limb, he picked up his clothes and turned back towards the shore. He was so feeble that he could scarcely walk through the snow that now lay thick on the short grass. When he reached the mouth of the gully he did not turn into the shed, but went on over the pebbles of the creek. His bloodshot eyes, which almost started from their sockets, glanced eagerly from side to side. At last he saw the thing he sought, and now that it was under him, within reach of his hand, he dare hardly look upon it.

At the foot of a jagged crag that hung heavily over from the cliff the body of Ewan Mylrea lay dead and cold. There was no mark of violence upon it save a gash on the wrist of the left hand, and over the wound there was a clot of blood. The white face lay deep in the breast, as if the neck had been dislocated. There were no other outward marks of injury from the fall. The body was outstretched on its back, with one arm – the left arm – lying half over the forehead, and the other, the right arm, with the hand open and the listless fingers apart, thrown loosely aside.

Dan knelt beside the body, and his heart was benumbed like ice. He tried to pray, but no prayer would come, and he could not weep.

'Ewan! Ewan!' he cried at length, and his voice of agony rolled round the corpse like the soughing of the wind.

'Ewan! Ewan!' he cried again; but only the sea's voice broke the silence that followed. Then his head fell on the cold breast, and his arms covered the lifeless body, and he cried upon God to have mercy on him and to lift up His hand against him and cut him off.

Presently he got on his feet, and, scarcely knowing what he was doing, he lifted the body in his arms, with the head lying backwards on his shoulder, and the white face looking up in its stony stare to the darkening heavens. As he did so his eyes were raised to the cliff, and there, clearly outlined over the black crags and against the somewhat lighter sky, he saw the figure of a man.

He toiled along towards the shed. He was so weak that he could scarce keep on his legs, and when he reached the little place at the mouth of the creek, he was more dead than alive. He put the body to lie on the bed of straw on which he had himself slept and dreamt an hour before. Then all at once he felt a low sort of cunning coming over him, and he went back to the door and shut it, and drew the long wooden bolt into its iron hoop on the jamb.

He had hardly done so when he heard an impatient footstep on the shingle outside. In another instant the latch was lifted and the door pushed heavily. Then there was a knock. Dan made no answer, but stood very still and held his breath. There was another knock, and another. Then in a low tremulous murmur there came the words,

'Where is he? God A'mighty! Where is he?' It was Davy Fayle. Another knock, louder, and still no reply.

'Mastha Dan, Mastha Dan, they're coming; Mastha Dan, God A'mighty! – '

Davy was now tramping restlessly to and fro. Dan was trying to consider what it was best to do, whether to open to Davy and hear what he had to say, or to carry it off as if he were not within, when another foot sounded on the shingle and cut short his meditations.

'Have you see Mr. Ewan – Parson Ewan?'

Dan recognized the voice. It was the voice of Jarvis Kerruish.

Davy did not answer immediately.

'Have you seen him, eh?'

'No, sir,' Davy faltered.

'Then why didn't you say so at once. It is very strange. The people said he was walking towards the creek. There's no way out in this direction, is there?'

'Way out – this direction. Yes, sir,' Davy stammered.

'How? show me the way.'

'By the sea, sir.'

'The sea! Simpleton, what are you doing here?'

'Waiting for the boat, sir.'

'What shed is this?'

Dan could hear that at this question Davy was in a fever of excitement.

'Only a place for bits of net and cable and all to that,' said Davy eagerly.

Dan could feel that Jarvis had stepped up to the shed, and that he was trying to look in through the little window.

'Do you keep a fire to warm your nets and cables?' he asked in a suspicious tone.

At the next moment he was trying to force the door. Dan stood behind. The bolt creaked in the hasp. If the hasp should give way, he and Jarvis would stand face to face.

'Strange – there's something strange about all this,' said the man outside. 'I heard a scream as I came over the Head. Did you hear anything?'

'I tell you I heard nothing,' said Davy sullenly.

Dan grew dizzy, and, groping for something to cling to, his hand scraped across the door.

'Wait! I could have sworn I heard something move inside. Who keeps the key of this shed?'

'Kay? There's never a kay at the like of it.'

'Then how is it fastened? From within? Wait – let me see.'

There was a sound like the brushing of a hand over the outside face of the door.

'Has the snow stopped up the keyhole, or is there no such thing? Or is the door fastened by a padlock?'

Dan had regained his self-possession by this time. He felt an impulse to throw the door open. He groped at his waist for the dagger, but belt and dagger were both gone.

'All this is very strange,' said Jarvis, and then he seemed to turn from the door and move away.

'Stop. Where is the man Dan – the captain?' he asked, from a little distance.

'I dunno,' said Davy stoutly.

'That's a lie, my lad.'

Then the man's footsteps went off in dull beats on the snow-clotted pebbles.

After a moment's silence there was a soft knocking; Davy had crept up to the door.

'Mastha Dan,' he whispered, amid panting breath.

Dan did not stir. The latch was lifted in vain.

'Mastha Dan, Mastha Dan.' The soft knocking continued.

Dan found his voice at last.

'Go away, Davy; go away,' he said hoarsely.

There was a short pause, and then there came from without an answer like a sob.

'I'm going, Mastha Dan.'

After that all was silent as death. Half an hour later, Dan Mylrea was walking through the darkness towards Ballamona. In his blind misery he was going to Mona. The snow was not falling now, and in the lift of the storm the sky was lighter than it had been. As Dan passed the old church, he could just descry the clock. The snow lay thick on the face, and clogged the hands. The clock had stopped. It stood at five exactly.

The blind leading that is here of passion by accident is everywhere that great tragedies are done. It is not the evil in man's heart more than the deep perfidy of circumstance that brings him to crime.

38   '*Jealousy*'

A. G. Rensham. From *Poems by A. G. R.*, 1892. Written 1888.

> He loves me, but I would that he would die;
>   I love him, but I would that he were dead,
> And that he, silent, evermore should lie,
>   Where the soft earth enfolds his clustering head.

Yes! die before another's arm entwine
    His strong, white neck; die, ere his heartstrings throb
On other bosoms, and those firm lips pine
    For kisses and the soul's enraptured sob,

Not mine! I could not bear to lie alone,
    Torn by fierce Jealousy's envenomed fang,
But I could sit beside his sculptured stone
    Nursing sad Memory's keen but gentler pang.

Dead, ere he wearied of my burning love,
    And those dear eyes had turned to one more dear;
Oh! better he should rest in Heaven above,
    Than leave me in such Hell as that I fear!

I may not love him as his darling should,
    I may not in his arms so happy lie;
I may not live the life of love I would,
    And therefore pray I God that he may die.

39   'Epithalamion'

Gerard Manley Hopkins. Written 1888. Published 1918.

Hark, hearer, hear what I do; lend a thought now, make believe
We are leafwhelmed somewhere with the hood
Of some branchy bunchy bushybowered wood,
Southern dene or Lancashire clough or Devon cleave,
That leans along the loins of hills, where a candycoloured,
    where a gluegold-brown
Marbled river, boisterously beautiful, between
Roots and rocks is danced and dandled, all in froth and
    water-blowballs, down.
We are there, when we hear a shout
That the hanging honeysuck, the dogeared hazels in the cover
Makes dither, makes hover
And the riot of a rout
Of, it must be, boys from the town
Bathing: it is summer's sovereign good.

By there comes a listless stranger: beckoned by the noise
He drops towards the river: unseen

Sees the bevy of them, how the boys
With dare and with downdolphinry and bellbright bodies
  huddling out,
Are earthworld, airworld, waterworld thorough hurled, all by
  turn and turn about.

This garland of their gambols flashes in his breast
Into such a sudden zest
Of summertime joys
That he hies to a pool neighbouring; sees it is the best
There; sweetest, freshest, shadowiest;
Fairyland; silk-beech, scrolled ash, packed sycamore, wild
  wychelm, hornbeam fretty overstood
By. Rafts and rafts of flake-leaves light, dealt so, painted on
  the air,
Hang as still as hawk or hawkmoth, as the stars or as the angels
  there,
Like the thing that never knew the earth, never off roots
Rose. Here he feasts: lovely all is! No more: off with – down he
  dings
His bleachèd both and woolwoven wear:
Careless these in coloured wisp
All lie tumbled-to; then with loop-locks
Forward falling, forehead frowning, lips crisp
Over finger-teasing task, his twiny boots
Fast he opens, last he offwrings
Till walk the world he can with bare his feet
And come where lies a coffer, burly all of blocks
Built of chancequarrièd, selfquainèd rocks
And the water warbles over into, filleted with glassy grassy
  quicksilvery shivès and shoots
And with heavenfallen freshness down from moorland still
  brims,
Dark or daylight on and on. Here he will then, here he will the
  fleet
Flinty kindcold element let break across his limbs
Long. Where we leave him, froliclavish, while he looks about
  him, laughs, swims.

Enough now; since the sacred matter that I mean
I should be wronging longer leaving it to float
Upon this only gambolling and echoing-of-earth note –
What is . . . the delightful dene?

Wedlock. What is water? Spousal love. . . .
Father, mother, brothers sisters, friends
Into fairy trees, wild flowers, wood ferns
Ranked round the bower. . . .

40 'Joy Standeth on the Threshold'

Richard C. Jackson. Written *c*. 1887–9. Subtitled 'A Reverie of Walter Pater'.
From Thomas Wright, *The Life of Walter Pater*, 1907. Appendix X.

Joy standeth on the threshold
    of each new delight,
As in that spirit true men
    take of roses white:
Of roses fill'd all through with
    joyaunces divine
As in that beauty rare I
    worship at its shrine.

Your darling soul I say is
    enflam'd with love of me:
Your very eyes do move, I
    cry, with sympathy:
Your darling feet and hands are
    blessings ruled by love,
As forth was sent from out the
    Ark a turtle dove!

Oh, how I watch'd the travail
    of your pensive soul,
Oh, sweetness unto sweetness
    grew to make me whole!
With lilies white thou shinest
    as fair Luna's brow;
The while thy latent thought, my
    joyaunce doth endow.

41 'Sonnet on a Picture by Tuke'

Charles Kains-Jackson. From *The Artist*, 1 May 1889. Full title 'On a picture
by H. S. Tuke in the present exhibition of the New English Art Club'.

Within this little space of canvas shut
    Are summer sunshine, and the exuberant glee

Of living light that laughs along the sea,
And freshness of kind winds; yet these are but
As the rich gem whereon the cameo's cut;
      The cameo's self, the boyish faces free
      From care, the beauty and the delicacy
Of young slim frames not yet to labour put.
The kisses that make red each honest face
      Are of the breeze and salt and tingling spray.
So, may these boys know never of a place
      Wherein, to desk or factory a prey,
That colour blanches slowly, nature's grace
      Made pale with life's incipient decay.

42   'Put on that Languor'

Mark André Raffalovich. From *It is Thyself*, 1889. No. cxx.

CXX

Put on that languor which the world frowns on,
That blamed misleading strangeness of attire,
And let them see that see us we have done
With their false worldliness and look up higher.
Because the world has treated us so ill
And brought suspicion near our happiness,
Let men that like to slander as they will;
It shall not be my fault if we love less.
Because we two who never did them harm,
And never dreamt of harm ourselves, find men
So eager to perplex us and alarm
And scare from us our dove-like thoughts, well then
      Since 'twixt the world and truth must be our choice,
      Let us seem vile, not be so, and rejoice.

43   'Ballade of Boys Bathing'

Frederick William Rolfe (Baron Corvo). From *The Art Review*, April 1890, vol. 1, no. 4.

(As dainty a sight as I wish to see.)
      Drifting along in a boat we were
On the coast of the land of the kilted knee,

Under the sea-cliffs' shadows, where
   A flock of boys, slender and debonnaire,
      Laugh in a lovely disarray,
Fear they know not, nor ever a care
        The boys who bathe in St. Andrew's Bay

Deep blue water as blue can be,
   Rocks rising high where the red clouds flare,
Boys of the colour of ivory,
   Breasting the wavelets, and diving there,
   White boys, ruddy, and tanned, and bare,
      With lights and shadows of rose and grey,
And the sea like pearls in their shining hair,
      The boys who bathe in St. Andrew's Bay.

A summer night, and a sapphire sea,
   A setting sun, and a golden glare:
Hurled from the height where the wild rocks be,
   Wondrous limbs in the luminous air,
   Fresh as white flame, flushed and fair,
      Little round arms in the salt sea spray,
And the sea seems alive with them everywhere,
      The boys who bathe in St. Andrew's Bay.

   Envoy
Andrea! Set me out tinctures rare
   Give me a palette, and while I may
I'll fix upon canvas, if so I may dare,
   The boys who bathe in St. Andrew's Bay.

44   'To W.J.M.'

George Gillett. From *The Artist*, 1 April 1890.

Guessed you but how I loved you, watched your smile
   Hungered to see the love-light in your eyes –
   That ne'er can wake for me – Would wild surprise
Or sheer disgust at passion you deem vile
Be your response? For you are free from guile
   While I, enraptured foolishly or wise
   Long but for you, till even yearning dies
Save to be near, you loving me the while.

In all the world this thing can never come
    And tho' I die, no word your soul shall shame.
    Mine by the punishment as mine the blame
And though in hopeless fear my heart is numb
At its renunciation, yet still dumb
    You shall not hear me even breathe your name.

45   'Sonnet'

S. S. Saale. From *The Artist*, 1 September 1890.

Upon the wall, of idling boys a row,
    The grimy barges not more dull than they
    When sudden in the midst of all their play
They strip and plunge into the stream below;
Changed by a miracle, they rise as though
    The youth of Greece burst on this later day,
    As on their lithe young bodies many a ray
Of sunlight dallies with its blushing glow.

Flower of clear beauty, naked purity,
    With thy sweet presence olden days return,
    Like fragrant ashes from a classic urn,
Flashed into life anew once more we see
Narcissus by the pool, or 'neath the tree
    Young Daphnis, and new pulses throb and burn.

46   *Teleny*

Anonymous. Written *c.* 1890. Full title *Teleny, or the Reverse of the Medal.*
These extracts are from the first edition of 1893.

As he came on, some few persons tried to cheer him by clapping their
hands, but a low murmur of disapproval, followed by a slight hissing
sound, stopped these feeble attempts at once. He seemed scornfully
indifferent to both sounds. He sat listlessly down, like a person worn
out by fever, but, as one of the musical reporters stated, the fire of art
began all at once to glow within his eyes. He cast a sidelong glance on
the audience, a searching look full of love and of thankfulness.

    Then he began to play, not as if his task were a weary one, but as
if he were pouring out his heavily-laden soul; and the music sounded

like the warbling of a bird which, in its attempt to captivate its mate, pants forth its floods of rapture, resolved either to conquer or to die in profuse strains of unpremeditated art.

It is needless to say that I was thoroughly overcome, whilst the whole crowd was thrilled by the sweet sadness of his song.

The piece finished, I hurried out – frankly, in the hope of meeting him. Whilst he had been playing, a mighty struggle had been going on within myself – between my heart and my brain; and the glowing senses asked cold reason, what was the use of fighting against an ungovernable passion? I was, indeed, ready to forgive him for all I had suffered, for after all, had I any right to be angry with him?

As I entered the room he was the first – nay, the only person I saw. A feeling of indescribable delight filled my whole being, and my heart seemed to bound forth towards him. All at once, however, all my rapture passed away, my blood froze in my veins, and love gave way to anger and hatred. He was arm-in-arm with Briancourt, who, openly congratulating him on his success, was evidently clinging to him like the ivy to the oak. Briancourt's eyes and mine met; in his there was a look of exultation; in mine, of withering scorn.

As soon as Teleny saw me, he at once broke loose from Briancourt's clutches, and came up to me. Jealousy maddened me, I gave him the stiffest and most distant of bows and passed on, utterly disregarding his outstretched hands.

I heard a slight murmur amongst the bystanders, and as I walked away I saw with the corner of my eye his hurt look, his blushes that came and went, and his expression of wounded pride. Though hot-tempered, he bowed resignedly, as if to say: 'Be it as you will,' and he went back to Briancourt, whose face was beaming with satisfaction.

Briancourt said, – 'He has always been a cad, a tradesman, a proud *parvenu!*' just loud enough for the words to reach my ear. 'Do not mind him.'

'No,' added Teleny, musingly, 'it is I who am to blame, not he.'

Little did he understand with what a bleeding heart I walked out of the room, yearning at every step to turn back, and to throw my arms around his neck before everybody, and beg his forgiveness.

I wavered for a moment, whether to go and offer him my hand or not. Alas! do we often yield to the warm impulse of the heart? Are we not, instead, always guided by the advice of the calculating, conscience-muddled, clay-cold brain?

It was early, yet I waited for some time in the street, watching for Teleny to come out. I had made up my mind that if he was alone, I would go and beg his pardon for my rudeness.

After a short time, I saw him appear at the door with Briancourt.

My jealousy was at once rekindled, I turned on my heels and walked off. I did not want to see him again. On the morrow I would take the first train and go – anywhere, out of the world if I could.

This state of feeling did not last long; and my rage being somewhat subdued, love and curiosity prompted me again to stop. I did so. I looked round; they were nowhere to be seen; still I had wended my steps towards Teleny's house.

I walked back. I glanced down the neighbouring streets; they had quite disappeared.

Now that he was lost to sight, my eagerness to find him increased. They had, perhaps, gone to Briancourt's. I hurried on in the direction of his house.

All at once, I thought I saw two figures like them at a distance. I hastened on like a madman. I lifted up the collar of my coat, I pulled my soft felt hat over my ears, so as not to be recognized, and followed them on the opposite side-walk.

I was not mistaken. Then they branched off; I after them. Whither were they going in these lonely parts?

So as not to attract their attention I stopped where I saw an advertisement. I slackened, and then quickened my pace. Several times I saw their heads come in close contact, and then Briancourt's arm encircled Teleny's waist.

All this was far worse than gall and wormwood to me. Still, in my misery, I had one consolation; this was to see that, apparently, Teleny was yielding to Briancourt's attentions instead of seeking them.

At last they reached the Quai de —, so busy in the daytime, so lonely at night. There they seemed to be looking for somebody, for they either turned round, scanned the persons they met, or stared at men seated on the benches that are along the quay. I continued following them.

As my thoughts were entirely absorbed, it was some time before I noticed that a man, who had sprung up from somewhere, was walking by my side. I grew nervous; for I fancied that he not only tried to keep pace with me but also to catch my attention, for he hummed and whistled snatches of songs, coughed, cleared his throat, and scraped his feet.

All these sounds fell upon my dreamy ears, but failed to arouse my attention. All my senses were fixed on the two figures in front of me. He therefore walked on, then turned round on his heels, and stared at me. My eyes saw all this without heeding him in the least.

He lingered once more, let me pass, walked on at a brisker pace, and was again beside me. Finally, I looked at him. Though it was cold, he was but slightly dressed. He wore a short, black velvet jacket and a pair of light grey, closely-fitting trousers marking the shape of the thighs and buttocks like tights.

As I looked at him he stared at me again, then smiled with that vacant, vapid, idiotic, facial contraction of a *raccrocheuse*. Then, always looking at me with an inviting leer, he directed his steps towards a neighbouring *Vespasienne*.

'What is there so peculiar about me?' I mused, 'that the fellow is ogling me in that way?'

Without turning round, however, or noticing him any further, I walked on, my eyes fixed on Teleny.

As I passed by another bench, someone again scraped his feet and cleared his throat, evidently bent on making me turn my head. I did so. There was nothing more remarkable about him than there is in the first man you meet. Seeing me look at him, he either unbuttoned or buttoned up his trousers.

After a while I again heard steps coming from behind; the person was close up to me. I smelt a strong scent – if the noxious odour of musk or of patchouli can be called a scent.

The person touched me slightly as he passed by. He begged my pardon; it was the man of the velvet jacket, or his Dromio. I looked at him as he again stared at me and grinned. His eyes were painted with khol, his cheeks were dabbed with rouge. He was quite beardless. For a moment, I doubted whether he was a man or a woman; but when he stopped again before the column I was fully persuaded of his sex.

Someone else came with mincing steps, and shaking his buttocks, from behind one of these *pissoirs*. He was an old, wiry, simpering man, as shrivelled as a frost-bitten pippin. His cheeks were very hollow, and his projecting cheek bones very red; his face was shaven and shorn, and he wore a wig with long, fair, flaxen locks.

He walked in the posture of the Venus de Medici; that is, with one hand on his middle parts, and the other on his breast. His looks were not only very demure, but there was an almost maidenly coyness about the old man that gave him the appearance of a virgin-pimp.

He did not stare, but cast a side-long glance at me as he went by. He was met by a workman – a strong and sturdy fellow, either a butcher or a smith by trade. The old man would evidently have slunk by unperceived, but the workman stopped him. I could not hear what they said, for though they were but a few steps away, they spoke in that hushed tone peculiar to lovers; but I seemed to be the object of their talk, for the workman turned and stared at me as I passed. They parted.

The workman walked on for twenty steps, then he turned on his heel and walked back exactly on a line with me, seemingly bent on meeting me face to face.

I looked at him. He was a brawny man, with massive features; clearly, a fine specimen of a male. As he passed by me he clenched his powerful fist, doubled his muscular arm at the elbow, and then moved it vertically hither and thither for a few times, like a piston-rod in action, as it slipped in and out of the cylinder.

Some signs are so evidently clear and full of meaning that no initiation is needed to understand them. This workman's sign was one of them.

Now I knew who all these night-walkers were. Why they so persistently stared at me, and the meaning of all their little tricks to catch my attention. Was I dreaming? I looked around. The workman had stopped, and he repeated his request in a different way. He shut his left fist, then thrust the forefinger of his right hand in the hole made by the palm and fingers, and moved it in and out. He was bluntly explicit. I was not mistaken. I hastened on, musing whether the cities of the plain had been destroyed by fire and brimstone.

As I learnt later in life, every large city has its particular haunts – its square, its garden for such recreation. And the police? Well, it winks at it, until some crying offence is committed; for it is not safe to stop the mouths of craters. Brothels of men-whores not being allowed, such trysting-places must be tolerated, or the whole is a modern Sodom or Gomorrah.

What! there are such cities now-a-days?

Aye! for Jehovah has acquired experience with age; so He has got to understand His children a little better than He did of yore, for He has either come to a righter sense of toleration, or, like Pilate, He has washed His hands, and has quite discarded them. . . .

The prostration which followed the excessive strain of the nerves had set in, when the carriage stopped before the door of Teleny's house – that door at which I had madly struck with my fist a short time before.

We dragged ourselves wearily out of the carriage, but hardly had the portal shut itself upon us than we were again kissing and fondling each other with renewed energy.

After some moments, feeling that our desire was too powerful to be withstood any longer, – 'Come,' said he, 'why should we linger any longer, and waste precious time here in the darkness and in the cold?'

'Is it dark and is it cold?' was my reply.

He kissed me fondly.

'In the gloom you are my light; in the cold you are my fire; the frozen wastes of the Pole would be a Garden of Eden for me, if you were there,' I continued.

We then groped our way upstairs in the dark, for I would not allow him to light a wax match. I therefore went along, stumbling against him; not that I could not see, but because I was intoxicated with mad desire as a drunken man is with wine.

Soon we were in his apartment. When we found ourselves in the small, dimly-lighted ante-chamber, he opened his arms and stretched them out towards me.

'Welcome!' said he. 'May this home be ever thine.' Then he added, in a low tone, in that unknown, musical tongue, 'My body hungereth for thee, soul of my soul, life of my life!'

He had barely finished these words before we were lovingly caressing each other.

After thus fondling each other for a few moments, – 'Do you know,' said he, 'that I have been expecting you today?'

'Expecting me?'

'Yes, I knew that sooner or later you would be mine. Moreover, I felt that you would be coming to-day.'

'How so?'

'I had a presentiment.'

'And had I not come?'

'I should have done what you were going to do when I met you, for life without you would have been unbearable.'

'What! drowned yourself?'

'No, not exactly: the river is too cold and bleak, I am too much of a Sybarite for that. No, I should simply have put myself to sleep – the eternal slumber of death, dreaming of you, in this room prepared to receive you, and where no man has ever set his foot.'

Saying these words he opened the door of a small chamber, and ushered me into it. A strong, overpowering smell of white heliotrope first greeted my nostrils.

It was a most peculiar room, the walls of which were covered over with some warm, white, soft, quilted stuff, studded all over with frosted silver buttons; the floor was covered with the curly white fleece of young lambs; in the middle of the apartment stood a capacious couch, on which was thrown the skin of a huge polar bear. Over this single piece of furniture, an old silver lamp – evidently from some Byzantine church or some Eastern synagogue – shed a pale glimmering light, sufficient, however, to light up the dazzling whiteness of this temple of Priapus whose votaries we were.

'I know,' said he, as he dragged me in, 'I know that white is your favourite colour, that it suits your dark complexion, so it has been fitted up for you and you alone. No other mortal shall ever set his foot in it.'

Uttering these words, he in a trice stripped me deftly of all my clothes – for I was in his hands like a slumbering child, or a man in a trance.

In an instant I was not only stark naked, but stretched on the bear-skin, whilst he, standing in front of me, was gloating upon me with famished eyes.

I felt his glances greedily fall everywhere; they sank in my brain, and my head began to swim; they pierced through my heart, whipping my blood up, making it flow quicker and hotter through all the arteries; they darted within my veins, and Priapus unhooded itself and lifted up its head violently so that all the tangled web of veins in its body seemed ready to burst.

Then he felt me with his hands everywhere, after which he began to press his lips on every part of my body, showering kisses on my breast, my arms, my legs, my thighs, and then, when he had reached my middle parts, he pressed his face rapturously on the thick and curly hair that grows there so plentifully.

He shivered with delight as he felt the crisp locks upon his cheek and neck; then, taking hold of my phallus, he pressed his lips upon it. That seemed to electrify him; and then the tip and afterwards the whole glans disappeared within his mouth. . . .

After a few moments' rest I uplifted myself on my elbow, and delighted my eyes with my lover's fascinating beauty. He was a very model of carnal comeliness; his chest was broad and strong, his arms rounded; in fact, I have never seen such a vigorous and at the same time agile frame; for not only was there not the slightest fat but not even the least superfluous flesh about him. He was all nerve, muscle, and sinew. It was his well-knit and supple joints that gave him the free, easy, and graceful motion so characteristic of the Felidae, of which he had also the flexibility, for when he clasped himself to you he seemed to entwine himself around you like a snake. Moreover, his skin was of a pearly almost iridescent whiteness, whilst the hair on the different parts of his body except the head was quite black.

Teleny opened his eyes, stretched his arms towards me, took hold of my hand, kissed, and then bit me on the nape of my neck; then he showered a number of kisses all along my back, which, following one another in quick succession, seemed like a rain of rose-leaves falling from some full-blown flower.

Then he reached the two fleshy lobes which he pressed open with his hands, and darted his tongue in that hole where a little while before he had thrust his finger. This likewise was for me a new and thrilling sensation.

This done, he rose and stretched forth his hand to lift me up.

'Now,' said he, 'let us go in the next room, and see if we can find something to eat; for I think we really require some food, though, perhaps, a bath would not be amiss before we sit down to supper. Should you like to have one?'

'It might put you to inconvenience.'

For all answer he ushered me into a kind of cell, all filled with ferns and feathery palms, that – as he showed me – received during the day the rays of the sun from a skylight overhead.

'This is a kind of make-shift for a hot-house and a bathroom, which every habitable dwelling ought to have. I am too poor to have either, still this hole is big enough for my ablutions, and my plants seem to thrive pretty well in this warm and damp atmosphere.'

'But it's a princely bathroom!'

'No, no!' said he, smiling; 'it's an artist's bathroom.'

We at once plunged into the warm water, scented with essence of heliotrope; and it was so pleasant to rest there locked in each other's arms after our last excesses.

'I could stay here all night,' he mused; 'it is so delightful to handle you in this warm water. But you must be famished, so we had better go and get something to satisfy the inward cravings.'

We got out, and wrapped ourselves up for a moment with hot *peignoirs* of Turkish towelling.

'Come,' said he, 'let me lead you to the dining-room.'

I stood hesitating, looking first at my nakedness, then upon his. He smiled, and kissed me.

'You don't feel cold, do you?'

'No, but – '

'Well, then, don't be afraid; there is no one in the house. Everyone is asleep on the other flats, and, besides, every window is tightly shut, and all the curtains are down.'

He dragged me with him into a neighbouring room all covered with thick, soft, and silky carpets, the prevailing tone of which was dull Turkish red.

In the centre of this apartment hung a curiously-wrought, star-shaped lamp, which the faithful – even now-a-days – light on Friday eve.

We sat down on a soft-cushioned divan, in front of one of those ebony Arab tables all inlaid with coloured ivory and iridescent mother-of-pearl.

'I cannot give you a banquet, although I expected you; still, there is enough to satisfy your hunger, I hope.'

There were some luscious Cancale oysters – few, but of an immense size; a dusty bottle of Sauterne, then a *pâté de foie gras* highly scented with Perigord truffles; a partridge, with *paprika* or Hungarian curry, and a salad made out of a huge Piedmont truffle, as thinly sliced as shavings, and a bottle of exquisite dry sherry.

All these delicacies were served in dainty blue old Delft and Savona ware, for he had already heard of my hobby for old majolica.

Then came a dish of Seville oranges, bananas, and pineapples, flavoured with Maraschino and covered with sifted sugar. It was a savoury, tasty, tart and sweet medley, combining together the flavour and perfume of all these delicious fruits.

After having washed it down with a bottle of sparkling champagne, we then sipped some tiny cups of fragrant and scalding Mocha coffee; then he lighted a narghilè, or Turkish water pipe, and we puffed at intervals the odorous Latakiah, inhaling it with our ever-hungry kisses from each other's mouths.

The fumes of the smoke and those of the wine rose up to our heads, and in our re-awakened sensuality we soon had between our lips a far more fleshy mouth-piece than the amber one of the Turkish pipe.

Our heads were again soon lost between each other's thighs. We had once more but one body between us, juggling with one another, ever seeking new caresses, new sensations, a sharper and more inebriating kind of lewdness, in our anxiety not only to enjoy ourselves but to make the other one feel. We were, therefore, very soon the prey of a blasting lust, and only some inarticulate sounds expressed the climax of our voluptuous state, until, more dead than alive, we fell upon each other – a mingled mass of shivering flesh.

After half an hour's rest and a bowl of arrak, curaçao and whisky punch, flavoured with many hot, invigorating spices, our mouths were again pressed together.

His moist lips grazed mine so very slightly that I hardly felt their touch; they thus only awakened in me the eager desire to feel their contact more closely, whilst the tip of his tongue kept tantalizing mine, darting in my mouth for a second and rapidly slipping out again. His hands in the meanwhile passed over the most delicate parts of my body as lightly as a soft summer breeze passes over the smooth surface of the waters, and I felt my skin shiver with delight.

I happened to be lying on some cushions on the couch, which thus elevated me to Teleny's height; he swiftly put my legs on his shoulders, then, bending down his head, he began first to kiss, and then to dart his pointed tongue in the hole of my bum, thrilling me with an ineffable pleasure. Then rising when he had deftly prepared the hole by lubricating it well all round, he tried to press the tip of his phallus into it, but though he pressed hard, still he could not succeed in getting it in'

'Let me moisten it a little, and then it will slip in more easily.'

I took it again in my mouth. My tongue rolled deftly all around it. I sucked it down almost to its very root, feeling it up to any little trick, for it was stiff, hard, and frisky.

'Now,' said I, 'let us enjoy together that pleasure which the gods themselves did not disdain to teach us.'

Thereupon the tips of my fingers stretched the edges of my unexplored little pit to their very utmost. It was gaping to receive the huge instrument that presented itself at the orifice.

He once more pressed the glans upon it; the tiny little lips protruded themselves within the gap; the tip worked its way inside, but the pulpy flesh bulged out all around, and the rod was thus arrested in its career.

'I am afraid I am hurting you?' he asked, 'had we not better leave it for some other time?'

'Oh, no! it is such a happiness to feel your body entering into mine.'

He thrust gently but firmly; the strong muscles of the anus relaxed; the glans was fairly lodged; the skin extended to such a degree that tiny, ruby beads of blood trickled from all around the splitting orifice; still, notwithstanding the way I was torn, the pleasure I felt was much greater than the pain. . . .

A few days afterwards we met Briancourt in the green room of the Opera. When he saw us, he looked away and tried to shun us. I would have done the same.

'No,' said Teleny, 'let us go and speak to him and have matters out. In such things never show the slightest fear. If you face the enemy boldly, you have already half vanquished him.' Then, going up to him and dragging me with him, – 'Well,' said he, stretching out his hand, 'what has become of you? It is some days since we have seen each other.'

'Of course,' replied he, 'new friends make us forget old ones.'

'Like new pictures old ones. By the bye, what sketch have you begun?'

'Oh, something glorious! – a picture that will make a mark, if any does.'

'But what is it?'

'Jesus Christ.'

'Jesus Christ?'

'Yes, since I knew Achmet, I have been able to understand the Saviour. You would love Him, too,' added he, 'if you could see those dark, mesmeric eyes, with their long and jetty fringe.'

'Love whom,' said Teleny, 'Achmet or Christ?'

'Christ, of course!' quoth Briancourt, shrugging his shoulders. 'You would be able to fathom the influence He must have had over the crowd. My Syrian need not speak to you, he lifts his eyes upon you and you grasp the meaning of his thoughts. Christ, likewise, never wasted His breath spouting cant to the multitude. He wrote on the sand, and could thereby "look the world to law." As I was saying, I shall paint Achmet as the Saviour, and you,' added he to Teleny, 'as John, the disciple He loved; for the Bible clearly says and continually repeats that He loved this favourite disciple.'

'And how will you paint Him?'

'Christ erect, clasping John, who hugs Him, and who leans his head on his friend's bosom. Of course there must be something lovably soft and womanly in the disciple's look and attitude; he must have your visionary violet eyes and your voluptuous mouth. Crouched at their feet there will be one of the many adulterous Marys, but Christ and the other – as John modestly terms himself, as if he were his Master's mistress – look down at her with a dreamy, half-scornful, half-pitiful expression.'

'And will the people understand your meaning?'

'Anybody who has any sense will. Besides, to render my idea clearer, I'll paint a pendant to it: "Socrates – the Greek Christ, with Alcibiades, his favourite disciple." The woman will be Xantippe.' Then turning to me, he added, 'But you must promise to come and sit for Alcibiades.'

'Yes,' said Teleny, 'but on one condition.'

'Name it.'

'Why did you write Camille that note?'

'What note?'

'Come – no gammon!'

'How did you know I wrote it?'

'Like Zadig, I saw the traces of the dog's ears.'

'Well, as you know it's me, I'll tell you frankly, it was because I was jealous.'

'Of whom?'

'Of you both. Yes, you may smile, but it's true.'

Then turning towards me, – 'I've known you since we both were but little more than toddling babies, and I've never had that from you,' – and he cracked his thumb-nail on his upper teeth – 'whilst he,' pointing to Teleny, 'comes, sees, and conquers. Anyhow, it'll be for some future time. Meanwhile, I bear you no grudge; nor do you for that stupid threat of mine, I'm sure.'

'You don't know what miserable days and sleepless nights you made me pass.'

'Did I? I'm sorry; forgive me. You know I'm mad – everyone says so,' he exclaimed, grasping both our hands; 'and now that we are friends you must come to my next symposium.'

'When is it to be?' asked Teleny.

'On Tuesday week.'

Then turning to me, – 'I'll introduce you to a lot of pleasant fellows who'll be delighted to make your acquaintance, and many of whom have long been astonished that you are not one of us.'

The week passed quickly. Joy soon made me forget the dreadful anxiety caused by Briancourt's card.

A few days before the night fixed for the feast, – 'How shall we dress for the symposium?' asked Teleny.

'How? Is it to be a masquerade?'

'We all have our little hobbies. Some men like soldiers, others sailors; some are fond of tightrope dancers, others of dandies. There are men who, though in love with their own sex, only care for them in women's clothes. *L'habit ne fait pas le moine* is not always a truthful proverb, for you see that even in birds the males display their gayest plumage to captivate their mates.'

'And what clothes should you like me to wear, for you are the only being I care to please?' said I.

'None.'

'Oh! but – '

'You'll feel shy, to be seen naked?'

'Of course.'

'Well, then, a tight-fitting cycling suit; it shows off the figure best.'

'Very well; and you?'

'I'll always dress exactly as you do.'

On the evening in question we drove to the painter's studio, the outside of which was, if not quite dark, at least very dimly lighted. Teleny tapped three times, and after a little while Briancourt himself came to open.

Whatever faults the general's son had, his manners were those of the French nobility, therefore perfect; his stately gait might even have graced the court of the *grand Monarque*; his politeness was unrivalled – in fact, he possessed all those 'small, sweet courtesies of life,' which, as Sterne says, 'beget inclinations to love at first sight.' He was about to usher us in, when Teleny stopped him.

'Wait a moment,' said he, 'could not Camille have a peep at your harem first? You know he is but a neophyte in the Priapean creed. I am his first lover.'

'Yes, I know,' interrupted Briancourt, sighing, 'and I cannot say sincerely, may you long be the last.'

'And not being inured to the sight of such revelry he will be induced to run away like Joseph from Mrs. Potiphar.'

'Very well, do you mind giving yourself the trouble to come this way?'

And with these words he led us through a dimly-lighted passage, and up a winding staircase into a kind of balcony made out of old Arab *moucharabiè*, brought to him by his father from Tunis or Algiers.

'From here you can see everything without being seen, so ta-ta for a while, but not for long, as supper will soon be served.'

As I stepped in this kind of loggia and looked down into the room, I was, for a moment, if not dazzled, at least perfectly bewildered. . . .

'But look there,' said I to Teleny; 'there are also women.'

'No,' replied he, 'women are never admitted to our revels.'

'But look at that couple there. See that naked man with his hand under the skirts of the girl clasped against him.'

'Both are men.'

'What! also that one with the reddish-auburn hair and brilliant complexion? Why, is it not Viscount de Pontgrimaud's mistress?'

'Yes, the Venus d'Ille, as she is generally called; and the Viscount is down there in a corner, but the Venus d'Ille is a man!'

I stared astonished. What I had taken for a woman looked, indeed, like a beautiful bronze figure, as smooth and polished as a Japanese cast *à cire perdue*, with an enamelled Parisian cocotte's head.

Whatever the sex of this strange being was, he or she had on a tight-fitting dress of a changing colour – gold in the light, dark green in the shade – silk gloves and stockings of the same tint as the satin of the dress, fitting so tightly on the rounded arms and most beautifully-shaped legs that these limbs looked as even and as hard as those of a bronze statue.

'And that other one there, with black ringlets, *accroche-cœurs*, in a dark blue velvet tea-gown, with bare arms and shoulders, is that lovely woman a man, too?'

'Yes, he is an Italian and a Marquis, as you can see by the crest on his fan. He belongs, moreover, to one of the oldest families of Rome. But look there. Briancourt has been repeatedly making signs to us to go down. Let us go.'

'No, no!' said I, clinging to Teleny; 'let us rather go away.'

Still, that sight had so heated my blood that, like Lot's wife, I stood there, gloating upon it.

'I'll do whatever you like, but I think that if we go away now you'll be sorry for it afterwards. Besides, what do you fear? Am I not with you? No one can part us. We shall remain all the evening together, for here it is not the same as in the usual balls, where men bring their wives in order that they may be clasped and hugged by the first comer who likes to waltz with them. Moreover, the sight of all those excesses will only give a zest to our own pleasure.'

'Well, let us go,' said I, rising; 'but stop. That man in a pearly-grey Eastern robe must be the Syrian; he has lovely almond-shaped eyes.'

'Yes, that is Achmet effendi.'

'Whom is he talking with? Is it not Briancourt's father?'

'Yes, the general is sometimes a passive guest at his son's little parties. Come, shall we go?'

'One moment more. Do tell me who is that man with eyes on fire? He seems, indeed, lust incarnate, and is evidently past-master in lewdness. His face is familiar, and still I cannot remember where I have seen him.'

'He is a young man who having spent his fortune in the most unbridled debauchery without any damage to his constitution, has enlisted in the Spahis to see what new pleasures Algiers could afford him. That man is indeed a volcano. But here is Briancourt.'

'Well,' said he, 'are you going to stay up here in the dark all the evening?'

'Camille is abashed,' said Teleny, smiling.

'Then come in masked,' said the painter, dragging us down, and giving us each a black velvet half-mask before ushering us in.

The announcement that supper was waiting in the next room had almost brought the revel to a stand-still.

As we entered the studio, the sight of our dark suits and masks seemed to throw a dampness on everyone. We were, however, soon surrounded by a number of young men who came to welcome and to fondle us, some of whom were old acquaintances.

After a few questions Teleny was known, and his mask was at once snatched off; but no one for a long time could make out who I was. I, in the meanwhile, kept ogling the middle parts of the naked men around me, the thick and curly hair of which sometimes covered the stomach and the thighs. Nay, that unusual sight excited me in such a way that I could hardly forbear handling those tempting organs; and had it not been for the love I bore Teleny, I should have done something more than finger them. . . .

. . .

Teleny returned me my kisses with the passionate eagerness of despair. His lips were on fire, his love seemed to have changed into a raging fever. I don't know what had come over me, but I felt that pleasure could kill, but not calm me. My head was all aglow!

There are two kinds of lascivious feelings, both equally strong and overpowering: the one is the fervent, carnal lust of the senses, enkindled in the genital organs and mounting to the brain, making human beings

> 'Swim in mirth, and fancy that they feel
> Divinity within them breeding wings
> Wherewith to scorn the earth.'

The other is the cold libidinousness of fancy, the keen and gall-like irradiation of the brain which parches the healthy blood.

The first, the strong concupiscence of lusty youth –

> 'as with new wine intoxicated,'

natural to the flesh, is satisfied as soon as men take largely

> 'their fill of love and love's disport,'

and the heavily-laden anther has sturdily shaken forth the seed that clogged it; and then they feel as our first parents did, when dewy sleep

> 'Oppressed them, wearied with their amorous play.'

The body then so delightfully light seems to rest on 'earth's freshest, softest lap,' and the slothful yet half-awakened mind broods over its slumbering shell.

The second, kindled in the head,

> 'bred of unkindly fumes,'

is the lechery of senility – a morbid craving, like the hunger of surfeited gluttony. The senses, like Messalina,

> 'lassata sed non satiata,'

ever tingling, keep hankering after the impossible. The spermatic ejaculations, far from calming the body, only irritate it, for the exciting influence of a salacious fancy continues after the anther has yielded all its seed. Even if acrid blood comes instead of the balmy, cream-like fluid, it brings with it nothing but a painful irritation. If, unlike as in satyriasis, an erection does not take place, and the phallus remains limp and lifeless, still the nervous system is no less convulsed by impotent desire and lechery – a mirage of the over-heated brain, no less shattering because it is effete.

These two feelings combined together are something akin to what I underwent as, holding Teleny clasped against my throbbing, heaving breast, I felt within me the contagion of his eager longing and of his overpowering sadness.

I had taken off my friend's shirt collar and cravat to see and to feel his beautiful bare neck, then little by little I stripped him of all his clothes, till at last he remained naked in my embrace.

What a model of voluptuous comeliness he was, with his strong and muscular shoulders, his broad and swelling chest, his skin of a pearly whiteness, as soft and as fresh as the petals of a waterlily, his limbs rounded like those of Leotard, with whom every woman was in love. His thighs, his legs and feet in their exquisite grace, were perfect models.

The more I looked upon him the more enamoured I was of him. But the sight was not enough. I had to heighten the visual delight by the sense of touch, I had to feel the tough and yet elastic muscles of the arm in the palm of my hand, to fondle his massive and sinewy breast, to paddle his back. From there my hands descended down to the round lobes of the rump, and I clasped him against me by the buttocks. Thereupon, tearing off my clothes, I pressed all his body on mine, and rubbed myself against him, wriggling like a worm. Lying over him as I was, my tongue was in his mouth, searching for his, that receded, and was darted out when mine retired, for they seemed to play a wanton, bickering game of hide-and-seek together – a game which made all the body quiver with delight.

Then our fingers twisted the crisp and curly hair that grew all around the middle parts, or handled the testicles, so softly and so gently that they were hardly sentient of the touch, and still they shivered in a way that almost made the fluid in them flow out before its time.

The most skilled of prostitutes could never give such thrilling sensations as those which I felt with my lover, for the tweake is, after all, only acquainted with the pleasures she herself has felt; whilst the keener emotions, not being those of her sex, are unknown to and cannot be imagined by her.

Likewise, no man is ever able to madden a woman with such over-powering lust as another tribade can, for she alone knows how to tickle her on the right spot just in the nick of time. The quintessence of bliss can, therefore, only be enjoyed by beings of the same sex.

Our two bodies were now in as close a contact as the glove is to the hand it sheathes, our feet were tickling each other wantonly, our knees were pressed together, the skin of our thighs seemed to cleave and to form one flesh.

Though I was loath to rise, still, feeling his stiff and swollen phallus throbbing against my body, I was just going to tear myself off from him, and to take his fluttering implement of pleasure in my mouth and drain it, when he – feeling that mine was now not only turgid, but moist and brimful to overflowing – clasped me with his arms and kept me down.

Opening his thighs, he thereupon took my legs between his own, and entwined them in such a way that his heels pressed against the sides of my calves. For a moment I was gripped as in a vice, and I could hardly move.

Then loosening his arms, he uplifted himself, placed a pillow under his buttocks, which were thus well apart – his legs being all the time widely open.

Having done this, he took hold of my rod and pressed it against his gaping anus. The tip of the frisky phallus soon found its entrance in the hospitable hole that endeavoured to give it admission. I pressed a little; the whole of the glans was engulfed. The sphincter soon gripped it in such a way that it could not come out without an effort. I thrust it slowly to prolong as much as possible the ineffable sensation that ran through every limb, to calm the quivering nerves, and to allay the heat of the blood. Another push, and half the phallus was in his body. I pulled it out half an inch, though it seemed to me a yard by the prolonged pleasure I felt. I pressed forward again, and the whole of it, down to its very root, was all swallowed up. Thus wedged I vainly endeavoured to drive it higher up – an impossible feat, and, clasped as I was, I felt it wriggling in its sheath like a baby in its mother's womb, giving myself and him an unutterable and delightful titillation.

So keen was the bliss that overcame me, that I asked myself if some ethereal, life-giving fluid were not being poured on my head, and trickling down slowly over my quivering flesh?

Surely the rain-awakened flowers must be conscious of such a sensation during a shower, after they have been parched by the scorching rays of an estival sun.

Teleny again put his arm round me and held me tight. I gazed at myself within his eyes, he saw himself in mine. During this voluptuous, lambent feeling, we patted each other's bodies softly, our lips cleaved together and my tongue was again in his mouth. We remained in this copulation almost without stirring, for I felt that the slightest movement would provoke a copious ejaculation, and this feeling was too exquisite to be allowed to pass away so quickly. Still we could not help writhing, and we almost swooned away with delight. We were both shivering with lust, from the roots of our hair to the tips of our toes; all the flesh of our bodies kept bickering luxuriously, just as placid waters of the mere do at noontide when kissed by the sweet-scented, wanton breeze that has just deflowered the virgin rose.

Such intensity of delight could not, however, last very long; a few almost unwilling contractions of the sphincter brandled the phallus, and then the first brunt was over; I thrust in with might and main, I wallowed on him; my breath came thickly; I panted, I sighed, I groaned. The thick burning fluid was spouted out slowly and at long intervals.

As I rubbed myself against him, he underwent all the sensations I was feeling; for I was hardly drained of the last drop before I was likewise bathed with his own seething sperm. We did not kiss each other any further; our languid, half-open, lifeless lips only aspired each other's breath. Our sightless eyes saw each other no more, for we fell into that divine prostration which follows shattering ecstasy.

47   'Comrade, my Comrade'

Hon. Roden Noel. From *Collected Poems*, 1903. Written at Brighton, October 1891. Also titled 'To J.H. – R.I.P.' Among unpublished poems.

Comrade, my comrade, they are calling names
Of epoch-making men about the town
Who died but now; and these are nought to me,
Who mourn my brother, lowly, poor, unknown,
Dead with them in thy manhood's flower; thee Death
Took using all thy strength to wrest a friend
From his cold clutch; but he would take you both.
No famous man hath ended better; God
Approveth, and thy comrade honours thee,
True child of ocean, whom wild wind and wave
Bronzed with much kissing, claiming for their own;
Convivial, improvident, free-handed,
Who more than once plucked human lives from waves
That would have whelmed in their tremendous play.

But life, alas! proves often hard to bear
For such as you, one warfare grim and long
With famine, daily want of those who lean
On you for daily needs, your children, wives;
And so, may be, the horror of cold gloom,
That unaware enshrouded my poor heart,
To thee was but the long-delayed, blithe sail,

SH–R

Scarce hoped for, dawning on the mariner
Who thirsts and hungers on a sullen sea;
For niggard Life had used thee hardly; Death
Relieves from burdens unendurable.

But, ah! my friend, I may not see thee more,
Nor hear, nor feel! whom now in this my dwelling
The very rooms with their appurtenances,
Inanimate and trivial, recall;
The frame well-knit, well-moulded, the deft hand,
That so disposed them even now; yon beach
That strews my garden speaks of thee
Who brought it; still I seek a face well-loved,
And listen for a well-remembered tone
Upon the stairway, in my private chamber;
Ah! who will do thine office for me now?
Nay, we may never more climb waves together
In bounding boats, nor ply the limber oar
Among those bounding billows; but I roam
Heart-wounded in chill twilight by the shore,
Like him of old of whom blind Homer sang,
How, reft of one he loved, disconsolate,
He went in silence by the sounding sea:
I hear that rhythmic breathing of the sea
And evermore the surge repeats thy name.
Even so Achilles mourned his friend Patroclus,
So Alexander wept Hephaestion.

O may thy soul repose in peace, my friend,
Nor any troubled dream disturb thy rest;
But from a maze of tranquil reverie
May one remembrance, light as a rose-petal,
Float to my world and wandering to me
Here by my side assume the form beloved!

48   *'Non Delebo Propter Decem'*

Herbert P. Horne. From *Diversi Colores*, 1891.

Ye priests of men, ye priests ordained
    By the pure hands of God alone,
Live on! for we, through you, have gained

Our stablishment, that else were gone.
Awake, ye silent priests, and move
    With power throughout the approaching years!
Ye sinews of all human love,
    Ye just of Sodom. Wrath appears!
Awake, awake, and gain for men
    Time yet, to lust and sin again!

49   'Antinous'

Charles Kains–Jackson. From *The Artist*, 1 October 1891. 'A translation from the French of Ernest Raymond'. Signed 'Philip Castle'.

Glory throughout the world thy conquering name
    Has celebrated, and through ages sung
The Asian youth whose cult's melodious flame
    Lends bitter-sweetness to the poet's tongue.
Thy love's keen darts strike languor through the frame,
    The aromatic odours of the south
    Breathe from the half-shut lotus of thy mouth,
Thy smile's strange power, our conquered hearts proclaim.
Thy amber flesh, the blood ambrosial
Were fashioned for the Gods' high festival,
A dream of Rubies 'neath transparent gold:
O thou, whom Hadrian didst, a star, behold
Opening afresh thine eyes on heaven's blue
In the strange hour ere day begins anew!

50   'To Kalon'

George Gillett. From *The Artist*, 1 December 1891. Sub-title 'Suggested by a portrait in a private collection'.

In the old Greek legends such a face was seen,
Flushing its carnations through the grey and green
Of the olive gardens, where the gods had been.

In the later stories, Plato has enshrined,
When the wondrous Sophist moved the youth to mind,
Such a look on Lysis' sunny face I find.

And the same sweet secret lives across the years,
Lights monastic cloisters with its smiles and tears
Fills the present moment with its hopes and fears.

In one fortress fostered, in one temple lord,
Banned elsewhere what matter, since with one accord
Artists through all ages have in soul adored?

While Art lives, thy Cult lives. By the crowd downtrod,
By the court neglected, or given to the rod;
Art in sight of *Beauty*, gains a glimpse of God.

Ask no foolish questions, Angel, youth or maid,
Virtuous or vicious, daring or afraid,
Beauty in mere being, having Love repaid.

Yet to him that giveth Love as a thing due,
Worship as of free will, Beauty lends the clue;
Whereby out of old things, Art makes all things new.

51   A Problem in Modern Ethics

John Addington Symonds. Extracts from *A Problem in Modern Ethics*, 1891.

IV

VULGAR ERRORS

Gibbon's remarks upon the legislation of Constantine, Theodosius, and Justinian supply a fair example of the way in which men of learning and open mind have hitherto regarded what, after all, is a phenomenon worthy of cold and calm consideration. 'I touch,' he says, 'with reluctance, and despatch with impatience, a more odious vice, of which modesty rejects the name, and nature abominates the idea.' After briefly alluding to the morals of Etruria, Greece, and Rome, he proceeds to the enactments of Constantine: 'Adultery was first declared to be a capital offence . . . the same penalties were inflicted on the passive and active guilt of paederasty; and all criminals, of free or servile condition, were either drowned, or beheaded, or cast alive into the avenging flames.'[1] Then, without further comment, he observes: 'The adulterers

---

[1] Vindices Flammae. [This note, and those throughout the essay, unless otherwise stated, are Symonds's.]

were spared by the common sympathy of mankind; but the lovers of their own sex were pursued by general and pious indignation.' 'Justinian relaxed the punishment at least of female infidelity: the guilty spouse was only condemned to solitude and penance, and at the end of two years she might be recalled to the arms of a forgiving husband. But the same Emperor declared himself the implacable enemy of unmanly lust, and the cruelty of his persecution can scarcely be excused by the purity of his motives. In defiance of every principle of justice he stretched to past as well as future offences the operations of his edicts, with the previous allowance of a short respite for confession and pardon. A painful death was inflicted by the amputation of the sinful instrument, or the insertion of sharp reeds into the pores and tubes of most exquisite sensibility.' One consequence of such legislation may be easily foreseen. 'A sentence of death and infamy was often founded on the slight and suspicious evidence of a child or a servant: the guilt of the green faction, of the rich, and of the enemies of Theodora, was presumed by the judges, and paederasty became the crime of those to whom no crime could be imputed.'

This state of things has prevailed wherever the edicts of Justinian have been adopted into the laws of nations. The Cathari, the Paterini, the heretics of Provence, the Templars, the Fraticelli, were all accused of unnatural crimes, tortured into confession, and put to death. Where nothing else could be adduced against an unpopular sect, a political antagonist, a wealthy corporation, a rival in literature, a powerful party-leader, unnatural crime was insinuated, and a cry of 'Down with the pests of society' prepared the populace for a crusade.

It is the common belief that all subjects of sexual inversion have originally loved women, but that, through monstrous debauchery and superfluity of naughtiness, tiring of normal pleasure, they have wilfully turned their appetites into other channels. This is true about a certain number. But the sequel of this Essay will prove that it does not meet by far the larger proportion of cases, in whom such instincts are inborn, and a considerable percentage in whom they are also inconvertible. Medical jurists and physicians have recently agreed to accept this as a fact.

It is the common belief that a male who loves his own sex must be despicable, degraded, depraved, vicious, and incapable of humane or generous sentiments. If Greek history did not contradict this supposition, a little patient enquiry into contemporary manners would suffice to remove it. But people will not take this trouble about a matter, which, like Gibbon, they 'touch with reluctance and despatch with impatience.' Those who are obliged to do so find to their surprise that 'among the men who are subject to this deplorable vice there are even quite intelligent, talented, and highly-placed persons, of excellent and even noble character.'[2] The vulgar expect to discover the objects of their outraged animosity in the scum of humanity. But these may be met with every day in drawing-rooms, law-courts, banks, universities, mess-rooms; on the bench, the throne, the chair of the professor; under the blouse of the workman, the cassock of the priest, the epaulettes of the officer, the smock-frock of the ploughman, the wig of the barrister, the mantle of the peer, the costume of the actor, the tights of the athlete, the gown of the academician.

It is the common belief that one, and only one, unmentionable act is what the lovers seek as the source of their unnatural gratification, and that this produces spinal disease, epilepsy, consumption, dropsy, and the like.[3] Nothing can be more mistaken, as the scientifically reported cases of avowed and adult sinners amply demonstrate. Neither do they invariably or even usually prefer the *aversa Venus*; nor, when this happens, do they exhibit peculiar signs of suffering in health.[4] Excess in any venereal pleasure will produce diseases of nervous exhaustion and imperfect nutrition. But the indulgence of inverted sexual instincts within due limits, cannot be proved to be especially pernicious. Were it so, the Dorians and Athenians, including Sophocles, Pindar, Aeschines, Epaminondas, all the Spartan kings and generals, the Theban legion, Pheidias, Plato, would have been one nation of rickety, phthisical, dropsical paralytics. The grain of truth contained in this vulgar error

[2] Stieber, *Practisches Lehrbuch der Criminal-Polizei*, 1860, cap. 19, quoted by Ulrichs, *Araxes*, p. 9. It is not necessary to multiply evidences upon a point so patent to every man of the world. But I will nevertheless translate a striking passage from Mantegazza (op. cit., p. 148). 'Nor is this infamous abomination confined to the vilest classes of our society. It soars into the highest spheres of wealth and of intelligence. Within the narrow range of my own experience I have known among the most scandalous sodomites a French journalist, a German poet, an Italian statesman, and a Spanish jurist; all of these men of exquisite taste and profound culture!' It would not be difficult to draw up a list of English kings, bishops, deans, nobles of the highest rank, poets, historians, dramatists, officers in the army and navy, civil servants, schoolmasters in the most fashionable schools, physicians, members of parliament, journalists, barristers, who in their lifetime were, as Dante says, 'd'un medesmo peccato al mondo lerci.' Many belonging to the past are notorious; and no good could come of mentioning the names of the living.

[3] This accusation against men who feel a sexual inclination for males loses some of its significance when we consider how common the practice of *Venus aversa* is among libertines who love women. Parent-Duchatelet asserts that no prostitute after a certain age has escaped it. Coffignon, in his book on *La Corruption à Paris* (p. 324), says: 'Chaque année, il passe en traitement à l'hôpital de Lourcine une centaine de femmes sodomistes. . . . Je suis persuadé qu'à l'hôpital de St. Lazare la proportion des sodomistes est encore beaucoup plus grande. . . . Les maîtresses de maison, professant cet odieux principe que la clientèle doit être satisfaite, ne permettent pas à une fille de se refuser à une acte de sodomie.' Tardieu (*Attentats*, &c., p. 198) observes: 'Chose singulière! c'est principalement des rapports conjugaux que se sont produits les faits de cette nature.'

[4] See Casper-Liman, vol. i., p. 182, at the end of Case 71.

is that, under the prevalent laws and hostilities of modern society, the inverted passion has to be indulged furtively, spasmodically, hysterically; that the repression of it through fear and shame frequently leads to habits of self-abuse; and that its unconquerable solicitations sometimes convert it from a healthy outlet of the sexual nature into a morbid monomania.[5] It is also true that professional male prostitutes, like their female counterparts, suffer from local and constitutional disorders, as is only natural.[6]

It is the common belief that boys under age are specially liable to corruption. This error need not be confuted here. Anyone who chooses to read the cases recorded by Casper-Liman, Casper in his Novellen, Krafft-Ebing, and Ulrichs, or to follow the development of the present treatise, or to watch the manners of London after dark, will be convinced of its absurdity. Young boys are less exposed to dangers from abnormal than young girls from normal voluptuaries.

It is the common belief that all subjects of inverted instinct carry their lusts written in their faces; that they are pale, languid, scented, effeminate, painted, timid, oblique in expression. This vulgar error rests upon imperfect observation. A certain class of such people are undoubtedly feminine. From their earliest youth they have shown marked inclination for the habits and the dress of women; and when they are adult, they do everything in their power to obliterate their

[5] While studying what Germans call the *Casuistik* of this question in medical, forensic, and anthropological works, we often meet with cases where inverted sexuality exhibits extraordinary symptoms of apparent craziness – strange partialities for particular kinds of dress, occupations in the beloved objects, nastinesses, and so forth. But it must be remarked first that the same symptoms are exhibited by sexually normal natures (Krafft-Ebing, *Observations* 27, 28, 29, 30, 31, 32, 33, 34, 35, 36, 37, 38, 39, and the cases recorded in footnote to page 71); and, secondly, that if they should appear to be more frequent in the abnormal, this can in a great measure be ascribed to the fact that these latter cases only come under the observation of medical men and judges when the patients have already for many years been suffering from all the pangs of a coerced and defrauded instinct. There is nothing in the copious history of Greece and Rome upon this subject to lead us to suppose that in a society which tolerated sexual inversion, its subjects were more conspicuous for filthy and degrading or insane proclivities than ordinary men and women were. Those who can bring themselves to enquire into such matters may convince themselves by reading Forberg's annotations to *Hermaphroditus*, Rosenbaum's *Lustseuche*, the pseudo-Meursius, and the pornographical dialogues of Aretino. It will appear conclusively that both in ancient and in modern times the normal sexual instinct has been subject to the wildest freaks and aberrations; not in actually diseased persons, but simply in lustful wantons and the epicures of new sensations. The curious things we know about flagellation and cruelty in connection with the ordinary appetite should also be remembered. As a final note on this topic, I will refer to a passage quoted by Tarnowsky from a work of Taxil, describing a peculiarly repulsive class of fashionable libertines in Paris called 'les stercoraires' (*op. cit.*, p. 70). Compare what Mantegazza reports of a 'gentile ufficiale francese' (*Gli amore degli uomini*, vol. i. p. 117).

[6] See upon this point Tardieu, *Attentats aux Moeurs*, Rosenbaum, *Die Lustseuche*.

manhood. It is equally true that such unsexed males possess a strong attraction for some abnormal individuals. But it is a gross mistake to suppose that all the tribe betray these attributes. The majority differ in no detail of their outward appearance, their physique, or their dress from normal men. They are athletic, masculine in habits, frank in manner, passing through society year after year without arousing a suspicion of their inner temperament. Were it not so, society would long ago have had its eyes opened to the amount of perverted sexuality it harbours.

The upshot of this discourse on vulgar errors is that popular opinion is made up of a number of contradictory misconceptions and confusions. Moreover, it has been taken for granted that 'to investigate the depraved instincts of humanity is unprofitable and disgusting.' Consequently the subject has been imperfectly studied; and individuals belonging to radically different species are confounded in one vague sentiment of reprobation. Assuming that they are all abominable, society is contented to punish them indiscriminately. The depraved debauchee who abuses boys receives the same treatment as the young man who loves a comrade. The male prostitute who earns his money by extortion is scarcely more contemned than a man of birth and breeding who has been seen walking with soldiers.

VIII

LITERATURE – HISTORICAL ANTHROPOLOGICAL

No one has yet attempted a complete history of inverted sexuality in all ages and in all races. This would be well worth doing. Materials, though not extremely plentiful, lie to hand in the religious books and codes of ancient nations, in mythology and poetry and literature, in narratives of travel, and the reports of observant explorers.

Gibbon once suggested that: 'A curious dissertation might be formed on the introduction of paederasty after the time of Homer, its progress among the Greeks of Asia and Europe, the vehemence of their passions, and the thin device of virtue and friendship which amused the philosophers of Athens. But,' adds the prurient prude, 'Scelera ostendi oportet dum puniuntur, abscondi flagitia.'

Two scholars responded to this call. The result is that the chapter on Greek love has been very fairly written by equally impartial, equally learned, and independent authors, who approached the subject from somewhat different points of view, but who arrived in the main at similar conclusions.

The first of these histories is M. H. E. Meier's article on 'Paederastie' in Ersch and Gruber's *Allgemeine Encyklopädie*: Leipzig, Brockhaus' 1837.

The second is a treatise entitled *A Problem in Greek Ethics*, composed by an Englishman in English. The anonymous author was not acquainted with Meier's article before he wrote, and only came across it long after he had printed his own essay. This work is extremely rare, ten copies only having been impressed for private use.[7]

Enquirers into the psychology and morality of sexual inversion should not fail to study one or other of these treatises. It will surprise many a well-read scholar, when he sees the whole list of Greek authorities and passages collected and co-ordinated, to find how thoroughly the manners and the literature of that great people were penetrated with paiderastia. The myths and heroic legends of prehistoric Hellas, the educational institutions of the Dorian states, the dialogues of Plato, the history of the Theban army, the biographies of innumerable eminent citizens – lawgivers and thinkers, governors and generals, founders of colonies and philosophers, poets and sculptors – render it impossible to maintain that this passion was either a degraded vice or a form of inherited neuropathy in the race to whom we owe so much of our intellectual heritage. Having surveyed the picture, we may turn aside to wonder whether modern European nations, imbued with the opinions I have described above in the section on Vulgar Errors, are wise in making Greek literature a staple of the higher education. Their motto is *Écrasez l'infame!* Here the infamous thing clothes itself like an angel of light, and raises its forehead unabashed to heaven among the marble peristyles and olive-groves of an unrivalled civilization.

Another book, written from a medical point of view, is valuable upon the pathology of sexual inversion and cognate aberrations among the nations of antiquity. It bears the title *Geschichte der Lustseuche im Alterthume*, and is composed by Dr. Julius Rosenbaum.[8] Rosenbaum attempts to solve the problem of the existence of syphilis and other venereal diseases in the remote past. This enquiry leads him to investigate the whole of Greek and Latin literature in its bearing upon sexual vice. Students will therefore expect from his pages no profound psychological speculations and no idealistic presentation of an eminently repulsive subject. One of the most interesting chapters of his work is devoted to what Herodotus called Νοῦσος θήλεια among the Scythians, a wide-spread effemination prevailing in a wild warlike and nomadic

[7] By Symonds himself; printed 1883, later included in H. Ellis and J. A. Symonds, *Sexual Inversion*, 1897, first edition (editor's note).
[8] Third edition. Halle a. S., 1882.

race. We have already alluded to Krafft-Ebing's remarks on this disease, which has curious points of resemblance with some of the facts of male prostitution in modern cities.[9]

Professed anthropologists have dealt with the subject, collecting evidence from many quarters, and in some cases attempting to draw general conclusions. Bastian's *Der Mensch in der Geschichte*[10] and Herbert Spencer's Tables deserve special mention for their encyclopaedic fullness of information regarding the distribution of abnormal sexuality and the customs of savage tribes.

In England an Essay appended to the last volume of Sir Richard Burton's *Arabian Nights* made a considerable stir upon its first appearance.[11] The author endeavoured to co-ordinate a large amount of miscellaneous matter, and to frame a general theory regarding the origin and prevalence of homosexual passions. His erudition, however, is incomplete; and though he possesses a copious store of anthropological details, he is not at the proper point of view for discussing the topic philosophically.[12] For example, he takes for granted that 'Pederasty,' as he calls it, is everywhere and always what the vulgar think it. He seems to have no notion of the complicated psychology of Urnings, revealed to us by their recently published confessions in French and German medical and legal works. Still his views deserve consideration.

Burton regards the phenomenon as 'geographical and climatic, not racial.' He summarizes the result of his investigations in the following five conclusions.[13]

'(1) There exists what I shall call a "Sotadic Zone," bounded westwards by the northern shores of the Mediterranean (N. lat. 43°) and by the southern (N. lat. 30°). Thus the depth would be 780 to 800 miles, including meridional France, the Iberian Peninsula, Italy and Greece, with the coast-regions of Africa from Morocco to Egypt.

'(2) Running eastward the Sotadic Zone narrows, embracing Asia Minor, Mesopotamia and Chaldaea, Afghanistan, Sind, the Punjab, and Kashmir.

[9] *Psych. Sex.*, p. 82.
[10] Leipzig, Wigand, 1860.
[11] *Arabian Nights*, 1885, vol. x., pp. 205–254.
[12] Burton's acquaintance with what he called 'le Vice' was principally confined to Oriental nations. He started on his enquiries, imbued with vulgar errors; and he never weighed the psychical theories examined by me in the foregoing section of this Essay. Nevertheless, he was led to surmise a crasis of the two sexes in persons subject to sexual inversion. Thus he came to speak of 'the third sex.' During conversations I had with him less than three months before his death, he told me that he had begun a general history of 'le Vice'; and at my suggestion he studied Ulrichs and Krafft-Ebing. It is to be lamented that life failed before he could apply his virile and candid criticism to those theories, and compare them with the facts and observations he had independently collected.
[13] I give the author's own text, p. 206.

'(3) In Indo-China the belt begins to broaden, enfolding China, Japan, and Turkistan.

'(4) It then embraces the South Sea Islands and the New World, where, at the time of its discovery, Sotadic love was, with some exceptions, an established racial institution.

'(5) Within the Sotadic Zone the vice is popular and endemic, held at the worst to be a mere peccadillo, whilst 'he races to the North and South of the limits here defined practise it only sporadically, amid the opprobrium of their fellows, who, as a rule, are physically incapable of performing the operation, and look upon it with the liveliest disgust.'

This is a curious and interesting generalization, though it does not account for what history has transmitted regarding the customs of the Kelts, Scythians, Bulgars, Tartars, Normans, and for the acknowledged leniency of modern Slavs to this form of vice.

Burton advances an explanation of its origin. 'The only physical cause for the practice which suggests itself to me, and that must be owned to be purely conjectural, is that within the Sotadic Zone there is a blending of the masculine and feminine temperaments, a crasis which elsewhere occurs only sporadically.'[14] So far as it goes, this suggestion rests upon ground admitted to be empirically sound by the medical writers we have already examined, and vehemently declared to be indisputable as a fact of physiology by Ulrichs, whom I shall presently introduce to my readers. But Burton makes no effort to account for the occurrence of this crasis of masculine and feminine temperaments in the Sotadic Zone at large, and for its sporadic appearance in other regions. Would it not be more philosophical to conjecture that the crasis, if that exists at all, takes place universally; but that the consequences are only tolerated in certain parts of the globe, which he defines as the Sotadic Zone? Ancient Greece and Rome permitted them. Modern Greece and Italy have excluded them to the same extent as Northern European nations. North and South America, before the Conquest, saw no harm in them. Since its colonization by Europeans they have been discountenanced. The phenomenon cannot therefore be regarded as specifically geographical and climatic. Besides, there is one fact mentioned by Burton which ought to make him doubt his geographical theory. He says that, after the conquest of Algiers, the French troops were infected to an enormous extent by the habits they had acquired there, and from them it spread so far and wide into civilian society that 'the vice may be said to have been democratized in cities and large towns.'[15] This surely proves that north of the Sotadic Zone males are neither physically incapable of the acts involved in

[14] P. 208.
[15] P. 251.

abnormal passion, nor gifted with an insuperable disgust for them. Law, and the public opinion generated by law and religious teaching, have been deterrent causes in those regions. The problem is therefore not geographical and climatic, but social. Again, may it not be suggested that the absence of 'the Vice' among the negroes and negroid races of South Africa, noticed by Burton,[16] is due to their excellent customs of sexual initiation and education at the age of puberty – customs which it is the shame of modern civilization to have left unimitated?

However this may be, Burton regards the instinct as natural, not *contre nature*, and says that its patients 'deserve, not prosecution but the pitiful care of the physician and the study of the psychologist.'[17]

Another distinguished anthropologist, Paolo Mantegazza, has devoted special attention to the physiology and psychology of what he calls 'I pervertimenti dell'amore.'[18] Starting with the vulgar error that all sexual inversion implies the unmentionable act of coition (for which, by the way, he is severely rebuked by Krafft-Ebing, *Psy. Sex.*, p. 92), he explains anomalous passions by supposing that the nerves of pleasurable sensation, which ought to be carried to the genital organs, are in some cases carried to the rectum.[19] This malformation makes its subject desire *coitum per anum*. That an intimate connection exists between the nerves of the reproductive organs and the nerves of the rectum, is known to anatomists and is felt by everybody. Probably some *cinaedi* are excited voluptuously in the mode suggested. Seneca, in his Epistles, records such cases; and it is difficult in any other way to account for the transports felt by male prostitutes of the Weibling type. Finally, writers upon female prostitution mention women who are incapable of deriving pleasure from any sexual act except *aversa venus*.

Mantegazza's observation deserves to be remembered, and ought to be tested by investigation. But, it is obvious, he pushes the corollary he draws from it, as to the prevalence of sexual inversion, too far.

He distinguishes three classes of sodomy: (1) Peripheric or anatomical, caused by an unusual distribution of the nerves passing from the spine to the reproductive organs and the rectum; (2) psychical, which he describes as 'specific to intelligent men, cultivated, and frequently neurotic,' but which he does not attempt to elucidate, though he calls it 'not a vice, but a passion'; (3) luxurious or lustful, when the *aversa venus* is deliberately chosen on account of what Mantegazza terms 'la desolante larghezza' of the female.[20]

16 P. 222.
17 Pp. 204, 209.
18 *Gli amori degli Uomini*, Milano, 1886, vol. i. cap. 5.
19 *Ibid.*, p. 149.
20 Pp. 148–154.

Mantegazza winds up, like Burton, by observing that 'sodomy, studied with the pitying and indulgent eye of the physician and the physiologist, is consequently a disease which claims to be cured, and can in many cases be cured.'[21]

After perusing what physicians, historians, and anthropologists have to say about sexual inversion, there is good reason for us to feel uneasy as to the present condition of our laws. And yet it might be argued that anomalous desires are not always maladies, not always congenital, not always psychical passions. In some cases they must surely be vices deliberately adopted out of lustfulness, wanton curiosity, and seeking after sensual refinements. The difficult question still remains then – how to repress vice, without acting unjustly toward the naturally abnormal, the unfortunate, and the irresponsible.

I pass now to the polemical writings of a man who maintains that homosexual passions, even in their vicious aspects, ought not to be punished except in the same degree and under the same conditions as the normal passions of the majority.

IX

LITERATURE – POLEMICAL

It can hardly be said that inverted sexuality received a serious and sympathetic treatment until a German jurist, named Karl Heinrich Ulrichs, began his long warfare against what he considered to be prejudice and ignorance upon a topic of the greatest moment to himself. A native of Hanover, and writing at first under the assumed name of Numa Numantius, he kept pouring out a series of polemical, analytical, theoretical, and apologetical pamphlets between the years 1864 and 1870. The most important of these works is a lengthy and comprehensive Essay entitled 'Memnon. Die Geschlechtsnatur des mann-liebenden Urnings. Eine naturwissenschaftliche Darstellung.' Schleiz 1868. Memnon may be used as the text-book of its author's theories; but it is also necessary to study earlier and later treatises – Inclusa, Formatrix, Vindex, Ara Spei, Gladius Furens, Incubus, Argonauticus, Prometheus, Araxes, Kritische Pfeile – in order to obtain a complete knowledge of his opinions, and to master the whole mass of information he has brought together.

The object of Ulrichs in these miscellaneous writings is twofold. He seeks to establish a theory of sexual inversion upon the basis of natural science, proving that abnormal instincts are inborn and healthy

[21] P. 154.

in a considerable percentage of human beings; that they do not owe their origin to bad habits of any kind, to hereditary disease, or to wilful depravity; that they are incapable in the majority of cases of being extirpated or converted into normal channels; and that the men subject to them are neither physically, intellectually, nor morally inferior to normally constituted individuals. Having demonstrated these points to his own satisfaction, and supported his views with a large induction of instances and a respectable show of erudition, he proceeds to argue that the present state of the law in many states of Europe is flagrantly unjust to a class of innocent persons, who may indeed by regarded as unfortunate and inconvenient, but who are guilty of nothing which deserves reprobation and punishment. In this second and polemical branch of his exposition, Ulrichs assumes, for his juristic starting-point, that each human being is born with natural rights which legislation ought not to infringe but to protect. He does not attempt to confute the utilitarian theory of jurisprudence, which regards laws as regulations made by the majority in the supposed interests of society. Yet a large amount of his reasoning is designed to invalidate utilitarian arguments in favour of repression, by showing that no social evil ensues in those countries which have placed abnormal sexuality upon the same footing as the normal, and that the toleration of inverted passion threatens no danger to the well-being of nations.

After this prelude, an abstract of Ulrichs' theory and his pleading may be given, deduced from the comparative study of his numerous Essays.

The right key to the solution of the problem is to be found in physiology, in that obscure department of natural science which deals with the evolution of sex. The embryo, as we are now aware, contains an undetermined element of sex during the first months of pregnancy. This is gradually worked up into male and female organs of procreation; and these, when the age of puberty arrives, are generally accompanied by corresponding male and female appetites. That is to say, the man in an immense majority of cases desires the woman, and the woman desires the man. Nature, so to speak, aims at differentiating the un-decided foetus into a human being of one or the other sex, the propagation of the species being the main object of life. Still, as Aristotle puts it, and as we observe in many of her operations, 'Nature wishes, but has not always the power': ἡ φύσις βούλεται μὲν ἀλλ' οὐ δύναται. Conse-quently, in respect of physical structure, there come to light imperfect individuals, so-called hermaphrodites, whose sexual apparatus is so far undetermined that many a real male has passed a portion of his life under a mistake, has worn female clothes, and has cohabited by prefer-ence with men. Likewise, in respect of spiritual nature, there appear males who, notwithstanding their marked masculine organization, feel from the earliest childhood a sexual proclivity toward men, with a corresponding indifference for women. In some of these abnormal, but natural, beings, the appetite for men resembles the normal appetite of men for women; in others it resembles the normal appetite of women for men. That is to say, some prefer effeminate males, dressed in feminine clothes and addicted to female occupations. Others prefer powerful adults of an ultra-masculine stamp. A third class manifest their predilection for healthy young men in the bloom of adolescence, between nineteen and twenty. The attitude of such persons toward women also varies. In genuine cases of inborn sexual inversion a positive horror is felt when the woman has to be carnally known; and this horror is of the same sort as that which normal men experience when they think of cohabitation with a male. In others the disinclination does not amount to repugnance; but the abnormal man finds considerable difficulty in stimulating himself to the sexual act with females, and derives a very imperfect satisfaction from the same. A certain type of man, in the last place, seems to be indifferent, desiring males at one time and females at another.

In order to gain clearness in his exposition, Ulrichs has invented names for these several species. The so-called hermaphrodite he dismisses with the German designation of *Zwitter*. Imperfect individuals of this type are not to be considered, because it is well known that the male or female organs are never developed in one and the same body. It is also, as we shall presently discover, an essential part of his theory to regard the problem of inversion psychologically.

The normal man he calls *Dioning*, the abnormal man *Urning*. Among Urnings, those who prefer effeminate males are christened by the name of *Mannling*; those who prefer powerful and masculine adults receive the name of *Weibling*; the Urning who cares for adolescents is styled a *Zwischen-Urning*. Men who seem to be indifferently attracted by both sexes, he calls *Uranodioninge*. A genuine Dioning, who, from lack of women, or under the influence of special circumstances, consorts with persons of his own sex, is denominated *Uraniaster*. A genuine Urning, who has put restraint upon his inborn impulse, who has forced himself to cohabit with women, or has perhaps contracted marriage, is said to be *Virilisirt* – a virilized Urning.

These outlandish names, though seemingly pedantic and superfluous, have their technical value, and are necessary to the understanding of Ulrichs' system. He is dealing exclusively with individuals classified by common parlance as males without distinction. Ulrichs believes that he can establish a real natural division between men proper, whom he calls *Dioninge*, and males of an anomalous sexual development, whom he calls *Urninge*. Having proceeded so far, he finds the necessity of distinguishing three broad types of the Urning, and of making out the crosses between Urning and Dioning, of which he also finds three species. It will appear in the sequel that, whatever may be thought about his psychological hypothesis, the nomenclature he has adopted is useful in discussion, and corresponds to well-defined phenomena, of which we have abundant information. The following table will make his analysis sufficiently plain:

The Human Male
- (1) Man or Dioning .. Uraniaster, when he has acquired the tastes of the Urning.
- (2) Urning ....
  - Mannling
  - Weibling
  - Zwischen-Urning
  - Virilized Urning
- (3) Uranodioning
- (4) Hermaphrodite

Broadly speaking, the male includes two main species: Dioning and Urning, men with normal and men with abnormal instincts. What then constitutes the distinction between them? How are we justified in regarding them as radically divergent?

Ulrichs replies that the phenomenon of sexual inversion is to be explained by physiology, and particularly by the evolution of the embryo.[22] Nature fails to complete her work regularly and in every

[22] The notion that human beings were originally hermaphroditic, is both ancient and widespread. We find it in the Book of Genesis, unless indeed there be a confusion here between two separate theories of creation. God is said to have first made man in his own image, male and female in one body, and to have bidden them multiply. Later on he created the woman out of part of this primitive man. The myth related by Aristophanes in Plato's *Symposium* has a curious bearing upon Ulrichs' speculations. There were originally human beings of three sexes: men, the children of the sun; women, the children of the earth; and hermaphrodites, the children of the moon. They were round, with two faces, four hands, four feet and two sets of reproductive organs apiece. In the case of the third sex, one set was male, the other female. Zeus, on account of their strength and insolence, sliced them into halves. Since that time the halves of each sort have always striven to unite with their corresponding halves, and have found some satisfaction in carnal congress – males with males, females with females, and males and females with each other: 'They who are a section of the male follow the male, and while they are young, being slices of the original man, they hang about men and embrace them, and they are themselves the best of boys and youths, because they have the most manly nature. And when they reach manhood, they are lovers of youth, and are not naturally inclined to marry or beget children, which they do, if at all, only in obedience to the law, but they are satisfied if they may be allowed to live with one another unwedded; and such a nature if prone to love and ready to return love, always embracing that which is akin to him.' (Symp. 191–2, Jowett's translation.) Then follows a glowing description of Greek Love, the whole reminding us very closely of the confessions made by Urnings in modern times, and preserved by medical or forensic writers on sexual inversion.

instance. Having succeeded in differentiating a male with full-formed sexual organs from the undecided foetus, she does not always effect the proper differentiation of that portion of the psychical being in which resides the sexual appetite. There remains a female soul in a male body. *Anima muliebris virili corpore inclusa*, is the formula adopted by Ulrichs; and he quotes a passage from the 'Vestiges of Creation,' which suggests that the male is a more advanced product of sexual evolution than the female. The male instinct of sex is a more advanced product than the female instinct. Consequently men appear whose body has been differentiated as masculine, but whose sexual instinct has not progressed beyond the feminine stage.

Ulrichs' own words ought to be cited upon this fundamental part of his hypothesis, since he does not adopt the opinion that the Urning is a Dioning arrested at a certain point of development; but rather that there is an element of uncertainty attending the simultaneous evolution of physical and psychical factors from the indeterminate ground-stuff. 'Sex,' says he, 'is only an affair of development. Up to a certain stage of embryonic existence all living mammals are hermaphroditic. A certain number of them advance to the condition of what I call man (Dioning), others to what I call woman (Dioningin), a third class become what I call *Urning* (including *Urningin*). It ensues therefrom that between these three sexes there are no primary, but only secondary differences. And yet true differences, constituting sexual species, exist as facts.'[23] Man, Woman, and Urning – the third being either a male or a female in whom we observe a real and inborn, not an acquired or a spurious, inversion of appetite – are consequently regarded by him as the three main divisions of humanity viewed from the point of view of sex. The embryonic ground-stuff in the case of each was homologous; but while the two former, Man and Woman, have been normally differentiated, the Urning's sexual instinct, owing to some imperfection in the process of development, does not correspond to his or her sexual organs.

The line of division between the sexes, even in adult life, is a subtle one; and the physical structure of men and women yields indubitable signs of their emergence from a common ground-stuff. Perfect men have rudimentary breasts. Perfect women carry a rudimentary penis in their clitoris. The raphé of the scrotum shows where the aperture, common at first to masculine and feminine beings, but afterwards only retained in the female vulva, was closed up to form a male. Other anatomical details of the same sort might be adduced. But these will suffice to make thinking persons reflect upon the mysterious

[23] *Memnon*, section xix.

dubiety of what we call sex. That gradual development, which ends in normal differentiation, goes on very slowly. It is only at the age of puberty that a boy distinguishes himself abruptly from a girl, by changing his voice and growing hair on parts of the body where it is not usually found in women. This being so, it is surely not surprising that the sexual appetite should sometimes fail to be normally determined, or in other words should be inverted.

Ulrichs maintains that the body of an Urning is masculine, his soul feminine, so far as sex is concerned. Accordingly, though physically unfitted for coition with men, he is imperatively drawn towards them by a natural impulse. Opponents meet him with this objection: 'Your position is untenable. Body and soul constitute one inseparable entity.' So they do, replies Ulrichs; but the way in which these factors of the person are combined in human beings differs extremely, as I can prove by indisputable facts. The body of a male is visible to the eyes, is mensurable and ponderable, is clearly marked in its specific organs. But what we call his soul — his passions, inclinations, sensibilities, emotional characteristics, sexual desires — eludes the observation of the senses. This second factor, like the first, existed in the undetermined stages of the foetus. And when I find that the soul, this element of instinct and emotion and desire existing in a male, has been directed in its sexual appetite from earliest boyhood toward persons of the male sex, I have the right to qualify it with the attribute of femininity. You assume that soul-sex is indissolubly connected and inevitably derived from body sex. The facts contradict you, as I can prove by referring to the veracious autobiographies of Urnings and to known phenomena regarding them.

Such is the theory of Ulrichs; and though we may not incline to his peculiar mode of explaining the want of harmony between sexual organs and sexual appetite in Urnings, there can be no doubt that in some way or other their eccentric diathesis must be referred to the obscure process of sexual differentiation.[24] Perhaps he antedates the moment at which the aberration sometimes takes its origin, not accounting sufficiently for imperative impressions made on the imagination or the senses of boys during the years which precede puberty.

However this may be, the tendency to such inversion is certainly inborn in an extremely large percentage of cases. That can be demonstrated from the reports of persons whose instincts were directed to the male before they knew what sex meant. It is worth extracting

[24] It might be queried whether this 'imperfect sexual differentiation,' or this 'congenital lack of balance between structures themselves healthy,' is not the result of an evolutionary process arriving through heredity and casual selection at an abnormal, but not of necessity a morbid, phenomenon in certain individuals.

passages from these confessions.[25] (1) 'As a schoolboy of eight years, I sat near a comrade rather older than myself; and how happy was I, when he touched me. That was the first indefinite perception of an inclination which remained a secret for me till my nineteenth year.' (2) 'Going back to my seventh year, I had a lively feeling for a school-fellow, two years older than myself; I was happy when I could be as close as possible to him, and in our games could place my head near to his private parts.' (3) 'At ten years of age he had a romantic attachment for a comrade; and the passion for people of his own sex became always more and more marked.' (4) Another confessed that 'already at the age of four he used to dream of handsome grooms.' (5) A fifth said: 'My passion for people of my own sex awoke at the age of eight. I used to enjoy my brother's nakedness; while bathing with other children, I took no interest at all in girls, but felt the liveliest attraction towards boys.' (6) A sixth dates his experience from his sixth or seventh year. (7) A seventh remembers that 'while yet a boy, before the age of puberty, sleeping in the company of a male agitated him to such an extent that he lay for hours awake.' (8) An eighth relates that 'while three years old, I got possession of a fashion book, cut out the pictures of men, and kissed them to tatters. The pictures of women I did not care to look at.' (9) A ninth goes back to his thirteenth year, and a school friendship. (10) A tenth records the same about his seventh year. (11) An eleventh says that his inverted instincts awoke in early childhood, and that from his ninth year onward he fell over and over again in love with adult men. (12) A twelfth spoke as follows: 'So far back as I can remember, I was always subject to this passion. Quite as a child, young men made a deeper impression on me than women or girls. The earliest sensual pertu bation of which I have any recollection was excited by a tutor, when I was nine or ten, and my greatest pleasure was to be allowed to ride astride upon his leg.' (13) A thirteenth: 'From the earliest childhood I have been haunted by visions of men, and only of men; never has a woman exercised the least influence over me. At school I kept these instincts to myself, and lived quite retired.' (14) A fourteenth can recollect 'receiving a distinctly sensual impression at the age of four, when the man-servants caressed him.' (15) A fifteenth says that at the age of thirteen, together with puberty, the inversion of appetite awoke in him. (16) A sixteenth confesses that he felt an un-conquerable desire for soldiers in his thirteenth year. (17) A seventeenth remembers having always dreamed only of men; and at school, he says, 'when my comrades looked at pretty girls and criticized them during

[25] The first two from Casper-Liman, *Handbuch der gerichtlichen Medicin*, vol. i. pp. 166–169. The others from Krafft-Ebing, *Psychopathia Sexualis*.

our daily promenades, I could not comprehend how they found anything to admire in such creatures.' On the other hand, the sight and touch of soldiers and strong fellows excited him enormously. (18) An eighteenth dates the awakening of passion in him at the age of eleven, when he saw a handsome man in church; and from that time forward his instinct never altered. (19) A nineteenth fell in love with an officer at the age of thirteen, and since then always desired vigorous adult males. (20) A twentieth confessed to having begun to love boys of his own age, sensually, while only eight years of age. (21) A twenty-first records that, when he was eight, he began to crave after the sight of naked men.

In addition to these cases a great many might be culled from the writings of Ulrichs, who has published a full account from his own early experience.[26] 'I was fifteen years and ten and a half months old,' he says, 'when the first erotic dream announced the arrival of puberty. Never before that period had I known sexual gratification of any kind whatever. The occurrence was therefore wholly normal. From a much earlier time, however, I had been subject to emotions, partly romantic, partly sensual, without any definite desire, and never for one and the same young man. These aimless yearnings of the senses plagued me in my solitary hours, and I could not overcome them. During my fifteenth year, while at school at Detmold, the vague longing took a twofold shape. First, I came across Normand's "Säulenordnungen," and there I was vehemently attracted by the figure of a Greek god or hero, standing in naked beauty. Secondly, while studying in my little room, or before going to sleep, the thought used suddenly and irresistibly to rise up in my mind – If only a soldier would clamber through the window and come into my room! I then painted in my fancy the picture of a splendid soldier of twenty to twenty-two years old. And yet I had no definite idea of why I wanted him; nor had I ever come in contact with soldiers. About two years after this, I happened to sit next a soldier in a post-carriage. The contact with his thigh excited me to the highest degree.' Ulrichs also relates that in his tenth year he conceived an enthusiastic and romantic friendship for a boy two years his senior.

That experiences of the kind are very common, every one who has at all conversed with Urnings knows well. From private sources of unquestionable veracity, these may be added. A relates that, before he was eight years old, reveries occurred to him during the day, and dreams at night, of naked sailors. When he began to study Latin and Greek, he dreamed of young gods, and at about the age of fourteen, became deeply enamoured of a photograph of the Praxitelean Erôs in the Vatican. He had a great dislike for physical contact with girls; and with

[26] *Memnon*, section lxxiii. p. 54.

boys was shy and reserved, indulging in no acts of sense. *B* says that during his tenderest boyhood, long before the age of puberty, he fell in love with a young shepherd on one of his father's farms, for whom he was so enthusiastic that the man had to be sent to a distant moor. *C*, at the same early age, conceived a violent affection for a footman; *D* for an officer, who came to stay at his home; *E* for the bridegroom of his eldest sister.

In nearly all the cases here cited, the inverted sexual instinct sprang up spontaneously. Only a few of the autobiographies record seduction by an elder male as the origin of the affection. In none of them was it ever wholly overcome. Only five out of the twenty-seven men married. Twenty declare that, tortured by the sense of their dissimilarity to other males, haunted by shame and fear, they forced themselves to frequent public women soon after the age of puberty. Some found themselves impotent. Others succeeded in accomplishing their object with difficulty, or by means of evoking the images of men on whom their affections were set. All, except one, concur in emphatically asserting the superior attraction which men have always exercised for them over women. Women leave them, if not altogether disgusted, yet cold and indifferent. Men rouse their strongest sympathies and instincts. The one exception just alluded to is what Ulrichs would call an Uranodioning. The others are capable of friendship with women, some even of aesthetic admiration and the tenderest regard for them, but not of genuine sexual desire. Their case is literally an inversion of the ordinary.

Some observations may be made on Ulrichs' theory. It is now recognized by the leading authorities, medical and medico-juristic, in Germany, by writers like Casper-Liman and Krafft-Ebing, that sexual inversion is more often than not innate. So far, without discussing the physiological or metaphysical explanations of this phenomenon, without considering whether Ulrichs is right in his theory of *anima muliebris inclusa in corpore virili*, or whether heredity, insanity, and similar general conditions are to be held responsible for the fact, it may be taken as admitted on all sides that the sexual diathesis in question is in a very large number of instances congenital. But Ulrichs seems to claim too much for the position he has won. He ignores the frequency of acquired habits. He shuts his eyes to the force of fashion and depravity. He reckons men like Horace and Ovid and Catullus, among the ancients, who were clearly indifferent in their tastes (as indifferent as the modern Turks) to the account of Uranodionings. In one word, he is so enthusiastic for his physiological theory that he overlooks all other aspects of the question. Nevertheless, he has acquired the right to an impartial hearing, while pleading in defence of those who are acknowledged by all investigators of the problem to be the subjects of an inborn mis-placement of the sexual appetite.

Let us turn then to the consideration of his arguments in favour of freeing Urnings from the terrible legal penalties to which they are at present subject, and, if this were possible, from the no less terrible social condemnation to which they are exposed by the repugnance they engender in the normally constituted majority. Dealing with these exceptions to the kindly race of men and women, these unfortunates who have no family ties knotted by bonds by mutual love, no children to expect, no reciprocity of passion to enjoy, mankind, says Ulrichs, has hitherto acted just in the same way as a herd of deer acts when it drives the sickly and the weakly out to die in solitude, burdened with contumely, and cut off from common sympathy.

From the point of view of morality and law, he argues, it does not signify whether we regard the sexual inversion of an Urning as morbid or as natural. He has become what he is in the dawn and first emergence of emotional existence. You may contend that he derives perverted instincts from his ancestry, that he is the subject of a psychical disorder, that from the cradle he is predestined by atavism or disease to misery. I maintain that he is one of nature's sports, a creature healthy and well organized, evolved in her superb indifference to aberrations from the normal type. We need not quarrel over our solutions of the problem. The fact that he is there, among us, and that he constitutes an ever-present factor in our social system, has to be faced. How are we to deal with him? Has society the right to punish individuals sent into the world with homosexual instincts? Putting the question at its lowest point, admitting that these persons are the victims of congenital morbidity, ought they to be treated as criminals? It is established that their appetites, being innate, are *to them* at least natural and undepraved; the common appetites, being excluded from their sexual scheme, are *to them* unnatural and abhorrent. Ought not such beings, instead of being hunted down and persecuted by legal bloodhounds, to be regarded with pitying solicitude as among the most unfortunate of human beings, doomed as they are to inextinguishable longings and life-long deprivation of that which is the chief prize of man's existence on this planet, a reciprocated love? As your laws at present stand, you include all cases of sexual inversion under the one denomination of crime. You make exceptions in some special instances, and treat the men involved as lunatics. But the Urning is neither criminal nor insane. He is only less fortunate than you are, through an accident of birth, which is at present obscure to our imperfect science of sexual determination.

So far Ulrichs is justified in his pleading. When it has been admitted that sexual inversion is usually a fact of congenital diathesis, the criminal law stands in no logical relation to the phenomenon. It is monstrous to punish people as wilfully wicked because, having been born with the same organs and the same appetites as their neighbours, they are doomed to suffer under the frightful disability of not being able to use these organs or to gratify these appetites in the ordinary way.

But here arises a difficulty, which cannot be ignored, since upon it is based the only valid excuse for the position taken up by society in dealing with this matter. Not all men and women possessed by abnormal sexual desires can claim that these are innate. It is certain that the habits of sodomy are frequently acquired under conditions of exclusion from the company of persons of the other sex – as in public schools, barracks, prisons, convents, ships. In some cases they are deliberately adopted by natures tired of normal sexual pleasure. They may even become fashionable and epidemic. Lastly, it is probable that curiosity and imitation communicate them to otherwise normal individuals at a susceptible moment of development. Therefore society has the right to say: those who are the unfortunate subjects of inborn sexual inversion shall not be allowed to indulge their passions, lest the mischief should spread, and a vicious habit should contaminate our youth. From the utilitarian point of view, society is justified in protecting itself against a minority of exceptional beings whom it regards as pernicious to the general welfare. From any point of view, the majority is strong enough to coerce the inborn instincts and to trample on the anguish of a few unfortunates. But, asks Ulrichs, is this consistent with humanity, is it consistent with the august ideal of impartial equity? Are people, sound in body, vigorous in mind, wholesome in habit, capable of generous affections, good servants of the state, trustworthy in all the ordinary relations of life, to be condemned at law as criminals because they cannot feel sexually as the majority feel, because they find some satisfaction for their inborn want in ways which the majority dislike?

Seeking a solution of the difficulty stated in the foregoing paragraph, Ulrichs finds it in fact and history. His answer is that if society leaves nature to take her course, with the abnormal as well as with the normal subjects of sexual inclination, society will not suffer. In countries where legal penalties have been removed from inverted sexuality, where this is placed upon the same footing as the normal – in France, Bavaria (?), the Netherlands (?) – no inconvenience has hitherto arisen.[27] There has ensued no sudden and flagrant outburst of a depraved habit, no dissemination of a spreading moral poison. On the other hand, in countries where these penalties exist and are enforced – in England,

[27] Since Ulrichs left off writing, Italy (by the *Nuovo Codicee Penal* of 1889) has adopted the principles of the Code Napoleon, and has placed sexual inversion under the same legal limitations as the normal sexual instinct.

for example, and in the metropolis of England, London – inverted sexuality runs riot, despite of legal prohibitions, despite of threats of prison, dread of exposure, and the intolerable pest of organized *chantage*. In the eyes of Ulrichs, society is engaged in sitting on a safety-valve, which if nature were allowed to operate unhindered would do society no harm, but rather good. The majority, he thinks, are not going to become Urnings, for the simple reason that they have not the unhappy constitution of the Urning. Cease to persecute Urnings, accept them as inconsiderable, yet real, factors, in the social commonwealth, leave them to themselves; and you will not be the worse for it, and will also not carry on your conscience the burden of intolerant vindictiveness.

Substantiating this position, Ulrichs demonstrates that acquired habits of sexual inversion are almost invariably thrown off by normal natures. Your boys at public schools, he says, behave as though they were Urnings. In the lack of women, at the time when their passions are predominant, they yield themselves up together to mutual indulgences which would bring your laws down with terrible effect upon adults. You are aware of this. You send your sons to Eton and to Harrow, and you know very well what goes on there. Yet you remain untroubled in your minds. And why? Because you feel convinced that they will return to their congenital instincts.

When the school, the barrack, the prison, the ship has been abandoned, the male reverts to the female. This is the truth about Dionings. The large majority of men and women remain normal, simply because they were made normal. They cannot find the satisfaction of their nature in those inverted practices, to which they yielded for a time through want of normal outlet. Society risks little by the occasional caprice of the school, the barrack, the prison, and the ship. Some genuine Urnings may indeed discover their inborn inclination by means of the process to which you subject them. But you are quite right in supposing that a Dioning, though you have forced him to become for a time an Uraniaster, will never in the long run appear as an Urning. The extensive experience which English people possess regarding such matters, owing to the notorious condition of their public schools, goes to confirm Ulrichs' position. Headmasters know how many Uraniasters they have dealt with, what excellent Dionings they become, and how comparatively rare, and yet how incorrigibly steadfast, are the genuine Urnings in their flock.

The upshot of this matter is that we are continually forcing our young men into conditions under which, if sexual inversion were an acquired attribute, it would become stereotyped in their natures. Yet it does not do so. Provisionally, because they are shut off from girls, because they find no other outlet for their sex at the moment of its most imperious claims, they turn toward males, and treat their younger school-fellows in ways which would consign an adult to penal servitude. They are Uraniasters by necessity and *faute de mieux*. But no sooner are they let loose upon the world than the majority revert to normal channels. They pick up women in the streets, and form connections, as the phrase goes. Some undoubtedly, in this fiery furnace through which they have been passed, discover their inborn sexual inversion. Then, when they cannot resist the ply of their proclivity, you condemn them as criminals in their later years. Is that just? Would it not be better to revert from our civilization to the manners of the savage man – to initiate youths into the mysteries of sex, and to give each in his turn the chance of developing a normal instinct by putting him during his time of puberty freely and frankly to the female? If you abhor Urnings, as you surely do, you are at least responsible for their mishap by the extraordinary way in which you bring them up. At all events, when they develop into the eccentric beings which they are, you are the last people in the world who have any right to punish them with legal penalties and social obloquy.

Considering the present state of the law in most countries to be inequitable toward a respectable minority of citizens, Ulrichs proposes that Urnings should be placed upon the same footing as other men. That is to say, sexual relations between males and males should not be treated as criminal, unless they be attended with violence (as in the case of rape), or be carried on in such a way as to offend the public sense of decency (in places of general resort or on the open street), or thirdly be entertained between an adult and a boy under age (the protected age to be decided as in the case of girls). What he demands is that when an adult male, freely and of his own consent, complies with the proposals of an adult person of his own sex, and their intercourse takes place with due regard for public decency, neither party shall be liable to prosecution and punishment at law. In fact he would be satisfied with the same conditions as those prevalent in France, and since June, 1889, in Italy.

If so much were conceded by the majority of normal people to the abnormal minority, continues Ulrichs, an immense amount of misery and furtive vice would be at once abolished. And it is difficult to conceive what evil results would follow. A defender of the present laws of England, Prussia, etc., might indeed reply: 'This is opening a free way to the seduction and corruption of young men.' But young men are surely at least as capable of defending themselves against seduction and corruption as young women are. Nay, they are far more able, not merely because they are stronger, but because they are not usually weakened by an overpowering sexual instinct on which the seducer plays. Yet the seduction and corruption of young women is tolerated, in spite of the attendant consequences of illegitimate childbirth, and all which that involves. This toleration of the seduction of women by men springs from the assumption that only the normal sexual appetite is natural. The seduction of a man by a male passes for criminal, because the inverted sexual instinct is regarded as unnatural, depraved, and wilfully perverse. On the hypothesis that individuals subject to perverted instincts can suppress them at pleasure or convert them into normal appetite, it is argued that they must be punished. But when the real facts come to be studied, it will be found: first, that these instincts are inborn in Urnings, and are therefore in their case natural; secondly, that the suppression of them is tantamount to life-long abstinence under the constant torture of sexual solicitation; thirdly, that the conversion of them into normal channels is in a large percentage of cases totally impossible, in nearly all where it has been attempted is only partially successful, and where marriage ensues has generally ended in misery for both parties. Ulrichs, it will be noticed, does not distinguish between Urnings, in whom the inversion is admitted to be congenital, and Uraniasters, in whom it has been acquired or deliberately adopted. And it would be very difficult to frame laws which should take cognizance of these two classes. The Code Napoleon legalizes the position of both, theoretically at any rate. The English code treats both as criminal, doing thereby, it must be admitted, marked injustice to recognized Urnings, who at the worst are morbid or insane, or sexually deformed, through no fault of their own.

In the present state of things, adds Ulrichs, the men who yield their bodies to abnormal lovers, do not merely do so out of compliance, sympathy, or the desire for reasonable reward. Too often they speculate upon the illegality of the connection, and have their main object in the extortion of money by threats of exposure. Thus the very basest of all trades, that of *chantage*, is encouraged by the law. Alter the law, and instead of increasing vice, you will diminish it; for a man who should then meet the advances of an Urning, would do so out of compliance, or, as is the case with female prostitutes, upon the expectation of a reasonable gain. The temptation to ply a disgraceful profession with the object of extorting money would be removed. Moreover, as regards individuals alike abnormally constituted, voluntary and mutually satisfying relations, free from degrading risks, and possibly permanent, might be formed between responsible agents. Finally, if it be feared that the removal of legal disabilities would turn the whole male population into Urnings, consider whether London is now so much purer in this respect than Paris?

One serious objection to recognizing and tolerating sexual inversion has always been that it tends to check the population. This was a sound political and social argument in the time of Moses, when a small and militant tribe needed to multiply to the full extent of its procreative capacity. It is by no means so valid in our age, when the habitable portions of the globe are rapidly becoming overcrowded.[28] Moreover, we must bear in mind that society, under the existing order, sanctions female prostitution, whereby men and women, the normally procreative, are sterilized to an indefinite extent. Logic, in these circumstances, renders it inequitable and ridiculous to deny a sterile exercise of sex to abnormal men and women, who are by instinct and congenital diathesis non-procreative.

As the result of these considerations, Ulrichs concludes that there is no real ground for the persecution of Urnings except such as may be found in the repugnance felt by the vast numerical majority for an insignificant minority. The majority encourages matrimony, condones seduction, sanctions prostitution, legalizes divorce, in the interest of its own sexual proclivities. It makes temporary or permanent unions illegal for the minority whose inversion of instinct it abhors. And this persecution, in the popular mind at any rate, is justified, like many other inequitable acts of prejudice or ignorance, by theological assumptions and the so-called mandates of revelation.

In the next place it is objected that inverted sexuality is demoralizing to the manhood of a nation, that it degrades the dignity of man, and that it is incapable of moral elevation. Each of these points may be taken separately. They are all of them at once and together contradicted by the history of ancient Greece. There the most warlike sections of the race, the Dorians of Crete and Sparta, and the Thebans, organized the love of male for male because of the social and military advantages they found in it. Their annals abound in eminent instances of heroic enthusiasm, patriotic devotion, and high living, inspired by homosexual passion. The fighting peoples of the world, Kelts in ancient story, Normans, Turks, Afghans, Albanians, Tartars, have been distinguished by the frequency among them of what popular prejudice regards as an effeminate vice.

---

[28] Dr. W. Ogle, on the 18th March, 1890, read a paper before the Statistical Society upon 'Marriage Rates and Ages.' The conclusion he arrived at, with regard to the rapidly-advancing over-population of England, was that, in order to equalize the death-rate with the birth-rate (or in other words, to maintain the population at its present level), we must look forward either to (1) an increase of emigration which would involve social revolution, or (2) to the advance of the average age at which women marry to the point of thirty years, or (3) to an exclusion of 45 per cent. of those who now marry from matrimony at any period of life. In the face of these calculations, after admitting their possible exaggeration, it seems illogical to punish with severe legal penalties those members of the male sex who do not want to marry, and who can satisfy their natural desires in ways which involve no detriment to the state and no violation of the rights of individuals.

With regard to the dignity of man, is there, asks Ulrichs, anything more degrading to humanity in sexual acts performed between male and male than in similar acts performed between male and female. In a certain sense all sex has an element of grossness which inspires repugnance. The gods, says Swinburne,

> Have strewed one marriage-bed with tears and fire,
> For extreme loathing and supreme desire.

It would not be easy to maintain that a curate begetting his fourteenth baby on the body of a worn-out wife is a more elevating object of mental contemplation than Harmodius in the embrace of Aristogeiton, or that a young man sleeping with a prostitute picked up in the Haymarket is cleaner than his brother sleeping with a soldier picked up in the Park. Much of this talk about the dignity of man, says Ulrichs, proceeds from a vulgar misconception as to the nature of inverted sexual desire. People assume that Urnings seek their pleasure only or mainly in an act of unmentionable indecency. The exact opposite, he assures them, is the truth. The act in question is no commoner between men and men than it is between men and women. Ulrichs, upon this point, may be suspected, perhaps, as an untrustworthy witness. His testimony, however, is confirmed by Krafft-Ebing, who, as we have seen, has studied sexual inversion long and minutely from the point of view of psychical pathology. 'As regards the nature of their sexual gratification,' he writes, 'it must be established at the outset that the majority of them are contented with reciprocal embraces; the act commonly ascribed to them they generally abhor as much as normal men do; and, inasmuch as they always prefer adults, they are in no sense specially dangerous to boys.'[29] This author proceeds to draw a distinction between Urnings, in whom sexual inversion is congenital, and old debauchees or half-idiotic individuals, who are in the habit of misusing boys. The vulgar have confounded two different classes; and everybody who studies the psychology of Urnings is aware that this involves a grave injustice to the latter.

'But, after all,' continues the objector, 'you cannot show that inverted sexuality is capable of any moral elevation.' Without appealing to antiquity, the records of which confute this objection overwhelmingly, one might refer to the numerous passages in Ulrich's writings where he relates the fidelity, loyalty, self-sacrifice, and romantic enthusiasm which frequently accompany such loves, and raise them above baseness. But, since here again he may be considered a suspicious witness, it will

[29] *Psych. Sex.*, p. 108. I have condensed the sense of four short paragraphs, to translate which in full would have involved a disagreeable use of medical language.

suffice, as before, to translate a brief passage from Krafft-Ebing. 'The Urning loves, idolizes his friend, quite as much as the normal man loves and idolizes his girl. He is capable of making for him the greatest sacrifices. He suffers the pangs of unhappy, often unreturned, affection; feels jealousy, mourns under the fear of his friend's infidelity.'[30] When the time comes for speaking about Walt Whitman's treatment of this topic, it will appear that the passion of a man for his comrade has been idealized in fact and deed, as well as in poetry. For the present it is enough to remark that a kind of love, however spontaneous and powerful, which is scouted, despised, tabooed, banned, punished, relegated to holes and corners, execrated as abominable and unmentionable, cannot be expected to show its best side to the world. The sense of sin and crime and danger, the humiliation and repression and distress, to which the unfortunate pariahs of inverted sexuality are daily and hourly exposed, must inevitably deteriorate the nobler elements in their emotion. Give abnormal love the same chance as normal love, subject it to the wholesome control of public opinion, allow it to be self-respecting, draw it from dark slums into the light of day, strike off its chains and set it free – and I am confident, says Ulrichs, that it will exhibit analogous virtues, checkered of course by analogous vices, to those with which you are familiar in the mutual love of male and female. The slave has of necessity a slavish soul. The way to elevate is to emancipate him.

'All that may be true,' replies the objector: 'it is even possible that society will take the hard case of your Urnings into consideration, and listen to their bitter cry. But, in the meanwhile, supposing these inverted instincts to be inborn, supposing them to be irrepressible and inconvertible, supposing them to be less dirty and nasty than they are commonly considered, is it not the plain duty of the individual to suppress them, so long as the law of his country condemns them?' No, rejoins Ulrichs, a thousand times no! It is only the ignorant antipathy of the majority which renders such law as you speak of possible. Go to the best books of medical jurisprudence, go to the best authorities on psychical deviations from the normal type. You will find that these support me in my main contention. These, though hostile in their sentiments and chilled by natural repugnance, have a respect for science, and they agree with me in saying that the Urning came into this world an Urning, and must remain till the end of his life an Urning still. To deal with him according to your code is no less monstrous than if you were to punish the colour-blind, or the deaf and dumb, or albinoes, or crooked-back cripples. 'Very well,' answers the objector: 'But I will quote the words of an eloquent living writer, and appeal to your generous

[30] *Psych. Sex.*, p. 107.

instincts and your patriotism. Professor Dowden observes that "self-surrender is at times sternly enjoined, and if the egoistic desires are brought into conflict with social duties, the individual life and joy within us, at whatever cost of personal suffering, must be sacrificed to the just claims of our fellows."[31] What have you to say to that?' In the first place, replies Ulrichs, I demur in this case to the phrases *egoistic desires, social duties, just claims of our fellows.* I maintain that in trying to rehabilitate men of my own stamp and to justify their natural right to toleration I am not egoistic. It is begging the question to stigmatize their inborn desires as selfish. The social duties of which you speak are not duties, but compliances to law framed in blindness and prejudice. The claims of our fellows, to which you appeal, are not just, but cruelly iniquitous. My insurgence against all these things makes me act indeed as an innovator; and I may be condemned, as a consequence of my rashness, to persecution, exile, defamation, proscription. But let me remind you that Christ was crucified, and that he is now regarded as a benefactor. 'Stop,' breaks in the objector: 'We need not bring most sacred names into this discussion. I admit that innovators have done the greatest service to society. But you have not proved that you are working for the salvation of humanity at large. Would it not be better to remain quiet, and to sacrifice your life and joy, the life and joy of an avowed minority, for the sake of the immense majority who cannot tolerate you, and who dread your innovation? The Catholic priesthood is vowed to celibacy; and unquestionably there are some adult men in that order who have trampled out the imperious appetite of the male for the female. What they do for the sake of their vow will not you accomplish, when you have so much of good to gain, of evil to escape?' What good, what evil? rejoins Ulrichs. You are again begging the question; and now you are making appeals to my selfishness, my personal desire for tranquillity, my wish to avoid persecution and shame. I have taken no vow of celibacy. If I have taken any vow at all, it is to fight for the rights of an innocent, harmless, down-trodden group of outraged personalities. The cross of a Crusade is sewn upon the sleeve of my right arm. To expect from me and from my fellows the renouncement voluntarily undertaken by a Catholic priest is an absurdity, when we join no order, have no faith to uphold, no ecclesiastical system to support. We maintain that we have the right to exist after the fashion in which nature made us. And if we cannot alter your laws, we shall go on breaking them. You may condemn us to infamy, exile, prison – as you formerly burned witches. You may degrade our emotional instincts and drive us into vice and misery. But you will not eradicate inverted sexuality. Expel nature with a fork, and you know what happens. 'That

[31] *Studies in Literature*, p. 119.

is enough,' says the objector: 'We had better close this conversation. I am sorry for you, sorry that you will not yield to sense and force. The Urning must be punished.'

X

LITERATURE – IDEALISTIC

To speak of Walt Whitman at all in connection with Ulrichs and sexual inversion seems paradoxical. At the outset it must be definitely stated that he has nothing to do with anomalous, abnormal, vicious, or diseased forms of the emotion which males entertain for males. Yet no man in the modern world has expressed so strong a conviction that 'manly attachment,' 'athletic love,' 'the high towering love of comrades,' is a main factor in human life, a virtue upon which society will have to rest, and a passion equal in its permanence and intensity to sexual affection.

He assumes, without raising the question, that the love of man for man co-exists with the love of man for woman in one and the same individual. The relation of the two modes of feeling is clearly stated in this poem:

> Fast-anchored, eternal, O love! O woman I love;
> O bride! O wife! More resistless than I can tell, the thought
>   of you
> Then separate, as disembodied, or another born,
> Ethereal, the last athletic reality, my consolation;
> I ascend – I float in the regions of your love, O man,
> O sharer of my roving life.

Neuropathical Urnings are not hinted at in any passage of his works. As his friend and commentator Mr. Burroughs puts it: 'The sentiment is primitive, athletic, taking form in all manner of large and homely out-of-door images, and springs, as anyone may see, directly from the heart and experience of the poet.'

This being so, Whitman never suggests that comradeship may occasion the development of physical desires. But then he does not in set terms condemn these desires, or warn his disciples against them. To a Western boy he says:

> If you be not silently selected by lovers, and do not silently
>   select lovers,
> Of what use is it that you seek to become eleve of mine.

Like Plato, in the *Phaedrus*, Whitman describes an enthusiastic type of masculine emotion, leaving its private details to the moral sense and special inclination of the person concerned.[32]

The language of 'Calamus' (that section of *Leaves of Grass* which is devoted to the gospel of comradeship) has a passionate glow, a warmth of emotional tone, beyond anything to which the modern world is used in the celebration of the love of friends. It recalls to our mind the early Greek enthusiasm – that fellowship in arms which flourished among Dorian tribes, and made a chivalry for prehistoric Hellas. Nor does the poet himself appear to be unconscious that there are dangers and diffi-culties involved in the highly-pitched emotions he is praising. The whole tenor of two mysterious compositions, entitled 'Whoever you are, Holding me now in Hand,' and 'Trickle, Drops,' suggests an under-lying sense of spiritual conflict. The following poem, again, is suffici-ently significant and typical to call for literal transcription:

> Earth, my likeness!
> Though you look so impressive, ample and spheric there,
> I now suspect that is not all;
> I now suspect there is something fierce in you, eligible to
>   burst forth;
> For an athletic is enamoured of me – and I of him,
> But toward him there is something fierce and terrible in me,
>   eligible to burst forth,
> I dare not tell it in words – not even in these songs.

The reality of Whitman's feeling, the intense delight which he derives from the personal presence and physical contact of a beloved man, find expression in 'A Glimpse,' 'Recorders ages hence,' 'When I heard at the Close of Day,' 'I saw in Louisiana a Live Oak growing,' 'Long I thought that Knowledge alone would content me,'[33] 'O Tan-faced Prairie Boy,' and 'Vigil Strange I kept on the Field one Night.'[34]

It is clear, then, that in his treatment of comradeship, or the impassioned love of man for man, Whitman has struck a keynote, to

---

[32] In this relation it is curious to note what one of Casper-Liman's correspondents says about the morals of North America (*op. cit.*, vol. i. p. 173). 'Half a year after my return I went to North America, to try my fortune. There the unnatural vice in question is more ordinary than it is here; and I was able to indulge my passions with less fear of punishment or persecution. The American's tastes in this matter resemble my own; and I discovered, in the United States, that I was always immediately recognized as a member of the confraternity.' The date of this man's visit to America was the year 1871–72. He had just returned from serving as a volunteer in the great Franco-German war of 1870–71.

[33] Not included in the *Complete Poems and Prose*. It will be found in *Leaves of Grass*, Boston, 1860–1861.

[34] The two last are from *Drum-Taps*.

11　Toto. From a photograph by
Frederick Rolfe (Baron Corvo), c. 1890
(Mr. Donald Weeks)

12　Boys on Lake Nemi. From a
photograph by Frederick Rolfe (Baron
Corvo), c. 1890 (Mr. Donald Weeks)

13   Italian boys. From a photograph by
Guglielmo Pluschow, Rome, c. 1900

the emotional intensity of which the modern world is unaccustomed. It therefore becomes of much importance to discover the poet-prophet's *Stimmung* – his radical instinct with regard to the moral quality of the feeling he encourages. Studying his works by their own light, and by the light of their author's character, interpreting each part by reference to the whole and in the spirit of the whole, an impartial critic will, I think, be drawn to the conclusion that what he calls the 'adhesiveness' of comradeship is meant to have no interblending with the 'amativeness' of sexual love. Personally, it is undeniable that Whitman possesses a specially keen sense of the fine restraint and continence, the cleanliness and chastity, that are inseparable from the perfectly virile and physically complete nature of healthy manhood. Still we may predicate the same ground-qualities in the early Dorians, those martial founders of the institution of Greek Love; and it is notorious to students of Greek civilization that the lofty sentiment of their chivalry was intertwined with singular anomalies in its historical development.

To remove all doubt about Whitman's own intentions when he composed 'Calamus,' and promulgated his doctrine of impassioned comradeship, I wrote to him, frankly posing the questions which perplexed my mind. The answer I received, dated Camden, New Jersey, U.S.A., August 19, 1890, and which he permits me to make use of, puts the matter beyond all debate, and confirms the conclusions to which I had been led by criticism. He writes as follows: 'About the questions on "Calamus," etc., they quite daze me. *Leaves of Grass* is only to be rightly construed by and within its own atmosphere and essential character – all its pages and pieces so coming strictly under. That the Calamus part has ever allowed the possibility of such construction as mentioned is terrible. I am fain to hope the pages themselves are not to be even mentioned for such gratuitous and quite at the time undreamed and unwished possibility of morbid inferences – which are disavowed by me and seem damnable.'

No one who knows anything about Walt Whitman will for a moment doubt his candour and sincerity. Therefore the man who wrote 'Calamus,' and preached the gospel of comradeship, entertains feelings at least as hostile to sexual inversion as any law-abiding humdrum Anglo-Saxon could desire. It is obvious that he has not even taken the phenomena of abnormal instinct into account. Else he must have foreseen that, human nature being what it is, we cannot expect to eliminate all sensual alloy from emotions raised to a high pitch of passionate intensity, and that permanent elements within the midst of our society will emperil the absolute purity of the ideal he attempts to establish.

These considerations do not, however, affect the spiritual nature

SH—T

of that ideal. After acknowledging, what Whitman has omitted to perceive, that there are inevitable points of contact between sexual inversion and his doctrine of comradeship, the question now remains whether he has not suggested the way whereby abnormal instincts may be moralized and raised to higher value. In other words, are those instincts provided in 'Calamus' with the means of their salvation from the filth and mire of brutal appetite? It is difficult to answer this question; for the issue involved is nothing less momentous than the possibility of evoking a new chivalrous enthusiasm, analogous to that of primitive Hellenic society, from emotions which are at present classified among the turpitudes of human nature.

Let us look a little closer at the expression which Whitman has given to his own feelings about friendship. The first thing that strikes us is the mystic emblem he has chosen for masculine love. That is the water-plant, or scented rush, called Calamus, which springs in wild places, 'in paths untrodden, in the growth by margins of pond-waters.' He has chosen these 'emblematic and capricious blades' because of their shyness, their aromatic perfume, their aloofness from the patent life of the world. He calls them 'sweet leaves, pink-tinged roots, timid leaves,' 'scented herbage of my breast.' Finally, he says:[35]

> Here my last words, and the most baffling,
> Here the frailest leaves of me, and yet my strongest-lasting,
> Here I shade down and hide my thoughts – I do not expose them
> And yet they expose me more than all my other poems.

The manliness of the emotion, which is thus so shyly, mystically indicated, appears in the magnificent address to soldiers at the close of the great war: 'Over the Carnage rose Prophetic a Voice.'[36] Its tenderness emerges in the elegy on a slain comrade:[37]

> Vigil for boy of responding kisses (never again on earth responding):
> Vigil for comrade swiftly slain – vigil I never forget, how as day brightened,
> I rose from the chill ground, and folded my soldier well in his blanket,
> And buried him where he fell.

Its pathos and clinging intensity transpire through the first lines of the following piece, which may have been suggested by the legends

[35] This I cannot find in 'Complete Poems and Prose.' It is included in the Boston edition, 1860–61, and the Camden edition, 1876.
[36] *Drum-Taps.* Complete Poems, p. 247.
[37] Ibid., p. 238.

of David and Jonathan, Achilles and Patroclus, Orestes and Pylades:[38]

> When I peruse the conquered fame of heroes, and the
>   victories of mighty generals,
> I do not envy the generals,
> Nor the President in his Presidency, nor the rich in his great
>   house;
> But when I read of the brotherhood of lovers, how it was
>   with them,
> How through life, through dangers, odium, unchanging, long
>   and long,
> Through youth, and through middle and old age, how un-
>   faltering, how affectionate and faithful they were,
> Then I am pensive – I hastily put down the book, and walk
>   away, filled with the bitterest envy.

But Whitman does not conceive of comradeship as a merely personal possession, delightful to the friends it links in bonds of amity. He regards it essentially as a social and political virtue. This human emotion is destined to cement society and to render commonwealths inviolable. Reading some of his poems, we are carried back to ancient Greece – to Plato's Symposium, to Philip gazing on the Sacred Band of Thebans after the fight at Chaeronea.[39]

> I dream'd in a dream, I saw a city invincible to the attacks of
>   the whole of the rest of the earth;
> I dream'd that was the new City of Friends;
> Nothing was greater there than the quality of robust love –
>   it led the rest;
> It was seen every hour in the actions of the men of that city,
> And in all their looks and words.

And again:[40]

> I believe the main purport of these States is to found a
>   superb friendship, exalté, previously unknown,
> Because I perceive it waits, and has been always waiting,
>   latent in all men.

And once again:[41]

[38] *Leaves of Grass. Complete Poems*, p. 107.
[39] *Complete Poems*, p. 109. Compare, 'I hear it was charged against me,' *ibid.*, p. 107.
[40] *Complete Poems*, p. 110.
[41] Camden edition, 1876, p. 127. *Complete Poems*, p. 99. Compare 'Democratic Vistas,' *Complete Prose*, p. 247, note

Come, I will make the continent indissoluble;
I will make the most splendid race the sun ever yet shone upon;
I will make divine magnetic lands,
　　With the love of comrades,
　　With the life-long love of comrades.
I will plant companionship thick as trees all along the rivers
　　of America, and along the shores of the great lakes, and
　　all over the prairies;
I will make inseparable cities, with their arms about each
　　other's necks;
　　　By the love of comrades,
　　　By the manly love of comrades.
For you these from me, O Democracy, to serve you ma femme!
For you, for you I am thrilling these songs.

In the company of Walt Whitman we are very far away from Gibbon and Carlier, from Tardieux and Casper-Liman, from Krafft-Ebing and Ulrichs. What indeed has this 'superb friendship, exalté, previously unknown,' which 'waits, and has been always waiting, latent in all men,' that 'something fierce in me, eligible to burst forth,' 'ethereal comradeship,' 'the last athletic reality' – what has all this in common with the painful topic of the preceding sections of my Essay?

It has this in common with it. Whitman recognizes among the sacred emotions and social virtues, destined to regenerate political life and to cement nations, an intense, jealous, throbbing, sensitive, expectant love of man for man: a love which yearns in absence, droops under the sense of neglect, revives at the return of the beloved; a love that finds honest delight in hand-touch, meeting lips, hours of privacy, close personal contact. He proclaims this love to be not only a daily fact in the present, but also a saving and ennobling aspiration. While he expressly repudiates, disowns, and brands as 'damnable' all 'morbid inferences' which may be drawn by malevolence or vicious cunning from his doctrine, he is prepared to extend the gospel of comradeship to the whole human race. He expects Democracy, the new social and political medium, the new religious ideal of mankind, to develop and extend 'that fervid comradeship,' and by its means to counterbalance and to spiritualize what is vulgar and materialistic in the modern world. 'Democracy,' he maintains, 'infers such loving comradeship, as its most inevitable twin or counterpart, without which it will be incomplete, in vain, and incapable of perpetuating itself.'[42]

If this be not a dream, if he is right in believing that 'threads of manly friendship, fond and loving, pure and sweet, strong and life-long,

---

[42] These prose passages are taken from *Democratic Vistas*, cited above.

carried to degrees hitherto unknown,' will penetrate the organism of society, 'not only giving tone to individual character, and making it unprecedentedly emotional, muscular, heroic, and refined, but having deepest relations to general politics' – then are we perhaps justified in foreseeing here the advent of an enthusiasm which shall rehabilitate those outcast instincts, by giving them a spiritual atmosphere, an environment of recognized and healthy emotions, wherein to expand at liberty and purge away the grossness and the madness of their pariahdom?

This prospect, like all ideals, until they are realized in experience, may seem fantastically visionary. Moreover, the substance of human nature is so mixed that it would perhaps be fanatical to expect from Whitman's chivalry of 'adhesiveness' a more immaculate purity than was attained by the mediaeval chivalry of 'amativeness.' Still that mediaeval chivalry, the great emotional product of feudalism, though it fell short of its own aspiration, bequeathed incalculable good to modern society by refining and clarifying the crudest of male appetites. In like manner, the democratic chivalry, announced by Whitman, may be destined to absorb, control, and elevate those darker, more mysterious, apparently abnormal appetites, which we have seen to be widely diffused and ineradicable in the ground-work of human nature.

Returning from the dream, the vision of a future possibili'y, it will at any rate be conceded that Whitman has founded comradeship, the enthusiasm which binds man to man in fervent love, upon a natural basis. Eliminating classical associations of corruption, ignoring the perplexed questions of a guilty passion doomed by law and popular antipathy to failure, he begins anew with sound and primitive humanity. There he discovers 'a superb friendship, exalté, previously unknown.' He perceives that 'it waits, and has been always waiting, latent in all men.' His method of treatment, fearless and uncowed by any thought of evil, his touch upon the matter, chaste and wholesome and aspiring, reveal the possibility of restoring in all innocence to human life a portion of its alienated or unclaimed moral birthright. The aberrations we have been discussing in this treatise are perhaps the morbid symptoms of suppression, of hypertrophy, of ignorant mis-regulation, in a genuine emotion capable of being raised to good by sympathetic treatment.

It were well to close upon this note. The half, as the Greeks said, is more than the whole; and the time has not yet come to raise the question whether the love of man for man shall be elevated through a hitherto unapprehended chivalry to nobler powers, even as the barbarous love of man for woman once was. This question at the present moment is deficient in actuality. The world cannot be invited to entertain it.[43]

SUGGESTIONS ON THE SUBJECT OF SEXUAL
INVERSION IN RELATION TO LAW AND EDUCATION

i

The laws in force against what are called unnatural offences derive from an edict of Justinian, A.D. 538. The Emperor treated these offences as criminal, on the ground that they brought plagues, famines, earthquakes, and the destruction of whole cities, together with their inhabitants, upon the nations who tolerated them.

ii

A belief that sexual inversion is a crime against God, nature, and the state pervades all subsequent legislation on the subject. This belief rests on (1) theological conceptions derived from the Scriptures; (2) a dread of decreasing the population; (3) the antipathy of the majority for the tastes of the minority; (4) the vulgar error that antiphysical desires are invariably voluntary, and the result either of inordinate lust or of satiated appetites.

iii

Scientific investigation has proved in recent years that a very large proportion of persons in whom abnormal sexual inclinations are manifested possess them from their earliest childhood, that they cannot divert them into normal channels, and that they are powerless to get rid of them. In these cases, then, legislation is interfering with the liberty of individuals, under a certain misconception regarding the nature of their offence.

iv

Those who support the present laws are therefore bound to prove that the coercion, punishment, and defamation of such persons are

---

[43] While these sheets were going through the press, I communicated Whitman's reply to a judicious friend, whose remarks upon it express my own opinion more clearly and succinctly than I have done above: 'I do not feel that this answer throws light on the really interesting question; does the sentiment of "Calamus" represent, in its own way, the ideal which we should aim at impressing on passionate affections between men, as certainly liable to take other objectionable forms? Is there sufficient affinity between the actual and the ideal for this to be practicable? That is what I have never felt sure about when we have discussed these matters. But I do not feel that my doubts have been resolved in any negative direction by Walt Whitman.'

justified either (1) by any injury which these persons suffer in health of body or mind, or (2) by any serious danger arising from them to the social organism.

v

Experience, confirmed by scientific observation, proves that the temperate indulgence of abnormal sexuality is no more injurious to the individual than a similar indulgence of normal sexuality.

vi

In the present state of over-population, it is not to be apprehended that a small minority of men exercising sterile and abnormal sexual inclinations should seriously injure society by limiting the increase of the human race.

vii

Legislation does not interfere with various forms of sterile inter-course between men and women: (1) prostitution, (2) cohabitation in marriage during the period of pregnancy, (3) artificial precautions against impregnation, (4) and some abnormal modes of congress with the consent of the female. It is therefore in an illogical position, when it interferes with the action of those who are naturally sterile, on the ground of maintaining the numerical standard of the population.

viii

The danger that unnatural vices, if tolerated by the law, would increase until whole nations acquired them, does not seem to be formidable. The position of women in our civilization renders sexual relations among us occidentals different from those of any country – ancient Greece and Rome, modern Turkey and Persia – where anti-physical habits have hitherto become endemic.

ix

In modern France, since the promulgation of the Code Napoleon, sexual inversion has been tolerated under the same restrictions as normal sexuality. That is to say, violence and outrages to public decency are punished, and minors are protected. But adults are allowed to dispose as they like of their own persons. The experience of nearly a century shows that in France, where sexual inversion is not criminal *per se*, there has been no extension of it through society. Competent observers, like agents of police, declare that London, in spite of our penal legislation, is no less notorious for abnormal vice than Paris.

x

Italy, by the Penal Code of 1889, adopted the principles of the Code Napoleon on this point. It would be interesting to know what led to this alteration of the Italian law. But it cannot be supposed that the results of the Code Napoleon in France were not fully considered.

xi

The severity of the English statutes render them almost incapable of being put in force. In consequence of this the law is not unfrequently evaded, and crimes are winked at.

xii

At the same time our laws encourage blackmailing upon false accusation; and the presumed evasion of their execution places from time to time a vile weapon in the hands of unscrupulous politicians, to attack the Government in office. Examples: the Dublin Castle Scandals of 1884, the Cleveland Street Scandals of 1889.

xiii

Those who hold that our penal laws are required by the interests of society must turn their attention to the higher education. This still rests on the study of the Greek and Latin classics, a literature impregnated with paederastia. It is carried on at public schools, where young men are kept apart from females, and where homosexual vices are frequent. The best minds of our youth are therefore exposed to the influences of a paederastic literature, at the same time that they acquire the knowledge and experience of unnatural practices. Nor is any trouble taken to correct these adverse influences by physiological instruction in the laws of sex.

xiv

The points suggested for consideration are whether England is still justified in restricting the freedom of adult persons, and rendering certain abnormal forms of sexuality criminal, by any real dangers to society: after it has been shown (1) that abnormal inclinations are congenital, natural, and ineradicable in a large percentage of individuals; (2) that we tolerate sterile intercourse of various types between the two sexes; (3) that our legislation has not suppressed the immorality in question; (4) that the operation of the Code Napoleon for nearly a century has not increased this immorality in France; (5) that Italy, with the experience of the Code Napoleon to guide her, adopted its principles in 1889; (6) that the English penalties are rarely inflicted to their full extent; (7) that their existence encourages blackmailing, and their non-enforcement gives occasion for base political agitation; (8) that our higher education is in open contradiction to the spirit of our laws.[44]

52   *Tim*

Howard Overing Sturgis. Closing passages from *Tim*, 1891.

> But sworn I have; and never must
> Your banished servant trouble you;
> For if I do, you may mistrust
> The vow I made to love you, too.
>
> HERRICK

The next time Carol came to the manor-house Tim was not to be found; he had run and hidden himself in the garden when he saw him coming. Crouching among the bushes, he could hear the dearly-loved voice calling him by the familiar nickname, and his courage nearly gave out; he pressed his hands over his mouth as though he would choke back the answering cry that rose naturally to his lips.

'Tim, Tim!' shouted Carol, 'where are you?'

Either there was, or Tim fancied there was, a tone of disappointment in the voice. Carol was in trouble; Carol had need of him, and he must hear him call and let him go unsatisfied away. It was his free act too; no one had compelled him to it. But it was for Carol's own sake; and in that thought alone he was strong.

For weeks afterwards, in the silence of the night, whenever he lay awake (and he lay awake a good deal in those nights), he heard that voice calling to him, 'Tim, Tim!' in saddest accents of one that sought something on which he had counted, and found it not. He felt that his one chance lay in avoiding a meeting with Carol, and the constant watch and care to do so told on him fearfully, making him nervous and excitable. He dreaded to stay at home, lest his friend should come and see him, and almost more to go out, lest he should come upon him unawares. He could settle to nothing; every step on the path, every

---

[44] It may not be superfluous to recapitulate the main points of English legislation on this topic. (1) Sodomy is a felony, defined as the carnal knowledge (per anum) of any man or of any woman by a male person; punishable with penal servitude for life as a maximum, for ten years as a minimum. (2) The attempt to commit sodomy is punishable with ten years' penal servitude as a maximum. (3) The commission, in public or in private, by any male person with another male person, of 'any act of gross indecency,' is punishable with two years' imprisonment and hard labour.

voice, every opening door, made him start and tremble, and when he could stand it no longer, and seized his hat to rush out no matter where, he would be taken with such an agony of apprehension before he had gone a hundred yards, that he had scarcely strength to get back to the house. No one will ever know what he suffered in those few days; and when his father, taking pity on his altered looks, offered to take him to the seaside till it should be time for him to return to Eton, he eagerly accepted. Not a word was spoken between them about Carol; the subject was avoided by tacit consent. William Ebbesley wondered not a little what had influenced his son to act as he had done, but he would not ask. He had long given up trying to understand the boy, who was as full of incomprehensible moods as a woman. He concluded that deference to his wishes had not had a large share in determining him, but there he did Tim injustice. Anyway his point was gained, and he could afford to be magnanimous; so the two went off to the sea together for the remaining week or ten days of Tim's holidays.

Poor Carol failed utterly at first to understand what had happened. Tim was never to be found when he went to the manor-house, never came to the Court. Then one day the answer to his enquiry was that Mr. Ebbesley and Tim were gone away to the seaside together. Tim was 'poorly,' the little maid who trembled under Mrs. Quitchett told him, 'needed change of air, the doctor had said.'

'And had he left no message for him?' Carol asked; 'was she sure there was none?'

Yes; the little maid thought she was sure there was none. Mrs. Quitchett was out, but she would ask her when she came in.

Carol went away sad at heart. Tim would write, he told himself, – was sure to write. He would not yet believe that Tim could mean anything. He was not well; he had had to go away suddenly; he would be sure to write in a day or two. So he waited the day or two, but still Tim made no sign. Then Carol got the address from Mrs. Quitchett, and wrote himself, but no answer came back. He began to grow anxious after that; to imagine all sorts of possibilities; he had not known how fond he was of his friend. He determined to go again to the manor-house, and ask if the accounts of Tim were good.

'Yes'; Mrs. Quitchett 'thanked him; she had had a letter from him that morning, and he said he was better. He liked the sea, and thought it was doing him good.'

'And was there any – any message or anything? in short, anything about *me* in the letter?' Carol asked with a little proud hesitation.

No, there was nothing; Mrs. Quitchett had noticed it and thought it strange. 'But doubtless he means to write you a long letter himself one of these days,' said the good-natured old woman; 'he knew his old nurse would be anxious, God bless him! and so he wrote to her first.'

But the letter Mrs. Quitchett predicted never came. 'If he is well enough to write to her,' Carol thought, 'he is surely up to sending me just a line, if only to say how he is; he might know I should be anxious.' And he felt, not unnaturally, a little hurt. He would not write again until Tim chose to answer his first letter, which had been all a kindly affectionate heart could make it, sympathy for his ill-health, regret at his going, and no hint of blame at the manner of it, not a word about himself. He had done what he could; now he would wait.

These were sad times for Carol; he was so unused to sorrow that it had all the added weight of strangeness. Violet seemed to have given him up, and now Tim – Tim, to whom he had turned in his grief with such implicit reliance, – just when most he needed the support of friendship and kindness, Tim had thrown him over too.

'I bored him with my troubles,' said the poor boy to himself a little bitterly; 'it was very natural; one could not expect a child like that to feel interest in such a subject. And yet he *seemed* so fond of me, and he never was quite like other boys of his age – older and younger at once, somehow. Well, well, who would have thought he was only a fair-weather friend after all!'

He did not know, poor fellow, all that the 'fair-weather friend' had borne, and was bearing, for his sake; he could not see him sitting gazing out to sea hour after hour, with eyes that saw nothing, and ears to which the long wash of the waves upon the beach kept always calling 'Tim, Tim!' in the never-to-be-forgotten tones that he had heard but the other day in the old manor-house garden.

But when things are at their worst they generally mend, and Carol presently found a star rising on his night that promised to comfort him not a little. It was about this time that Miss Markham Willis, finding that the *rôle* she had assumed was anything but an easy or pleasant one, finding too that the obnoxious Tim had gone away, and seeing that Carol looked delightfully miserable as he made her a fine sarcastic bow when they occasionally met in their walks or rides, began wisely to consider that it did not make her domestic worries easier to bear to cut herself off from her principal extraneous source of enjoyment, and so determined to take pity on her lover, and show him some signs of kindness. At first these only took the form of a few gracious smiles. Then finding that these had not quite the effect she desired, she made her mother take her to call at the Court, and there, as she had hoped, was Carol.

'Why, Lily dear, – I mean Violet!' cried old Mrs. Darley, 'I declare you are quite a stranger; where have you hidden yourself all these days?'

'Oh! there has been so much to do at home, dear Mrs. Darley,' answered Violet, all radiant with smiles, and glowing on Carol at second-hand through grandmamma. 'You know Fräulein has gone away for a holiday, so I have all the children on my hands from morning till night. I never appreciated poor Fräulein before; but now I have had a taste of what her life is, I feel quite differently towards her; if it was only the bread-and-butter. I assure you, I rival Goethe's Charlotte in the art of cutting bread-and-butter.'

'Dear, dear, do young folks read the sorrows of What's-his-name nowadays? My poor dear mother never would allow us to. She said it was a dreadful book, and that when it first came out it made all the young men commit suicide. To tell the truth, when I did read it, I didn't think it very interesting, but perhaps I am not a good judge. You *do* take sugar, Mrs. Wilkins, don't you?'

'Please yes, a little; thank you, quite enough. I *do* hope, Mrs. Darley, I haven't let Violet read anything improper; what you said just now about that book, you know. But Fräulein told me all young ladies read it in Germany as being a classic. I don't read German myself, but I placed reliance on her.'

Carol meanwhile held obstinately in the background, looking black as a thunder-cloud, and strongly inclined to compare himself with the other unfortunate who was cursed with love for a woman that cut bread-and-butter. But when the visitors rose to take leave, while the elders were making their little farewell speeches, Violet took occasion to say to him in an undertone, and with a look of gentlest expostulation –

'Are you angry with me, Carol? you haven't been to see us for an age; won't you come and see us again?'

Had he been dreaming? he wondered; was it all a mistake of his, this fancied coldness on her part? She spoke with such entire innocence, a little justly hurt, but ready to forgive, that he began to think it must have been his fault. His resentment was not proof against this; he pressed the little hand she held out to him, and promised to come next day.

'I am going primrosing in the morning,' she said, 'in Fern Dingle, so it is no good coming then.'

And on the way home she seemed in such high spirits, that her mother stole her hand into hers and asked her what she had said to Carol. But Violet for all answer trilled out the words of an old catch –

The falling out of faithful friends, renewal is of love,

until the woods echoed to her bright clear singing; and then, putting her arm round her mother, she said, 'Silly mamma,' and kissed her.

Of course Carol vowed to himself that nothing should tempt him to go near Fern Dingle the next morning, and of course he went; and there, over the big half-filled basket of primroses, the lovers made up this not very terrible quarrel. Violet was half contrite, half reproachful, wholly gentle and charming.

'Had she been sulky? she half feared so; but she had been dreadfully busy, and the children had been a little tiresome sometimes, and she had been rather out of sorts. Carol must forgive her if she had unwittingly hurt him; how *could* he suppose she meant anything; he ought to have *known* she didn't.'

And Carol, we may be sure, was not very hard to melt. He began, on the contrary, to feel that it was he who was in the wrong for having doubted Violet's constancy; but for this he, in his turn, received absolution, and was presently taken back into favour.

As to Tim, his name was not mentioned between them; if they thought about him at all, which is unlikely, they certainly did not waste these precious moments in talking about him. Violet's little spurt of indignation against him was of the most transitory nature; had she recollected it, it would have been to be rather ashamed of it; besides, he was gone away, and that was enough; and Carol would certainly not have introduced a subject on which he was feeling a little sore. Violet was restored to him; the first cloud that had shadowed his young brightness had rolled away; and nothing else seemed to matter much. He went back to Cambridge in a far more peaceful frame of mind, and plunged with robust cheerfulness into all the pleasures of the May term.

One day the old Squire, meeting Mr. Ebbesley on the road, stopped his pony to ask after Tim.

'Sorry to hear your boy was not quite strong, Ebbesley,' he said kindly.

'Thank you,' said Mr. Ebbesley; 'he is quite well again now, and gone back to school.'

'Ah! I must tell Carol when I write; he'll be glad to hear it; the boys are fond of one another; but most likely the young 'un will be writing to him himself.'

'Ah! by the way, Mr. Darley, that reminds me, if you are writing to your grandson, will you kindly say my boy hopes he will excuse his not writing to him at present? he has to read rather hard for his upper division trials, and by the doctor's advice, I discourage his working his brain in other ways, too.'

'Quite right, quite right. When I was a lad we didn't write letters much. To be sure, it was before the penny post; but I can't say I should have used it much if it had been invented. I never was a good correspondent; I don't think I ever wrote to my poor dear father when I was a lad except when I wanted money, which I generally didn't get. Well, good-bye. Can you come and dine with us, Tuesday?'

'Thank you, but I am obliged to go to town again tomorrow.'

And so the two men separated; and, the Squire's memory not being of the best, Carol never got the message.

It was quite true; Tim was trying very hard to drown in work the recollection of his troubles. It is not easy to take bodily out of one's life a sentiment, the growth of nearly eight years, and not feel the change; and Tim's was not a nature to which changes came easily. To take his devotion to Carol *out* of his life, did I say? Why, it *was* his life; it had begun when he first began to feel anything, and had grown with his growth ever since. In some fantastic way everything else in the world seemed to cluster round that central point; nothing was of interest until he had somehow brought it into relation with this ruling and pervading sentiment. And it was this that he had undertaken to cast from him and forget. He felt as some flower might which a child had plucked from its root, and then stuck back in the ground expecting it to go on growing as heretofore.

As often happens, after the very cold winter came an unusually hot summer. The air seemed to pulse and vibrate. Scarcely a leaf stirred of the lime-trees before the chapel, heavy and odorous with their wealth of blossom, and drowsy with the hum of innumerable bees. The boys grew languid and listless over their lessons, and even over their games. They fell asleep in three o'clock school, an offence with which the masters could not in their hearts but feel a secret sympathy. The dust seemed to spring eternal, almost from under the very hose of the water-cart that went ceaselessly to and fro through the highways of the old school, and the pelargoniums and fuchsias drooped in the window-boxes, because their owners had not the energy to water them. Eton is a healthy place, in spite of all its enemies say to the contrary, and the life there is for most boys the healthiest that could be devised. But Tim was not as most boys. To him, to eat, sleep, and study in one small room, to wear a high hat and a tight black cloth coat, with the thermometer at something fabulous in the shade, was very trying. The heat that made other lads drowsy and languid, roused him to unnatural and feverish alertness; so far from sleeping in school, he did not sleep at all. When we reflect that in addition to this he was fretting day and night over his hidden sorrow, – a sorrow from which he was persistently trying to find escape in extra hard work, in spite of headaches and other warning signs, – the result is not difficult to foretell. What wonder if he broke down? He never went in for those upper division trials. One day he did not come to dinner, he the soul of regularity; and when they went to look for him they found him stretched on the floor of his room, his face white and set, his eyes open, but with no consciousness in them. They put him to bed and sent for the doctor, who pronounced it a curious case.

'It is no doubt partly the heat,' he said, 'and he has been working too hard; but he must have been in a wretched state of health to begin with; neither the weather nor his work is enough to account for it.'

'He has never been very strong,' answered his tutor, 'and lately I have noticed that he has been working very hard, harder than was necessary even. I have had once or twice to put on the drag, a thing I am very seldom forced to do.'

'He must have perfect rest and quiet, and must not write or read even the lightest books for a long time to come; when he is able to bear the move, he had better be taken home.'

So the tutor went and wrote a kind sympathetic letter to Mr. Ebbesley, telling him his son was ill. How ill he thought him he took care not to say, but he did say enough to carry an awful dread to the father's heart. A chill foreboding seized upon him, and would not be shaken off, – a presentiment that he was to lose his child, that child so zealously longed for, so little appreciated, and yet in a way so deeply loved.

William Ebbesley was in no sense of the word religious; the rough struggle with the world that had filled his early years had not tended to bring him into the devotional attitude, nor had he ever been visited by one of those overwhelming joys that sweep the soul, whatever the nature of its beliefs, with an imperious necessity for giving thanks. And great and terrible as had been some of his sorrows, they had been such as harden and embitter rather than the reverse. But now he felt in some dim way a kind of wonder if this were intended as a punishment to him for the little regard he had paid to the one blessing of his life, which, in that it did not bless him in strict accord with his own notions of what he desired, he had flung from him so carelessly, the priceless gem of his child's love. How that child could love, he had seen; and till now the thought that the love was not for him but another, had chafed and angered him. Now he was humbled by it. Who could say but that had he tried, he might have turned at least some streamlet of those freshening waters into his own parched and rugged field?

There was an old woman once to whom certain kind friends of mine used to send her dinner. She was quite past work, and absolutely destitute, except for what was bestowed upon her in charity, but if the victuals were not to her taste she would send them back. Was it that by so doing she got better ones? On the contrary, the alternative was to fast, and indeed to risk offending the givers, and so cutting herself off from the alms for ever. The proverb that half a loaf is better than no bread, is one to which we all give assent with our lips, but few people, if any, are found willing to make it a rule of conduct. They will have a whole loaf, new and soft, of the finest wheaten flour, and baked just as they choose, or they will eat no bread, though they starve for it. These are perhaps somewhat homely illustrations for the state of mind of a father half wild with grief and self-reproach over a dying son. For something told him, as I have said, that the gift which he had so reck-lessly cast aside, would never be his now. His boy would die, and would never know how much he really loved him. If he could only win him back to life, only make him think a little more kindly of his father, he felt that nothing else mattered.

He went and fetched Tim home himself, and when he saw how ill and fragile the lad looked, his heart died within him; he longed to fall on his knees by him and tell him how he loved him, and implore him not to leave him. But the doctor had cautioned him to betray no emo-tion, and to conceal as far as possible any shock he might experience at his son's appearance.

At first for a few days Tim suffered from a raging pain in the head; he could bear no light and no sound, and they feared that he would have brain fever. Then suddenly the pain left him, but left him so exhausted that he hardly seemed alive. Still, weak as he was, the doctor thought he had better be taken away from school, and his father carried him back to the old manor-house where his childhood had past. As though to mock William Ebbesley's grief by violent contrast to the pale and feeble Tim, it was the time of year when the earth is most instinct with buoyant and vibrating life, – July, when the last crowning touch has been put to the long work of spring, while no foreshadowing of the yet distant autumn has fallen on any leaf. The lilies were in their tallest, whitest majesty, the roses blushed and glowed in the old garden, where, a few weeks before, Tim had hidden himself from the voice of his friend.

'I never see such a year, sir,' said the gardener; 'everything is a-doing better than I've ever known it since I've lived here.'

Yes. Everything. Everything but that one blossom for which he would gladly have bartered all the wealth of sunny fruit and folded petals, and on which a frosty hand had been laid in the midst of all the warmth of summer. For Mrs. Quitchett's old friend the doctor, who had known Tim from a baby, did not dare conceal from the poor father his belief that the lad would die. How soon he could not say; he might even be wrong, and Tim might take a turn and begin to gain strength; but he was afraid to hope it. The little stock of life in him seemed to be ebbing away. He might go on for a year, or it might be much sooner; it was impossible to say.

14 J. G. Nicholson and
A. Melling as a boy.
From a photograph,
c. 1892 (Mr. Donald
Weeks)

15 'August Blue'. From a painting by H. S. Tuke, R.A., 1894 (The Tate Gallery,
London)

16   Aleister Crowley. From the
frontispiece to a selection of his poems,
Ambergris, London, 1911

'And could nothing be done?' asked the father. 'Were there no new remedies he could try, no learned men to consult, no places or climates in which the flickering young life would have a better chance to reassert itself?'

The old doctor's voice trembled as he answered. He was almost as fond of the child himself, and he grasped Mr. Ebbesley's hand and spoke very gently. 'I should only be deceiving you if I said "yes"; of course consult any one you will, if it will be any comfort to you; but they will only say the same thing. There is no organic disease; he is dying of sheer weakness, and to drag him about the world will only use up the little stock of strength he has left. If, as God grant, he takes a turn and lives till the winter, then I don't say but it would be well to try a better climate. But at present he is as well off here as anywhere.'

So, then, there was no help for it; nothing to do but to watch his child fade slowly from him, to see him grow whiter, thinner, more easily tired day by day.

The Darleys were all away, and Violet was with them. The Court was shut up, and Tim might have wandered up there without any fear of meeting Carol. But he found, when he tried it, that even this walk, short as it was, was beyond his powers, and this, coming upon him with a vague surprise, was the first intimation to him of how ill he really was. He thought of the old childish days when he had skimmed across the fields for miles round his home, and the Court woods had been but the beginning of his rambles.

Mrs. Quitchett thought of those days too, and wept when she compared the child, small and frail, it is true, but lithe and active as a young squirrel, with the figure of the slim lad of sixteen that moved so slowly round the garden paths. 'Who would ha' thought, who would ha' thought that see'd us two,' sobbed the poor old woman, 'that he was the one the Lord would take first to Himself!' But to Tim she showed a smiling front, watching every sign, indefatigable in her zeal to miss no attention that might do good, and never admitting for a moment that he was not getting better.

As the Ethiopian cannot change his skin, so was it not given to William Ebbesley in an instant to alter his whole nature; such changes do not happen in real life; and even now he caught himself sometimes speaking half-sharply to Tim, when the struggle within him was almost more than he could bear. But the boy did not feel afraid of him any longer; it seemed as though he had some intuition of all that his father was suffering and had suffered on his account; he was beginning to understand him, and in the place of his old fear there welled up in his heart an infinite pity.

One day, when Mr. Ebbesley had brought out cushions with which to make the garden seat easy and soft for him, and was turning to go, as he usually did after shyly proffering some such little act of tenderness, Tim laid one of his thin white hands on his, saying, 'You are very good to me, father.'

'Oh! my boy, my little son,' burst out the poor man, 'I have been a very hard father to you. I see it all now; I thought, I meant to do what was right, but I have been very cruel. Oh! if I could only atone! but you will never forgive me, never love me now.'

The cry that had been stifling him was uttered at last, the proud man had humbled himself, the thin partition that for eight years had kept these two apart had crumbled and let them find one another.

Tim for all answer put up his other arm and drew his father's head down upon his breast, and so for a little space they sat quite silent. After a time Tim said very simply, 'Do you remember the talk we had about my grandmother? You said all her family died young; I think *I* shall die this summer.'

His father could not speak: he could not contradict him, he could only fold him more closely in his arms; and it was Tim who spoke again.

'You mustn't fret for me, father; I am surprised myself to find how little I mind the thought; I think I am rather glad. But there is something I have wanted to say. I am afraid I have not been all you wished; I have disappointed and vexed you. Do you forgive me?'

Still his father could not trust himself to answer save by that convulsive hold; the words meant to ask pardon set themselves in array against him like accusing angels. What words could he find strong enough to express all he was feeling? But Tim smiled and was satisfied. He seemed as though he understood.

CHAPTER XIII

. . . Even the weariest river
Winds, somewhere, safe to sea.
    SWINBURNE's *Garden of Proserpine*.

As the weeks succeeded each other, one thought was ever present in the mind of Tim. 'Shall I see him again before I die? It can do him no harm now. I shall so soon be out of the way; I cannot come between him and his love any more.'

As his poor hands, whose hold on this world was loosening day by day, grew thinner and more transparent, his face paler, his step slower upon the gravel, his heart yearned ever with a patient longing for just one more sight of the friend to whom his whole life had been true. But he had given the crowning proof of his devotion – renunciation. The arms that should have been upholding him in his last sore struggle, he had himself unclasped; the dear lips and eyes that should even now be smiling on his sick-bed, his own free act had sent far away from him.

'He will never know that I was true to him. I shall never see him again.' Through all the long empty hours this one cry repeats itself in his soul. All the little life that is left to him seems concentrated in this one intense longing for Carol. To see his face, to hear his loved voice again, if only for a moment; to tell him the truth at last; only once, just once, before he died. And yet even now he could not put his thought into words, – could not bring himself to make this last request to his father.

As for Mr. Ebbesley, he too was troubled by one thought which he could not find the courage to speak. He was always with Tim now. It was his arm which supported the boy into the garden where he loved to sit, and back to the house; no tending could have been more loving, more sympathetic. But, as I have said, no one changes his whole nature at a leap, even in the great crises of life; and there was yet one struggle to be made with his pride before perfect ease and confidence could exist between them.

Hour after hour would Tim lie silent and uncomplaining, yearning for Carol, but dreading to endanger the new-found treasure of his father's love; dreading to see the old cloud settle on the face that he was watching, the hard look grow round the mouth, as it was wont to do when in the old days he had been obliged to mention his friend's name. And William Ebbesley would sit beside him all the while, divining his thoughts, knowing there was one supreme proof of his affection to be given to his son, one sacrifice that he could make for him, one happiness that he could give him, and longing to make the effort, yet ever just kept from it by some strange inexplicable shyness and reserve. For a long time he hoped that Tim would break the silence, would be the first to approach the subject; but at last he saw that that was not to be hoped, and he was half angry with himself for the cowardice that made him wish to shift this burthen to those poor weak shoulders. No. It was clearly for him to take the first step; had he not ardently desired some way of showing his devotion to his son, and when he had it, was it possible that he should hesitate?

So one evening when they had been watching the sunset, which had left a sham glow on Tim's white cheeks, William Ebbesley, holding his son's hand, and with face half-turned away, said suddenly, 'Tim, dear, you have not everything you want; there is one thing I have not done for you.'

There was a real glow in Tim's cheeks now; the sunset light had faded, but in its place an inward radiance, brighter but almost as transient, had spread over the delicate face. Feeling his grasp tighten, his father stole a look at him, and even then a pang shot through him at the thought of the love that had called forth this happy flush at the bare chance of a meeting, the love that was not for him, that might perhaps have been his.

'Oh, father! you mean – ' Tim began tremulously, and paused; he dared hardly complete the sentence even in his own mind.

William Ebbesley choked down the last touch of the old jealousy. 'I will write tonight,' he said quietly, answering the other's unspoken thought.

But a new trouble had fallen on Tim. 'Will he come?' he said half to himself; and then, 'Oh yes. If I know him for the kind, generous Carol I think him, he will surely come.'

Then he asked, 'Father, may *I* write?'

'You know, dear boy, the doctor has forbidden you to write a word.'

'Yes, I know; but this will do me good. I shall not be easy unless I may.'

'Won't it do if you dictate to me?'

'No. I must write myself; nothing else will do.'

'Well, if you are sure it will not tire you.' And he went and brought the writing things.

Tim took them eagerly, and was beginning to write, when he stopped suddenly and looked up. 'Father, forgive me; I am selfish. You are sorry at this.'

It was so unexpected, the little impulse of unselfish consideration, that at its contact the last drop of bitterness fell from the father's heart, and in his eyes for the first time for more years than he could remember shone the blessed healing tears to which he had so long been a stranger.

'No, no, my darling,' he faltered hastily; 'whatever makes you happy – I – ' then his voice broke, and he could not finish.

'God bless you, dear dear father. I am quite happy now.'

And this was Tim's letter: 'I am very ill, Carol – dying, I think. Dear Carol, if I have seemed ungrateful, can you and will you forgive me? I could explain to you if I had you here, but I can't write. Come to me, Carol dear. – Your loving TIM.'

'Father.'

'Yes, dear.'

'Do you want to see what I have written?'

'No, my boy, no.'

Mr. Ebbesley took the letter and sealed it; then he sent it to the address that he had already got from the servants at the Court.

Whether it was the reaction from the tense longing in which he had been living or merely that as his strength decreased the change in him grew more apparent, Tim seemed to get worse much more quickly after his letter had gone.

The doctor came and went, shaking his head sadly, and saying, 'It is quicker than I thought,' and despair settled down upon the two watchers by the sick boy.

But still Tim waited day by day for the answer that was to bring peace to his soul. Life was slipping away too fast. 'Oh! come, Carol,' he would whisper, 'or it may be too late; she will surely spare you just for a little.'

Tim had been at home nearly a month now; the blazing July weather had ended in a rather wet August. All around, the harvest lay beaten down by the rain; not the only grain stricken ere it had come to maturity. One evening, after a more than usually dreary day, the clouds had broken, giving place to a gorgeous sunset. Tim had been placed on a sofa in the open window, from which he could watch the purple and crimson and gold, and the delicate green and lilac tints of the western sky; the same sofa on which he had lain eight years before, pondering on his 'angel,' and had seen Carol come in with his offering of grapes.

'Father.'

'Yes, my boy.' He knew too well what question was coming.

'Has the postman been?'

'Yes, dear.'

Alas! no letter. Tim did not even ask, knowing that if there were one, it would be given to him at once. He closed his eyes and lay quite still. His father looked wearily out of the window; he knew what was passing in the lad's mind, and had come to desire the letter almost as much as the sick boy himself.

The air was cool and fresh. The garden was yielding a thousand scents to the soft touch of the summer rain. The setting sun lit little coloured lamps in the large drops that hung from every leaf of the grateful trees and shrubs; the birds kept up a drowsy twittering. A few knowing old blackbirds and thrushes, well aware that the moisture brings out the fine fat worms, were hopping about on the grass-plot in search of their supper. All sounds were strangely distinct that evening.

Hark! what was that? surely a step on the wet gravel; not old Richard the gardener's step. No, it was a young foot that struck the ground lightly, and scrunched stoutly along the little approach to the house. Tim's ears had caught the sound, and he started up from his pillows, his cheeks aflame, his eyes bright and eager, while his heart beat loud and fast. He would know that dear step among a thousand.

He had come – at last, at last!

Mr. Ebbesley stole noiselessly away, with a heavy dull ache in his heart, and I am afraid neither of the friends noticed his absence. In the same room, in the same place, in the same attitudes in which they had met as children, they had come together again.

'Oh, Carol! are you come to me?'

'Oh, my poor dear Tim!'

Carol could say no more. He was shocked at the havoc these few short weeks had wrought. A sacred silence rested between them for a few minutes. Enough for Tim that he was there; no need of words. Carol was the first to speak; his voice was hushed and full of awe.

'I was not with my family when your letter came, dear Tim, and they did not know where to forward it to me, as I was moving about; so I never got it for nearly ten days, or I should have been here long ago.'

'Oh, Carol! how good of you to come. I half thought sometimes – forgive me for doubting you – but I thought you might not come at all – after – after the way I treated you.'

'Don't let's talk of that now, Tim; it's past and gone. I don't want you to explain; I am content not to understand. I remember only the dear good friend of the old days, who is come back to me.'

'But I *must* talk of it, please, Carol; I must tell you how it was. It can do no harm now, and I can't leave you thinking hardly of me, for you know I have not very long to live; something tells me you are come only just in time.'

'Oh! dear dear boy, for God's sake, don't talk like that,' said Carol, with a great lump rising in his throat. 'You are not going to – to – ' He felt all the repugnance of the young and strong to face the thought, or say the word.

'To die.' Tim finished the sentence for him quite simply. 'Yes, I think so.'

'No, no; you will get well and strong. You must, for all our sakes.'

Tim smiled and shook his head; it did not seem to him worth while to argue the point; that was not what he wanted to say.

'Never mind,' he said gently, in a way that put the subject aside as unimportant. 'If I had lived I could not have had you with me now. I could never have told you what I am going to tell you. Carol, will you believe me when I say that I never wavered for an instant in my love for you; never loved you better than when I seemed to give you up?' Tim was getting excited, and Carol, fearing it would be bad for him, tried in vain to stop him. 'Oh, Carol! it was for your sake I did it; will you believe me when I tell you all this?'

'For my sake, dear old boy? I don't understand you.' He thought his friend's mind was wandering, but he was very patient and tender with him, humouring him, as one would a sick child.

'She said – I heard her say – that I came between you. You know, Carol, it was when you were so unhappy; and then I saw that I was the cause of it all; and so I determined not to come between you any more; and, indeed, indeed, dear Carol, I would have held my tongue for ever, only there is no more need now. I could not die and leave you thinking ill of me. I suppose I ought to have, but I couldn't do it.'

A new light was breaking in upon Carol. 'And did you do all this for me?' he asked wonderingly. 'Why, Tim, I knew you liked me absurdly, much more than I deserved, but I never dreamt you cared as much for me as that.'

'And you understand now, Carol, don't you, why I didn't answer your dear letter? See, I have it here; it never leaves me.'

'I was a beast and a fool to doubt you, Tim. How could I ever have done it? but it *did* seem as though you must be bored with me and my affairs. And all the time you were doing this for me!'

'Carol, did she mind your coming to me? Tell me I have not made fresh mischief between you?'

'She was very unhappy when I told her how ill you were, and she said, "Oh! go at once to him; I can guess what it would be to be ill and wanting you; and he has been waiting so long already." And then she cried, and said a great deal I did not understand at the time about having been jealous of my friendship for you, and having had hard thoughts of you sometimes, and that she was so ashamed of herself now that you were so ill. I was to be sure and tell you, and to ask if you would ever forgive her.'

'There is nothing to forgive,' Tim answered indifferently.

'But how did you guess,' Carol continued, 'how could you imagine that she felt anything of the sort?'

Then Tim told him all that he had overheard Violet say, only softening it off, and generalizing a little with fine tact. And then, the floodgates once open, he went on with sudden eloquence, the more touching from its sheer simplicity, and told all the long story of his constant love, but with as little mention as possible of his father throughout, and of the part he had played in it. And this short hour, which some may think was a sad one, was just the happiest of Tim's whole life.

Carol listened in wonder and awe, not unmingled with compunction, as the description of the feeling he had so unconsciously excited unrolled itself before him. He forgot himself, Violet, his love for her, everything for the moment in contemplation of this devotion, so single-hearted, so lofty, so pure and so unselfish, which had been his, all his, and at which he had been so far from guessing.

'I had no idea of anything of the kind,' he said, more to himself than to Tim. 'I knew the old people were awfully fond of me, God bless them; and I understand what I feel for Violet. But this beats me; I've always been what's called popular, I suppose. I never thought much about it, but fellows have always been jolly to me, and seemed to like me. Oh! my dear friend, what have I ever done that you should care about me like this?'

Tim's face lit up exultingly. ' "Passing the love of women," ' he said; 'that was it, Carol, wasn't it? "Thy love to me was wonderful, passing the love of women." Do you remember the day when they read it in the lesson in chapel at Eton?'

Carol had forgotten, but Tim's words brought back the scene with strange distinctness: the big chapel in its stillness, the silence of a great crowd, and of a crowd unused to be still, the little flecks of light from the air-holes in the roof, the ugly picture of the finding of Moses in the window opposite his seat, the droning voice of the reader, and the flash of the little face that turned up to his, with the expression that had puzzled him at the time.

'Yes, I remember,' he answered.

'I have thought of it so often since. It would be grand for one's friend to be able to say that of one, after one was dead. Put your strong arms round me, Carol, and raise me a little; I can talk better so.'

Carol lifted the poor thin body as easily as a baby, and propped it up on the cushions.

'Thank you, that is better. Ah! don't take your arms away; let me feel them round me for a little. Carol, when I am buried, I want those words to be put on the stone. My father will let it be so, I know, if I wish it; I shall ask him the last thing. But you must remind him.'

'Oh! Tim, I can't bear to hear you talk so. You mustn't die; we all want you so much.'

'Don't cry, Carol; you will do as I wish, won't you? And, Carol, tell her how I tried to make things happy for her and you; I want her to think kindly of me too.'

He laid his head on his friend's breast and closed his eyes; the effort of talking so much had tired him. Carol thought he was asleep, and dared not move for fear of waking him; but by and by he said, 'Do you remember, Carol? I lay on this sofa when you first came to see me after the accident. I had been dreaming of you without knowing it; I thought you were an angel. And then I turned and saw you standing there in the doorway. You kissed me that day, Carol. Will you kiss me now?'

Carol bowed his head without a word and kissed him. And thus their friendship was sealed at either end.

'Father,' said Tim, after a little, 'are you there?'

'Yes, my boy.' He had come in, and was standing a little apart in the deepening twilight, humbly watching the friends. How unlike the proud man who had so bitterly resented his little son's preferring another to himself!

'Will you come here, father? I cannot see you there.' He came round the sofa, and Tim held out his hand to him. 'You and Carol must love one another,' he said, looking from one to the other, 'for my sake.' Silently the two men clasped hands over the couch.

'You must leave us now, Carol dear,' Tim went on; 'I must be alone with my father.'

Carol longed to say something, but could not; he went out without a word. Tim watched him walk away with eyes that knew they were taking their last look. Then a satisfied smile lit up his face as he turned it to his father.

53   'Of Boys' Names'

John Gambril Nicholson. From *Love in Earnest*, 1892. Dedicated 'To W.E.M.'

> Old memories of the Table Round
>   In Percival and Lancelot dwell,
> Clement and Bernard bring the sound
>   Of anthems in the cloister-cell,
>   And Leonard vies with Lionel
> In stately step and kingly frame,
>   And Kenneth speaks of field and fell,
> And Earnest gets my heart a-flame.
>
> One name can make my pulses bound,
>   No peer it owns, nor parallel,
> By it is Vivian's sweetness drowned,
>   And Roland, full as organ-swell;
>   Though Frank may ring like silver bell,
> And Cecil softer music claim,
>   They cannot work the miracle, –
> 'Tis Earnest gets my heart a-flame.
>
> Cyril is lordly, Stephen crowned
>   With deathless wreaths of asphodel,
> Oliver whispers peace profound,
>   Herbert takes arms his foes to quell,

Eustace with sheaves is laden well,
    Christopher has a nobler fame,
And Michael storms the gates of Hell,
    But Earnest gets my heart a-flame.

Envoy

My little Prince, Love's mystic spell
    Lights all the letters of your name,
And you, if no one else, can tell
    Why Earnest gets my heart a-flame.

54   'Sonnet IV. Held in Bondage'

John Gambril Nicholson. From *Love in Earnest*, 1892.

The happy day – my brightest and my best –
    You kissed me playfully, – a mere mad freak
    Of which you will not, and I dare not speak,
And all it meant to me you never guessed;
For when with hopeless doubt I am oppressed,
    Knowing my love so strong and yours so weak,
    Once more I feel your lips upon my cheek,
And this one comfort lulls my care to rest.

You love me not, and yet (why should it be?)
    You are my Life and Death, my Fate and Fere!
    What makes the sun control this whirling sphere? –
What makes the moon command the patient sea? –
As little know I why you are to me
    So strangely incommunicably dear!

55   'St William of Norwich'

Frederick William Rolfe (Baron Corvo) and John Gambril Nicholson.
From *Love in Earnest*, 1892.

When twilight wrapped the tall cathedral spire,
    With eyes uplifted in adoring mood
    To the white Christ upon the Holy Rood

He sang at Vespers in the darkening choir;
Now, as the midnight-moon mounts ever higher,
    With outstretched arms he hangs within the wood,
    The awful wings of Death above him brood –
Martyred to glut the Hebrews' foul desire.

Fair as the Boy that Mary loved was he
    In chanter's garb, nor has the beauty fled
    From his still form with blood-stained limbs outspread;
The shadows deepen round the lonely tree,
But through the gathering gloom the angels see
    The nimbus forming round his drooping head.

56   'The Destroyer of a Soul'

Lionel Johnson. From *Poems*, 1895. Written 1892.

I hate you with a necessary hate.
First, I sought patience: passionate was she:
My patience turned in very scorn of me,
That I should dare forgive a sin so great,
As this, through which I sit disconsolate;
Mourning for that live soul, I used to see;
Soul of a saint, whose friend I used to be:
Till you came by! a cold, corrupting, fate.

Why come you now? You, whom I cannot cease
With pure and perfect hate to hate? Go, ring
The death-bell with a deep, triumphant toll!
Say you, my friend sits by me still? Ah, peace!
Call you this thing my friend? this nameless thing?
This living body, hiding its dead soul?

57   'Si vous croyez que je vais dire'

Francis William Bourdillon. From *Love in a Mist*, 1892.

My lips must say not
My eyes betray not
    My heart's hid treasure;

My hands must deaden,
My feet go leaden,
   Not leap in measure.

For how they would rate me,
Preach me and prate me,
   Scoff at and scold me,
Should they discover
Who is my lover,
   And what he has told me!

58   'Daphnis'

E. Bonney-Steyne. From *The Artist*, 1 November 1892.

To all the world what you may seem
   I know not neither do I care
To me you are a waking dream
   Fulfilling all things sweet and fair.

The world may prize you or disdain,
   You are my world; the only thing
That sways my life, one perfect gain
   The only pleasure without sting.

Your love shines on me like a sun
   And in its rays reveals my youth,
For one I live, and love that one
   With loyalty and perfect truth.

59   'Heartsease and Orchid'

Percy Osborn. From *The Spirit Lamp*, vol. 3, 17 February 1893. Written December 1892.

Heartsease it was from his dear hand I took,
A dainty flower that loves the garden air,
Breathing the freshness of his boyhood fair.
So it was treasured in a golden book.

There came another with a far-off look,
His hand an orchid gave; 'twas strange and rare,
And caught my senses in a beauteous snare,
Till sunlight for the furnace I forsook.

My heart grew drowsy with a sweet disease;
And fluttered in a cage of fantasy;
And I remembered how his face was pale,
Yet by its very paleness more did please;
Now hath the orchid grown a part of me,
But still the heartsease tells its olden tale.

60   'By the Aegean'

'Saloninus'. From *The Artist*, 2 January 1893.

Beauty long sought for, incarnate, consummate
Found but in marble serenely quiescent
Wayward impetuously leapt into being
                              With you and in you.

Rapturous, exquisite past all concealment
Love in a sigh breathed to perfect fruition
Seeing unclothed unashamed in the sunlight
                              Glad adolescence.

Tremulous flesh in its riotous beauty
Flashing yet delicate past all expressing
The mirth of the world, and the joy of mere being;
                              Life at its zenith.

Eyes that fulfill all the yearnings of twilight
Mouth that steals open like dawn o'er the ocean
Figure more beautiful than (dared one imagine it)
                              God in his boyhood.

Now in thy nakedness, radiant, triumphant
Known by the salt waves in amorous transport
Kissed by the warm wind, caressed by the wavelets
                              Monarch of beauty.

Thus to have seen you is light for all ages
Just to have dreamed you were rapture for ever
But to have loved you is moment for lasting
                    For ever immortal.

Vibrant the future responds to your movement
Sinuous curves round all living to loving
Perfect contentment at last is accomplished
                    Full and sufficient.

61   'To a Sicilian Boy'

Theodore Wratislaw. From *The Artist*, 1 August 1893.

Love, I adore the contours of thy shape,
Thine exquisite breasts and arms adorable;
The wonders of thine heavenly throat compel
Such fire of love as even my dreams escape:
I love thee as the sea-foam loves the cape,
Or as the shore the sea's enchanting spell:
In sweets the blossoms of thy mouth excel
The tenderest bloom of peach or purple grape.

I love thee, sweet! Kiss me, again, again!
Thy kisses soothe me, as tired earth the rain;
Between thine arms I find my only bliss;
Ah let me in thy bosom still enjoy
Oblivion of the past, divinest boy,
And the dull ennui of a woman's kiss!

62   'We Have Forgot'

James Morgan Brown. From *Verses*, 1893.

We have forgot what we have been,
        And what we are we little know;
We fancy new events begin,
        But all has happened long ago.

Full oft my feelings make me start,
    Like footprints on a foreign shore,
As if the chambers of my heart,
    Had heard their shadowy step before.

So, looking into thy clear eyes,
    Strange memories come to me, as though
Somewhere – perchance in Paradise –
    I had adored thee long ago.

63   'Many are Dreams'

Eric, Count Stenbock. From *The Shadow of Death*, 1893.

Octave I

Many are dreams that one should tell thereof,
    But I have only one dream – I and he,
    His arms wound all around me tenderly,
Treading on air, and flower-lit fields we rove.

Sucked down into the abyss of my great love;
    I think, beloved! thou mightest cease to be,
    And we, being made as one eternally,
Walk a twin star along the light above.

64   'I Love him Wisely'

John Gambril Nicholson. From *A Chaplet of Southernwood*, 1896. Chaplet III.
Written 1893.

I love him wisely if I love him well,
    And so I let him keep his innocence;
    I veil my adoration with pretence
Since he knows nothing of Love's mystic spell;
I dare not for his sake my passion tell
    Though strong desire upbraid my diffidence; –
    To buy my happiness at his expense
Were folly blind and loss unspeakable.

Suspicious of my simplest acts I grow;
    I doubt my passing words, however brief;
    I catch his glances feeling like a thief.
Perchance he wonders why I shun him so, –
It would be strange indeed if he should know
    I love him, love him, love him past belief!

65   *'Ah, would that I in Dreamland'*

John Gambril Nicholson. From *A Chaplet of Southernwood*, 1896.
Chaplet IV. Written 1892.

Ah, would that I in Dreamland aye might dwell,
    Since Dreamland brings my Prince divinely near!
    In Dreamland I know neither doubt nor fear –
I only know I love him passing well.
We meet in Dreamland, and its wondrous spell
    Makes all my love's perplexing issues clear,
    And there I whisper boldly in his ear
The things that I elsewhere may never tell.

And many a time I wonder, when I wake,
    If happy dreams are sent me for a sign
    That cloudless love may yet be his and mine;
Then for the torturing day fresh courage take,
And hush my heart to silence for his sake,
    Till Dreamland brings again the anodyne.

66   *'You Wonder Why'*

John Gambril Nicholson. From *A Chaplet of Southernwood*, 1896. Chaplet V.
Written 1894.

You wonder why I love my Prince so well:
    'Tis not (*you* say) for face, or form, or wit,
    Or speech, or mood, or manner, – you admit
None of these motives for the miracle;
'Tis not (by observation *you* can tell)
    Because he loves me, as would best befit;
    A mystery then, and you would fathom it –
What beauty makes him so desirable?

A lover's reason shall my answer be: –
I cannot tell you where his beauty lies,
I cannot make you see him with my eyes;
'Tis not because he's beautiful to me
I love him; but because I love him, he
Is beautiful. How foolish! And how wise!

67 'The Age of Athletic Prizemen'

Walter Pater. From *Greek Studies*, 1895. Written February 1894.

Myron was a native of Eleutherae, and a pupil of Ageladas of Argos. There is nothing more to tell by way of positive detail of this so famous artist, save that the main scene of his activity was Athens, now become the centre of the artistic as of all other modes of life in Greece. *Multiplicasse veritatem videtur*, says Pliny. He was in fact an earnest realist or naturalist, and rose to central perfection in the portraiture, the idealized portraiture, of athletic youth, from a mastery first of all in the delineation of inferior objects, of little lifeless or living things. Think, however, for a moment, how winning such objects are still, as presented on Greek coins; – the ear of corn, for instance, on those of Metapontum; the microscopic cockle-shell, the dolphins, on the coins of Syracuse. Myron, then, passes from pleasant truth of that kind to the delineation of the worthier sorts of animal life, – the ox, the dog – to nothing short of illusion in the treatment of them, as ancient connoisseurs would have you understand. It is said that there are thirty-six extant epigrams on his brazen cow. That animal has her gentle place in Greek art, from the Siren tomb, suckling her young there, as the type of eternal rejuvenescence, onwards to the procession of the Elgin frieze, where, still breathing deliciously of the distant pastures, she is led to the altar. We feel sorry for her, as we look, so lifelike is the carved marble. The sculptor who worked there, whoever he may have been, had profited doubtless by the study of Myron's famous work. For what purpose he made it, does not appear, – as an architectural ornament; or a votive offering; perhaps only because he liked making it. In hyperbolic epigram, at any rate, the animal breathes, explaining sufficiently the point of Pliny's phrase regarding Myron – *Corporum curiosus*. And when he came to his main business with the quoit-player, the wrestler, the runner, he did not for a moment forget that they too were animals, young animals, delighting in natural motion, in free course through the yielding air, over uninterrupted space, according to Aristotle's definition of pleasure: – 'the unhindered exercise of one's natural force.' *Corporum tenus curiosus*: – he was a 'curious workman' as far as the living body is concerned. Pliny goes on to qualify that phrase by saying that he did not express the sensations of the mind – *animi sensus*. But just there, in fact, precisely in such limitation, we find what authenticates Myron's peculiar value in the evolution of Greek art. It is of the essence of the athletic prizeman, involved in the very ideal of the quoit-player, the cricketer, not to give expression to mind, in any antagonism to, or invasion of, the body; to mind as anything more than a function of the body, whose healthful balance of functions it may so easily perturb; – to disavow that insidious enemy of the fairness of the bodily soul as such.

Yet if the art of Myron was but little occupied with the reasonable soul (*animus*), with those mental situations the expression of which, though it may have a pathos and a beauty of its own, is for the most part adverse to the proper expression of youth, to the beauty of youth, by causing it to be no longer youthful, he was certainly a master of the animal or physical soul there (*anima*); how it is, how it displays itself, as illustrated, for instance, in the *Discobolus*. Of voluntary animal motion the very soul is undoubtedly there. We have but translations into marble of the original in bronze. In that, it was as if a blast of cool wind had congealed the metal, or the living youth, fixed him imperishably in that moment of rest which lies between two opposed motions, the *backward* swing of the right arm, the movement *forwards* on which the left foot is in the very act of starting. The matter of the thing, the stately bronze or marble, thus rests indeed; but the artistic form of it, in truth, scarcely more, even to the eye, than the rolling ball or disk, may be said to rest, at every moment of its course, – just meta-physically, you know.

This mystery of combined motion and rest, of rest in motion, had involved, of course, on the part of the sculptor who had mastered its secret, long and intricate consideration. Archaic as it is, primitive still in some respects, full of the primitive youth it celebrates, it is, in fact, a learned work, and suggested to a great analyst of literary style, singular as it may seem, the 'elaborate' or 'contorted' manner in litera-ture of the later Latin writers, which, however, he finds 'laudable' for its purpose. Yet with all its learned involution, thus so oddly charac-terized by Quintilian, so entirely is this quality subordinated to the proper purpose of the *Discobolus* as a work of art, a thing to be looked at rather than to think about, that it makes one exclaim still, with the poet of athletes, 'The natural is ever best!' – τὸ δὲ φυᾷ ἅπαν κράτιστον. Perhaps that triumphant, unimpeachable naturalness is after all the reason why, on seeing it for the first time, it suggests no new view of the beauty of human form, or point of view for the regarding of it; is acceptable rather as embodying (say, in one perfect flower) all one has ever fancied or seen, in old Greece or on Thames' side, of the unspoiled body of youth, thus delighting itself and others, at that perfect, because unconscious, point of good-fortune, as it moves or rests just there for a moment, between the animal and spiritual worlds. 'Grant them,' you pray in Pindar's own words, 'grant them with feet so light to pass through life!'

The face of the young man, as you see him in the British Museum for instance, with fittingly inexpressive expression, (look into, look at the curves of, the blossomlike cavity of the opened mouth) is beautiful, but not altogether virile. The eyes, the facial lines which they gather into one, seem ready to follow the coming motion of the *discus* as those of an onlooker might be; but that head does not really belong to the *Discobolus*. To be assured of this you have but to compare with that version in the British Museum the most authentic of all derivations from the original, preserved till lately at the Palazzo Massimi in Rome. Here, the vigorous head also, with the face, smooth enough, but spare, and tightly drawn over muscle and bone, is sympathetic with, yields itself to, the concentration, in the most literal sense, of all beside; – is itself, in very truth, the steady centre of the *discus*, which begins to spin; as the source of will, the source of the motion with which the *discus* is already on the wing, – that, and the entire form. The *Discobolus* of the Massimi Palace presents, moreover, in the hair, for instance, those survivals of primitive manner which would mark legitimately Myron's actual pre-Pheidiac stand-point; as they are congruous also with a certain archaic, a more than merely athletic, spareness of form generally – delightful touches of unreality in this realist of a great time, and of a sort of conventionalism that has an attraction in itself.

Was it a portrait? That one can so much as ask the question is a proof how far the master, in spite of his lingering archaism, is come already from the antique marbles of Aegina. Was it the portrait of one much-admired youth, or rather the type, the rectified essence, of many such, at the most pregnant, the essential, moment, of the exercise of their natural powers, of what they really were? Have we here, in short, the sculptor Myron's reasoned memory of many a quoit-player, of a long flight of quoit-players; as, were he here, he might have given us the cricketer, the passing generation of cricketers, *sub specie eternitatis*, under the eternal form of art?

Was it in that case a commemorative or votive statue, such as Pausanias found scattered throughout Greece? Was it, again, designed to be part only of some larger decorative scheme, as some have supposed of the Venus of Melos, or a work of *genre* as we say, a thing intended merely to interest, to gratify the taste, with no further purpose? In either case it may have represented some legendary quoit-player – Perseus at play with Acrisius fatally, as one has suggested; or Apollo with Hyacinthus, as Ovid describes him in a work of poetic *genre*.

And if the *Discobolus* is, after all, a work of *genre* – a work merely imitative of the detail of actual life – for the adornment of a room in a private house, it would be only one of many such produced in Myron's day. It would be, in fact, one of the *pristae* directly attributed to him by Pliny, little congruous as they may seem with the grandiose motions of his more characteristic work. The *pristae*, the sawyers, – a celebrated creation of the kind, – is supposed to have given its name to the whole class of like things. No age, indeed, since the rudiments of art were mastered, can have been without such reproductions of the pedestrian incidents of every day, for the mere pleasant exercise at once of the curiosity of the spectator and the imitative instinct of the producer. The *Terra-Cotta* Rooms of the Louvre and the British Museum are a proof of it. One such work indeed there is, delightful in itself, techni-cally exquisite, most interesting by its history, which properly finds its place beside the larger, the full-grown, physical perfection of the *Discobolus*, one of whose alert younger brethren he may be, – the *Spinario* namely, the boy drawing a thorn from his foot, preserved in the so rare, veritable antique bronze at Rome, in the Museum of the Capitol, and well known in a host of ancient and modern reproductions.

There, or elsewhere in Rome, tolerated in the general destruction of ancient sculpture – like the 'Wolf of the Capitol,' allowed by way of heraldic sign, as in modern Siena, or like the equestrian figure of Marcus Aurelius doing duty as Charlemagne, – like those, but like very few other works of the kind, the *Spinario* remained, well-known and in honour, throughout the Middle Age. Stories like that of Ladas the famous runner, who died as he reached the goal in a glorious foot-race of boys, the subject of a famous work by Myron himself, (the 'last breath', as you saw, was on the boy's lips) were told of the half-grown bronze lad at the Capitol. Of necessity, but fatally, he must pause for a few moments in his course; or the course is at length over, or the breathless journey with some all-important tidings; and now, not till now, he thinks of resting to draw from the sole of his foot the cruel thorn, driven into it as he ran. In any case, there he still sits for a mo-ment, for ever, amid the smiling admiration of centuries, in the agility, in the perfect *naïveté* also as thus occupied, of his sixteenth year, to which the somewhat lengthy or attenuated structure of the limbs is conformable. And then, in this attenuation, in the almost Egyptian proportions, in the shallowness of the chest and shoulders especially, in the Phoenician or old Greek sharpness and length of profile, and the long, conventional, wire-drawn hair of the boy, arching formally over the forehead and round the neck, there is something of archaism, of that archaism which survives, truly, in Myron's own work, blending with the grace and power of well-nigh the maturity of Greek art. The blending of interests, of artistic alliances, is certainly delightful.

68   'The New Chivalry'

Charles Kains-Jackson. From *The Artist*, 2 April 1894. Signed 'By P.C.'

'Cet état sera toujours pauvre si sa peuple excède les moyens de vivre, et il sera toujours florissant si, contenue dans les justes bornes, il peut traffiquer de son superflu.' These are the words of the Marquis de Sade written in 1791. They anticipate all the conclusions of Malthus and have in the century which has elapsed since their publication entirely changed the destinies of France. They explain at once the defeat of the French by Germany in 1870 and that wonderful recovery which four and twenty years afterwards place the vanquished in a financial, social, and economic position far superior to that of the victors. The other view of the case is the more familiar to Englishmen. The Psalmist thought that the man with many children was blessed in that he would not fear to speak with his enemy in the gate and the enlightened, if somewhat trite and irritating commonsense of the Eighteenth Century, warned us in one of the most familiar of quotations of what happens to that country 'where wealth accumulates and men decay.'

For the last five hundred years the existence of England as a separate nation has been bound up with an acceptance of the Hebraic code of morality, not because that code had any universal application, but because climatic and other reasons had combined to place the England of the middle ages in the same position as that occupied by the people of ancient Judea. The protection of the Hebraic race consisted in the desert and the mountain, that of England has always consisted in the sea, but whether the march be on the mountain or on 'the mountain-wave' some militant force to hold the frontier was ever needed, behind the mountain and beyond the sea. The Jews were neighbours, but for the deserts and mountains, of two much more numerous peoples, the Egyptians and Persians, the English, but for the sea were equally – still are – neighbours of the French and Germans. Now the present population of the United Kingdom is equal to that of France and is not dangerously inferior to that of Germany. But this has not been so before. In the times of the Plantagenets England had but one fighting man against France's five, and the Hundred years war was practically the one Englishman backed by a couple of decadent Frenchmen; Burgundian and Breton or Burgundian and Gascon or Breton and Gascon against the other three Frenchmen. It was only by dividing that we conquered and we were always terribly in danger from the enormous preponderance of fighting force possessed by a United France. Between 1356 the date of Crecy, and 1793 the date of the last war with France, conditions did not vary very greatly, in the latter year the French still outnumbered us by more than two to one. This was the abiding and prime danger of these 437 years and there were interludes of the Germanic danger, as from 1558 to 1660, when Spain from time to time obtained command of the military force of Central Europe and the Teutonic peoples. The danger from the Armada was the danger of being outnumbered, Philip II drawing upon a fighting population more than five times that of Great Britain and Teutonico-Spanish coalitions against us being always possible until internecine religious wars splintered Central Europe into fragments which even 1866 and 1870 failed wholly to reunite.

Thus England has only now emerged into conditions favourable to a real civilization and a high moral code. For 437 years at least there has been a necessity for increasing the population, a necessity on which the national existence depended. Necessity makes its own laws, and makes its own morals. It dictates what form religion shall assume and decides what classes of a religious code shall be enforced or left in-operative by the civil law. We accordingly find that any contract in restraint of marriage during this period of defective population as compared with our neighbours has been held invalid at law as 'contrary to public policy.' *Salus populi suprema lex.* We find that second marriages have always been allowed, that a celibate priesthood has been legally discouraged, that marriages however much of affection, are null at law unless 'consummated' in other words that not love or fidelity, but a physical act is 'of the essence of the contract.' Yet the sense of humour always inherent in the English people has kept them from such curious exhibitions of nasty mindedness and truculence as marked the Jewish laws of family marriages and as express themselves in the Levitical books, in such passages as 'Habeo duas filias – vobit placuerit.' (Gen. xix., 8), and 'Ingredere – cum Dominus' (Gen. xxxviii., 8–10); Semitic influences however, continue to secure that the work containing these cold-blooded incitements to phallic filthiness is actually allowed to be published at the leading seats of learning, as well as in the metropolis. Even health and science when their teachings clashed with this desire for population have had to go to the wall, and despite the increase of insanity resulting, the marriage of first cousins is permitted – so jealous has the State been of any restraint, even that of hygiene, on marriage.

That the next century, at all events, will have to be lived for Englishmen under widely different circumstances than the last five have been is a point which hardly requires to be enforced. Time and circumstances have conspired to remove the dangers which affected the past. Even a hundred years ago either France or Germany would have conquered England twice over if valour were merely equal. We had frightful arrears of fighting strength to make up. Today even without our colonies we are too numerous for this to happen and it is probable that we should be assisted by England oversea. The problem therefore is shifted and from the dangers foreseen in the Middle Ages in England, from the dangers to which the Jews eventually succumbed, we have now to turn and confront the new series of perils involved in 'the people exceeding the means to live contentedly.'

Again, will necessity effect our laws, our morals, the enforcement or non-enforcement of different sections of a religious code. It will not be all gain; no change ever is. But we can at least make the best of it; as can the wise of all changes. Wherefore just as the flower of the early and imperfect civilization was in what we may call the Old Chivalry, or the exaltation of the youthful feminine ideal, so the flower of the adult and perfect civilization will be found in the New Chivalry or the exaltation of the youthful masculine ideal. The time has arrived when the eternal desire for Love which nature has implanted in the breast of man requires to be satisfied without such an increase in population as has characterized the past. The methods connected with the agreeable names of Bradlaugh, Besant and Drysdale need no notice here. We need not consider the degree of viciousness involved in what is known as 'French vice.' It will suffice for us that it is essentially bourgeois, that it is not only lacking in the aesthetic element but is directly anti-pathetic thereto. To the aesthete a smirched flower is worse than no flower at all, and the intrusion of chill precaution upon the heat of passion can only result in that lukewarm condition which aestheticism rejects as forcibly as ever orthodoxy did Laodicea.

The new ideal therefore will be one which unites true fancies and a lofty aspiration with a freedom from the two classes of evils already considered. The direction in which it is to be found is indicated by the natural tendencies which secure the survival of the fittest. The animal ideal is to secure immortality by influencing the body. The spiritual is that addition by which we are differentiated from the animal. And the law of evolution is addition, is change. Wherefore the human animal to which the spiritual has been added, will eventually find the line of proper and ultimate evolution is emphasizing that which has been added. The men of most influence on their fellows will be those who are the most spiritual, not those who are the most animal. At the same time the majority will always lag behind the more advanced type, a provision by which the perpetuation of the species is adequately secured. For five centuries in England the necessity that the race should increase and multiply has been paramount, but these five centuries of assistance have now secured their result, and we need at the present time no more than not to go back in numbers, at the same time that we greatly need to increase in the average of wealth. 'Il faut traffiquer de notre superflu.'

The New Chivalry then is also the new necessity. Happily it is already with us. The advanced – the more spiritual types of English manhood already look to beauty first. In the past the beauty has been conditioned and confined to such beauty as could be found in some fair being *capable of increasing the population*. The condition italicized is now for the intelligent, removed. The New Chivalry therefore will not ask that very plain question of the Marriage Service. 'Will it lead to the procreation of children?' It will rest content with beauty – God's outward clue to the inward Paradise. No animal consideration of mere sex will be allowed to intrude on the higher fact. A beautiful girl will be desired before a plain lad, but a plain girl will not be considered in the presence of a handsome boy. Where boy and girl are of equal outward grace the spiritual ideal will prevail over the animal and the desire of influencing the higher mind, the boy's, will prevail over the old desire to add to the population. The higher form of influence will be chosen.

The gain in human happiness will be direct and immediate. It has been obvious in the past that the praiseworthy attempts of women to be beautiful have in the next generation been half abolished by the want of such attempt in their husbands. Thus the human animal in England got 'no forwarder' in physical beauty. But the New Chivalry inducing boys to be beautiful as well as girls, will remedy this. The whole species will move on, and a type of higher beauty will be evolved.

The gain in human intelligence will be direct, for love will impart with the eagerness of joy all its most treasured intellectual acquisitions, all its experiences of life. It will not fear to bare its errors to loving eyes and will not grudge even shame if so be it may save the beloved from the like. As in Sparta so once more, will the lover be the inbreather – eispnêlos, the beloved 'the listener,' – aïtes. A royal road to learning will be found. The gain in human physique will be direct. For the carelessness of fathers, the sexual impossibilities of mother and sisters, the more than indifference of brothers, the watchful and devoted discipline of the lover will be substituted. The boy will find exactly the words, the cautions, he requires, the incentives which best stimulate in the converse of the lover still young and strong enough to preach by act, and finding as in Sir Frederick Leighton's admirable canvas no greater glory than in guiding younger and well loved hands to the mark.

That comparisons are not popular has been affirmed by many authorities and in cases where evolution is working out its silent inevitable course they are also unnecessary. There are, however, two matters wherein the New Chivalry inspires us with a new hope. It is evident that in the Old Chivalry there was always a certain absence of freewill, in other words its essential element, a refusal to take by force and for ought than love, was at best imperfect. A married woman blessed with children is cajoled by nature itself, as it were, into tolerating the husband for the sake of the children even where but for the Baconian 'hostages to fortune' no such tolerance would be possible. And the marriage contract adds for the same sake a proviso which is not of chivalry or even – except for the good of the community as expressed in increase of population – of common sense. 'Till death us do part' is the phrase. 'Till Love us do part' is the obvious logic of the situation. The New Chivalry imposes no irksome or fatuous ties. It is genuine or it is nothing. Where love upholds its banner the heathen may rage in vain; and it is

So strong

That should its own hands dig its grave
The wide world's power and pity shall not save.

The chief drawback is that under the New Chivalry all the plots of the French dramatists would disappear. Lovers while loving would not care for the 'world outside' and when they ceased to love there would be neither incongruity or scandal in their going apart.

A gain to the world of a new nature, but all the more important in an age when poverty of purse, not of population, is the danger, exists in the decrease of idleness involved by the New ideal. No woman wants to work. Every girl of the least personal attractiveness nourishes the hope of being kept in idleness. Above a certain class the proviso 'by a husband' is added. But the new lovers will both work and will be the happier for both working. The newer and intenser love will see its way to avoid the separation of hours, of interests and of resources which is the inevitable destiny of ninety-nine married couples out of every hundred. The desire of the male to express itself in action, will be fully satisfied in each case, age will make no difference. The ideal partnership indeed will more frequently than not be accomplished, the elder having the greater capital to balance the lesser physical energy, the younger having greater power of physical endurance, the younger too having greater powers of physical endurance under due direction. Had it but this single recommendation, the new ideal would still be adding enormously to the wealth and happiness of the country.

This is at best a brief and superficial note on a vast subject. The stimulating experiences of ancient Hellas, the wisdom of Saadi and Omar Khayyam have not been drawn upon for a single analogy or argument; there are, however, two facts, one suggested by nature and one by religion, which in their direct and immediate bearing on the issues already raised, cannot possibly be overlooked.

The one is that of the unique aid to be rendered through unity of sex. This is Nature's witness to the New Chivalry. Be a man ever so devotedly attached to his wife there will always remain 'a great gulf fixed.' Were this gulf unbridgeable by humanity it were easy to bear it, but far from this being so it is a beaten highway trod by every other woman. The slatternly charwoman may tread it or the painted Lais of the Haymarket, but the husband may not, the lover is shut out. Nature's most intimate and instructive bond of sympathy is denied to the old love; it is opened to the new.

Of companionship also there is much to be said. Here it is enough to ask how much do ordinary engaged couples, how much even do husband and wife, see of each other? How much may not lovers see if man and youth, if youth and boy? The joys of palaestra, of the river, of the hunt and of the moor, the evening tent-pitching of campers out, and the exhilaration of the early morning swim, for one pleasure of life and physical delight in each other's presence, touch and voice which man and woman ordinarily share, it is not too much to say that the new chivalry has ten. Intimacy of constant companionship, of physical and personal knowledge is also a power of help and aid which cannot be put into words.

And the other fact which we have in mind as essential to what has been said is that of the highest Ideal of all. 'For man is still God's dearest minion' says Sylvester. In the development of adolescent powers both of body and of soul the highest ideal is surely set. That the most beautiful is not always the most intellectual also is the fault of our negligence and misunderstanding in a past, when it was wholly by the intellectual that man made his way, and moral differences were not weighed against absolute cleverness. Canon Liddon once said to a friend 'Well, the Devil is exceedingly clever, and beautiful people are sometimes quite stupid, but cleverness and beauty only come together where The Third, Goodness, is there also.'

The mind of adolescent manhood being the development stage of potentially greater powers, must needs be capable under stimulus and guidance, of sweeter and fuller flower than that of girlhood, sweet as is that flower, and while no woman wishes to be loved for her intellect, youth is proud to be helped to learn. Nor is handsome youth less disposed towards knowledge than youth which is not handsome.

The possibility of having to fight life's intellectual and physical battles side by side and shoulder to shoulder is full of a new inspiration, an inspiration which the old ideal could not take to itself, which the Old Chivalry never knew. When Love enters, then Possibility will become Desire, and Like will be drawn to Like by each attempting to attain, for the sake of greater worthiness, to that which in the other is the Best.

That the tenderness of elder for younger, of one who has endured for him that has yet to endure, of the strong for the weak, the developed for the developing, is retained in all fulness, while these other things are added, is perhaps that note which gives its highest value to the New Chivalry.

69   'Narcissus'

Eric, Count Stenbock. From *Studies of Death*, 1894.

My father died before I was born, and my mother in giving birth to me, so I was born at once to a title and a fortune. I merely mention this to show that Fortune, in a way, seemed from the first to smile upon me. The one passion of my life was beauty, and I thought myself specially *fortunate* that I realized my own ideal in myself. Even now that I am writing I look round the room, and see portraits of myself at various stages of my life: as a child, a boy, and a young man. Never have I seen a face as lovely as my own was. That glorious classic outline, those large, lustrous, dark blue eyes, that curled gold hair, like woven sunshine, that divinely curved mouth and exquisite grace of lips, that splendid poise of neck and throat! I was not vain in the proper sense of the word, for vanity means desire for the approbation of others, and getting up oneself to please others. But I, on the contrary, did not care what others thought; I would remain for hours before the mirror in a kind of ecstasy. No! no single picture I had ever seen could come up to me!

I was spoilt as a child. At school my life was made easy for me. Others did my impositions, and masters overlooked my peccadilloes; and if the boys of my own form hated and envied me, they knew that if they dared lift a finger against me, they would have their lives thrashed out of them by my champions in the upper forms. I do not mean to say by this that my school career was not a success in the ordinary sense of the word; because, besides being beautiful, I was brilliantly clever, and learnt in a day what it would take others months to learn. And if I say I was spoilt, I at least was not pettish and fretful as spoilt children usually are; on the contrary, I was invariably amiable, perhaps because my will was never gainsaid. Unlike most in whom the aesthetic sense is abnormally developed, I had absolutely no passions. I did not love anyone – but then, I allowed myself very gracefully to be loved, and always sought to please those who loved me, so that I actually got the reputation of being unselfish.

This was all very well as a boy. When I became of age I was launched into society. Women, one and all, appeared to fall in love with me. I don't mean fortune-seekers and tuft-hunters, but such as had the same wealth and social position as myself. I was congratulated on my conquests, and told that my admirers were celebrated beauties. Beauties, indeed! What was their beauty to mine? I did not understand women or their sentiments at all; but I had read several novels, and tried to be amiable to one and all, and make love to them in the conventional way, as I had read. One time there appeared on the scene a girl who was considered dazzlingly beautiful. She really was rather handsome. She was the daughter of a Mexican millionaire, and, of course, was sought after by everyone. Indeed, I was reminded at the time of the Bab Ballad, 'Dukes with the humble maiden dealt,' and, unlike Duke Baily and Duke Humphey, they were willing to cast their coronets and their lands at her feet. But she, unlike the heroine of the Bab Ballad, preferred my 'miserable and grovelling' self. I must say here that my *vanity* was this time rather flattered; it rather pleased me to think that they should be put in the background for my sake, and I was as amiable to her as possible, and used to take her out everywhere. She was certainly clever, but there was a certain savage passionateness about her nature that jarred upon me.

One day her father said to me, 'You can't think how glad I am to hear that you are engaged to my daughter. As we happen to be alone together, perhaps you wouldn't mind if we settle all the particulars of this business. I intend to behave very handsomely to her, and will give her a dowry of – .' (Good heavens! This parvenu!)

'Engaged to your daughter!' I cried, 'there has been no such understanding between us. I am extremely sorry, but I cannot imagine who could have been your informant. The information is wholly and entirely false.'

'What?' he said, 'not engaged to Enriqueta? What on earth do you mean? Do you suppose I should have allowed you to go about with my girl as you have been doing? Again, I ask, what do you mean?'

'I am sorry,' I replied, 'that you should have been labouring under such a misapprehension. In proof that I mean what I say, I will avoid all intercourse with your daughter for the future. And I can scarcely believe she is under the same misapprehension as yourself.' With that remark I left the house abruptly.

A short time afterwards, when I was seated by the fire in my drawing-room reading, who should walk in suddenly but Enriqueta herself, with furiously flashing eyes. She looked like a fiend incarnate. The emblem of anger in the abstract. I remember at that moment the words of the proverb flashing across me, 'Non est ira sicut ira mulieris.'

'So,' she said, 'this is how you behave! Well, then, take that!' and saying this, she threw a fluid from a glass phial into my face. It was not vitriol; that would have blinded me: this, unfortunately, did not!

A sudden smart on one side of the face, then gradually the whole face corroded. The cheeks fell in, the flesh part of the nose dropped off, the hair came out in handfuls, several of the teeth dropped out, the mouth contorted into a ghastly grin, the eyes became cavernous and horrible, denuded of eyebrows and lashes. I saw myself in a mirror *once*; anything more loathsome it would be impossible to imagine.

Some friends called to sympathize with me, but on no consideration would I admit anyone. I had every mirror in the house broken and thrown away, and could scarcely bear to look into a washing-basin. I spoke to my servants from behind a screen, and lived utterly alone, and by night. I had only one opportunity of air and exercise, so I managed to bribe the policeman to let me into Hyde Park just before the gates closed at night, and there I would wander about all night through, till at dawn the gates opened again, when I would hurry home.

One night, when I was going on my usual lonely walk, the wailing voice of a child came out of the darkness.

'Do please help me,' it cried, 'mother left me here, and said she would come back directly, and now I have heard the clock strike the hour four times, and mother hasn't come back, and I am blind, quite blind.'

I lit my lantern; it was a child of about nine or ten years old. It was clad in rags – yet the voice had the accent of a gentleman.

I said, 'It's impossible to get out now; you must wait till the gates open in the morning. Come and sit here? Are you hungry?'

'Yes,' said the child simply.

'Well, then, let's have something to eat.' Then I undid my knapsack, wherein I always took with me provisions of various dainties, and wine, for my nocturnal meal, and spreading a napkin, prepared a repast.

Then the child told me his story. I cannot repeat it in the artless way he told it; I can only give the gist of it. He was very delicate-looking, with a very sweet face, and an infinite pathos in the expression of the closed eyes. It appeared he lived alone with his mother. His name, he

said, was Tobit: that he had been born blind, and did not know what
seeing anything meant. He did not think he had any surname; his
mother was always called 'Bonny Bess,' because people said she was so
handsome.

'What does handsome mean?' he asked. I shuddered.

'Oh!' I said, 'it means good-looking; but it's no use being handsome. It's better to be good.'

He said his mother was very unkind to him, and was always
beating him; but there was a gentleman, who used to come about every
three months, who was very kind to him, and used to bring him presents, and give his mother money. The gentleman was an officer, he said.
He always knew when the gentleman was coming, because his mother
did not beat him for three weeks beforehand, because one time the
gentleman had seen some bruises on him, and had been very angry, and
had beaten his mother. And when the gentleman had gone, his mother
had said: 'If you dare to tell the gentleman anything about me again,
I'll thrash you within an inch of your life.'

The gentleman used to talk to him, and take him out for walks.
But all toys the gentleman brought him his mother would take away
from him, and sell them in order to get drink. Twice he had taken him
to a place called 'the country' for a whole week. There were flowers
and birds singing; then he was really happy.

'The only thing she didn't take away from me,' he said, 'is this,'
and from his pocket he produced a penny whistle, 'because she said she
could not get anything for it, and I might go and play it in the street.
Then, perhaps, people would give me pennies.' Then he proceeded to
perform on the penny whistle. Good heavens! I had no idea that out of
a thing like that so much tone could be elicited! He began with a well-
known organ-grinder tune, then came variations filled with roulades.
I was simply astounded.

'A great many people give me pennies,' he said, naïvely, 'but
mother takes them all away from me.'

One day he had overheard the gentleman quarrelling with his
mother. 'Then why don't you make me an honest woman?' she had
said.

'It would be quite impossible to make *you* an honest woman. Shut
up your cant. You know perfectly well I can't marry you. Even if I
could, I wouldn't. I only wish to God I could take poor little Tobit
away with me.'

'Rob a mother of her only child,' said the mother, whimpering,
'fortunately the law of England does not allow that.'

'Blast your infernal humbug!' said the gentleman, 'I know you
don't care a hang about the child. You only want the money. I feel

quite certain that you ill-treat him, though he has never said a word to me about it. Bah! you talk of being an *honest* woman. Look how the child is dressed – look how you are!'

As soon as the gentleman had gone his mother seized upon him, and beat him so severely that he screamed for help. A man came in, and seized her arms and pinned her to the ground.

'Look here,' the man had said, 'that's enough of that, you she-devil! If you try that sort of game again you'll get the worst of it!'

The last time he saw the gentleman he had been more tender than ever before. He had felt hot tears falling on his face.

'Poor little Tobit!' he had said. 'I am going away to a far country, and perhaps may never see you again.'

Then he had heard the gentleman talking to his mother. 'Look here, Bess,' he said, 'this is all the money I can scrape together, and this must last you out while I am away. But I hope to be back soon, and then I shall have higher pay.'

He had cried for many days afterwards, which made his mother very angry. One day, after waiting some time, he had asked when the gentleman would be coming back again from the far country. 'He won't be coming back again at all,' answered his mother snappishly. 'He's dead – got shot in Africa, blast him! Get out and play the whistle.'

He had gone out in the streets, and cried very much at first, and then it seems he put his grief into music: 'Because,' he said, 'he had got more pennies than he had ever got before.' A little while after he had heard his mother whispering to a man. 'Damn it!' said the man, 'we can't take that bloody brat with us.'

'Oh, I'll manage that,' the mother had said. And that evening his mother had taken him out into the park, and had told him she wanted to speak with somebody, and was coming back directly, and told him to stay there. He had heard a man's voice, but his mother had never come back again.

Fortunately, as soon as the child had finished his story he went fast asleep. I do not know what I should have said. Its utter loathsomeness reminded me of the one sight I had had of my own face. At dawn I woke the child up. Putting down my thick black veil I turned home, taking the child with me. I sent a servant to make inquiries, and the result was as I had expected – the mother had decamped with all her possessions, and not paid the rent.

So at last one consolation was sent me. After having been so long alone, at last I had a companion – one who would not recoil from the sight of me. I determined to give up my nocturnal life, and managed to secure a cottage in a remote and desolate part of the country, where one could walk for miles without seeing anyone, and in mercy to my servants, stationed them in the nearest town, requiring them only to bring me provisions and do the house once a day.

The child was delighted with the country. His placid, absolute happiness, in all his blindness, was much more than I had ever experienced in the delight in beauty by the sense of sight. He was very intelligent and phenomenally good, and I managed to teach him music, in which he took the keenest pleasure. The piano, of course, was a thing unknown to him before. His only instrument had been a penny whistle!

One day I read in the paper that an operation had been successfully performed by a certain eminent oculist on a person born blind. An awful struggle rose in my mind; supposing the child could be made to see! I thought of the frightful blank all things which to me had seemed of the greatest value must be to him, and was I to deprive him of that? Then, if he could see, and saw me, he would recoil from me in horror. But then I knew that my health was failing – that I should not live long, and was I, just to gratify my own selfishness for a short time, to condemn him to perpetual darkness, when it lay within my reach to save him? It was, as I said before, a frightful struggle. At last I decided I would consult the oculist. I took the child to London.

The oculist came, and said in his case the operation would be quite simple – not nearly so difficult as the case mentioned in the papers. It would merely require – well, I don't know what. I know nothing of medical terms, so I consented to have the operation performed. The child was given chloroform, and, the operation completed, his eyes were bound with bandages, which I was told to take off on the third day.

On the third day I did so. I had always thought that the blind, even though born blind, made visual images of things. In his case it was not so. The operation had been successful, and he could see. He knew well enough, by the touch, what a chair or a table was, but I had the greatest difficulty in explaining this or that was a chair or table as he saw it. He seemed quite dazed. Then he said ultimately:

'And you are the most beautiful person in all the world!'

70   Homogenic Love

Edward Carpenter. 1894.

Of all the many forms that Love delights to take, perhaps none is more interesting (for the very reason that it has been so inadequately considered) than that special attachment which is sometimes denoted by the word Comradeship. In general we may say that the passion of love provides us with at once the deepest problems and the highest manifestations of life, and that to its different workings can be traced the farthest-reaching threads of human endeavor. In one guise, as the mere semi-conscious Sex-love, which runs through creation and is common to man and the lowest animals and plants, it affords a kind of organic basis for the unity of all creatures; in another, as for instance the love of the Mother for her offspring (also to be termed a passion) it seems to pledge itself to the care and guardianship of the growing race; then again in the Marriage of man and woman it becomes a thing of mystic and eternal import, and one of the corner-stones of human society; while in the form of the Comrade-love with which this paper is concerned, it has uses and functions which we trust will clearly appear as we proceed.

To some perhaps it may appear a little strained to place this last-mentioned form of attachment on a level of importance with the others, and such persons may be inclined to deny to the homogenic or homo-sexual love[1] (as it has been called) that intense, that penetrating, and at times overmastering character which would entitle it to rank as a great human passion. But in truth this view, when entertained, arises from a want of acquaintance with the actual facts; and it may not be amiss here, in the briefest possible way, to indicate what the world's History, Literature and Art has to say to us on the whole subject, before we go on to any further considerations of our own. Certainly, if the confronting of danger and the endurance of pain and distress for the sake of the loved one, if sacrifice, unswerving devotion and life-long union, constitute proofs of the reality and intensity (and let us say *healthiness*) of an affection, then these proofs have been given in numberless cases of such attachment, not only as existing between men, but as between women, since the world began. The records of chivalric love, the feats of enamored knights for their ladies' sakes, the stories of Hero and Leander, etc., are easily paralleled, if not surpassed, by the stories of the Greek comrades-in-arms and tyrannicides – of Cratinus and Aristo-demus, who offered themselves together as a voluntary sacrifice for the purification of Athens; of Chariton and Melanippus,[2] who attempted to assassinate Phalaris, the tyrant of Agrigentum; of Diocles who fell fighting in defence of his loved one; or of Cleomachus who in like manner, in a battle between the Chalkidians and Eretrians, being entreated to charge the latter, 'asked the youth he loved, who was standing

---

[1] 'Homosexual,' generally used in scientific works, is of course a bastard word. 'Homogenic' has been suggested, as being from two roots, both Greek, *i.e.*, *homos* 'same,' and *genos* 'sex.' [Carpenter's notes here and throughout.]

[2] *Athenaeus*, xiii., c. 78.

SH–Y

by, whether he would be a spectator of the fight; and when he said he would, and affectionately kissed Cleomachus and put his helmet on his head, Cleomachus with a proud joy placed himself in the front of the bravest of the Thessalians and charged the enemy's cavalry with such impetuosity that he threw them into disorder and routed them; and the Eretrian cavalry fleeing in consequence, the Chalkidians won a splendid victory.'[3]

The annals of all nations contain similar records – though probably among none has the ideal of this love been quite so enthusiastic and heroic as among the post-Homeric Greeks. It is well known that among the Polynesian Islanders – for the most part a very gentle and affectionate people, probably inheriting the traditions of a higher culture than they now possess – the most romantic male friendships are (or were) in vogue. Says Herman Melville in *Omoo* (ch. 39), 'The really curious way in which all Polynesians are in the habit of making bosom friends is deserving of remark. ... In the annals of the island (Tahiti) are examples of extravagant friendships, unsurpassed by the story of Damon and Pythias – in truth much more wonderful; for notwithstanding the devotion – even of life in some cases – to which they led, they were frequently entertained at first sight for some stranger from another island.' So thoroughly recognized indeed were these unions that Melville explains (in *Typee*, ch. 18) that if two men of hostile tribes or islands became thus pledged to each other, then each could pass through the enemy's territory without fear of molestation or injury; and the passionate nature of these attachments is indicated by the following passage from *Omoo*: – 'Though little inclined to jealousy in [ordinary] love-matters, the Tahitian will hear of no rivals in his *friendship*.'

Even among savage races lower down than these in the scale of evolution, and who are generally accused of being governed in their love-relations only by the most animal desires, we find a genuine sentiment of comradeship beginning to assert itself – as among the Balonda[4] and other African tribes, where regular ceremonies of the betrothal of comrades take place, by the transfusion of a few drops of blood into each other's drinking bowls, by the exchange of names,[5] and the mutual gift of their most precious possessions; but unfortunately, owing to the obtuseness of current European opinion on this subject, these and other such customs have been but little investigated and have by no means received the attention that they ought.

When we turn to the poetic and literary utterances of the more

[3] See Plutarch *Eroticus*, § xvii.
[4] See *Natural History of Man* by J. G. Wood. Vol: 'Africa,' p. 419.
[5] See also Livingstone's *Expedition to the Zambesi*, Murray, 1865, p. 148.

civilized nations on this subject we cannot but be struck by the range and intensity of the emotions expressed – from the beautiful threnody of David over his friend whose love was passing the love of women, through the vast panorama of the Homeric Iliad, of which the heroic friendship of Achilles and his dear Patroclus forms really the basic theme, down to the works of the great Greek age – the splendid odes of Pindar burning with clear fire of passion, the lofty elegies of Theognis, full of wise precepts to his beloved Kurnus, the sweet pastorals of Theocritus, the passionate lyrics of Sappho, or the more sensual raptures of Anacreon. Some of the dramas of Aeschylus and Sophocles – as the *Myrmidones* of the former and the *Lovers of Achilles* of the latter – appear to have had this subject for their motive;[6] and many of the prose-poem dialogues of Plato were certainly inspired by it.

Then coming to the literature of the Roman age, whose materialistic spirit could only with difficulty seize the finer inspiration of the homogenic love, and which in such writers as Catullus and Martial could only for the most part give expression to its grosser side, we still find in Virgil a noble and notable instance. His second Eclogue bears the marks of a genuine passion; and, according to some,[7] he there under the name of Alexis immortalizes his own love for the youthful Alexander. Nor is it possible to pass over in this connection the great mass of Persian literature, and the poets Sadi, Hafiz, Jami, and many others, whose names and works are for all time, and whose marvellous love-songs ('Bitter and sweet is the parting kiss on the lips of a friend') are to a large extent if not mostly addressed to those of their own sex.[8]

Of the medieval period in Europe we have of course but few literary monuments. Towards its close we come upon the interesting story of Amis and Amile (thirteenth century), unearthed by Mr. W. Pater from the *Bibliotheca Elzeviriana*.[9] Though there is historic evidence of the prevalence of the passion we may say of this period that its *ideal* was undoubtedly rather the chivalric love than the love of comrades. But with the Renaissance in Italy and the Elizabethan period in England the latter once more comes to evidence in a burst of poetic utterance,[10] which culminates perhaps in the magnificent sonnets of Michel Angelo and of Shakespeare; of Michel Angelo whose pure beauty of expression lifts the enthusiasm into the highest region as the

---

[6] Though these two plays, except for some quotations, are lost.
[7] Mantegazza and Lombroso. See Albert Moll, *Conträre Sexual-empfinding*, second ed., p. 36.
[8] Though in translations this fact is often by pious fraudulence disguised.
[9] W. Pater's *Renaissance*, pp. 8–16.
[10] Among *prose* writers of this period Montaigne, whose treatment of the subject is enthusiastic and unequivocal, should not be overlooked. See Hazlitt's *Montaigne*, ch. xxvii.

direct perception of the divine in mortal form;[11] and of Shakespeare – whose passionate words and amorous spirituality of friendship have for long enough been a perplexity to hide-bound commentators. Thence through minor writers (not overlooking Winckelmann[12] in Germany) we pass to quite modern times – in which, notwithstanding the fact that the passion has been much misunderstood and misinterpreted, two names stand conspicuously forth – those of Tennyson, whose 'In Memoriam' is perhaps his finest work, and of Walt Whitman, the enthusiasm of whose poems on Comradeship is only paralleled by the devotedness of his labours for his wounded brothers in the American Civil War.

It will be noticed that here we have some of the very greatest names in all literature concerned; and that their utterances on this subject equal if they do not surpass, in beauty, intensity, and humanity of sentiment, whatever has been written in praise of the other more ordinarily recognized love.

And when again we turn to the records of Art, and compare the way in which man's sense of Love and Beauty has expressed itself in the portrayal of the male form and the female form respectively, we find exactly the same thing. The whole vista of Greek statuary shows the male passion of beauty in high degree. Yet though the statues of men and youths (by male sculptors[13]) preponderate probably considerably, both in actual number and in devotedness of execution, over the statues of female figures, it is, as J. A. Symonds says in his *Life of*

[11] I may be excused for quoting here the sonnet No. 54, from J. A. Symonds' translation of the sonnets of Michel Angelo:

From thy fair face I learn, O my loved lord,
    That which no mortal tongue can rightly say;
    The soul, imprisoned in her house of clay,
    Holpen by Thee to God hath often soared:
And though the vulgar, vain, malignant horde
    Attribute what their grosser wills obey,
    Yet shall this fervent homage that I pay,
    This love, this faith, pure joys for us afford.
Lo, all the lovely things we find on earth,
    Resemble for the soul that rightly sees,
    That source of bliss divine which gave us birth;
Nor have we first-fruits or remembrances
    Of heaven elsewhere. Thus, loving loyally,
    I rise to God, and make death sweet by thee.

The labours of von Scheffler, followed by J. A. Symonds, have now pretty conclusively established the pious frauds of the nephew, and the fact that the love-poems of the elder Michel Angelo were, for the most part, written to male friends.

[12] See an interesting paper in W. Pater's *Renaissance*.

[13] I am not aware of any cases in the plastic arts, which strongly illustrate the homogenic sentiment as between women by the loving portrayal of female beauty by artists of the same sex – as by Sappho in literature – though no doubt there are such cases.

Michel Angelo, remarkable that in all the range of the former there are hardly two or three that show a base or licentious expression, such as is not so very uncommon in the female statues. Knowing as we do the strength of the male physical passion in the life of the Greeks, this one fact speaks strongly for the sense of proportion which must have characterized this passion – at any rate in the most productive age of their Art.

In the case of Michel Angelo we have an artist who with brush and chisel portrayed literally thousands of human forms; but with this peculiarity, that while scores and scores of his male figures are obviously suffused and inspired by a romantic sentiment there is hardly one of his female figures that is so, – the latter being mostly representative of woman in her part as mother, or sufferer, or prophetess or poetess, or in old age, or in any aspect of strength or tenderness, except that which associates itself especially with passionate love. Yet the cleanliness and dignity of Michel Angelo's male figures are incontestable, and bear striking witness to that nobility of the sentiment in him, which we have already seen illustrated in his sonnets.

This brief sketch may suffice to give the reader some idea of the place and position in the world of the particular sentiment which we are discussing; nor can it fail to impress him – if any reference is made to the authorities quoted – with a sense of the dignity and solidity of the sentiment, at any rate as handled by some of the world's greatest men. At the same time it will be sure to arouse further questions. It will be evident from the instances given – and there would be no object in ignoring this fact – that this kind of love, too, like others, has its physical side; and queries will naturally arise as to the exact place and purport of the physical in it.

This is a subject which we shall have occasion to consider more in detail in the second part of this paper; but here a few general remarks may be made. In the first place we may say that to all love and indeed to all human feeling there must necessarily be a physical side. The most delicate emotion which plays through the mind has, we cannot but perceive, its corresponding subtle change in the body, and the great passions are accompanied by wide-reaching disturbances and transformations of corporeal tissue and fluid. Who knows (it may be asked) how deeply the mother-love is intertwined with the growth of the lacteal vessels and the need of the suckled infant? or how intimately even the most abstract of desires – namely the religious – is rooted in the slow hidden metamorphosis by which a new creature is really and physically born within the old? Richard Wagner, in a pregnant little passage in his *Communication to my Friends*, says that the essence of human love 'is the longing for utmost physical reality, for fruition in an object which can be grasped by all the senses, held fast with all the force of actual being.' And if this is a somewhat partial statement it yet puts into clear language one undoubted relation between the sensuous and the emotional in all love, and the sweet *excuse* which this relation may be said to provide for the existence of the actual world – namely that the latter is the means whereby we become conscious of our most intimate selves.[14]

But if this is true of love in general it must be true of the Homogenic Love; and we must not be surprised to find that in all times this attachment has had some degree of physical expression. The question however as to *what* degree of physical intimacy may be termed in such a case fitting and natural – though a question which is sure to arise – is one not easy to answer: more especially as in the common mind any intimacy of a bodily nature between two persons of the same sex is so often (in the case of males) set down as a sexual act of the crudest and grossest kind. Indeed the difficulty here is that the majority of people, being incapable perhaps of understanding the *inner* feeling of the homogenic attachment,[15] find it hard to imagine that the intimacy has any other object than the particular form of sensuality mentioned (i.e. the *Venus aversa*, which appears, be it said, to be rare in all the northern countries), or that people can be held together by any tie except the most sheerly material one – a view which of course turns the whole subject upside down, and gives rise to violent and no doubt very natural disapprobation; and to endless recriminations and confusion.

Into this mistake we need not fall. Without denying that sexual intimacies do exist; and while freely admitting that, in great cities, there are to be found associated with this form of attachment prostitution and other evils comparable with the evils associated with the ordinary sex-attachment; we may yet say that it would be a great error to suppose that the homogenic love takes as a rule the extreme form vulgarly supposed; and that it would also be a great error to overlook the fact that in a large number of instances the relation is not distinctively sexual at all, though it may be said to be physical in the sense of embrace and endearment. While it is not my object in this paper to condemn special acts or familiarities between lovers (since these things must no doubt be largely left to individual judgement, aided by whatever light Science or Physiology may in the future be able to throw upon the subject) – still I am anxious that it should be clearly understood that the glow of a really human and natural love between two persons of the same sex may be, and often is, felt without implying (as

---

[14] See pamphlet, *Sex-Love*, p. 7.
[15] As indeed the majority of people have a difficulty in appreciating the inner feeling of most love.

is so often assumed) mere depravity of character or conduct. No one can read the superb sonnets, already mentioned, of Shakespeare and Michel Angelo without feeling, beneath the general mass of emotional utterance, the pulsation of a distinct bodily desire; and even Tennyson, somewhat tenuous and Broad-churchy as he is, is too great a master and too true a man not to acknowledge in his great comrade-poem 'In Memoriam' (see Cantos xiii., xviii., etc.) the passionateness of his attach-ment – for doing which indeed he was soundly rated by the *Times* at the time of its publication; yet it would be monstrous to suppose that these men, and others, because they were capable of this kind of feeling and willing to confess its sensuous side, were therefore particularly licentious.

With these few general remarks, and the conclusion, so far, that while the homogenic feeling undoubtedly demands *some* kind of physical expression, the question what degree of intimacy is in all cases fitting and natural may not be a very easy one to decide – we may pass on to consider what light is thrown on the whole subject by some recent scientific investigations.

That passionate attachment between two persons of the same sex is, as we have seen, a phenomenon widespread through the human race, and enduring in history, has been always more or less recognized; and once at least in history – in the Greek age – the passion rose into distinct consciousness, and justified, or even it might be said glorified, itself; but in later times – especially perhaps during the last century or two of European life – it has generally been treated by the accredited thinkers and writers as a thing to be passed over in silence, as associated with mere grossness and mental aberration, or as unworthy of serious attention.

In latest times however – that is, during the last thirty years or so – a group of scientific and capable men in Germany, France, and Italy – among whom are Dr. Albert Moll of Berlin; Krafft-Ebing, one of the leading medical authorities of Vienna, whose book on *Sexual Psycho-pathy* has passed into its eighth edition; Dr. Paul Moreau (*des Aber-rations du sens Génésique*); Cesare Lombroso, the author of various works on Anthropology; Tarnowski; Mantegazza; K. H. Ulrichs, and others – have made a special and more or less impartial study of this subject: with the result that a quite altered complexion has been given to it; it being indeed especially noticeable that the change of view among the scientists has gone on step by step with the accumulation of reliable information, and that it is most marked in the latest authors, such as Krafft-Ebing and Moll.

It is not possible here to go into anything like a detailed account of the works of these various authors, their theories, and the immense number of interesting cases and observations which they have contributed; but some of the general conclusions which flow from their researches may be pointed out. In the first place their labours have established the fact, known hitherto only to individuals, that *sexual inversion* – that is the leaning of sexual desire to one of the same sex – is in a vast number of cases quite instinctive and congenital, mentally and physically, and therefore twined in the very roots of individual life and practically ineradicable. To Men or Women thus affected with an innate homosexual bias, Ulrichs gave the name of Urning,[16] since pretty widely accepted by scientists. Too much emphasis cannot be laid on the distinction between these born lovers of their own sex, and that class of persons, with whom they are so often confused, who out of mere carnal curiosity or extravagance of desire, or from the dearth of opportunities for a more normal satisfaction (as in schools, barracks, etc.) adopt some homosexual practices. In the case of these latter the attraction towards their own sex is merely superficial and temptational, so to speak, and is generally felt by those concerned to be in some degree morbid. In the case of the former it is, as said, so deeply rooted and twined with the mental and emotional life that the person concerned has difficulty in imagining himself affected otherwise than he is; and to him at least the homogenic love appears healthy and natural, and indeed necessary to the concretion of his individuality.

In the second place it has become clear that the number of individuals affected with 'sexual inversion' in some degree or other is very great – much greater than is generally supposed to be the case. It is however very difficult or perhaps impossible to arrive at satisfactory figures on the subject, for the simple reasons that the proportions vary so greatly among different peoples and even in different sections of society and in different localities, and because of course there are all possible grades of sexual inversion to deal with, from that in which the instinct is *quite exclusively* directed towards the same sex,[17] to the other extreme in which it is normally towards the opposite sex but capable occasionally and under exceptional attractions, of inversion towards its own – this last condition being probably among some peoples very widespread, if not universal.

In the third place, by the tabulation and comparison of a great number of cases and 'confessions,' it has become pretty well established that the individuals affected with inversion in marked degree do not after all differ from the rest of mankind, or womankind, in any other

[16] From Uranos – because the celestial love was the daughter of Uranos (see Plato's *Symposium*, speech of Pausanias).

[17] With regard to the number of these *quite exclusive* homosexuals (supposably born so) estimates vary, from one man in every 50 to one in every 500. See Moll. *Conträre Sexual-empfinding*, second edn., p. 75.

physical or mental particular which can be distinctly indicated.[18] No congenital association with any particular physical conformation or malformation has yet been discovered; nor with any distinct disease of body or mind. Nor does it appear that persons of this class are usually of a gross or specially low type, but if anything rather the opposite – being often of refined sensitive nature and including, as Krafft-Ebing points out (*Psychopathia Sexualis*, seventh ed., p. 227) a great number 'highly gifted in the fine arts, especially music and poetry,' and, as Mantegazza says,[19] many persons of high literary and social distinction. It is true that Krafft-Ebing insists on the generally strong sexual equipment of this class of persons (among men), but he hastens to say that their emotional love is also 'enthusiastic and exalted,'[20] and that, while bodily congress is desired, the special act with which they are vulgarly credited is in most cases repugnant to them.[21]

The only distinct characteristic which the scientific writers claim to have established is a marked tendency to nervous development in the subject, not infrequently associated with nervous maladies; but – as I shall presently have occasion to show – there is reason to think that the validity even of this characteristic has been exaggerated.

Taking the general case of men with a marked exclusive preference for their own sex, Krafft-Ebing says (*P.S.*, p. 256) 'The sexual life of these Homosexuals is *mutatis mutandis* just the same as in the case of normal sex-love. . . . The Urning loves, deifies his male beloved one, exactly as the woman-wooing man does *his* beloved. For him, he is capable of the greatest sacrifice, experiences the torments of unhappy, often unrequited, love, of faithlessness on his beloved's part, of jealousy, and so forth. His attention is enchained only by the male form. . . . The sight of feminine charms is indifferent to him, if not repugnant.' Then he goes on to say that many such men, notwithstanding their actual aversion to intercourse with the female, do ultimately marry – whether from ethical, as sometimes happens, or from social considerations. But very remarkable – as illustrating the depth and tenacity of the homogenic instinct[22] – and pathetic too, are the records that he gives of these cases; for in many of them a real friendship and regard between the married pair was still of no avail to overcome the distaste on the part of one to sexual intercourse with the other, or to prevent the experience of actual physical distress after such intercourse, or to check the continual

[18] Though there is no doubt a general *tendency* towards femininity of type in the male Urning, and towards masculinity in the female.
[19] *Gli amori degli uomini.*
[20] *Psychopathia Sexualis*, seventh ed., p. 227.
[21] *Ibid*: pp. 229 and 258.
[22] 'How deep congenital sex-inversion roots may be gathered from the fact that the pleasure-dream of the male Urning has to do with male persons, and of the female with females.' (Krafft-Ebing *P.S.* seventh ed., p. 228.)

flow of affection to some third person of the same sex; and thus un-
willingly, so to speak, this bias remained a cause of suffering to the
end.

This very brief summary of scientific conclusions, taken in conjunction with the fact (which we have already referred to) that the whole
literature and life of the greatest people of antiquity – the Greeks of the
Periclean age – was saturated with the passion of homogenic or comrade-
love, must convince us that this passion cannot be lightly dismissed as
of no account – must convince us that it has an important part to play
in human affairs. On the one hand we have anathemas and execrations,
on the other we have the sublime enthusiasm of a man like Plato – one
of the leaders of the world's thought for all time – who puts, for example, into the mouth of Phaedrus (in the *Symposium*) such a passage
as this:[23] 'I know not any greater blessing to a young man beginning life
than a virtuous lover, or to the lover than a beloved youth. For the
principle which ought to be the guide of men who would nobly live –
that principle, I say, neither kindred, nor honour, nor wealth, nor any
other motive is able to implant so well as love. Of what am I speaking?
Of the sense of honour and dishonour, without which neither states
nor individuals ever do any good or great work. . . . For what lover
would not choose rather to be seen of all mankind than by his beloved,
either when abandoning his post or throwing away his arms? He would
be ready to die a thousand deaths rather than endure this. Or who
would desert his beloved or fail him in the hour of danger? The veriest
coward would become an inspired hero, equal to the bravest, at such a
time; love would inspire him. That courage which, as Homer says, the
god breathes into the soul of heroes, love of his own nature inspires
into the lover.' Or again in the *Phaedrus* Plato makes Socrates say:[24] –
'In like manner the followers of Apollo and of every other god, walking
in the ways of their god, seek a love who is to be like their god, and
when they have found him, they themselves imitate their god, and
persuade their love to do the same, and bring him into harmony with
the form and ways of the god as far as they can; for they have no feelings
of envy or jealousy towards their beloved, but they do their utmost to
create in him the greatest likeness of themselves and the god whom
they honour. Thus fair and blissful to the beloved when he is taken, is
the desire of the inspired lover, and the initiation of which I speak into
the mysteries of true love, if their purpose is effected.' And yet Plato
throughout his discourses never suggests for a moment that the love of
which he is speaking is any other than the homogenic passion, nor
glosses over or conceals its strong physical substructure.

[23] Jowett's *Plato* (second ed.) Vol. II., p. 30
[24] Jowett, op. cit., Vol. II., p. 130.

II

We have now I think said enough to show from the testimony of History, Literature, Art, and even of Modern Science, that the homogenic passion is capable of splendid developments; and that a love and capacity of love of so intimate, penetrating and inspiring a kind – and which has played so important a part in the life-histories of some of the greatest races and individuals – is well worthy of respectful and thoughtful consideration. And I think it has become obvious that to cast a slur upon this kind of love because it may in cases lead to aberrations and extravagances would be a most irrational thing to do – since exactly the same charges, of possible aberration and extravagance, might be brought, and the same conclusion enforced, against the ordinary sex-love.

It is however so often charged against the sentiment in question that it is essentially unnatural and *morbid* in character, that it may be worth while, though we have already touched on this point, to consider it here at greater length. I therefore propose to devote a few more pages to the examination of the scientific position on this subject, and then to pass on to a consideration of the general place and purpose of the homogenic or comrade-love (its sanity being granted) in human character and social life.

It might be thought that the testimonies of History, Literature and Art, above referred to, would be quite sufficient of themselves to dispose of the charge of essential morbidity. But as mankind in general is not in the habit of taking bird's eye views of History and Literature, and as it finds it easy to assume that anything a little exceptional is also morbid, so it is not difficult to see how this charge (in countries where the sentiment *is* exceptional) has arisen and maintained itself. Science, of course, is nothing but common observation organized and systemized, and so we naturally find that with regard to this subject it started on its investigations from the same general assumptions that possessed the public mind. It may safely be said that until the phenomena of homogenic Love began to be calmly discussed by the few scientific men already mentioned, the subject had never since classical times been once fairly faced in the arena of literature or public discussion, and had as a rule been simply dismissed with opprobrious epithets well suited to give an easy victory to prejudice and ignorance. But the history of even these few years of scientific investigation bears with it a memorable lesson. For while at the outset it was easily assumed that the homogenic instinct was thoroughly morbid in itself, and probably always associated with distinct disease, either physical or mental, the progress of the inquiry has – as already pointed out – served more and more to dissipate this view; and it is noticeable that Krafft-Ebing and

Moll – the latest of the purely scientific authorities – are the least disposed to insist upon the theory of morbidity. It is true that Krafft-Ebing clings to the opinion that there is generally some *neurosis*, or degeneration of a nerve-centre, or *inherited tendency in that direction*, associated with the instinct; see p. 190 (seventh ed.), also p. 227, where he speaks, rather vaguely, of 'an hereditary neuropathic or psychopathic tendency' – *neuro(psycho)pathische Belastung*. But it is an obvious criticism on this that there are few people in modern life, perhaps none, who could be pronounced absolutely free from such a *Belastung*! And whether the Dorian Greeks or the Polynesian Islanders or the Kelts (spoken of by Aristotle, *Pol.*, ii. 7) or the Normans or the Albanian mountaineers, or any of the other notably hardy races among whom the passion has been developed, were particularly troubled by nervous degeneration we may well doubt![25]

As to Moll, though he speaks[26] of the instinct as morbid (feeling perhaps in duty bound to do so), it is very noticeable that he abandons the ground of its association with other morbid symptoms – as this association, he says, is by no means always to be observed; and is fain to rest his judgement on the *dictum* that the mere failure of the sexual instinct to propagate the species is itself pathological – a *dictum* which in its turn obviously springs from that pre-judgement of scientists that generation is the sole object of love,[27] and which if pressed would involve the good doctor in awkward dilemmas, as for instance that every worker-bee is a pathological specimen.

With regard to the nerve-degeneration theory, while it may be allowed that sexual inversion is not uncommonly found in connection with the specially nervous temperament, it must be remembered that its occasional association with nervous troubles or disease is quite another matter; since such troubles ought perhaps to be looked upon as the *results* rather than the causes of the inversion. It is difficult of course for outsiders not personally experienced in the matter to realize the great strain and tension of nerves under which those persons grow up from boyhood to manhood – or from girl to womanhood – who find their deepest and strongest instincts under the ban of the society around them; who before they clearly understand the drift of their own natures discover that they are somehow cut off from the sympathy and understanding of those nearest to them; and who know that they can never give expression to their tenderest yearnings of affection without exposing

[25] It is interesting, too, to find that Walt Whitman, who certainly had the homogenic instinct highly developed, was characterized by his doctor, W. B. Drinkard, as having 'the most natural habits, bases, and organization he had ever met with or ever seen' in any man. *In re Walt Whitman*, p. 115.

[26] *Conträre Sexual-empfindung*, second ed., p. 269.

[27] See *Sex-Love*, p. 23.

themselves to the possible charge of actions stigmatized as odious crimes.[28] That such a strain, acting on one who is perhaps already of a nervous temperament, should tend to cause nervous prostration or even mental disturbance is of course obvious; and if such disturbances are really found to be commoner among homogenic lovers than among ordinary folk we have in these social causes probably a sufficient explanation of the fact.

Then again in this connection it must never be forgotten that the medico-scientific enquirer is bound on the whole to meet with those cases that *are* of a morbid character, rather than with those that are healthy in their manifestation, since indeed it is the former that he lays himself out for. And since the field of his research is usually a great modern city, there is little wonder if disease colours his conclusions. In the case of Dr. Moll, who carried out his researches largely under the guidance of the Berlin police (whose acquaintance with the subject would naturally be limited to its least satisfactory sides), the only marvel is that his verdict is so markedly favourable as it is. As Krafft-Ebing says in his own preface 'It is the sad privilege of Medicine, and especially of Psychiatry, to look always on the reverse side of life, on the weakness and wretchedness of man.'

Having regard then to the direction in which science has been steadily moving in this matter, it is not difficult to see that the epithet 'morbid' will probably before long be abandoned as descriptive of the homogenic bias – that is, of the general sentiment of love towards a person of the same sex. That there are excesses of the passion – cases, as in ordinary sex-love, where mere physical desire becomes a mania – we may freely admit; but as it would be unfair to judge of the purity of marriage by the evidence of the Divorce courts, so it would be monstrous to measure the truth and beauty of the attachment in question by those instances which stand most prominently perhaps in the eye of the modern public; and after all deductions there remains, we contend, the vast body of cases in which the manifestation of the instinct has on the whole the character of normality and healthfulness – sufficiently so in fact to constitute this *a distinct variety of the sexual passion*. The question, of course, not being whether the instinct is *capable* of morbid and extravagant manifestation – for this can easily be proved of any instinct – but whether it is capable of a healthy and sane expression And this, we think, it has abundantly shown itself to be.

[28] 'Though then before my own conscience I cannot reproach myself, and though I must certainly reject the judgment of the world about us, yet I suffer greatly. In very truth I have injured no one, and I hold my love in its nobler activity for just as holy as that of normally disposed men, but under the unhappy fate that allows us neither sufferance nor recognition I suffer often more than my life can bear.' – (Extract from a letter given by Krafft-Ebing.)

Anyhow the work that Science has practically done has been to destroy the dogmatic attitude of the former current opinion from which itself started, and to leave the whole subject freed from a great deal of misunderstanding, and much more open than before. Its labours – and they have been valuable in this way – have been chiefly of a negative character. While unable on the one hand to characterize the physical attraction in question as definitely morbid or the result of morbid tendencies, it is unable on the other hand to say positively at present what physiological or other purpose is attained by the instinct.

This question of the physiological basis of the homogenic love – to which we have more than once alluded – is a very important one; and it seems a strange oversight on the part of Science that it has hitherto taken so little notice of it. The desire for corporeal intimacy of some kind between persons of the same sex existing as it does in such force and so widely over the face of the earth, it would seem almost certain that there must be some physiological basis for the desire: but until we know more than we do at present as to what this basis may be, we are necessarily unable to understand the desire itself as well as we might wish. It may be hoped that this is a point to which attention will be given in the future. Meanwhile, though the problem is a complex one, it may not be amiss here to venture a suggestion or two.

In the first place it may be suggested that an important part of *all* love-union, mental or physical, is its influence personally on those concerned. This influence is, of course, subtle and hard to define; and one can hardly be surprised that Science, assuming hitherto in its consideration of ordinary sexual relations that the mutual actions and reactions were directed solely to the purpose of generation and the propagation of the species, has almost quite neglected the question of the direct influences on the lovers themselves. Yet everyone is sensible practically that there is much more in an intimacy with another person than the question of children alone; that even setting aside the effects of actual sex-intercourse there are subtle elements passing from one to another which are indispensable to personal well-being, and which make some such intimacy almost a necessary condition of health. It may be that there are some persons for whom these necessary reactions can only come from one of the same sex. In fact it is obvious there are such persons. 'Successful love,' says Moll (p. 125) 'exercises a helpful influence on the Urning. His mental and bodily condition improves, and capacity of work increases – just as it often happens in the case of a normal youth with *his* love.' And further on (p. 173) in a letter from a man of this kind occur these words: 'The passion is I suppose so powerful, just because one looks for everything in the loved man – Love, Friendship, Ideal, and Sense-satisfaction. . . . As it is at present

I suffer the agonies of a deep unresponded passion, which wake me like a nightmare from sleep. And I am conscious of physical pain in the region of the heart.' In such cases the love, in some degree physically expressed, of another person of the same sex, is clearly as much a necessity and a condition of healthy life and activity, as in more ordinary cases is the love of a person of the opposite sex.

It has probably been the arbitrary limitation of the function of love to child-breeding which has (unconsciously) influenced the popular mind against the form of love which we are considering. That this kind of union was not concerned with the propagation of the race was in itself enough to make people look askance at it; that any kind of love-union could exist in which the sex-act might possibly *not* be the main object was an incredible proposition. And, in enforcing this view, no doubt the Hebraic and Christian tradition has exercised a powerful influence – dating, as it almost certainly does, from far-back times when the multiplication of the tribe was one of the very first duties of its members, and one of the first necessities of corporate life; though nowadays when the need has swung round all the other way it is not unreasonable to suppose that a similar revolution will take place in people's views of the place and purpose of the non-child-bearing love. We find in some quarters that even the most naïve attachments between youths are stigmatized as 'unnatural' (though, inconsistently enough, not those between girls) – and this can only well be from an assumption that all familiarities are meant by Nature to lead up to generation and race-propagation. Yet no one – if fairly confronted with the question – would seriously maintain that the mutual stimulus, physical, mental and moral, which flows from embrace and endearment is nothing, and that because these things do not lead to actual race propagation therefore they must be discountenanced. If so, must even the loving association between man and wife, more than necessary for the breeding of children, or after the period of fertility has passed, be also discountenanced? Such questions might be multiplied indefinitely. They only serve to show how very crude as yet are all our theories on these subjects, and how necessary it is in the absence of more certain knowledge to suspend our judgement.[29]

Summarizing then some of our conclusions on this rather difficult question we may say that the homogenic love, as a distinct variety of the sex-passion, is in the main subject to the same laws as the ordinary love; that it probably demands and requires some amount of physical intimacy; that a wise humanity will quite recognize this; but that the

[29] 'The truth is that we can no more explain the inverted sex-feeling than we can the normal impulse; all the attempts at explanation of these things, and of Love, are defective.' (Moll, second ed. p. 253.)

degree of intimacy, in default of more certain physiological knowledge than we have, is a matter which can only be left to the good sense and feeling of those concerned; and that while we do not deny for a moment that excesses of physical appetite exist, these form no more reason for tabooing all expression of the sentiment than they do in the case of the more normal love. We may also say that if on the side of science much is obscure, there is no obscurity in the principles of healthy morality involved; that there is no exception here to the law that sensuality apart from love is degrading and something less than human; or to the law that love – true love – seeks nothing which is not consistent with the welfare of the loved one; and that here too the principle of Trans-mutation applies[30] – the principle that Desire in man has its physical, emotional and spiritual sides, and that when its outlet is checked along one channel, it will, within limits, tend to flow with more vehemence along the other channels – and that reasonable beings, perceiving this, will (again within limits) check the sensual and tend to throw the centre of their love-attraction upwards.

Probably in this, as in all love, it will be felt in the end by those who devote themselves to each other and to the truth, to be wisest to concentrate on the *real thing*, on the enduring deep affection which is the real satisfaction and outcome of the relation, and which like a young sapling they would tend with loving care till it grows into a mighty tree which the storms of a thousand years cannot shake; and those who do so heartily and truly can leave the physical to take care of itself. This indeed is perhaps the only satisfactory touchstone of the rightness and fitness of human relations generally, in sexual matters. People, not unnaturally, seek for an absolute rule in such matters, and a *fixed* line between the right and the wrong; but may we not say that there is no rule except that of Love – Love making use, of course, of whatever certain knowledge Science may from time to time be able to provide?

And speaking of the law of Transmutation and its importance, it is clear, I think, that in the homosexual love – whether between man and man or between woman and woman – the physical side, from the very nature of the case, can never find expression quite so freely and perfectly as in the ordinary heterosexual love; and therefore that there is a 'natural' tendency for the former love to run rather more along emotional channels.[31] And this no doubt throws light on the fact that love of the homogenic type has inspired such a vast amount of hero-ism and romance – and is indeed only paralleled in this respect (as J. Addington Symonds has pointed out in his paper on 'Dantesque and

[30] See *Sex-Love*, p. 8.
[31] See *Marriage*, p. 7.

Platonic ideals of Love)[32] by the loves of Chivalry, which of course owing to their special character, were subject to a similar transmutation.

It is well-known that Plato in many passages in his dialogues gives expression to the opinion that the love which at that time was common among the Greek youths had, in its best form, a special function in educational social and heroic work. I have already quoted a passage from the *Symposium*, in which Phaedrus speaks of the inspiration which this love provides towards an honourable and heroic life. Pausanias in the same dialogue says:[33] 'In Ionia and other places, and generally in countries which are subject to the barbarians, the custom is held to be dishonourable; loves of youths share the evil repute of philosophy and gymnastics *because they are inimical to tyranny*, for the interests of rulers require that their subjects should be poor in spirit, and that there should be no strong bond of friendship or society between them – which love above all other motives, is likely to inspire, as our Athenian tyrants learned by experience.' This is a pretty strong statement of the political significance of this kind of love.

Richard Wagner in his pamphlet *The Art-work of the Future*[34] has some interesting passages to the same effect – showing how the conception of the beauty of manhood became the formative influence of the Spartan State. He says: 'This beauteous naked man is the kernel of all Spartanhood; from genuine delight in the beauty of the most perfect human body – that of the male – arose that spirit of comradeship which pervades and shapes the whole economy of the Spartan State. This love of man to man, in its primitive purity, proclaims itself as the noblest and least selfish utterance of man's sense of beauty, for it teaches man to sink and merge his entire self in the object of his affection;' and again: 'The higher element of that love of man to man consisted even in this: that it excluded the motive of egoistic[35] physicalism. Nevertheless it not only included a purely spiritual bond of friendship, but this spiritual friendship was the blossom and the crown of the physical friendship. The latter sprang directly from delight in the beauty, aye in the material bodily beauty of the beloved comrade; yet this delight was no egoistic yearning, but a thorough stepping out of self into unreserved sympathy with the comrade's joy in himself; involuntarily betrayed by his life-glad beauty-prompted bearing. This love, which had its basis in the noblest pleasures of both eye and soul – not like our modern postal correspondence of sober friendship, half

[32] See *In the Key of Blue* by J. A. Symonds (Published by Elkin Matthews, 1893).
[33] Jowett's *Plato*, second ed. vol. ii. p. 33.
[34] Prose-works of Richard Wagner, translated by W. A. Ellis.
[35] The emphasis is on the word *egoistic*.

businesslike, half sentimental – was the Spartan's only tutoress of youth, the never-ageing instructress alike of boy and man, the ordainer of common feasts and valiant enterprises; nay the inspiring helpmeet on the battle-field. For this it was that knit the fellowship of love into battalions of war, and fore-wrote the tactics of death-daring, in rescue of the imperilled or vengeance for the slaughtered comrade, by the infrangible law of the soul's most natural necessity.'

The last sentence in this quotation is well illustrated by a passage from a 'privately printed' pamphlet entitled *A Problem in Greek Ethics*, in which the author endeavors to reconstruct as it were the genesis of comrade-love among the Dorians in early Greek times. Thus: 'Without sufficiency of women, without the sanctities of established domestic life, inspired by the memory of Achilles and venerating their ancestor Herakles,[36] the Dorian warriors had special opportunity for elevating comradeship to the rank of an enthusiasm. The incidents of emigration into a distant country – perils of the sea, passages of rivers and mountains, assaults of fortresses and cities, landings on a hostile shore, night vigils by the side of blazing beacons, foragings for food, picquet service in the front of watchful foes – involved adventures capable of shedding the lustre of romance on friendship. These circumstances, by bringing the virtues of sympathy with the weak, tenderness for the beautiful, protection for the young, together with corresponding qualities of gratitude, self-devotion, and admiring attachment into play, may have tended to cement unions between man and man no less firm than that of marriage. On such connections a wise captain would have relied for giving strength to his battalions, and for keeping alive the flames of enterprise and daring.' The author then goes on to suggest that though in such relations as those indicated the physical probably had its share, yet it did not at that time overbalance the emotional and spiritual elements, or lead to the corruption and effeminacy of a later age.

At Sparta the lover was called *Eispnélos*, the inspirer, and the younger beloved *Aïtes*, the hearer. This alone would show the partly educational aspects in which comradeship was conceived; and a hundred passages from classic literature might be quoted to prove how deeply it had entered into the Greek mind that this love was the cradle of social chivalry and heroic life. Finally it seems to have been Plato's favourite doctrine that the relation if properly conducted led up to the disclosure of true philosophy in the mind, to the divine vision or mania, and to the remembrance or rekindling within the soul of all the forms of celestial beauty. He speaks of this kind of love as causing a 'generation

[36] Whose tomb on account of his attachment to Iolaus was a place where Comrades swore troth to each other (Plutarch on *Love*, section xvii).

in the beautiful'[37] within the souls of the lovers. The image of the beloved one passing into the mind of the lover and upward through its deepest recesses reaches and unites itself to the essential forms of divine beauty there long hidden – the originals as it were of all creation – and stirring them to life excites a kind of generative descent of noble thoughts and impulses, which thenceforward modify the whole cast of thought and life of the one so affected.

I have now said enough I think to show that though Science has not as yet been able to give any decisive utterance on the import of the physical and physiological side of the homogenic passion (and it must be remembered that its real understanding of this side of the ordinary sex-love is very limited), yet on its ethical and social sides – which cannot of course, in the last resort, be separated from the physiological – the passion is pregnant with meaning, and has received at various times in history abundant justification. And in truth it seems the most natural thing in the world that just as the ordinary sex-love has a special function in the propagation of the race, so the other love should have its special function in social and heroic work, and in the generation – not of bodily children – but of those children of the mind, the philosophical conceptions and ideals which transform our lives and those of society. This without limiting too closely. In each case the main object may be said to be union. But as all love is also essentially creative, we naturally look for the creative activities of different kinds of love in different directions – and seem to find them so.

If there is any truth – even only a grain or two – in these speculations, it is easy to see that the love with which we are specially dealing is a very important factor in society, and that its neglect, or its repression, or its vulgar misapprehension, may be matters of considerable danger or damage to the common-weal. It is easy to see that while on the one hand the ordinary marriage is of indispensable importance to the State as providing the workshop as it were for the breeding and rearing of children, another form of union is almost equally indispensable to supply the basis for social activities of other kinds. Every one is conscious that without a close affectional tie of some kind his life is not complete, his powers are crippled, and his energies are inadequately spent. Yet it is not to be expected (though it may of course happen) that the man or woman who have dedicated themselves to each other and to family life should leave the care of their children and the work they have to do at home in order to perform social duties of a remote and less obvious, though may-be more arduous, character. Nor is it to be expected that a man or woman single-handed, without the counsel of

[37] *Symposium*: speech of Socrates.

a helpmate in the hour of difficulty, or his or her love in the hour of need, should feel equal to these wider activities. If – to refer once more to classic story – the love of Harmodius had been for a wife and children at home, he would probably not have cared, and it would hardly have been his business, to slay the tyrant. And unless on the other hand each of the friends had had the love of his comrade to support him, the two could hardly have nerved themselves to this audacious and ever-memorable exploit. So it is difficult to believe that anything except that kind of comrade-union which satisfies and invigorates the two lovers and yet leaves them free from the responsibilities and *impedimenta* of family life can supply the force and liberate the energies required for social and mental activities of the most necessary kind.

For if the slaughter of tyrants is not the chief social duty nowadays, we have with us hydra-headed monsters at least as numerous as the tyrants of old, and more difficult to deal with, and requiring no little courage to encounter. And beyond the extirpation of evils we have solid work waiting to be done in the patient and life-long building up of new forms of society, new orders of thought, and new institutions of human solidarity – all of which in their genesis will meet with opposition, ridicule, hatred, and even violence. Such campaigns as these – though different in kind from those of the Dorian mountaineers described above – will call for equal hardihood and courage and will stand in need of a comradeship as true and valiant. It may indeed be doubted whether the higher heroic and spiritual life of a nation is ever quite possible without the sanction of this attachment in its institutions; and it is not unlikely that the markedly materialistic and commercial character of the last age of European civilized life is largely to be connected with the fact that the *only* form of love and love-union that it has recognized has been one founded on the quite necessary but comparatively materialistic basis of matrimonial sex-intercourse and child-breeding.[38]

Walt Whitman, the inaugurator, it may almost be said, of a new world of democratic ideals and literature, and – as one of the best of our critics[39] has remarked – the most Greek in spirit and in performance of modern writers, insists continually on this social function of 'intense and loving comradeship, the personal and passionate attachment of

[38] It is interesting in this connection to notice the extreme fervor, almost of romance, of the bond which often unites lovers of like sex over a long period of years, in an unfailing tenderness of treatment and consideration towards each other, equal to that shown in the most successful marriages. The love of many such men, says Moll (p. 119), 'developed in youth lasts at times the whole life through. I know of such men, who had not seen their first love for years, even decades, and who yet on meeting showed the old fire of their first passion. In other cases a close love-intimacy will last unbroken for many years.'

[39] J. A. Symonds.

man to man.' 'I will make,' he says, 'the most splendid race the sun ever shone upon, I will make divine magnetic lands. . . . I will make inseparable cities with their arms about each others necks, by the love of comrades.' And again, in *Democratic Vistas*, 'It is to the development, identification, and general prevalence of that fervid comradeship (the adhesive love at least rivalling the amative love hitherto possessing imaginative literature, if not going beyond it), that I look for the counterbalance and offset of materialistic and vulgar American Democracy, and for the spiritualization thereof. . . . I say Democracy infers such loving comradeship, as its most inevitable twin or counterpart, without which it will be incomplete, in vain, and incapable of perpetuating itself.'

Yet Whitman could not have spoken, as he did, with a kind of authority on this subject, if he had not been fully aware that through the masses of the people this attachment was already alive and working – though doubtless in a somewhat suppressed and unselfconscious form – and if he had not had ample knowledge of its effects and influence in himself and others around him. Like all great artists he could but give form and light to that which already existed dim and inchoate in the heart of the people. To those who have dived at all below the surface in this direction it will be familiar enough that the homogenic passion ramifies widely through all modern society, and that among the masses of the people as among the classes, below the stolid surface and reserve of British manners, letters pass and enduring attachments are formed, differing in no very obvious respect from those correspondences which persons of opposite sexes knit with each other under similar circumstances; but that hitherto while this passion has occasionally come into public notice through the police reports, etc., in its grosser and cruder forms, its more sane and spiritual manifestations – though really a moving force in the body politic – have remained unrecognized.

It is hardly needful in these days when social questions loom so large upon us to emphasize the importance of a bond which by the most passionate and lasting compulsion may draw members of the different classes together, and (as it often seems to do) none the less strongly because they are members of different classes. A moment's consideration must convince us that such a comradeship may, as Whitman says, have 'deepest relations to general politics.' It is noticeable, too, in this deepest relation to politics that the movement among women towards their own liberation and emancipation which is taking place all over the civilized world has been accompanied by a marked development of the homogenic passion among the female sex. It may be said that a certain strain in the relations between the opposite sexes which has come about owing to a growing consciousness among women that they have been oppressed and unfairly treated by men,[40] and a growing unwillingness to ally themselves unequally in marriage – that this strain has caused the womankind to draw more closely together and to cement alliances of their own. But whatever the cause may be it is pretty certain that such comrade-alliances – and of a quite passionate kind – are becoming increasingly common, and especially perhaps among the more cultured classes of women, who are working out the great cause of their sex's liberation; nor is it difficult to see the importance of such alliances in such a campaign. In the United States where the battle of women's independence has been fought more vehemently perhaps than here, the tendency mentioned is even more strongly marked.

In conclusion there are a few words to be said about the legal aspect of this important question. It has to be remarked that the present state of the Law – arising as it does partly out of some of the misapprehensions above alluded to, and partly out of the sheer unwillingness of legislators to discuss the question – is really quite impracticable and unjustifiable, and will no doubt have to be altered.

The Law, of course, can only deal, and can only be expected to deal, with the outward and visible. It cannot control feeling; but it tries – in those cases where it is concerned – to control the expression of feeling. It has been insisted on in this essay that the Homogenic Love is a valuable social force, and, in cases, an indispensable factor of the noblest human character; also that it has a necessary root in the physical and sexual organism. This last is the point where the Law steps in. 'We know nothing' – it says – 'of what may be valuable social forces or factors of character, or of what may be the relation of physical things to things spiritual; but when you speak of a sexual element being present in this kind of love, we can quite understand that; and that is just what we mean to suppress. That sexual element is nothing but gross indecency, *any form of which by our Act of 1885 we make criminal.*'

Whatever substantial ground the Law may have had for previous statutes on this subject – dealing with a specific act (sodomy) – it has surely quite lost it in passing so wide-sweeping a condemnation on all relations between male persons.[41] It has undertaken a censorship over private morals (entirely apart from social results) which is beyond its province, and which – even if it were its province – it could not possibly fulfil; it has opened wider than ever before the door to a real social evil and crime – that of blackmailing; and it has thrown a shadow over even

[40] See *Woman*, p. 11, etc.
[41] Though, inconsistently enough, making no mention of females.

the simplest and most natural expressions of an attachment which may, as we have seen, be of the greatest value in national life.[42]

That the homosexual passion may be improperly indulged in, that it may lead, like the heterosexual, to public abuses of liberty and decency we of course do not deny; but as, in the case of persons of opposite sex, the law limits itself on the whole to the maintenance of public order, the protection of the weak from violence and insult[43] and, of the young from their inexperience: so it should be here. Whatever teaching may be thought desirable on the general principles of morality concerned must be given – as it can only be given – by the spread of proper education and ideas, and not by the clumsy bludgeon of the statute-book.[44]

We have shown the special functions and really indispensable import of the homogenic or comrade love, in some form, in national life, and it is high time now that the modern States should recognize this in their institutions – instead of (as is also done in schools and places of education) by repression and disallowance perverting the passion into its least satisfactory channels. If the dedication of love were a matter of mere choice or whim, it still would not be the business of the State to compel that choice; but since no amount of compulsion can ever change the homogenic instinct in a person, where it is innate, the State in trying to effect such a change is only kicking vainly against the pricks of its own advantage – and trying, in view perhaps of the conduct of a licentious few, to cripple and damage a respectable and valuable class of its own citizens.

71   'August Blue'

Alan Stanley. From *Love Lyrics*, 1894. Otherwise titled 'The Dawn Nocturne'. Line 22 'grow' is an error for 'glow' and was later corrected, but this Freudian error seems better.

> Silver mists on a silver sea,
> And white clouds overhead
> Sailing the grey sky speedily
> To where the east turns red.

[42] Dr. Moll maintains (second ed., pp. 314, 315) that if familiarities between those of the same sex are made illegal, as immoral, self-abuse ought much more to be so made.

[43] Though it is doubtful whether the marriage-laws even do this!

[44] In France, since the adoption of the Code Napoleon, sexual inversion is tolerated under the same restrictions as normal sexuality; and according to Carlier, formerly Chief of the French Police, Paris is not more depraved in this matter than London. Italy in 1889 also adopted the principles of the Code Napoleon on this point.

And one lone boat her sails has spread,
Sails of the whitest lawn,
That seem to listen for the tread
Of the tender feet of dawn.

The risen sun now makes the sky
An arching roof of gold,
Amber the clouds turn as they fly
Uncurling fold on fold;
The sun a goblet seems to hold
A draught of fervid wine,
And the young day no longer cold
Glows with a fire divine.

Stripped for the sea your tender form
Seems all of ivory white,
Through which the blue veins wander warm
O'er throat and bosom slight,
And as you stand, so slim, upright
The glad waves grow and yearn
To clasp you circling in their might,
To kiss with lips that burn.

Flashing limbs in the waters blue
And gold curls floating free;
Say, does it thrill you through and through
With ardent love, the sea?
A very nymph you seem to be
As you glide and dive and swim,
While the mad waves clasp you fervently
Possessing every limb.

King of the Sea, triumphant boy,
Nature itself made thrall
To God's white work without alloy
On whom no stain doth fall.
Gaze on him, slender, fair, and tall,
And on the yearning sea
Who deigns to creep and cling, and crawl,
His worshipper to be.

72   *'A Summer Hour'*

Bertram Lawrence (pseud. of J. F. Bloxam). From *The Artist*, October 1894
(new Style). Written August 1894.

> Love tarried for a moment on his way,
> Against my cheek his curly head he lay;
> He said that he would never leave my breast
> If I would give him what I valued best.
> Mine arms went out to greet him then and there,
> What heart had I to cast out one so fair?
>
> He whispered that his little feet were sore,
> He was so weary he could go no more,
> He showed the wounds upon his tender flesh,
> And, as he whispered, bound me in his mesh.
> He whispered in mine ear his piteous tale,
> What heart had I to cast out one so frail?
>
> I kissed his little hands, his lips, his hair,
> And kissing gave my soul into his care,
> Love laughed a little, like a child at play, –
> 'Regretted that he could no longer stay,
> He had so many things to do today,' –
> Another moment Love was far away.

73   *'The Priest and the Acolyte'*

John Francis Bloxam. From *The Chameleon*, December 1894. Written
June 1894.

> *Honi soit qui mal y pense*

> Part One

'Pray, father, give me thy blessing, for I have sinned.'

The priest started; he was tired in mind and body; his soul was
sad and his heart heavy as he sat in the terrible solitude of the confessional ever listening to the same dull round of oft-repeated sins. He
was weary of the conventional tones and matter-of-fact expressions.
Would the world always be the same? For nearly twenty centuries the

Christian priests had sat in the confessional and listened to the same old tale. The world seemed to him no better; always the same, the same. The young priest sighed to himself, and for a moment almost wished people would be worse. Why could they not escape from these old wearily-made paths and be a little original in their vices, if sin they must? But the voice he now listened to aroused him from his reverie. It was so soft and gentle, so diffident and shy.

He gave the blessing, and listened. Ah, yes! he recognized the voice now. It was the voice he had heard for the first time only that very morning: the voice of the little acolyte that had served his Mass.

He turned his head and peered through the grating at the little bowed head beyond. There was no mistaking those long soft curls. Suddenly, for one moment, the face was raised, and the large moist blue eyes met his; he saw the little oval face flushed with shame at the simple boyish sins he was confessing, and a thrill shot through him, for he felt that here at least was something in the world that was beautiful, something that was really true. Would the day come when those soft scarlet lips would have grown hard and false? when the soft shy treble would have become careless and conventional? His eyes filled with tears, and in a voice that had lost its firmness he gave the absolution.

After a pause, he heard the boy rise to his feet, and watched him wend his way across the little chapel and kneel before the altar while he said his penance. The priest hid his thin tired face in his hands and sighed wearily. The next morning, as he knelt before the altar and turned to say the words of confession to the little acolyte whose head was bent so reverently towards him, he bowed low till his hair just touched the golden halo that surrounded the little face, and he felt his veins burn and tingle with a strange new fascination.

When that most wonderful thing in the whole world, complete soul-absorbing love for another, suddenly strikes a man, that man knows what heaven means, and he understands hell: but if the man be an ascetic, a priest whose whole heart is given to ecstatic devotion, it were better for that man if he had never been born.

When they reached the vestry and the boy stood before him reverently receiving the sacred vestments, he knew that henceforth the entire devotion of his religion, the whole ecstatic fervour of his prayers, would be connected with, nay, inspired by, one object alone. With the same reverence and humility as he would have felt in touching the consecrated elements he laid his hands on the curl-crowned head, he touched the small pale face, and, raising it slightly, he bent forward and gently touched the smooth white brow with his lips.

When the child felt the caress of his fingers, for one moment everything swam before his eyes; but when he felt the light touch of the tall

priest's lips, a wonderful assurance took possession of him: he understood. He raised his little arms, and, clasping his slim white fingers
around the priest's neck kissed him on the lips. With a sharp cry the
priest fell upon his knees, and, clasping the little figure clad in scarlet
and lace to his heart, he covered the tender flushing face with burning
kisses. Then suddenly there came upon them both a quick sense of
fear; they parted hastily, with hot trembling fingers folded the sacred
vestments, and separated in silent shyness.

The priest returned to his poor rooms and tried to sit down and
think, but all in vain: he tried to eat, but could only thrust away his
plate in disgust: he tried to pray, but instead of the calm figure on the
cross, the calm, cold figure with the weary, weary face, he saw continually before him the flushed face of a lovely boy, the wide star-like
eyes of his new-found love.

All that day the young priest went through the round of his
various duties mechanically, but he could not eat nor sit quiet, for
when alone, strange shrill bursts of song kept thrilling through his
brain, and he felt that he must flee out into the open air or go mad.

At length, when night came, and the long, hot day had left him
exhausted and worn out, he threw himself on his knees before his
crucifix and compelled himself to think.

He called to mind his boyhood and his early youth; there returned
to him the thought of the terrible struggles of the last five years. Here
he knelt, Ronald Heatherington, priest of Holy Church, aged twenty-
eight: what he had endured during these five years of fierce battling
with those terrible passions he had fostered in his boyhood, was it all
to be in vain? For the last year he had really felt that all passion was
subdued, all those terrible outbursts of passionate love he had really
believed to be stamped out for ever. He had worked so hard, so unceasingly, through all these five years since his ordination – he had
given himself up solely and entirely to his sacred office; all the intensity
of his nature had been concentrated, completely absorbed, in the
beautiful mysteries of his religion. He had avoided all that could affect
him, all that might call up any recollection of his early life. Then he
had accepted this curacy, with sole charge of the little chapel that stood
close beside the cottage where he was now living, the little mission-
chapel that was the most distant of the several grouped round the old
Parish Church of St. Anselm. He had arrived only two or three days
before, and, going to call on the old couple who lived in the cottage, the
back of which formed the boundary of his own little garden, had been
offered the services of their grandson as acolyte.

'My son was an artist fellow, sir,' the old man had said: 'he never was satisfied here, so we sent him off to London; he was made a lot of there, sir, and married a lady, but the cold weather carried him off one winter, and his poor young wife was left with the baby. She brought him up and taught him herself, sir, but last winter she was taken too, so the poor lad came to live with us – so delicate he is, sir, and not one of the likes of us; he's a gentleman born and bred, is Wilfred. His poor mother used to like him to go and serve at the church near them in London, and the boy was so fond of it himself that we thought, supposing you did not mind, sir, that it would be a treat for him to do the same here.'

'How old is the boy?' asked the young priest.

'Fourteen, sir,' replied the grandmother.

'Very well, let him come to the chapel tomorrow morning,' Ronald had agreed.

Entirely absorbed in his devotions, the young man had scarcely noticed the little acolyte who was serving for him, and it was not till he was hearing his confession later in the day that he had realized his wonderful loveliness.

'Ah God! help me! pity me! After all this weary labour and toil, just when I am beginning to hope, is everything to be undone? am I to lose everything? Help me, help me, O God!'

Even while he prayed; even while his hands were stretched out in agonized supplication towards the feet of that crucifix before which his hardest battles had been fought and won; even while the tears of bitter contrition and miserable self-mistrust were dimming his eyes – there came a soft tap on the glass of the window beside him. He rose to his feet, and wonderingly drew back the dingy curtain. There in the moonlight, before the open window, stood a small white figure – there, with his bare feet on the moon-blanched turf, dressed only in his long white night-shirt, stood his little acolyte, the boy who held his whole future in his small childish hands.

'Wilfred, what are you doing here?' he asked in a trembling voice.

'I could not sleep, father, for thinking of you, and I saw a light in your room, so I got out through the window and came to see you. Are you angry with me, father?' he asked, his voice faltering as he saw the almost fierce expression in the thin ascetic face.

'Why did you come to see me?' The priest hardly dared recognize the situation, and scarcely heard what the boy said.

'Because I love you, I love you – oh, so much! but you – you are angry with me – oh, why did I ever come! why did I ever come! – I never thought you would be angry!' and the little fellow sank on the grass and burst into tears.

The priest sprang through the open window, and seizing the slim little figure in his arms, he carried him into the room. He drew the curtain, and, sinking into the deep arm-chair, laid the little fair head upon his breast, kissing his curls again and again.

'O my darling! my own beautiful darling!' he whispered, 'how could I ever be angry with you? You are more to me than all the world. Ah, God! how I love you, my darling! my own sweet darling!'

For nearly an hour the boy nestled there in his arms, pressing his soft cheek against his; then the priest told him he must go. For one long last kiss their lips met, and then the small white-clad figure slipped through the window, sped across the little moonlit garden, and vanished through the opposite window.

When they met in the vestry next morning, the lad raised his beautiful flower-like face, and the priest, gently putting his arms round him, kissed him tenderly on the lips.

'My darling! my darling!' was all he said; but the lad returned his kiss with a smile of wonderful almost heavenly love, in a silence that seemed to whisper something more than words.

'I wonder what was the matter with the father this morning?' said one old woman to another, as they were returning from the chapel; 'he didn't seem himself at all; he made more mistakes this morning than Father Thomas made in all the years he was here.'

'Seemed as if he had never said a Mass before!' replied her friend, with something of contempt.

And that night, and for many nights after, the priest, with the pale tired-looking face, drew the curtain over his crucifix and waited at the window for the glimmer of the pale summer moonlight on a crown of golden curls, for the sight of slim boyish limbs clad in the long white night-shirt, that only emphasized the grace of every movement, and the beautiful pallor of the little feet speeding across the grass. There at the window, night after night, he waited to feel tender loving arms thrown round his neck, and to feel the intoxicating delight of beautiful boyish lips raining kisses on his own.

Ronald Heatherington made no mistakes in the Mass now. He said the solemn words with a reverence and devotion that made the few poor people who happened to be there speak of him afterwards almost with awe; while the face of the little acolyte at his side shone with a fervour which made them ask each other what this strange light could mean. Surely the young priest must be a saint indeed, while the boy beside him looked more like an angel from heaven than any child of human birth.

Part Two

The world is very stern with those that thwart her. She lays down her precepts, and woe to those who dare to think for themselves, who venture to exercise their own discretion as to whether they shall allow their individuality and natural characteristics to be stamped out, to be obliterated under the leaden fingers of convention.

Truly, convention is the stone that has become head of the corner in the jerry-built temple of our superficial, self-assertive civilization.

'And whosoever shall fall on this stone shall be broken: but on whomsoever it shall fall, it will grind him to powder.'

If the world sees anything she cannot understand, she assigns the basest motives to all concerned, supposing the presence of some secret shame, the idea of which, at least, her narrow-minded intelligence is able to grasp.

The people no longer regarded their priest as a saint, and his acolyte as an angel. They still spoke of them with bated breath and with their fingers on their lips; they still drew back out of the way when they met either of them; but now they gathered together in groups of twos and threes and shook their heads.

The priest and his acolyte heeded not; they never even noticed the suspicious glances and half-suppressed murmurs. Each had found in the other perfect sympathy and perfect love: what could the outside world matter to them now? Each was to the other the perfect fulfilment of a scarcely preconceived ideal; neither heaven nor hell could offer more. But the stone of convention had been undermined; the time could not be far distant when it must fall.

The moonlight was very clear and very beautiful; the cool night air was heavy with the perfume of the old-fashioned flowers that bloomed so profusely in the little garden. But in the priest's little room the closely drawn curtains shut out all the beauty of the night. Entirely forgetful of all the world, absolutely oblivious of everything but one another, wrapped in the beautiful visions of a love that far outshone all the splendour of the summer night, the priest and the little acolyte were together.

The little lad sat on his knees with his arms closely pressed round his neck and his golden curls laid against the priest's close-cut hair; his white night-shirt contrasting strangely and beautifully with the dull black of the other's long cassock.

There was a step on the road outside – a step drawing nearer and nearer; a knock at the door. They heard it not; completely absorbed in each other, intoxicated with the sweetly poisonous draught that is the gift of love, they sat in silence. But the end had come: the blow had fallen at last. The door opened, and there before them in the doorway stood the tall figure of the rector.

Neither said anything; only the little boy clung closer to his beloved, and his eyes grew large with fear. Then the young priest rose slowly to his feet and put the lad from him.

'You had better go, Wilfred,' was all he said.

The two priests stood in silence watching the child as he slipped through the window, stole across the grass, and vanished into the opposite cottage.

Then the two turned and faced each other.

The young priest sank into his chair and clasped his hands, waiting for the other to speak.

'So it has come to this!' he said: 'the people were only too right in what they told me! Ah, God! that such a thing should have happened here! that it has fallen on me to expose your shame – our shame! that it is I who must give you up to justice, and see that you suffer the full penalty of your sin! Have you nothing to say?'

'Nothing – nothing,' he replied softly. 'I cannot ask for pity: I cannot explain: you would never understand. I do not ask you anything for myself, I do not ask you to spare me; but think of the terrible scandal to our dear Church.'

'It is better to expose these terrible scandals and see that they are cured. It is folly to conceal a sore: better show all our shame than let it fester.'

'Think of the child.'

'That was for you to do: you should have thought of him before. What has his shame to do with me? it was your business. Besides, I would not spare him if I could: what pity can I feel for such as he—?'

But the young man had risen, pale to the lips.

'Hush!' he said in a low voice; 'I forbid you to speak of him before me with anything but respect'; then softly to himself, 'with anything but reverence; with anything but devotion.'

The other was silent, awed for the moment. Then his anger rose.

'Dare you speak openly like that? Where is your penitence, your shame? have you no sense of the horror of your sin?'

'There is no sin for which I should feel shame,' he answered very quietly. 'God gave me my love for him, and He gave him also his love for me. Who is there that shall withstand God and the love that is His gift?'

'Dare you profane the name by calling such a passion as this "love"?'

'It was love, perfect love: it is perfect love.'

'I can say no more now; tomorrow all shall be known. Thank God, you shall pay dearly for all this disgrace,' he added, in a sudden outburst of wrath.

'I am sorry you have no mercy; – not that I fear exposure and punishment for myself. But mercy can seldom be found from a Christian,' he added, as one that speaks from without.

The rector turned towards him suddenly, and stretched out his hands.

'Heaven forgive me my hardness of heart,' he said. 'I have been cruel; I have spoken cruelly in my distress. Ah, can you say nothing to defend your crime?'

'No: I do not think I can do any good by that. If I attempted to deny all guilt, you would only think I lied: though I should prove my innocence, yet my reputation, my career, my whole future, are ruined for ever. But will you listen to me for a little? I will tell you a little about myself.'

The rector sat down while his curate told him the story of his life, sitting by the empty grate with his chin resting on his clasped hands.

'I was at a big public school, as you know. I was always different from other boys. I never cared much for games. I took little interest in those things for which boys usually care so much. I was not very happy in my boyhood, I think. My one ambition was to find the ideal for which I longed. It has always been thus: I have always had an indefinite longing for something, a vague something that never quite took shape, that I could never quite understand. My great desire has always been to find something that would satisfy me. I was attracted at once by sin: my whole early life is stained and polluted with the taint of sin. Sometimes even now I think that there are sins more beautiful than anything else in the world. There are vices that are bound to attract almost irresistibly anyone who loves beauty above everything. I have always sought for love: again and again I have been the victim of fits of passionate affection: time after time I have seemed to have found my ideal at last: the whole object of my life has been, times without number, to gain the love of some particular person. Several times my efforts were successful; each time I woke to find that the success I had obtained was worthless after all. As I grasped the prize, it lost all its attraction – I no longer cared for what I had once desired with my whole heart. In vain I endeavoured to drown the yearnings of my heart with the ordinary pleasures and vices that usually attract the young. I had to choose a profession. I became a priest. The whole aesthetic tendency of my soul was intensely attracted by the wonderful mysteries of Christianity, the artistic beauty of our services. Ever since my ordination I have been striving to cheat myself into the belief that peace had come at last – at last my yearning was satisfied: but all in vain. Unceasingly I have struggled with the old cravings for excitement, and, above all, the weary, incessant thirst for a perfect love. I have found, and still find, an exquisite delight in religion: not in the regular duties of a religious life, not in the ordinary round of parish organizations; – against these I chafe incessantly; – no, my delight is in the aesthetic beauty of the services, the ecstasy of devotion, the passionate fervour that comes with long fasting and meditation.'

'Have you found no comfort in prayer?' asked the rector.

'Comfort? – no. But I have found in prayer pleasure, excitement, almost a fierce delight of sin.'

'You should have married. I think that would have saved you.'

Ronald Heatherington rose to his feet and laid his hand on the rector's arm.

'You do not understand me. I have never been attracted by a woman in my life. Can you not see that people are different, totally different, from one another? To think that we are all the same is impossible; our natures, our temperaments, are utterly unlike. But this is what people will never see; they found all their opinions on a wrong basis. How can their deductions be just if their premisses are wrong? One law laid down by the majority, who happen to be of one disposition, is only binding on the minority *legally*, not *morally*. What right have you, or anyone, to tell me that such and such a thing is sinful for me? Oh, why can I not explain to you and force you to see?' and his grasp tightened on the other's arm. Then he continued, speaking fast and earnestly:

'For me, with my nature, to have married would have been sinful: it would have been a crime, a gross immorality, and my conscience would have revolted.' Then he added, bitterly: 'Conscience should be that divine instinct which bids us seek after that our natural disposition needs – we have forgotten that; to most of us, to the world, nay, even to Christians in general, conscience is merely another name for the cowardice that dreads to offend against convention. Ah, what a cursed thing convention is! I have committed no moral offence in this matter; in the sight of God my soul is blameless; but to you and to the world I am guilty of an abominable crime – abominable, because it is a sin against convention, forsooth! I met this boy: I loved him as I had never loved anyone or anything before: I had no need to labour to win his affection – he was mine by right: he loved me, even as I loved him, from the first: he was the necessary complement to my soul. How dare the world presume to judge us? What is convention to us? Nevertheless, although I really knew that such a love was beautiful and blameless, although from the bottom of my heart I despised the narrow judgement of the world, yet for his sake and for the sake of our Church, I tried at first to resist. I struggled against the fascination he possessed for me. I would never have gone to him and asked his love; I would have struggled on till the end: but what could I do? It was he that came to me, and offered me the wealth of love his beautiful soul possessed. How could I tell to such a nature as his the hideous picture the world would paint? Even as you saw him this evening, he has come to me night by night, – how dare I disturb the sweet purity of his soul by hinting at the horrible suspicions his presence might arouse? I knew what I was doing. I have faced the world and set myself up against it. I have openly scoffed at its dictates. I do not ask you to sympathize with me, nor do I pray you to stay your hand. Your eyes are blinded with a mental cataract. You are bound, bound with those miserable ties that have held you body and soul from the cradle. You must do what you believe to be your duty. In God's eyes we are martyrs, and we shall not shrink even from death in this struggle against the idolatrous worship of convention.'

Ronald Heatherington sank into a chair, hiding his face in his hands, and the rector left the room in silence.

For some minutes the young priest sat with his face buried in his hands. Then with a sigh he rose and crept across the garden till he stood beneath the open window of his darling.

'Wilfred,' he called very softly.

The beautiful face, pale and wet with tears, appeared at the window.

'I want you, my darling; will you come?' he whispered.

'Yes, father,' the boy softly answered.

The priest led him back to his room; then, taking him very gently in his arms, he tried to warm the cold little feet with his hands.

'My darling, it is all over.' And he told him as gently as he could all that lay before them.

The boy hid his face on his shoulder, crying softly.

'Can I do nothing for you, dear father?'

He was silent for a moment. 'Yes, you can die for me; you can die with me.'

The loving arms were about his neck once more, and the warm, loving lips were kissing his own. 'I will do anything for you. O father, let us die together!'

'Yes, my darling, it is best: we will.'

Then very quietly and very tenderly he prepared the little fellow for his death; he heard his last confession and gave him his last absolution. Then they knelt together, hand in hand, before the crucifix.

'Pray for me, my darling.'

Then together their prayers silently ascended that the dear Lord would have pity on the priest who had fallen in the terrible battle of life. There they knelt till midnight, when Ronald took the lad in his arms and carried him to the little chapel.

'I will say Mass for the repose of our souls,' he said.

Over his night-shirt the child arrayed himself in his little scarlet cassock and tiny lace cotta. He covered his naked feet with the scarlet sanctuary shoes; he lighted the tapers and reverently helped the priest to vest. Then before they left the vestry the priest took him in his arms and held him pressed closely to his breast; he stroked the soft hair and whispered cheeringly to him. The child was weeping quietly, his slender frame trembling with the sobs he could scarcely suppress. After a moment the tender embrace soothed him, and he raised his beautiful mouth to the priest's. Their lips were pressed together, and their arms wrapped one another closely.

'Oh, my darling, my own sweet darling!' the priest whispered tenderly.

'We shall be together for ever soon; nothing shall separate us now,' the child said.

'Yes, it is far better so; far better to be together in death than apart in life.'

They knelt before the altar in the silent night, the glimmer of the tapers lighting up the features of the crucifix with strange distinctness. Never had the priest's voice trembled with such wonderful earnestness, never had the acolyte responded with such devotion, as at this midnight Mass for the peace of their own departing souls.

Just before the consecration the priest took a tiny phial from the pocket of his cassock, blessed it, and poured the contents into the chalice.

When the time came for him to receive from the chalice, he raised it to his lips, but did not taste of it.

He administered the sacred wafer to the child, and then he took the beautiful gold chalice, set with precious stones, in his hand; he turned towards him; but when he saw the light in the beautiful face he turned again to the crucifix with a low moan. For one instant his courage failed him; then he turned to the little fellow again, and held the chalice to his lips:

'*The Blood of our Lord Jesus Christ, which was shed for thee, preserve thy body and soul unto everlasting life.*'

Never had the priest beheld such perfect love, such perfect trust, in those dear eyes as shone from them now; now, as with face raised upwards he received his death from the loving hands of him that he loved best in the whole world.

The instant he had received, Ronald fell on his knees beside him and drained the chalice to the last drop. He set it down and threw his arms round the beautiful figure of his dearly loved acolyte. Their lips met in one last kiss of perfect love, and all was over.

When the sun was rising in the heavens it cast one broad ray upon the altar of the little chapel. The tapers were burning still, scarcely half-burnt through. The sad-faced figure of the crucifix hung there in its majestic calm. On the steps of the altar was stretched the long, ascetic frame of the young priest, robed in the sacred vestments; close beside him, with his curly head pillowed on the gorgeous embroideries that covered his breast, lay the beautiful boy in scarlet and lace. Their arms were round each other; a strange hush lay like a shroud over all.

'And whosoever shall fall on this stone shall be broken: but on whomsoever it shall fall, it will grind him to powder.'

74   'Two Loves'

Lord Alfred Douglas. From *The Chameleon*, December 1894.

> I dreamed I stood upon a little hill,
> And at my feet there lay a ground, that seemed
> Like a waste garden, flowering at its will
> With buds and blossoms. There were pools that dreamed
> Black and unruffled; there were white lilies
> A few, and crocuses, and violets
> Purple or pale, snake-like fritillaries
> Scarce seen for the rank grass, and through green nets
> Blue eyes of shy pervenche winked in the sun.
> And there were curious flowers, before unknown,
> Flowers that were stained with moonlight, or with shades
> Of Nature's wilful moods; and here a one
> That had drunk in the transitory tone
> Of one brief moment in a sunset; blades
> Of grass that in an hundred springs had been
> Slowly but exquisitely nurtured by the stars,
> And watered with the scented dew long cupped
> In lilies, that for rays of sun had seen
> Only God's glory, for never a sunrise mars
> The luminous air of Heaven. Beyond, abrupt,
> A grey stone wall, o'ergrown with velvet moss

Uprose; and gazing I stood long, all mazed
To see a place so strange, so sweet, so fair.
And as I stood and marvelled, lo! across
The garden came a youth; one hand he raised
To shield him from the sun, his wind-tossed hair
Was twined with flowers, and in his hand he bore
A purple bunch of bursting grapes, his eyes
Were clear as crystal, naked all was he,
White as the snow on pathless mountains frore,
Red were his lips as red wine-spilth that dyes
A marble floor, his brow chalcedony.
And he came near me, with his lips uncurled
And kind, and caught my hand and kissed my mouth,
And gave me grapes to eat, and said, 'Sweet friend,
Come I will show thee shadows of the world
And images of life. See from the South
Comes the pale pageant that hath never an end.'
And lo! within the garden of my dream
I saw two walking on a shining plain
Of golden light. The one did joyous seem
And fair and blooming, and a sweet refrain
Came from his lips; he sang of pretty maids
And joyous love of comely girl and boy,
His eyes were bright, and 'mid the dancing blades
Of golden grass his feet did trip for joy;
And in his hand he held an ivory lute
With strings of gold that were as maidens' hair,
And sang with voice as tuneful as a flute,
And round his neck three chains of roses were.
But he that was his comrade walked aside;
He was full sad and sweet, and his large eyes
Were strange with wondrous brightness, staring wide
With gazing; and he sighed with many sighs
That moved me, and his cheeks were wan and white
Like pallid lilies, and his lips were red
Like poppies, and his hands he clenched tight,
And yet again unclenched, and his head
Was wreathed with moon-flowers pale as lips of death.
A purple robe he wore, o'erwrought in gold
With the device of a great snake, whose breath
Was fiery flame: which when I did behold
I fell a-weeping, and I cried, 'Sweet youth,
Tell me why, sad and sighing, thou dost rove

These pleasant realms? I pray thee speak me sooth
What is thy name?' He said, 'My name is Love.'
Then straight the first did turn himself to me
And cried, 'He lieth, for his name is Shame,
But I am Love, and I was wont to be
Alone in this fair garden, till he came
Unasked by night; I am true Love, I fill
The hearts of boy and girl with mutual flame.'
Then sighing, said the other, 'Have thy will,
I am the love that dare not speak its name.'

75   'In Praise of Shame'

Lord Alfred Douglas. From *The Chameleon*, December 1894.

Last night unto my bed methought there came
Our lady of strange dreams, and from an urn
She poured live fire, so that mine eyes did burn
At sight of it. Anon the floating flame
Took many shapes, and one cried: I am Shame
That walks with Love, I am most wise to turn
Cold lips and limbs to fire; therefore discern
And see my loveliness, and praise my name.

And afterwards, in radiant garments dressed
With sound of flutes and laughing of glad lips,
A pomp of all the passions passed along
All the night through; till the white phantom ships
Of dawn sailed in. Whereat I said this song,
'Of all sweet passions Shame is loveliest.'

76   The Portrait of Mr. W.H.

Oscar Wilde. Written 1889–95. Published (New York) 1921.

I

I had been dining with Erskine in his pretty little house in Birdcage
Walk, and we were sitting in the library over our coffee and cigarettes,
when the question of literary forgeries happened to turn up in conversation. I cannot at present remember how it was that we struck upon

this somewhat curious topic, as it was at that time, but I know we had a long discussion about Macpherson, Ireland, and Chatterton, and that with regard to the last I insisted that his so-called forgeries were merely the result of an artistic desire for perfect representation; that we had no right to quarrel with an artist for the conditions under which he chooses to present his work; and that all Art being to a certain degree a mode of acting, an attempt to realize one's own personality on some imaginative plane out of reach of the trammelling accidents and limitations of real life, to censure an artist for a forgery was to confuse an ethical with an aesthetical problem.

Erskine, who was a good deal older than I was, and had been listening to me with the amused deference of a man of forty, suddenly put his hand upon my shoulder and said to me, 'What would you say about a young man who had a strange theory about a certain work of art, believed in his theory, and committed a forgery in order to prove it?'

'Ah! that is quite a different matter,' I answered.

Erskine remained silent for a few moments, looking at the thin grey threads of smoke that were rising from his cigarette. 'Yes,' he said, after a pause, 'quite different.'

There was something in the tone of his voice, a slight touch of bitterness perhaps, that excited my curiosity. 'Did you ever know anybody who did that?' I cried.

'Yes,' he answered, throwing his cigarette into the fire – 'a great friend of mine, Cyril Graham. He was very fascinating, and very foolish, and very heartless. However, he left me the only legacy I ever received in my life.'

'What was that?' I exclaimed laughing. Erskine rose from his seat, and going to a tall inlaid cabinet that stood between the two windows, unlocked it, and came back to where I was sitting, carrying a small panel picture set in an old and somewhat tarnished Elizabethan frame.

It was a full-length portrait of a young man in late sixteenth-century costume, standing by a table, with his right hand resting on an open book. He seemed about seventeen years of age, and was of quite extraordinary personal beauty, though evidently somewhat effeminate. Indeed, had it not been for the dress and the closely cropped hair, one would have said that the face, with its dreamy, wistful eyes and its delicate scarlet lips, was the face of a girl. In manner, and especially in the treatment of the hands, the picture reminded one of François Clouet's later work. The black velvet doublet with its fantastically gilded points, and the peacock-blue background against which it showed up so pleasantly, and from which it gained such luminous value of

colour, were quite in Clouet's style; and the two masks of Tragedy and
Comedy that hung somewhat formally from the marble pedestal had
that hard severity of touch – so different from the facile grace of the
Italians – which even at the Court of France the great Flemish master
never completely lost, and which in itself has always been a characteristic
of the northern temper.

'It is a charming thing,' I cried; 'but who is this wonderful young
man whose beauty Art has so happily preserved for us?'

'This is the portrait of Mr. W.H.,' said Erskine, with a sad smile.
It might have been a chance effect of light, but it seemed to me that his
eyes were swimming with tears.

'Mr. W.H.!' I repeated; 'who was Mr. W.H.?'

'Don't you remember?' he answered; 'look at the book on which
his hand is resting.'

'I see there is some writing there, but I cannot make it out,' I
replied.

'Take this magnifying-glass and try,' said Erskine, with the same
sad smile still playing about his mouth.

I took the glass, and moving the lamp a little nearer, I began to
spell out the crabbed sixteenth-century handwriting. 'To The Onlie
Begetter Of These Insuing Sonnets.' . . . 'Good heavens!' I cried, 'is
this Shakespeare's Mr. W.H.?'

'Cyril Graham used to say so,' muttered Erskine.

'But it is not a bit like Lord Pembroke,' I rejoined. 'I know the
Wilton portraits very well. I was staying near there a few weeks ago.'

'Do you really believe then that the Sonnets are addressed to Lord
Pembroke?' he asked.

'I am sure of it,' I answered. 'Pembroke, Shakespeare, and Mrs.
Mary Fitton are the three personages of the Sonnets; there is no doubt
at all about it.'

'Well, I agree with you,' said Erskine, 'but I did not always think
so. I used to believe – well, I suppose I used to believe in Cyril Graham
and his theory.'

'And what was that?' I asked, looking at the wonderful portrait,
which had already begun to have a strange fascination for me.

'It is a long story,' he murmured, taking the picture away from
me – rather abruptly I thought at the time – 'a very long story; but if
you care to hear it, I will tell it to you.'

'I love theories about the Sonnets,' I cried; 'but I don't think I am
likely to be converted to any new idea. The matter has ceased to be a
mystery to anyone. Indeed, I wonder that it ever was a mystery.'

'As I don't believe in the theory, I am not likely to convert you to
it,' said Erskine, laughing; 'but it may interest you.'

'Tell it to me, of course,' I answered. 'If it is half as delightful as the picture, I shall be more than satisfied.'

'Well,' said Erskine, lighting a cigarette, 'I must begin by telling you about Cyril Graham himself. He and I were at the same house at Eton. I was a year or two older than he was, but we were immense friends, and did all our work and all our play together. There was, of course, a good deal more play than work, but I cannot say that I am sorry for that. It is always an advantage not to have received a sound commercial education, and what I learned in the playing fields at Eton has been quite as useful to me as anything I was taught at Cambridge. I should tell you that Cyril's father and mother were both dead. They had been drowned in a horrible yachting accident off the Isle of Wight. His father had been in the diplomatic service, and had married a daughter, the only daughter, in fact, of old Lord Crediton, who became Cyril's guardian after the death of his parents. I don't think that Lord Crediton cared very much for Cyril. He had never really forgiven his daughter for marrying a man who had no title. He was an extraordinary old aristocrat, who swore like a costermonger, and had the manners of a farmer. I remember seeing him once on Speech-day. He growled at me, gave me a sovereign, and told me not to grow up a 'damned Radical' like my father. Cyril had very little affection for him, and was only too glad to spend most of his holidays with us in Scotland. They never really got on together at all. Cyril thought him a bear, and he thought Cyril effeminate. He was effeminate, I suppose, in some things, though he was a capital rider and a capital fencer. In fact he got the foils before he left Eton. But he was very languid in his manner, and not a little vain of his good looks, and had a strong objection to football, which he used to say was a game only suitable for the sons of the middle classes. The two things that really gave him pleasure were poetry and acting. At Eton he was always dressing up and reciting Shakespeare, and when we went up to Trinity he became a member of the A.D.C. his first term. I remember I was always very jealous of his acting. I was absurdly devoted to him; I suppose because we were so different in most things. I was a rather awkward, weakly lad, with huge feet, and horribly freckled. Freckles run in Scotch families just as gout does in English families. Cyril used to say that of the two he preferred the gout; but he always set an absurdly high value on personal appearance, and once read a paper before our Debating Society to prove that it was better to be good-looking than to be good. He certainly was wonderfully handsome. People who did not like him, Philistines and college tutors, and young men reading for the Church, used to say that he was merely pretty; but there was a great deal more in his face than mere prettiness. I think he was the most splendid creature I ever saw, and nothing could exceed the grace of his movements, the charm of his manner. He fascinated everybody who was worth fascinating, and a great many people who were not. He was often wilful and petulant, and I used to think him dreadfully insincere. It was due, I think, chiefly to his inordinate desire to please. Poor Cyril! I told him once that he was contented with very cheap triumphs, but he only tossed his head, and smiled. He was horribly spoiled. All charming people, I fancy, are spoiled. It is the secret of their attraction.

'However, I must tell you about Cyril's acting. You know that no women are allowed to play at the A.D.C. At least they were not in my time. I don't know how it is now. Well, of course Cyril was always cast for the girls' parts, and when "As You Like It" was produced he played Rosalind. It was a marvellous performance. You will laugh at me, but I assure you that Cyril Graham was the only perfect Rosalind I have ever seen. It would be impossible to describe to you the beauty, the delicacy, the refinement of the whole thing. It made an immense sensation, and the horrid little theatre, as it was then, was crowded every night. Even now when I read the play I can't help thinking of Cyril; the part might have been written for him, he played it with such extraordinary grace and distinction. The next term he took his degree, and came to London to read for the Diplomatic. But he never did any work. He spent his days in reading Shakespeare's Sonnets, and his evenings at the theatre. He was, of course, wild to go on the stage. It was all that Lord Crediton and I could do to prevent him. Perhaps, if he had gone on the stage he would be alive now. It is always a silly thing to give advice, but to give good advice is absolutely fatal. I hope you will never fall into that error. If you do, you will be sorry for it.

'Well, to come to the real point of the story, one afternoon I got a letter from Cyril asking me to come round to his rooms that evening. He had charming chambers in Piccadilly overlooking the Green Park, and as I used to go to see him almost every day, I was rather surprised at his taking the trouble to write. Of course I went, and when I arrived I found him in a state of great excitement. He told me that he had at last discovered the true secret of Shakespeare's Sonnets; that all the scholars and critics had been entirely on the wrong track; and that he was the first who, working purely by internal evidence, had found out who Mr. W.H. really was. He was perfectly wild with delight, and for a long time would not tell me his theory. Finally, he produced a bundle of notes, took his copy of the Sonnets off the mantelpiece, and sat down and gave me a long lecture on the whole subject.

'He began by pointing out that the young man to whom Shakespeare addressed these strangely passionate poems must have been somebody who was a really vital factor in the development of his dramatic art, and that this could not be said of either Lord Pembroke or Lord Southampton. Indeed, whoever he was, he could not have been anybody of high birth, as was shown very clearly by Sonnet XXV, in which Shakespeare contrasts himself with men who are "great princes' favourites"; says quite frankly –

> Let those who are in favour with their stars
> Of public honour and proud titles boast,
> Whilst, I whom fortune of such triumph bars,
> Unlooked for joy in that I honour most;

and ends the sonnet by congratulating himself on the mean state of him he so adored:

> Then happy I, that love and am beloved
> Where I may not remove nor be removed.

This sonnet Cyril declared would be quite unintelligible if we fancied that it was addressed to either the Earl of Pembroke or the Earl of Southampton, both of whom were men of the highest position in England and fully entitled to be called "great princes"; and he in corroboration of his view read me Sonnets CXXIV and CXXV, in which Shakespeare tells us that his love is not "the child of state," that it "suffers not in smiling pomp," but is "builded far from accident." I listened with a good deal of interest, for I don't think the point had ever been made before; but what followed was still more curious, and seemed to me at the time to dispose entirely of Pembroke's claim. We know from Meres that the Sonnets had been written before 1598, and Sonnet CIV informs us that Shakespeare's friendship for Mr. W.H. had been already in existence for three years. Now Lord Pembroke, who was born in 1580, did not come to London till he was eighteen years of age, that is to say till 1598, and Shakespeare's acquaintance with Mr. W.H. must have begun in 1594, or at the latest in 1595. Shakespeare, accordingly, could not have known Lord Pembroke till after the Sonnets had been written.

'Cyril pointed out also that Pembroke's father did not die till 1601; whereas it was evident from the line,

> You had a father, let your son say so,

that the father of Mr. W.H. was dead in 1598; and laid great stress on the evidence afforded by the Wilton portraits which represent Lord Pembroke as a swarthy dark-haired man, while Mr. W.H. was one whose hair was like spun gold, and whose face the meeting-place for the "lily's white" and the "deep vermilion in the rose"; being himself "fair," and "red," and "white and red," and of beautiful aspect. Besides it was absurd to imagine that any publisher of the time, and the preface is from the publisher's hand, would have dreamed of addressing William Herbert, Earl of Pembroke, as Mr. W.H.; the case of Lord Buckhurst being spoken of as Mr. Sackville being not really a parallel instance, as Lord Buckhurst, the first of that title, was plain Mr. Sackville when he contributed to the "Mirror for Magistrates," while Pembroke, during his father's lifetime, was always known as Lord Herbert. So far for Lord Pembroke, whose supposed claims Cyril easily demolished while I sat by in wonder. With Lord Southampton Cyril had even less difficulty. Southampton became at a very early age the lover of Elizabeth Vernon, so he needed no entreaties to marry; he was not beautiful; he did not resemble his mother, as Mr. W.H. did –

> Thou art thy mother's glass, and she in thee
> Calls back the lovely April of her prime;

and, above all, his Christian name was Henry, whereas the punning sonnets (CXXXV and CXLIII) show that the Christian name of Shakespeare's friend was the same as his own – *Will*.

'As for the other suggestions of unfortunate commentators, that Mr. W.H. is a misprint for Mr. W.S., meaning Mr. William Shakespeare; that "Mr. W.H. all" should be read "Mr. W. Hall"; that Mr. W.H. is Mr. William Hathaway; that Mr. W.H. stands for Mr. Henry Willobie, the young Oxford poet, with the initials of his name reversed; and that a full stop should be placed after "wisheth," making Mr. W.H. the writer and not the subject of the dedication, – Cyril got rid of them in a very short time; and it is not worth while to mention his reasons, though I remember he sent me off into a fit of laughter by reading to me, I am glad to say not in the original, some extracts from a German commentator called Barnstorff, who insisted that Mr. W.H. was no less a person than "Mr. William Himself." Nor would he allow for a moment that the Sonnets are mere satires on the work of Drayton and John Davies of Hereford. To him, as indeed to me, they were poems of serious and tragic import, wrung out of the bitterness of Shakespeare's heart, and made sweet by the honey of his lips. Still less would he admit that they were merely a philosophical allegory, and that in them Shakespeare is addressing his Ideal Self, or Ideal Manhood, or the Spirit of Beauty, or the Reason, or the Divine Logos, or the Catholic Church. He felt, as indeed I think we all must feel, that the Sonnets are addressed to an individual, to a particular young man whose personality for some reason seems to have filled the soul of Shakespeare with terrible joy and no less terrible despair.

'Having in this manner cleared the way, as it were, Cyril asked me to dismiss from my mind any preconceived ideas I might have formed on the subject, and to give a fair and unbiased hearing to his own theory. The problem he pointed out was this: Who was that young man of Shakespeare's day who, without being of noble birth or even of noble nature, was addressed by him in terms of such passionate adoration that we can but wonder at the strange worship, and are almost afraid to turn the key that unlocks the mystery of the poet's heart? Who was he whose physical beauty was such that it became the very corner-stone of Shakespeare's art; the very source of Shakespeare's inspiration; the very incarnation of Shakespeare's dreams? To look upon him as simply the object of certain love-poems was to miss the whole meaning of the poems: for the art of which Shakespeare talks in the Sonnets is not the art of the Sonnets themselves, which indeed were to him but slight and secret things – it is the art of the dramatist to which he is always alluding; and he to whom Shakespeare said –

> Thou art all my art, and dost advance
> As high as learning my rude ignorance,

he to whom he promised immortality,

> Where breath most breathes, even in the mouths of men,

he who was to him the tenth "muse" and

> Ten times more in worth
> Than those old nine which rhymers invocate,

was surely none other than the boy-actor for whom he created Viola and Imogen, Juliet and Rosalind, Portia and Desdemona, and Cleopatra herself.'

'The boy-actor of Shakespeare's plays?' I cried.

'Yes,' said Erskine. 'This was Cyril Graham's theory, evolved as you see purely from the Sonnets themselves, and depending for its acceptance not so much on demonstrable proof or formal evidence, but on a kind of spiritual and artistic sense, by which alone he claimed could the true meaning of the poems be discerned. I remember his reading to me that fine sonnet –

> How can my Muse want subject to invent,
> While thou dost breathe, that pour'st into my verse
> Thine own sweet argument, too excellent
> For every vulgar paper to rehearse?

> O give thyself the thanks, if aught in me
> Worthy perusal stand against thy sight;
> For who's so dumb that cannot write to thee,
> When thou thyself does give invention light?

– and pointing out how completely it corroborated his view; and indeed he went through all the Sonnets carefully, and showed, or fancied that he showed, that, according to his new explanation of their meaning, things that had seemed obscure, or evil, or exaggerated, became clear and rational, and of high artistic import, illustrating Shakespeare's conception of the true relations between the art of the actor and the art of the dramatist.

'It is of course evident that there must have been in Shakespeare's company some wonderful boy-actor of great beauty, to whom he intrusted the presentation of his noble heroines; for Shakespeare was a practical theatrical manager as well as an imaginative poet; and Cyril Graham had actually discovered the boy-actor's name. He was Will, or, as he preferred to call him, Willie Hughes. The Christian name he found of course in the punning sonnets, CXXXV and CXLIII; the surname was, according to him, hidden in the eighth line of Sonnet XX, where Mr. W.H. is described as –

> A man in hew, all *Hews* in his controwling.

'In the original edition of the Sonnets "Hews" is printed with a capital letter and in italics, and this, he claimed, showed clearly that a play on words was intended, his view receiving a good deal of corroboration from those sonnets in which curious puns are made on the words "use" and "usury," and from such lines as –

> Thou art as fair in knowledge as in hew.

Of course I was converted at once, and Willie Hughes became to me as real a person as Shakespeare. The only objection I made to the theory was that the name of Willie Hughes does not occur in the list of the actors of Shakespeare's company as it is printed in the first folio. Cyril, however, pointed out that the absence of Willie Hughes' name from this list really corroborated the theory, as it was evident from Sonnet LXXXVI, that he had abandoned Shakespeare's company to play at a rival theatre, probably in some of Chapman's plays. It was in reference to this that in the great sonnet on Chapman Shakespeare said to Willie Hughes –

> But when your countenance filled up his line,
> Then lacked I matter; that enfeebled mine –

the expression "when your countenance filled up his line" referring clearly to the beauty of the young actor giving life and reality and added charm to Chapman's verse, the same idea being also put forward in Sonnet LXXIX:

> Whilst I alone did call upon thy aid,
> My verse alone had all thy gentle grace,
> But now my gracious numbers are decayed,
> And my sick Muse doth give another place;

and in the immediately preceding sonnet, where Shakespeare says,

> Every alien pen hath got my *use*
> And under thee their poesy disperse,

the play upon words (use = Hughes) being of course obvious, and the phrase, "under thee their poesy disperse," meaning "by your assistance as an actor bring their plays before the people."

'It was a wonderful evening, and we sat up almost till dawn reading and re-reading the Sonnets. After some time, however, I began to see that before the theory could be placed before the world in a really perfected form, it was necessary to get some independent evidence about the existence of this young actor, Willie Hughes. If this could be once established, there could be no possible doubt about his identity with Mr. W.H.; but otherwise the theory would fall to the ground. I put this forward very strongly to Cyril, who was a good deal annoyed at what he called my Philistine tone of mind, and indeed was rather bitter upon the subject. However, I made him promise that in his own interest he would not publish his discovery till he had put the whole matter beyond the reach of doubt; and for weeks and weeks we searched the registers of City churches, the Alleyn MSS. at Dulwich, the Record Office, the books of the Lord Chamberlain – everything, in fact, that we thought might contain some allusion to Willie Hughes. We discovered nothing, of course, and each day the existence of Willie Hughes seemed to me to become more problematical. Cyril was in a dreadful state, and used to go over the whole question again and again, entreating me to believe; but I saw the one flaw in the theory, and I refused to be convinced till the actual existence of Willie Hughes, a boy-actor of the Elizabethan stage, had been placed beyond the reach of doubt or cavil.

'One day Cyril left town to stay with his grandfather, I thought at the time, but I afterwards heard from Lord Crediton that this was not the case; and about a fortnight afterwards I received a telegram from him, handed in at Warwick, asking me to be sure to come and dine with him in his chambers, that evening at eight o'clock. When I arrived, he said to me, "The only apostle who did not deserve proof was St. Thomas, and St. Thomas was the only apostle who got it." I asked him what he meant. He answered that he had been able not merely to establish the existence in the sixteenth century of a boy-actor of the name of Willie Hughes, but to prove by the most conclusive evidence that he was the Mr. W.H. of the Sonnets. He would not tell me anything more at the time; but after dinner he solemnly produced the picture I showed you, and told me that he had discovered it by the merest chance nailed to the side of an old chest that he had bought at a farmhouse in Warwickshire. The chest itself, which was a very fine example of Elizabethan work, and thoroughly authentic, he had, of course, brought with him, and in the centre of the front panel the initials W.H. were undoubtedly carved. It was this monogram that had attracted his attention, and he told me that it was not till he had had the chest in his possession for several days that he had thought of making any careful examination of the inside. One morning, however, he saw that the right-hand side of the chest was much thicker than the other, and looking more closely, he discovered that a framed panel was clamped against it. On taking it out, he found it was the picture that is now lying on the sofa. It was very dirty, and covered with mould; but he managed to clean it, and, to his great joy, saw that he had fallen by mere chance on the one thing for which he had been looking. Here was an authentic portrait of Mr. W.H. with his hand resting on the dedicatory page of the Sonnets, and on the corner of the picture could be faintly seen the name of the young man himself written in gold uncial letters on the faded *bleu de paon* ground, "Master Will Hews."

'Well, what was I to say? It is quite clear from Sonnet XLVII that Shakespeare had a portrait of Mr. W.H. in his possession, and it seemed to me more than probable that here we had the very "painted banquet" on which he invited his eye to feast; the actual picture that awoke his heart "to heart's and eye's delight." It never occurred to me for a moment that Cyril Graham was playing a trick on me, or that he was trying to prove his theory by means of a forgery.'

'But is it a forgery?' I asked.

'Of course it is,' said Erskine. 'It is a very good forgery; but it is a forgery none the less. I thought at the time that Cyril was rather calm about the whole matter; but I remember he kept telling me that he himself required no proof of the kind, and that he thought the theory complete without it. I laughed at him, and told him that without it the entire theory would fall to the ground, and I warmly congratulated him on his marvellous discovery. We then arranged that the picture should be etched or facsimiled, and placed as the frontispiece to Cyril's edition of the Sonnets; and for three months we did nothing but go over each poem line by line, till we had settled every difficulty of text or meaning. One unlucky day I was in a print-shop in Holborn, when I saw upon the counter some extremely beautiful drawings in silverpoint. I was so attracted by them that I bought them; and the proprietor of the place, a man called Rawlings, told me that they were done by a young painter of the name of Edward Merton, who was very clever, but as poor as a church mouse. I went to see Merton some days afterwards, having got his address from the print-seller, and found a pale, interesting young man, with a rather common-looking wife, – his model, as I subsequently learned. I told him how much I admired his drawings, at which he seemed very pleased, and I asked him if he would show me some of his other work. As we were looking over a portfolio, full of really very lovely things, – for Merton had a most delicate and delightful touch, – I suddenly caught sight of a drawing of the picture of Mr. W.H. There was no doubt whatever about it. It was almost a facsimile, – the only difference being that the two masks of Tragedy and Comedy were not lying on the floor at the young man's feet, as they were in the picture, but were suspended by gilt ribands. "Where on earth did you get that?" I asked. He grew rather confused, and said, – "Oh, that is nothing. I did not know it was in this portfolio. It is not a thing of any value." "It is what you did for Mr. Cyril Graham," exclaimed his wife; "and if this gentleman wishes to buy it, let him have it." "For Mr. Cyril Graham?" I repeated. "Did you paint the picture of Mr. W.H.?" "I don't understand what you mean," he answered, growing very red. Well, the whole thing was quite dreadful. The wife let it all out. I gave her five pounds when I was going away. I can't bear to think of it, now; but of course I was furious. I went off at once to Cyril's chambers, waited there for three hours before he came in, with that horrid lie staring me in the face, and told him I had discovered his forgery. He grew very pale, and said, – "I did it purely for your sake. You would not be convinced in any other way. It does not affect the truth of the theory." "The truth of the theory!" I exclaimed; "the less we talk about that the better. You never even believed in it yourself. If you had, you would not have committed a forgery to prove it." High words passed between us; we had a fearful quarrel. I daresay I was unjust, and the next morning he was dead.'

'Dead!' I cried.

'Yes, he shot himself with a revolver. By the time I arrived, – his servant had sent for me at once, – the police were already there. He had left a letter for me, evidently written in the greatest agitation and distress of mind.'

'What was in it?' I asked.

'Oh, that he believed absolutely in Willie Hughes; that the forgery of the picture had been done simply as a concession to me, and did not in the slightest degree invalidate the truth of the theory; and that in order to show me how firm and flawless his faith in the whole thing was, he was going to offer his life as a sacrifice to the secret of the Sonnets. It was a foolish, mad letter. I remember he ended by saying that he intrusted to me the Willie Hughes theory, and that it was for me to present it to the world, and to unlock the secret of Shakespeare's heart.'

'It is a most tragic story,' I cried, 'but why have you not carried out his wishes?'

Erskine shrugged his shoulders. 'Because it is a perfectly unsound theory from beginning to end,' he answered.

'My dear Erskine,' I exclaimed, getting up from my seat, 'you are entirely wrong about the whole matter. It is the only perfect key to Shakespeare's Sonnets that has ever been made. It is complete in every detail. I believe in Willie Hughes.'

'Don't say that,' said Erskine, gravely; 'I believe there is something fatal about the idea, and intellectually there is nothing to be said for it. I have gone into the whole matter, and I assure you the theory is entirely fallacious. It is plausible up to a certain point. Then it stops. For heaven's sake, my dear boy, don't take up the subject of Willie Hughes. You will break your heart over it.'

'Erskine,' I answered, 'it is your duty to give this theory to the world. If you will not do it, I will. By keeping it back you wrong the memory of Cyril Graham, the youngest and the most splendid of all the martyrs of literature. I entreat you to do him this bare act of justice. He died for this thing, – don't let his death be in vain.'

Erskine looked at me in amazement. 'You are carried away by the sentiment of the whole story,' he said. 'You forget that a thing is not necessarily true because a man dies for it. I was devoted to Cyril Graham. His death was a horrible blow to me. I did not recover from it for years. I don't think I have ever recovered from it. But Willie Hughes! There is nothing in the idea of Willie Hughes. No such person ever existed. As for bringing the matter before the world, – the world thinks that Cyril Graham shot himself by accident. The only proof of his suicide was contained in the letter to me, and of this letter the public never heard anything. To the present day Lord Crediton is under the impression that the whole thing was accidental.'

'Cyril Graham sacrificed his life to a great idea,' I answered; 'and if you will not tell of his martyrdom, tell at least of his faith.'

'His faith,' said Erskine, 'was fixed in a thing that was false, in a thing that was unsound, in a thing that no Shakespearian scholar would accept for a moment. The theory would be laughed at. Don't make a fool of yourself, and don't follow a trail that leads nowhere. You start by assuming the existence of the very person whose existence is the thing to be proved. Besides, everybody knows that the Sonnets were addressed to Lord Pembroke. The matter is settled once for all.'

'The matter is not settled,' I exclaimed. 'I will take up the theory where Cyril Graham left it, and I will prove to the world that he was right.'

'Silly boy!' said Erskine. 'Go home, it is after three, and don't think about Willie Hughes any more. I am sorry I told you anything about it, and very sorry indeed that I should have converted you to a thing in which I don't believe.'

'You have given me the key to the greatest mystery of modern literature,' I answered; 'and I will not rest till I have made you recognize, till I have made everybody recognize, that Cyril Graham was the most subtle Shakespearian critic of our day.'

I was about to leave the room when Erskine called me back. 'My dear fellow,' he said, 'let me advise you not to waste your time over the Sonnets. I am quite serious. After all, what do they tell us about Shakespeare? Simply that he was the slave of beauty.'

'Well, that is the condition of being an artist!' I replied.

There was a strange silence for a few moments. Then Erskine got up, and looking at me with half closed eyes, said, 'Ah! how you remind me of Cyril! He used to say just that sort of thing to me.' He tried to smile, but there was a note of poignant pathos in his voice that I remember to the present day, as one remembers the tone of a particular violin that has charmed one, the touch of a particular woman's hand. The great events of life often leave one unmoved; they pass out of consciousness, and, when one thinks of them, become unreal. Even the scarlet flowers of passion seem to grow in the same meadow as the poppies of oblivion. We reject the burden of their memory, and have anodynes against them. But the little things, the things of no moment, remain with us. In some tiny ivory cell the brain stores the most delicate, and the most fleeting impressions.

As I walked home through St. James's Park, the dawn was just breaking over London. The swans were lying asleep on the smooth surface of the polished lake, like white feathers fallen upon a mirror of black steel. The gaunt Palace looked purple against the pale green sky, and in the garden of Stafford House the birds were just beginning to sing. I thought of Cyril Graham, and my eyes filled with tears.

II

It was past twelve o'clock when I awoke, and the sun was streaming in through the curtains of my room in long dusty beams of tremulous gold. I told my servant that I would not be at home to anyone, and after I had discussed a cup of chocolate and a *petit-pain*, I took out of the library my copy of Shakespeare's Sonnets, and Mr. Tyler's facsimile edition of the Quarto, and began to go carefully through them. Each poem seemed to me to corroborate Cyril Graham's theory. I felt as if I had my hand upon Shakespeare's heart, and was counting each separate throb and pulse of passion. I thought of the wonderful boy-actor, and saw his face in every line.

Previous to this, in my Lord Pembroke days, if I may so term them, I must admit that it had always seemed to me very difficult to understand how the creator of Hamlet and Lear and Othello could have addressed in such extravagant terms of praise and passion one who was merely an ordinary young nobleman of the day. Along with most students of Shakespeare, I had found myself compelled to set the Sonnets apart as things quite alien to Shakespeare's development as a dramatist, as things possibly unworthy of the intellectual side of his nature. But now that I began to realize the truth of Cyril Graham's theory, I saw that the moods and passions they mirrored were absolutely essential to Shakespeare's perfection as an artist writing for the Elizabethan stage, and that it was in the curious theatric conditions of that stage that the poems themselves had their origin. I remember what joy I had in feeling that these wonderful Sonnets,

> Subtle as Sphinx; as sweet and musical
> As bright Apollo's lute, strung with his hair,

were no longer isolated from the great aesthetic energies of Shakespeare's life, but were an essential part of his dramatic activity, and revealed to us something of the secret of his method. To have discovered the true name of Mr. W.H. was comparatively nothing: others might have done that, had perhaps done it: but to have discovered his profession was a revolution in criticism.

Two sonnets, I remember, struck me particularly. In the first of these (LIII) Shakespeare, complimenting Willie Hughes on the versatility of his acting, on his wide range of parts, a range extending, as we know, from Rosalind to Juliet, and from Beatrice to Ophelia, says to him:

> What is your substance, whereof are you made,
> That millions of strange shadows on you tend?
> Since every one hath, every one, one shade,
> And you, but one, can every shadow lend –

lines that would be unintelligible if they were not addressed to an actor, for the word 'shadow' had in Shakespeare's day a technical meaning connected with the stage. 'The best in this kind are but shadows,' says Theseus of the actors in the *Midsummer Night's Dream*;

> Life's but a walking shadow, and poor player
> That struts and frets his hour upon the stage,

cries Macbeth in the moment of his despair, and there are many similar allusions in the literature of the day. This sonnet evidently belonged to the series in which Shakespeare discusses the nature of the actor's art, and of the strange and rare temperament that is essential to the perfect stage-player. 'How is it,' says Shakespeare to Willie Hughes, 'that you have so many personalities?' and then he goes on to point out that his beauty is such that it seems to realize every form and phase of fancy, to embody each dream of the creative imagination, – an idea that is still further expanded in the sonnet that immediately follows, where, beginning with the fine thought,

> O, how much more doth beauty beauteous seem
> By that sweet ornament which *truth* doth give!

Shakespeare invites us to notice how the truth of acting, the truth of visible presentation on the stage, adds to the wonder of poetry, giving life to its loveliness, and actual reality to its ideal form. And yet, in Sonnet LXVII, Shakespeare calls upon Willie Hughes to abandon the stage with its artificiality, its unreal life of painted face and mimic costume, its immoral influences and suggestions, its remoteness from the true world of noble action and sincere utterance.

> Ah, wherefore with infection should he live,
> And with his presence grace impiety,
> That sin by him advantage should receive,
> And lace itself with his society?
> Why should false painting imitate his cheek,
> And steal dead seeing of his living hue?
> Why should poor beauty indirectly seek
> Roses of shadow, since his rose is true?

It may seem strange that so great a dramatist as Shakespeare, who realized his own perfection as an artist and his full humanity as a man on the ideal plane of stage-writing and stage-playing, should have written in these terms about the theatre; but we must remember that in Sonnets CX and CXI, Shakespeare shows us that he too was wearied of the world of puppets, and full of shame at having made himself 'a motley to the view.' Sonnet CXI is especially bitter:

> O, for my sake do you with Fortune chide,
> The guilty goddess of my harmful deeds,
> That did not better for my life provide
> Than public means which public manners breeds.
> Thence comes it that my name receives a brand,
> And almost thence my nature is subdued
> To what it works in, like the dyer's hand:
> Pity me, then, and wish I were renewed –

and there are many signs of the same feeling elsewhere, signs familiar to all real students of Shakespeare.

One point puzzled me immensely as I read the Sonnets, and it was days before I struck on the true interpretation, which indeed Cyril Graham himself seemed to have missed. I could not understand how it was that Shakespeare set so high a value on his young friend marrying. He himself had married young and the result had been unhappiness, and it was not likely that he would have asked Willie Hughes to commit the same error. The boy-player of Rosalind had nothing to gain from marriage, or from the passions of real life. The early sonnets with their strange entreaties to love children seemed to be a jarring note.

The explanation of the mystery came on me quite suddenly and I found it in the curious dedication. It will be remembered that this dedication was as follows:

TO . THE . ONLIE . BEGETTER . OF .

THESE . INSUING . SONNETS .

MR. W.H. ALL . HAPPINESSE .

AND . THAT . ETERNITIE .

PROMISED . BY .

OUR . EVER-LIVING . POET .

WISHETH .

THE . WELL-WISHING .

ADVENTURER . IN .

SETTING .

FORTH .

T.T.

Some scholars have supposed that the word 'begetter' here means simply the procurer of the Sonnets for Thomas Thorpe the publisher; but this view is now generally abandoned, and the highest authorities are quite agreed that it is to be taken in the sense of inspirer, the metaphor being drawn from the analogy of physical life. Now I saw that the same metaphor was used by Shakespeare himself all through the poems, and this set me on the right track. Finally I made my great discovery.

The marriage that Shakespeare proposes for Willie Hughes is the 'marriage with his Muse,' an expression which is definitely put forward in Sonnet LXXXII where, in the bitterness of his heart at the defection of the boy-actor for whom he had written his greatest parts, and whose beauty had indeed suggested them, he opens his complaint by saying –

> I grant thou wert not married to my Muse.

The children he begs him to beget are no children of flesh and blood, but more immortal children of undying fame. The whole cycle of the early sonnets is simply Shakespeare's invitation to Willie Hughes to go upon the stage and become a player. How barren and profitless a thing, he says, is this beauty of yours if it be not used:

> When forty winters shall besiege thy brow,
> And dig deep trenches in thy beauty's field,
> Thy youth's proud livery, so gazed on now,
> Will be a tattered weed, of small worth held;
> Then being asked where all thy beauty lies,
> Where all the treasure of thy lusty days,
> To say, within thine own deep-sunken eyes,
> Were an all-eating shame and thriftless praise.

You must create something in art: my verse 'is thine and *born* of thee'; only listen to me, and I will '*bring forth* eternal numbers to outlive long date,' and you shall people with forms of your own image the imaginary world of the stage. These children that you beget, he continues, will not wither away, as mortal children do, but you shall live in them and in my plays: do but –

> Make thee another self, for love of me,
> That beauty still may live in thine or thee!

Be not afraid to surrender your personality, to give your 'semblance to some other':

> To give away yourself keeps yourself still,
> And you must live, drawn by your own sweet skill.

I may not be learned in astrology, and yet, in those 'constant stars' your eyes,

> I read such art
> As truth and beauty shall together thrive,
> If from thyself to store thou wouldst convert.

What does it matter about others?

> Let those whom Nature hath not made for store,
> Harsh, featureless, and rude, barrenly perish:

With you it is different, Nature –

> carv'd thee for her seal, and meant thereby
> Thou shouldst print more, nor let that copy die.

Remember, too, how soon Beauty forsakes itself. Its action is no stronger than a flower, and like a flower it lives and dies. Think of 'the stormy gusts of winter's day,' of the 'barren edge of Death's eternal cold,' and –

> ere thou be distilled,
> Make sweet some vial; treasure thou some place
> With beauty's treasure, ere it be self-killed.

Why, even flowers do not altogether die. When roses wither,

> Of their sweet deaths are sweetest odours made:

and you who are 'my rose' should not pass away without leaving your form in Art. For Art has the very secret of joy.

> Ten times thyself were happier than thou art,
> If ten of thine ten times refigur'd thee.

You do not require the 'bastard signs of fair,' the painted face, the fantastic disguises of other actors:

> . . . the golden tresses of the dead,
> The right of sepulchres,

need not be shorn away for you. In you –

> . . . those holy antique hours are seen,
> Without all ornament, itself and true,
> Making no summer of another's green.

All that is necessary is to 'copy what in you is writ'; to place you on the stage as you are in actual life. All those ancient poets who have written of 'ladies dead and lovely knights' have been dreaming of such a one as you, and –

> All their praises are but prophecies
> Of this our time, all you prefiguring.

For your beauty seems to belong to all ages and to all lands. Your shade comes to visit me at night, but, I want to look upon your 'shadow' in the living day, I want to see you upon the stage. Mere description of you will not suffice:

> If I could write the beauty of your eyes,
> And in fresh numbers number all your graces,
> The age to come would say, 'This poet lies;
> Such heavenly touches ne'er touched earthly faces.'

It is necessary that 'some child of yours,' some artistic creation that embodies you, and to which your imagination gives life, shall present you to the world's wondering eyes. Your own thoughts are your children, offspring of sense and spirit; give some expression to them, and you shall find –

> Those children nursed, delivered from thy brain.

My thoughts, also, are my 'children.' They are of your begetting and my brain is –

> the womb wherein they grew.

For this great friendship of ours is indeed a marriage, it is the 'marriage of true minds.'

I collected together all the passages that seemed to me to corroborate this view, and they produced a strong impression on me, and showed me how complete Cyril Graham's theory really was. I also saw that it was quite easy to separate those lines in which Shakespeare speaks of the Sonnets themselves, from those in which he speaks of his great dramatic work. This was a point that had been entirely overlooked by all critics up to Cyril Graham's day. And yet it was one of the most important in the whole series of poems. To the Sonnets Shakespeare was more or less indifferent. He did not wish to rest his fame on them. They were to him his 'slight Muse,' as he calls them, and intended, as Meres tells us, for private circulation only among a few, a very few, friends. Upon the other hand he was extremely conscious of the high artistic value of his plays, and shows a noble self-reliance upon his dramatic genius. When he says to Willie Hughes:

> But thy eternal summer shall not fade,
> Nor lose possession of that fair thou owest;
> Nor shall Death brag thou wander'st in his shade,
> When in *eternal lines* to time thou growest:
> So long as men can breathe or eyes can see,
> So long lives this and this gives life to thee; –

the expression 'eternal lines' clearly alludes to one of his plays that he was sending him at the time, just as the concluding couplet points to his confidence in the probability of his plays being always acted. In his address to the Dramatic Muse (Sonnets C and CI) we find the same feeling.

> Where art thou, Muse, that thou forget'st so long
> To speak of that which gives thee all thy might?
> Spend'st thou thy fury on some worthless song,
> Darkening thy power to lend base subjects light?

he cries, and he then proceeds to reproach the mistress of Tragedy and Comedy for her 'neglect of truth in beauty dyed,' and says –

> Because he needs no praise, wilt thou be dumb?
> Excuse not silence so; for 't lies in thee
> To make him much outlive a gilded tomb,
> And to be praised of ages yet to be.
> Then do thy office, Muse, I teach thee how,
> To make him seem long hence as he shows now.

It is, however, perhaps in Sonnet LV that Shakespeare gives to this idea its fullest expression. To imagine that the 'powerful rhyme' of the second line refers to the sonnet itself was entirely to mistake Shakespeare's meaning. It seemed to me that it was extremely likely, from the general character of the sonnet, that a particular play was meant, and that the play was none other but *Romeo and Juliet*.

> Not marble, nor the gilded monuments
> Of princes shall outlive this powerful rhyme;
> But you shall shine more bright in these contents
> Than unswept stone besmeared with sluttish time.
> When wasteful war shall statues overturn,
> And broils root out the work of masonry,
> Not Mars his sword nor war's quick fire shall burn
> The living record of your memory.
> 'Gainst death and all-oblivious enmity
> Shall you pace forth; your praise shall still find room
> Even in the eyes of all posterity
> That wear this world out to the ending doom.
> So, till the judgment that yourself arise,
> You live in this, and dwell in lovers' eyes.

It was also very suggestive to note how here as elsewhere Shakespeare promised Willie Hughes immortality in a form that appealed to men's eyes – that is to say, in a spectacular form, in a play that is to be looked at.

For two weeks I worked hard at the Sonnets, hardly ever going out, and refusing all invitations. Every day I seemed to be discovering something new, and Willie Hughes became to me a kind of spiritual presence, an ever-dominant personality. I could almost fancy that I saw him standing in the shadow of my room, so well had Shakespeare drawn him, with his golden hair, his tender flower-like grace, his dreamy deep-sunken eyes, his delicate mobile limbs, and his white lily hands. His very name fascinated me. Willie Hughes! Willie Hughes! How musically it sounded! Yes; who else but he could have been the master-mistress of Shakespeare's passion,[1] the lord of his love to whom he was bound in vassalage,[2] the delicate minion of pleasure,[3] the rose of the whole world,[4] the herald of the spring,[5] decked in the proud livery of youth,[6] the lovely boy whom it was sweet music to hear,[7] and whose beauty was the very raiment of Shakespeare's heart,[8] as it was the keystone of his dramatic power? How bitter now seemed the whole tragedy of his desertion and his shame! – shame that he made sweet and lovely[9] by the mere magic of his personality, but that was none the less shame. Yet as Shakespeare forgave him, should not we forgive him also? I did not care to pry into the mystery of his sin or of the sin, if such it was, of the great poet who had so dearly loved him. 'I am that I am,' said Shakespeare in a sonnet of noble scorn –

> I am that I am, and they that level
> At my abuses reckon up their own;
> I may be straight, though they themselves be bevel;
> By their rank thoughts my deeds must not be shown.

Willie Hughes' abandonment of Shakespeare's theatre was a different matter, and I investigated it at great length. Finally I came to the conclusion that Cyril Graham had been wrong in regarding the rival dramatist of Sonnet LXXX as Chapman. It was obviously Marlowe who was alluded to. At the time the Sonnets were written, which must have been between 1590 and 1595, such an expression as 'the proud full sail of his great verse' could not possibly have been used of Chapman's work, however applicable it might have been to the style of his later Jacobean plays. No; Marlowe was clearly the rival poet of whom Shakespeare spoke in such laudatory terms; the hymn he wrote in Willie Hughes' honour was the unfinished *Hero and Leander*, and that

> Affable familiar ghost
> Which nightly gulls him with intelligence,

was the Mephistophilis of his *Doctor Faustus*. No doubt, Marlowe was fascinated by the beauty and grace of the boy-actor, and lured him away from the Blackfriars Theatre, that he might play the Gaveston of his *Edward II*. That Shakespeare had some legal right to retain Willie

---

[1] Sonnet XX. 2. [4] Sonnet CIX. 14. [7] Sonnet VIII. 1.
[2] Sonnet XXVI. 1. [5] Sonnet I. 10. [8] Sonnet XXII. 6.
[3] Sonnet CXXVI. 9. [6] Sonnet II. 3. [9] Sonnet XCV. 1.

Hughes in his own company seems evident from Sonnet LXXXVII, where he says:

> Farewell! thou art too dear for my possessing,
> And like enough thou know'st thy estimate:
> The *charter of thy worth* gives thee releasing;
> My *bonds* in thee are all determinate.
> For how do I hold thee but by thy granting?
> And for that riches where is my deserving?
> The cause of this fair gift in me is wanting,
> *And so my patent back again is swerving.*
> Thyself thou gav'st, thy own worth then not knowing,
> Or me, to whom thou gav'st it, else mistaking;
> So thy great gift, upon misprision growing,
> Comes home again, on better judgment making.
> Thus have I had thee, as a dream doth flatter,
> In sleep a king, but waking no such matter.

But him whom he could not hold by love, he would not hold by force. Willie Hughes became a member of Lord Pembroke's company, and perhaps in the open yard of the Red Bull Tavern, played the part of King Edward's delicate minion. On Marlowe's death, he seems to have returned to Shakespeare, who, whatever his fellow-partners may have thought of the matter, was not slow to forgive the wilfulness and treachery of the young actor.

How well, too, had Shakespeare drawn the temperament of the stage-player! Willie Hughes was one of those –

> That do not do the thing they most do show,
> Who, moving others, are themselves as stone.

He could act love, but could not feel it, could mimic passion without realizing it.

> In many's looks the false heart's history
> Is writ in moods and frowns and wrinkles strange,

but with Willie Hughes it was not so. 'Heaven,' says Shakespeare, in a sonnet of mad idolatry –

> Heaven in thy creation did decree
> That in thy face sweet love should ever dwell;
> Whate'er thy thoughts or thy heart's workings be,
> Thy looks should nothing thence but sweetness tell.

In his 'inconstant mind' and his 'false heart' it was easy to recognize the insincerity that somehow seems inseparable from the artistic nature, as in his love of praise, that desire for immediate recognition that characterizes all actors. And yet, more fortunate in this than other actors, Willie Hughes was to know something of immortality. Intimately connected with Shakespeare's plays, he was to live in them, and by their production.

> Your name from hence immortal life shall have,
> Though I, once gone, to all the world must die:
> The earth can yield me but a common grave,
> When you entombed in men's eyes shall lie.
> Your monument shall be my gentle verse,
> Which eyes not yet created shall o'er-read,
> And tongues to be your being shall rehearse,
> When all the breathers of this world are dead.

Nash with his venomous tongue had railed against Shakespeare for 'reposing eternity in the mouth of a player,' the reference being obviously to the Sonnets.

But to Shakespeare, the actor was a deliberate and self-conscious fellow-worker who gave form and substance to a poet's fancy, and brought into Drama the elements of a noble realism. His silence could be as eloquent as words, and his gesture as expressive, and in those terrible moments of Titan agony or of god-like pain, when thought outstrips utterance, when the soul sick with excess of anguish stammers or is dumb, and the very raiment of speech is rent and torn by passion in its storm, then the actor could become, though it were but for a moment, a creative artist, and touch by his mere presence and personality those springs of terror and of pity to which tragedy appeals. This full recognition of the actor's art, and of the actor's power, was one of the things that distinguished the Romantic from the Classical Drama, and one of the things, consequently, that we owed to Shakespeare, who, fortunate in much, was fortunate also in this, that he was able to find Richard Burbage and to fashion Willie Hughes.

With what pleasure he dwelt upon Willie Hughes' influence over his audience – the 'gazers' as he calls them; with what charm of fancy did he analyse the whole art! Even in the 'Lover's Complaint' he speaks of his acting, and tells us that he was of a nature so impressionable to the quality of dramatic situations that he could assume all 'strange forms' –

> Of burning blushes, or of weeping water,
> Or swooning paleness:

explaining his meaning more fully later on where he tells us how Willie Hughes was able to deceive others by his wonderful power to –

> Blush at speeches rank, to weep at woes,
> Or to turn white and swoon at tragic shows.

It had never been pointed out before that the shepherd of this lovely pastoral, whose 'youth in art and art in youth' are described with such subtlety of phrase and passion, was none other than the Mr. W.H. of the Sonnets. And yet there was no doubt that he was so. Not merely in personal appearance are the two lads the same, but their natures and temperaments are identical. When the false shepherd whispers to the fickle maid –

> All my offences that abroad you see
> Are errors of the blood, none of the mind;
> Love made them not:

when he says of his lovers,

> Harm have I done to them, but ne'er was harmed;
> Kept hearts in liveries, but mine own was free,
> And reigned, commanding in his monarchy:

when he tells us of the 'deep-brained sonnets' that one of them had sent him, and cries out in boyish pride –

> The broken bosoms that to me belong
> Have emptied all their fountains in my well:

it is impossible not to feel that it is Willie Hughes who is speaking to us. 'Deep-brained sonnets,' indeed, had Shakespeare brought him, 'jewels' that to his careless eyes were but as 'trifles,' though –

> each several stone,
> With wit well blazoned, smiled or made some moan;

and into the well of beauty he had emptied the sweet fountain of his song. That in both places it was an actor who was alluded to, was also clear. The betrayed nymph tells us of the 'false fire' in her lover's cheek, of the 'forced thunder' of his sighs, and of his 'borrowed motion': of whom, indeed, but of an actor could it be said that to him 'thought, characters, and words' were 'merely Art,' or that –

> To make the weeper laugh, the laugher weep,
> He had the dialect and different skill,
> Catching all passions in his craft of will?

The play on words in the last line is the same as that used in the punning sonnets, and is continued in the following stanza of the poem, where we are told of the youth who –

> did in the general bosom reign
> Of young, of old; and sexes both enchanted,

that there were those who –

> . . . dialogued for him what he would say,
> Asked their own wills, and made their Wills obey.

Yes: the 'rose-cheeked Adonis' of the Venus poem, the false shepherd of the 'Lover's Complaint,' the 'tender churl,' the 'beauteous niggard' of the Sonnets, was none other but a young actor; and as I read through the various descriptions given of him, I saw that the love that Shakespeare bore him was as the love of a musician for some delicate instrument on which he delights to play, as a sculptor's love for some rare and exquisite material that suggests a new form of plastic beauty, a new mode of plastic expression. For all Art has its medium, its material, be it that of rhythmical words, or of pleasurable colour, or of sweet and subtly-divided sound; and, as one of the most fascinating critics of our day has pointed out, it is to the qualities inherent in each material, and special to it, that we owe the sensuous element in Art, and with it all that in Art is essentially artistic. What then shall we say of the material that the Drama requires for its perfect presentation? What of the Actor, who is the medium through which alone the Drama can truly reveal itself? Surely, in that strange mimicry of life by the living which is the mode and method of Theatric art, there are sensuous elements of beauty that none of the other arts possess. Looked at from one point of view, the common players of the saffron-strewn stage are Art's most complete, most satisfying instruments. There is no passion in bronze, nor motion in marble. The sculptor must surrender colour, and the painter fullness of form. The epos changes acts into words, and music changes words into tones. It is the Drama only that, to quote the fine saying of Gervinus, uses all means at once, and, appealing both to eye and ear, has at its disposal, and in its service, form and colour, tone, look, and word, the swiftness of motion, the intense realism of visible action.

It may be that in this very completeness of the instrument lies the secret of some weakness in the art. Those arts are happiest that employ a material remote from reality, and there is a danger in the absolute identity of medium and matter, the danger of ignoble realism and unimaginative imitation. Yet Shakespeare himself was a player, and wrote for players. He saw the possibilities that lay hidden in an art that up to his time had expressed itself but in bombast or in clowning. He has left us the most perfect rules for acting that have ever been written. He created parts that can be only truly revealed to us on the stage, wrote plays that need the theatre for their full realization, and we cannot marvel that he so worshipped one who was the interpreter of his vision, as he was the incarnation of his dreams.

There was, however, more in this friendship than the mere delight of a dramatist in one who helps him to achieve his end. This was indeed a subtle element of pleasure, if not of passion, and a noble basis for an artistic comradeship. But it was not all that the Sonnets revealed to us. There was something beyond. There was the soul, as well as the language, of neo-Platonism.

'The fear of the Lord is the beginning of wisdom,' said the stern Hebrew prophet: 'The beginning of wisdom is Love,' was the gracious message of the Greek. And the spirit of the Renaissance, which already touched Hellenism at so many points, catching the inner meaning of this phrase and divining its secret, sought to elevate friendship to the high dignity of the antique ideal, to make it a vital factor in the new culture, and a mode of self-conscious intellectual development. In 1492 appeared Marsilio Ficino's translation of the *Symposium* of Plato, and this wonderful dialogue, of all the Platonic dialogues perhaps the most perfect, as it is the most poetical, began to exercise a strange influence over men, and to colour their words and thoughts, and manner of living. In its subtle suggestions of sex in soul, in the curious analogies it draws between intellectual enthusiasm and the physical passion of love, in its dream of the incarnation of the Idea in a beautiful and living form, and of a real spiritual conception with a travail and a bringing to birth, there was something that fascinated the poets and scholars of the sixteenth century. Shakespeare, certainly, was fascinated by it, and had read the dialogue, if not in Ficino's translation, of which many copies found their way to England, perhaps in that French translation by Leroy to which Joachim du Bellay contributed so many graceful metrical versions. When he says to Willie Hughes,

> he that calls on thee, let him bring forth
> Eternal numbers to outlive long date,

he is thinking of Diotima's theory that Beauty is the goddess who presides over birth, and draws into the light of day the dim conceptions of the soul: when he tells us of the 'marriage of true minds,' and exhorts his friend to beget children that time cannot destroy, he is but repeating the words in which the prophetess tells us that 'friends are married by a far nearer tie than those who beget mortal children, for fairer and more immortal are the children who are their common offspring.' So, also, Edward Blount in his dedication of *Hero and Leander* talks of Marlowe's works as his 'right children,' being the 'issue of his brain'; and when Bacon claims that 'the best works and of greatest merit for the public have proceeded from the unmarried and childless men, which both in affection and means have married and endowed the public,' he is paraphrasing a passage in the *Symposium*.

Friendship, indeed, could have desired no better warrant for its permanence or its ardours than the Platonic theory, or creed, as we might better call it, that the true world was the world of ideas, and that these ideas took visible form and became incarnate in man, and it is only when we realize the influence of neo-Platonism on the Renaissance that we can understand the true meaning of the amatory phrases and words with which friends were wont, at this time, to address each other. There was a kind of mystic transference of the expressions of the physical sphere to a sphere that was spiritual, that was removed from gross bodily appetite, and in which the soul was Lord. Love had, indeed, entered the olive garden of the new Academe, but he wore the same flame-coloured raiment, and had the same words of passion on his lips.

Michael Angelo, the 'haughtiest spirit in Italy' as he has been called, addresses the young Tommaso Cavalieri in such fervent and passionate terms that some have thought that the sonnets in question must have been intended for that noble lady, the widow of the Marchese di Pescara, whose white hand, when she was dying, the great sculptor's lips had stooped to kiss. But that it was to Cavalieri that they were written, and that the literal interpretation is the right one, is evident not merely from the fact that Michael Angelo plays with his name, as Shakespeare plays with the name of Willie Hughes, but from the direct evidence of Varchi, who was well acquainted with the young man, and who, indeed, tells us that he possessed 'besides incomparable personal beauty, so much charm of nature, such excellent abilities, and such a graceful manner, that he deserved, and still deserves, to be the better loved the more he is known.' Strange as these sonnets may seem to us now, when rightly interpreted they merely serve to show with what intense and religious fervour Michael Angelo addressed himself to the worship of intellectual beauty, and how, to borrow a fine phrase from Mr. Symonds, he pierced through the veil of flesh and sought the divine idea it imprisoned. In the sonnet written for Luigi del Riccio on the death of his friend, Cecchino Bracci, we can also trace, as Mr. Symonds points out, the Platonic conception of love as nothing if not spiritual, and of beauty as a form that finds its immortality within the lover's soul. Cecchino was a lad who died at the age of seventeen, and when Luigi asked Michael Angelo to make a portrait of him, Michael Angelo answered, 'I can only do so by drawing you in whom he still lives.'

> If the beloved in the lover shine,
> Since Art without him cannot work alone,
> Thee must I carve, to tell the world of him.

The same idea is also put forward in Montaigne's noble essay on Friendship, a passion which he ranks higher than the love of brother for brother, or the love of man for woman. He tells us – I quote from Florio's translation, one of the books with which Shakespeare was familiar – how 'perfect amitie' is indivisible, how it 'possesseth the soule, and swaies it in all soveraigntie,' and how 'by the interposition of a spiritual beauty the desire of a spiritual conception is engendered in the beloved.' He writes of an 'internall beauty, of difficile knowledge, and abstruse discovery' that is revealed unto friends, and unto friends only. He mourns for the dead Etienne de la Boëtie, in accents of wild grief and inconsolable love. The learned Hubert Languet, the friend of Melanchthon and of the leaders of the reformed church, tells the young Philip Sidney how he kept his portrait by him some hours to feast his eyes upon it, and how his appetite was 'rather increased than diminished by the sight,' and Sidney writes to him, 'the chief hope of my life, next to the everlasting blessedness of heaven, will always be the enjoyment of true friendship, and there you shall have the chiefest place.' Later on there came to Sidney's house in London, one – some day to be burned at Rome, for the sin of seeing God in all things – Giordano Bruno, just fresh from his triumph before the University of Paris. 'A filosofia è necessario amore' were the words ever upon his lips, and there was something in his strange ardent personality that made men feel that he had discovered the new secret of life. Ben Jonson writing to one of his friends subscribes himself 'your true lover,' and dedicates his noble eulogy on Shakespeare 'To the memory of my Beloved.' Richard Barnfield in his 'Affectionate Shepherd' flutes on soft Virgilian reed the story of his attachment to some young Elizabethan of the day. Out of all the Eclogues, Abraham Fraunce selects the second for translation, and Fletcher's lines to Master W. C. show what fascination was hidden in the mere name of Alexis.

It was no wonder then that Shakespeare had been stirred by a spirit that so stirred his age. There had been critics, like Hallam, who had regretted that the Sonnets had ever been written, who had seen in them something dangerous, something unlawful even. To them it would have been sufficient to answer in Chapman's noble words:

> There is no danger to a man that knows
> What Life and Death is: there's not any law
> Exceeds his knowledge: neither is it lawful
> That he should stoop to any other law.

But it was evident that the Sonnets needed no such defence as this, and that those who had talked of 'the folly of excessive and misplaced affection' had not been able to interpret either the language or the spirit of these great poems, so intimately connected with the philosophy and the art of their time. It is no doubt true that to be filled with an absorbing passion is to surrender the security of one's lover life, and yet in such surrender there may be gain, certainly there was for Shakespeare. When Pico della Mirandola crossed the threshold of the villa of Careggi, and stood before Marsilio Ficino in all the grace and comeliness of his wonderful youth, the aged scholar seemed to see in him the realization of the Greek ideal, and determined to devote his remaining years to the translation of Plotinus, that new Plato, in whom, as Mr. Pater reminds us, 'the mystical element in the Platonic philosophy had been worked out to the utmost limit of vision and ecstasy.' A romantic friendship with a young Roman of his day initiated Winckelmann into the secret of Greek art, taught him the mystery of its beauty and the meaning of its form. In Willie Hughes, Shakespeare found not merely a most delicate instrument for the presentation of his art, but the visible incarnation of his idea of beauty, and it is not too much to say that to this young actor, whose very name the dull writers of his age forgot to chronicle, the Romantic Movement of English Literature is largely indebted.

III

One evening I thought that I had really discovered Willie Hughes in Elizabethan literature. In a wonderfully graphic account of the last days of the great Earl of Essex, his chaplain, Thomas Knell, tells us that the night before the Earl died, 'he called William Hewes, which was his musician, to play upon the virginals and to sing. "Play," said he, "my song, Will Hewes, and I will sing it myself." So he did it most joyfully, not as the howling swan, which, still looking down, waileth her end, but as a sweet lark, lifting up his hands and casting up his eyes to his God, with this mounted the crystal skies, and reached with his un-wearied tongue the top of highest heavens.' Surely the boy who played on the virginals to the dying father of Sidney's Stella was none other than the Will Hews to whom Shakespeare dedicated the Sonnets, and who he tells us was himself sweet 'music to hear.' Yet Lord Essex died in 1576, when Shakespeare was but twelve years of age. It was impossible that his musician could have been the Mr. W.H. of the Sonnets. Perhaps Shakespeare's young friend was the son of the player upon the virginals? It was at least something to have discovered that Will Hews was an Elizabethan name. Indeed the name Hews seemed to have been closely connected with music and the stage. The first English actress was the lovely Margaret Hews, whom Prince Rupert so madly adored. What more probable than that between her and Lord Essex' musician had come the boy-actor of Shakespeare's plays? In 1587 a certain Thomas Hews brought out at Gray's Inn a Euripidean tragedy entitled 'The Misfortunes of Arthur,' receiving much assistance in the arrangement of the dumb shows from one Francis Bacon, then a student of law. Surely he was some near kinsman of the lad to whom Shakespeare said –

'Take all my loves, my love, yea, take them all'; the 'profitless usurer' of 'unused beauty,' as he describes him. But the proofs, the links – where were they? Alas! I could not find them. It seemed to me that I was always on the brink of absolute verification, but that I could never really attain to it. I thought it strange that no one had ever written a history of the English boy-actors of the sixteenth and seventeenth centuries, and determined to undertake the task myself, and to try and ascertain their true relations to the drama. The subject was, certainly, full of artistic interest. These lads had been the delicate reeds through which our poets had sounded their sweetest strains, the gracious vessels of honour into which they had poured the purple wine of their song. Foremost, naturally, amongst them all had been the youth to whom Shakespeare had intrusted the realization of his most exquisite creations. Beauty had been his, such as our age has never, or but rarely seen, a beauty that seemed to combine the charm of both sexes, and to have wedded, as the Sonnets tell us, the grace of Adonis and the loveliness of Helen. He had been quick-witted, too, and eloquent, and from those finely curved lips that the satirist had mocked at had come the passionate cry of Juliet, and the bright laughter of Beatrice, Perdita's flower-like words, and Ophelia's wandering songs. Yet as Shakespeare himself had been but as a god among giants, so Willie Hughes had only been one out of many marvellous lads to whom our English Renaissance owed something of the secret of its joy, and it appeared to me that they also were worthy of some study and record.

In a little book with fine vellum leaves and damask silk cover – a fancy of mine in those fanciful days – I accordingly collected such information as I could about them, and even now there is something in the scanty record of their lives, in the mere mention of their names, that attracts me. I seemed to know them all: Robin Armin, the goldsmith's lad who was lured by Tarlton to go on the stage: Sandford, whose performance of the courtezan Flamantia Lord Burleigh witnessed at Gray's Inn: Cooke, who played Agrippina in the tragedy of *Sejanus*: Nat. Field, whose young and beardless portrait is still preserved for us at Dulwich, and who in *Cynthia's Revels* played the 'Queen and Huntress chaste and fair': Gil. Carie, who, attired as a mountain nymph, sang in the same lovely masque Echo's song of mourning for Narcissus: Parsons, the Salmacis of the strange pageant of *Tamburlaine*: Will. Ostler, who was one of 'The Children of the Queen's Chapel,' and accompanied King James to Scotland: George Vernon, to whom the King sent a cloak of scarlet cloth, and a cape of crimson velvet: Alick Gough, who performed the part of Caenis, Vespasian's concubine, in Massinger's *Roman Actor*, and three years later that of Acanthe, in the same dramatist's *Picture*: Barrett, the heroine of Richards' tragedy of *Messalina*: Dicky Robinson, 'a very pretty fellow,' Ben Jonson tells us, who was a member of Shakespeare's company, and was known for his exquisite taste in costume, as well as for his love of woman's apparel: Salathiel Pavy, whose early and tragic death Jonson mourned in one of the sweetest threnodies of our literature: Arthur Savile, who was one of 'the players of Prince Charles,' and took a girl's part in a comedy by Marmion: Stephen Hammerton, 'a most noted and beautiful woman actor,' whose pale oval face with its heavy-lidded eyes and somewhat sensuous mouth looks out at us from a curious miniature of the time: Hart, who made his first success by playing the Duchess in the tragedy of *The Cardinal*, and who in a poem that is clearly modelled upon some of Shakespeare's Sonnets is described by one who had seen him as 'beauty to the eye, and music to the ear': and Kynaston, of whom Betterton said that 'it has been disputed among the judicious, whether any woman could have more sensibly touched the passions,' and whose white hands and amber-coloured hair seem to have retarded by some years the introduction of actresses upon our stage.

The Puritans, with their uncouth morals and ignoble minds, had of course railed against them, and dwelt on the impropriety of boys disguising as women, and learning to affect the manners and passions of the female sex. Gosson, with his shrill voice, and Prynne, soon to be made earless for many shameful slanders, and others to whom the rare and subtle sense of abstract beauty was denied, had from pulpit and through pamphlet said foul or foolish things to their dishonour. To Francis Lenton, writing in 1629, what he speaks of as –

> loose action, mimic gesture
> By a poor boy clad in a princely vesture,

is but one of the many –

> tempting baits of hell
> Which draw more youth unto the damned cell
> Of furious lust, than all the devil could do
> Since he obtained his first overthrow.

Deuteronomy was quoted and the ill-digested learning of the period laid under contribution. Even our own time had not appreciated the artistic conditions of the Elizabethan and Jacobean drama. One of the most brilliant and intellectual actresses of this century had laughed at the idea of a lad of seventeen or eighteen playing Imogen, or Miranda, or Rosalind. 'How could any youth, however gifted and specially trained, even faintly suggest these fair and noble women to an audience? . . . One quite pities Shakespeare, who had to put up with seeing his brightest creations marred, misrepresented, and spoiled.' In his book on *Shakespeare's Predecessors* Mr. John Addington Symonds also had talked of 'hobbledehoys' trying to represent the pathos of Desdemona and Juliet's passion. Were they right? Are they right? I did not think so then. I do not think so now. Those who remember the Oxford production of the *Agamemnon*, the fine utterance and marble dignity of the Clytemnestra, the romantic and imaginative rendering of the prophetic madness of Cassandra, will not agree with Lady Martin or Mr. Symonds in their strictures on the condition of the Elizabethan stage.

Of all the motives of dramatic curiosity used by our great playwrights, there is none more subtle or more fascinating than the ambiguity of the sexes. This idea, invented, as far as an artistic idea can be said to be invented, by Lyly, perfected and made exquisite for us by Shakespeare, seems to me to owe its origin, as it certainly owes its possibility of life-like presentation, to the circumstance that the Elizabethan stage, like the stage of the Greeks, admitted the appearance of no female performers. It is because Lyly was writing for the boy-actors of St. Paul's that we have the confused sexes and complicated loves of Phillida and Gallathea: it is because Shakespeare was writing for Willie Hughes that Rosalind dons doublet and hose, and calls herself Ganymede, that Viola and Julia put on pages' dress, that Imogen steals away in male attire. To say that only a woman can portray the passions of a woman, and that therefore no boy can play Rosalind, is to rob the art of acting of all claim to objectivity, and to assign to the mere accident of sex what properly belongs to imaginative insight and creative energy. Indeed, if sex be an element in artistic creation, it might rather be urged that the delightful combination of wit and romance which characterizes so many of Shakespeare's heroines was at least occasioned if it was not actually caused by the fact that the players of these parts were lads and young men, whose passionate purity, quick mobile fancy, and healthy freedom from sentimentality can hardly fail to have suggested a new and delightful type of girlhood or of womanhood. The very difference of sex between the player and the part he represented must also, as Professor Ward points out, have constituted 'one more demand upon the imaginative capacities of the spectators,' and must have kept them from that over-realistic identification of the actor with his *rôle*, which is one of the weak points in modern theatrical criticism.

This, too, must be granted, that it was to these boy-actors that we owe the introduction of those lovely lyrics that star the plays of Shakespeare, Dekker, and so many of the dramatists of the period, those 'snatches of bird-like or god-like song,' as Mr. Swinburne calls them. For it was out of the choirs of the cathedrals and royal chapels of England that most of these lads came, and from their earliest years they had been trained in the singing of anthems and madrigals, and in all that concerns the subtle art of music. Chosen at first for the beauty of their voices, as well as for a certain comeliness and freshness of appearance, they were then instructed in gesture, dancing, and elocution, and taught to play both tragedies and comedies in the English as well as in the Latin language. Indeed, acting seems to have formed part of the ordinary education of the time, and to have been much studied not merely by the scholars of Eton and Westminster, but also by the students at the Universities of Oxford and Cambridge, some of whom went afterwards upon the public stage, as is becoming not uncommon in our own day. The great actors, too, had their pupils and apprentices, who were formally bound over to them by legal warrant, to whom they imparted the secrets of their craft, and who were so much valued that we read of Henslowe, one of the managers of the Rose Theatre, buying a trained boy of the name of James Bristowe for eight pieces of gold. The relations that existed between the masters and their pupils seem to have been of the most cordial and affectionate character. Robin Armin was looked upon by Tarlton as his adopted son, and in a will dated 'the fourth daie of Maie, anno Domini 1605,' Augustine Phillips, Shakespeare's dear friend and fellow-actor, bequeathed to one of his apprentices his 'purple cloke, sword, and dagger,' his 'base viall,' and much rich apparel, and to another a sum of money and many beautiful instruments of music, 'to be delivered unto him at the expiration of his terme of yeres in his indenture of apprenticehood.' Now and then, when some daring actor kidnapped a boy for the stage, there was an outcry or an investigation. In 1600, for instance, a certain Norfolk gentleman of the name of Henry Clifton came to live in London in order that his son, then about thirteen years of age, might have the opportunity of attending the Bluecoat School, and from a petition which he presented to the Star Chamber, and which has been recently brought to light by Mr. Greenstreet, we learn that as the boy was walking quietly to Christ Church cloister one winter morning he was waylaid by James Robinson, Henry Evans, and Nathaniel Giles, and carried off to the Blackfriars Theatre, 'amongste a companie of lewde and dissolute mercenarie players,' as his father calls them, in order that he might be trained 'in acting of parts in base playes and enterludes.' Hearing of his son's misadventure, Mr. Clifton went down at once to the theatre, and demanded his surrender, but 'the sayd Nathaniel Giles, James Robinson and Henry Evans most arrogantlie then and there answered that they had authoritie sufficient soe to take any noble man's sonne in this land,' and handing the young schoolboy 'a scrolle of paper, conteyning parte of one of their said playes and enterludes,' commanded him tolearn it by heart. Through a warrant issued by Sir John Fortescue, however, the boy was restored to his father the next day, and the Court of Star Chamber seems to have suspended or cancelled Evans' privileges.

The fact is that, following a precedent set by Richard III, Elizabeth had issued a commission authorizing certain persons to impress into her service all boys who had beautiful voices that they might sing for her in her Chapel Royal, and Nathaniel Giles, her Chief Commissioner, finding that he could deal profitably with the managers of the Globe Theatre, agreed to supply them with personable and graceful lads for the playing of female parts, under colour of taking them for the Queen's service. The actors, accordingly, had a certain amount of legal warrant on their side, and it is interesting to note that many of the boys whom they carried off from their schools or homes, such as Salathiel Pavy, Nat. Field, and Alvery Trussell, became so fascinated by their new art that they attached themselves permanently to the theatre, and would not leave it.

Once it seemed as if girls were to take the place of boys upon the stage, and among the christenings chronicled in the registers of St. Giles', Cripplegate, occurs the following strange and suggestive entry: 'Comedia, base-born, daughter of Alice Bowker and William Johnson, one of the Queen's plaiers, 10 Feb. 1589.' But the child upon whom such high hopes had been built died at six years of age, and when, later on, some French actresses came over and played at Blackfriars, we learn that they were 'hissed, hooted, and pippin-pelted from the stage.' I think that, from what I have said above, we need not regret this in any way. The essentially male culture of the English Renaissance found its fullest and most perfect expression by its own method, and in its own manner.

I remember I used to wonder, at this time, what had been the social position and early life of Willie Hughes before Shakespeare had met with him. My investigations into the history of the boy-actors had made me curious of every detail about him. Had he stood in the carved stall of some gilded choir, reading out of a great book painted with square scarlet notes and long black key-lines? We know from the Sonnets how clear and pure his voice was, and what skill he had in the art of music. Noble gentlemen, such as the Earl of Leicester and Lord Oxford, had companies of boy-players in their service as part of their household. When Leicester went to the Netherlands in 1558 he brought with him a certain 'Will' described as a 'plaier.' Was this Willie

Hughes? Had he acted for Leicester at Kenilworth, and was it there that Shakespeare had first known him? Or was he, like Robin Armin, simply a lad of low degree, but possessing some strange beauty and marvellous fascination? It was evident from the early sonnets that when Shakespeare first came across him he had no connection whatsoever with the stage, and that he was not of high birth has already been shown. I began to think of him not as the delicate chorister of a Royal Chapel, not as a petted minion trained to sing and dance in Leicester's stately masque, but as some fair-haired English lad whom in one of London's hurrying streets, or on Windsor's green silent meadows, Shakespeare had seen and followed, recognizing the artistic possibilities that lay hidden in so comely and gracious a form, and divining by a quick and subtle instinct what an actor the lad would make could he be induced to go upon the stage. At this time Willie Hughes' father was dead, as we learn from Sonnet XIII, and his mother, whose remarkable beauty he is said to have inherited, may have been induced to allow him to become Shakespeare's apprentice by the fact that boys who played female characters were paid extremely large salaries, larger salaries, indeed, than were given to grown-up actors. Shakespeare's apprentice, at any rate, we know that he became, and we know what a vital factor he was in the development of Shakespeare's art. As a rule, a boy-actor's capacity for representing girlish parts on the stage lasted but for a few years at most. Such characters as Lady Macbeth, Queen Constance and Volumnia, remained of course always within the reach of those who had true dramatic genius and noble presence. Absolute youth was not necessary here, not desirable even. But with Imogen, and Perdita, and Juliet, it was different. 'Your beard has begun to grow, and I pray God your voice be not cracked,' says Hamlet mockingly to the boy-actor of the strolling company that came to visit him at Elsinore; and certainly when chins grew rough and voices harsh much of the charm and grace of the performance must have gone. Hence comes Shakespeare's passionate preoccupation with the youth of Willie Hughes, his terror of old age and wasting years, his wild appeal to time to spare the beauty of his friend:

> Make glad and sorry seasons as thou fleet'st,
> And do whate'er thou wilt, swift-footed time,
> To the wide world and all her fading sweets;
> But I forbid thee one most heinous crime:
> O carve not with thy hours my Love's fair brow
> Nor draw no lines there with thine antique pen;
> Him in thy course untainted do allow
> For beauty's pattern to succeeding men.

Time seems to have listened to Shakespeare's prayers, or perhaps Willie Hughes had the secret of perpetual youth. After three years he is quite unchanged:

> To me, fair friend, you never can be old,
> For as you were when first your eye I eyed,
> Such seems your beauty still. Three winters' cold
> Have from the forests shook three summers' pride,
> Three beauteous springs to yellow autumn turned,
> In process of the seasons have I seen,
> Three April perfumes in three hot Junes burned,
> Since first I saw you fresh which yet are green.

More years pass over, and the bloom of his boyhood seems to be still with him. When, in *The Tempest*, Shakespeare, through the lips of Prospero, flung away the wand of his imagination and gave his poetic sovereignty into the weak, graceful hands of Fletcher, it may be that the Miranda who stood wondering by was none other than Willie Hughes himself, and in the last sonnet that his friend addressed to him, the enemy that is feared is not Time but Death.

> O thou, my lovely boy, who in thy power
> Dost hold time's fickle glass, his sickle hour;
> Who hast by waning grown, and therein show'st
> Thy lovers withering as thy sweet self grow'st;
> If Nature, sovereign mistress over wrack,
> As thou goest onwards, still will pluck thee back,
> She keeps thee to this purpose, that her skill
> May Time disgrace and wretched minutes kill.
> Yet fear her, O thou minion of her pleasure!
> She may detain, but not still keep, her treasure.
> Her audit, though delay'd answer'd must be,
> And her quietus is to render thee.

IV

It was not for some weeks after I had begun my study of the subject that I ventured to approach the curious group of Sonnets (CXXVII–CLII) that deal with the dark woman who, like a shadow or thing of evil omen, came across Shakespeare's great romance, and for a season stood between him and Willie Hughes. They were obviously printed out of their proper place and should have been inserted between Sonnets XXXIII and XL. Psychological and artistic reasons necessitated this change, a change which I hope will be adopted by all future editors, as without it an entirely false impression is conveyed of the nature and final issue of this noble friendship.

Who was she, this black-browed, olive-skinned woman, with her amorous mouth 'that Love's own hand did make,' her 'cruel eye,' and her 'foul pride,' her strange skill on the virginals and her false, fascinating nature? An over-curious scholar of our day had seen in her a symbol of the Catholic Church, of that Bride of Christ who is 'black but comely.' Professor Minto, following in the footsteps of Henry Brown, had regarded the whole group of Sonnets as simply 'exercises of skill undertaken in a spirit of wanton defiance and derision of the commonplace.' Mr. Gerald Massey, without any historical proof or probability, had insisted that they were addressed to the celebrated Lady Rich, the Stella of Sir Philip Sidney's sonnets, the Philoclea of his 'Arcadia,' and that they contained no personal revelation of Shakespeare's life and love, having been written in Lord Pembroke's name and at his request. Mr. Tyler had suggested that they referred to one of Queen Elizabeth's maids-of-honour, by name Mary Fitton. But none of these explanations satisfied the conditions of the problem. The woman that came between Shakespeare and Willie Hughes was a real woman, black-haired, and married, and of evil repute. Lady Rich's fame was evil enough, it is true, but her hair was of –

> fine threads of finest gold,
> In curled knots man's thought to hold,

and her shoulders like 'white doves perching.' She was, as King James said to her lover, Lord Mountjoy, 'a fair woman with a black soul.' As for Mary Fitton, we know that she was unmarried in 1601, the time when her amour with Lord Pembroke was discovered, and besides, any theories that connected Lord Pembroke with the Sonnets were, as Cyril Graham had shown, put entirely out of court by the fact that Lord Pembroke did not come to London till they had been actually written and read by Shakespeare to his friends.

It was not, however, her name that interested me. I was content to hold with Professor Dowden that 'To the eyes of no diver among the wrecks of time will that curious talisman gleam.' What I wanted to discover was the nature of her influence over Shakespeare, as well as the characteristics of her personality. Two things were certain: she was much older than the poet, and the fascination that she exercised over him was at first purely intellectual. He began by feeling no physical passion for her. 'I do not love thee with mine eyes,' he says:

> Nor are mine ears with thy tongue's tune delighted;
> Nor tender feeling to base touches prone,

Nor taste, nor smell, desire to be invited
To any sensual feast with thee alone.

He did not even think her beautiful:

My mistress' eyes are nothing like the sun;
Coral is far more red than her lips' red:
If snow be white, why then her breasts are dun;
If hairs be wires, black wires grow on her head.

He has his moments of loathing for her, for, not content with enslaving
the soul of Shakespeare, she seems to have sought to snare the senses of
Willie Hughes. Then Shakespeare cries aloud, –

Two loves I have of comfort and despair,
Which like two spirits do suggest me still:
The better angel is a man right fair,
The worser spirit a woman colour'd ill.
To win me soon to hell, my female evil
Tempteth my better angel from my side,
And would corrupt my saint to be a devil,
Wooing his purity with her foul pride.

Then he sees her as she really is, the 'bay where all men ride,' the
'wide world's common place,' the woman who is in the 'very refuse' of
her evil deeds, and who is 'as black as hell, as dark as night.' Then it is
that he pens that great sonnet upon Lust ('Th' expense of spirit in a
waste of shame'), of which Mr. Theodore Watts says rightly that it is
the greatest sonnet ever written. And it is then, also, that he offers to
mortgage his very life and genius to her if she will but restore to him
that 'sweetest friend' of whom she had robbed him.

    To compass this end he abandons himself to her, feigns to be full
of an absorbing and sensuous passion of possession, forges false words
of love, lies to her, and tells her that he lies.

My thoughts and my discourse as madmen's are,
At random from the truth vainly express'd;
For I have sworn thee fair, and thought thee bright,
Who art as black as hell, as dark as night.

Rather than suffer his friend to be treacherous to him, he will himself be
treacherous to his friend. To shield his purity, he will himself be vile.
He knew the weakness of the boy-actor's nature, his susceptibility to
praise, his inordinate love of admiration, and deliberately set himself
to fascinate the woman who had come between them.

    It is never with impunity that one's lips say Love's Litany. Words have their mystical power over the soul, and form can create the feeling from which it should have sprung. Sincerity itself, the ardent, momentary sincerity of the artist, is often the unconscious result of style, and in the case of those rare temperaments that are exquisitely susceptible to the influences of language, the use of certain phrases and modes of expression can stir the very pulse of passion, can send the red blood coursing through the veins, and can transform into a strange sensuous energy what in its origin had been mere aesthetic impulse, and desire of art. So, at least, it seems to have been with Shakespeare. He begins by pretending to love, wears a lover's apparel and has a lover's words upon his lips. What does it matter? It is only acting, only a comedy in real life. Suddenly he finds that what his tongue had spoken his soul had listened to, and that the raiment that he had put on for disguise is a plague-stricken and poisonous thing that eats into his flesh, and that he cannot throw away. Then comes Desire, with its many maladies, and Lust that makes one love all that one loathes, and Shame, with its ashen face and secret smile. He is enthralled by this dark woman, is for a season separated from his friend, and becomes the 'vassal-wretch' of one whom he knows to be evil and perverse and unworthy of his love, as of the love of Willie Hughes. 'O, from what power,' he says –

> hast thou this powerful might,
> With insufficiency my heart to sway?
> To make me give the lie to my true sight,
> And swear that brightness does not grace the day?
> Whence hast thou this becoming of things ill,
> That in the very refuse of thy deeds
> There is such strength and warrantise of skill
> That, in my mind, thy worst all best exceeds?

He is keenly conscious of his own degradation, and finally, realizing that his genius is nothing to her compared to the physical beauty of the young actor, he cuts with a quick knife the bond that binds him to her, and in this bitter sonnet bids her farewell:

> In loving thee thou know'st I am forsworn,
> But thou art twice forsworn, to me love swearing;
> In act thy bed-vow broke, and new faith torn,
> In vowing new hate after new love bearing.
> But why of two oaths' breach do I accuse thee,
> When I break twenty? I am perjur'd most;
> For all my vows are oaths but to misuse thee,
> And all my honest faith in thee is lost:
> For I have sworn deep oaths of thy deep kindness,

Oaths of thy love, thy truth, thy constancy;
And, to enlighten thee, gave eyes to blindness,
Or made them swear against the thing they see;
For I have sworn thee fair; more perjur'd I,
To swear against the truth so foul a lie!

His attitude towards Willie Hughes in the whole matter shows at once the fervour and the self-abnegation of the great love he bore him. There is a poignant touch of pathos in the close of this sonnet:

Those pretty wrongs that liberty commits,
When I am sometime absent from thy heart,
Thy beauty and thy years full well befits,
For still temptation follows where thou art.
Gentle thou art, and therefore to be won,
Beauteous thou art, therefore to be assailed;
And when a woman woos, what woman's son
Will sourly leave her till she have prevailed?
Ay me! but yet thou mightst my seat forbear,
And chide thy beauty and thy straying youth,
Who lead thee in their riot even there
Where thou art forc'd to break a two-fold truth, –
Hers, by thy beauty tempting her to thee,
Thine, by thy beauty being false to me.

But here he makes it manifest that his forgiveness was full and complete:

No more be griev'd at that which thou hast done:
Roses have thorns, and silver fountains mud;
Clouds and eclipses stain both moon and sun,
And loathsome canker lives in sweetest bud.
All men make faults, and even I in this,
Authorizing thy trespass with compare,
Myself corrupting, salving thy amiss,
Excusing thy sins more than thy sins are;
For to thy sensual fault I bring in sense, –
Thy adverse party is thy advocate, –
And 'gainst myself a lawful plea commence:
Such civil war is in my love and hate,
That I an accessary needs must be
To that sweet thief which sourly robs from me.

Shortly afterwards Shakespeare left London for Stratford (Sonnets XLIII–LII), and when he returned Willie Hughes seems to have grown tired of the woman who for a little time had fascinated him. Her name is never mentioned again in the Sonnets, nor is there any allusion made to her. She had passed out of their lives.

But who was she? And, even if her name has not come down to us, were there any allusions to her in contemporary literature? It seems to me that although better educated than most of the women of her time, she was not nobly born, but was probably the profligate wife of some old and wealthy citizen. We know that women of this class, which was then first rising into social prominence, were strangely fascinated by the new art of stage playing. They were to be found almost every afternoon at the theatre, when dramatic performances were being given, and *The Actors' Remonstrance* is eloquent on the subject of their amours with the young actors.

Cranley in his *Amanda* tells us of one who loved to mimic the actor's disguises, appearing one day 'embroidered, laced, perfumed, in glittering show . . . as brave as any Countess,' and the next day, 'all in mourning, black and sad,' now in the grey cloak of a country wench, and now 'in the neat habit of a citizen.' She was a curious woman, 'more changeable and wavering than the moon,' and the books that she loved to read were Shakespeare's *Venus and Adonis*, Beaumont's *Salmacis and Hermaphroditus*, amorous pamphlets, and 'songs of love and sonnets exquisite.' These sonnets, that were to her the 'bookes of her devotion,' were surely none other but Shakespeare's own, for the whole description reads like the portrait of the woman who fell in love with Willie Hughes, and, lest we should have any doubt on the subject, Cranley, borrowing Shakespeare's play on words, tells us that, in her 'proteus-like strange shapes,' she is one who –

Changes hews with the chameleon.

Manningham's Table-book, also, contains a clear allusion to the same story. Manningham was a student at the Middle Temple with Sir Thomas Overbury and Edmund Curle, whose chambers he seems to have shared; and his Diary is still preserved among the Harleian MSS. at the British Museum, a small duodecimo book written in a fair and tolerably legible hand, and containing many unpublished anecdotes about Shakespeare, Sir Walter Raleigh, Spenser, Ben Jonson and others. The dates, which are inserted with much care, extend from January 1600–1 to April 1603, and under the heading 'March 13, 1601,' Manningham tells us that he heard from a member of Shakespeare's company that a certain citizen's wife being at the Globe Theatre one afternoon, fell in love with one of the actors, and 'grew so farre in liking with him, that before shee went from the play shee appointed him to come that night unto hir,' but that Shakespeare 'overhearing their conclusion' anticipated his friend and came first to the lady's house, 'went before and was entertained,' as Manningham puts it, with some added looseness of speech which it is unnecessary to quote.

It seemed to me that we had here a common and distorted version of the story that is revealed to us in the Sonnets, the story of the dark woman's love for Willie Hughes, and Shakespeare's mad attempt to make her love him in his friend's stead. It was not, of course, necessary to accept it as absolutely true in every detail. According to Manningham's informant, for instance, the name of the actor in question was not Willie Hughes, but Richard Burbage. Tavern gossip, however, is proverbially inaccurate, and Burbage was, no doubt, dragged into the story to give point to the foolish jest about William the Conqueror and Richard the Third, with which the entry in Manningham's Diary ends. Burbage was our first great tragic actor, but it needed all his genius to counterbalance the physical defects of low stature and corpulent figure under which he laboured, and he was not the sort of man who would have fascinated the dark woman of the Sonnets, or would have cared to be fascinated by her. There was no doubt that Willie Hughes was referred to, and the private diary of a young law student of the time thus curiously corroborated Cyril Graham's wonderful guess at the secret of Shakespeare's great romance. Indeed, when taken in conjunction with *Amanda*, Manningham's Table-book seemed to me to be an extremely strong link in the chain of evidence, and to place the new interpretation of the Sonnets on something like a secure historic basis, the fact that Cranley's poem was not published till after Shakespeare's death being really rather in favour of this view, as it was not likely that he would have ventured during the lifetime of the great dramatist to revive the memory of this tragic and bitter story.

This passion for the dark lady also enabled me to fix with still greater certainty the date of the Sonnets. From internal evidence, from the characteristics of language, style, and the like, it was evident that they belonged to Shakespeare's early period, the period of *Love's Labour's Lost* and *Venus and Adonis*. With the play, indeed, they are intimately connected. They display the same delicate euphuism, the same delight in fanciful phrase and curious expression, the artistic wilfulness and studied graces of the same 'fair tongue, conceit's expositor.' Rosaline, the –

> whitely wanton with a velvet brow,
> With two pitch-balls stuck in her face for eyes,

who is born 'to make black fair,' and whose 'favour turns the fashion of the days,' is the dark lady of the Sonnets who makes black 'beauty's successive heir'. In the comedy as well as in the poems we have that half-sensuous philosophy that exalts the judgement of the senses 'above all slower, more toilsome means of knowledge,' and Berowne is perhaps, as Mr. Pater suggests, a reflex of Shakespeare himself 'when he has just become able to stand aside from and estimate the first period of his poetry.'

Now though *Love's Labour's Lost* was not published till 1598, when it was brought out 'newlie corrected and augmented' by Cuthbert Burby, there is no doubt that it was written and produced on the stage at a much earlier date, probably, as Professor Dowden points out, in 1588–9. If this be so, it is clear that Shakespeare's first meeting with Willie Hughes must have been in 1585, and it is just possible that this young actor may, after all, have been in his boyhood the musician of Lord Essex.

It is clear, at any rate, that Shakespeare's love for the dark lady must have passed away before 1594. In this year there appeared, under the editorship of Hadrian Dorell, that fascinating poem, or series of poems, *Willobie his Avisa*, which is described by Mr. Swinburne as the one contemporary book which has been supposed to throw any direct or indirect light on the mystic matter of the Sonnets. In it we learn how a young gentleman of St. John's College, Oxford, by name Henry Willobie, fell in love with a woman so 'fair and chaste' that he called her Avisa, either because such beauty as hers had never been seen, or because she fled like a bird from the snare of his passion, and spread her wings for flight when he ventured but to touch her hand. Anxious to win his mistress he consults his familiar friend W.S., 'who not long before had tried the curtesy of the like passion, and was now newly recovered of the like infection.' Shakespeare encourages him in the siege that he is laying to the Castle of Beauty, telling him that every woman is to be wooed, and every woman to be won; views this 'loving comedy' from far off, in order to see 'whether it would sort to a happier end for this new actor than it did for the old player,' and 'enlargeth the wound with the sharpe razor of a willing conceit,' feeling the purely aesthetic interest of the artist in the moods and emotions of others. It is unnecessary, however, to enter more fully into this curious passage in Shakespeare's life, as all that I wanted to point out was that in 1594 he had been cured of his infatuation for the dark lady, and had already been acquainted for at least three years with Willie Hughes.

My whole scheme of the Sonnets was now complete, and, by placing those that refer to the dark lady in their proper order and position, I saw the perfect unity and completeness of the whole. The drama – for indeed they formed a drama and a soul's tragedy of fiery passion and of noble thought – is divided into four scenes or acts. In the first of these (Sonnets I–XXXII) Shakespeare invites Willie Hughes to go upon the stage as an actor, and to put to the service of Art his

SH–D2

wonderful physical beauty, and his exquisite grace of youth, before passion has robbed him of the one, and time taken from him the other. Willie Hughes, after a time, consents to be a player in Shakespeare's company, and soon becomes the very centre and keynote of his inspiration. Suddenly, in one red-rose July (Sonnets XXXIII–LII, LXI, and CXXVII–CLII) there comes to the Globe Theatre a dark woman with wonderful eyes, who falls passionately in love with Willie Hughes. Shakespeare, sick with the malady of jealousy, and made mad by many doubts and fears, tries to fascinate the woman who had come between him and his friend. The love, that is at first feigned, becomes real, and he finds himself enthralled and dominated by a woman whom he knows to be evil and unworthy. To her the genius of a man is as nothing compared to a boy's beauty. Willie Hughes becomes for a time her slave and the toy of her fancy, and the second act ends with Shakespeare's departure from London. In the third act her influence has passed away. Shakespeare returns to London, and renews his friendship with Willie Hughes, to whom he promises immortality in his plays. Marlowe, hearing of the wonder and grace of the young actor, lures him away from the Globe Theatre to play Gaveston in the tragedy of *Edward II*, and for the second time Shakespeare is separated from his friend. The last act (Sonnets C–CXXVI) tells us of the return of Willie Hughes to Shakespeare's company. Evil rumour had now stained the white purity of his name, but Shakespeare's love still endures and is perfect. Of the mystery of this love, and of the mystery of passion, we are told strange and marvellous things, and the Sonnets conclude with an envoi of twelve lines, whose motive is the triumph of Beauty over Time, and of Death over Beauty.

And what had been the end of him who had been so dear to the soul of Shakespeare, and who by his presence and passion had given reality to Shakespeare's art? When the Civil War broke out, the English actors took the side of their king, and many of them, like Robinson foully slain by Major Harrison at the taking of Basing House, laid down their lives in the king's service. Perhaps on the trampled heath of Marston, or on the bleak hills of Naseby, the dead body of Willie Hughes had been found by some of the rough peasants of the district, his gold hair 'dabbled with blood,' and his breast pierced with many wounds. Or it may be that the Plague, which was very frequent in London at the beginning of the seventeenth century, and was indeed regarded by many of the Christians as a judgement sent on the city for its love of 'vaine plaies and idolatrous shewes,' had touched the lad while he was acting, and he had crept home to his lodging to die there alone, Shakespeare being far away at Stratford, and those who had flocked in such numbers to see him, the 'gazers' whom, as the Sonnets tell us, he had 'led astray,' being too much afraid of contagion to come near him. A story of this kind was current at the time about a young actor, and was made much use of by the Puritans in their attempts to stifle the free development of the English Renaissance. Yet, surely, had this actor been Willie Hughes, tidings of his tragic death would have been speedily brought to Shakespeare as he lay dreaming under the mulberry tree in his garden at New Place, and in an elegy as sweet as that written by Milton on Edward King, he would have mourned for the lad who had brought such joy and sorrow into his life, and whose connection with his art had been of so vital and intimate a character. Something made me feel certain that Willie Hughes had survived Shakespeare, and had fulfilled in some measure the high prophecies the poet had made about him, and one evening the true secret of his end flashed across me.

He had been one of those English actors who in 1611, the year of Shakespeare's retirement from the stage, went across sea to Germany and played before the great Duke Henry Julius of Brunswick, himself a dramatist of no mean order, and at the Court of that strange Elector of Brandenburg, who was so enamoured of beauty that he was said to have bought for his weight in amber the young son of a travelling Greek merchant, and to have given pageants in honour of his slave all through that dreadful famine year of 1606–7, when the people died of hunger in the very streets of the town, and for the space of seven months there was no rain. The Library at Cassel contains to the present day a copy of the first edition of Marlowe's *Edward II*, the only copy in existence, Mr. Bullen tells us. Who could have brought it to that town, but he who had created the part of the king's minion, and for whom indeed it had been written? Those stained and yellow pages had once been touched by his white hands. We also know that *Romeo and Juliet*, a play specially connected with Willie Hughes, was brought out at Dresden in 1613, along with *Hamlet* and *King Lear*, and certain of Marlowe's plays, and it was surely to none other than Willie Hughes himself that in 1617 the death-mask of Shakespeare was brought by one of the suite of the English ambassador, pale token of the passing away of the great poet who had so dearly loved him. Indeed there was something peculiarly fitting in the idea that the boy-actor, whose beauty had been so vital an element in the realism and romance of Shakespeare's art, had been the first to have brought to Germany the seed of the new culture, and was in his way the precursor of the *Aufklärung* or Illumination of the eighteenth century, that splendid movement which, though begun by Lessing and Herder, and brought to its full and perfect issue by Goethe, was in no small part helped on by a young actor – Friedrich Schroeder – who awoke the popular consciousness, and by means of the feigned passions and mimetic methods of the stage showed the intimate, the vital, connection between life and literature. If this was so, – and there was certainly no evidence against it, – it was not improbable that Willie Hughes was one of those English comedians (*mimi quidam ex Britannia*, as the old chronicle calls them), who were slain at Nuremberg in a sudden uprising of the people, and were secretly buried in a little vineyard outside the city by some young men 'who had found pleasure in their performances, and of whom some had sought to be instructed in the mysteries of the new art.' Certainly no more fitting place could there be for him to whom Shakespeare said 'thou art all my art,' than this little vineyard outside the city walls. For was it not from the sorrows of Dionysos that Tragedy sprang? Was not the light laughter of Comedy, with its careless merriment and quick replies, first heard on the lips of the Sicilian vine-dressers? Nay, did not the purple and red stain of the wine-froth on face and limbs give the first suggestion of the charm and fascination of disguise? – the desire for self-concealment, the sense of the value of objectivity, thus showing itself in the rude beginnings of the art. At any rate, wherever he lay – whether in the little vineyard at the gate of the Gothic town, or in some dim London churchyard amidst the roar and bustle of our great city – no gorgeous monument marked his resting place. His true tomb, as Shakespeare saw, was the poet's verse, his true monument the permanence of the drama. So had it been with others whose beauty had given a new creative impulse to their age. The ivory body of the Bithynian slave rots in the green ooze of the Nile, and on the yellow hills of the Cerameicus is strewn the dust of the young Athenian; but Antinous lives in sculpture, and Charmides in philosophy.

V

A young Elizabethan, who was enamoured of a girl so white that he named her Alba, has left on record the impression produced on him by one of the first performances of *Love's Labour's Lost*. Admirable though the actors were, and they played 'in cunning wise,' he tells us, especially those who took the lovers' parts, he was conscious that everything was 'feigned,' that nothing came 'from the heart,' that though they appeared to grieve they 'felt no care,' and were merely presenting 'a show in jest.' Yet, suddenly, this fanciful comedy of unreal romance became to him, as he sat in the audience, the real tragedy of his life. The moods of his own soul seemed to have taken shape and substance, and to be moving before him. His grief had a mask that smiled, and his sorrow wore gay raiment. Behind the bright and quickly-changing pageant of the stage, he saw himself, as one sees one's image in a fantastic glass. The very words that came to the actors' lips were wrung out of his pain. Their false tears were of his shedding.

There are few of us who have not felt something akin to this. We become lovers when we see *Romeo and Juliet*, and *Hamlet* makes us students. The blood of Duncan is upon our hands, with Timon we rage against the world, and when Lear wanders out upon the heath the terror of madness touches us. Ours is the white sinlessness of Desdemona, and ours, also, the sin of Iago. Art, even the art of fullest scope and widest vision, can never really show us the external world. All that it shows us is our own soul, the one world of which we have any real cognizance. And the soul itself, the soul of each one of us, is to each one of us a mystery. It hides in the dark and broods, and consciousness cannot tell us of its workings. Consciousness, indeed, is quite inadequate to explain the contents of personality. It is Art, and Art only, that reveals us to ourselves.

We sit at the play with the woman we love, or listen to the music in some Oxford garden, or stroll with our friend through the cool galleries of the Pope's house at Rome, and suddenly we become aware that we have passions of which we have never dreamed, thoughts that make us afraid, pleasures whose secret has been denied to us, sorrows that have been hidden from our tears. The actor is unconscious of our presence: the musician is thinking of the subtlety of the fugue, of the tone of his instrument; the marble gods that smile so curiously at us are made of insensate stone. But they have given form and substance to what was within us; they have enabled us to realize our personality; and a sense of perilous joy, or some touch or thrill of pain, or that strange self-pity that man so often feels for himself, comes over us and leaves us different.

Some such impression the Sonnets of Shakespeare had certainly produced on me. As from opal dawns to sunsets of withered rose I read and re-read them in garden or chamber, it seemed to me that I was deciphering the story of a life that had once been mine, unrolling the record of a romance that, without my knowing it, had coloured the very texture of my nature, had dyed it with strange and subtle dyes. Art, as so often happens, had taken the place of personal experience. I felt as if I had been initiated into the secret of that passionate friendship, that love of beauty and beauty of love, of which Marsilio Ficino tells us, and of which the Sonnets, in their noblest and purest significance, may be held to be the perfect expression.

Yes: I had lived it all. I had stood in the round theatre with its open roof and fluttering banners, had seen the stage draped with black for a tragedy, or set with gay garlands for some brighter show. The young gallants came out with their pages, and took their seats in front of the tawny curtain that hung from the satyr-carved pillars of the inner scene. They were insolent and debonair in their fantastic dresses. Some of them wore French love-locks, and white doublets stiff with Italian embroidery of gold thread, and long hose of blue or pale yellow silk. Others were all in black, and carried huge plumed hats. These affected the Spanish fashion. As they played at cards, and blew thin wreaths of smoke from the tiny pipes that the pages lit for them, the truant prentices and idle schoolboys that thronged the yard mocked them. But they only smiled at each other. In the side boxes some masked women were sitting. One of them was waiting with hungry eyes and bitten lips for the drawing back of the curtain. As the trumpet sounded for the third time she leant forward, and I saw her olive skin and raven's-wing hair. I knew her. She had marred for a season the great friendship of my life. Yet there was something about her that fascinated me.

The play changed according to my mood. Sometimes it was *Hamlet*. Taylor acted the Prince, and there were many who wept when Ophelia went mad. Sometimes it was *Romeo and Juliet*. Burbage was Romeo. He hardly looked the part of the young Italian, but there was a rich music in his voice, and passionate beauty in every gesture. I saw *As You Like It*, and *Cymbeline*, and *Twelfth Night*, and in each play there was someone whose life was bound up into mine, who realized for me every dream, and gave shape to every fancy. How gracefully he moved! The eyes of the audience were fixed on him.

And yet it was in this century that it had all happened. I had never seen my friend, but he had been with me for many years, and it was to his influence that I had owed my passion for Greek thought and art, and indeed all my sympathy with the Hellenic spirit. Φιλοσοφεῖν μετ᾽ ἐρῶτος! How that phrase had stirred me in my Oxford days! I did not understand then why it was so. But I knew now. There had been a presence beside me always. Its silver feet had trod night's shadowy meadows, and the white hands had moved aside the trembling curtains of the dawn. It had walked with me through the grey cloisters, and when I sat reading in my room, it was there also. What though I had been unconscious of it? The soul had a life of its own, and the brain its own sphere of action. There was something within us that knew nothing of sequence or extension, and yet, like the philosopher of the Ideal City, was the spectator of all time and of all existence. It had senses that quickened, passions that came to birth, spiritual ecstasies of contemplation, ardours of fiery-coloured love. It was we who were unreal, and our conscious life was the least important part of our development. The soul, the secret soul, was the only reality.

How curiously it had all been revealed to me! A book of sonnets, published nearly three hundred years ago, written by a dead hand and in honour of a dead youth, had suddenly explained to me the whole story of my soul's romance. I remembered how once in Egypt I had been present at the opening of a frescoed coffin that had been found in one of the basalt tombs at Thebes. Inside there was the body of a young girl swathed in tight bands of linen, and with a gilt mask over the face. As I stooped down to look at it, I had seen that one of the little withered hands held a scroll of yellow papyrus covered with strange characters. How I wished now that I had had it read to me! It might have told me something more about the soul that hid within me, and had its mysteries of passion of which I was kept in ignorance. Strange, that we knew so little about ourselves, and that our most intimate personality was concealed from us! Were we to look in tombs for our real life, and in art for the legend of our days?

Week after week, I pored over these poems, and each new form of knowledge seemed to me a mode of reminiscence. Finally, after two months had elapsed, I determined to make a strong appeal to Erskine to do justice to the memory of Cyril Graham, and to give to the world his marvellous interpretation of the Sonnets – the only interpretation that thoroughly explained the problem. I have not any copy of my letter, I regret to say, nor have I been able to lay my hand upon the original; but I remember that I went over the whole ground, and covered sheets of paper with passionate reiteration of the arguments and proofs that my study had suggested to me.

It seemed to me that I was not merely restoring Cyril Graham to his proper place in literary history, but rescuing the honour of Shakespeare himself from the tedious memory of a commonplace intrigue. I put into the letter all my enthusiasm. I put into the letter all my faith.

No sooner, in fact, had I sent it off than a curious reaction came over me. It seemed to me that I had given away my capacity for belief in the Willie Hughes theory of the Sonnets, that something had gone out of me, as it were, and that I was perfectly indifferent to the whole subject. What was it that had happened? It is difficult to say. Perhaps, by finding perfect expression for a passion, I had exhausted the passion itself. Emotional forces, like the forces of physical life, have their positive limitations. Perhaps the mere effort to convert anyone to a theory involves some form of renunciation of the power of credence. Influence is simply a transference of personality, a mode of giving away what is most precious to one's self, and its exercise produces a sense, and, it may be, a reality of loss. Every disciple takes away something from his master. Or perhaps I had become tired of the whole thing, wearied of its fascination, and, my enthusiasm having burnt out, my reason was left to its own unimpassioned judgement. However it came about, and I cannot pretend to explain it, there was no doubt that Willie Hughes suddenly became to me a mere myth, an idle dream, the boyish fancy of a young man who, like most ardent spirits, was more anxious to convince others than to be himself convinced.

I must admit that this was a bitter disappointment to me. I had gone through every phase of this great romance. I had lived with it, and it had become part of my nature. How was it that it had left me? Had I touched upon some secret that my soul desired to conceal? Or was there no permanence in personality? Did things come and go through the brain, silently, swiftly, and without footprints, like shadows through a mirror? Were we at the mercy of such impressions as Art or Life chose to give us? It seemed to me to be so.

It was at night-time that this feeling first came to me. I had sent my servant out to post the letter to Erskine, and was seated at the window looking out at the blue and gold city. The moon had not yet risen, and there was only one star in the sky, but the streets were full of quickly-moving and flashing lights, and the windows of Devonshire House were illuminated for a great dinner to be given to some of the foreign princes then visiting London. I saw the scarlet liveries of the royal carriages, and the crowd hustling about the sombre gates of the courtyard.

Suddenly, I said to myself: 'I have been dreaming, and all my life for these two months has been unreal. There was no such person as Willie Hughes.' Something like a faint cry of pain came to my lips as I began to realize how I had deceived myself, and I buried my face in my hands, struck with a sorrow greater than any I had felt since boyhood. After a few moments I rose, and going into the library took up the Sonnets, and began to read them. But it was all to no avail. They gave me back nothing of the feeling that I had brought to them; they revealed to me nothing of what I had found hidden in their lines. Had I merely been influenced by the beauty of the forged portrait, charmed by that Shelley-like face into faith and credence? Or, as Erskine had suggested, was it the pathetic tragedy of Cyril Graham's death that had so deeply stirred me? I could not tell. To the present day I cannot understand the beginning or the end of this strange passage in my life.

However, as I had said some very unjust and bitter things to Erskine in my letter, I determined to go and see him as soon as possible, and make my apologies to him for my behaviour. Accordingly, the next morning I drove down to Birdcage Walk, where I found him sitting in his library, with the forged picture of Willie Hughes in front of him.

'My dear Erskine!' I cried, 'I have come to apologize to you.'

'To apologize to me?' he said. 'What for?'

'For my letter,' I answered.

'You have nothing to regret in your letter,' he said. 'On the contrary, you have done me the greatest service in your power. You have shown me that Cyril Graham's theory is perfectly sound.'

I stared at him in blank wonder.

'You don't mean to say that you believe in Willie Hughes?' I exclaimed.

'Why not?' he rejoined. 'You have proved the thing to me. Do you think I cannot estimate the value of evidence?'

'But there is no evidence at all,' I groaned, sinking into a chair. 'When I wrote to you I was under the influence of a perfectly silly enthusiasm. I had been touched by the story of Cyril Graham's death, fascinated by his artistic theory, enthralled by the wonder and novelty of the whole idea. I see now that the theory is based on a delusion. The only evidence for the existence of Willie Hughes is that picture in front of you, and that picture is a forgery. Don't be carried away by mere sentiment in this matter. Whatever romance may have to say about the Willie Hughes theory, reason is dead against it.'

'I don't understand you,' said Erskine, looking at me in amazement. 'You have convinced me by your letter that Willie Hughes is an absolute reality. Why have you changed your mind? Or is all that you have been saying to me merely a joke?'

'I cannot explain it to you,' I rejoined, 'but I see now that there is really nothing to be said in favour of Cyril Graham's interpretation. The Sonnets may not be addressed to Lord Pembroke. They probably are not. But for heaven's sake don't waste your time in a foolish attempt to discover a young Elizabethan actor who never existed, and to make a phantom puppet the centre of the great cycle of Shakespeare's Sonnets.'

'I see that you don't understand the theory,' he replied.

'My dear Erskine,' I cried, 'not understand it! Why, I feel as if I had invented it. Surely my letter shows you that I not merely went into the whole matter, but that I contributed proofs of every kind. The one flaw in the theory is that it presupposes the existence of the person whose existence is the subject of dispute. If we grant that there was in Shakespeare's company a young actor of the name of Willie Hughes, it is not difficult to make him the object of the Sonnets. But as we know that there was no actor of this name in the company of the Globe Theatre, it is idle to pursue the investigation further.'

'But that is exactly what we don't know,' said Erskine. 'It is quite true that his name does not occur in the list given in the first folio; but, as Cyril pointed out, that is rather a proof in favour of the existence of Willie Hughes than against it, if we remember his treacherous desertion of Shakespeare for a rival dramatist. Besides,' and here I must admit that Erskine made what seems to me now a rather good point, though, at the time, I laughed at it, 'there is no reason at all why Willie Hughes should not have gone upon the stage under an assumed name. In fact it is extremely probable that he did so. We know that there was a very strong prejudice against the theatre in his day, and nothing is more likely than that his family insisted upon his adopting some *nom de plume*. The editors of the first folio would naturally put him down under his stage name, the name by which he was best known to the public, but the Sonnets were of course an entirely different matter, and in the dedication to them the publisher very properly addresses him under his real initials. If this be so, and it seems to me the most simple and rational explanation of the matter, I regard Cyril Graham's theory as absolutely proved.'

'But what evidence have you?' I exclaimed, laying my hand on his. 'You have no evidence at all. It is a mere hypothesis. And which of Shakespeare's actors do you think that Willie Hughes was? The "pretty fellow" Ben Jonson tells us of, who was so fond of dressing up in girls' clothes?'

'I don't know,' he answered rather irritably. 'I have not had time to investigate the point yet. But I feel quite sure that my theory is the true one. Of course it is a hypothesis, but then it is a hypothesis that explains everything, and if you had been sent to Cambridge to study science, instead of to Oxford to dawdle over literature, you would know that a hypothesis that explains everything is a certainty.'

'Yes, I am aware that Cambridge is a sort of educational institute,' I murmured. 'I am glad I was not there.'

'My dear fellow,' said Erskine, suddenly turning his keen grey eyes on me, 'you believe in Cyril Graham's theory, you believe in Willie Hughes, you know that the Sonnets are addressed to an actor, but for some reason or other you won't acknowledge it.'

'I wish I could believe it,' I rejoined. 'I would give anything to be able to do so. But I can't. It is a sort of moonbeam theory, very lovely, very fascinating, but intangible. When one thinks that one has got hold of it, it escapes one. No: Shakespeare's heart is still to us "a closet never pierc'd with crystal eyes," as he calls it in one of the sonnets. We shall never know the true secret of the passion of his life.'

Erskine sprang from the sofa, and paced up and down the room. 'We know it already,' he cried, 'and the world shall know it some day.'

I had never seen him so excited. He would not hear of my leaving him, and insisted on my stopping for the rest of the day.

We argued the matter over for hours, but nothing that I could say could make him surrender his faith in Cyril Graham's interpretation. He told me that he intended to devote his life to proving the theory, and that he was determined to do justice to Cyril Graham's memory.

I entreated him, laughed at him, begged of him, but it was to no use. Finally we parted, not exactly in anger, but certainly with a shadow between us. He thought me shallow, I thought him foolish. When I called on him again, his servant told me that he had gone to Germany. The letters that I wrote to him remained unanswered.

Two years afterwards, as I was going into my club, the hall porter handed me a letter with a foreign postmark. It was from Erskine, and written at the Hôtel d'Angleterre, Cannes. When I had read it, I was filled with horror, though I did not quite believe that he would be so mad as to carry his resolve into execution. The gist of the letter was that he had tried in every way to verify the Willie Hughes theory, and had failed, and that as Cyril Graham had given his life for this theory, he himself had determined to give his own life also to the same cause. The concluding words of the letter were these: 'I still believe in Willie Hughes; and by the time you receive this I shall have died by my own hand for Willie Hughes' sake: for his sake, and for the sake of Cyril Graham, whom I drove to his death by my shallow scepticism and ignorant lack of faith. The truth was once revealed to you, and you rejected it. It comes to you now, stained with the blood of two lives, – do not turn away from it.'

It was a horrible moment. I felt sick with misery, and yet I could not believe that he would really carry out his intention. To die for one's theological opinions is the worst use a man can make of his life; but to die for a literary theory! It seemed impossible.

I looked at the date. The letter was a week old. Some unfortunate chance had prevented my going to the club for several days, or I might have got it in time to save him. Perhaps it was not too late. I drove off to my rooms, packed up my things, and started by the night mail from Charing Cross. The journey was intolerable. I thought I would never arrive.

As soon as I did, I drove to the Hôtel d'Angleterre. It was quite true. Erskine was dead. They told me that he had been buried two days before in the English cemetery. There was something horribly grotesque about the whole tragedy. I said all kinds of wild things, and the people in the hall looked curiously at me.

Suddenly Lady Erskine, in deep mourning, passed across the vestibule. When she saw me she came up to me, murmured something about her poor son, and burst into tears. I led her into her sitting room. An elderly gentleman was there, reading a newspaper. It was the English doctor.

We talked a great deal about Erskine, but I said nothing about his motive for committing suicide. It was evident that he had not told his mother anything about the reason that had driven him to so fatal, so mad an act. Finally Lady Erskine rose and said, 'George left you something as a memento. It was a thing he prized very much. I will get it for you.'

As soon as she had left the room I turned to the doctor and said, 'What a dreadful shock it must have been for Lady Erskine! I wonder that she bears it as well as she does.'

'Oh, she knew for months past that it was coming,' he answered.

'Knew it for months past!' I cried. 'But why didn't she stop him? Why didn't she have him watched? He must have been out of his mind.'

The doctor stared at me. 'I don't know what you mean,' he said.

'Well,' I cried, 'if a mother knows that her son is going to commit suicide—'

'Suicide!' he answered. 'Poor Erskine did not commit suicide. He died of consumption. He came here to die. The moment I saw him I knew that there was no chance. One lung was almost gone, and the other was very much affected. Three days before he died he asked me was there any hope. I told him frankly that there was none, and that he had only a few days to live. He wrote some letters, and was quite resigned, retaining his senses to the last.'

I got up from my seat, and going over to the open window I looked out on the crowded promenade. I remember that the brightly-coloured umbrellas and gay parasols seemed to me like huge fantastic butterflies fluttering by the shore of a blue-metal sea, and that the heavy odour of violets that came across the garden made me think of that wonderful sonnet in which Shakespeare tells us that the scent of these flowers always reminded him of his friend. What did it all mean? Why had Erskine written me that extraordinary letter? Why when standing at the very gate of death had he turned back to tell me what was not true? Was Hugo right? Is affectation the only thing that accompanies a man up the steps of the scaffold? Did Erskine merely want to produce a dramatic effect? That was not like him. It was more like something I might have done myself. No: he was simply actuated by a desire to reconvert me to Cyril Graham's theory, and he thought that if I could be made to believe that he too had given his life for it, I would be deceived by the pathetic fallacy of martyrdom. Poor Erskine! I had grown wiser since I had seen him. Martyrdom was to me merely a tragic form of scepticism, an attempt to realize by fire what one had failed to do by faith. No man dies for what he knows to be true. Men die for what they want to be true, for what some terror in their hearts tells them is not true. The very uselessness of Erskine's letter made me doubly sorry for him. I watched the people strolling in and out of the cafés, and wondered if any of them had known him. The white dust blew down the scorched sunlit road, and the feathery palms moved restlessly in the shaken air.

At that moment Lady Erskine returned to the room carrying the fatal portrait of Willie Hughes. 'When George was dying, he begged me to give you this,' she said. As I took it from her, her tears fell on my hand.

This curious work of art hangs now in my library, where it is very much admired by my artistic friends, one of whom has etched it for me. They have decided that it is not a Clouet, but an Ouvry. I have never cared to tell them its true history, but sometimes, when I look at it, I think there is really a great deal to be said for the Willie Hughes theory of Shakespeare's Sonnets.

77   'Rondeau'

Lord Alfred Douglas. From *Poems* (Paris) 1896. Written August 1895.
This poem written at Sorrento not long after the Wilde drama, refers to the absence of Wilde himself, who was, of course, in prison.

If he were here, this glorious sky,
This sweet blue sea, these ships that lie
On the bay's bosom, like white sheep
On English fields, these hours that creep
Golden in summer's panoply,
This wind that seems a lover's sigh,
Would make a heaven of peace as high
As God's great love, a bliss as deep.
If he were here.

This great peace does but magnify
My great unrest that will not die,
My deep despair that may not reap
One poppy, one poor hour of sleep,
Nor aught but pain to wake and cry
'If he were here!'

78   'Tulip of the Twilight'

Mark André Raffalovich. From *The Thread and the Path*, 1895.

> How often have the onyx skies, pale tulip of the twilight,
> Failed quite as when thy paling eyes fail, tulip of the twilight,
> To teach thy teacher, guide thy guide and lead him to thy
>   chamber
> Unknown to friend and foe, to spy's tale, tulip of the twilight,
> As to the loving silence of thy most discreet disciple!
> I love their greyness, thine, and I sail, tulip of the twilight,
> Into their pallor, memory's or else oblivion's,
> I know not! till I see surprise scale, tulip of the twilight,
> The battlements of Heaven, and people them with all an army
> The army of my Love, and wise hale, tulip of the twilight,
> I seize thy meaning and I grasp thy secret, and I hold thee.
> Though all the blighting world despise, rail, tulip of the twilight,
> I love thee as I know thee, and I know thee as I love thee.
> Hail, tulip of Love's paradise, hail, tulip of the twilight.

79   'Stories Toto Told Me: About Beata Beatrice and the Mama of San Pietro'

Frederick William Rolfe (Baron Corvo). From *The Yellow Book*, vol. ix,
April 1896.

'Ah, sir, don't be angry with me, because I really do love her so! What else can I do when she is as pretty as that, and always good and cheerful and patient? And when I met her last evening by the boat-house I took her into my arms asking her to kiss me, and, sir, she did. And then I told her that I loved her dearly, and she said she loved me too. And I said that when I grew up I would marry her, and when I looked into her eyes they were full of tears so I know she loves me; but she is ashamed because she is so poor and her mamma such a hag. But do I mind her being poor – the little pigeon? Ma che! for when I feel her soft arms round me and her breath in my hair, then I kiss her on the lips and neck and bosom, and I know it is Beatrice, her body and her soul, that I want and that I care for, not her ragged clothes.'

Toto jumped off the tree trunk and stood before me, with all his lithe young figure tense and strung up as he went on with his declamatory notices.

'Has not your Excellency said that I am strong like an ox, and will it not be my joy to work hard to make my girl happy and rich and grand as the sun? Do you think that I spend what you give me at the wine-shop or the tombola? You know that I don't. Yes, I have always saved, and now I shall save more, and in a year or two I shall ask your permission to marry her. No, I don't want to go away, or to leave you. May the devil fly away with me to the pit of hell and burn me for ever with his hottest fire if I do! Nor will Beatrice make any difference to your Excellency; you need never see her, you need never even know that there is such a flower of Paradise, such an angel, living near you if you don't wish to know it. And I can assure you that Beatrice has the greatest respect for you, and if you will only be so good and so kind as to let us make each other happy she will be quite proud and glad to serve you as well as I do, and to help me to serve you too. And, sir, you know how fond you are of a fritto? Ah well, Beatrice can make a *rigaglie* so beautiful that you will say it must have come straight from Heaven; and this I know because I have tried it myself.'

He flung himself down on the ground and kissed my hands, and kissed my feet, and wept, and made me an awful scene.

I told him to get up and not be a young fool. I said that I didn't care what he did, and asked if I had ever been a brute to him, or denied him anything that was reasonable.

He swore that I was a saint, a saint from Heaven, that I always had been and always should be, because I could not help myself; and was going down on his knees again, when I stopped that, and said he had better bring me the girl and not make me hotter than I was with his noise.

'To tell you the truth, sir,' he replied, 'I was always quite sure that you would have pity upon us when you knew how very much we loved each other. And when you caught us last night I told Beatrice that now I must let you know everything, because I was certain that as long as I did not deceive you (and you know that I have never done so) there was nothing to be afraid of; and I told her you would without doubt like to see her to give her good counsel, because she was my friend; and she said she would call that too much honour. Then I felt her trembling against my heart, so I kissed her for a long time and said she must be brave like I am; and, sir, as you are so gracious as to want to see her, I have taken the liberty of bringing her and she is here.'

I had always admired the cleverness of this lad, and was not much surprised at his last announcement.

'Where?' I said.

'I put her behind that tree, sir,' and he pointed to a big oak about twenty yards away. I could not help laughing at his deepness; and he took courage, I suppose, from my auspicious aspect. All sorts of clouds of hesitation, uncertainty and doubt moved out of his clear brown eyes, while his face set in a smile absurd and complacently expectant. 'Shall I fetch her, sir?'

I nodded. I had had some experience of his amours before; but this was a new phase, and I thought I might as well be prepared for *anything*. He went a few paces away, and disappeared behind the oak tree. There was a little rustle of the underwood, and some kissing for a minute or two. Then he came out again, leading his companion by the hand. I said I was prepared for anything, but I confess to a little gasp at what I saw. It was not a boy and girl who approached me, but a couple of boys – apparently, at least. They came and stood beside the hammock in which I was lying. Toto, you know, was sixteen years old, a splendid, wild (*discolo*) creature, from the Abruzzi, a figure like Cellini's Perseus; skin brown, with real red blood under it; smooth as a peach, and noble as a god. He had a weakness for sticking a dead-white rose in the black waves of hair over his left ear, and the colour of that rose against his cheeks, flushed as they were now, was something to be truly thankful for. I used to make him wear white clothes on these hot summer days down by the lake – a silk shirt with all the buttons undone and the sleeves rolled up, showing his broad brown chest and supple arms, and short breeches of the same, convenient for rowing. (He had half-a-dozen creatures like himself under his command, and their business was to carry my photographic and insect-hunting apparatus, and to wait upon me while I loafed the summers away in the Alban hills or along the eastern coast.) The seeming boy, whom he had called Beatrice, looked about fourteen years old, and far more delicately dainty even than he was. The bold magnificent independence of his carriage was replaced in her by one of tenderness and softness, quite as striking in its way as the other. She wore her hair in a short silky mop like Toto, and her shirt was buttoned up to the spring of her pretty throat. She was about as high as her boy's shoulder, and stood waiting before me with her poor little knees trembling, and a rosy blush coming and going over her face. They were so exquisitely lovely, in that sun-flecked shade with the blue lake for a background, that I could not help keeping them waiting a few minutes. Such pictures as this are not to be seen every day. Presently he put his arm round her neck, and she put hers round his waist, and leaned against him a little. But he never took his eyes off mine.

'Go on, Toto,' I said, 'what were you going to say?'

'Ah, well, sir, you see I thought if Beatrice came to live with us – with me, I mean – it would be more convenient for you if she looked like the rest of us, because then she would be able to do things for you as well as we can, and people will not talk.'

It struck me immediately that Toto was right again as usual; for, upon my word, this girl of his would pass anywhere for a very pretty boy, with just the plump roundness of the Florentine Apollino, and no more.

'So I got some clean clothes of Guido's, and brought them here early this morning, and then I fetched Beatrice and put them on her, and hid her behind the tree, because I knew you would scold me about her when you came down to read your newspapers; and I determined to tell you everything, and to let you know that the happiness of both of us was in your hands. And I only wanted you to see her like this, in order that you might know that you will not be put to any discomfort or inconvenience if you are so kind as to allow us to love each other.'

This looked right enough; but, whether or not, there was no good in being nasty-tempered just then, so I told them to be as happy as they liked, and that I would not interfere with them as long as they did not interfere with me. They both kissed my hands, and I kissed Beatrice on the forehead, and cheeks and lips, Toto looking on as proud as a peacock. And then I told him to take her away and send her home properly dressed, and return to me in half an hour.

I could see very well that all these happenings were natural enough, and that it was not a part I cared to play to be harsh or ridiculous, or to spoil an idyll so full of charm and newness. Besides, I have reason to know jolly well the futility of interfering between the male animal and his mate.

So when Toto came back I said nothing discouraging or *ennuyant* beyond reminding him that he ought to make quite sure of possessing an enduring love for this girl, a love which would make him proud to spend his life with and for her, and her only. I told him he was very young, which was no fault of his, and that if he would take my advice he would not be in a hurry about anything. He said that my words were the words of wisdom, and that he would obey me just as he would the Madonna del Portone in her crown of glory if she came down and told him things then and there; that he had known Beatrice since they had been babies together, and had always loved her far better than his sisters, and in a different way too, if I could only understand. Last night when he had held her in his arms he told her that he knew she wished him well, and felt himself so strong and she so weak, looking so tender and so tempting, that all of a minute he desired her for his own, and to give somebody a *bastonata* of the finest for her, and to take her out of the clutches of that dirty mean old witch-cat of a mamma of hers who never gave her any pleasure, kept her shut up whenever there was a festa, and, Saints of Heaven! sometimes beat her simply because she envied her for being beautiful and delicate, and bright as a young primrose. 'What a hag of a mamma it was to be cursed with, and what could the Madonna be thinking about to give such a *donnicciuola* of a mamma to his own *bellacuccia*! Not but what the Madonnina was some-times inattentive, but then, of course, she had so many people to look after or she could not have given such a mamma to San Pietro as she did.'

Here I saw a chance of changing the subject, and remarked that it would be nice to know what sort of a mamma the Madonna had given to San Pietro.

'Ah, well, sir, you must know that the mamma of San Pietro was the meanest woman that ever lived – scraping and saving all the days of her life, and keeping San Pietro and his two sisters (the nun and the other one, of whom I will tell you another time) for days together with nothing to eat except perhaps a few potato-peelings and a cheese rind. As for acts of kindness and charity to her neighbours, I don't believe she knew what they were, though of course I am not certain; and what-ever good San Pietro had in him he must have picked up somewhere else. As soon as he was old enough to work he became a fisherman, as you know, because when the Santissimo Salvatore wanted a Pope to govern the Church, He went down to the seaside and chose San Pietro, because He knew that as San Pietro was a fisherman he would be just the man to bear all kinds of hardships, and to catch people's souls and take them to Paradise, just as he had been used to catch fish and take them to the market. And so San Pietro went to Rome, and reigned there for many years. And at last the Pagans settled that all the Catholics had to be killed. And the Catholics thought that though they had no objec-tion to being killed themselves it would be a pity to waste a good Pope like San Pietro, who had been chosen and given to them by the Lord God Himself. Therefore they persuaded San Pietro to run away on a night of the darkest, and to hide himself for a time in a lonely place outside the gates of the city. After he had gone a little way along the Via Appia – and the night was very dark – he saw a grey light on the road in front of him, and in the light there was the Santissimo Himself; and San Pietro was astonished, for His Majesty was walking towards Rome. And San Pietro said: "O Master, where do you go?" And the Face of the Santissimo became very sad, and He said: "I am going to Rome to be crucified again." And then San Pietro knew it was not a noble thing that he was doing to run away on the sly like this, because a shepherd doesn't leave his sheep when wolves come – at least, no shepherd worth a *baiocco*.

'Then San Pietro turned round and went back himself to Rome, and was crucified with much joy between two posts in the Circus of Nero; but he would not be crucified like the Santissimo, because he wished to make amends for his weakness in trying to run away, and he begged and prayed to be crucified with his head where his feet ought to be. The Pagans said most certainly if he liked it that way, it was all the same to them. And so San Pietro made no more ado but simply went straight to Heaven. And, of course, when he got there his angel gave him a new cope and a tiara and his keys, and the Padre Eterno put him to look after the gate, which is a very great honour, but only his due, because he had been of such high rank when he lived in the world. Now after he had been there a little while his mamma also left the world, and was not allowed to come into Paradise, but because of her meanness she was sent to hell. San Pietro did not like this at all, and when some of the other saints chaffed him about it he used to grow angry. At last he went to the Padre Eterno, saying that it was by no means suitable that a man of his quality should be disgraced in this way; and the Padre Eterno, Who is so good, so full of pity, and of mercy that He would do anything to oblige you if it is for the health of your soul, said He was sorry for San Pietro and He quite understood his position. He suggested that perhaps the case of San Pietro's mamma had been decided hurriedly, and He ordered her Angel Guardian to bring the book in which had been written down all the deeds of her life, good or bad.

' "Now," said the Padre Eterno, "We will go carefully through this book and if We can find only one good deed that she has done We will add to that the merits of Our Son and of hers so that she may be delivered from eternal torments."

'Then the Angel read out of the book, and it was found that in the whole of her life she had only done one good deed; for a poor starving beggar-woman had once asked her, for the love of God, to give her some food, and she had thrown her the top of an onion which she was peeling for her own supper.

'And the Padre Eterno instructed the Angel Guardian of San Pietro's mamma to take that onion-top and to go and hold it over the pit of hell, so that if by chance she should boil up with the other damned souls to the top of that stew, she might grasp the onion-top and by it be dragged up to Heaven.

'The Angel did as he was commanded and hovered in the air over the pit of hell holding out the onion-top in his hand, and the furnace flamed, and the burning souls boiled and writhed like *pasta* in a copper pot, and presently San Pietro's mamma came up thrusting out her hands in anguish, and when she saw the onion-top she gripped it, for she was a very covetous woman, and the Angel began to rise into the air carrying her up towards Heaven.

'Now when the other damned souls saw that San Pietro's mamma was leaving them, they also desired to escape and they hung on to the skirts of her gown hoping to be delivered from their pain, and still the Angel rose, and San Pietro's mamma held the onion-top, and many tortured souls hung on to her skirts, and others to the feet of those, and again others on to them, and you would surely have thought that hell was going to be emptied straight away. And still the Angel rose higher and the long stream of people all hanging to the onion-top rose too, nor was the onion-top too weak to bear the strain. But when San Pietro's mamma became aware of what was going on and of the numbers who were escaping from hell along with her, she didn't like it: and, because she was a nasty selfish and cantankerous woman, she kicked and struggled, and took the onion-top in her teeth so that she might use her hands to beat off those who were hanging to her skirts. And she fought so violently that she bit through the onion-top, and tumbled back for always into hell flame.

'So you see, sir, that it is sure to be to your own advantage if you are kind to other people and let them have their own way so long as they don't interfere with you.'

I chuckled at Toto's moral reflections.

80   'All Souls' Night'

Percy Addleshaw. From *The Happy Wanderer and Other Verses*, 1896.
This poem was written under the pseudonym Percy Hemingway.

This All Souls' night, to solace my desire,
The board with meats and heartening wines is spread,

For I, in joyful terror, by the fire
Would see some shadowy lover leave the dead.

Lo, I would gather from this noiseless breath
The wisdom stored the further side of Death,

While the mysterious, wistful, midnight gloom
Should palpitate with passions from the tomb.

But 'tis no phantom wooes me on this night,
My lover's limbs are strong, his heart is light,

He thinks with lusty songs to please my ear,
He dreams that burning kisses scorch the tear,

Nor does he guess I cheat my eyes to see
The ghost of what I once thought love to be.

81   '*Look Not in my Eyes*'

A. E. Housman. From *A Shropshire Lad*, 1896.

> Look not in my eyes, for fear
>   They mirror true the sight I see,
> And there you find your face too clear
>   And love it and be lost like me.
> One the long nights through must lie
>   Spent in star-defeated sighs,
> But why should you as well as I
>   Perish? gaze not in my eyes.
>
> A Grecian lad, as I hear tell,
>   One that many loved in vain,
> Looked into a forest well
>   And never looked away again.
> There, when the turf in springtime flowers,
>   With downward eye and gazes sad,
> Stands amid the glancing showers
>   A jonquil, not a Grecian lad.

82   '*If Truth in Hearts that Perish*'

A. E. Housman. From *A Shropshire Lad*, 1896.

> If truth in hearts that perish
>   Could move the powers on high,
> I think the love I bear you
>   Should make you not to die.

Sure, sure, if stedfast meaning,
    If single thought could save,
The world might end tomorrow,
    You should not see the grave.

This long and sure-set liking,
    This boundless will to please,
– Oh, you should live for ever
    If there were help in these.

But now, since all is idle,
    To this lost heart be kind,
Ere to a town you journey
    Where friends are ill to find.

83   'Shot? so Quick, so Clean an Ending?'

A. E. Housman. From *A Shropshire Lad*, 1896.

Shot? so quick, so clean an ending?
    Oh that was right, lad, that was brave:
Yours was not an ill for mending,
    'Twas best to take it to the grave.

Oh you had forethought, you could reason,
    And saw your road and where it led,
And early wise and brave in season
    Put the pistol to your head.

Oh soon, and better so than later
    After long disgrace and scorn,
You shot dead the household traitor,
    The soul that should not have been born.

Right you guessed the rising morrow
    And scorned to tread the mire you must:
Dust's your wages, son of sorrow,
    But men may come to worse than dust.

Souls undone, undoing others, –
    Long time since the tale began.
You would not live to wrong your brothers:
    Oh lad, you died as fits a man.

Now to your grave shall friend and stranger
    With ruth and some with envy come:
Undishonoured, clear of danger,
    Clean of guilt, pass hence and home.

Turn safe to rest, no dreams, no waking;
    And here, man, here's the wreath I've made:
'Tis not a gift that's worth the taking,
    But wear it and it will not fade.

84   'With Whom, then, should I Sleep?'

George Ives. From *A Book of Chains*, 1897. Written in Hampshire, August 1896.

With whom, then, should I sleep? perhaps with thee,
And gaze into those eyes, those deep sad eyes,
Feeling the drowsy touch of thy vast wings.

Thy brother Sleep I know, with him have lain
Many a night, forgetting all the day
And every pain in that sweet comradeship.

Ah, he is younger, gay, capricious oft,
Dwelling with some for hours, or else away,
As with my friend, for lonely days and nights.

But thou, angel of night, youth of the silent glance,
All sleep with thee, but yet how diversely,
And but the very few hail thee with gladness.

Say would there be a telling of our tryst,
A wild Greek meeting with my spirit free,
Or would it be but rest, a heavy sleeping?

I fancy I could echo sighs with thee,
Picturing all the sights that thou hast seen,
And flying in my thought where thou hast flown.

85   'Rouge et Noir'

John Le Gay Brereton (the Younger). From *The Song of Brotherhood*.
Written in Australia, published 1896.

Why should I be thus shaken by a dream,
Than which a baby's babble has more meaning,
Unless the tedious thoughts that I have traced
Of late to where they lose themselves in the sea
Have wronged my sense? And that my friendship, too,
Should lay the spell on me. To think that love
Like mine should send a clap of misery
To cling upon me like a shadowy plague
That baffles grappling!
                          Under a sloping roof
Of twining branches, as I thought, I lay
And read, and in among the perfect green
Of new-burst leaves the sunlight pierced and threw
Round splashes of lilac colour on the book,
Twinned circles wavering to the sleepy sigh
Of noontide, and the gladioles were stirred
To half-heard rustlings in their yellowing blades
And light seed-bearing wands; the lizard sunned
His grace of bronze beside the crisping leaves
That the last storm had torn from the trees; afar
The steam-boat panted on the river. While
I lay with fettered senses, lazily
Following Gautama's golden words and deeds,
I heard a sound of slowly-wending feet
Approaching, so I rose and thrust apart
The boughs and looked; a sad-faced company
Of men and maids and children walked adown
The hillside with its rust of perished ferns,
And each of them was clad in spotless white
And crowned with faded leaves, and in their midst
Four young men bare a coffin, over which
Was spread a blood-red pall. There as they went
The shrubs and flowers drooped behind them. Then
With reverent head I stood, and while they passed
I plucked the hindmost by the sleeve to ask
Whose body lay beneath yon crimson pall;
For answer came two whispered words that struck
My soul to dulness, but I watched them go,

With one thought in my heart, and on my lips
One single phrase – 'He was my friend, my friend!'
Before the words had died away, the bush
Had vanished, but the thought remained unchanged.

Now I was in my sleeping-room, and there
With a keen knife I pierced a purple vein
Within my arm, and lay awaiting death,
And listening to the dripping of the blood
That redly marked the passing time. I heard
The bees at work in the blossoming tree before
My window, and I heard a lumbering cart
Toil up the road with picnickers, and still
My blood flowed and my strength ebbed, but I thought
Of him, the boy I loved, and was content
To die, for we might meet beyond the bourne,
Or, though we met not, dreamless sleep were better
Than waking misery. A distant clock
Tolled out the hour, and a cow lowed far away,
And farther still it seemed to me, my ears
Being blunted so that the sound of ruddy drops
Scarce entered, and my strength was almost null;
All will or power to move had faded out,
Till I was ripe for the end. Then suddenly
Before the darkness fell I heard a laugh
Out in the sunshine, and my name was cried
In joyous tones; his foot scattered the gravel
As he ran through the garden, but I lay
Powerless, and the horror beats amain
At my temples as I write; I crushed my force
Into a single knot for one last cry,
To shout his name, and, with the effort, woke.

86   'Dédicace'

Aleister (Edward Alexander) Crowley. From *White Stains*, 1898.

You crown me king and queen. There is a name
    For whose soft sound I would abandon all
    This pomp. I liefer would have had you call
Some soft sweet title of beloved shame.
Gold coronets be seemly, but bright flame

I choose for diadem; I would let fall
All crowns, all kingdoms, for one rhythmical
Caress of thine, one kiss my soul to tame.

You crown me king and queen: I crown thee lover!
I bid thee hasten, nay, I plead with thee,
    Come in the thick dear darkness to my bed.
Heed not my sighs, but eagerly uncover,
    As our mouths mingle, my sweet infamy,
    And rob thy lover of his maidenhead.

Lie close; no pity, but a little love.
    Kiss me but once and all my pain is paid.
Hurt me or soothe, stretch out one limb above
    Like a strong man who would constrain a maid.
Touch me; I shudder and my lips turn back
    Over my shoulder if so be that thus
My mouth may find thy mouth, if aught there lack
    To thy desire, till love is one with us.

God! I shall faint with pain, I hide my face
    For shame. I am disturbed, I cannot rise,
I breathe hard with thy breath; thy quick embrace
    Crushes; thy teeth are agony – pain dies
In deadly passion. Ah! you come – you kill me!
Christ! God! Bite! Bite! Ah Bite! Love's fountains fill me.

87   *'Go into the Highways'*

Aleister (Edward Alexander) Crowley. From *White Stains*, 1898. Full title
'Go into the Highways and Hedges and compel them *to come in*'.

Let my fond lips but drink thy golden wine,
    My bright-eyed Arab, only let me eat
    The rich brown globes of sacramental meat
Steaming and firm, hot from their home divine,
And let me linger with thy hands in mine,
    And lick the sweat from dainty dirty feet
    Fresh with the loose aroma of the street,
And then anon I'll glue my mouth to thine.

> This is the height of joy, to lie and feel
>   Thy spicéd spittle trickle down my throat;
> This is more pleasant than at dawn to steal
>   Towards lawns and sunny brooklets, and to gloat
>   Over earth's peace, and hear in ether float
> Songs of soft spirits into rapture peal.

88 Jaspar Tristram

E. A. W. Clarke. Extracts from *Jaspar Tristram*, 1899.

Now more than once already Jaspar had felt inclined to take it ill that he, who at Scarisbrick had been a great personage, should here have suddenly become of absolutely no consequence; and the change had grown doubly distasteful since Orr had appeared, and at every turn he saw him treated as well by dons as boys with a respect which made his own insignificance still harder to bear than before. Nor did his old enemy act generously and try to break his fall, as, had their positions been reversed, he felt sure he would have done himself. He did nothing certainly to make it worse, but this, far from mending matters, was only an additional aggravation. At their old school he had bullied him, it was true, but that he did so showed at least that he considered him as one with whom it was necessary to count; while here, for all that appeared to the contrary, he was not even aware of his existence. But Jaspar's chief reason for hating him was that he had dared to come between him and Els, having already altered the course of their outward life, and even, it might be, diverted some small portion of the boy's affections: for several times of late it had struck him that there had been a certain constraint in the other's manner, such as he did not remember to have previously noticed. It was clearly then no more than prudent at once to do what he could to render his position too strong to be assailed with any hope of success; for even if Orr had no intention of trying to supplant him with Els, it would still be not amiss to make his hold over him even more secure if possible than it was already, and so render it a matter of indifference whether or no any attack was delivered from without. And the wisest plan to attain this end would surely be to assume the part of mentor; so best would he at once relieve that feeling of anger he could not choose but entertain at seeing himself left without the smallest share in the attentions lavished upon Els, and perhaps even prevail on this latter to be more chary of accepting them. Besides, by so doing he would both humiliate Elsie's new friends by

showing on what terms of intimacy he lived with one, even a few minutes of whose conversation *they* had to look on as a favour; and afford
such a demonstration of his ascendancy as must certainly discourage
any attempt to put him from his place; and lastly, by thus warning Els
of the dangers attending association with Orr and his set, it would
enable him to deal his enemy a blow all the more effective because
delivered on such disinterested grounds.

Yet so far was he all this time from entertaining any serious fears
on the subject of his friendship, that he was rather afraid lest, in thus
acting, he might be falling into the mistake of an excess of precaution;
and so for a while gave less of his thoughts to Els and Orr than to
Young. It really seemed as if this latter were trying to revenge himself
on him for being on such easy terms with one towards whom his own
attitude had to be that of sucking up. Not that he actually bullied him;
that of course he would not have stood for a moment; but he never let
slip a chance of worrying him in some petty fashion or another, shoving
against him roughly when they met, or knocking off his cap or catching
hold of him by his gown or standing in his way when he wanted to pass
through a door; all which was not only in itself irritating, but kept him
in a perpetual state of trying to make up his mind as to whether or no
it was worth while to resist.

But his attention was soon recalled to Els by the way in which he
saw him advancing in general favour. For not only was he extraordinarily popular with the set – *the* set of the school – he had been
introduced into by Orr; but those of his own age and standing were, if
possible still more devoted to him, blindly following in whatever his
high spirits and daring suggested; though indeed, when he was leader
of the escapade, being caught by no means entailed such consequences
as you might think in the way of punishment; for on such rare occasions
as his quick wits and ready resource were not enough to get him and
his companions out of the scrape he had led them into, there were very
few dons and fewer prefects, who had the heart to punish him, when he
looked up into your face with that gaze which, as the story ran, when it
had been tried on him, had made even the austere Cator in angry
surprise at his own weakness, ask what he meant by having such eyes;
and of course those with him had necessarily to be let off as well. And
in proportion as he thus daily became more popular with the rest of the
school, so did Jaspar, by the increasing severity of his remarks, seek to
defend himself against charms which to him also appeared to be constantly growing more difficult to resist. It was partly too to the same end,
and in part to be beforehand with the ridicule he was always so ready
to expect, that he now adopted a depreciatory tone in speaking of him,
and all the more if, as was usually the case, he heard him referred to in

terms of the most exaggerated praise. He never indeed could help looking on it as a liberty that anyone but himself should venture to talk of him at all. Besides, he found a curious pleasure in the fact that what with his lips he blamed that in his heart he most approved. And all the time he was observing him with great attention, and pondering the inner significance, not only of what he said, but of his looks and tones and gestures.

So still for a while he persevered in the plan on which he had originally decided; but at length growing frightened, as it seemed to him that Elsie's manner insensibly altered, he resolved to try whether a change might not be productive of good effect. Hitherto, while his one anxiety had been to secure a firmer foothold, he had only slipped the more; now he would see what would be the result of stopping still. Besides it was altogether beneath him to force his affection upon anyone, be he who he might. If Els chose to remain friends, why, well and good; if not, he would certainly never engage in any scuffle for his affections. His dearest wish, no doubt, was to be all in all for his friend, but he must be so of the boy's own free will, and not as a result of anything he himself might do or leave undone. And while he conceived that he would be best consulting his own dignity by adopting this method of letting alone; he was not without hope that after all in other respects as well it would turn out the best. It would give Els a foretaste of what he would lose in losing him, and might perhaps beget in him a desire to merit a trust so nobly given. Only a few days ago up in form he had read in his Livy: '*habita fides ipsam plerumque fidem obligat.*' Why should not the maxim serve him? And not only would he release Els from all claims upon his time, but he would show him that he was free to do as he liked. So, whenever they met in Covered Passage or Hall, in School or Dormitory, he was careful not to say a word which could lead him to suspect that anything he did was known, much less either blamed or approved. But all the while he kept his eyes open, and flattered himself there was not much the boy did of which he remained long in ignorance.

So matters continued for a while. But presently, despite the resolves he had made that he would wait for the first advances to come from Els, he found he could hold out no longer; and that evening at tea sent a servitor with a note – the boy was always receiving them – to ask if the next morning after breakfast he would once more come for a walk. With this step, however, jealousy, he assured himself, had nothing to do; he had certainly no such feeling towards Elsie's friends and least of all towards Orr; he would never condescend to bestow so much as a single thought on one to whom he himself was of such little concern: and, besides, he had already gained his object, since Els by this time must surely have seen that he was far from being so indispensable as no doubt he had thought. But he presently discovered that it was easier to drop than to pick up the thread. It was not altogether without difficulty that he persuaded him again to take him as his companion in the morning stroll; and even then they had now no subjects of conversation in common, since he could hardly speak of amusements with which he had nothing to do, or of those with whom Els shared them, who, he felt, were either loftily ignorant of his very existence, or knew him merely as one of that crowd of Lower Boys whom with a few exceptions, such as Els himself, they disdainfully lumped all together in their minds as smugs. Indeed, in every way Els seemed to have greatly changed. Even his clothes were now of a number and sort, and worn with such an air that he who had only one every-day suit and one for Sunday-best – made at the little village tailor's corner-shop in Rottingdean – could not help feeling as if he were suddenly become one of an inferior class. As for the boy's manners, winning as they had always been, they had now, so Jaspar thought, acquired 'a sovereign and radiant grace,' which seemed, however, after all no more than the complement of his altered life and ways and finer clothes.

Thus irritated at once and pleased; anxious to assert himself as being on equal terms, and yet at the same time more than ever convinced that Els was of different and superior clay; but, above all, eager to maintain that place in his affections which he grew the more desirous of keeping as the possibility of losing it increased; his memory fondly went back to the day when he was not as yet distracted by all these conflicting emotions, and he began to talk of the life they had led together at Scarisbrick; he was half afraid that never again would he be so happy as he had been then. Meanwhile, the recollection gave him courage in face of Elsie's new greatness and charms by assuring him that once they had been friends, and by letting him fancy he was showing him that nothing now could ever get over the fact of their having had a common past. Then, when he saw him obviously bored, he would ask what was the matter:

'Oh, nothing!' Els would answer. 'Why?'

Or would burst out with a 'Do you care for me?'

'Oh, yes, of course!' responded Els.

'As much as you used to?' he persisted, trying to get the other to look him in the face.

'Oh yes, I suppose so!' said Els, and for a moment raised his eyes, but only to turn away again and move a little aside so as to shake off the hand laid upon his shoulder. And then for a little while Jaspar would let himself sink into a fit of despair; it seemed as if just as his affection for Els grew, so Elsie's for him waned, while every effort he made to secure his position only resulted in his losing ground. But by and by, and often while they were still together, he would begin to hope for better luck next time, and so would leave him but to count the moments till they met again, and he should have another chance. The worst of it was that whenever he essayed to express his feelings, if he did not simply weary Els, it appeared as if there were something in him stronger than himself that either forced him to speak in so vague a way there was no understanding what he meant, or else gave such an air of irony to what he said that even to himself it sounded as though he were laughing in his sleeve. For a while, indeed, he tried what making him presents would do; but though he ran into debt for every sort of thing from tuck at Shop to a pair of silver and coral links from the jeweller's in the neighbouring town, it did not take him long to see that not only did Els himself not care for all these offerings, but that, even had he done so, it was little good for him with his small means to try and rent, as it were, the affections of one, to whom there were half a dozen big chaps at least who would have been only too glad to have given anything he wanted – not to mention that he himself had always any amount of tin.

Thus was it Els who was the first to break through the custom they had only of late resumed of walking together after breakfast. But when Chapel bells began to ring, and Jaspar saw it was no use waiting any longer, angry though he was at being thus thrown over, it was by no means without pleasure that he found himself able to look forward to another quarrel; he only hoped that when next he met Els it would be in public, that so he might astonish such as happened to be by by insulting one to whom he was known to be attached, and whom, as he was well aware, he still held dearer than anybody in the world. Nor was it long before he got the chance he asked. That very afternoon he was going down Covered Passage, talking as he went to his form-master Toady Maude, when Els with another chap passed by, half-walking, half-running, yet still not so fast but that this latter had time to shoot at him a laughing glance. This he, upon his side, succeeded in meeting with a stare of cold surprise, though he was very glad the other's eyes had been so quickly taken off, for in another moment they would have overcome him; as it was, his legs felt as if they were giving way. For a little he walked bravely on, but they had scarce gone a dozen yards before he found it so much more than he could bear, thus to be going at every step farther and farther from Els, that he plucked up courage enough to break through etiquette and suggest to Toady Maude they should turn back. There was, he recognized, little or no chance of catching Els up, but still there would be some comfort in following the road he had taken.

'Why?' asked Toady Maude in some surprise.

'Oh, I don't know, sir!' he murmured; 'I only thought—' and so stopped, confused.

But at last he managed to get free, and hurried back to the spot where he had seen that swift-passing vision of laughing eyes, hoping indeed against all hope that there would Els still be found. But no such luck was his. And so he began aimlessly to wander about, not going far, but staying always near the place where they had met; it was just where Covered Passage proper ends and the round arch that supports the Infirmary vaults the way; and from Covered Passage he would go out on to the path that, running past Hades with its low terra-cotta battlements and shrubs, forms an outdoor communication between the Market Place and Hall, and through the porch into the Big Schoolroom, out by the little side door and so back into Covered Passage once again. Sometimes, thinking that the longer he was away, the greater would be his chance of finding Els when he returned, he would go all round by Mother Collins's old garden, the shrubbery, and Chapel, and so back once more by the entrance close to Hall, which he and Els had always used when first they had gone for their after-breakfast walks. Then, as he came near, he would resolutely keep his eyes fixed on the ground, raising them suddenly again at the last with a sort of hope that they would meet what so ardently they desired to see. At length however, tired out, he let himself drop into a window-seat close to the spot he found it impossible to get away from, and taking a book out of his pocket began to read. And there he remained till the bell commenced ringing for Roll, though during the hour that intervened, each time he heard footsteps he would jump up to see if by good luck it was Els.

The next morning after breakfast as Jaspar was passing through Middle Hall he stopped for a moment to speak to a chap who was standing, one of a group, by the marble mantelpiece, warming himself at the great fire roaring up from its huge basket-grate. And presently, as he lingered, appeared Els; and at once he grew so self-conscious there was nothing he did from the attitude in which he stood to the way he talked – but he scarce knew what he said – that was not done with an eye to his friend. Yet he flattered himself that to all outward seeming he was still the same, and even affected not to know the boy was there. Suddenly, as, leaning back against the jamb, he was opening one hand to the blaze, he felt it touched, and, looking round, met Elsie's eyes, and in that instant it seemed to him, not so much that they were reconciled, as that their friendship somehow passed into a different stage. Yet even then, as he caught sight of the boy's hands, he recognized, with a curious pleasure at the incongruity of such a reflection at such a time, that they were large and coarse; in particular was he unpleasantly affected by what yet he had seen countless times before – the swelling on the top of the forefinger of the right, which, as he knew, was due to an accident that he had had years ago as a child. Then, as they went away, with a gesture that filled him with pleasure, Els slipped his hand affectionately through his arm and began to talk; he even proposed that they should go for a long walk that afternoon. And presently he referred to Bagley Wood.

'Where's that?' asked Jaspar; but 'Where you and I are going this afternoon!' was all the answer he got.

So they separated on the best of terms, and after dinner, as soon as he was flannelized, he made haste down to the Market-Place where they had arranged to meet. But time went on and still there was no Els, until at last, his patience gone, he went off to his place in School, using all the little devices he was master of to hide, as well from himself as from any by whom he might have been seen, the fact that he had been waiting, and waiting in vain. But his suspicions were so quick that when in the distance he saw a group of loudly-laughing boys, he thought it could only be at him they were mocking, and he even fancied that among them he recognized Els. And as he sat alone at his desk there rang in his ears, 'Where you and I are going this afternoon! Where you and I are going this afternoon!' Yet some little consolation there was to be found in promising himself that he would be revenged. But when on the following morning he came out of the Library, where, since breakfast, he had been keeping out of the way in the hope that Els all the time was waiting for him in the Music School, he had the mortification of overhearing someone say that the boy had been with Orr in his study.

So resolved that none should ever have a chance of saying that he had begged for love, and least of all that he had begged in vain; and equally determined that he would never stoop to remind Els of what he had done for him in days gone by, and so seek to obtain from gratitude what affection denied; he made up his mind once more that, happen what might, the first offer at reconciliation should not come from him; and this time he would keep his word. Meanwhile he would so act as to show the boy, what perhaps it was partly his own fault had been forgotten – that he had no notion of being friends unless upon equal terms; and again he murmured to himself the old refrain – if Els did not care for him, he did not care for Els. And he took every opportunity of putting himself in his way, and letting him see by his loud laughter and talk that at any rate it was not he who was pining to have their quarrel made up. He even tried to excite his jealousy by taking up with young Clavering, but dropped him again when he saw that Els was not even aware of what he was about; besides, though he wasn't going to push and scuffle for a share in anyone's affections, he found it equally little to his taste to appear as wanting what scarce anyone else desired. However, he was quite content so long as, constantly meeting Els, he was able by his demeanour to prove to him in a way it was impossible to mistake, not only that he had ceased to care for him, but, if that might be, that he had never done so at all. He would doubtless have been happier could he have perceived in him any signs of being sorry for what he had done; but, unfortunately, far from this being the case, he more than once had actually seen him laugh, and having felt sure it had been at him, had replied in the only way he could, by assuming as he passed an air of killing scorn and dignity. More especially did he put this on when, as was generally the case, he met him in company with Orr, when he would give the pair a rapid look of as much insolence as he judged safe, and so continue on his way without even a pause that anybody but himself could perceive. Yet every time a pang shot through his heart as he plunged on into the darkness – such was his phrase – now only made more dense by the glimpse he had obtained of light. He had often thought it was that black devil, who was chiefly responsible for the way he and Els had quarrelled, and the hate he had borne him so long was now increased. What would he not gladly have done and suffered, could he only have had revenge! And yet he was powerless, it seemed, and must console himself with nursing his vengeance till they should meet in after-life. And then it would be his turn! Then *he* would be the greater of the two! For *he* when he came of age would have, if not a large fortune, one at least which would allow of his choosing his own profession, while as for Orr, he would be a nobody – a city clerk perhaps, or something of that sort. Yet while hatred and contempt were what alone he would have liked to feel, he could not choose but recognize that for the present they were largely mixed with envy and admiration; and the knowledge this was so intensified a hate, which was still further increased by his enemy's obstinate affectation of ignoring his very existence. But worse than all was the curious sense of physical submission that ever since old Scarisbrick days, not only Orr's actual presence, but even the mere thought of him never failed of producing; for while in all other respects his passions proceeded outwards, in this they appeared to return against himself.

Meanwhile, instead of trying to avoid Young, or at the least to keep him at arm's-length, suddenly he veered about, and did everything that he was asked. Partly he wanted to be free to give his entire thoughts to Els, and partly he was inclined to think that once out of the boy's favour, it really was no matter what he did. But he had never expected as the first result of his new complaisance that he would be treated with contempt. However, he only smiled, and was pleased to think that in so doing he showed that his real self could remain unaffected by any slight put upon it from outside: indeed he considered that he was even more superior to Young than ever in that, while this latter was doubtless of opinion that he was now still more to be despised, he knew that in his own eyes his surrender was a matter of no account. . . .

Jaspar knew however that in Chapel that evening he would see the boy again, and hear him too, since it was he who was to take the solo in the anthem. He had already grown to like the fashion after which it was the custom at Bridwell to celebrate the various festivals of the Church, and never failed to display the utmost seriousness and dignity in acting such part in them as fell to his share. He was only sorry it was always so small, being indeed but to mount to his place, but he tried to forget that he was nothing more than a boy with the rest, and loved to conceit himself rather a king at his coronation, the central figure in the eyes of God and man in some great pageant of religion and state. And so now, as proud and erect, he stood and waited in his stall, the organ in the gallery above began to play, and while the full notes were rolling tumultuously down, filling his ears with the magnificent thunder of their music, in two long undulating white lines, their surplices swelling and rustling about them, he saw the Choir come streaming down Ante-Chapel steps. Els led the Cantoris side, and as he advanced, not so much walking as borne in a sort of floating pace over the soft crimson carpet, the level rays of the setting sun shot through the west window and, taking the gorgeous colours of its saints' robes as they passed, flamed like a halo round his fair head and dyed his wide turn-down collar and the spotless folds of his surplice in all the colours of the rainbow. But a few hours before, as he had watched him at the Sports, he had appeared extraordinarily good-looking no doubt, but still a boy; now he was an angel descending from the clouds.

So while the last notes of the organ were still rumbling among the dark timbers of the roof, Jaspar knelt down and, bending over the desk, pressed the palms of his hands hard against his eyes. It was only for a moment that he so remained, but when, at the general rustling with which the others regained their feet, he also rose and, with a half-dazed glance, looked round, it seemed as if the place had undergone some sudden and mysterious change. From out the blackness that brooded heavily overhead and even shrouded the aspiring finials of the tabernacle-work above the stalls, there loomed the great carved stone angels who bore up the roof; only walled-in up to the waist, with half their bodies they hung in air above, and their arms devoutly crossed on their breasts, their mighty wings outstretched behind them, sphinx-like and unmoved, they fulfilled their eternal task. Below, on his own level,

ranged in three tiers, motionless and dazzling, there stretched away on
either hand long lines of surpliced boys, his schoolfellows now no more,
but rather part of that great multitude he had read of as standing,
clothed with white robes, before the Throne of God. And the throne
was the altar, upraised on its marble steps and shut off in mystic
seclusion alone within its low gilt rails. From among the strange tropic
flowers and innumerable twinkling candles with which at the back it
was banked high, there rose aloft, solemn and awful, a great cross of
polished brass that seemed not so much to reflect as to radiate light,
and to be, if not a deity itself, at least a symbol on which some effluence
of the Divinity had been poured out. And while from his lofty canopied
stall the Warden read, his musical full voice giving an expression to his
words of sonorous grace and stately magnificence; and while the Choir
in alternate strophe and antistrophe chanted the Psalms; Jaspar clasped
his hands together in an agony of supplication and, turning his eyes in
passionate appeal toward the Holy of Holies, brilliant now, as he
thought, with a more than earthly light, prayed, yet not in words, for
he knew not what, to he knew not whom.

Presently, as once more they were standing waiting, the organ
began its prelude, now exulting as if in triumph, and pealing forth
louder and yet more loud till the massive framework of the roof seemed
to be actually quivering in response; and now letting its notes, tender
and pathetic, go floating gently down until at last, growing fainter by
degrees and more remote, they trembled for a moment, and then softly
died away upon the air, and everything was absolutely still. Then
suddenly there stole on his expectant ears, familiar at once and strange,
a voice that somehow appeared as if it came from far away, from out
heaven's gates themselves. Low at the first and soft, it quickly gathered
strength, as higher and higher it went, now for an instant held in pause,
now soaring fresh and clear once more, as if every rest but served for a
foothold from which to spring each time to loftier flight. And as he
listened, all the solemn-burning lights melted together into one dazzling
and unearthly blaze, chapel and boys disappeared, and, rapt on high,
he grew faint with desire for a happiness he had never had, home-sick
for a heaven he had never known. And all the time he derived a curious
sensation of pleasure from the thought that it was none other than
Elsie's, this voice which was so strangely moving him, and from the
contrast between what the boy really was and what his looks and function would have had him be, with a soul as white as the spotless robe
of innocence that he was wearing. He resolved he would lose no time
in seeking reconciliation with one who, already endowed with every
mortal charm, was proving now that he had those of the angels as well.
Then, while he was still half on earth and half in heaven, the rest of

the Choir took up the tale, and with one triumphant burst of melody the anthem ended.

As he came out of Chapel, still under the influence of all the various emotions which, one after another, he had gone through within its walls, he seemed suddenly to have been raised so high above all mean and petty things that he found it hard to conceive how he had ever given a moment's consideration to such foolish trifles as those upon account of which he had quarrelled with Els. Indeed, it required some little effort of thought to persuade him that their reconciliation was so far from being already completed that, if it was to be at all, it must be brought about before they separated for the holidays on the following day. What a pity it was that the last Sunday of the half had gone by; otherwise, they could have celebrated their *reintegratio amoris* by taking the Communion together, and so marked its final character by uniting themselves after a fashion which, while not unlike that of their interchange of blood at Rose Hill, would, by its being really sacramental, have better responded to the manner in which since then his notions had grown.

But bed-time came, and though more than once he had seen Els, on not one of these occasions had they been alone. He was just behind him indeed as they went upstairs, yet could not speak, for standing in the arched doorway of Upper Dormitory was a noisy group of exactly such of Elsie's friends as he hated most. And as the boy would have passed, he saw one of them stretch out a hand and ruffle over his hair, while another called out: 'Good night, sweet re—' but he heard no more, for, seeing his enemies' attention thus taken up, he thought he had better not let slip so good a chance of getting past unperceived. Yet still he refused to give up, and, having undressed, stood shivering, partly with excitement and partly with cold, listening with all his ears to what was going on on the other side of his cubicle-curtain, but not daring even to peep out. And now the various noises of the other fellows undressing had nearly ceased when, by the darkness that suddenly fell upon Recess, he knew that the servitor had begun to put out the lights. And nearer and nearer the blackness came and swallowed up the two gas-jets opposite his own cubicle, and went on until at last, as that which burned over the entrance disappeared and the heavy door clanged-to, from end to end it shrouded the whole place. And still he stood and waited. Presently here and there away on the right and on the opposite side sounds of snoring arose, a sign, he thought, that now at last he might venture forth upon the perilous expedition he had resolved to undertake to Elsie's cubicle. Slowly and cautiously he slipped out, taking especial care not to disarrange his curtain, so that should anyone pass, there might appear no reason to suspect him not to be in bed, and as he went he kept as close in to the side as he could. He had already reached his journey's end when suddenly, lightly as he stepped, a board creaked under his tread. His heart was in his mouth; it seemed as if the entire dormitory must have been woke by such a noise; and for a few moments he remained poised on one foot and holding his breath. But when the precipitate thumping of his own heart was still the only sound to be heard; and when the only light that could be seen was still that of the watch-lamp glimmering, solitary and mournful, in the midst of the vast black waste; and when the long rows of cubicle-curtains which stretched away on either hand into the thick darkness, remained motionless and mysterious, his courage returned and he slipped in.

'Who's that?' asked Els in a whisper, and sat up in bed.

'It's me!' he answered, and began to move cautiously forward.

'I'm very sorry!' he said, and, as he heard himself speak, he was struck with the noble simplicity of his own tone and words: 'I'm very sorry! It's been my fault!'

'Oh, all right, old chap!' answered Els. 'It doesn't matter!'

For a moment he was so taken aback at the small success of his magnanimous confession that he found himself actually wishing he had never come, but soon recovering, he began to talk; he hoped every moment to arrive at that perfect understanding they surely once had lived in, to return to which had but a short while ago seemed so easy. But so far he had got nothing from Els beyond the vaguest answers, when suddenly he heard him whisper: 'Sh! what's that?' and in an instant was outside the curtain; behind him, he heard the rings rattle slightly on their pole as, with long strides, a-tiptoe, he hastened back.

On the following day the school broke up, and he went home. But, though thus separated from Els before he had in any way benefited by the reconciliation he had been so anxious to bring about, he was not altogether sorry to have three quiet weeks to himself, in which to reflect on all the errors of his conduct and to form resolutions for a more prudent behaviour in the future. Besides, the holidays would form a sort of break to divide his old life which had been filled with mistakes, from that he was going to lead when he returned. Innumerable indeed, as he could now perceive, had been his errors; but they all, he thought, might be referred to the attempt to keep Els to himself, in which he had unfortunately engaged. He wondered how he could have been such a fool: he surely might have known that so outrageous a pretension could not have ended otherwise than in disaster: certainly Els, in resenting such behaviour on his part, had but acted as in like case he would have done himself. But the next time he would be wiser, and not only avoid the cardinal error he had fallen into in the past, but walk, as it were, so carefully as to render it absolutely impossible that anything he did should give offence. And having thus satisfactorily found out, as he imagined, the cause of their estrangement, and having made all sorts of resolves as to how he would behave in the future, he grew impatient for the holidays to come to an end, being anxious to see how the plans he had thus formed in peace would stand the strain of actual warfare. And then at last the long looked-for day arrived and he went back. . . .

But this was only the beginning of a period during which he was obliged to be a spectator of Orr's triumph, the rival to whom, at first despised, then hated as he saw him beginning to gain ground, he had now at last been compelled to leave the field. Nor was it only occasionally that he met the two together; at all hours and everywhere he had to see his enemy occupying that place in Elsie's life which not so very long ago had belonged to him.

If he went down to the river they were there. Now it was Els alone who would be sculling in his whiff, made more charming than ever by the serious air with which he was obviously doing his best, being rather frightened, as it seemed, of Orr who, bare-headed and bare-legged, came racing at full speed along the towing-path, keeping his head turned towards him and, as he ran, shouting out words of command, exhortation, and abuse; and now it was the Eight that would go leaping past over the water, Orr rowing stroke and Els over against him, his every faculty absorbed in steering, the lines tight-grasped in his hands, and bending backwards and forwards with the rest of the crew as with a clockwork regularity they rose and fell. Then, as he himself continued on his lonely way, once more there descended upon everything the silence that had for a moment given place to this rush of life, but now was only broken by the soft whisper of the stream among the reeds. Sometimes, as he went up by the field-path through the standing corn, he would stop for a moment and look back: to the left the river flowed away towards the Lydiat woods, and, just below, the mill, bestriding the rushing water with its two dark arches, shot its tall tapering, chimney-shaft, all black at the top, into the air. Then, as he waited, Orr and Els, one after the other, came climbing over the stile; round the latter's neck was wrapped a soft white woollen scarf, the loose ends of which were flung picturesquely over his shoulders; his jacket was open, and his almost transparent jersey, pulled down outside his shorts, lent to his figure something of that indescribable charm possessed by those pictures of mediaeval pages whose jewelled belts you always saw worn low over their hips. And once again, in Upper Dormitory, as he passed along the broad central aisle to his own cubicle, he would find them still together: Orr's head was round the corner of Elsie's curtain; the boy's delightful laugh mingled with the splashing of water. Just above, there hung forward a large picture of the Crucifixion, in which everything but the bowed head of Our Lord and His outstretched arms was lost in deep brown shade.

But it was on Sundays that he suffered most. As soon as dinner was over, he would take a book and go off to the bowling-green, where, stretching himself out full length upon the grass, he would prop his chin in the hollow of his hands and begin to read. High overhead the tall limes met and, shutting out with interarching boughs the garish rays of the hot sun, only let through a subdued and mysterious light that well accorded with the drowsy murmurous hum of bees and the ceaseless rustling of leaves which filled his ears, and presently sent him into a waking dream. Then, looking up, there were Orr and Els and half a dozen of their friends coming in his direction. The boy was bare-headed, and behind his ear was stuck a rose – after the fashion, was it not, of the gallants of Elizabeth's court? His tie was of that pale-blue silk the school affected, the delicate tint and material of which for the most part made the wearer's complexion dark and coarse, but his only more soft and fair; his turn-down collar worn outside his Eton jacket was wide and spotlessly white, and the lines down the middle of his trousers had somehow the same effect as those on the steel legpieces of the young St. George of whom an engraving hung over the mantelpiece in the Butcher's study. But as down at the bathing-place he appeared so perfectly formed as no more to want a covering than does a statue; now you scarcely stopped to consider the clothes for the body which, as it were, shone through them. So, his old untidy gown swaying as he came with a rhythmic grace, with a delightful boyish swagger he advanced over the sun-flecked turf, the youngest and smallest of them all, yet certainly the one whom first a stranger would have noticed. For while he walked a little in front of the rest, as though not so much an equal as a prince at the head of his court, the resemblance was continued by the way in which each there was evidently trying emulously to find favour in his sight above the others. And though for one brief moment Jaspar made an effort to persuade himself it was contempt he ought to feel for him, and felt; the next, as the group passed by so close that the gown of the nearest almost touched his head as he lay on the grass, he caught a word, from which he knew that Els was telling one of his stories, and his thoughts were once more in a tumult and beyond his control. He himself had only heard a few, but those, now for ever forcing themselves upon him, coloured all his motions of life, so great had been the effect produced by the union of matter, already strange and troubling by itself, with a manner in which an air of cherub innocence and a voice of extraordinary sweetness combined to force you to think twice before you could understand what had been really meant. And then, laughing loudly, they all disappeared up the steps at the farther end.

Of course he knew that, in spite of all he said to the contrary, he could easily have avoided these encounters; but so far from attempting anything of the kind, rather he took every opportunity of throwing himself in the boy's way. And often, just as he was setting out for a walk, the mere sight of something belonging to Els – a cap – a book – would be enough to bring him up with a sudden shock, and to keep him hanging about for hours, in the hope of one of these same meetings which, over in a second, never failed to leave him more restless and unhappy than before. But indeed the boy was hardly ever out of his thoughts, which had always the same refrain: 'Et tu, Brute! Et tu, Brute!' Anything else he could have borne, but not this having been forsaken by his own familiar friend. He must then after all be no more than human, this boy-god, whom he had adored for so long and with such noble constancy! But even to himself it was only, as it were, under his breath that he made this acknowledgment; as far as others were concerned, he still was careful not to let slip a single word that might lead them to suspect his faith was shaken; on the contrary, he rather enjoyed being laughed at for the way in which he persisted in speaking of one who had treated him so very ill. He affected too a kind of generous anger in denying the truth of the things that now were said about the boy. Not that for a moment he really thought his soul was as immaculate as the white and red of his cheeks; but somehow it pleased him to believe that to be false, which all the time his reason told him was true. . . .

So when evening arrived and it was time for the Play to begin, he felt too down at heart to care to go; yet, as he liked still less the prospect of being left alone in the silent and deserted schoolroom, he resolved to follow the others. The night was sultry and starless, but from the open door of Gymnasium streamed a long shaft of light, for which he made across the wide open gravel-space the end of School abuts upon. Outside this sort of path, all was thick blackness through which could just be seen looming, vast and mysterious, the building itself, and the tall dark motionless trees on either side. But resolved still to keep to himself as much as possible, he took his place at the back, and so, in shadow and with no one near, was free to give way to those thoughts of melancholy and desire and nightmare-apprehension, which were oppressing him. And as he sat, he felt himself turning to stone, while even his eyes, life's last retreat, could only look straight out in front with a fixed and unblinking stare. Figures he could see were moving to and fro on the stage, gesticulating and talking, but he gave them little heed, every faculty being absorbed in the gaze he had fastened on the set-piece at the back. And momentarily this grew in brightness and size, the while the rest of the building appeared with equal pace to fade away into darkness and insignificance. It evidently represented some town upon the coast of Italy or Greece: to the left, a mass of yellow houses with green jalousies and ribbed red tiles descended in terraces to the harbour's edge where floated a crowd of gaily-painted boats; they and their sails alike were of a shape and colour quite different from those of the dull lettered and numbered fishing-smacks he had so often seen drawn up on the narrow steep beach at Rottingdean, or, from the cliffs, caught sight of, as they moved slowly over the leaden waters of the Channel; to the right, a deep-blue sea stretched, far as the eye could reach, until it met the cloudless sky: and on all was a light that, neither of sun nor lamp, seemed more appropriate than either to a land which was surely that of the fulfilment of hope. And his heart ached with longing after a place where, under new and fairer skies, happiness would at once be his, and he would live in that perfect union he had always aimed at with an Els who would be different from the boy he knew and yet the same.

Then suddenly there appeared upon the stage a figure which was the very embodiment of his dream. Never had Els appeared so hand-some; while his everyday clothes – and even they had seemed better than those of others – had been exchanged for a costume as much more delightful to look upon as he than his ordinary self. It was a page's suit of blue and white satin, all a-flutter with ribbons and bows; over the Vandyke collar fell, in great loosely-curling rings, long love-locks of soft gold hair; his slim and shapely legs were cased in delicate white silk stockings, and he wore high-heeled satin shoes with huge rosettes; one hand carried a plumed hat, the other pressed down the hilt of his sword; and here and there he moved with a gallant grace and spoke his words, the while his short cloak swung this way and that from his shoulders. All at once, darting to the front of the stage, from its scabbard of silver and blue velvet he whipped his rapier, and shaking it with a gesture of defiance above his head till it flashed again in the light, burst full-throated into his song. It was that of the School, and scarce had he finished the first line than they one and all, as if swept out of themselves, sprang to their feet and with an absolute roar chimed in. But Jaspar still kept his seat; not that he was not moved, but he wished to prove to himself he was above the vulgar passions that swayed others. Then, as he sat in his corner at the back, his eyes wide open, yet seeing nothing but one great blaze of light and, in its midst, that beautiful and dazzling figure; and his ears filled with the thunder of those hundreds of voices, slowly, as if under the compulsion of some outside force, he began to rise, and leaning forward, clutched at the rail of the chair in front, the while it seemed to him as if his soul, straining towards the heaven that had opened before it, was trying to drag his body after.

Suddenly the curtain fell; and as he made his way back, jostled in the semi-darkness among the noisy crowd of fellows who were streaming out, his former notions of pride and honour fell away, and, abandoning all thought, not only of reigning alone in Elsie's heart, but even of doing so on equal terms with Orr, he told himself he would be more than content if still he might keep a part, however small, in the vision which yet dazzled his eyes.

It would be impossible, he knew, to get a word with the boy that night, or even to send him a note, but he thought it would ease his mind if, before he went to bed, he composed one to despatch next day; and so, no sooner was he back in his cubicle than, taking a piece of paper, he placed it up against the partition, so as to get the benefit of the light which from the gas in the middle fell over the curtain-pole, and wrote:

> My dearest Els, – I am ridiculously foolish I know, but
> still I do not want to quarrel with you altogether; and so I
> beg you to forgive me. But before you forgive me, I must
> inform you of a few facts, which I can only do by word of
> mouth. If you forgive me, therefore, tell me as soon as
> possible. If I am not told I am forgiven before tea, I shall
> know I am not. – Till then, believe me, yours penitently, J.T.

So, content now he had done all that was for the moment possible, he fell asleep.

The next morning at breakfast he gave the precious folded paper to one of the servitors to take: he would have liked, had he only dared, to have warned the man to be very careful not to lose it, nor to let it fall into any other hands than those for which it was intended; but he let it go with a careless air, as if it had been of no more account than the dozens of others which were daily sent about at meals. And then in school he began to talk of Els to his next-door neighbour on the form. It was not the first time by many that he had done so, and the other had on each occasion warned him how much better it would be to give up thinking of one who so little deserved regard, and he had listened with pleasure, feeling comfortably superior the while in being able to have relations at all with one who occupied such a distinguished position; nor did he ever fail to let it be understood they were much closer than was really the case. Now, as he talked of his desire to be reconciled, and heard the other point out how well he was rid of the boy, and how very silly it would be of him to allow himself again to be entangled, it pleased him to think that he had already written and despatched a note which must presently bring about the very state of things thus earnestly deprecated. Meanwhile he answered, yes, he knew all that, but he could not help it; and on this theme he proceeded to expatiate with the greatest warmth, wishing to astonish his friend, and feeling there was something fine in such a weakness, and spurred on by the sound of his own voice. Besides the fact that, morally speaking, Els was unworthy his love, far from diminishing, only increased it; and whatever he might have done had the boy been all he should, he found it as it was quite impossible to give him up.

Then, once alone, his thoughts flew back to the note. Had he said too much? Or not enough? And from these reflections he was always being roused by fancying that some servitor whom he saw in the distance, was surely bringing him the reply. So, as the day wore on and still no answer came, he began to set his wits to work to prepare some loop-hole through which, should none arrive before the hour he had fixed, he might still escape and take refuge in hope. Was it not tea-time on the following day that he had settled as the term beyond which he would not wait? Perhaps the note had never reached Els after all? Or was it the answer that had gone astray?

And then at last the bell began to ring for tea, and he went off to Upper Hall. This was a meal of which he had come to be very fond. The great high room was always cool, kept so by its thick walls and by the outside blinds which were let down the moment the afternoon sun began to fall on that side of the house. And while it thus afforded a pleasant contrast to the heat out of doors, the soft dim light that filled it was grateful after the glare. Just opposite where he sat, one of the tall windows, wide open, showed under the semi-circle of its blind, a small piece of the bright green turf of the lawn; round the edges trailed two or three loose branches of a climbing rose that now and again would gently wave as they were stirred for a moment by some puff of wind; and this, with the hair of the boys about him still wet and their faces freshly dipped from bathing, filled him with a delightful sense of summer life; not as he had known it at Telscombe, baking and breathless, at the bottom of a valley close shut in, and in a tiny stuffy room, but as a thing of cool shining rivers, wide smooth lawns, shady avenues and rustling trees. From the lofty walls, panelled to the ceiling with squares of dark lustrous oak, here and there looked down, from out their frames of tarnished gold and the impenetrable blackness of their backgrounds, half a dozen or so heads of those benefactors for whom in their Grace they daily prayed. Over the stately mantelpiece of marble, pillared and carved, was affixed a trophy of the College Arms, a dove striking down a serpent with its claws, and the legend 'Sicut Columbae' round about. Opposite him sat Young; and now, when they were half-way through their meal:

'Rosy,' he said.

But he gave no sign that he had heard.

'Rosy!' the other cried again, and letting himself slip a little under the table, but clinging still with his hands to the bare massive edge of oak, he kicked at him underneath. But still he said nothing, only tucking his legs out of danger under the form.

'Rosy!' once again cried Young.

'Well, what is it?' Jaspar asked, but did not take his eyes off his book.

'I've got something for you from Els!' he said.

'Have you?' he returned, in what he hoped was an indifferent and unmoved voice, though he could not but fear that his excitement must be generally obvious.

'Will you have it now,' continued Young, 'or wait till you get it?' and with that he stretched out his hand across the table, showing from out his tightly-doubled fist a corner of what looked like an envelope. For a moment Jaspar sat quite still, affecting not to care, until at last, Young's hand being now quite near, he made a sudden grab. But the other was too quick for him:

'Oh no, you don't!' he cried, and drew back. And then, as through the doorway into Middle Hall he saw that behind the Warden's great chair of state the servitor was standing with his trencher-cap ready to hand him so soon as he should rise for Grace; and by that sign knew that the end of the meal was near:

'Well, here you are then!' he said with a generous air, and gave the envelope which Jaspar received with an elaborate affectation of indifference, so that if after all it should turn out to be a sell, he might be able to pretend that he had never been taken in. Recognizing, how-ever, Elsie's hand outside, he opened it, and was preparing to draw out its content, when he perceived that there was nothing inside but the scraps of his own note. Surprised, he raised his head to look at Young, and, as he did so, met his eyes fixed on him with an air of the most malicious mockery and triumph; and just as the words, *Per Jesum Christum Dominum Nostrum!* came booming in in the Butcher's mellow voice, he seized his tea-cup, and in a gust of disappointment and rage, hurled it straight at the other's head. But Young had time to step a little aside, and it went crash against the wall behind. The noise was partly lost in the slight confusion that always attended the passage of the dons through Upper Hall on their way out; but the Prefect, whose table it was, had seen him.

'Five hundred lines, Tristram!' he called out.

But Jaspar scarcely heard, as he stood there trembling with passion, and feeling as if in another moment he would have flown at Young with one of the knives that lay there on the table so ready to hand. Indeed this latter was so alarmed at his air that he did nothing more to revenge the insult than bluster, declaring with much affectation of magnanimity that since the young squit had got his lines he was content, and would not himself punish him any more for an attempt which after all had failed. But Jaspar, though he heard him speaking, understood not a word, and only walked slowly out of the room.

Of course Jaspar's wiser judgment told him that all possibility of reconciliation was now at an end, but still for a little he clung to the hope that some change for the better in his relations with Els might even yet be brought about, were he to take the one step his dignity allowed of, and return the old silver pencil-case which, though he knew he had really bought it of the boy, he had always tried to make believe was a sort of Essex's ring. And if he sent back Elsie's presents, surely Els must send back his; and there were any amount of things he had given him that he would be very glad to have himself.

But before he could arrive at any decision on the point, he found that he had sunk into such a state of torpor he could hardly force himself to get up and dress in the morning or, when once he had sat down, to move. And so far now was he from ever knowing his lessons that he did not even try to learn them, doing nothing in Preparation, but, with a fixed, vacant stare, gaze at the book open before him till the whole page was blurred; while when impot followed impot in such quick succession that before one was finished he had always another to do, he was rather glad to be able so to get through his time as to give his recollections no chance of rushing in, which only waited for an instant's emptiness to flood his mind. He even began to look forward with a silly curiosity to the moment, now surely near at hand, when he would be sent up to the Butcher to be swished. Perhaps, too, they would take away his scholarship – he had heard of such things being done – but it appeared no more than right that, as that which had enabled him to gain it had been lost, so the prize itself should pass also out of his possession. And the worse he could make his case, the better he was pleased; it seemed as if, in so doing, he were somehow revenging himself on Els.

'I can't make out what's come to you of late!' said Toady Maude one day. 'Aren't you well?' But answering not a word, with a half-stubborn, half sleepy face, he kept his eyes still fixed on his book.

'Oh, well,' observed the don with a resigned air, 'I suppose you'd better write out the lesson as usual!'

And without even an attempt at protest he sat down, and leaning back against the wall closed his eyes, and with much ostentation affected to go to sleep.

'Tristram!' cried the don. And as he looked up with a pretended start: 'Why don't you attend, you silly fellow?' he said. Yet far from being grateful that his cheek should be thus forgiven, Jaspar was only angry his heroics should so have missed of their effect.

'I can easily get a crib!' he muttered. Toady however, with a kindness which only irritated him the more, pretended not to have heard, and the lesson went on. But when it was over, and most of the form were indeed already out of the room, he called him back, as, slowly, the last, he followed, and essayed once more to find out to what was due the change that had of late come over him.

'What's the matter?' he asked. 'Is it anything in which I can help you?'

And standing there before the desk with sullen face and hanging head, Jaspar thought how glad he would have been to have opened himself to such unexpected sympathy; but something in him, which was quite beyond his control, compelled him still to answer with a 'Nothing, sir! why?' which, even as he spoke, he knew was tantamount to a definite rejection of the assistance the don proffered; who indeed appeared to consider it as such, for he said nothing more, but presently looking up from the mark book he was busy over: 'I don't want any-thing!' he said in the coldest of tones. 'You can go!' And Jaspar turned and went slowly off. Now that all chance of doing so was over, he would have given much to have accepted this offer of help: and vexed with himself on this account, he was no less ashamed. Not only had he wantonly rejected the sympathy that he needed so much, but, by his behaviour up in form, had traded most unworthily on Toady's for-bearance; for, of course he never would have dared to show his temper like that to anyone, whether master or boy, who he was not sure would put up with it. . . .

But indeed, as they wandered together over the Chase, now under the lichen-dappled beeches of Solomon's Mound, now under red-scaled pines knee-deep in bracken, where the dry slippery ground crunched under their feet as they went up; and now again in some little open dell scattered with sombre yews and may-trees overgrown with honeysuckle and blackberry, she was for ever crying out to him to look at something or other which, but for her sharp eyes, he would have missed; at a rabbit as it skirried away, its white scut glancing up and down, or some deer as, startled, they tripped off and stopped and stood at gaze. And this keen interest on her part in things about which he thought no girl would either have known or cared, presently confirmed him in that fancy he had at first conceived on the river, that she had in her something of a boy. And once this notion had taken hold of him, there was nothing, from the way she went scrambling about to that in which she whistled to Hector, that did not seem but another proof that he was right. Even her dress, as in the boat so now, contributed to this effect, for her thick boots with their brass hooks and thongs of leather looked, especially when covered with mud, exactly like those that Els had worn when they had played football together long ago. But indeed it was always of her brother that she reminded him; not of the brother he had known in more recent times, but rather of that young Prince Charming his fond imagination had already begun to insist had been his friend in those far-off Scarisbrick days. For though not nearly so good-looking, she had yet the same broken eyebrows which in him he had been so fond of and the same laughing eyes; even the few tiny freckles which Els had had and which had exercised upon him such a curious charm, were now reproduced in her and with the same effect. He compared them fantastically to those that speckled the warm apricots upon the long south wall. It was true that it was framed in heavy curls, this face which was so troublingly like that of the boy to whom, a boy, he had been devoted; but even this was not enough to persuade him of her being really a girl, for Elsie's lovelocks in the theatricals had been as long; and it was only when he helped her over some many-barred and bramble-topped gate or some battlemented clinker-built paling of grey rattling oak, and felt how small and pliant was her waist and how meltingly soft her dress, that he knew her not to be of his own sex. But this was not a thing that often happened, for if she could she would always jump; and then, more than ever, she reminded him of her brother, snatching off, like him, her cricket-cap and crumpling it in her little clenched fist as, setting her face, she took her run. For her language, that too, like everything else about her, had in it something of both sexes, and he found an extraordinary charm in hearing her at one time talk like a small girl and at another make use of such very boyish expressions as 'beastly,' and 'jolly,' and 'stalky,' 'feign I!' and 'no fear!' Nor while thus perpetually comparing his present relations with her to those that had once existed between him and her brother, did he forget that, still now as then, he could enjoy the consciousness that his intellect was, as he phrased it, 'stooping its lofty crest' before one in every way its inferior. And ever since he could remember anything it had been a favourite notion with him, this, of strength obeying weakness and one which several times he had carried into execution. It was a matter of indifference whether, as the former, he voluntarily submitted to the caprice of one who was pretty and younger and weaker than he, or played this latter part himself, supplying by force of character and what else he could, that which he wanted in good looks.

89   'Bored'

Horatio Brown. From *Drift*, 1900. Sub-titled 'At a London Music'.

Two rows of foolish faces blent
In two blurred lines; the compliment,
The formal smile, the cultural air,
The sense of falseness everywhere.
Her ladyship superbly dressed –
    I liked their footman, John, the best.

The tired musicians' ruffled mien,
Their whispered talk behind the screen,
The frigid plaudits, quite confined
By fear of being unrefined
His lordship's grave and courtly jest –
    I liked their footman, John, the best.

Remote I sat with shaded eyes,
Supreme attention in my guise,
And heard the whole laborious din,
Piano, 'cello, violin;
And so, perhaps, they hardly guessed
    I liked their footman, John, the best.

Index

Jackson, Richard C., 35

Jaspar Tristram (Clarke), 51, 53

Jocelyn, Percy, Bishop of Clogher, 23

Johnson, Lionel, 39, 40, 46

Jopling, Louise, 20 [n17], 52 [n62]

Jowett, Benjamin, 19

Kains-Jackson, Charles, 6, 40, 41 [n44], 42–47, 51, 53

Kennerley, Mitchell, 29

Known Signatures (Gawsworth), 35 [n34]

Kottabos, 28 [n27]

Lamborne, Lionel, 18 [n14]

Lane, John (Publisher), 28, 33

'Lawrence, Bertram', *see* Bloxam, J. F.

Leaves of Grass (Whitman), 3, 17, 23

Lefroy, Edward Cracroft, 29, 30, 40

Le Gallienne, Richard, 23

Leighton, Sir Frederick (Lord Leighton), 30

Lesbia Brandon (Swinburne), 14 [n9]

Letters of Oscar Wilde, The (Hart-Davis), 25 [n25], 46 [n56], 51 [n60]

Leverson, Ada, 53

Life of Walter Pater, The (Wright), 35 [n35]

Louÿs, Pierre, 47

Love in Earnest (Nicholson), 43

Lyra Viginti Cordarum (Symonds), 22 [n20]

McCarthy, Justin Huntly, 41

Mademoiselle de Maupin (Gautier), 14

Marcus, Steven, 2 [n1]

Marillier, Henry C., 25

Marius the Epicurean (Pater), 20, 32, 35

Marvell, Arthur (Clifton), 41

Mason, Stuart, 25 [n26], 27 [n27]

Mathews, Elkin (Publisher), 33

Maupassant, Guy de, 18

Memoirs of a Misspent Youth (Richards), 47 [n57]

Memoirs of Arthur Hamilton, The (Benson), 35

Merrill, George, 24

Meynell, Alice, 14

Michelangelo, 19

Melling, W. A., 44

Miles, Francis, 25

Morality in Public Schools and its Relation to Religion (Wilson), 4 [n2]

Morrison, Palgrave, 41

Mountmorres, Lord, 45

Mulready, William, 16

My Secret Life, 49

Myers, F. W. H., 21, 30

Narcissus and Other Poems (Carpenter), 23

Newbolt, Henry, 10

New Chivalry, The (Bradford), 6, 54

New Chivalry, The (Kains-Jackson), 6, 45, 46

Newman, John Henry, 4, 11, 29

New Republic, The (Mallock), 19

New Review, The, 29 [n28]

Nicholson, John Gambril, 43, 44, 47, 51, 53

Noel, The Hon. Roden, 21, 22, 23

Old and Young, 44

Old Mortality club, 19

Omar Khayyam, 5

Osborn, Percy, 47, 53

Other Victorians, The (Marcus), 2 [n1]

Oxford Apostles (Faber), 4, 5 [n3]

Oxford Book of Modern Verse, The (ed. W. B. Yeats), 38 [n39]

Oxford Movement, 4, 10, 11, 19, 20, 29

Packard, Vance, 54

Paget, Violet (Vernon Lee), 32

Pall Mall Gazette, The, 41

Park (Gray), 33

Pater, Walter, 18–20, 32, 35, 36

Patience (Gilbert), 31

Perverts, the, 11

Picture of Dorian Gray, The (Wilde), 25, 33

Pillar of the Cloud, The (Newman), 4

Platen, August von, 34

Plato, 9

Playgoers Club, 33

Pluschow, Guglielmo, 43

Poems and Ballads (Swinburne), 13 [n7], 17